Sybex's Quick Tour of Windows 95

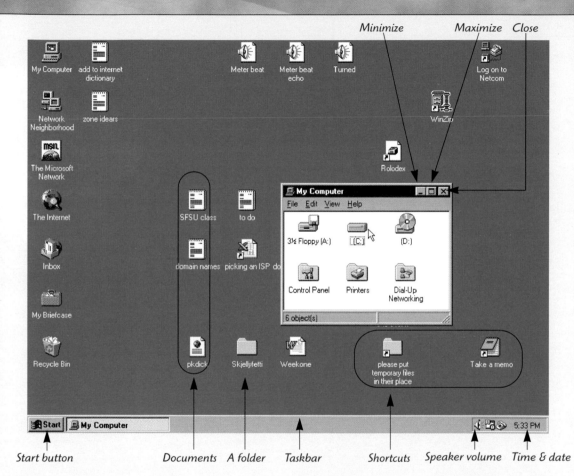

Minimize Maximize Close

Start button   Documents   A folder   Taskbar   Shortcuts   Speaker volume   Time & date

The Desktop *is where your programs, files, and shortcuts reside.*

My Computer *allows you to browse the contents of your computer, open folders, open documents, and run programs.*

Network Neighborhood *gives you direct access to other computers (and shared resources, such as printers).*

The Microsoft Network *dials up your connection to Microsoft's online service.*

The Internet *starts up the Internet Explorer, a World Wide Web browser (available only with Plus!).*

Inbox *starts Microsoft Exchange and opens your inbox, so you can see if you have any new mail.*

My Briefcase *is a new feature for keeping documents consistent as you move them between computers.*

Recycle Bin *makes it easy to delete and undelete files.*

The Start button *the Start menu, you can run just program.*

The Taskbar *displays a button for every running program.*

Create **shortcuts** *on your Desktop for frequently used programs and documents.*

D0813625

FORMATTING A FLOPPY DISK

To format a floppy disk, first double-click the My Computer icon. Put the floppy in the disk drive. Then right-click the 3½ Floppy icon in the My Computer window and choose Format. The Format dialog box appears.

If you want some density other than the standard 1.44MB, click the Capacity drop-down list box and choose another option. To give the disk a label, click in the Label box and type one. Then click Start.

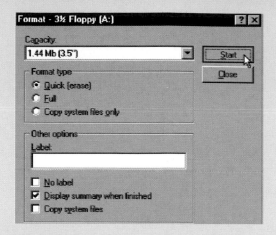

USEFUL KEYBOARD SHORTCUTS

TASK	KEYSTROKE
Get help	F1
Quit a program	Alt+F4
Pop up shortcut menu for selected item	Shift+F10
Pop up the Start menu	Ctrl+Esc
Cut a selection	Ctrl+X
Copy a selection	Ctrl+C
Paste a selection	Ctrl+V
Delete a selection	Delete
Undo the last action	Ctrl+Z
Select all items in window	Ctrl+A
Refresh a window	F5
Open folder one level up from current one	Backspace
Close a folder and all its parents	Shift and click Close button
Rename a selection	F2
Find a file starting with current folder	F3
Delete a selection without putting it in Recycle Bin (be careful!)	Shift+Delete
View a selection's properties	Alt+Enter or Alt+double-click
Copy an icon	Ctrl+click and drag
Create a shortcut from an icon	Ctrl+Shift+click and drag

Sybex Inc.
2021 Challenger Drive
Alameda, CA 94501
Tel: 510-523-8233 · 800-227-2346
Fax: 510-523-2373

SYBEX®

You have all kinds of control over the appearance of Windows. You can get to the Display Properties dialog box to change the look via the Control Panel, but the easiest shortcut is to right-click in any empty area of the Desktop and select Properties. The Display Properties dialog box comes up with the Background tab selected.

- *Choose a desktop pattern or wallpaper design.*

- *Choose **Screen Saver** to select a screen saver or stop using one.*

- *Choose **Appearance** to change the look of the windows and dialog boxes.*

- *Choose **Settings** to change the color palette or screen resolution.*

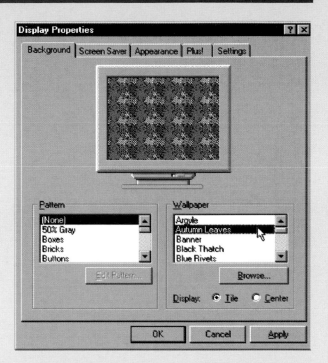

No one likes having to set up a printer, but Windows has made it fairly unthreatening. Choose Start ➢ Settings ➢ Printer (or open My Computer and double-click Printers). Your Printers window will open.

- *To modify an existing Printer, right-click it and choose Properties.*

- *To create a new Printer, double-click the Add Printer icon and follow the instructions in the Add Printer Wizard.*

- *To change the default printer, right-click a printer and choose Set as Default.*

Sybex's Quick Tour of Windows 95

Just press the Start button to do almost anything.

- *Choose a program or program group from a submenu.*
- *Reopen one of the last 15 documents you've worked on.*
- *Change the way Windows is set up or add a printer.*
- *Search for a missing document, folder, or program.*
- *Get online help.*
- *Run a program directly, the old-fashioned (DOS) way.*
- *Turn off or restart your computer.*

Running a Program

To start a program, click Start ➢ Programs, choose a program folder (if necessary), and then point to a program.

Putting a Program, Folder, or Document on the Start Menu

First, open the folder that contains the program you want to put on the Start menu. Then click the program icon and drag it onto the Start button. (If you want to get a look at the hierarchy of the programs on the Start submenus—so that you can move things around—right-click on the Start button and choose Open.)

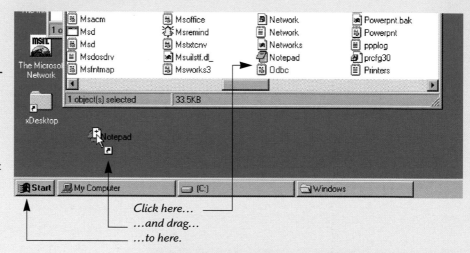

Click here...
...and drag...
...to here.

Finding Files and Folders Quickly

Unlike Windows 3.1's cumbersome Search command in the File Manager, Windows 95 has a simple-to-use Find command. To try it, select Start ➢ Find ➢ Files or Folders.

Type the name of the file you're looking for (or just part of it), then click Find Now.

A window will open, showing the files as Windows finds them.

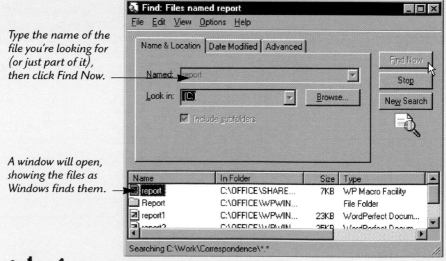

Sure, Windows 3.1 enabled you to use the mouse to scroll, click menus, and interact with dialog boxes, but now just about every feature of Windows can be clicked on (with either button), double-clicked, and/or dragged.

Selecting Things

Click most things to select them. Shift-click to add all intervening items to a selection. Ctrl-click to add an individual item to a selection. Click and drag to lasso and select several items (click in an empty space before starting to drag—otherwise, you'll drag the item itself).

Right-Click Dragging

If you click with the left button and drag, Windows 95 will either copy the icon (for example, when dragging from or to a floppy) or move the icon (for example, when dragging from one folder to another).

For more control, right-click on an icon and drag it. When you release the mouse button, a menu pops up.

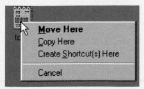

Things You Can Right-Click On

Right-click on an item to pop up a shortcut menu. Every icon's shortcut menu has Properties as its last choice —each object on your computer has a set of properties associated with it, which you can view or change.

■ My Computer

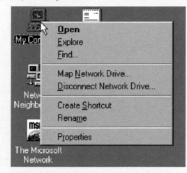

Explore displays a File Manager–like view of folders and files.

■ Any folder, document, or program icon

Send To sends documents directly to a floppy, printer, or fax machine.

■ The Start button

Open lets you make changes to the Start menu.

■ The Recycle Bin

■ The Desktop

Arrange Icons sorts them by name, type, size, or date.

New creates a new folder, document, or shortcut on the Desktop.

■ The Taskbar

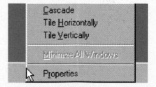

■ A Taskbar button

■ Undo
After you move, copy, create a shortcut from, or delete an icon, the next time you right-click anywhere you can undo your last action. The menu will have a choice like Undo Move or Undo Delete.

Every running program, open folder, and drive gets a button on the Taskbar. Dialog boxes do not.

You can switch to any task by clicking its button. When you get a lot of things going at once, the Taskbar can get crowded, as you can see in example 1 below.

Making the Taskbar Bigger

To make more room on the Taskbar, click it along its top edge and drag it up. You'll get something more like example 2.

Moving the Taskbar

If you'd prefer to have the Taskbar at the top of the screen, so the Start menu will pull down like a menu on the menu bar, just click the Taskbar (not one of the buttons on it) and drag it to the top of the screen. It will look similar to example 3.

You can also put the Taskbar at the left or right edge of the screen to get something that looks like the taskbars shown to the right. In either position, the Taskbar can be stretched up to half the width of the screen.

Changing the Way the Taskbar Works

You can customize the Taskbar by right-clicking on an empty portion of it and choosing Properties. This brings up the Properties dialog box.

Check or uncheck the options (the preview area shows you the effects of your choices). Uncheck **Always on top** if you want the Taskbar to be covered by other windows. Check **Auto hide** if you want the Taskbar to stay hidden until you move your mouse toward it.

Task-Switching with Alt+Tab

Another easy way to switch from task to task is to hold down the Alt key and press Tab repeatedly. This worked in Windows 3.1 too. But now when you do this, a plaque will appear showing all the running programs as

icons, with the currently selected one labeled in a box at the bottom of the plaque. Press Tab until the program you want is highlighted and then release both the Tab and the Alt keys.

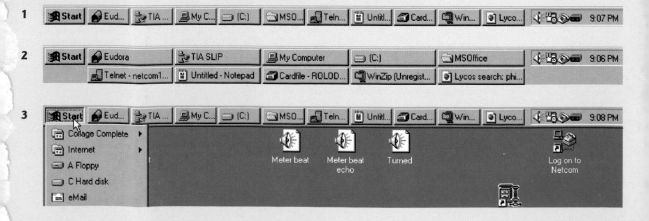

The basic routine for poking around your computer is to double-click on folder icons and select programs or documents from folder windows.

Starting with My Computer

Usually, you'll start by double-clicking My Computer, which gives you a view of all the drives and devices attached to your computer. Double-click the C: icon to look at the contents of your hard disk.

Then double-click one of the folders in the C: window to open another window, and so on, and so on.

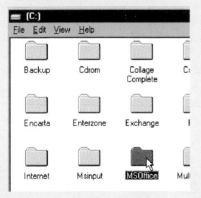

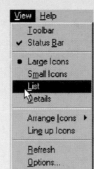

Besides the Large Icons view, you can also choose List view (shown below). Or you can choose Details view to see more information about a folder or file, such as size, type of file it is, and date it was last changed.

If you'd prefer that each new folder opens up in the same window, instead of creating a new window (which can get very irritating when you end up with numerous open windows on your screen), select View ➢ Options ➢ Browse folders by using a single window.

Renaming, Copying, or Moving an Icon

In Windows 95, an icon can represent a document, folder, program, or shortcut. The rules for manipulating an icon are the same no matter what the icon corresponds to.

To rename an icon, select it and click in the label below it (wait a few seconds for the text in the label to become highlighted). Then type a new name (up to 255 characters, including spaces if you like) and press Enter.

To copy an icon, the easiest way is to right-click on it and select Copy. Then move to the destination, right-click again, and select Paste. To move an icon, right-click on it and select Cut. Then move to the destination, right-click, and select Paste.

This is a big change from Windows 3.1! Before, the convenience of cutting, copying, and pasting was limited to the text and other contents of application windows. Now just about every item on the screen can be dragged, dropped, cut, copied, and pasted.

Or, you can just hold down Ctrl and drag a copy of an icon to a new location. (A safer way to copy an icon is to right-click on it, drag to a new location, and then choose Copy from the menu that pops up.)

One of the best new features of Windows 95 is shortcuts. Each shortcut you create takes up only a small amount of disk space, but can save you time and energy by opening a program or document that you'd otherwise have to hunt around for. You can recognize a shortcut by the little doubling-back arrow in the bottom-left corner of its icon.

Putting a Shortcut on the Desktop

There are many ways to do this. If you have a document or program already visible on the screen and want to create a shortcut to it on the desktop, right-click on the icon, drag it onto the Desktop, and then choose Create Shortcut(s) Here. You can also start from the Desktop when the "target" of your shortcut-to-be is not readily available.

Right-click on the Desktop, select New, and then Shortcut.

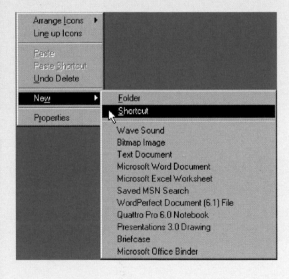

This brings up the Create Shortcut wizard. If you don't know the command line for the program you want, click the Browse button. This brings up an Open-style dialog box; work your way through various folders until you find the program you want to make a shortcut to. Then click the Open button, click Next (or type a different name for the shortcut and click Next), and click Finish when you're done. Voila! Your shortcut appears on the Desktop.

Making a Keyboard Shortcut

Once you've created a shortcut icon, you can also set up a keyboard shortcut to launch the program (or open the document) automatically.

Right-click the shortcut icon and choose Properties. Click the Shortcut tab in the Properties dialog box, click inside the Shortcut Key box, and then press the keyboard shortcut you want. It will appear in the box as you press it.

Shows the default folder for the program

Controls how the program's window appears when you first run it (other choices are Minimized and Maximized)

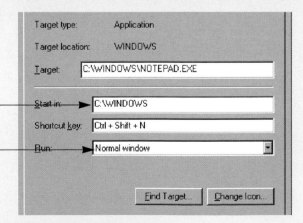

Mastering Microsoft Office Professional for Windows 95

Mastering Microsoft® Office Professional for Windows® 95

Lonnie E. Moseley
David M. Boodey

SYBEX

San Francisco • Paris • Düsseldorf • Soest

Acquisitions Manager: Kristine Plachy
Developmental Editor: James Sumser
Editors: Doug Robert, Marilyn Smith, Dusty Bernard, Pat Coleman, Laura Arendal
Project Editor: Doug Robert
Technical Editors: Frank Seidel, Ann Hoang Seidel, Sandra Teng
Book Designer: Helen Bruno, adapted by Jan Haseman
Desktop Publishers: Thomas Goudie Bonasera at SYBEX; Dave Bryant at London Road Design
Production Coordinator: Renée Avalos
Indexer: Ted Laux
Cover Designer: Design Site
Cover Photographer: David Bishop

Library of Congress Card Number: 95-71028
ISBN: 0-7821-1747-3

Manufactured in the United States of America
10 9 8 7 6 5 4 3

Acknowledgments

We would like to thank the many people who contributed their effort and support to the creation of this book.

We cannot say enough about Jim Sumser, our Developmental Editor, who has been with us with support and enthusiasm for our ideas throughout the entire process.

One thing is for certain and that is if it were not for Doug Robert and his editorial team, including Marilyn Smith, Dusty Bernard, Pat Coleman, and Laura Arendal, this book would not have been as polished and smooth as it turned out.

Technically, this book has been honed by a pleasantly scrutinizing bunch that included Frank Seidel, Ann Hoang Seidel, Sandra Teng, and Dan Tauber, and we are ever grateful for knowing that our technical "fact checkers" were there for us.

Putting the scads of files, figures, and edits together was the unthankful (until now) job of a great group of professionals who are responsible for the layout, style, and general appearance of the book. Thanks to Renée Avalos, Thomas Goudie, and others at SYBEX, and the folks at London Road in Palo Alto who stepped in to pinch hit in the final rush.

Special thanks go to Kristine Plachy, Cordell Sloan, Michael Lee, Michelle Moore, Denise Leo, and Millie Burton for their invaluable time, professional contributions, and pervasive good humor.

Our special thanks and gratitude to business partners and friends Cordell Sloan and Terry Zurzola who saw the potential for this project long before we did.

We would also like to thank some very important people who have touched our lives with their support, encouragement, forbearance, and belief.

▶ William and Wynn Moseley, Bill, David, and Anthony Moseley, Michael Valenoti, Ray Trost, Dave Olson, Deborah Batt, Rona Barufkin, Barbara Grinnell, Mary Powell, Deborrah Wilkinson, Connie Bell, Maurice Henry, Doris and John Zurzola, Steve Woodland, Susan Greco, Mary Sloan, Brenda Kienan, Dwight Miller, Holly Hewlett, Peggy DeVito, Sharon Leib, Inez Gibbs, Ruth and André Ferber, Linda and Allen Hammond, Obra Kernodle, Harry Watts, Ed Nickerson, Frank Spezzano, Rashida Sule, and Bernard Watson.

▶ Robert Boodey, Mickey Boodey, Diana Boodey, Grandmom Francis and all of her wonderful children and grandchildren, Martha, Leon, Mike and Alice Boodey, The Greenwalds, The Petersons, Nadine Medbery, Bryan Becker, Lisa and Larry Grady, and Darren Fromal.

Contents at a Glance

Table of Contents

Introduction

Business software integration has come into its own with the release of Microsoft Office 95, which combines a new common look and a more polished interface, thanks to Windows 95, with a seamless exchange of information between the Office applications to enable us to focus on our documents rather than on the intricacies of the software that creates them.

The components that make up the integrated Office suite include:

Word
In addition to using Word for anything you'd use a word processor for, you can use it as the foundation for creating letters, memos, reports, and any other document that will include or be included in documents from the other Office applications. For example, you can use a Word document as the basis for an Excel chart or a PowerPoint slide, or within a Word document you can merge data from Schedule+ or Access.

Excel
Use Excel to formulate and analyze numbers, manage and sort lists, and create graphs, maps, and pivot tables. The lists and numbers can be created and stored in Excel or in an external source, such as an Access database.

Power-Point
Use PowerPoint to present your thoughts, ideas, and plans to various audiences—for example, your board of directors, sales prospects, students, or any other group. Multimedia, animation, and links to your Office data make PowerPoint ideal for timely information and powerful presentations.

Schedule+   Use Schedule+ to manage pertinent information about your contacts and facilitate the scheduling of your time. A welcome addition to the Office suite, Schedule+ provides quick access to your contact data for inclusion in a single letter or a mass mailing. Schedule+ also integrates well with other users' Schedule+ schedules when you need to find the best time that a group of people can get together for a meeting.

Access   Use Access to store, track, and report information. Membership lists, client data, student registrations, inventory tracking, and customer invoicing are among the many uses of Access. As a member of the Office, Access can utilize the tools of Excel to analyze and map the data stored. Access also contributes greatly to the other products by working seamlessly with Word when you need to merge data for mass mailings, or when you want to use PowerPoint to show data that substantiates the points being made in a presentation, and when you want to make Access forms and reports available for use with Excel.

NOTE   Microsoft Office Professional includes Access, but Microsoft Office Standard does not. The Standard version, however, integrates seamlessly with the stand-alone version of Access 95 if you want to purchase it separately.

Our Approach

Our approach when writing this book was to focus on the skills that you would need when you are on your own in the real world trying to get a job done. The features that we present are the ones that we felt were the most important in order for you to gain a strong understanding of the software, so that you can best use your computer to accomplish your job.

At the end of each of the seven parts of the book is a chapter on integration, focusing on how to use the program with the other applications in the Office suite. These wrap-up chapters provide step-by-step solutions to common business projects. By substituting your documents for the sample documents used in the examples, many of your tasks that could take advantage of the Office as a whole have been laid out for you as a reference.

Part 1: Welcome to Your New Office

Included in this section is an orientation to your Office environment. This orientation includes an introduction to the individual applications, a primer on the new Windows 95 environment, and the tools made available to facilitate the integration of the Office applications.

Part 2: Business Processing— Communicating with Word

This section covers in depth the features necessary to provide you with the knowledge to create polished and professional documents, like letters, proposals, integrated reports that incorporate information from other Office applications, and reusable templates that help make your document creation more efficient.

The integration chapter at the end of this section outlines the process for combining multiple Word documents created by multiple users. The compiled documents also demonstrate how to incorporate Excel charts and PowerPoint slides.

Part 3: Business Processing— Analyzing with Excel

This section delves into the creation of Excel financial workbooks, which allow you to use mathematical expressions and formulas to generate answers from raw data. Also explored are the analyzing, charting, and mapping of your numbers. Other chapters in this section teach you how to use Excel's powerful list and database features to sort, subtotal, and filter the data.

The integration chapter of this section takes a growing Word table, imports it into Excel for list management, and uses forms and reports while linking the information to Access.

Part 4: Business Processing— Presenting with PowerPoint

This section covers the fundamentals needed for creating colorful and effective slide presentations using PowerPoint. Features explored include everything from the use of Wizards and templates for quickly getting presentations ready to the new animation and multimedia effects that will make your presentations stand out.

The integration chapter of this section follows the process of a user who needs to create a presentation that incorporates data and charts from Word and Excel.

Part 5: Business Processing— Organizing with Schedule+

In this section the features of the newest member of the Office are introduced, with special attention devoted to its vital integration with Word. The features of Schedule+ are explored to provide you with the ability to create and manage appointments, projects, and to-do lists.

The integration chapter of this section details the process of importing contact information from other Office applications and how to use the contacts stored in Schedule+ for mass mailings.

Part 6: Business Processing— Data Management with Access

Making a relational database has never been easier than it is now with this most recent release of Access. This section explains how you can create very powerful relational databases. From basic concepts and helpful Wizards to advanced tips, we cover basic database design and implementation. Quicker and easier development of forms, reports, and query development are the hallmark of this release.

The integration section examines the possible needs of the fictional NorthWind Traders company, addressing the company's needs to merge Access data with Word for a monthly mailing, to substantiate presentation points using data stored in Access, and using an Excel pivot table on an Access form to analyze the data stored in Access.

Part 7: WordMail and OLE (Object Linking and Embedding)

In this short section we explore how to use electronic mail within Office, with tips on using Word as your mail editor, and we explain the powerful features afforded by object linking and embedding (OLE).

Conventions Used in This Book

We've used some standard conventions and typographer's tricks to make this book easier to read. While most of them will be obvious, you should scan the next few paragraphs just in case.

Keyboard Notations

To simplify instructions and make them easier to follow, we've used a special kind of shorthand notation:

▶ Whenever you need to hold down one key, then press another, you'll see the keys separated by plus signs. For instance, Ctrl+S means hold down the Ctrl key while pressing the S key.

▶ Boldface text usually indicates text you are expected to type.

▶ Some keys (the arrow keys and the Enter key, to be precise) are indicated by symbols, especially in lists where we're trying to save space. The symbol for the Enter key is a crooked arrow, ↵, as found on many keyboards.

So, if you are being asked to type a file name and then press the Enter key in an example, you'll read something like the following:

Type **readme.doc** then press ↵.

The ▶ Symbol for Menu Commands

As a shortcut and an eye-catcher, we've used a special convention to indicate menu commands. When we want you to choose a command from the menu bar, it will follow this pattern: *menu name* ▶ *command*. For instance, "Choose File ▶ Save" is a shorter, neater way of saying "Choose the File command from the menu bar, then choose the Save command from the File menu." Sometimes you'll even see a sequence of commands that goes three or four levels deep into subcommands.

Welcome to Your New Office

Included in this part is an orientation to your Office environment.

This orientation includes an introduction to the individual

applications, a primer on the new Windows 95 environment, and

the tools made available to facilitate the integration of the Office

applications.

Chapter 1

Introducing You around the Office

Featuring

Before you jump into working at your desk with your hand glued to the mouse, your head arched at an awkward angle toward the monitor and your eyes riveted on a font that is much too small, take a minute and read this overview of what's in store when working with Microsoft Office for Windows 95. Once you realize the capabilities of this powerful and revolutionary product, I am sure you will begin to relax as you begin an incredible computing experience.

What You Can Look Forward To

The new Office is an excellent group of compatible programs written by the Microsoft programming teams; teams known for their innovative and user-tested software-interface designs. The group of Office programs includes:

▶ Word

▶ Excel

▶ PowerPoint

▶ Access (included only in the Professional Edition of office)

▶ Schedule+

All of the products have been written to run optimally under Microsoft's new operating system, Windows 95. This new and long-awaited graphical operating system is the next version of Microsoft's flagship product, which, in its earlier incarnation as Windows 3.1, pushed the PC marketplace to levels of use unparalleled in the industry.

Who Is in the Office?

The Professional Edition of Office's product suite includes word processing (Word), spreadsheet (Excel), business presentation (PowerPoint), personal-information management (Schedule+), and business data management and tracking (Access) programs, updated for Office for Windows 95. Each program can function independently or interact seamlessly, depending on your needs.

Columns of numbers created in Excel can be placed within a Word report and then placed within a PowerPoint Presentation or become the basis for a database in Access. Tables of information created in Word can be copied directly into Excel as the data for a new spreadsheet. Letters typed in Word can be used as the basis of a mail merge of names and addresses contained in Excel or Access.

Architectures of the Future

New to Office is the ability to combine documents from multiple Office applications into one "virtual document." These documents form sections within an Office Binder, which will provide you with a way to more easily handle large projects.

The Comfort of Team Work

The possibilities are boundless. Never has it been easier to revolutionize the way we perform our work. The Office programs share a look and feel, so as you continue to work in one product, you are already becoming familiar with all of the others because of the commonality between menus, toolbars, and other design elements.

The Office programs share common spelling dictionaries and shortcut word libraries—called AutoCorrect libraries—so productivity tools you create in one application are automatically used in the other applications.

Also available "across the Office" is a special feature called an Answer Wizard that allows you to query the Help system with your own words instead of trying to think of what the exact help listing may be. The Answer Wizard is part of the Microsoft IntelliSense technology—which borders on artificial intelligence—built into your Office team members.

You'll Be Glad You Joined This Office

With the new design of Windows 95, you can easily start multiple programs by clicking on the Start button on the Taskbar. Regardless of the program in which you are working at the moment, all the names of the open programs appear on the Windows 95 Taskbar. You can easily switch between open programs by clicking on their names on the Taskbar, or you can tile the applications to see all four programs and their data at one time.

The bottom line is: you will be extremely pleased with your choice of the Microsoft Office suite of products as the tools for redesigning business in the '90s. Figure 1.1 shows Word, Excel, PowerPoint, and Schedule+ open in memory and tiled so a part of each is displayed.

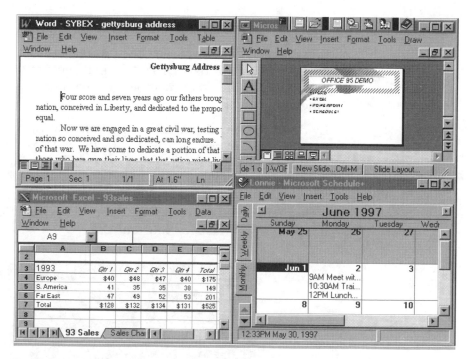

Figure 1.1   *The Office programs work together better than ever before.*

How Much Space Does the Office Need?

The requirements for the Typical Install of the Standard Edition of Office is 55MB of disk space and a recommended 8MB of RAM. If you bought the Professional Edition of Office, which includes Access, you will need an additional 40MB of hard disk space. See Appendix A for complete installation procedures for Office.

Introducing the Office Staff

Even though in the subsequent pages of this book you will be sitting down individually with each member of Office to find out exactly how each one can help you with your work, a general introduction is in order so you can decide which member you want to meet with first.

OMSB—The Office Manager

It is a good idea to meet the Office Manager—officially titled the Office Manager Shortcut Bar (OMSB)—first, because the OMSB can quickly help you find the other members of the office and even organize their functions for you.

By default, the Office Manager is present at the top right-hand side of the screen. You can, however, "dock" or "float" the Office Manager anywhere you want by dragging the toolbar to a new position. You can even make the Office Manager appear and disappear depending on where you hover your mouse pointer. See Chapter 3 for directions for activating and customizing the Office Manager. Figure 1.2 displays a floating Office Manager Shortcut Bar.

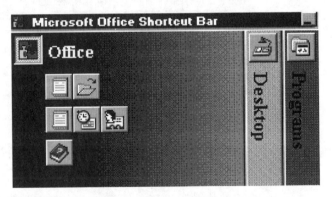

Figure 1.2   *The Office Manager Shortcut Bar can be floated and customized.*

Word—The Staff Writer

Word for Windows 95 is a seasoned word-processing program, and you can customize Word so it virtually writes your letters, memos, and proposals, composes tables, generates monthly reports, and outlines your articles and book chapters. Capable of producing newsletters, brochures, mail-merge letters, and envelopes, you will find virtually every writing feature you might need to produce a wide variety of document types.

Once you have typed information into the Word program, you can always reuse the information by storing it as an AutoText or AutoCorrect selection. When you choose File ➤ New from the menu bar, you will be provided with *Wizards*: already designed fax forms, agenda meeting forms, calendars, and memos. Word tells you exactly where you should type specific information in case you don't have a background in business typing standards. You will think that it's magic when you see how quickly you can get up and running with this powerful member of the Office team. See Chapter 4 for a full introduction to Word.

You will be quite happy with the way Word works with the Finance staff member (Excel) to produce documents that combine technical information with the charts, graphs, and numbers that back up the information. Figure 1.3 shows a multiple-page print preview of a proposal report that includes Excel budgetary numbers.

Excel—The Analyst

An equally powerful member of the Office team is Excel, your Analyst. Capable of building spreadsheets in a single bound; automatically summing columns of numbers; presenting a graphical representation of your

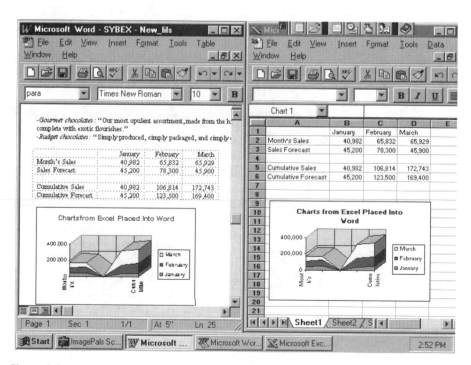

Figure 1.3 Word works seamlessly with Excel to produce reports that include numbers and graphs created in Excel.

data in the form of Pie, Bar, Line Charts, and more; and allowing quick sorts and subtotal tallying, you will be immensely grateful for this member of the team as you begin to work through your budgets, proposals, and other financial documents. Figure 1.4 shows an Excel financial document with the AutoFormat feature applied to the table of numbers.

Completely compatible with the other members, Excel can create numerical analyses that you can then take into a Word report, a PowerPoint presentation, or an Access database. Some of your most pleasurable times at the office will be spent with Excel as you explore the "what-if" possibilities generated by the formulas you create.

Excel incorporates a powerful feature called the Pivot Table, an innovative approach that *flips* and *sums* data in seconds, allowing you to see your financial numbers from various perspectives. You can also design your own screen forms and completely program Excel to automatically perform repetitive monthly tasks. But long before you get to the programming stage with Excel, you will be creating custom toolbars to

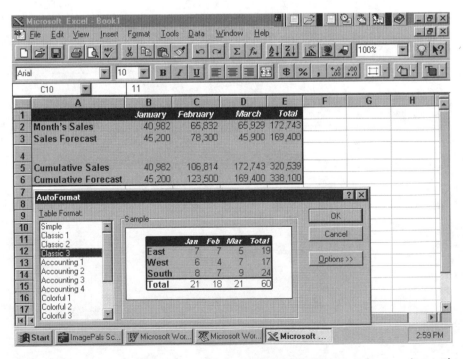

Figure 1.4   You can pick from among sixteen different AutoFormat styles to enhance the attractiveness of your tables.

include the operation buttons you want to use on a daily basis. See Chapter 14 for the hands-on meeting with Excel.

PowerPoint—The Graphic and Presentation Designer

If you failed Straight Line Drawing 101 in school, you will be immensely impressed with the next member of your team, PowerPoint, your presentation designer. Because you may not have the time or the background to figure out design elements and the proper color scheme for presentations, PowerPoint is a built-in designer that will give you suggestions on how to lay out and organize your on-screen slide presentations, audience handouts, and 35mm slides.

PowerPoint works with your Finance Assistant, Excel, to use numbers and charts in its slide presentation. Also very friendly with Word, the writer, PowerPoint automatically generates a complete slide show from the outlines generated by Word in Outline mode. PowerPoint then will suggest color, flourish, and maybe some clip art pictures to emphasize what you are writing.

Once all of the parts are together, PowerPoint will help you decide how dramatic you want your slide show to be by allowing words and bullet points to zoom in from the top or bottom of the screen and sounds and music to generate from a point highlighted on the screen. You will even be able to write directly on your slide show screen as you are presenting so you can add emphasis to a particular point.

When your show is over, PowerPoint will store the presentation for future use and for you to insert into Word as part of the monthly report information you provide management. See Chapter 25 for a run-through of your designer's capabilities.

Schedule+—The Personal Information Manager

More and more responsibilities are being heaped on our personal and business shoulders. Keeping appointments and to-do tasks straight has become a full-time job, one for which we need some sort of software tool. In walks Schedule+ for Windows 95, a very different entity than it was in the Windows for Workgroups software program. Here in Windows 95 you have a true personal information manager that can assist you with your daily, weekly, and monthly scheduling of appointments and tasks. Also acting as a business contact manager, Schedule+ lets you track address and other information about business and personal contacts (date of birth, last meeting date, whether follow-up is needed, and so on).

With Schedule+ working to keep you organized, you can designate certain tasks as recurring and only list them once. Schedule+ will make sure that these tasks and appointments appear on your calendar for as long as you specify. Tasks are allowed different percentages of completion, and you can sort by any category in a to-do list or business contact list.

Schedule+ will let you print and type into monthly, weekly, and daily calendar grid layouts. You can then use print preview to see exactly how your calendars will look printed. Figure 1.5 shows appointments being entered directly into a monthly calendar grid.

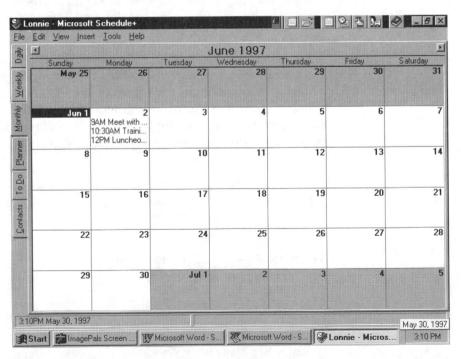

Figure 1.5   Schedule+ now has an on-screen monthly calendar in which you can directly enter your appointments and tasks.

As any true manager knows how to do, Schedule+ works with the other members of the team, and as you are writing a letter with Word, you can directly insert Schedule+ addresses from the business-contact section into the letter you are creating. Schedule+ will even grab the information you have been storing in the Windows Card File and make these entries part of your business contact list. See Chapter 32 to make an appointment with your personal information manager, Schedule+.

Access—The Data Master

Access rounds out the Office suite by providing powerful and simple-to-use data-management tools. With Access you can enter client information, track legal cases, design a mailing list, register participants for events and training—any tasks that involve asking questions and getting answers will be handled by Access. Aligned with its other Office partners, Access can display a form for data entry in Excel, mail-merge customer names using Word, print catalogs and directories using Word's beautiful word-processing features, embed a PowerPoint slide in a field, and take information from Schedule+. Designed so anyone can create categories, forms, questions, and reports for their data, Access sits in the corner office of the suite.

WordMail—The Mail Thing

Political correctness dictates that gender-specific nouns be as few as possible in a book geared toward a broad audience of women and men. Instead of having a Mail man or Mail woman or even a Mail person, you have in Windows 95 a Mail thing: WordMail.

WordMail allows you to compose and edit your mail messages using the full power of Word's various word-processing features. Microsoft Exchange will send your messages through the network to other users.

Turn to Chapter 47 to see how you can use the WordMail system within the Office suite of products and within Windows 95. Word, Excel, PowerPoint, and Schedule+ can all send their documents through the mail system to other users. Word will allow you to route the same document through a series of users so corrections and edits can be done.

Windows 95

Before you sit down with each of the Office program members, you should understand the layout of the offices, meaning the underlying environment: Windows 95. This new operating system offers functionality that lets the Office members work seamlessly with each other. Think of fancier intercom systems and internetworking capability as being like some of the things Windows 95 supplies to the Office members.

You also need to understand this innovative, productivity-enhancing technology so you can better direct the members of the Office team to use the new "toys" of Windows 95 to their advantage: link data together, grab back deleted information, receive information from the Internet, route mail around the office, and much more.

The next chapter gives you a tour of the environment before you actually meet the individual Office team members. Get familiar with your new and enhanced environment first; then you can make the most of your team of support members.

Chapter 2

Your Office Environment: An Overview of Windows 95

FEATURING

N ew and experienced users alike will need to take a minute and examine their cyber-office environment when beginning to use Microsoft Office for Windows 95. The software packages included with Office are some of the first applications written to take advantage of Windows 95, Microsoft's new version of its popular Windows operating system. New users who are working with computers for the first time will need to understand the basics of working within a Windows environment. Seasoned users will need to rethink how they perform certain functions that have become second nature.

New Users   If you are new to computers, take a deep breath and … relax. Microsoft has designed an operating system that is much easier to learn than its predecessors. Once pointed in the right direction, and made aware of a few of the core navigating tools (which allow you to move from program to program and to manage your files), you will be able to perform a multitude of business tasks more easily than you ever could before.

Users Familiar with Windows 3.x   Users already familiar with Windows will have a slightly different experience when switching to Windows 95. When taking Windows 95 out for a spin for the first time, you will probably experience a fair amount of frustration, as it's only natural to approach Windows 95 as if it were Windows 3.1, and of course there are differences. For most people, though, the initial frustration turns into familiarity and, eventually, after a few hours of use, an enthusiastic recognition of the benefits that the changes bring. In fact, after reaching a level of comfort with the interface, you will probably find you want to burrow deeper into the offerings of Windows 95 to discover what other enhancements have been made.

What Is Windows 95?

Windows 95 at the most simplistic level is a new version of the Windows operating system. At the highest level, it is a complete retooling of not only Windows' user interface and feature set but also its internal architecture. Windows 95 provides the ability to run 32-bit applications that take advantage of today's newer hardware technologies while also maintaining backward compatibility with "legacy" (existing Windows-compatible) hardware and existing DOS and Windows software.

Starting from the Beginning

NOTE   To avoid getting into too much technical information in these introductory chapters, we must assume that you already have Windows 95 installed on your machine. This helps to keep the order of the topics on track, as this chapter offers only an introduction to using Windows 95 as it applies to Microsoft Office. For your convenience, we have placed installation instructions for Office 95 in an appendix at the back of the book.

When your system boots up for the first time with Windows 95, you find yourself facing *the desktop*, where you will be spending quite a bit of time. Depending on which options you chose during installation, you will see some or all of the objects in Figure 2.1, which are described in Table 2.1.

Figure 2.1   The Windows 95 desktop

Icon	Purpose
My Computer	Provides direct access to all of your local drives, printers, Control Panel and the Dial-Up Networking utility
Network Neighborhood	Access to shared resources on your machine and computers on your LAN and WAN
Recycle Bin	Provides you with drag-and-drop deletion of files from folders or your desktop, and provides a second chance to recover files deleted from your hard drive
Inbox	Universal in-box for all of your mail sources including faxes, Microsoft Mail and Exchange, and others
Start	Provides single-click access to all of the options you need to manipulate Windows applications and tools
Taskbar	Displays all open applications and windows

Table 2.1 **Windows 95 Desktop Icons**

Start Button and Taskbar

By default, the Taskbar is on the bottom of the screen, with the Start button on the left-hand side. The Taskbar can, if you desire, be placed on the top or either side of the screen. The Start button and the Taskbar work together to make managing your applications and open windows easier. Figure 2.2 shows the main options you receive when you click on the Start button.

Program Submenu

Moving your mouse pointer over the Programs item on the Start menu will pop up another menu. The function of this submenu is to organize your programs. If you're familiar with earlier versions of Windows this will look like a listing of *program groups*. In fact, if you installed Windows 95 over a previous version of Windows, most of your old program groups will now appear in this list. Once you have Microsoft Office installed,

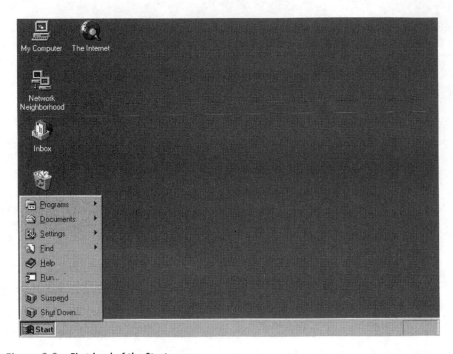

Figure 2.2   **First level of the Start menu**

you will be able to access all of your programs from the Program submenu of the Start-button menu, much as they are being accessed in Figure 2.3.

Because you can very easily open programs and files on top of other programs on files on the desktop, thus obscuring your view of what you have running, Windows 95 keeps track of all your open windows and lists them on the Taskbar. Even if an application window is minimized on the desktop, it can still be accessed from the Taskbar. The benefit of the Taskbar is that when you have multiple applications open at the same time you can see all of them listed in the foreground, whether or not they are hidden by another window. By clicking on an application's window on the Taskbar you can bring that application to the front of the other windows, and restore it if it was minimized. This is a pleasant change for experienced users who have had to cope with windows being "lost" behind other windows and not being sure what applications were open. In Windows 3.1, in order to see a list of currently running programs, you would have to press Ctrl and Esc at the same time to bring up the Task List, which had a functionality similar to the Windows 95 Taskbar. The

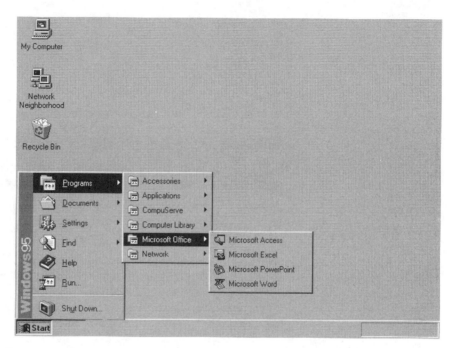

Figure 2.3   *You have quick access to Microsoft Office programs from the Start button.*

problem with the Task List was that the vast majority of users never knew that it existed, because it was not as intuitive and accessible.

The more windows you open, the more items that will be listed on the Taskbar. If you find that you are having more than five windows open at a time, you can increase the size of the Taskbar to allow for multiple lines of open items.

You increase the height of the Taskbar by placing the mouse pointer over its top border, at which point the pointer turns into a double-headed sizing arrow. Then click and hold your primary mouse button (usually the left one) and drag up as illustrated in Figure 2.4.

TIP   If you click your right mouse button on the Taskbar and select Properties from the menu that pops up, you can access the properties of the Taskbar. From here, you can check off Auto Hide on the Taskbar options tab so that the Taskbar disappears when your mouse pointer is not within its area. By selecting this option, you will provide yourself more screen real estate while working within your applications.

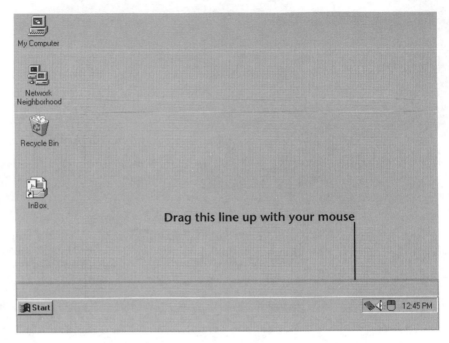

Figure 2.4 *Increasing the size of your Taskbar with the mouse to allow for multiple lines*

Document Submenu

The Documents option of the Start-button menu makes available the last 15 documents that you had open in any application (Figure 2.5). The documents are listed alphabetically, not by use, and will be listed whether you open them from within an application or from the folder where they are stored. If the list fills with irrelevant documents that you know that you will not want to access, you can clear the list by right-clicking on the Taskbar to bring up the Taskbar Properties window and then clicking on the Clear button in the Documents Menu section (Figure 2.6—if the tab page named Start Menu Programs isn't open in the properties window, click on its tab to display it).

Settings Submenu

The Settings option of the Start menu gives you access to the Control Panel, your printers, and the Properties window for the Taskbar. The Control Panel, seen in Figure 2.7, is where you can do most of your customizing of your Windows environment. It contains a great many more options than were available in the Control Panel in earlier versions

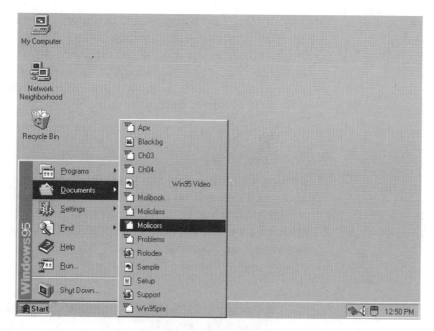

Figure 2.5   Most-recently-used-document list, accessed from the Start button

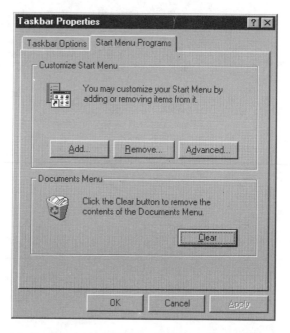

Figure 2.6   You can clear the documents list by clicking on Clear in this window, available by
right-clicking on the Taskbar.

of Windows. The Printers option shows you your installed printers and the Add Printer Wizard, which assists you in installing new printers. Double-clicking on any of the installed printers will open a window similar to Figure 2.8, showing the current print jobs sent to the printer and a number of menu options available to manipulate the printer and its jobs. The printer windows are the Windows 95 equivalent to the Print Manager in Windows 3.1.

Find Submenu

Windows 95 provides a universal find option for all of your applications. When you select Find on the Start-button menu, you can use it to find a file or folder located on your computer, on a computer on your network, or in areas of interest on *the Microsoft Network*. (The Microsoft Network is an online service that Microsoft provides access to through an interface bundled with Windows 95.)

Figure 2.7   Start ➤ Settings brings up the Control Panel.

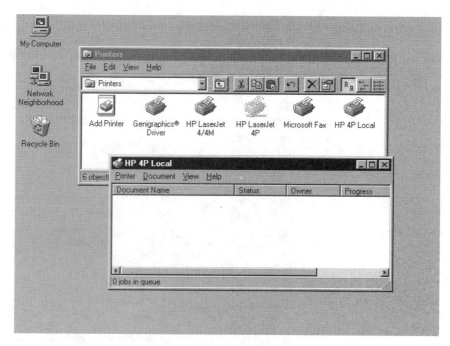

Figure 2.8 A printer window opened by double-clicking on an installed printer in the printer window

The file system in Windows 95 is broken down into *folders* and files. For those already familiar with Windows 3.1 or DOS, folders translate into what you previously knew as *directories*. Those new to computers should consider folders as places to store files, as well as other folders. Folders are used to group files and folders that are used together. For instance, the files used to run your Microsoft Office programs are stored in individual program folders, which are themselves stored in one main folder labeled Microsoft Office or Msoffice (or Office95, depending on if you kept a previous version of Office on your machine when Office was installed). This is illustrated in Figures 2.9 through 2.11.

Selecting files and folders from the Find submenu is how you can easily search for files located on local or network drives. Within the Find window (Figure 2.12) you can search for a file by providing anything from part of the file name to some of the text that you are looking for.

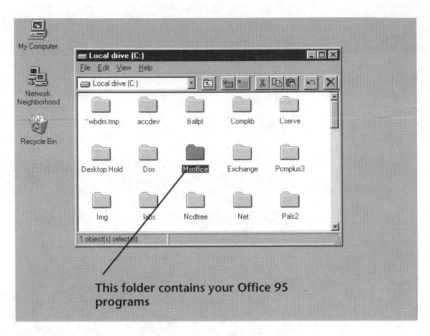

Figure 2.9   Msoffice, the Microsoft Office main folder

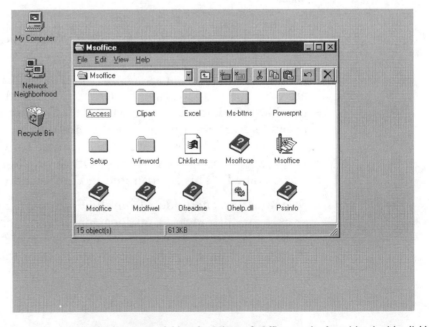

Figure 2.10   Individual program folders for Microsoft Office can be found by double-clicking on the Msoffice folder.

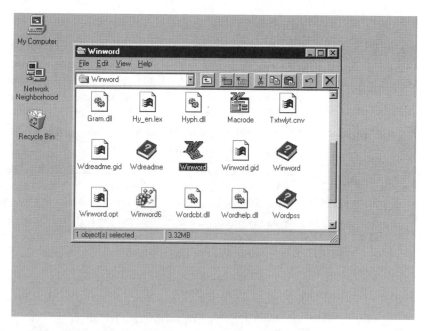

Figure 2.11   *Some of the files and folders found in the Winword folder*

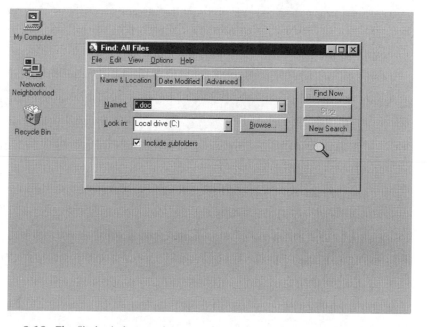

Figure 2.12   *The Find window used to search for files and folders that might meet certain specifications*

Quick Viewing a File

It is frequently the case when you are looking for files that you do not necessarily know which file contains the information you need. For this reason, looking for and finding the *right* file can be a long and arduous task if you need to continually open and close files to track down your information. In an effort to provide a more efficient search pattern, Windows 95 has a multipurpose *file viewer* called **Quick View** that displays the data content of any application file your find operation turns up.

 NOTE   Quick View is not part of the "recommended installation" when you first install Windows 95 onto your system, so depending on how Windows was installed, you might or might not see Quick View when you right-click on a file name. Go to Start ➤ Settings and check out the Add/Remove Programs item in the Control Panel to install Quick View.

If a find operation results in, say, five files that might or might not contain what you're looking for, you can use Quick View to take a peek at each of the files without having to start the application that created it. (Depending on your machine and its current resources, starting an application can take a few seconds; Quick View is instantaneous.) If you click your right mouse button on any of the files returned, you will get a menu of actions to perform, including the option to open the file in Quick View, like the example in Figure 2.13.

Once you have a file open in Quick View, you can view it from a number of levels of Zoom (magnification). In Figure 2.14 you can see a file that was created in Excel being viewed with Quick View.

If the file is the one you are looking for, you can open it in the application that created it by clicking the Open File for Editing button of the Quick View toolbar.

Viewing your files with Quick View is not an option limited to use while performing a find operation. If you right-click on a file name, whether it is in Find, the Desktop, or another system navigating option (like My Computer, Network Neighborhood, or Windows Explorer, all discussed later in this chapter), you will have the option to Quick View your file.

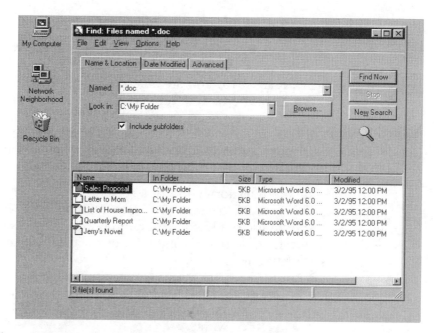

Figure 2.13 *Successful find operation with five file possibilities.*

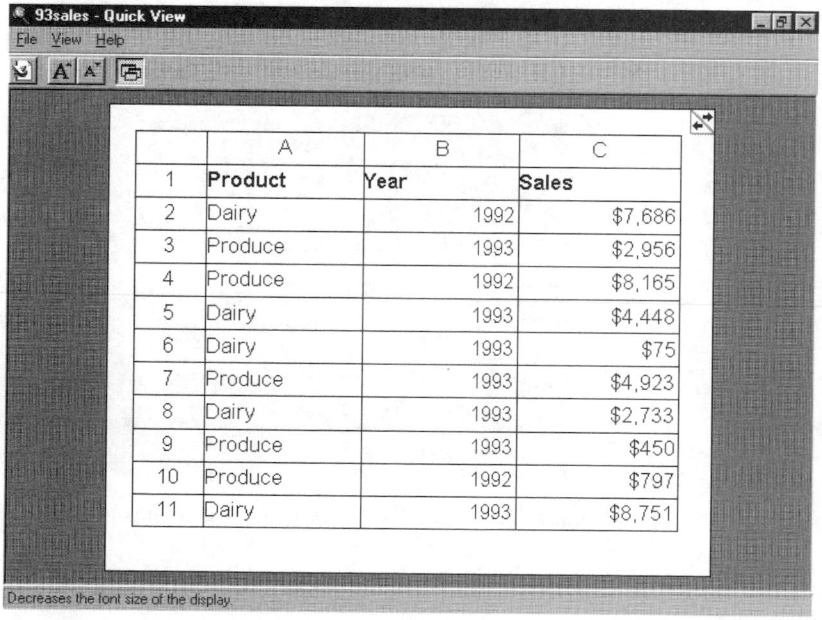

	A	B	C
1	**Product**	Year	Sales
2	Dairy	1992	$7,686
3	Produce	1993	$2,956
4	Produce	1992	$8,165
5	Dairy	1993	$4,448
6	Dairy	1993	$75
7	Produce	1993	$4,923
8	Dairy	1993	$2,733
9	Produce	1993	$450
10	Produce	1992	$797
11	Dairy	1993	$8,751

Decreases the font size of the display.

Figure 2.14 *An Excel file being viewed with Quick View*

Help Option

You can find answers to your questions about Windows 95 by selecting Help on the Start-button menu, which opens the Help window shown in Figure 2.15. You are able to search for help about Windows 95 by typing in the desired topic in the text box at the top of the Index tab page. As you type your topic, the help index will try to zero in on your help topic. If it does not come up with what you are searching for, try typing another combination of words under which your topic could be listed.

If your questions concern a specific application that you are using with Windows 95 (for example, Microsoft Office, or Word, or Excel, etc.), you should use the Help item found on the menu bar for the application in question, or by pressing F1 from within that application for context-sensitive help.

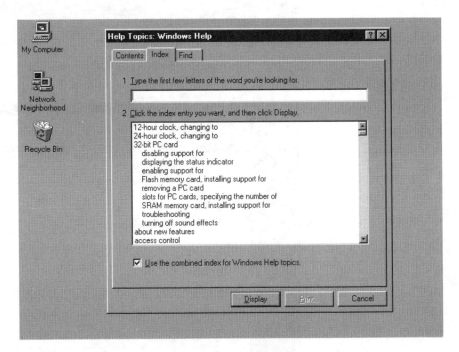

Figure 2.15   Windows 95 Help, accessed from Help on the Start-button menu

Run

The Run option on the Start menu is generally an option for the more experienced user. Selecting Run brings up the Run window where you can type the name of a file or folder that you wish to open, as shown in Figure 2.16.

If you don't know the entire *path* of folders within which the file or folder can be found, you can click on the Browse button within this window to find what you're looking for. Although this is generally not the quickest way to open a document or run a program, sometimes it simply seems more direct than opening a sequence of folders to get to the one you need.

Shut Down

You should "shut down" Windows 95 before you turn your machine off or before you change certain aspects of your "presence" on the system—for example, before you log on to your network with a different user name. Believe it or not, to shut down, you go to the Start button. (Part of Microsoft's idea of what users would find intuitive, no doubt.) Figure 2.17 displays the options presented when you choose Start ➤ Shut Down.

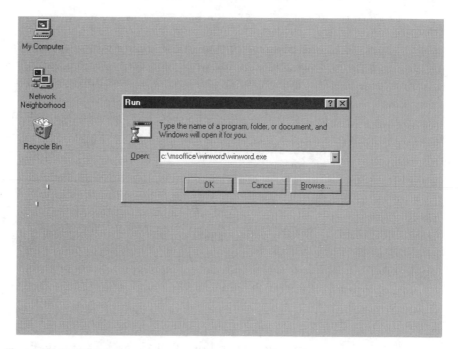

Figure 2.16 Run Window

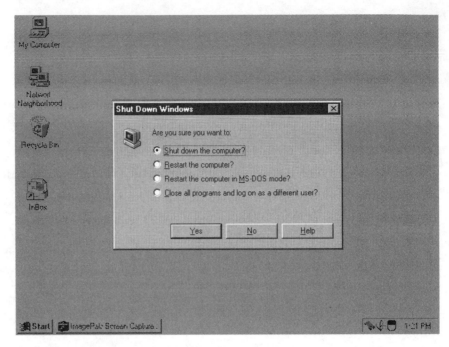

Figure 2.17   **The options in the Shut Down window**

The primary option in the dialog window is to *Shut down the computer*. This option is for when you are simply finished using the machine for the day, or for occasions when Windows has advised you to shut down and reboot. It may take a few seconds for Windows to carry out the shutdown command; once your computer shuts down, Windows will tell you when it is safe to turn your machine off (i.e., to actually flick the power switch on your computer) or reboot (by pressing Ctrl+Alt+Delete at the same time).

The other options are for more specialized circumstances. For example, the second option, *Restart the computer*, will close all programs, clear everything from memory, and start the computer in Windows mode. This may be necessary if the system seems to become unstable for any reason or if you change certain system settings.

The third option is to *Restart the computer in MS-DOS mode*. Experienced users who are coming from the age of DOS may need to have the comfort of its command prompt to perform certain operations. Everything *most* users need to do, however, should be able to be done through windows, including the running of DOS sessions in either a Window or full screen.

Finally, if you are in a network environment, you have the option to close all open applications and log on as a different user. This will be a common operation if you're using a machine that is being shared by a number of people in a network environment where login names and passwords are essential for restricting access to network resources.

Window Appearance

Among its changes to the operating system, Windows 95 includes a minor modification to its basic window structure. New users will simply accept it as "This is a window"; experienced users will notice some definite changes—not major ones, but changes nonetheless. In either case, an identification of the parts will be helpful.

All application windows have the same basic components. Figure 2.18 and Table 2.2 use a window in Word as an example.

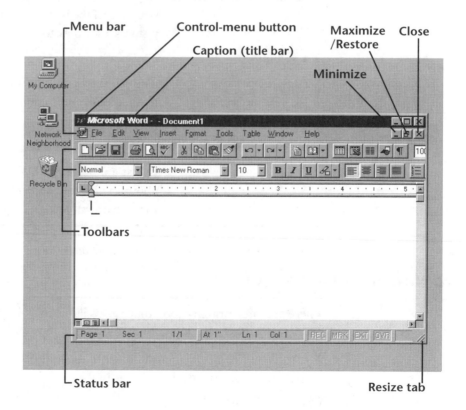

Figure 2.18   A window in Word

Component	Purpose
Control-menu button	This button is used to open the window's Control menu, with which you can size, move, or close the window
Caption	The caption, also known as the *title bar*, displays the application name and the name of the active document if there is one
Menu bar	Almost all of an application's functionality can be accessed through its menu bar. To display a menu, click on its name on the menu bar.
Minimize button	Minimizes your window to the Taskbar
Maximize/Restore button	Expands a window so that it takes up the entire screen, or if the window is already maximized, restores a window to its previous dimensions
Close button	Closes a window
Toolbars	The buttons on toolbars provide quick access to an application's commands
Resize tab	Clicking and dragging this corner will allow you to stretch or shrink the size of a window.
Status bar	(Most applications) Displays information about the current state of your application and the document you have open

Table 2.2   The Components of a Window in Windows 95

Taking a Look Around

There are three primary tools that are available to assist you in finding the files, folders, and other resources on your local machine and network. These are:

▶ My Computer

▶ Network Neighborhood

▶ Windows Explorer

My Computer, which is located on your desktop, is provided to give you easy access to your *local resources* (the ones available on your machine).

Network Neighborhood, which is installed only if your machine is used in a networking environment, is similar in function to My Computer except it is able to view the printers and directories shared by the owners of computers available to you through your *local area network* (LAN), regardless of network provider (e.g., Windows NT Server or Novell Netware).

The Windows Explorer, which is available from the Programs submenu of the Start-button menu, combines the features of My Computer and Network Neighborhood by providing you with an outline view of all of your resources, local and over the network. Explorer can be considered an enhancement to and replacement of the File Manager found in earlier versions of Windows.

My Computer

My computer will allow you to look at the resources available to you on your local machine. If you have network drives mapped as local drives, they will also show up here. Figure 2.19 shows what a common top-level window of My Computer may display.

The top level contains all of your lettered drives, local or networked, a folder for access to the Control Panel, a folder for access to your printers, and a Dial-Up Networking folder containing dial-up (modem) connections, if you installed this option at the time of setup.

Double-clicking on a drive in the top level of My Computer will open another window containing the main folders on the selected drive. Figure 2.20 shows the top level of the My Computer window and the window showing the available folders of a local drive.

Double-clicking on the folders in the drive window will continue to "drill down" into the local drive until there are no more folders left in the current folder or you find the file you need.

Double-clicking on either the Control Panel folder or the Printers folder in the My Computer window will let you manipulate the settings for your computer or printer the same way that you would if you were accessing them from the Start menu.

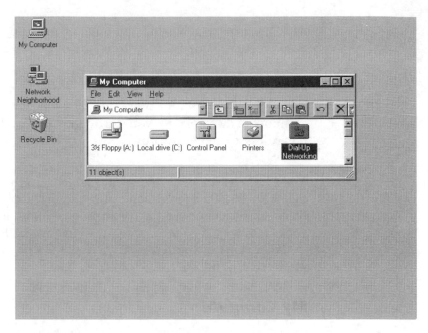

Figure 2.19   **My Computer (opening window)**

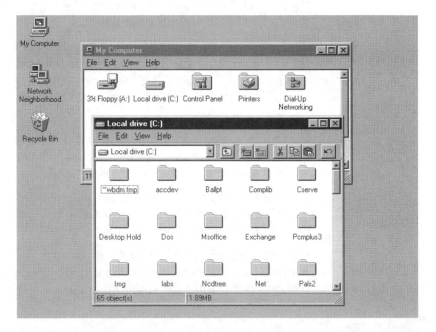

Figure 2.20   *Top-level window of My Computer and a Local Drive window with available folders*

Make Keeping Track of Open Windows Easy!

The process of drilling down into folders of a drive tends to yield a lot of open windows, which can become increasingly difficult to keep track of. Here are a couple of techniques to minimize the confusion.

First, remember you don't have to go looking for windows all over the desktop. Every window that is open will be listed on the Taskbar; you can simply click on the window you want on the Taskbar to bring it to the front of all of the other windows.

Second, if you select View ➤ Options from the My Computer menu bar, you can choose to have your drilling down into folders and other resources done through a *single window*—thereby eliminating the overcrowding of your desktop with windows you are only opening so you can get to another window. If you select this option, you can easily get back to the windows you opened on your way to the current one by using the Backspace key or the Up One Level button on the drive window's toolbar to backtrack through the windows one at a time.

Double-clicking on the Dial-Up Networking folder will open a window with saved settings for network connections that you make with your modem, and a Make A New Connection Wizard that will assist you in adding new dial-up network connections. Figure 2.21 illustrates the first step of the Make A New Connection Wizard.

My Computer may very well become your preferred method of accessing everything from folders and files to the Control Panel simply because of its convenient location on the desktop and its ability to provide direct access to many of the resources you will use on a regular basis.

Network Neighborhood

Network Neighborhood takes the abilities of My Computer and extends them one step further by providing you with the ability to view all of the computers in your workgroup or network, and see what drives or printers may be available for your use. The first window in Network Neighborhood is presented in Figure 2.22.

When you first open Network Neighborhood, a list of the computers within your workgroup are listed along with an Entire Network icon. If you double-click on one of the computers, any resources that computer shares with others in the workgroup, like drives, directories, or printers, will be listed. If you double-click on the Entire Network icon instead, all

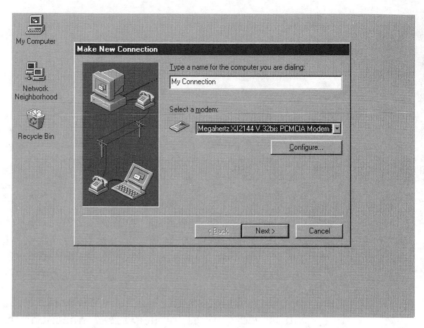

Figure 2.21   The first screen of the Make A New Connection Wizard

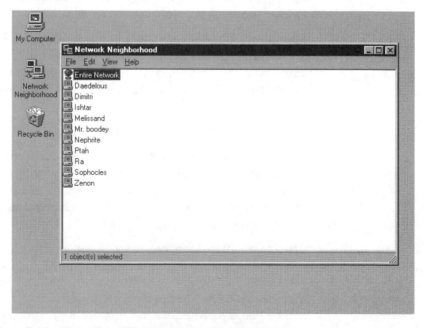

Figure 2.22   The opening window of Network Neighborhood

of the domains or workgroups on the entire network will be listed. Double-clicking on one of these items reveals the computers that can be accessed through that workgroup or domain; from there you can check any resources made available by those computers.

Windows Explorer

Windows Explorer may very well end up being a primary tool for you if you are an advanced user with needs to manipulate your resources at a deeper level than is provided by My Computer or Network Neighborhood alone. In addition to drive, folder, and file listings, Windows Explorer can display information such as:

▶ the current print jobs for available printers,

▶ identifying comments about other computers in the Network Neighborhood,

▶ descriptions of Control Panel tools,

▶ and the amount of space available on local and networked drives.

Whereas My Computer and Network Neighborhood provide you with viewing options from Large Icons (no detail) to Detail (extensive detail), Explorer provides a two-pane approach that permits you to investigate the detail of a section in the right pane while at the same time manipulating the outline view of the available resources in the left pane; Figure 2.23 shows this two-pane approach by showing detail information in the right pane about a Word folder while still providing the ability to manipulate the outline on the left. This approach, which in previous versions of Windows required multiple windows in File Manager, and which provided only some of the information now available with Explorer, is ideal for drag-and-drop copying from one location to another.

Recycle Bin

The Recycle Bin is where your files go when you delete them from your hard drive. You can access the bin to restore or "undelete" any files you inadvertently deleted. You can also drag and drop files onto the Recycle Bin for quick deleting.

The very name *Recycle* Bin suggests that when you delete files, they really do not get deleted. It's a safety feature, built in to protect you against the possibility of deleting something you shouldn't have. Files you have deleted are out of use, and might as well be nonexistent, but should you

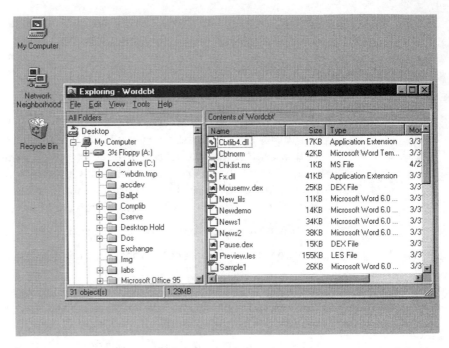

Figure 2.23   **Windows Explorer viewing files from one folder in the right pane while looking at the outline of available folders in the left pane**

decide you need to retrieve one of them from the bin, it will be there …, that is, until you *empty* the Recycle Bin, at which time the files are truly gone and cannot be recovered.

Of course, what this means is that deleted files in the Recycle Bin still take up disk space. You need to remember, then, to occasionally empty it. To empty your Recycle Bin, right-click on the bin icon and, from the shortcut menu that appears (Figure 2.24), select Empty Recycle Bin.

TIP   If you want to absolutely, positively delete something from your system and bypass the Recycle Bin altogether, select the file, then press Shift+Delete (i.e., hold down the Shift key and press Delete while you still have the Shift key depressed).

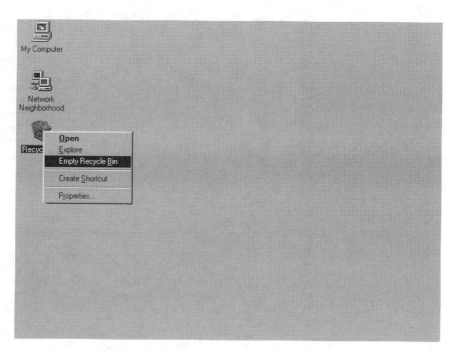

Figure 2.24   *Emptying the Recycle Bin*

Inbox

Windows 95 comes with Microsoft's new Exchange software that provides a universal in-box (called Inbox) for all of your e-mail sources, including your office e-mail, mail from the Internet, and mail from most online services, including Microsoft Network.

You can set up Inbox so that it can retrieve your mail when you are connected to your various mail sources. Figure 2.25 shows the Inbox Window. If you have had experience with Microsoft Mail, the basic layout of this window should look familiar. The layout of the window is similar to that of the Explorer: here you have folders, in this case mail folders, in the left pane, and the specific mail pieces contained in a folder are listed in the right pane.

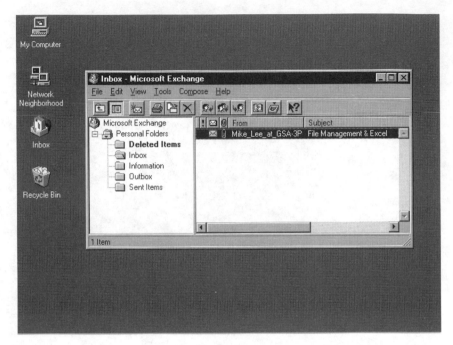

Figure 2.25   Use Microsoft Exchange Inbox to collect e-mail from a variety of sources.

From the "You Should Know This" Category...

ShortCuts

The icons that you will eventually arrange on your desktop in Windows 95 are fundamentally different from the icons that appeared in the Program Manager in earlier versions of Windows—and not just in appearance. The Windows 95 interface presents a "true" desktop. What this means is that when you click on an icon and delete it, the file(s) or programs that the icon represents *are* in fact deleted; they're not merely "de-iconized" (removed from the desktop) as was the case in Program Manager. You may not have even known that this was the way Program Manager considered icons, but if you did, knowing that Windows 95 considers them differently is a very important distinction to keep in mind.

NOTE In earlier versions of Windows, you couldn't delete files and pro-grams from Program Manager. You had to go to File Manager (or the long and complicated Find File option in Word), and select by name and directory the files to be deleted.

Because Windows 95 makes it so easy to delete files and programs merely by clicking on their icons, you may be reluctant to move them onto the desktop in the first place. Anticipating this concern, Windows 95 allows you to create "shortcut" icons, which work rather like the icons found in Program Manager, only better. For one thing, unlike the icons in Program Manager, shortcut icons *keep track* of the files they refer to. If you move a file that you have a shortcut pointing to, Windows 95 will attempt to find it in your system, so that the next time you use the shortcut, it will still open the file or folder that you intended. Previous versions of Windows could not keep track of such changes.

There are a number of ways to create a shortcut to a file in Windows 95. Figure 2.26 shows the most direct route: right-click on the file you want to create a shortcut for and, from the menu that appears, select Create Shortcut.

Once you create a shortcut icon, you can double-click on it to open the file or folder that it is attached to. You can also drag it to wherever it is convenient for you, whether it be another folder or your desktop. You will always be able to pick a shortcut icon out of a group of regular icons because it will be the one with a little arrow in the bottom left-hand corner.

TIP You can create a shortcut and drag it to your desired location at the same time by clicking and dragging the file or folder while holding both the Ctrl key and the Shift key.

Special Key Combinations

Table 2.3 lists some keyboard combinations that you may find useful. No matter how devoted you become to your mouse, using key combi-nations for some of your most frequent tasks will help improve your efficiency while working in Windows.

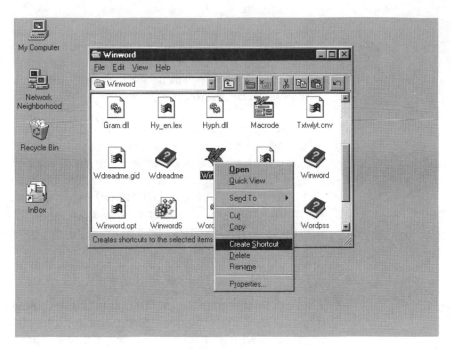

Figure 2.26   **Creating a shortcut by right-clicking on the original file.**

Key(s)	Purpose	Where Used
F1	Call up help for the specific situation you are in	Anywhere in Windows
Alt+F4	Close an application	Anywhere in Windows
Ctrl+Esc	Pop up Start menu	Anywhere in Windows
Alt+Tab	Switch to the last window that you were in	Anywhere in Windows
Shift+F10	View the Shortcut menu for the selected object	Anywhere in Windows
F2	Rename an object	Desktop or Windows Explorer

Table 2.3   **Special Key Combinations for Windows 95**

Key(s)	Purpose	Where Used
F3	Find a file or folder	Desktop or Windows Explorer
Alt+Enter	View object properties	Desktop or Windows Explorer
F5	Refresh (update) the view in a window	My Computer or Windows Explorer
Ctrl+Z	Undo file-management actions	My Computer or Windows Explorer
Backspace	View folder one level back	My Computer or Windows Explorer
Ctrl+Tab or Ctrl+Shift+Tab	Move to next tab in a dialog box	Dialog boxes

Table 2.3   **Special Key Combinations for Windows 95 (continued)**

Summary

You should now have a basic understanding of the workings of the Windows 95 desktop interface. Although you may have misgivings at first, as you continue to work within the Windows 95 environment you will become more and more comfortable. And as you become more comfortable, you will begin to customize the desktop, the way you perform basic functions, and the overall way you interact with your computer. The best feature of Windows 95 is that it is so customizable that no two people have to use it exactly alike.

Chapter 3

Microsoft Office's Integrated Tools

FEATURING

What makes Microsoft Office stand out the most from its peers is the level of integration between its individual applications. The integration is made possible through common interfaces, shared tools, the ability to link and embed data from one application into another, and the newest, perhaps the biggest, stride towards document integration, the Office Binder, which allows you to keep all of your Office documents for one project in a single file.

Taking a broad look at Microsoft Office will be the goal of this chapter. We will start with investigating the unique contributions of each product and then move the focus towards the features of Office that will allow you to marry these features to accomplish your document chores.

The Power of One

The integration of applications is understandably the primary area of interest among application users these days. Before you can talk about integration, however, you must know what there is to integrate. And with the applications contained within Office there is plenty to integrate. Word, Excel, PowerPoint, and Schedule+ are all valuable resources in their own right, providing the quality ingredients of integrated Office solutions.

Word

The most familiar application among the members of the Office suite is Word. With Word you can accomplish all of your basic word-processing duties and fulfill most of your desktop publishing needs. You will be using Word to generate all of your memos, letters, reports, and other text-intensive documents. Word's most valuable contribution to Office is its flexibility with text and its ability to incorporate data from the other Office applications in their original format to produce comprehensive documents.

Within a Word document, some specific tools you can take advantage of are:

▶ Built-in and custom templates that allow fast document creation based on boilerplate text and styles, Auto Text, macros, and toolbars stored with individual templates

▶ Master Document View that allows you to manage very large documents by incorporating smaller, "sub" documents into one primary "master" document

▶ The ability to insert fields that make your documents more dynamic by facilitating user input, system input for data (like the current date), and other special features that need to be updated regularly

▶ Large-Document management features, like the ability to easily create tables of contents, indexes, tables of authorities, tables of figures, and cross references

▶ Mail-Merge Helper that allows you to quickly create merge documents like mass mailings or mailing labels

▶ Easy table creation and formatting that includes Table AutoFormat, which allows you to focus on your data and let Word handle the formatting

▶ Automation through the means of macro creation with Word's powerful WordBasic programming language

▶ AutoCorrect and AutoFormat features that can catch many typographical errors automatically and use predefined shortcuts and typing patterns to quickly format your documents

Excel

Excel is the Office application that you will want to focus on when number crunching and analyzing raw data is a concern. While Excel can be classified as a spreadsheet program, it is misleading to limit Excel by such a definition. Excel can perform all of the general spreadsheet operations with extended functionality in the areas of data entry, data analyzing, and sheer capacity.

Excel is a perfect companion for Word and PowerPoint, letting them provide the presentation while Excel provides the numbers to back it all up. Some of the features of Excel that are used to provide the numbers to you and to the other Office applications are:

▶ Templates that you can use to standardize data entry files that may contain complex formulas

▶ Charting and mapping tools that allow you to graphically represent your data

▶ The ability to record or edit macros for repetitive tasks with the Visual Basic for Applications language

▶ The ability to quickly sort and filter lists of information

▶ Subtotaling and grouping features that give you the chance to see your data in a concise form

▶ Importing and exporting tools that help you upscale your data into Excel, or out of Excel and into Access or another database application

▶ Scenario tools like Goal Seek and Solver that assist in "What if..." calculations

▶ The Pivot Table Wizard, which creates interactive tables that summarize your data every way possible

PowerPoint

When it comes time to make a presentation, whether it is to prospective clients or your own Board of Directors, PowerPoint is the application that you will want to have on your side. With PowerPoint, you will be able to get your point across whether it is through a slide show of your presentation on the computer or by using printed overhead slides. PowerPoint will take a combination of the results of your efforts in Word and Excel and add some of its splashy effects to really get your point across. Features that provide PowerPoint with its presentation power include:

▶ AutoContent Wizards to walk you through the development of common presentations

▶ Templates with over 36 fully designed text and graphical slide formats

▶ AutoLayouts, which provide standardized slide formats, reducing the time to build most standard slides

▶ Extensive Clip Art library with an Auto Launch button from the standard toolbar

▶ The ability to add multimedia sound and video to your presentations

▶ Animation effects for true incremental display of feature graphics

▶ Meeting Minder feature that allows users to annotate presentations during group meetings with action items or minutes of the meeting

▶ The ability to create and insert organizational charts into your presentations with Microsoft Organization Chart

Schedule+

A welcome new member to the Office suite is Schedule+. Previously included with Windows for WorkGroups, the newest version of Schedule+ included with Office brings true contact management functionality to Office. Schedule+ now not only allows you to schedule your time, it also facilitates the management of both your personal and business contacts. With the inclusion of Schedule+ in Office, Microsoft is recognizing the need to include the information that we store about our contacts with the software we use to be productive. The newest integration in Office will make itself most evident in Word where you will find the ability to insert names stored with Schedule+ into your documents. Some of the features in Schedule+ that will assist you in time and contact management include:

▶ The ability to record tasks, appointments, projects, and events

▶ Onscreen daily, weekly, monthly, yearly, and planner views of your schedule

▶ The ability to print your schedule in many formats, including popular planner formats

▶ Store your contact information, from name and address to multiple phone numbers, as well as birthdays and anniversaries

▶ Allow others on the network to have various levels of viewing rights of your schedule

▶ Schedule meetings with others using the Meeting Wizard, which finds available time for all participants

The Common Threads That Bind

One of the barriers that many users face when working with multiple software packages is having to remember how each separate system functions. Which key combinations work in *this* application? Where are the font commands on *this* menu bar? And so on. With Microsoft Office, this barrier to productive computing is reduced, by centering each of the applications around a core of common user interfaces. Also available to make computing easier in the Office are tools that are common across all of the applications. Having these tools available in all of the applications provides a familiarity that is conducive to faster learning.

Menu Bars

Probably the most noticeable similarity between the Office applications is the common menu bar. The menu bars, as seen in Figure 3.1, are identical in Word, Excel, and PowerPoint, with the exception of only one menu item that is different in each; and even that item appears in the same place on all of the menu bars. (Schedule+ also has the common menu bar; it just has fewer menu items due to the simple fact that it has less functionality.)

Shared Tools

If the words that you are typing are not common words, or are words that are particular to your field of study, chances are that they will not be stored in the dictionaries that come with your applications. You can add the words during a spell check to the dictionaries of the individual applications. Without Office, however, if you add the word to one application, you will still need to add it to the other applications that you use. Microsoft has pulled the Office applications together in this area as well.

The Office applications all share the same spell-check engine and dictionaries. If you add a word in one application, that word will be recognized in all of your Office applications. In addition, the AutoCorrect feature, which was previously available only in Word, is now a tool in Word, Excel, and PowerPoint. AutoCorrect automatically corrects common spelling errors, both built-in and those that you specify, and allows

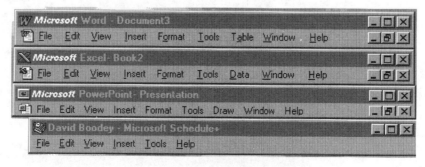

Figure 3.1 *Common menu bars available in the Office applications*

you to use shorthand combinations that you can define yourself to quickly insert common sections of text or special characters. To get an idea of the shared spelling checker and AutoCorrect, follow these steps:

1. Launch Excel from the Start button.

2. In cell A1 type **Wunderbar**.

3. Run the Spell Checker by pressing F7. If you are prompted to decide if the spell check should start at the beginning of the document, click on Yes.

4. The Spell Checker will not recognize Wunderbar as a word. Choose Cancel in the Spelling dialog box, as seen in Figure 3.2.

5. Close Excel and launch Word from the Start button.

6. In the blank document opened with Word, type **Wunderbar**.

7. Press F7 to spell-check the document.

8. When Word prompts you to make a decision about Wunderbar, click on the Add button.

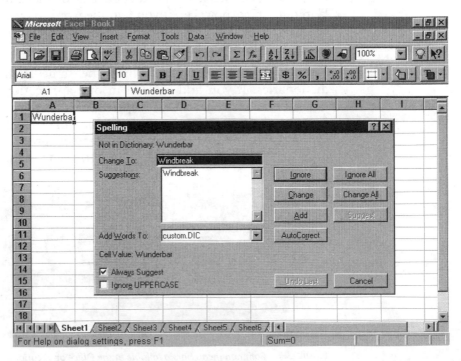

Figure 3.2   Excel spell-checking the word Wunderbar

9. After the spell check is finished, on a new line type **(C)**. AutoCorrect will replace the characters with a copyright symbol.

10. Your Word screen should look like Figure 3.3

11. Close Word, and don't save the changes.

12. Launch Excel.

13. In cell A1 type **Wunderbar** again. Spell-check the workbook by pressing F7, and notice that because you added the word in the spelling dictionary in Word (step 8), Excel now also recognizes the word.

14. In cell A2 try the AutoCorrect shortcut of step 9; that is, type **(C)**. Notice that Excel also has AutoCorrect: the (C) is automatically changed to a copyright symbol. (Figure 3.4)

15. In Excel, select Tools ➤ AutoCorrect from the menu bar.

16. In the AutoCorrect dialog box type **g!** in the Replace text box and **!!!GREAT!!!** in the With text box, as in Figure 3.5.

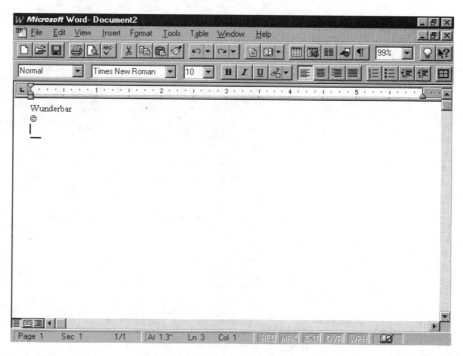

Figure 3.3   *Word screen with Wunderbar and a copyright symbol created with AutoCorrect*

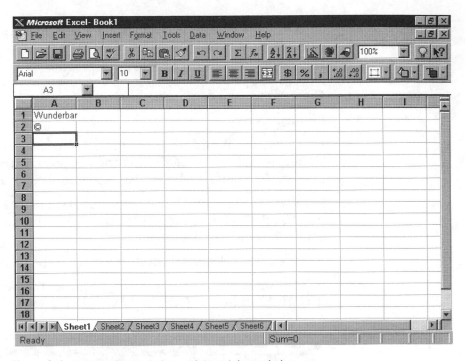

Figure 3.4   Excel with Wunderbar and Copyright symbol

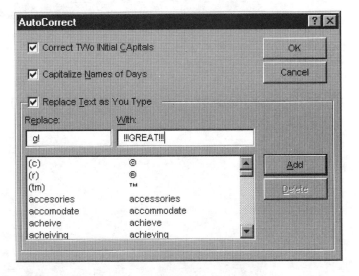

Figure 3.5   Adding an AutoCorrect entry in Excel

17. Click on the Add button and then close Excel; don't worry about saving any of the changes.

18. Open PowerPoint and get to a section of a slide where you can enter text.

19. Type **g** with an **!** after it.

20. Figure 3.6 shows the result. The custom AutoCorrect item assigned in Excel (step 16: the g! changing to !!!GREAT!!!) is available in Power-Point.

The above exercise is a good simple sampling of how the shared tools of Office work together. It is the cooperation of features like these that help make your efforts much more productive and efficient.

Answer Wizard and Online Help

Another feature that is available in all of your applications is a big advance in online assistance. This advance is the Answer Wizard, which

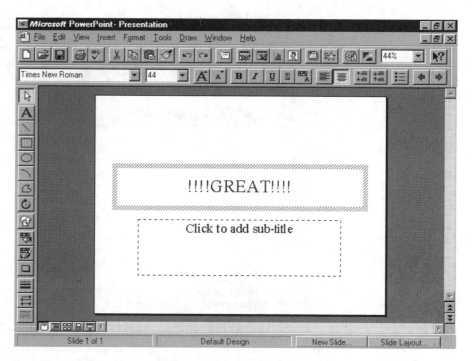

Figure 3.6   !!!GREAT!!! quickly inserted into PowerPoint with AutoCorrect

is launched from the Help menu of whatever application you are in. Open Word and select Help ➤ Answer Wizard from the menu bar. You will see the Answer Wizard window shown in Figure 3.7.

The Answer Wizard allows you to request help about the features of a product in your own words. For instance, you can ask "How do I apply an underline to text?" and the Answer Wizard will come up with three categories of help.

The first category of help is the *How Do I* section which lists possible answers to your question. If you choose one of the items in this category, the Answer Wizard will show you how to do the selected item. To try this, run Answer Wizard, type the question "How do I apply an underline to text", click on the Search button, and double-click on the first item under the How Do I section. (You don't need to type the quotation marks around the question. For that matter, you don't need to type the question mark at the end, either.) Notice how the Answer Wizard assists you in applying underlines in your document.

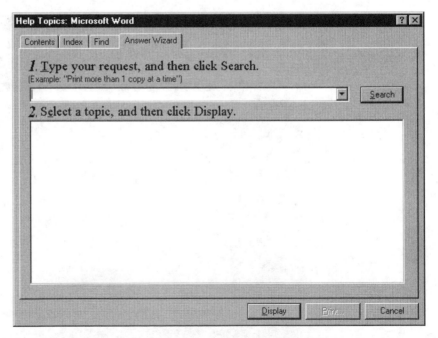

Figure 3.7   *Answer Wizard is available in all of your Office applications.*

The second category is the *Tell Me About* section. The items listed under this category provide you with more of an overview explanation of the areas that the Answer Wizard thinks that you are asking about. An example of this can be seen if, after asking the Answer Wizard the same question we asked above, you chose an item under the Tell Me About section, for example, "Tell Me About Character Formatting." An interactive information screen like the one in Figure 3.8 would open, and you could click on the various pieces of help and information to receive more specific help.

Finally, all of your Answer Wizard questions will come with a Programming and Language Reference category. Under this category are lists of items that direct you to key statements or functions that you can use in WordBasic to automate tasks. The screen in Figure 3.9 shows you information about the Underline statement and function.

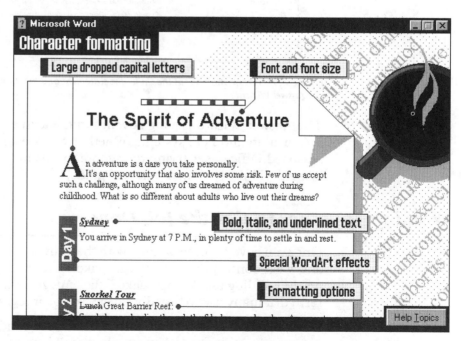

Figure 3.8   A "Tell Me About" information screen on the topic of character formatting

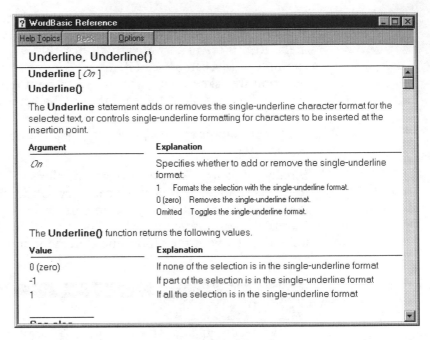

Figure 3.9 *Information about the Underline statement and function, reached by going through the Answer Wizard*

The Answer Wizard is a big advance in the features available for online information and help systems. Whether you are a new user or simply a seasoned Office user trying to migrate to this new version, the Answer Wizard will prove to be a valuable guide.

Working Together to Get the Job Done

Once you have become familiar with the individual components of Office and what contributions they can make to your projects, you can focus on the building blocks that make Office integration possible. OLE is the term that many use to broadly categorize the integration of applications.

OLE, which originally stood for Object Linking and Embedding, is now an umbrella term used when people are talking not just about the linking and embedding of objects from one application into another, but also about the ability to programmatically automate and manipulate those objects.

Because the terminology of OLE can quickly become an overwhelming onslaught of information, we want to take the rest of this chapter to pick apart the pieces of OLE and spend time with each one to make it easier to understand the whole.

Objects

At the center of OLE are *objects*. What are objects? Well, you can say that objects are things that have certain characteristics, like size and color, that are created in one program but can be manipulated by other applications. Objects that you may be familiar with are Excel workbooks, Excel charts, Word documents, PowerPoint slides, WordArt, and Paintbrush pictures. There is a quick way that you can get a more comprehensive, though far from complete, list of objects you can use within your Office applications.

1. Launch Word.

2. Select Insert ➤ Object from the menu bar.

3. On the Create New tab page, scroll through the list of objects, which you can see in Figure 3.10. (When you've gotten a feel for the number and variety of objects available, click on Cancel.)

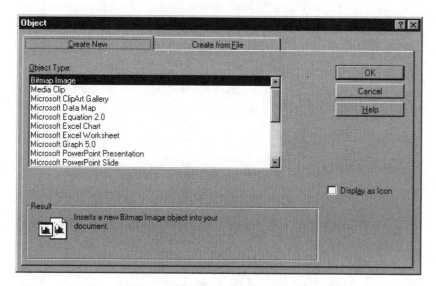

Figure 3.10 *The Create New tab page, available from the Insert ➤ Object menu option*

The list of objects on the Create New tab page is an ever growing list. It expands as you add applications to your computer. Using the Insert ➤ Object menu item is not the only way to get application objects from their native application into another application (say, for example, an Excel chart into a Word document). You can simply make use of the Windows *Clipboard*. By using variations of the Edit ➤ Paste Special command, you can achieve the next part of OLE, Linking and embedding.

Linking

Linking is one method of placing an object from one application into another. What sets linking apart from embedding, and what you should immediately think of when you hear the word, is that *live data from the original application is being used*. For example, you may have numbers in Excel that you need to present in a Word document. You can copy those numbers from Excel and Paste Link them into a Word document. Since you linked the information (the numbers: the objects), when the numbers change in the original Excel workbook, they will be updated in the Word document as well. This quick exercise will show you the power of linking.

1. Launch Excel.

2. Put 100 into cell A1. Put 100 into cell A2. Place the formula =A1+A2 into cell A3.

3. Save the workbook as Excel Link Test with the worksheet looking like Figure 3.11.

4. Select the range A1 through A3, and select Edit ➤ Copy from the menu bar.

5. Launch Word.

6. Select Edit ➤ Paste Special from the Word menu bar.

7. In the Paste Special dialog box, select Paste Link and Microsoft Excel Worksheet Object so that the one on your screen looks like the one in Figure 3.12.

8. Click on OK to paste link the object, then switch to Excel by clicking on its button on the Taskbar.

9. Change the contents of cell A1 to **200**.

10. Switch back to Word. Figure 3.13 shows the changes updated in Word.

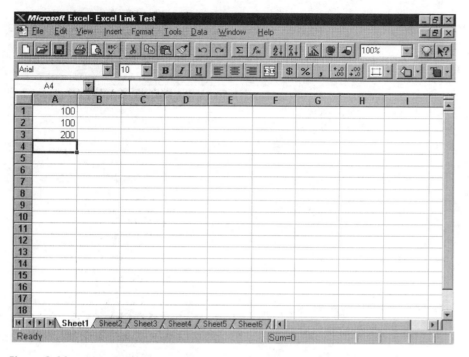

Figure 3.11 **Excel workbook with three cells containing information**

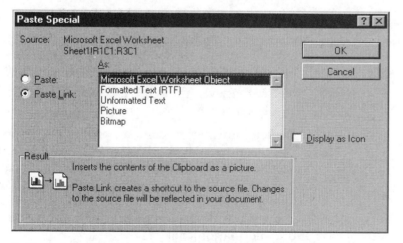

Figure 3.12 **Paste Special dialog box set to link an Excel worksheet object**

11. Save the document as **Word Link Test** and close Word.

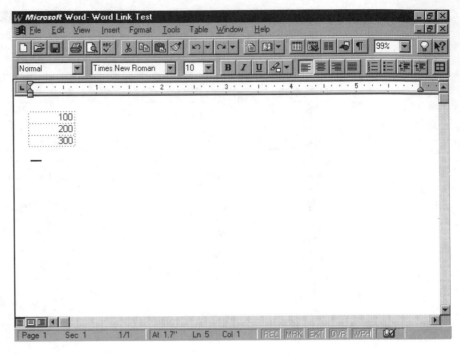

Figure 3.13   **Excel data linked into Word**

12. In Excel, change the value of cell A2 to **400**.

13. Save the workbook and close Excel.

14. Launch Word and open the Word Link Test file.

15. Notice that even though Word was closed when the changes were made and Excel is now closed, the information is still updated.

Linked information can be updated either manually or automatically. The default is for the link to be updated automatically. If you have a number of linked objects in your document, you may want to select Edit ➤ Links from the menu bar and change your links to manual (by highlighting the links and clicking the Manual Updating button), so that you will not be frequently interrupted by your links updating whenever the information changes.

The Print and General tab pages of the Options dialog box also have options that help you with linked data. The Print tab page has an option where you can Update Links just before printing. On the General tab page you can specify whether or not to update links when the file is opened.

When working with linked data, you can edit the linked object by double-clicking on the object. When you double-click on a linked object, the application that created that data will be opened, and the file that contains the data will also be opened. In the above example, if you double-clicked on the linked Excel data in Word, Excel would launch and the Excel Link Test file would open so that you could edit it.

WARNING   When working with linked data, be sure not to move the file where the linked data originated. When you link information, you are specifying a path to the file. If you move the file, the path is no longer valid. Unlike the shortcuts in Windows 95 that find the files they are pointing to even if they are moved, OLE does not facilitate file paths automatically being updated. If a linked document does in fact get moved, however, all is not lost. If you need to modify the path of a linked file, select Edit ➤ Links from the menu bar and click on the Change Source button to update the link.

Embedding

Embedding an object into a document is similar in process to linking an object. While the initial appearance of embedded and linked data is the same, the underlying data is quite different. When you embed an object, you are taking a copy of the original data from one application and placing it into another application. When you embed the object, you are able to edit the object with the original application's menu bar and toolbars. The biggest difference between linking and embedding is that there is *no connection to the original file* in embedding. If you make changes to the original file or to the embedded object, the other will not be affected. When you double-click on an embedded object, the menu and toolbars from the original application are brought into the application in which the object is embedded. Use the Excel Link Test file you created above with the steps below to see embedding in action.

1. Open the Excel Link Test file.
2. Select the range A1 through A3.
3. Select Edit ➤ Copy from the menu bar.
4. Launch Word.

5. Select Edit ➤ Paste Special from the menu bar.

6. In the Paste Special dialog box, modify the options so that Word is set to Paste (not Paste Link) a Microsoft Excel Worksheet Object, as in Figure 3.14, and then click on OK.

7. Save the Document as **Word Embed Test**.

8. Switch to Excel and change the value of cell A1 to **50**.

9. Save the workbook and switch to Word. Notice that the information in the Word document did not change. There is no link to the original file.

10. Double-click on the embedded object in Word. Note the changes in the toolbar and menu bar that are illustrated in Figure 3.15: the Excel toolbars and menu bar have replaced those of Word.

11. Make changes to one of the cells in the object.

12. Click in the document outside of the object. Note how your interface returns to normal (that is, to the Word interface).

The biggest benefit of embedding versus linking an object is that with embedding you need not worry about the location of the original file; everything you need is stored within the one file. You will want to be careful about embedding objects, however, if file *size* is an issue. When you embed an Excel Worksheet Object into Word, for example, *the entire workbook is embedded*, not just the selected portion that you see in Word!

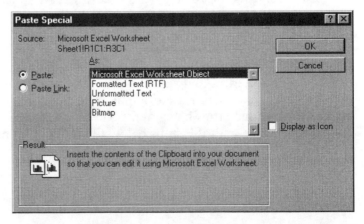

Figure 3.14   **Paste Special dialog box set to embed a Microsoft Excel Worksheet Object**

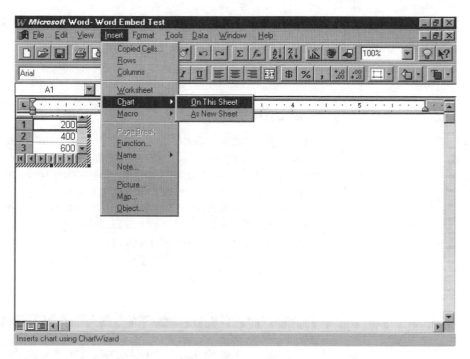

Figure 3.15   Embedded Excel object being edited in Word. Not only has the Excel object been activated, but the Excel toolbars and menu bar are now on screen, making it possible for you to perform Excel operations on it.

A once-small Word document can quickly grow very large with only a couple of embedded objects.

Automation

OLE *automation* is the ability to control an object programmatically. For example, you can not only run a macro that performs an end-of-month function on a workbook, you can add to that macro to have it then create a Word document, format the document, insert some relevant end-of-month text, place the monthly numbers into the document, print the document, and then end without the user ever having to go into Word.

OLE automation requires rather deep coding in WordBasic and/or VBA, so it is beyond the scope of this book, and while a quick and understandable example is not really possible in the static pages of a book, you can get a better sense of what's involved by asking "What is OLE automation" in the Word Answer Wizard and then selecting the *Using OLE Automation with Word* item under the Wizard's Programming and Language Reference section.

The Office Binder

Microsoft Office Binder is probably the best example of the power of OLE. This application allows you to combine all of the individual documents for a project you are working on into a single entity—a binder. The Office Binder interface, seen in Figure 3.16, consists of two panes, a very narrow "contents" column on the left and a regular document pane on the right. The left pane functions like tabs in a notebook, showing you the constituent elements—the *sections*—of the Office Binder file. The right pane is where you can work on the element selected in the left pane.

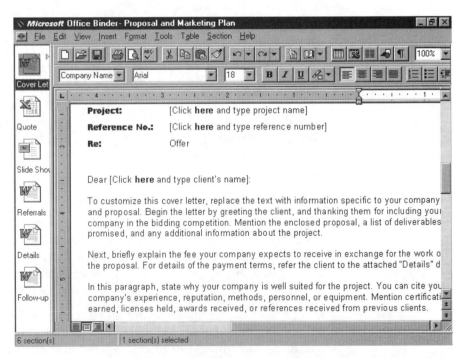

Figure 3.16   A binder in Microsoft Office Binder, containing multiple "sections" (Office files)

Part
1

Welcome to Your
New Office

Office Binder allows you to edit your section files either directly in a binder itself, or as a separate document outside of the binder. The binders are easy to create, maintain, and distribute. For a quick introduction to Office Binder, walk through these groups of steps.

1. From the Start button, launch Microsoft Office Binder. A new binder will open up.

2. From the Section menu on the menu bar, select Add.

3. Select Word Document from the Add Section dialog box.

4. Your binder will now have a Word Document section, which shows up as a Section 1 icon in the left pane. Your binder should look similar to Figure 3.17.

5. Select File ➤ Save from the Office Binder menu bar.

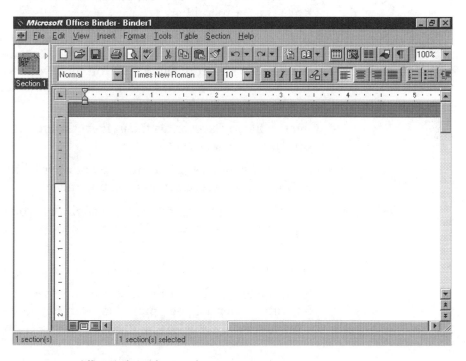

Figure 3.17   Office Binder with a Word Document section

6. Save the binder as **Test Binder.**

7. Type **Main Heading** in the right pane of the binder—the binder's document screen.

8. Center the Main Heading text by clicking on the center-alignment button on the Formatting toolbar.

9. Say to yourself, "Neat, I'm working in this Word section of my binder as if it were a regular Word document!"

Although working in a binder section is almost exactly like working on the document in its original application, there may be occasions when you need to work on a section outside of the binder to use one of the few functions of a program not available when you are inside the binder. Print Previewing a section, for example, requires you to release a section from the binder. To do this, select Section ➤ View Outside from the Office Binder menu bar.

Files can also be inserted from existing files. From the Section menu on the Office Binder menu bar, you can select Add from File to insert existing files into your binder. If you have your windows tiled in a way that you can see your files and the binder, you can even click and drag the file into the binder:

1. Create a file in Excel and a file in PowerPoint, save them, and then close both Excel and PowerPoint.

2. Using the Section ➤ Add from File option from the Office Binder menu bar, find your Excel document and add it to your binder.

3. Using My Computer, find the PowerPoint file you created, and click and drag the file from the My Computer window into the left pane of the binder.

4. Your binder should look similar to the one in Figure 3.18.

When you are ready to print out the contents of the binder, it will provide you with sequential page numbers from beginning to end if you want, or maintain individual pagination for each section separately.

Figure 3.18   *Office Binder with Word, Excel, and PowerPoint documents in it*

Office Binder will play a key role in your organization of Office documents into projects. In fact, Office Binder may prove to be the best feature addition to Office for this version.

Business Processing: Communicating with Word

This part covers in depth the features necessary to provide you with the knowledge to create polished and professional documents, like letters, proposals, integrated reports that incorporate information from other Office applications, and reusable templates that help make your document creation more efficient.

The integration chapter at the end of this part outlines the process for combining multiple Word documents created by multiple users. The compiled documents also demonstrate how to incorporate Excel charts and PowerPoint slides.

Chapter 4
The Road Map

FEATURING

Word for Windows 95 encompasses a vast territory of word-processing capabilities. Whether you want to type a one-page letter or create a one-hundred-page proposal with Excel numbers and charts embedded on multiple pages, this program can move at whatever speed you desire.

This overview chapter was created for the many new users to Word and for those migrating from other word-processing programs. Having a clear sense of the tremendous power of Word from the beginning will help you to search out and use many of the shortcuts and features early on in your travels with this wonderful program.

Overview of Word

Word is a program that allows you to type letters, reports, memos, proposals, newsletters, brochures—virtually all the documents of communication commonly found in business. We say "virtually" because some documents—such as brochures or magazine-quality page layouts—may be easier to create with programs—such as Microsoft Publisher, Corel Ventura, Aldus/Adobe Pagemaker, and so forth—specifically designed for these types of complex documents.

Word will not disappoint you, however, and you will be happy with the rich and varied features and tools you can use. From typing a short, simple letter to designing a complex newsletter, Word will astonish you with its easy-to-use, state-of-the-art commands and capabilities.

Jump-Start into Word for Windows 95

To get you started quickly with the actions and functions needed to produce a document, here are the steps to get you jump-started. See Chapter 5 for a thorough discussion of the wonderful possibilities Word offers you.

Starting Word

You must launch or start Word before you can begin to type a letter or other kind of document. There are a number of ways to start the Word program; the keystroke steps listed below launch Word from the Start button on the Taskbar.

▶ Click on the Start button on the Taskbar.

▶ Move the mouse to the Programs item. A submenu will open.

▶ Move the mouse to the Office 95 item (if you upgraded from Office 4.2 or a previous version, this item will be called Microsoft Office).

▶ Move to the Word item. Figure 4.1 shows the sequence of items.

Starting a New Document

To begin typing a new document, you must have a blank page on which to type your thoughts. Here are the steps for launching a new page.

1. When you first launch Word, an empty screen will come up ready for you to begin typing on. If you're already in Word, choose File ➤ New from the menu bar to start a new document. The New dialog box appears; click on the General tab and double-click on the Normal template. The blank typing screen represents an $8\frac{1}{2}$-by-11-inch piece of paper with left and right margins of $1\frac{1}{4}$ inches and top and bottom margins of 1 inch.

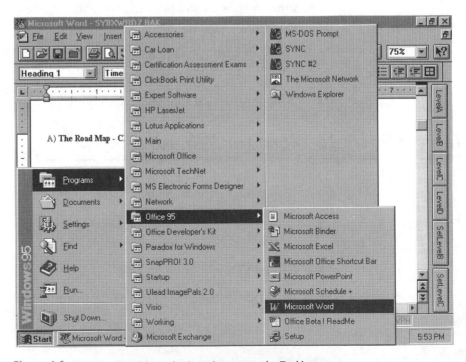

Figure 4.1   *Starting Word from the Start button on the Taskbar*

2. Look around the screen to get your bearings. Hover the mouse for a few seconds over each button that appears on the top rows of the screen. A tip shows what each button does.

3. Begin typing. When you reach the right margin, the text will automatically wrap around to the next line. Press the Enter key only when you have finished typing a paragraph of information or short lines of address information. Figure 4.2 shows the toolbars and the typing area with sample lines of typing.

Correcting Your Document

Corrections are a necessary part of creating and editing documents. Word provides excellent correcting methods and tools. The most common of these methods are listed below.

▶ Use the Backspace key (located above the Enter key) to back over your typos immediately after you make them. Do not use the Backspace key to back over a whole line of good typing just to correct a few letters.

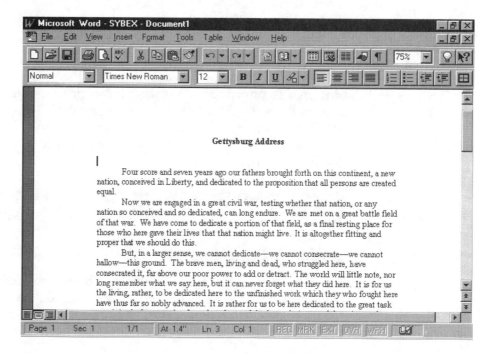

Figure 4.2 *A Word screen with sample typing*

▶ Click the mouse where you find the typos. Use the Delete key (located to the right of the Enter key) and/or the Backspace key to remove the typos. Click and drag the mouse (*select*) across and/or down multiple words or lines and then press the Delete key to remove the highlighted block (the Backspace key deletes the character to the left of the cursor, and the delete key deletes the character to the right).

Enhancing Your Work

You will want to give emphasis to particular words by using the bold, italic, or underline formatting features. You may also want to center a line of text as you are typing. The fastest method for enhancing and aligning text is to use the commands on the Formatting toolbar. This is the toolbar that shows the capital B, I, and U (bold, italic, underline). If you do not see this toolbar, choose View ➤ Toolbars and click on the check box next to Formatting or right-click anywhere in the toolbar area and select Formatting from the pop-up menu.

▶ To bold, italicize, or underline, select the word or words to be formatted. Click on the appropriate button to add the desired format. To remove the formatting, click on the same key to remove it. This on and off effect is called a *toggle*.

▶ To center a line of text, select the text and click on the Center button (the button with the centered lines next to the bold, italic, and underline buttons). To return the text to the left margin, click on the left-alignment button. Below you'll see the Formatting toolbar used to change the style, typeface, point size, formats and alignments, bullets, numbering, and indentation. Bold, italics, and underline are the most frequently used document formats.

Undoing Problems

You can reverse the last ninety-nine actions you have done using the Undo feature. When you perform an unintended action, choose Edit ➤ Undo, Ctrl+Z (hold down the Ctrl key and tap the letter Z), or click on the Undo button on the Standard toolbar to activate the Undo feature.

Repeat as many times as necessary to undo up to ninety-nine of your previous actions. The Edit ➤ Undo command is shown at right.

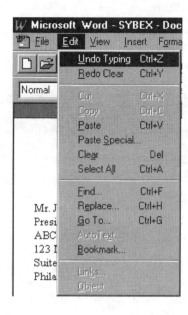

 NOTE If you close the file without saving, you can't undo it. You also cannot undo saving over a file.

Saving Your Work

Many times it is necessary to store a permanent copy of your work. The typing on the screen disappears from the computer's memory when the computer is shut down. You must, therefore, manually store or save your work on a disk. This disk can be the hard disk that always resides inside your computer, or it can be a small disk that you insert into your computer's disk drive. You may be a member of a workgroup on a network, in which case your disk is not near you at all and is called the network drive. Regardless of the medium, save your work as often as you can to avoid losing data through accidents and power loss. Save at any point at any time.

1. Choose File ➤ Save.

Part 2

Communicating with Word

2.   Type a name for your document. You are allowed to use spaces, periods, and numbers, as well as letters in your name. You can have a maximum of 255 characters in the name.

You only name the file the first time you save it. After you've saved once, when you choose File ➤ Save Word automatically saves without asking you for a name. The Save As dialog box is displayed below.

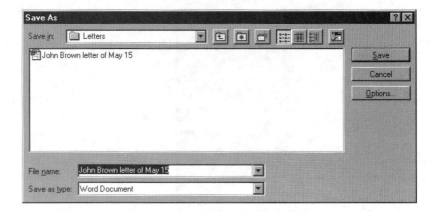

Backing Up Your Work

You may want an additional copy of each of your documents. The Backup option tells Word to always make two copies of everything you do. Although having a backup is a safeguard, you do take up twice the disk space because Word keeps two copies: your original and a backup. For mission-critical work, it is necessary to have a backup copy. To start creating backup copies, follow these steps:

1.   Choose Tools ➤ Options from the menu bar.

2.   Click on the Save tab and make sure the Always Create Backup Copy option has a check mark (the Allow Fast Saves check box will clear itself). Whenever you manually save, a backup will be created.

3. Click on OK. The Save tab of the Options dialog box is shown below.

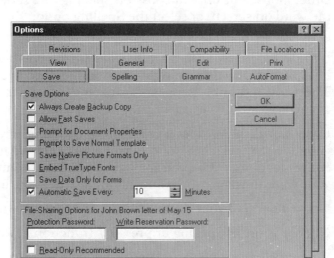

 NOTE To create a backup, you must manually save your document. AutoSave (see Chapter 20) will not create a backup.

Spell Checking Your Work

Word has designed a unique feature into its spell-checking command: If you choose Tools ➤ Options ➤ Spelling and check Automatic Spell Checking, Word will automatically check your spelling as you are typing.

When an incorrect word is typed (or a word not in Word's dictionary, such as the name of a person or a company), Word will immediately underline the word with a wavy red line and the Tip Wizard will activate a flashing lightbulb and explain what to do next. You can activate the Speller's suggested word list by right-clicking on the underlined word or double-clicking on the Speller icon in the Status bar.

Hover the mouse over the underlined word and *right-click* (click the button opposite what you usually click—usually the right button) on it.

You will see a list of possible spellings. Click on the correct spelling with either mouse button. If no possible spellings are shown, tap Esc and edit the word on screen, or select the Spelling option from the bottom of the pop-up dialog box and use the Change Text area to edit the word.

If the word you type is not a misspelled word but is being flagged because it is not in the dictionary, right-click on the word and choose Ignore All. The wavy red line disappears from underneath the word, and future occurrences of this word will not be flagged.

Even though Word does a great job of checking as you type, it is still a good idea to spell check once again after you have finished typing your entire document. Use the spell-checking feature after you have saved your work to ensure that you will not lose data during spell checking.

1. Go to the top of your document. Save your work with File ➤ Save.

2. Choose Tools ➤ Spelling or press F7 (function key number 7).

3. When spell checking starts, notice the words it stops on. If the word is correct, click on the Ignore All option. If the word is not correct and you see the correct spelling in the Suggestions box, click on the correct spelling and choose the Change option or double-click on the desired spelling in the Suggestions box.

4. If the word is not correct and you do not see the correct spelling in the suggestions box, click on the word in the document and correct it or make the changes in the Change To box and click on the Change button. Click on the Resume button to continue spell checking your document. Figure 4.3 displays the spelling dialog box.

Previewing and Printing Your Work

Rarely does the first printing of a document meet your expectations. You can reduce the number of printings, however, by previewing the document before printing. Once you decide which layout is most desirable, you can print your work.

1. Choose File ➤ Print Preview. Your document will appear as a small page.

    - You can edit the page; for instance, as long as the Magnifier button is toggled off, you can add more lines by pressing the Enter key multiple times or take out lines by pressing the Delete key multiple times.

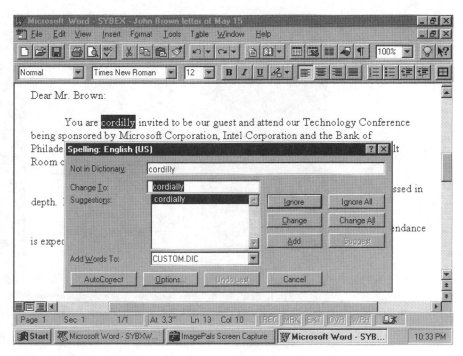

Figure 4.3   *You can easily correct typos using the spell-checking feature.*

- You can change the viewing percentage to a larger size, perhaps to 50 percent so you can fully proof the screen.

- If your document runs over a couple of lines to the second page and you want your work to fit on one page, click on the Shrink to Fit button on the Preview toolbar to force the document to one page.

2. When everything looks fine, click on the Print button on the toolbar or press Ctrl+P to send the work to the printer. Click on the Close button to return to Normal view. Figure 4.4 shows the Print Preview screen and the toolbar buttons.

Printing an Envelope for Your Work

If you have completed a letter, you may wish to print the address on an envelope. Most laserjet and deskjet printers will allow you to place an envelope

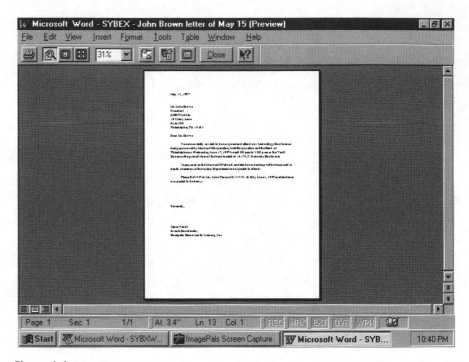

Figure 4.4 *The File ➤ Print Preview screen shows how your document will look before it is printed. Click on the screen to increase the magnification.*

on top of the paper tray. The feeder on these printers has been programmed to take the envelope when printing the address.

1. Select the entire address of the person to whom the letter is being sent.

2. Choose Tools ➤ Envelopes and Labels. The top part of the dialog box shows the recipient's address. The bottom half of the window shows the return address, if you desire one. You can click on Omit and choose not to have a return address for envelopes that already have a return address.

3. Position the envelope in the printer and click on Print. If the return address should be the default return address for the next envelope printing, chose Yes from the message box that appears. The envelope will print. Make sure you save your work again (File ➤ Save or Ctrl+S). The Envelopes and Labels dialog box is displayed as seen on the following page.

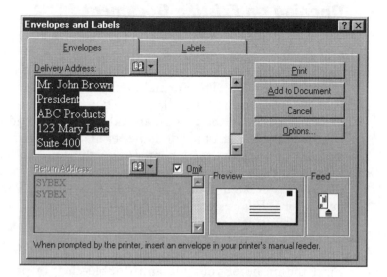

Closing/Clearing Your Work from the Screen

When you have completed a document or you have finished working on a document, you will clear it from the screen. This is called closing the document. You should have saved your work before closing, but in case you have not, you will be reminded when Word closes your document.

1. Save your work first.

2. Choose File ➤ Close. If you have already saved your work, your file will close. If you have not saved your work, you will be asked to save. If you want to save your work, choose Yes and, if necessary, think up a file name. If not, choose No. A blank screen will appear once this operation is completed. The dialog box below shows a message similar to the one you will see if you have not saved your work before closing the file.

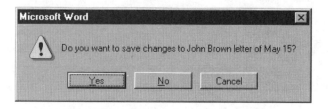

Opening an Existing Document

When you have saved and closed your work, you will sometimes need to reopen the document (retrieve it) back into the computer's memory (onto the screen). You can open as many different documents as your memory will allow. The normal method for opening a file is to use the File ➤ Open option from the menu bar. Another method is to choose the File option on the menu bar and look at the end of the File menu for the list of the last four documents that were open. (You can set this number up to nine—see Chapter 9.) A third method is to use the Start button to view the Documents folder so you can see the last fifteen documents created in all Office programs (Excel, PowerPoint, Access, and so on). Figures 4.5, 4.6, and 4.7 show the different ways you can open an existing document.

1. Choose File ➤ Open or press Ctrl+O to see the list of files on your disk.

2. Find the name of your file and double-click on it or click once and choose OK.

   or

1. Choose File from the menu bar.

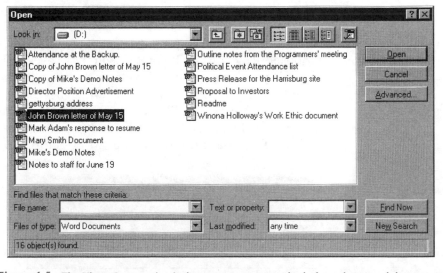

Figure 4.5   The File ➤ Open option is the most common method of opening stored documents.

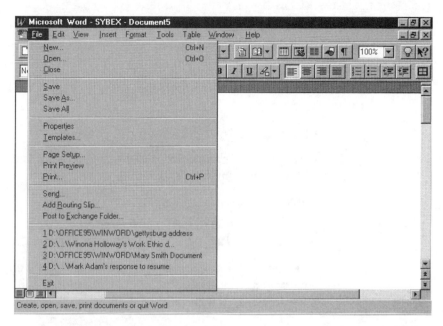

Figure 4.6   *Use the File menu to see a list of the last four files you were working on in Word.*

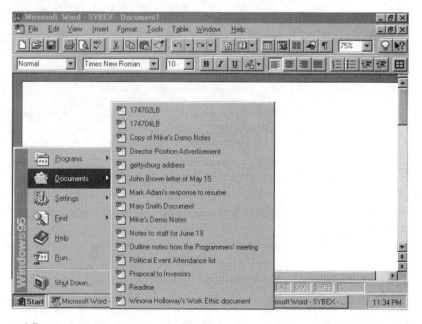

Figure 4.7   *Windows 95 remembers the last fifteen documents you were working on among all programs.*

2. Look for your file at the bottom of the File menu. You will see the last four documents created in Word (you can see up to nine previously open documents here; this option is covered in Chapter 9).

3. Click on the name of your file.

or

1. Click on the Start button on the Taskbar.

2. Choose the Documents folder to see a list of the last fifteen documents you were working on among all programs.

3. Click on the name of the document.

Switching between Multiple Open Documents

You can switch to any other open document by choosing Window on the menu bar. A list of the open documents will appear. Click on the document you wish to make active. To close these documents, switch to

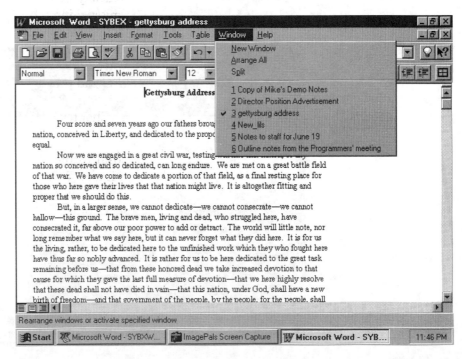

Figure 4.8   You can have multiple documents open and switch between them using the Window menu option.

each one and chose File ➤ Close (make sure you save your work when prompted). Figure 4.8 shows the drop-down list of open documents.

Possibilities

Imagine storing all your frequently typed phrases, sentences, letter headings and closings, addresses for envelopes, and pictures (such as logos and clip art). Word has an *AutoText* feature, which allows you unlimited storage of your frequently used electronic words. Once stored, you can bring these phrases forward by typing whatever name you gave to the stored information and tapping the F3 key. The time reductions are tremendous. The consistency maintained in style and format gives your work a polished and professional appearance. See Chapter 11 for how to activate the AutoText feature.

Imagine the computer correcting your typos as you type. Maybe one of your common typos is *adn* (instead of *and*). Word is preprogrammed to recognize this typo and change it for you. You can also tell Word about any other typos you wish to have automatically changed, and Word for Windows 95 will automatically correct your misspellings with its *AutoCorrect* feature. This wonderful tool also allows you to create a shorthand word that stands for a real word or phrase. For example, suppose your company name is American Business Corporation; you could assign it the abbreviation ABC. Then when you type the letters *ABC* and press the spacebar, Word would automatically substitute *American Business Corporation*. AutoCorrect is located on the Tools menu. See Chapter 11 for how to activate the AutoCorrect feature.

Imagine writing a business proposal using Word and including a projected budget and pie chart from Excel. Word and Excel work together to allow you to copy and link the Excel numbers and charts. The copied budget information can be placed onto any page within the Word proposal. You can then link the data so every time you change a number in the Excel budget, the Word proposal is automatically updated to reflect the most current version of the budget. With linking, you can be confident that you are printing the most up-to-date numbers and charts. See Chapter 20 for the steps for these types of linkages.

The interactive possibilities within Word extend to the entire Microsoft Office suite, including Access databases, PowerPoint slides, and Schedule+. As you read the book, you will be given the steps and techniques needed to perform these powerful integration features of Word and Microsoft Office for Windows 95.

What Dedicated Word-Processors Need to Know

Individuals who come to Word with years of experience working with other word-processing programs bring with them concepts and techniques inherited from the other systems they used. There is nothing more frustrating than attempting to use another word processor's strategy on a new word-processing program only to find that the two different programs are based on very different methods for accomplishing the same tasks. The following sections are tips for current word-processing users and new users (although new users don't bring as many preconceptions to Word) about the premises from which Word operates.

Paragraph-Based Formatting

Word uses a paragraph-format point of view rather than a page point of view. The paragraph-format point of view doesn't allow you to position your cursor just anywhere on the page, issue a formatting command, and expect the program to format the rest of the page or document. If your cursor is in a paragraph, only that paragraph will be affected by the command. Once paragraphs are already typed, you must select the paragraphs you want to format and then issue the commands. You can tell where a paragraph ends by its paragraph marker. Click on the Show/Hide Paragraph symbol (shown at left) to see the paragraph (hard return) markers.

Word considers a single line a paragraph if you press Enter at the end of the line. Each paragraph symbol contains the genetic code of its paragraph (the formats, styles, and alignments). You can copy one paragraph symbol to another paragraph using the Format Painter, and Word will copy the first paragraph's genetic code to the new paragraph.

Tabs

To change tabs for text that is already typed, you must select the text that has already been tabbed (the tab-setting markers are displayed on the ruler), and then you can change the tabs by dragging the tab markers around on the ruler.

Styles

Default fonts, point sizes, and alignments (left, right, center, full) are held within a style. On the Formatting toolbar, there is a drop-down list box with the word "Normal" in it. *Normal* is the name of a style that Word uses for a simple business style. If you click on the drop-down-list arrow to the right of the word "Normal," you will see a number of other styles. If you hold down Shift and click on the drop-down-list arrow, you will see a list of all of the other styles contained in the program. A list of styles is displayed at left.

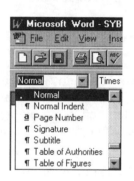

When you click anywhere in a paragraph and choose another style, Word will change the paragraph's style to what you selected. If you want multiple paragraphs to receive the new style, select all of the paragraphs to be changed and then choose the new style.

When you merge one paragraph into another, the second paragraph gives the previous paragraph its genetic code. Because the first paragraph loses its paragraph marker, the styles and alignments coded in the second paragraph's paragraph marker will determine the newly merged paragraph's style.

Sections

Word uses *sections* to control different page layouts. If you want one page Portrait ($8\frac{1}{2}$ by 11 inches) and another page Landscape (11 by $8\frac{1}{2}$ inches), you can choose File ➤ Page Setup. At the bottom of the resulting Page Setup dialog box, you'll find an Apply To option; here you can decide whether to apply your changes to the Whole Document, from This Point Forward, or to the Selected Text.

You can insert your own *breaks* into a document to create your own sections (choose Insert ➤ Break ➤ Section Breaks). You can make a section that has very different margins than another section, or you may wish to have different sets of headers and footers for different sections of your document. The Section Breaks option group allows variations on whether you will be starting a new page or starting a new section on the same page. Starting a new section on the same page is frequently used in documents where you need multiple-column layouts on one page. For example, imagine a newsletter that requires three columns in the top part of the page and two columns in the bottom part of the page. You would use the Section Break feature to control where the different layout begins.

Next Page section breaks are needed when you must start a group of pages with a new page number; for example, the first five pages might be preface pages with lowercase Roman numerals, but you want to begin page six with the Arabic number one. It will be necessary to insert a Next Page section break to create a new next page. On the new page, choose Insert ➤ Page Numbers ➤ Format to assign "1" as the new Start At number.

Multiple Documents

Word allows you to open as many documents as memory allows and then view them through the Window option on the menu bar. You can switch back and forth between multiple documents by tapping Ctrl+F6 or by choosing a document from the list of open documents you see when you click on Window on the menu bar.

You can arrange to view the multiple documents all at once with Window ➤ Arrange All. To return an open document to a full screen, click on the Maximize button to the right of the Title bar (see Chapter 2 if you don't know which is the Maximize button).

Sights and Attractions

Word allows you to type text in many different layouts, such as: letters, memos, minutes, agendas, multiple-page reports, manuscripts, brochures, newsletters, legal documents, pleadings, briefs, columns, landscape, postcards, labels, envelopes, dissertations, bibliographies, documentation, and movie scripts.

Here is a list of some of the things you can do in Word:

Place pictures anywhere in a document	Insert ➤ Picture
Stretch and contort words to produce special effects	Insert ➤ Object ➤ Microsoft WordArt 2.0
Bold	Ctrl+B
Italicize	Ctrl+I
Underline	Ctrl+U
Double underline	Shift+Ctrl+D
Words-only underline	Shift+Ctrl+W
Format an entire document that has multiple headings	Format ➤ AutoFormat
Find and Replace words	Edit ➤ Find; Ctrl+F or Edit ➤ Replace; Ctrl+H
Abbreviate or type shorthand words that Word then replaces with their full meaning	Tools ➤ AutoCorrect
Spell check your work	Tools ➤ Spelling
Grammar check	Tools ➤ Grammar
Thesaurus check	Tools ➤ Thesaurus
Use pre-designed and pre-typed faxes, agendas, resumes, memos, letters	File ➤ New
Save files with names that have as many as 255 characters and may include spaces in the name	File ➤ Save As
Undo any typo or problem	Edit ➤ Undo

Part 2

Communicating with Word

Mark a special place in the document to go to	Edit ➤ Bookmark
Reduce the size of your screen to a tiny piece of paper to check layout	View ➤ Page Layout ➤ View ➤ Zoom ➤ Whole Page or click on the Print Preview button.
Design custom on-screen forms where a typist can choose items from a list	Insert ➤ Form Field
Footnote a word	Insert ➤ Footnote
Place copyright, registered, trademark, cents, and other symbols	Insert ➤ Symbol
Number or bullet paragraphs automatically	Format ➤ Bullets and Numbering
Place document names in Headers or Footers	View ➤ Header and Footer ➤ Insert ➤ Field ➤ Document Information ➤ file name
Automatically produce a Table of Contents when you use Heading 1, Heading 2, Heading 3, etc. styles	Insert ➤ Index and Tables
Draw text boxes, rectangles, squares, circles, and lines	View ➤ Toolbars ➤ Drawing
Outline and shadow a paragraph	Format ➤ Borders and Shading
Type text in columns using the Table command	Table ➤ Insert Table
Beautify tables with shading and/or white letter on black backgrounds	Table ➤ Table AutoFormat

Copy a Word table into an Excel spreadsheet	Table ➤ Select Table ➤ Edit ➤ Copy, start Excel, choose Edit ➤ Paste
Sort columns in a table or words typed on each line	Table ➤ Sort
Adjust color to text	Format ➤ Font ➤ Color
Customize toolbars with your own buttons	View ➤ Toolbars ➤ New
Outline items in Word using Heading styles	View ➤ Outline
Convert Word headings into PowerPoint styles	In PowerPoint, choose File ➤ Open ➤ All Outlines

Chapter 5

The Launch and Tour

FEATURING

Windows 95 offers many ways to start your applications. For example, you can start Word by launching it from the Programs item on the Start-button menu, or you can activate a Word-created document from the Documents item on the Start-button menu, or you can have Word start automatically whenever Windows 95 starts. In this chapter we'll present all of the possible ways in which you can start Word.

We'll also give you a quick tour of Word's most important features, and point out a few special features that you might not immediately recognize from their pictures on the toolbars.

Starting Word through the Start Button

Whether you have just turned on your computer and are viewing the desktop or you are currently working in another program, you can easily start Word or any other program by clicking on the Start button and choosing the program you want from the Programs submenu.

Figure 5.1 provides a visual representation of the Windows 95 menuing system: you click on an item that brings up a menu, and click on an item within that menu to bring up a submenu. Notice in this figure that the Start button is at the bottom left side of the screen. The default behavior for the Start button is to remain visible on the screen regardless of what programs are currently running in memory.

To locate and start Word:

1. Click on the Start button.

2. In the menu that pops up, point to the Programs item. Another menu appears.

3. In this submenu, point to the Office95 folder item. Another menu appears.

4. Within the Office95 menu you will see Microsoft Word. Click on it to launch the program.

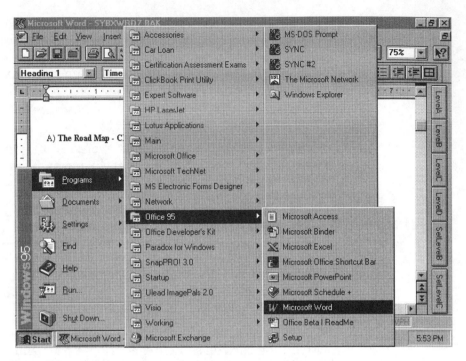

Figure 5.1   Windows 95 Start button and program menuing system

Starting Word with a Document

On the Start-button menu you can see a Documents folder. Point to this item to see the names of the most recent 15 documents you created or opened using Windows 95. Documents are files created from any Windows program (Word, Excel, PowerPoint, etc.). If you click on a document that was created using Word, for example, the document and Word will launch together. This feature allows you to quickly start both the program and the file on which you were last working. Figure 5.2 shows an example of the Documents folder's contents.

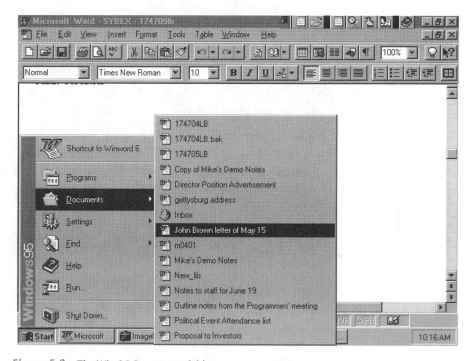

Figure 5.2   *The Win 95 Documents folder*

Starting Word Automatically When Windows 95 Starts

If you use Word as your main Windows program, you may want Word to start automatically when Windows 95 starts. This can save you from having to go through the steps above every time you turn on your computer, but to set up Word to launch automatically you must be able to locate the folder that contains the Word program file. You can browse around on your hard disk looking for the program when you are at step 5 in the setup. Follow these steps to start Word each time Windows starts:

1. Click on the Start button.

2. On the Start-button menu, point to the Settings item. A menu appears next to it. On this menu, click on the Taskbar item.

3. When the Taskbar dialog box appears, click on the Start Menu Programs tab.

4. Click on the Add button.

5. When prompted for the command line for the program, click on the Browse button, and use the Browse window to find the Microsoft Word program. Depending on how Office was installed on your system, the Word shortcut file may be located in your Microsoft Office, Msoffice, or Office95 folder.

 NOTE   You may have to change to another drive in the Browse window in order to find the folder containing the Office programs.

6. When you find Word, double-click on it. The Create Shortcut dialog box will open, and the Command Line option will be filled in with the address (path) of the Word program/shortcut.

7. Click on the Next button in the dialog box.

8. In this next dialog box you are being asked to select the folder into which to place the program. Since you want Word to start whenever you start Windows 95, scroll down until you find the StartUp folder (you will be looking alphabetically down the list). Double-click on the StartUp folder name.

9. In the Select A Title For The Program dialog box that opens, you can now enter the name you want to see for Word on the StartUp menu. You can leave the default name that Windows 95 provides or you can change it to "My Word Processor" (or anything you like).

10. Click on the Finish button, then click on the OK Button.

To find out if you have successfully performed the steps, click on the Start button on the Taskbar and then point to the Programs folder, as shown in Figure 5.3. Point to the StartUp menu item to see the names of all the programs that will start automatically when Windows 95 starts.

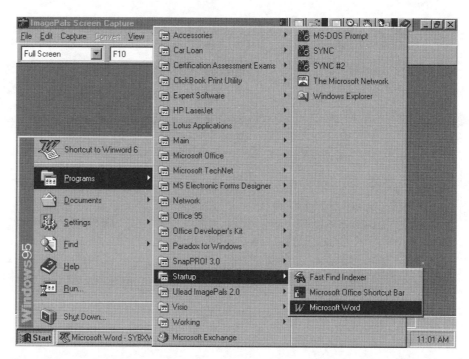

Figure 5.3   *From the Start button, go to the Programs folder, then the StartUp menu to display all the programs that are set to start automatically whenever Windows 95 starts.*

A Tour of the Word Screen

The Word screen/window contains a variety of objects. We'll describe Word's default appearance here.

To see the screen more or less as shown in Figure 5.4, click on the *New* button (the first button on the left) on the strip of buttons identified in the figure as the *Standard toolbar* (the first strip of buttons across the top of the Word screen).

Starting at the top of the window are four rows of objects: *title bar*, *menu bar*, *Standard toolbar*, and *Formatting toolbar*. Depending on your View menu settings, you may also see a *ruler* below the toolbars. Below these upper rows is the *typing area*, which may show a *scroll bar* along the right side and across the bottom. Below the typing area is the *Status bar*. All of these items will be described in the following paragraphs, and are identified in Figure 5.4.

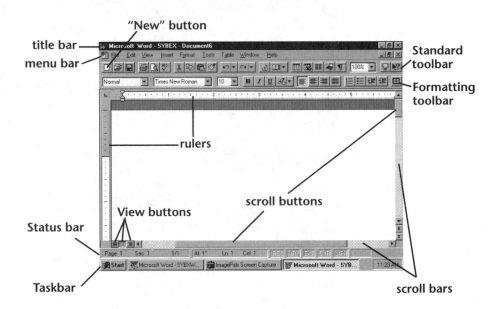

Figure 5.4   *The elements of the Word screen*

NOTE   If you do not see the toolbars (the two strips of buttons along the top of the Word window) as shown in Figure 5.4, select View ➤ Toolbars from the menu bar. Make sure there is a checkmark beside the toolbars named Standard and Formatting. (If the checkmark is not present, click the mouse in the empty box to make a checkmark.) Then click on the OK button. Similarly, if you don't see the ruler as shown in Figure 5.4, select View ➤ Ruler.

Title Bar

The title bar displays the name of the program in which you are working: *Microsoft Word.* The bar also displays the name under which you registered the software. If the next word is *Document* followed by a number, what you see in the window represents a new, unsaved document. Once you save the document you can give it a more descriptive name than Document1 or Document2.

Menu Bar

The menu bar displays the names of the *menus* (lists of commands) in Word. You can activate a menu by clicking on its name with the mouse, which drops down the list of commands. Click on a command to initiate it. (If the command appears only dimly, it cannot be initiated under the present circumstances.)

For typists who prefer using keyboard commands over the mouse, there are key combinations for activating each menu: hold down the Alt key and tap the key for the underscored letter of the menu bar item. For example, Alt+F will activate the File menu, and Alt+O will activate the Format menu.

Once the menu is activated, any of the menu's commands that have underscored letters can then be activated by pressing the key for that letter. (But don't hold down the Alt key while you're doing this; if you do, Word will think you want to drop down another menu.)

WARNING Using the keyboard to initiate a menu command is slightly different from using it to activate an option in a dialog box. While a menu command that contains an underscored letter can be initiated simply by typing that letter, a dialog box option that contains an underscored letter requires you to press Alt along with the underscored letter. (If you type the letter without pressing the Alt key, Word will think that you are entering text—for example, a file name—into a text box in the dialog box.)

Toolbars

The *Standard* toolbar (the first strip of buttons in Figure 5.4) is relatively consistent across all of the Office programs, which is to say that most of the buttons you see in this toolbar when you're working in Word will also appear when you're working in Excel or PowerPoint. The Standard toolbar contains buttons that represent functions that are common to many of the Office programs. For example, clicking on the Printer button will quickly print a copy of the entire current document.

The *Formatting* toolbar (the strip with the buttons lettered B, I, U—for bold, italic, underline) is also consistent across all of the Office applications. The Formatting toolbar contains buttons that represent common actions for changing the appearance of your work.

For example, the four buttons that look like "scratch marks" represent the different text alignments (left-justified, center, right-justified, and full justification). Notice that the left-alignment button appears "pushed in." A pushed in or depressed button lets you know that the format is applied. You will like the fact that when a formatting action is "on," you can see multiple depressed buttons. When a button is depressed, clicking on the button again turns the action off. Figure 5.5 displays the four alignment buttons.

There are nine toolbars that come with Microsoft Word. You can also create your own toolbars and populate them with the buttons of your choice. Others may appear on an as-needed basis (for example, when you are in Print Preview mode or Outline view).

Figure 5.5   *Paragraph alignment buttons—Left, Center, Right, and Full Justification*

Just to get familiar with the default toolbars, select View ➤ Toolbars and checkmark every toolbar on the list to make them all appear on the screen, then click on OK.

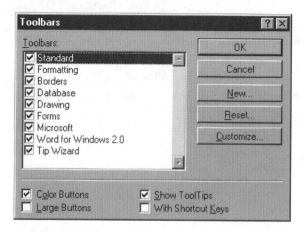

After a time, you can return to this dialog box and click again on the toolbars you won't be needing for a while—leaving only the Standard and Formatting toolbars checkmarked.

The Ruler

The ruler displays a horizontal scale that reflects the width of your typing area. When the Word screen is set to Page Layout view, the ruler also shows the height of the typing area. (If you don't see the ruler, click on View ➤ Ruler.) The ruler is invaluable when you want to quickly set tabs, margins and indents. Figure 5.6 shows a typical ruler in Page Layout view.

NOTE To see both the horizontal and vertical rulers make sure that you are in Page Layout view (select View ➤ Page Layout). Normal view shows only the horizontal ruler when View ➤ Ruler is selected.

For the rest of this introduction, let's deactivate the ruler in order to unclutter the screen. Click on View ➤ Ruler to turn the ruler off, and switch to Normal view by selecting View ➤ Normal.

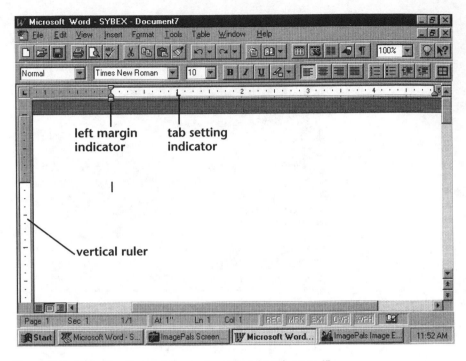

Figure 5.6   *This ruler shows a left margin at 0″ and a tab set at 1″.*

The Typing Area

The open area below the rulers and toolbars is the writing or typing area. This is your "piece of paper" on which you type and place your thoughts, procedures, tasks, graphics, etc. If the ruler is showing, you can make the area somewhat larger by getting rid of the ruler. From the menu bar, select View ➤ Ruler to deactivate the ruler.

There are certain objects that are a permanent part of the typing area. The insertion point and some version of the mouse pointer are always visible. The end-of-document marker (an underline character) is only visible at the end of the document when you are in Normal view (View ➤ Normal). Figures 5.7 and 5.8 show the typing area with a simple sentence typed in both the Normal and the Page Layout view.

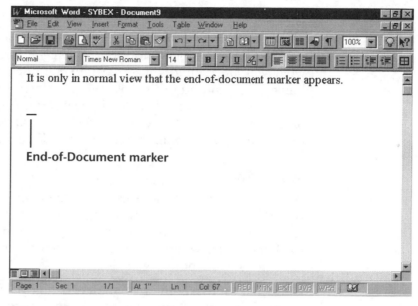

Figure 5.7 Normal view with a simple sentence typed

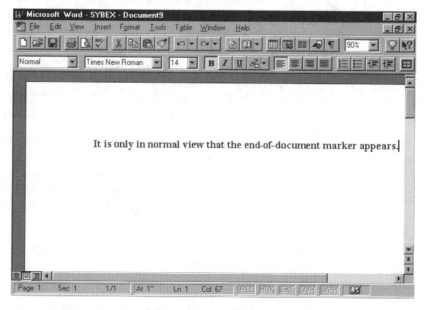

Figure 5.8 Page Layout view with a simple sentence typed

Insertion Point

The black vertical blinking line that is initially at the top left side of the typing area is the guide for your typing—it indicates the place where what you are typing is inserted into the document. As you type, the blinking line continuously moves along. When you tap the up, down, left, or right arrows on your keyboard, the insertion point moves accordingly, one character or line at a time in the typing area. Note that you cannot move the insertion point below the end-of-document marker.

Mouse Pointer

When you move the mouse around in the typing area, the mouse pointer is in the shape of a thin I-beam. (You can see it at the end of the typed line in Figure 5.8.) As you move the mouse near the menu line and toolbars (or anywhere outside of the typing area), the mouse pointer becomes a white pointing arrow.

Move the mouse pointer to some existing piece of text and click the mouse. This action will bring the insertion point to that spot in the text.

TIP   When there is only a short distance to move the insertion point, use the right, left, up, or down arrow keys on your keyboard instead of using the mouse. It is easier to move two or three letters to the right or left with the arrow keys than to reach over, position your hand on the mouse, steady your hand, and click at the exact spot two characters away from where the insertion point already is.

End-of-Document Marker

The horizontal line situated like a short underline at the end of the document is seen only when Word is in Normal view, as shown in Figure 5.7. As its name makes clear, the end-of-document marker lets you know where the end of the document occurs. It stays below your typing as you go, and remains at the very end of the document when you are finished typing.

Vertical Scrolls

The typing area is bordered on the right side by the vertical scroll bar with a scroll button and arrows. In Normal view, the scroll bar shows a single up-arrow button and a single down-arrow button. Click on these to move your document up or down one line at a time. The position of the bar or button in the middle of the scroll bar represents where the screen is in relation to the top and bottom of the document. (The size of the bar represents the relative size of the screen as a part of the complete document. When the bar is long, the document itself is not much longer than what you see on the screen. When the bar is short, or looks more like a button, the document as a whole is many times longer than what you can currently see on the screen.) Click and drag this bar or button to move quickly to the top or bottom of the document.

In Page Layout view, the scroll bar also shows a double up-arrow and a double down-arrow, which are useful for moving up or down a page at a time in long documents. The double up-arrow jumps to the page above, and the double down-arrow jumps to the page below.

Horizontal Scrolls

The first bar along the bottom of the typing area is the horizontal scroll bar. Use the left and right arrow buttons on this bar to see text that is off the right or left side of the screen. The position of the bar or button in the middle of the scroll bar represents where the screen is in relation to the left and right margins of the document. (The size of the bar represents the relative size of the screen between the margins.) Click and drag the horizontal scroll button to move quickly to the left or right margins. (You'll find that you have to use this horizontal scroll button to reset your view after you have performed an indent.)

View Buttons

To the left side of the horizontal scroll arrow at the bottom of the window are the three document view buttons: Normal View, Page Layout View, and Outline.

Normal view allows you to see your document in a traditional word processing fashion. No real margins are shown, page and section breaks appear as a dashed line across the screen, and there is no promise that you are seeing an actual graphic representation of how the page will look when printed. Because there is no memory taken up to show you a graphical representation, Normal view provides for faster scrolling than Page Layout view.

The Page Layout View button changes the screen to a graphical representation of your document, more or less as it will appear when printed. Margins and page breaks are more obvious in Page Layout view than in Normal view. At a Zoom setting of 75% or less (select View ➤ Zoom or click on the Zoom box on the Standard toolbar), you can see both the right and left edges of a standard $8^{1}/_{2} \times 11''$ page. In addition, if you choose View ➤ Zoom ➤ Many Pages while in Page Layout view, you can view many tiny pages in your document simultaneously.

NOTE Word will actually alert you that you cannot perform certain commands unless your document is in Page Layout view, and will ask permission to switch you over to this view. Other times, Word will automatically switch you to Page Layout mode (for example, when you start working with headers and footers).

Use the Outline button to create or view documents as outlines, which lets you choose how many "levels" of content you want to display. You can use Outline view to show only the headings in a document so that you can see at a glance how the document is organized. Whenever you want, you can show or hide the subheads and/or the regular text. One attractive use of outlines is to open them in PowerPoint to be shown as slides.

NOTE You can also use the third button to display Master Documents instead of Outline view, by selecting View ➤ Master Document. This lets you work with multiple documents that you might want to treat as subdocuments to a larger, master document.

Status Bar

At the bottom of the typing area, below the horizontal scroll bar if the scroll bar is showing, is a Status bar displaying information about the current page number, the position of the insertion point, and the status of certain settings. Figure 5.9 focuses on the Status bar.

TIP Double-click on the page number on the Status bar as a shortcut procedure for activating the Go To command. This brings up a dialog box that allows you to type in a specific page number (among other locations) to go to.

Figure 5.9 *The Status bar provides valuable information regarding the position of the insertion point in the document.*

The Status bar is divided into three sections.

▶ The left portion of the bar shows the page number of the current screen, the section number, and the page number as a fraction of the total number of pages in the document (for example, 1/12 for page 1 of 12).

▶ When the insertion point is on the current screen, the middle portion of the bar shows its vertical position on the page as measured in inches as well as in lines, and its horizontal position as measured in columns. These readings can be quite helpful when you are trying to place characters or other elements very precisely, as when you are working with tables or graphics.

▶ The right side of the bar contains abbreviations for settings that you can turn on and off by double-clicking the mouse on them. Table 5.1 provides the meaning of each of the Status bar's abbreviations.

The Status bar also serves as an information banner, describing the function of each button on a toolbar. The information is in addition to the name and shortcut key that appears in a small yellow tag when you let the mouse pointer linger on a toolbar button. Unless you've deactivated this "Tool Tips" feature, the additional information appears in the Status bar, temporarily replacing the information about the page and cursor locations.

The Taskbar

Although technically not part of the Word screen, you can't miss the importance of the Windows 95 *Taskbar*, which by default remains on the screen whenever Windows 95 is running. (You can override this default behavior by selecting Auto Hide as one of the Taskbar settings. With Auto Hide on, the Taskbar only appears when you bring the mouse pointer to its hidden location.) The Taskbar displays the Start button and other buttons for any application programs that are currently open in memory. You can click on the Start button to find another program to start while you are in Word, or click on another Taskbar button to switch to a program that is already open.

Abbreviation	Explanation
REC	Macro Record on/off. Turns on and off the recording of *macros*, which are short programs that you can create to record and play back any steps you perform frequently while working in Word.
MRK	Revision Marking on/off. Turns on and off the the marking of revisions that are being made during the editing of a document.
EXT	Extend Selection on/off. When EXT is displayed, everything between the current location of the insertion point and the point where you turn off the EXT indicator will be highlighted (selected). Double-click again on the EXT indicator, or press the **Esc** key, to turn off the EXT feature, leaving the selection on screen, ready to be moved or copied or deleted.
OVR	Overtype on/off. Turns on and off the ability to type over text, in effect replacing text a character at a time alongside the insertion point (rather than the default of inserting text without destroying the text alongside it). Works the same as the **INSERT** key on the keyboard.
WP/WPH/WPN	WordPerfect keystrokes, WordPerfect Help, WordPerfect Navigation keystrokes. For users who are migrating to Word from WordPerfect. Activates options to let you use WordPerfect keystrokes to perform many Word tasks, to provide WordPerfect Help (identifying equivalent keystrokes in Word), or to just let you use WordPerfect navigation (cursor-movement) keys. Double-click on the indicator and then click on the desired options when the dialog box comes up. You can uncheck the Help and Navigation keys in this dialog box to turn off the automatic WordPerfect keystrokes and Help.

Table 5.1 **Status Bar Abbreviations**

NOTE The Windows 95 Taskbar and Start button are described more fully in Chapter 2.

At the far right side of the Taskbar, the time appears. If you let the mouse pointer linger on the time, Windows 95 will display the date and the day of the week. When you double-click on the time, Windows 95 will display a calendar and a combination analog/digital clock. Word automatically enters the date and time into the file details of your individual documents. You can see the dates and times that you created and last revised a document by selecting File ➤ Properties ➤ Statistics from the Word menu bar. Figure 5.10 shows the Windows 95 clock screen that is displayed when you click on the Taskbar's time readout.

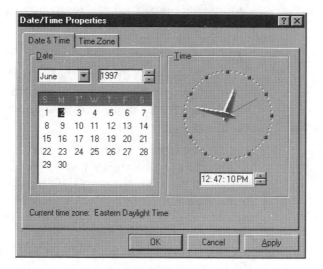

Figure 5.10 **The Windows 95 Clock**

Templates and Magical Wizards

Word contains a number of predesigned documents called *templates* that you can use as the basis for your documents. The templates include fax forms, calendars, and layouts for multipage reports, newsletters, legal pleadings, letters, and meeting agendas. Word may set the specific margins, point size, typeface, indentations, and even graphics for each of these types of documents. You can enter your own text into the example documents without being concerned with setting up the layout and formatting. Word has completely managed the details so that you can concentrate on typing out your thoughts.

Some of the templates are programmed to "walk you through the steps" of creating your document. The step-by-step procedures are called *Wizards*. Word maintains its Wizards in a number of classifications, including Publications, Reports, Memos, Letters & Faxes, Other Documents, and General.

The Normal Template   When you create a new document, the default choice of template is the predesigned *Normal* template: the margins on the left and right are 1.25″, the top and bottom margins are 1″, the tab stops are set every half inch, and the paper is positioned in a portrait orientation (as opposed to a landscape orientation). You may not think of these settings as fancy, and in fact they're intended to serve as a generic layout. There are, however, many other templates that Word has created for you to use.

1. Choose File ➤ New from the menu bar.

2. Click on each tab in the New dialog box to familiarize yourself with what is available in each category. When you click on one of the templates or Wizards, a sample document will appear in the Preview portion of the dialog box.

3. Double-click on any document that has the "magic wand" across the button. These are the Wizard templates mentioned above that are programmed to go through the steps of asking what you would like in your document design. (Remember, you can always choose File ➤ Close and close it down without saving after you have looked at the design.) If you like the design, go ahead and use it as the basis for a document and save your work as you would normally (select File ➤ Save and name the document as you wish).

Figure 5.11 shows the Other Documents category of templates, which contains a number of Wizards to try.

NOTE   For the above exercise, make sure in step 1 that you select File ➤ New from Word's menu bar to locate the Wizards and templates. If you click on the New button instead (the first button on the Standard toolbar), you will be given the general, default new document which uses the Normal template's layout. You will not see the dialog box that offers you more choices.

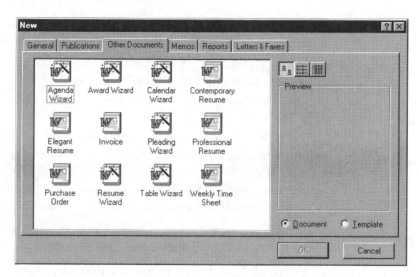

Figure 5.11   Word's Wizards walk you through the steps of working with some very useful

Useful Features and Commands
That Are Not Obvious

Word includes many features that are not obvious from the pictures on
their buttons or their menu descriptions, but which nonetheless provide
capabilities you may need during your work with the program. In this
section we'll show you some of these more subtle capabilities of Word.

► View the returns, tabs, and spaces in a document: Click on the paragraph
symbol button at the right end of the Standard toolbar (which is usually
the first toolbar at the top of the Word screen), or use the
Ctrl+Shift+8 keyboard combination. This feature can help you
troubleshoot layout problems caused by hidden returns or tabs.

► List all the formatting options that have been set for a paragraph: Click
on the Help button (question mark with the black arrow,
located at the right end of the Standard toolbar) and then click
on any word within the paragraph.

► Create an instant database for mail-merge or Rolodex reference by
simply typing the categories of your database separated by a tab (for
example, FirstName➡LastName➡Title➡Company➡ etc.)
and choosing View ➤ Toolbars ➤ Database. Click the Data
Form button, the first button on the Database toolbar, then at

the Header Record Delimiters dialog box, click on OK. You will see a data entry form to use in typing the data for your categories.

▶ If you repeatedly select Edit ➤ Undo or click on the Undo button on the Standard toolbar, Word will incrementally back up, one action at a time, to as many as 99 actions, or to the last time you saved the file, whichever comes first.

▶ To return to the location in the document where you last performed some editing or entered some text, press Shift+F5. (This works even if you've just reopened a file you haven't worked on in days.) If you've had the file open for numerous edits, you can press Shift+F5 repeatedly to cycle through the last four edit/entry locations.

And here are a couple of minor problems that can be mystifying until you discover the simple cause for the effect:

▶ Problem: You notice a little late that what you've been typing is coming out with the upper and lower case letters transposed. This is usually the result of accidentally pressing CAPS Lock when you began typing. You can change what you've typed back to the correct case by selecting the text (highlighting it) and choosing Format ➤ Change Case ➤ tOGGLE cASE.

▶ Problem: When you select text and choose Copy from the menu bar, nothing special seems to happen. This is because the copy has gone into a part of the computer's memory called the "Clipboard." It reappears only when you position the pointer where you want the copy to appear and choose Edit ➤ Paste (or click the Clipboard Paste button on the Standard toolbar). Remember, you can copy a table in one program (Word for example), and paste it into another (Excel, for example). If you need to verify what's in the clipboard before you paste it, you can view the Clipboard using the Windows 95 accessory, Clipboard Viewer.

Chapter 6

Functions Common to All Word Documents

Featuring

As you work in Word, you'll find that there are numerous functions and processes common to any and all documents. These functions and processes include:

▶ Deciding document layout

▶ Typing/editing

▶ Saving often

▶ Formatting to enhance appearance

▶ Checking text

▶ Printing

▶ Customizing the environment for future work

▶ Reusing parts of documents

▶ Sharing information among programs

First off, when you create a new document, there are the default layout settings:

▶ Printing

▶ Customizing the environment for future work

▶ Reusing parts of documents

▶ Sharing information among programs

When you create a new document, there are the default layout settings: the paper size is $8^1/_2''$ by $11''$, the margins are at least 1 inch, and the typeface is a generic business typeface, like 10-point Times New Roman. When you begin other types of documents—proposals, newsletters, or pleadings, for example—you will probably want to change the page layout and size, typeface, and point size.

This chapter reviews the features and functions that you will encounter during your document production and the considerations you must bring to each document you create.

Word's Document Defaults

New documents in Word have predefined settings called *defaults*. The type of defaults depends on the type of document you chose. If you picked one of the predesigned documents (called *templates*) from the

New dialog box (File ➤ New), your margins, spacing, and other settings may be quite different from the settings for a generic document. The list below displays the default settings for the Normal template.

Paper size	$8^1/2" \times 11"$
Orientation	Portrait
Top margin	1"
Bottom margin	1"
Left margin	1.25"
Right margin	1.25"
Alignment	Left-aligned text
Page numbering	None
Sections	One
Tabs	Set every half inch
Typeface	Times New Roman (depends on printer type)
Point size	10 points (depends on printer type)
Paper bin	Upper tray in printer (if printer has multiple trays)

Starting a New Document

When you begin a new document in Word, a blank page appears with the generic name *Document#* (as in Document2) in the title bar. This is how Word refers to the document until you save your work with a better name.

Your job is to decide what kind of document you are creating. Is it a single- or multiple-page letter or memo? Is it a report or proposal? Does your letterhead paper require certain margins at the left side or at the top? Will the document be laid out sideways (landscape)? Does the document require page numbers? What about repeating text at the top or bottom of each page (headers or footers)? Should you be typing in side-by-side tables?

Word makes it very easy to change your page settings to match the type of document you are going to type. We advise you to change these settings before beginning, because it could drastically affect the appearance of the document layout. For example, if you know that your document needs to be printed sideways on paper, it might be easier to type the document in landscape mode from the beginning rather than changing it to landscape later.

Table 6.1 lists the keystrokes needed to change the page settings of a document before beginning to type.

Feature	Menu Commands to Use
Margins	File ➤ Page Setup ➤ Margins
Paper size	File ➤ Page Setup ➤ Paper Size
Paper orientation	File ➤ Page Setup ➤ Paper Size
See margins and/or page breaks	View ➤ Page Layout. When you go to a different page, you will see a gray separation. Margins are seen in a smaller, graphical page view.
See a graphical page	View ➤ Zoom ➤ 75%. You can see a whole page by choosing Whole Page, but it will be difficult to type in this small view. 100% is the normal view.
Add page numbers	Insert ➤ Page Numbers. If you don't want page numbers to begin on the first page, click on the Show Number on First Page check box to uncheck this feature.
Headers and footers	View ➤ Header and Footer. For repeating words at the top, start typing within the Header. For repeating words at the bottom, click on the first button in the Header and Footer toolbar (called the *Switch between Header and Footer button*).
Turn on Automatic Save	Tools ➤ Options ➤ Save ➤ Automatic Save Every *x* Minutes.

Table 6.1 **Settings** for Your Documents

NOTE You can also make any of these changes after you have created and typed a document.

Getting Around the Document

It is important to learn early on how to move around quickly and efficiently so you can concentrate on your thoughts and not on the mechanics of the software.

The temptation is to constantly use the mouse, even to move short distances. However, when you wish to move down multiple lines, don't press Enter; tap the down arrow multiple times. The arrow keys move much more quickly through short distances than does the mouse.

Vertical Scrolls

For moving longer distances, use the mouse and the vertical scroll bars on the right side of the screen.

If you are in Page Layout view (choose View ➤ Page Layout), you will be able to see the document's margins and page breaks. You will also see two sets of up and down arrows on the vertical scroll bar to the right side of the screen. Clicking on the single down arrow will move you down one line at a time (it is still quicker to tap the keyboard down arrow). The double up and down arrows move you to the previous page and the next page, respectively.

Clicking in the space above or below the scroll box (the *elevator*) moves you nearer the top or bottom of the page. Each click moves you up or down one screen. Approximately four clicks in the elevator positions you on a new page. Look at your Status bar to see what page you are on.

If you drag the scroll box (the *slide*) up and down, Word shows the page number you are on as you slide. Figure 6.1 shows an excerpt from Maya Angelou's "Inaugural Poem" on page 15 of our document.

Remember, when you use the vertical scrolls you must click on the screen to reposition the insertion point.

Tables 6.2 and 6.3 provide quick references to some of the ways to reposition the insertion point on different lines, paragraphs, and pages within your document.

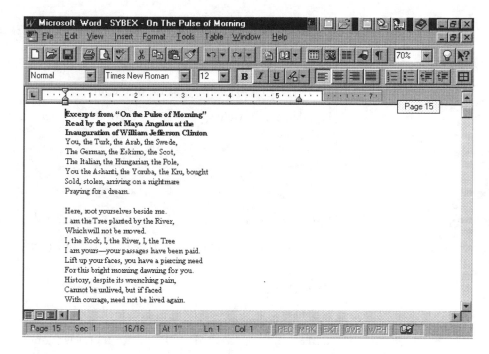

Figure 6.1 *When you drag the vertical scroll box, the page number is indicated.*

Spacebar

Use the spacebar as a separator for your words and sentences. Don't use the spacebar to move the insertion point across a line of text. The spacebar works on a typewriter as a way of moving across a line, but not in word processing. If you use the spacebar to move, Word will make additional spaces (gaps in your text), which you'll then have to delete.

To type text in columns, avoid using the spacebar to position across the line; use the Tab key instead. Text that has been separated by more than a couple of spaces tends not to align correctly when printed. If you have spaced your text into columns, delete the spaces between the words and re-tab the words across a line.

TIP Use the Table feature (Table ➤ Insert Table) if you want to designate a specific number of columns and rows in which to type your columnar text.

Keyboard Combinations	The Insertion Point Repositions At...
Home	Beginning of the line
End	End of the line
Up, down, left, right arrow keys	Lines up or down or characters left or right
Ctrl+← or →	Words right or left
Ctrl+↑ or ↓	One paragraph up or down
PgUp or PgDn	Screens up or down
Previous pages or next pages	Ctrl+Alt+PgUp or PgDn
Ctrl+Home	Top of document
Ctrl+End	End of document
Ctrl+F and type a word	The word that was found
Ctrl+G or F5 and type a page number	Top of that page
Shift+F5	Previous four locations where changes occurred

Table 6.2   **Positioning the Insertion Point Using the Keyboard**

Mouse Movements	Repositions the Screen How...
Vertical Scroll buttons	Up and down lines
Vertical Scroll bar	Proportionately positions at the top, middle, or bottom of the document
Vertical Page buttons	Previous and next pages
Vertical Slider	Slide up or down to see the page number

Table 6.3   **Positioning the Insertion Point Using the Mouse**

Typing the Text

If you are not a touch typist, you may want to increase your typing speed by purchasing a typing program. If you have no experience at all in typing documents, you might want to speak with a typist or someone who creates electronic documents to get a sense of the issues involved with typing. This section will help you get comfortable with the typing objects and concepts you will encounter using Word, but general business typing information can be best gleaned from someone with a background in generating office documents.

The Insertion Point

The blinking vertical line that sits at the beginning of a new document is called the *insertion point* and is a guide for your typing. It remains in a document at all times. It is also called the *cursor* in other programs.

To position the insertion point so you can make a change or add or delete words, click the primary mouse button (usually the left mouse button) on the spot where you want the insertion point. You can also tap the up, down, left, or right arrow keys to move the insertion point.

When the insertion point is to the left of a letter, think of the insertion point as being "on top of" that letter (even though it does not look that way). This means if you type a new letter, the new letter will go to the left of the insertion point. If you tap the Delete key, Word will delete the letter to the right of the insertion point. Figure 6.2 shows a sentence with the insertion point positioned on the line.

Repositioning the Insertion Point

Word provides many methods for quickly repositioning the insertion point using either the mouse or the keyboard. For instance, it takes much longer to move your hand to the mouse and click one letter to the left than it does to press the left arrow once. See *Selecting Text* later in this chapter to learn all the tricks.

Quick Typing Tips

Experience has taught all users of word-processing programs that there are concepts you need to know sooner rather than later. Here are the

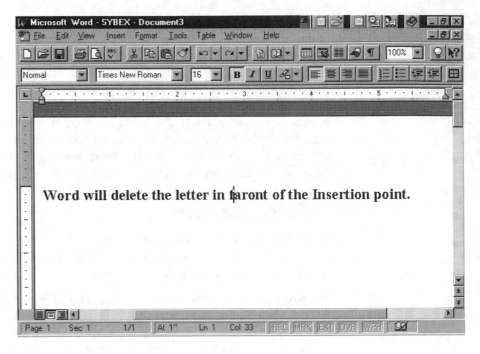

Figure 6.2   *The insertion point is a vertical line that indicates where typing will occur.*

most common word-processing concepts you should know or remember regardless of your level of Word usage.

Word Wrap

You can start typing your document as you would with a typewriter or any other word processor. Unlike a typewriter, however, you do not press Enter at the end of each line. Continue to let your text wrap around until you are ready to start a new and separate paragraph.

You must press Enter after typing short lines, such as those found on the inside address of a letter or on a list of items.

Centering Text

Use the Center button on the Formatting toolbar or press Ctrl+E (think "Even" between the margins) to center a line, then type your text and press Enter. To return the text to the left margin, click on the Align Left button on the toolbar or press Ctrl+L. See Chapter 7 for a full discussion of line alignment.

Quick Corrections

As you type, the automatic spell checker will display a wavy red underline under words that are not in the dictionary. This red underline will not print. If you know the correct spelling, you can quickly correct your typos right after you make them by tapping the Backspace key (located above Enter)—or right-click on the word and select the possible correct spelling from the shortcut menu that appears. The Backspace key "backs over" any characters to the left of the insertion point, acting like an eraser. You can then type in the correct spelling.

If you inadvertently hit Enter in the middle of a line and break the line, tap the Backspace key to back up the broken line.

WARNING The Caps key can be a source of frustration if you accidentally hit it when typing. When Caps is on (look for the indicator light on your keyboard), all of your typing will be in uppercase. If you hold down the Shift key, the computer toggles Caps, and you will type in lowercase. Normally, you will want to turn Caps off and type capital letters with the Shift key.

NOTE The AutoCorrect feature is on by default in Word and will automatically correct such misspellings as *teh* when you meant to type *the*. Choose Tools ➤ AutoCorrect to see the list of words that will automatically be corrected. See Chapter 11 for directions for adding your own words.

Paragraph Markers

You may find it easier to type when you can see where the returns, spaces, and tabs are in your document. If so, click on the Show/Hide Paragraph symbol to display the marks. Click on the symbol again to hide them.

TIP If you've inadvertently typed a bit of text with the Caps key in the on state, causing your upper and lower case to be transposed, select the text and choose Format ➤ Change Case ➤ tOGGLE cASE to change the case back to normal.

Selecting Text

When you want Word to change particular characters, words, lines, sentences, paragraphs, or pages, you must show the software the specific text to which you are referring by selecting it. Text must also be selected before such actions as formatting, copying, deleting, moving, or adding borders and shading can be done.

There are a number of techniques for selecting text, detailed below.

WARNING   When text is selected, it is vulnerable to deletion. Selected text can be easily replaced by other characters by tapping any key on the keyboard. For example, if you select a page of text and inadvertently tap the spacebar, Word thinks you want to replace the selected page with a space! (If this happens, immediately press Undo or choose Edit ➤ Undo.) Try not to keep text selected after you have performed an operation on the text. Click the mouse on the screen to unselect the text.

Selection Bar

There is an invisible vertical area on the left side of the screen called the *selection bar*. You can see this area only by noticing how the mouse changes from an I-beam to a left arrow. Sweep your mouse slowly to the left side of the document screen and watch how it changes from an I-beam to a left arrow. When it changes, click the mouse button to select a line of text. Double-click to select a paragraph.

Mouse Techniques

The following list gives shortcuts, tips, and techniques for selecting text with the mouse.

▶ Select characters by clicking and dragging the mouse over the characters.

▶ Select a line by moving the mouse to the left side of the line until the I-beam turns into an arrow, then click once.

▶ Select a word by double-clicking on it.

▶ Select a sentence by holding down the Ctrl key and clicking anywhere in the sentence.

► Select a paragraph by triple-clicking within the paragraph or double-clicking in the selection bar next to the paragraph.

► Select a page by pressing the mouse button and dragging down the page (no shortcuts).

► Select the entire document by Ctrl-clicking or triple-clicking in the selection bar or tapping Ctrl+A.

► Select a rectangular area by holding down the Alt key and clicking and dragging the mouse pointer across and down the text. Figure 6.3 displays text selected using Alt.

Keyboard Techniques

The following list describes some of the techniques you can use with the Shift key.

► Select characters one at a time by holding down the Shift key and tapping the right (→) or left (←) arrows.

► Select from the cursor to the beginning or end of a word by holding down the Shift key and pressing Ctrl+← or Ctrl+→.

► Select from the cursor to the end of a line by holding down the Shift key and pressing End.

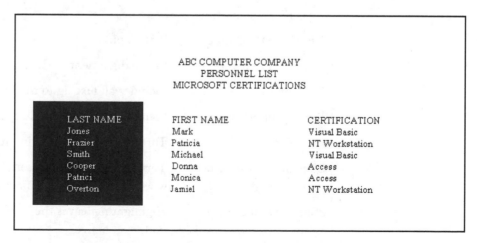

Figure 6.3   *You can make a rectangular text selection by holding down the Alt key while you click and drag.*

▶ Select from the cursor to the same position on the next line by holding down the Shift key and pressing ↑ or ↓.

▶ Select from the cursor to the beginning or end of a paragraph by holding down the Shift key and pressing Ctrl+↑ or Ctrl+↓.

▶ Select screens by holding down the Shift key and pressing PgUp or PgDn.

▶ Select the entire document by pressing Ctrl+A or Ctrl+5 (on the number pad).

F8 Function Key Technique

The F8 key is an interesting selection key: It functions similarly to the F12 or Alt+F4 key in WordPerfect for DOS. The F8 key selects a unit of text each time you tap the key. Table 6.4 is a reference guide for effectively using the F8 key.

F8 Key Combination	Selection
Press F8 first time	Turns on the F8 selector
Once on, press F8 once	Word
Press F8 a second time	Sentence
Press F8 a third time	Paragraph
Press F8 a fourth time	Entire document
Tap a period	Includes all text up to the first period
Tap any letter/character	Includes all text up to that letter/character
Press Esc	Turns off F8, but selection remains
Click the mouse or tap an arrow key	Turns off F8, but selection remains, up to where you had clicked the mouse
Press Esc and click the mouse or tap an arrow key	Highlighting leaves the selection (selection is no longer active)

*Table 6.4   **The F8 Key Reference Guide***

Correcting Text

You can easily correct text and proof your work using Word. There are a number of strategies and techniques for correcting typos and making changes quickly as you type.

Manually Correcting As You Type

When you are typing a line of text and you make a typo, the automatic spell check will alert you with a wavy red line under the typo. The easiest way to correct the word is to immediately tap the Backspace key and back over the typo. Do not tap the left arrow and then press Delete; that's too many keystrokes. The Backspace key is similar to correction tape on a typewriter and requires only one or two keys.

Undo

We also suggest that you use the Undo feature (Edit ➤ Undo) to immediately reverse the typo. Be careful: it might undo the entire line you just typed. And if you use the mouse and click on the Undo button on the Standard toolbar or choose Edit ➤ Undo from the menu bar, you have performed too many keystrokes. Use the keyboard combination for Undo: Ctrl+Z.

Redo

The Undo feature can reverse up to ninety-nine actions. If you wish to redo what you have undone, tap Ctrl+Y to bring back your last Undo or click on the Redo button on the Standard toolbar.

If you click on the drop-down list arrow next to the Undo button, you will see the list of previous Undo actions. If you click on the drop-down list arrow next to the Redo button, you will see the actions you can do again.

Backspace and Delete Techniques

A more advanced method for backing over words as you type is to use the Ctrl+Backspace key combination. Instead of tapping the Backspace key multiple times, hold down Ctrl and tap Backspace once; Word will remove the whole previous word.

When you need to correct a word that is further back in the line, don't backspace over correct characters to get to the incorrect character. Click on the incorrect word, or tap the left or right arrow keys to position the insertion point by the typo. Or use the Ctrl key with the left and right arrow keys to jump from word to word in either direction.

If you are positioned at the beginning of the word, use Delete to remove the characters, not Backspace. Remember, Backspace backs over the letters to the left of the insertion point. Use Delete to remove characters to the right of the insertion point.

An advanced deletion method is to combine Delete with Ctrl to delete the whole word to the right of the insertion point. Ctrl+Delete is faster than lifting your hands from the keyboard, picking up the mouse, selecting the word, and tapping Delete.

Deleting Blank Lines

Extra lines in your text can be quickly deleted by telling Word to display the paragraph symbols, which indicate where the Enter key was typed. Click on the Show/Hide ¶ button near the end of the Standard toolbar. Word will display the paragraph and spacing symbols so you can tell where too many Enter keys have been pressed.

Select all the blank lines (represented by the paragraph symbols) and tap Delete. You can also delete the symbols one line at a time by tapping Delete repeatedly.

Automatically Correcting As You Go Along

If there are specific typos that you always type, such as *don;t* where you mean to type *don't*, you can add them to the AutoCorrect list so it will automatically change your typos as you type.

To add your typos to the AutoCorrect list, follow these steps:

1. Choose Tools ➤ AutoCorrect.

2. In the Replace box (where the insertion point is blinking), type the typo that Word should look out for in the future.

3. Press Tab or click in the With box and type the correct spelling.

4. Click on Add on the right side of the AutoCorrect dialog box.

5. Click on OK.

Now, when you make that particular typo, Word will automatically change it to the correct spelling after you have pressed the spacebar or the Enter key. You will have more fun with AutoCorrect in Chapter 11.

Inserting a Page

Click at the beginning of the line where the new page is to begin and press Ctrl+Enter or choose Insert ➤ Break ➤ Page Break ➤ OK. A new page break will appear. If you change your mind and don't want a page break, tap Ctrl+Z or Edit ➤ Undo or click on the Undo arrow on the Standard toolbar. If the page break is not the last action performed and you are unable to use Undo, position your cursor before the beginning character of the page and press Backspace.

Typing over Text

Typing over existing text (using Overstrike rather than Insert) is risky business because you must watch the screen carefully to make sure that you are not typing over good text as you are typing over the old text. It requires too much monitoring.

We recommend that you delete your old text and add your new text, rather than turning on the Overstrike option. This feature is toggled off and on when you tap the Insert key (OVR—on the left side of the Status bar—will appear bold when Overstrike is on).

Replacing Text

Replacing text requires that you select the word(s) you wish to replace (double-click on the word or use Shift+→ or Shift+← to select the word). Then type your next text. The selected text will be replaced by the new typing, and you won't type over any good text.

Moving and Copying Text

Part of the editing process is the ability to move or copy text to other sections of your document. Use the copy and cut commands to eliminate the re-keying of text at other locations in your document.

When you copy or cut text, the text is stored in an area of memory called the Clipboard. In the Clipboard, Word only remembers the last text you copied or moved. (If you need to manage multiple text selections, check out the Windows 95 Clipbook Viewer, which is a more advanced utility, and slightly more difficult to get the hang of. The following discussion of copy and cut techniques assumes you are using the Clipboard.)

Menu Method

All Windows programs use the same menu and keyboard commands for moving and copying text. The procedure for cutting or copying text is to select the text first, then choose Edit ➤ Copy for copying or Edit ➤ Cut for moving text. Reposition the insertion point at the new location. Choose Edit ➤ Paste to paste (retrieve) the text from the Clipboard.

Shortcut Menu Method

Word makes use of the mouse button opposite the one you usually click. The secondary mouse button (usually the right button) displays a shortcut menu, which has Cut, Copy, and Paste options.

The procedure for using Cut, Copy, and Paste is the same: select the text, keep your pointer on the selected text, click the secondary mouse button (*right-click*), and choose Copy or Cut from the menu. Reposition your insertion point at the new location. Right-click and choose Paste from the shortcut menu. You can also choose paragraph formats through this menu. On the left you'll see the options available to you on the shortcut menu.

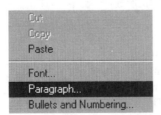

Keyboard Method

The fast keyboard method for cutting or copying and pasting text is to select the text and then tap Ctrl+X for cut or Ctrl+C for copy. Then reposition your cursor at the new location and tap Ctrl+V to paste. This method eliminates reaching for the mouse and using the toolbar.

Toolbar Method

If you use the mouse to select the text, it is more efficient to use the Cut, Copy, and Paste buttons on the toolbar. Select the text and then click on the Cut button (with scissors) to cut or the Copy button (with two sheets of paper) to copy. The selected text goes on the Clipboard. Reposition at the new location and click on the Paste button (with a clipboard) to paste the text.

Remember, once you have moved or copied text onto the Clipboard, you can paste the same text again and again until you cut or copy another selection.

Drag-and-Drop Method

The drag-and-drop method eliminates placing text onto the Clipboard. (You can activate or deactivate this feature through Tools ➤ Options ➤ Edit on the menu bar.) To use drag-and-drop, you select the text, click on the selected text without letting up, and drag the selected text to the new location. You will see a small, gray outline box attached to your cursor as you drag to the new location. When you release the mouse button, the text will be moved from its original location to the new location (marked by the I-beam).

To copy the text instead of moving it, hold down the Ctrl key as you drag. You will see a small, gray outline box with a plus sign attached to the cursor as you drag the copy to its new location.

WARNING Drag and drop can be unwieldy, as the mouse moves very quickly when you move to the new location. Often you will find yourself continuously running past the location where you are trying to drop off the text. If drag-and-drop does not go well, immediately press the Undo key to return the document to its previous state.

The Importance of the Clipboard in Windows 95

As a user of Office 95 desiring to integrate data among the multiple Office 95 programs, you must understand the role of the Clipboard. When you cut or copy a selection into memory, it goes into a part of memory called the *Clipboard*. This storage area holds the last selection you cut or copied. When you cut or copy a new selection, the previous selection is overwritten.

Once a selection is on the Clipboard, it is available to other Windows programs. You can start another program and paste or "paste special" the contents of the Clipboard.

If you paste the selection contents, you are pasting a copy of the selection. Any future changes made to the original selection in the source program are not updated in the destination program. The destination has a copy (a static snapshot), that is all. For example, if you create a budget using Excel and then copy and paste that budget onto a page within a Word report, this is only a copy of the Excel budget. If later on you change some numbers in the Excel budget, they will *not* be reflected in your Word report. You will have to recopy and paste the selection to reflect the new changes in your numbers.

However, if you use Edit ➤ Paste Special after you have copied the selection, you can specify that you wish the copied text to be linked to the source's selection. When a destination program contains a linked selection from a source program, any changes in the source document are updated in the destination document. If you choose Edit ➤ Paste Special to place an Excel budget into a Word report and request a link, when you change the Excel budget, these changes are automatically updated in the Word report. See Chapter 15 for more about linking.

Table 6.5 is a quick-reference list of the methods described for correcting, editing, cutting, and pasting.

Action	Method
Insert text	Click on location for new text; begin typing
Replace text	Select text to be replaced; type new text.
Delete previous word(s)	Press Backspace or Ctrl+Backspace
Delete the next word(s)	Press Delete or Ctrl+Delete
Delete multiple words	Select text; press Delete
Delete a sentence	Ctrl+click in sentence; press Delete
Delete a paragraph	Triple-click in paragraph; press Delete
Delete a page	Select page (click and drag); press Delete
Move word(s)	Select words, press Ctrl+X or Cut button, reposition, and paste by clicking on Ctrl+V or the Paste button
Copy word(s)	Select the words, press Ctrl+C or Copy button, reposition, and paste by clicking on Ctrl+V or the Paste button

Table 6.5 **Editing Reference Guide**

Checking Text

The Spelling feature (Tools ➤ Spelling or F7) is a word-processing tool for electronically checking your document for misspellings and irregular case problems. Word also has an automatic spell-check feature that is turned on when you begin Word. The automatic spell check will underline any misspelled words with a wavy red line as you type. If this feature is not turned on and you would like automatic spell check as you type, follow these steps:

1. Choose Tools ➤ Options.
2. Click on the Spelling tab.
3. Check the first box to activate Automatic Spell Checking.
4. Click on OK.

Once activated, the spell checker will place a wavy red line under words *not* in its dictionary, and the Tip Wizard will flash to alert you to right-click on the misspelled word. This does not always mean that the word it stopped on is incorrectly spelled. It only means that the word is not in the dictionary.

Many proper names, street names, company names, and company-specific words are not in the dictionary. You can tell the software to ignore the word and go on, change the word to another spelling, or add the word to the dictionary so when you use the word in future sentences, Word will know that it is correct.

Homonym problems such as *for* and *four* or *their* and *there* will not be picked up by the spell checker. Homonym problems are spotted by the grammar checker.

If Word alerts you that a word is misspelled and you are not sure of the correct spelling, you can choose from the suggested correct spellings. Right-click on the word that has been underlined and look at the suggestions. Click on the correct spelling. If the correct spelling is not listed, click anywhere in the document to get rid of the shortcut menu, backspace over the word, and try another spelling to see if you get attacked again by the wavy red underline. Below you'll see the automatic-spell-checker shortcut menu with a suggested correct spelling.

We would like to annunce

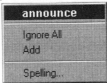

The Spell Checker

To check the spelling of some or all of the text in your document:

1. Select the text to be spell checked (for partial document checking) or start with the insertion point at the top of the document (really, you can start anywhere in the document and the spell checker will wrap around).

2. Press F7 or choose Tools ➤ Spelling to activate the spell checker.

If there are no typos or words about which Word is confused, you will not see the Spell Check dialog box. Word will just display a message telling you that the spell check is complete, as shown at left.

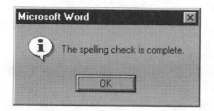

 TIP   If you activate full-blown spell checking (press F7 or click on the Spelling button—with ABC on it—on the Standard toolbar), you can correct a typo and add the typo and its correction to a list of your common typos and corrections. Word's AutoCorrect feature (Tools ➤ AutoCorrect) is an option in the Spelling dialog box that opens when you start the spell check. See *Adding an AutoCorrect Entry during Spell Checking*, below.

Changing or Ignoring Incorrect Words

When Word finds text that is not in either its own dictionary or the added custom dictionaries, it will stop on the text and offer you options for handling the word.

Type the following sentence on a blank line, misspellings and all:

This is a hapy occassion for Bob Ziegler, his fmily and the entire Bromberg community.

Ignore the wavy red underlining that shows up as you are typing. Start the spell check by clicking on the Spelling button on the Standard toolbar or by pressing F7. Figure 6.4 shows the Spelling dialog box displaying the first typo in the sentence.

Word, of course, correctly identifies the first typo, *hapy*, as not being in its dictionaries and displays a list of suggestions for what we might have been trying to spell. Because Word's first suggestion is the correct one, you do not have to type the correction yourself. Click on the Change button, and Word will automatically change the spelling to the highlighted suggestion. Word then goes to the next problem word; you can now change *occassion* to *occasion*.

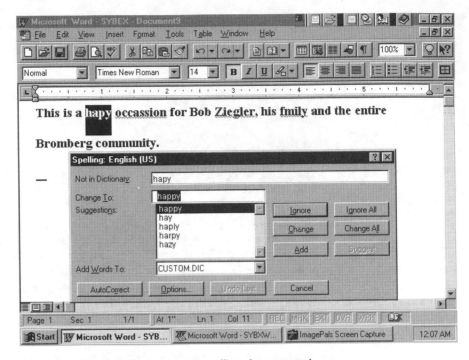

Figure 6.4   **The Spell Checker suggests spellings for your words.**

When Word gets to *Bob Ziegler*, it stops because *Ziegler* is not in Word's dictionaries and Word has no possible suggestions for you. To tell Word that *Ziegler* is correct and to ignore the fact that the word is not in its dictionaries, click on Ignore. Word moves on to the next word.

> **TIP**   If you have multiple occurrences of the same word in one document and you don't want Word to stop again, choose Ignore All so Word will not stop each time it encounters this word in this document.

Adding an AutoCorrect Entry during Spell Checking

Suppose the word *fmily* is a common typo you make, and you see it all the time when you are spell checking documents. During this spell checking, you are going to tell Word to make this typo an AutoCorrect option so when you type *fmily* in future documents Word will automatically correct it.

At this point in the exercise, spell check has stopped on *fmily*. Make sure you have highlighted *family* in the Suggestions box. Click on the AutoCorrect button. Word adds the typo to its list of AutoCorrect words and moves on to the next word. We will manage the next word by adding it to the custom dictionary.

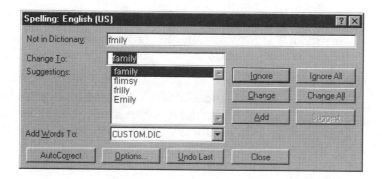

The Custom Dictionary

Many times there are words that are proper names; business acronyms; or technical, medical, or legal words that may not be in Word's dictionary. Although you cannot make changes to Word's dictionary, you can add to and edit words in the custom dictionary.

During the installation process, a dictionary is created for you to add your own words to. The default name of this dictionary is Custom.dic, and it resides in the Windows\MSapps\Proof folder of your hard disk or network drive. This is a folder that all of the Office products share.

Adding to the Custom Dictionary   You are going to add *Bromberg*, the next problem word in our sentence, to Custom.dic by clicking on the Add button on the Spelling dialog box.

In the next section you will take the word out of the custom dictionary, but for right now, add the word so there is something to see in this dictionary. Follow these steps to add a word to the custom dictionary:

1. Activate the Spelling command (F7, or click on the Spelling button, or choose Tools ➤ Spelling).

2. When Word pauses on a word that is not in its dictionary that you think should be part of the custom dictionary (right now it's *Bromberg*), click on the Add button on the right side of the dialog box.

Part
2

Communicating
with Word

3. Repeat the previous step for as many words as you wish to add. If you inadvertently add a word that you don't want, you can edit the custom dictionary and take out the word, as detailed below.

    Editing the Custom Dictionary   Word allows you to see, add, or change the words that are in Custom.dic. There will be times when you add words to the custom dictionary that you did not mean to add. You can easily take out these words or change them in the custom dictionary.

    Word also gives you the ability to create multiple custom dictionaries. You could create a dictionary of legal or medical terms and tell Word to use that specific dictionary in addition to its own dictionary and the custom dictionary. In the next section you will create an additional customized dictionary.

    You are now going to take the word *Bromberg* out of your custom dictionary:

1. Choose Tools ➤ Options. The Options dialog box appears.

2. Choose the Spelling tab.

3. In the bottom left corner of the page, click on the Custom Dictionaries button. This will open a dialog box that lists the names of any custom dictionaries. (Usually there is one Custom.dic. It will be checked because it is currently open and being used in conjunction with the Word dictionary during the spell check.)

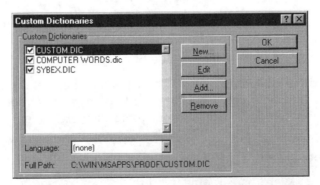

4. On the right side of the Custom Dictionaries dialog box are options. Click on Edit (do not choose Remove). The custom dictionary will open, and you can now add, edit, and delete words. The items in your custom dictionary will be unique to your work and not the ones reflected in the

example above, but you should have the word *Bromberg* in your custom dictionary.

```
Ashanti
Audrey
Boodey
Borland
Bromberg
Centex
Christoper
Coutant
Dann
Dupont
Hegman
Kru
Nollet
Phila
Rita
```

NOTE When you edit the custom dictionary, Word notifies you that automatic spell checking will be turned off while you are editing the dictionary. After you finish with the dictionary, make sure you turn automatic spell checking back on by choosing Tools ➤ Options ➤ Spelling and rechecking the Automatic Spell Checking option.

5. Double-click on *Bromberg* and press Delete.

6. Save the custom dictionary. Click on the Save button on the Standard toolbar or choose File ➤ Save from the menu. Word will save over the previous version of the dictionary.

7. Choose File ➤ Close.

8. You will be asked if formatting should be saved to the file. Click on No.

New Dictionaries

You can create additional dictionaries (as many as you want) to store words that you may want to group together, such as legal or computer words. You create these new dictionaries for Word to refer to when spell checking your documents.

Creating New Dictionaries   The steps for creating your own custom dictionary are easy to follow; Word has made this multidictionary feature the best among all the word-processing programs.

1. Choose Tools ➤ Options to activate the Options dialog box.

2. Click on the Spelling tab.

3. Click on the Custom Dictionaries option.

4. Click on New. Word opens the subfolder where all of the dictionaries are filed.

5. At the bottom of the Create Custom Dictionary dialog box, the insertion point is blinking in the File Name text box; type a name for your dictionary (e.g., **COMPUTER WORDS**) here. Click on Save. Word appends the .dic extension to the name so it knows this is a dictionary file. Figure 6.5 shows the Create Custom Dictionary dialog box.

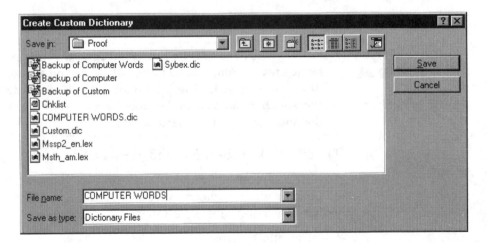

Figure 6.5   **The Create Custom Dictionary dialog box**

6. When you have clicked on Save, make sure that your new dictionary is checked in the Custom Dictionaries dialog box so Word knows to use it as well as Custom.dic during the spell check. Click on OK until you return to document window. The Spelling dialog box below shows three dictionaries in the dialog box.

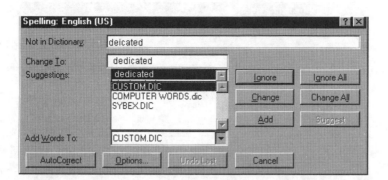

Adding Words to a New Dictionary during the Spell Check Word gives you the ability to add words to a particular custom dictionary. You can then open that particular dictionary during a spell check so Word will know to use your dictionary as well as its own.

1. Start a new document (click on the New button or choose File ➤ New ➤ OK).

2. Type the following words in the blank document and don't worry about the wavy red underlines. If these lines do not appear, the Automatic Spell Checking option has not been reset; choose Tools ➤ Options ➤ Spelling to set it.

   Internet

   gigabyte

   subdirectory

   Microsoft

3. Position your cursor at the beginning of the list and start the spell check.

4. When Word stops on the first word, *Internet*, notice at the bottom of the dialog box that Word is telling you what dictionary it will add words to.

5. In the Add Words To box, click on the drop-down list arrow and choose the name of your new dictionary.

6. Click on the Add button to add *Internet* to your new custom dictionary. Continue adding all the words to the dictionary. When the spell check is complete, click on OK. Figure 6.6 shows *Internet* being added to the Computer Words dictionary.

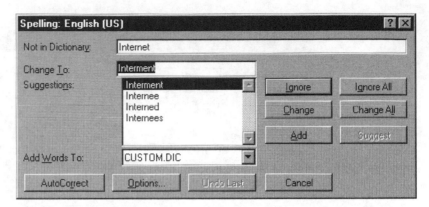

Figure 6.6 *You can add words to your custom dictionary.*

You do not have to tell Word to use a particular custom dictionary when spell checking. It will do that automatically based on your custom dictionary settings. You do have to specify a custom dictionary when you want to add specific words to it.

NOTE   Microsoft has included a spelling feature in the other Office products and has designed all of the spellers to use the same Custom.dic. Excel can also use any of the custom dictionaries you create in Word.

AutoCorrect Checking

The AutoCorrect option is an extremely helpful tool, not only for the automatic correction of typos, but also for its ability to store any phrases, paragraphs, letters, and graphics.

Adding Words to AutoCorrect

Although Word has created a list of the common typos that are created during word-processing sessions, these typos may not be the ones you make. You can easily add your own typo corrections without spell checking:

1.   Choose Tools ➤ AutoCorrect. The insertion point will be blinking in the Replace box, which is where you will type the typo.

2.   Type **corect** (this is a common typo).

3.   Press the Tab key to move to the With box. Here you will tell the software with what word it should replace *corect*.

4. Type **correct**.

5. Click on the Add button on the lower right side of the dialog box.

6. Click on OK.

7. Test your typo. On a blank line, type the incorrect spelling **corect**. Tap the spacebar or press Enter; Word automatically corrects the typo. Figure 6.7 shows the entry in the list of AutoCorrect words.

   In Chapter 11, you will be given more invaluable uses for the AutoCorrect feature. Right now, add in as many typos as you can think of.

> **NOTE**   The entries you make in AutoCorrect, either through spell checking or through Tools ➤ AutoCorrect, are available to you in the rest of the Office products. So if you make the same kind of typos in the other Office programs, they will automatically be corrected.

The Thesaurus

Effective writing means finding words that precisely express your meaning and thoughts. Word's built-in thesaurus displays multiple synonyms for 90 percent of the words you will use in writing. When Word displays

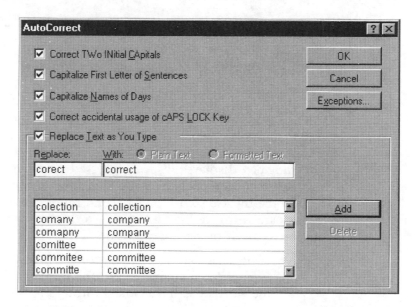

Figure 6.7   *The AutoCorrect list of replacement words*

a list of synonyms, you can easily replace a word in your document with one of them.

Click on any word and choose Tools ➤ Thesaurus or press Shift+F7, and Word will display the synonyms for that word and, in some cases, the antonyms (opposite meanings).

Below you'll see the list of synonyms for the word *dedicated*, used in the first sentence of the Gettysburg Address, spoken by Abraham Lincoln at the consecration of the Gettysburg cemetery in 1863.

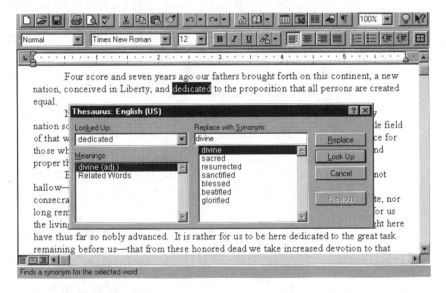

The word being looked up appears on the left side of the Thesaurus dialog box in the Looked Up box. Below the Looked Up box is the Meanings list, which displays a short definition of the word, the part of speech, and sometimes the antonym for the word. The right side of the dialog box displays a list of suggested synonyms to replace the word in your document. If you double-click on one of the synonyms, it will become the Looked Up word, and more synonyms and meanings will appear. To move back through words that were selected, click on the Previous button on the right side of the dialog box.

To return to the list of synonyms for the first word you were using, click on the drop-down arrow next to the Looked Up box, and you will see all of the words you have looked through in this session.

If you see the word you want, click on it once and then click on the Replace button on the right side of the Thesaurus dialog box.

If you change your mind and don't want to use any of the suggested synonyms, click on the Cancel button.

The Grammar Checker

If you are concerned about the readability of your document or want Word to check for correct word usage, you will find the grammar checker to be helpful but not always accurate.

Word's grammar checker uses rules to identify problems in your writing, such as passive verbs, pronoun errors, possessive noun errors, homonym problems (like *there* and *their*), double negatives, and even political incorrectness.

The grammar checker is set up by default to check your writing for a business audience and will check both spelling and grammar. If you do not want the grammar checker to check spelling, choose Tools ➤ Options, click on the Grammar tab, and uncheck the Check Spelling option. You can also customize the settings and rules by which the grammar checker checks your document.

The results of a grammar check of the first sentence in the Gettysburg Address are shown below. The grammar checker has flagged the sentence for being gender specific or, as we say in the '90s, politically incorrect.

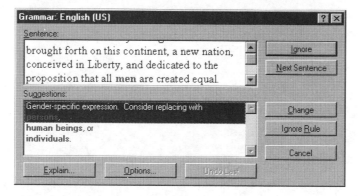

To check the grammar in your document, choose Tools ➤ Grammar from the menu bar. The grammar checker will stop on the first word that violates one of its rules. You can ignore the suggestion by pressing Ignore or, if the Change button is active, tell the grammar checker to change the word or sentence. Sometimes the checker will show you the grammar rule to consider, and you can choose to have the checker ignore the rule for the rest of the document by pressing Ignore Rule.

If you ask the grammar checker to change your writing and then decide you do not like the change, tap the Undo Last button in the Grammar dialog box.

If the sentence is too long, Word may be unable to process it for its grammatical structure and will tell you so in the suggestion. For most people, this should be taken as a hint to shorten the sentence.

When the grammar checker has finished checking your document, you will be given some Readability Statistics to ponder: the number of words, sentences, and paragraphs used and the grade level for which the writing was appropriate. After you have read the statistics, you can press Esc, or click on the X in the upper right corner of the Statistics dialog box, or simply click on OK.

TIP You can select a portion of your document to be grammar checked. Highlight the text to be checked and choose Tools ➤ Grammar from the menu bar.

Chapter 7

Enhancing Documents with Character and Paragraph Formats

Featuring

Enhancing a document's appearance is Word's specialty. In seconds, you can create professional-looking documents.

Text and document enhancements are called *formats*. Word offers a tremendous amount of formatting options: multiple typefaces and point sizes (depending on your printer); easy-to-apply type styles, such as bold, italics, single and double-underline; and many text alignment, indentation, and spacing options.

This chapter describes how to set character and paragraph formats manually. Word provides many special tools to automate formatting, such as Template Wizards, discussed in Chapter 9, and the AutoFormat and Style commands, discussed in Chapter 10. With these tools, you can create beautiful documents without doing much more than typing the headings and text, and letting Word do the rest for you.

Word also provides many other features that take you into the realm of desktop publishing, such as multiple-column newsletter layouts. These features are covered in Chapter 10.

How to Format Text

Word provides a number of methods for changing formats. The Formatting toolbar contains buttons for the most common text formats:

Keyboard shortcuts are also available for some formats. The Font dialog box offers the standard character formats, as well as other options, such as colors for your text and special effects. The Paragraph dialog box contains the paragraph formats, including indent, spacing, and alignment choices.

When you want to apply a format to text that is already typed, you must select the text first and then apply the format. Use all of your selection shortcuts—double-clicking to select an entire word, Ctrl-clicking to select a sentence, using the selection bar to select a line, and so on.

You can also turn on the formats before you type, so that as you type, the formatting will be applied. For example, if you press Ctrl+B to turn on bold type, any text you type will be bold until you tap Ctrl+B again to turn off this type style.

Formatting Characters

Word's formats can be applied to any characters. Character formats don't affect the entire paragraph unless you select an entire paragraph. When you bold a word within a paragraph, the entire paragraph does not become bold. On the other hand, alignments (centered, left-aligned, right-aligned, and justified) affect entire paragraphs. For example, when you center a word within a paragraph, the entire paragraph becomes centered.

The simplest formats applied to text are font changes, point size changes, and adding the type styles of bold, italics, and underline. Word supplies a comprehensive dialog box to display all of the fonts, sizes, and styles. Choose the Format ➤ Font command, or right-click the mouse on the text and select Font from the shortcut menu to access all of your options at once. Figure 7.1 shows the Font dialog box.

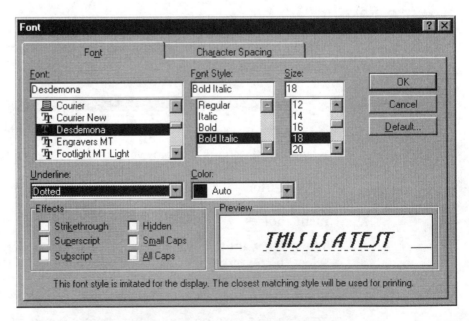

Figure 7.1   **The Font dialog box contains all the character-formatting options.**

In this dialog box, special effects such as strikethrough and different flavors of underline are listed. The option to apply color to your text is also available. The Preview section in the lower-right corner of the Font dialog box shows a small preview of the results of your changes. This lets you experiment and see what you are going to get before making a final selection.

Changing the Default Font

Through the Font dialog box, you can specify a different default font or font size for your current document and all new, future documents. Choose the desired font and size and click the Default button in the Font dialog box. When Word asks you to confirm the change, choose Yes.

Your selection will be used as the default font for all new documents. The new font and point size will not affect documents you have already typed and stored on the disk.

> **TIP**   Despite the fact that you can't see the punctuation marks in Times New Roman, there are business professionals who find the default typeface (font) of Times New Roman a good choice for business typing. For editing choose Courier New. The default point size (height of the typeface) is 10 points, which you might want to change to a larger, easier-to-read size (9 to 12 points is the business typing point size range; 12 points is a good reading size).

Changing the Font

It is fun to experiment with different fonts. Your choices depend on the audience for your document (you wouldn't pick the same font for a newsletter as you would for a serious proposal).

You can change the font for your document or selected text through the Font dialog box or Formatting toolbar. To use the Formatting toolbar, click the drop-down arrow next to the font name. The additional fonts available to your printer are listed:

The shortcut key combination of Shift+Ctrl+F also activates the font option on the Formatting toolbar. Tap a down arrow key after pressing Shift+Ctrl+F to select from the list of fonts displayed.

Changing the Font Size

The size of the font is measured in *points*. There are 72 points to an inch. Dramatic headlines on newspapers can be as large as 216 points, or 3 inches. Normal business typing font sizes are between 9 and 12 points.

To change the point size of your document or of selected text, use the Format ➤ Font dialog box or click the drop-down arrow next to the font size on the Formatting toolbar.

The shortcut key combination of Shift+Ctrl+P allows for quick font size changes. After you press this combination, type in a new size or tap a down arrow to select from the list of point sizes displayed. See Figure 7.2 for examples of different point sizes.

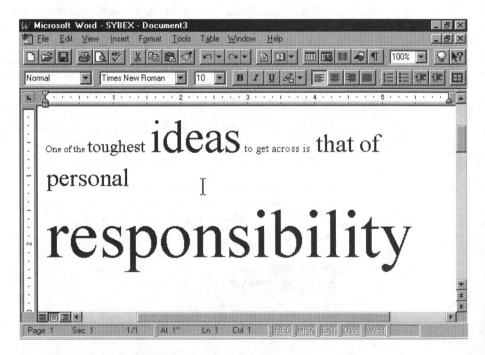

Figure 7.2　　**Multiple point sizes in a sentence**

TIP You can designate point sizes not shown in the drop-down list of font point sizes. When you click the drop-down list arrow on the toolbar or press Shift+Ctrl+P, type in any number for a point size, such as 15, 17, or 52.

Changing the Type Style

The three most common character formats in business documents are bold, italics, and underline. You can set these styles in the following ways:

▶ Display the Font dialog box (Format ➤ Font) and select from the Font Style list box. You can also select special styles in the Effects section of this dialog box, which includes Strikethrough, Superscript, Subscript, Hidden, Small Caps, and All Caps options.

▶ The Formatting toolbar includes the buttons B, I, and U, for bold, italics, and underline.

▶ The shortcut key combinations, such as Ctrl+B for bold, Ctrl+I for italics, and Ctrl+U for underline, are as easy to use as the buttons on the Formatting toolbar. Table 7.1 lists those character formats that have shortcut key combinations.

Format	Keyboard Shortcut
Bold	Ctrl+B
Italic	Ctrl+I
Underline	Ctrl+U
Words only underline	Shift+Ctrl+W
Double continuous underline	Shift+Ctrl+D
All caps	Shift+Ctrl+A
Uppercase, propercase, lowercase	Shift+F3
Superscript	Shift+Ctrl+Plus Sign
Subscript	Ctrl+Equal Sign

Table 7.1 Character Formats and Their Shortcuts

Part 2

Communicating with Word

Remember, most of these character formats are toggles—tap the key combination once to turn the format on or off. If a format is not a toggle, click the Undo button to reverse the action of applying the format. Multiple formats can be applied at the same time; for example, you can make a word bold, italic, and underlined.

> **TIP**   To create a few lines on a page for printing purposes only, for example for signature block lines, click the Underline button or press Ctrl+U and then press the Tab key repeatedly. The insertion point will jump to each tab stop, dragging the underline with it. This creates an even line, and you can do this to print multiple lines. Make sure you press Ctrl+U or click the Formatting toolbar button to turn off the underline feature when you're finished. Don't type on these lines, or you will push the underline to the right.

Highlighting Characters

Word has added a new character-formatting command: Highlight. This format applies color to text. Like the yellow highlighter markers we use to highlight words in a book or manual, you can now "yellow marker" (highlight) words in your document. If you don't have a color printer, the different highlight colors will print in different shades of gray.

This is a great feature in a workgroup environment where you route a document to other individuals. Highlighted words can be used as discussion points. Even if you are in a single PC environment, you can use the highlight feature to dramatically emphasize words in a printed document or use the highlight as on-screen reminders for yourself. Figure 7.3 shows a sentence where specific words are highlighted.

Word supplies four colors and the None color for highlighting. Note that you must have existing text in the document in order to apply the highlight. Unlike other formats that can be turned on before typing, the highlighter can only be applied to existing text.

Follow these steps to use the highlight feature:

1. To select the highlighter, click the drop-down arrow to the right of the highlight button on the Formatting toolbar.

2. Choose a color. Hover the mouse over your document typing area. Notice that the I-beam cursor now also has a marker symbol.

3. Click and drag across the word(s) you want to highlight.

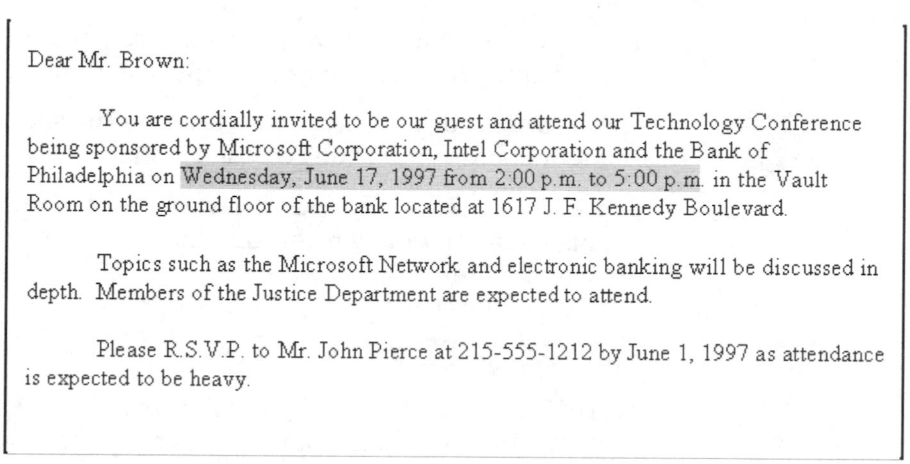

Dear Mr. Brown:

    You are cordially invited to be our guest and attend our Technology Conference being sponsored by Microsoft Corporation, Intel Corporation and the Bank of Philadelphia on Wednesday, June 17, 1997 from 2:00 p.m. to 5:00 p.m. in the Vault Room on the ground floor of the bank located at 1617 J. F. Kennedy Boulevard.

    Topics such as the Microsoft Network and electronic banking will be discussed in depth. Members of the Justice Department are expected to attend.

    Please R.S.V.P. to Mr. John Pierce at 215-555-1212 by June 1, 1997 as attendance is expected to be heavy.

Figure 7.3 **Using the highlight feature to emphasize text**

4. To turn off the highlight feature, press Esc or click the highlight marker button again. Note that if you drag across highlighted text with the same color, the text becomes unhighlighted.

Setting Alignment Formats

Alignment formats, such as centering, indenting, and tab stops, are applied to paragraphs rather than to individual characters. For example, you cannot center one word within a line of words without centering the entire line.

Remember, a paragraph is defined as any amount of text ending with a paragraph mark. You can click the show/hide paragraph button on the Standard toolbar (or use the keyboard shortcut, Ctrl+Shift+*) to see where the paragraph marks are in your document. When you apply paragraph-based formats, all of the text within the paragraph and before the paragraph mark receive the formats. This is in contrast to character formats, which you can apply to one character or word without affecting the other text in the paragraph.

The ability to center a line with heading or date text has long been available with typewriters and word processors. Word's capabilities include center, right, left, and justified alignments. Figure 7.4 shows examples of all four text-alignment positions. The default alignment is left; when the line word wraps or you press the Enter key, the insertion point returns to the left margin (unless an indent is set).

You can set these alignments by pressing the shortcut keys or by using the four alignment buttons on the Formatting toolbar:

You can also select alignments, as well as the other paragraph formats discussed in this chapter, through the Format ➤ Paragraph dialog box, shown in Figure 7.5.

Centering Text

Word's centered alignment centers text between the left and right margins. Here is a quick way to center your text:

1. Position the cursor on a new blank line or click on an existing line of text that ends in a return (paragraph mark). If you click into a single existing line of text, only that one paragraph becomes centered. Select multiple paragraphs to center all of them at the same time.

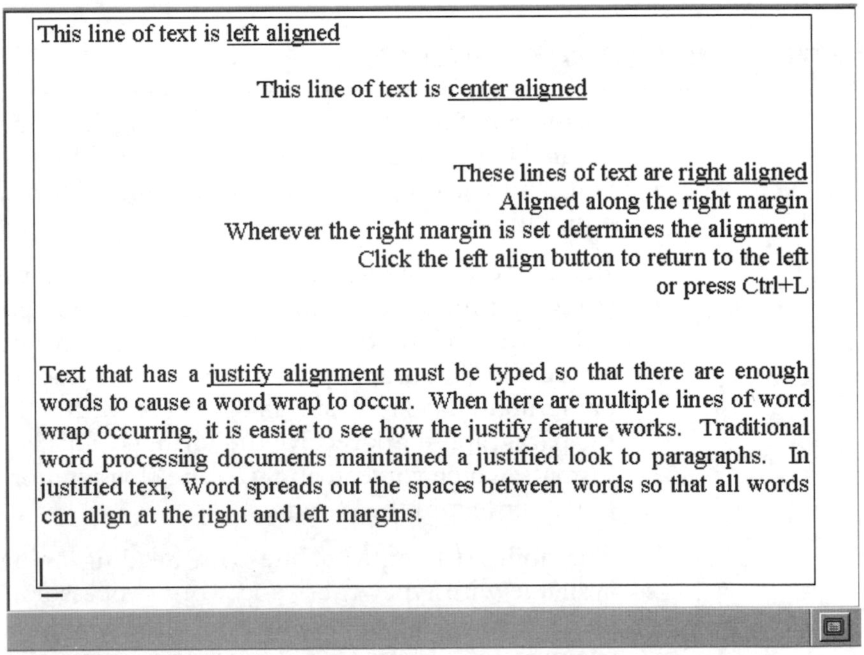

This line of text is <u>left aligned</u>

This line of text is <u>center aligned</u>

These lines of text are <u>right aligned</u>
Aligned along the right margin
Wherever the right margin is set determines the alignment
Click the left align button to return to the left
or press Ctrl+L

Text that has a <u>justify alignment</u> must be typed so that there are enough words to cause a word wrap to occur. When there are multiple lines of word wrap occurring, it is easier to see how the justify feature works. Traditional word processing documents maintained a justified look to paragraphs. In justified text, Word spreads out the spaces between words so that all words can align at the right and left margins.

Figure 7.4   ***Word's four paragraph alignments***

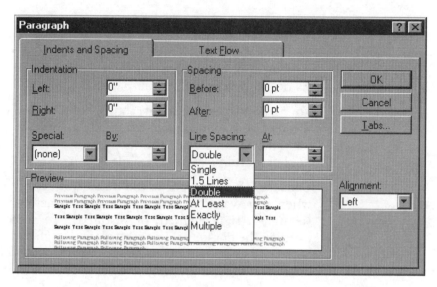

Figure 7.5 *The Paragraph Format dialog box contains all the paragraph-formatting options.*

2. Click the center button on the Formatting toolbar or press Ctrl+E (think of E as *Even* between the margins).

3. Type the text to be centered and press Enter. If you continue typing now, the next line will also be centered.

4. When you are ready to type a line of text with a different alignment, choose the button or press the key combination for that alignment. For example, click the left alignment button or press Ctrl+L to return to the left margin of the document.

TIP Even if the text does not look centered on the screen, it should print centered on the page. To get a realistic view of the centering, use the File ➤ Print Preview option to see how the document will look when it's printed.

When you want to center all the text vertically on the page, not just horizontally on a line, use the Layout menu's Center option for Vertical Alignment. To get to this menu item, choose File ➤ Page Setup ➤ Layout ➤ Vertical Alignment—Center. For example, you may want to use a Center page alignment for a title page, where the text must be centered between the top and bottom margins as well as between the left and right margins.

Left-Aligning Text

Left alignment means the text will be aligned at the left margin of the document or the temporary left margin made by an indent command. As noted earlier, the default paragraph format is left alignment.

Your left margin (or indent) settings of your document determine where the text will align on the left. For example, if your left margin is the default of 1.25 inches, the text will line up at 1.25 inches. You can set the left margin by choosing File ➤ Page Setup ➤ Margin.

Because left alignment is the default, it is only necessary to tell Word when you want to return to left alignment from another alignment (centered, right-aligned, or justified). To switch to left-aligned text, position the cursor on a new blank line or click on an existing line of text that ends in a return (paragraph mark). Then click the left alignment button on the Formatting toolbar or press Ctrl+L.

Right-Aligning Text

When you choose right alignment, you will start typing the text at the right margin, but the text "pulls back" to the left as you type, so that the right side of each line aligns with the right margin. The left side of the text is not aligned.

To right-align text, position the cursor on a new blank line or click on an existing line of text that ends in a return (paragraph mark), and then click the right alignment button on the Formatting toolbar or press Ctrl+R. If you click into a single existing line of text, only that line will be right aligned. Select multiple lines before issuing the command to right align them all at the same time.

Type the text to be right aligned and press Enter. If you continue typing, the next line will also be right aligned. Click the left alignment button or press Ctrl+L to return to the left side of the margin.

Justifying Text

Word's Justify format aligns both the left and right side of text to the left and right margins. This alignment gives the text a typeset look, where the text is squared off similar to the text lines on a newspaper.

NOTE Keep in mind that Justify alignment can give a professional but somewhat static appearance to a document. It is generally easier to read text that is not justified.

To justify text, click anywhere in a paragraph that should be justified or select multiple paragraphs. Then click the justify button on the Formatting toolbar or press Ctrl+J. The left and right sides of the text will align with the margins. To return to left alignment, click the left alignment button on the Formatting toolbar or press Ctrl+L.

Copying Formats with Format Painter

Once you have formatted a series of characters or a paragraph, you can easily copy these formats to other characters or paragraphs. You no longer need to remember which formats (font, point size, and so on) you applied to a word(s). Copying these formats to other words makes it easy to reapply formatting. You can now create documents that have a more consistent look to them.

The Format Painter is a unique feature within Word that allows you to copy the formats of characters or paragraphs and apply these same formats to other locations. Imagine that you have bolded, underlined, and small-capped a word. You want the same formats applied to another word without manually selecting them again. Or suppose you have a heading that is in a different typeface and font size, as well as bold, italic, and centered. The next two headings in your document should have the same formats, but you don't wish to create a style because you will never use this heading format again. This is when you would use the Format Painter.

The Format Painter can manage the copying of formats applied to both characters and paragraphs.

To copy a format, follow these steps:

1. Click into the word that already has the character formats or select the line that already has the paragraph formats.

 2. Click (one-time copy) or double-click (multiple copies) the Format Painter button on the Standard toolbar:

   When you hover the mouse back onto the screen, the I-beam cursor now also shows a paintbrush.

3. Click once on a single word or select the multiple words or lines that should receive the format copy.

4. Turn off the Format Painter by clicking the Format Painter button again or by pressing the Esc key.

Setting Tabs

Setting tab stops has been the traditional method for lining up multiple lines of text on a typewriter. Word provides both column and table features to make it easy to produce tabular formats. Tabs do not allow you the full flexibility you can have with tables. You cannot insert text in one tabbed column without affecting the alignment of all the tabbed columns. Tabs are recommended for the indentation of the first line of text and for small amounts of text that need to be typed in multiple columns. For more complex formatting, use columns or tables, which are discussed in Chapter 10.

The default unit of measurement when setting tabs is inches. Instead of inches, you can use centimeters (cm), points (pt), or picas (pi). When you type in the measurement, use the letters *cm, pt,* or *pi* after the number. Word will convert it to inches.

Tab Types

Word offers four types of tab stop alignments:

▶ The default tabs are left-aligned. When you press the Tab key, the insertion point jumps to the first tab stop, and text aligns so that its left side lines up at the tab stop.

▶ With a right-aligned tab, after you press Tab, any typed text aligns so that its right side lines up at the tab stop.

▶ A center tab causes the text to be centered on either side of the tab stop.

▶ Decimal tabs allow you to line up numbers on their decimal points.

A special type of tab stop is created with the bar alignment tab. This tab causes a vertical bar to appear at the tab stop, giving an effect similar to border lines in a table, as shown in the example in Figure 7.6.

Bar tabs add a vertical line so that each tabbed line appears to have a line divider. Set the bar tab in the same way that you would set the other tabs. When you have tabbed to that set position, a bar appears. Usually, you will not want to type right at the bar. Instead, press Tab again so that the bar stands alone.

Word also allows you to set leaders for your tabs. Leaders help the reader's eye move across a tabbed line of text or numbers. When you set a tab (left, right, center, or decimal tab), you can give that tab a leader attribute of dots (periods), dashes, underline, or none. The default attribute is none (for no leader). Figure 7.7 shows a document that includes tab leaders.

ABC COMPUTER COMPANY
PERSONNEL LIST
MICROSOFT CERTIFICATIONS

LAST NAME	FIRST NAME	CERTIFICATION
Jones	Mark	Visual Basic
Frazier	Patricia	NT Workstation
Smith	Michael	Visual Basic
Cooper	Donna	Access
Patrici	Monica	Access
Overton	Jamiel	NT Workstation

Figure 7.6   Bar tabs create vertical bars at their tab stops.

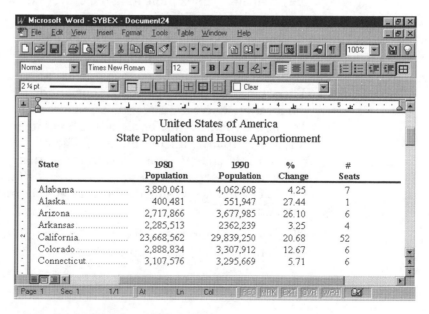

Figure 7.7   Tab leaders help guide the reader's eye.

The tab types are *relative to the margin,* in that they are set from the left margin of your document. For example, a tab stop at 2" is a tab 2 inches in from the already set left margin. If your left margin is the default 1.25 inches, the tab at 2" is 2 inches from the existing 1.25-inch left margin. The tab is actually set at 3.25 inches, measuring from the left edge of the piece of paper instead of from the margin.

Setting New Default Tabs

View the ruler (View ➤ Ruler) and notice the small tick marks at every half an inch:

Word sets the default tabs at every half inch so that you do not need to "space over" when you need to move across a line. Press the Tab key to move the insertion point to the next half-inch mark on the ruler. Always use the Tab key instead of the spacebar to line up your columnar work (or use Words's column and table features, described in Chapter 10).

To change the default tabs, choose Format ➤ Tabs to see the Tabs dialog box. You will not see the list of default tab stops; the dialog box shows only a small text box indicating the current default tab settings. Change the default from .5" to any other increment. You can set default tab settings as low as every .01" and as high as every 22". Click OK to save your changes. Figure 7.8 shows the Tabs dialog box set with a new default of 1".

These tab stops only apply for the current document you are in and from the location where the insertion point was when you set the new default. To change the defaults for already tabbed items, select all the lines first (drag over them with the mouse). Then set the new default tabs. To permanently change your tab settings so that all new documents have the default tabs that you desire, open the Normal.dot template. Change your tab defaults by using the Format ➤ Tabs menu option and save the changes.

When you are working with tabs, keep in mind that the tab set information is held in the paragraph marker at the end of each line.

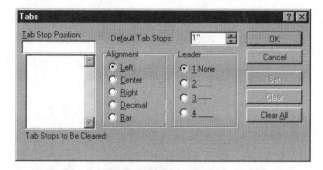

Figure 7.8   The Tabs Dialog box with the default tab settings

Setting Multiple Tab Stops

Word allows you to set tabs using either the Tabs dialog box or visually by clicking on the ruler. In this section, we will go through the steps for creating the business sample shown in Figure 7.9. For this example, we will use the Tabs command on the Format menu. Setting tabs on the ruler is discussed a little later in the chapter.

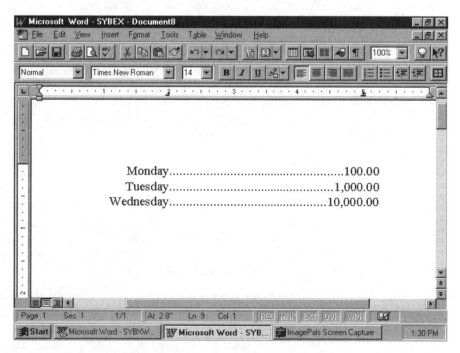

Figure 7.9   A sample business document using multiple tabs

To create the sample business document, follow these steps:

1. Position the cursor on a blank line and choose Format ➤ Tabs.

2. Type the number **2** in the Tab Stop Position text box. This sets a tab stop at 2".

3. Click the Right radio button in the Alignment section.

4. Click the Set button on the right side of the dialog box. Do not click OK yet.

5. Type the number **5** to set a tab stop at 5".

6. Click the Decimal radio button.

7. Click the Leader radio button next to 2 (the dotted leader).

8. Click the Set button on the right side of the dialog box.

9. Click OK to signal you are finished.

10. When you return to the document, press the Tab key and type the word **Monday**.

11. Press the Tab key once to jump to position 5". Notice the dots leading over to this tab stop.

12. Type **100.00** and press Enter.

13. Tab to the second line and type **Tuesday**.

14. Press Tab and type **1,000.00**.

15. Tab to the third line, type **Wednesday**, press Tab, and type **10,000.00**.

Clearing Tabs

To clear a specific tab stop for text that is currently using the tab, you must first select all of the text. Remember, each paragraph mark holds the information about the previously set tabs. You must select all of the tabbed lines before making a change to the tab stop. If you are removing a tab set for new text that has not yet been typed, just position the cursor on a new blank line before clearing the tab.

After you've selected the text or positioned the cursor, choose Format ➤ Tabs. In the left side of the dialog box, click on the tab stop you want to clear, then on the Clear button on the right side of the dialog box. If you click Clear All by mistake, choose the Cancel button and start all over again. Repeat this process for each tab stop you want to clear. Click OK to signal you are finished.

Clear All is the button to use when you want to remove all of your custom tabs. When you choose Clear All, the default tab stops become operational again.

NOTE   Another way of thinking about clearing all tabs is that you are setting the default tab stops all over again. With Word, you always have tab stops. Either you have at least one of your own custom tab stops, or you have some type of default tabs.

Setting Tabs Using the Ruler

As you've seen, the ruler (View ➤ Ruler) displays the tick marks for the default left tabs. The ruler shows other tab marker symbols when you have set your own custom tabs (through the Tabs dialog box or by clicking on the ruler).

To set a tab on the ruler, display the ruler and click once on the position on the ruler where you want to set a tab. A small tab symbol, resembling a left angle (it looks like an L for left) will appear on the ruler line:

This is the default left-aligned tab setting.

If you want to set a different type of tab, first change the tab type symbol on the furthest left side of the ruler (at the left corner of the ruler). Click on this symbol to cycle through the four possible tab marker symbols:

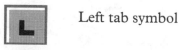   Left tab symbol

Right tab symbol

   Center tab symbol

Decimal tab symbol

Click the tab symbol until you find the representation of the tab that you want. Then click further down on the ruler at the number of the tab position where you would like this type of tab to be set. For example, click until you get a center tab symbol and then click at 3" on the ruler to set a center tab 3 inches in from the left margin of the page. Figure 7.10 shows an example with a center tab set on the ruler and some text formatted with that custom tab.

Note that if you did click to set a custom tab at 3", any default tabs that appeared on the ruler before will be gone—Word figures that you want your first tab stop to be at 3". You can set other tab stops, before or after 3", by clicking to change the tab symbol (if necessary), and then clicking on that position in the ruler.

TIP   To get to the Tabs dialog box quickly, double-click the tab set number on the ruler.

If the tab that you set by clicking on the ruler is not where you want it to be, you do not need to remove it and start again. You can move the tab around on the ruler until you see the layout you desire. When you have already typed the text, the only trick to moving tabs on the ruler is

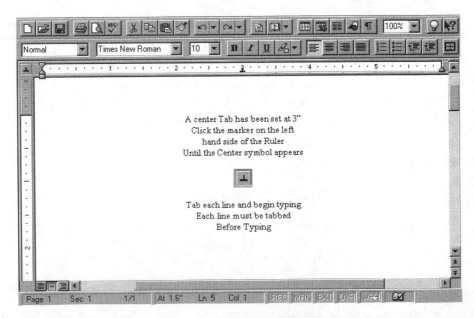

Figure 7.10   You can click the left side of the ruler to change the tab symbol type.

to make sure that you have first selected (dragged the mouse over) all of the text lines that are currently using this tab stop. Once you have selected the lines of text, click and drag the symbol for the particular tab stop to the right or left to reposition the tab where you want it to appear.

To remove a tab from the ruler, you can use Format ➤ Tab and clear the individual tabs you have set, as described earlier. You can also simply drag the tab stop off of the ruler. The tab symbol (and setting) will disappear. Use Undo if you inadvertently pull off the wrong tab stop.

Setting Multiple Alignments on a Single Line

You may want to format a single line of text with different alignments. For example, you might want some text aligned at the left, some text centered, and some text aligned on the right side of a line, as shown in Figure 7.11. You can't do this by using the paragraph-formatting commands of left, center, and right, because Word allows a paragraph or line to have only one type of alignment at a time—not all three on one line. However, you can set up multiple alignments on a single line by using the tab stops and the ruler.

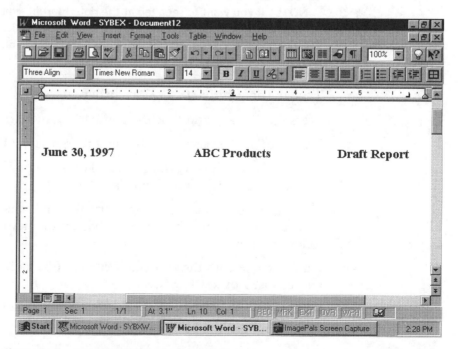

Figure 7.11   Multiple alignments on a single line

To set the alignments shown in Figure 7.11, you need to set a center tab stop in the middle of the margins and a right tab at the right side of the margin (you don't need a left tab stop because the regular left margin will take care of that alignment). Follow these steps:

1. Position the cursor on a blank line.

2. Click the tab symbol on the left side of the ruler until the center tab appears.

3. Click at 3" further down the ruler to set a center tab stop at 3". This is the middle of the page for the default margins of 1.25" on both sides. The calculation is 8.5-inch paper with 2.5-inch left and right margins gives a typing area of 6 inches. Half of 6 inches is 3 inches. Find your own center between the margins for your page layout.

4. Click back on the tab symbol on the left side of the ruler until the right tab appears.

5. Find position 5.5" and then click the second space after 5.5" (this is really 5.75", not quite at 6").

NOTE   If you want to set a tab at the right margin, you may want to use the Tabs dialog box instead of the ruler. It is difficult to click directly on the right margin marker and have the program "hear" that you want to set a tab at the right margin.

6. Type the date **June 30, 1997** at the left margin.

7. Press the Tab key and type the company name **ABC Products**.

8. Press the Tab key again. At the right margin, type **Draft Report.**

9. Press Enter when you are finished. There are now three alignments on the same line: left, center, and right.

   If you think that you will want to use the three-alignment tab set again in future documents, make a new style for them, by continuing with the following steps.

10. Click the line with the text (the text won't be copied; only the tab sets) and choose Format ➤ Style.

11. Click the New button. In the next dialog box, type over the name Style1 to give your style a name (such as **Three Align**).

12. Click on the Add to Template checkbox, so that this style will be there for future documents.

13. Click the OK button, then the Close button.

If you created a style for the three alignments, you can easily apply them again. Click the drop-down arrow next to the style box on the Formatting toolbar and choose Three Align:

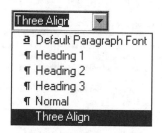

Then you can immediately tab to the different alignments and type your text. For more information about Word styles, see Chapter 10.

Indenting Paragraphs

If you want to indent text at the beginning of a paragraph, you can press the Tab key before you start typing. A tab will push the first line of the paragraph in by one tab stop (one-half inch, by default). Using the Tab key is preferable to spacing over (pressing the spacebar to insert space characters in the text). The tabbed paragraph, however, is not considered an indented paragraph.

If you want to indent more than the first line of text or set special types of indents, you can use Word's Indent commands. Figure 7.12 shows three paragraphs with different formatting: tabbed, indented, and hanging-indent.

You can click the Formatting toolbar buttons, press key combinations, or directly drag the indent markers on the ruler to set indents. You can also set indents through the Format ➤ Paragraph dialog box, in the Indentation section (see Figure 7.5, shown earlier). The following sections describe the various types of indents available in Word and how to set them.

Our American Government

What form of government do we have in the United States? (TAB PARAGRAPH)

The United States, under its Constitution, is a Federal, democratic republic, an indivisible union of 50 sovereign States. With the exception of town meetings, a form of pure democracy, we have at the local, state, and national levels a government which is "democratic" because the people govern themselves; "representative" because the people choose elected delegates by free and secret ballot; and "republican" because government derives its power from the will of the people.

What form of government do we have in the United States? (INDENTED PARAGRAPH)

The United States, under its Constitution, is a Federal, democratic republic, an indivisible union of 50 sovereign States. With the exception of town meetings, a form of pure democracy, we have at the local, state, and national levels a government which is "democratic" because the people govern themselves; "representative" because the people choose elected delegates by free and secret ballot; and "republican" because government derives its power from the will of the people.

What form of government do we have in the United States? (HANGING INDENT)

The United States, under its Constitution, is a Federal, democratic republic, an indivisible union of 50 sovereign States. With the exception of town meetings, a form of pure democracy, we have at the local, state, and national levels a government which is "democratic" because the people govern themselves; "representative" because the people choose elected delegates by free and secret ballot; and "republican" because government derives its power from the will of the people.

Figure 7.12   Tab, indent, and hanging-indent paragraphs

WARNING   Do not press the Enter key at the end of a line and then press the Tab key in order to produce an indented paragraph. Use the increase indent and decrease indent buttons at the end of the Formatting toolbar to indent text in and out from the left margin. Using the Tab key on each line will cause editing problems later. Large tab gaps will appear between words later when you are editing the paragraph. You will need to find and delete the gaps manually with the Delete key.

Increasing and Decreasing Indents

You may need to produce documents in which entire paragraphs are indented from the normal left margin. You can set a temporary left margin by using the increase indent button on the Formatting toolbar, and remove the indent by clicking the decrease indent button.

The entire paragraph moves in one-half inch for each click of the increase indent button or the Ctrl+M keyboard shortcut. To increase the indentation of a paragraph, first click into or select the paragraph(s) that should be indented. Then click the increase indent button or press Ctrl+M for each indent increment. The paragraph moves in one tab set. All the lines in the paragraph are indented. If you want the first line to stay at the left margin but the rest of the word-wrapped paragraph lines to be indented, use a hanging-indent format (Ctrl+T), as described in the next section.

To decrease the indentation, click the decrease indent button or press Shift+Ctrl+M for each indent decrement.

TIP   Use Word's automatic numbering feature to create numbered lines and paragraphs. Use Format ➤ Bullets and Numbering or the numbering button on the right side of the Formatting toolbar to produce a hanging-indent effect for your paragraphs. See Chapter 10 for details.

Formatting Hanging Indents

Hanging indents use a temporary left margin for the word wrapped lines but not for the first line of the paragraph, which is flush with the left margin.

Before you begin typing a paragraph, press the keyboard shortcut of Ctrl+T (think of Ctrl+T as a *Controlled Tab*). As you type, each wrapped line of text will remain indented. Remember, the first line stays at the left margin.

Ctrl+T affects only the indentation of the wrapped lines. The wrapped lines will indent for each tab stop (default tab stops are at each half inch). Press Shift+Ctrl+T to bring the indent back to the left margin (decrease each indent).

WordPerfect's Indent

You can combine a tab stop with a hanging indent to produce simple numbered paragraphs similar in appearance to the effect produced by the F4-indent feature in WordPerfect. Type a number at the left margin. Press the Tab key once. Press Ctrl+T once. Type your lines of text. The wrapped lines will remain indented, while the first line with the number "hangs" back at the left margin.

Remember, once activated, the hanging indent remains in effect for the rest of the document. Each new paragraph will have the wrapped lines indented. To return to a normal left margin, press Shift+Ctrl+T.

If you want to fully emulate the multiple levels of indentation found in WordPerfect with the F4-indent key, use Word's multilevel numbering feature (Format ➤ Bullets and Numbering ➤ Multilevel). See Chapter 10 for the steps to create documents with multilevel numbering.

Formatting a Two-Column Hanging Indent

You can also use Word's hanging-indent format to produce simple but effective two-column typing layouts, as follows:

1. Display the ruler (View ➤ Ruler). (It is helpful to have the ruler on the first couple of times you use the indent feature with Word so that you can fully understand—and therefore control—the indent operation).

2. Type the first column's text normally at the left margin.

3. Press Tab once. (Don't worry that the tab does not go over far enough; the Ctrl+T keypress will handle this.)

4. Press Ctrl+T six times. The bottom indent marker will position itself at 3" on the ruler.

5. Begin typing the second column's text. When the line wraps down to the next one, the text correctly indents.

6. Press Enter only when you're finished typing the paragraph.

7. Type your next paragraph's first line back at the left margin.

8. Press Tab once. The insertion point is automatically positioned at 3". You do not need to press Ctrl+T again. Remember, every new paragraph will have its wrapped lines start at 3" unless you press Shift+Ctrl+T to turn off the hanging indent.

Figure 7.13 shows an example of a format created this way. Note on the ruler the position of the triangular indent symbol on the *second line*. The top triangular indent represents the first line. The first line of typing is at the left margin; but the second line of typing will wrap at 3". The next section describes the indent markers on the ruler.

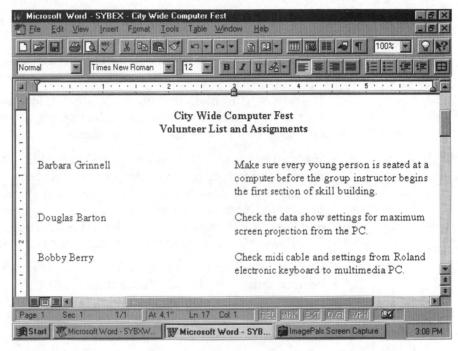

Figure 7.13 *A simple two-column format created by using the hanging-indent feature*

Using the Ruler to Set Indents

On the ruler, the indent markers are normally positioned at the left margin. The top indent marker represents the first line of typing of a paragraph. The bottom indent marker is divided into two sections: a triangle and a square. When you indent text, these markers move to show you where the indentations will occur on the page.

The increase and decrease indent operations cause the markers to move together. This arrangement indicates that the first line and the wrapped lines of a paragraph will both be at a new setting. Here is the ruler with a regular indent setting:

The hanging-indent operation (Ctrl+T) causes the bottom indent marker to move to the next tab stop and the top indent marker to stay at the left margin. This arrangement indicates that the first line of the paragraph will remain at the left margin (hang back), and the wrapped lines will become indented. Here is a hanging-indent setting on the ruler:

If you drag the markers yourself (rather than using the keyboard or button shortcuts) to change the indent position, you can get somewhat confused about the bottom indent marker.

When the top and bottom indent markers start off lined up at the left margin and you drag the *square section of the bottom indent marker*, both the top and bottom markers move together. If you drag the *triangular section of the bottom indent marker*, only the bottom indent marker moves. This layout indicates that only the wrapped lines will be indented; the first line of the paragraph will remain at the left margin.

Once the markers are not aligned and you drag the square section of the bottom indent marker, both markers move together in the same relationship but they remain unaligned. To realign the markers, drag the bottom indent marker's triangular section to line up with the top marker. Then start again.

Setting Left and Right Indents

Left and right indents (sometimes called *double* indents) are activated through the Format ➤ Paragraph ➤ Indents and Spacing tab. For example, double indents are often used for long quotes that must be indented on both sides. Figure 7.14 shows a paragraph that has a left indentation of 1 inch and a right indentation of 1 inch.

Note on the ruler where the triangular indent markers appear. The markers on the first and second lines of the ruler indicate that the first line of text and any wrapped lines of text will be at 1". The right marker has pulled in the right margin so that the word wrap occurs at 1 inch in from the right margin, which would place the right margin marker at 5".

To set left and right indents, choose Format ➤ Paragraph ➤ Indents and Spacing tab. Change the values for the left and right indents in the Indentation section of the Paragraph dialog box (see Figure 7.5, shown earlier), and then click OK. When you return to the writing area, there is a different (temporary) left margin. Begin typing lines of text that will wrap around. Notice how the line wraps short of the right margin.

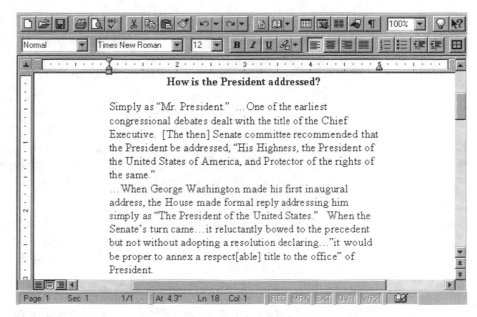

Figure 7.14   Text formatted with indents on the left and right

Spacing Paragraph Lines

Single spacing is the default spacing when you begin new documents in Word. You can easily change the spacing of paragraphs of text to double, one and one-half, or any other amount you desire. Spacing can be measured in points or in lines.

Setting Paragraph Line Spacing

The line spacing in your document depends on the size of your typed text. When you change the point size of your fonts, the spacing between lines increases.

You can use two methods for changing the spacing within your document:

▶ Use the keyboard shortcut. Select the lines of text or click into a single paragraph whose spacing will be changed. Press Ctrl+2 for double spacing, Ctrl+5 for one and one-half spacing, or Ctrl+1 for single spacing. (Hold down the Ctrl key and tap the numbers that are above the letters of the keyboard.)

▶ Through the menu. Choose Format ➤ Paragraph ➤ Indents and Spacing tab. In the Line Spacing list (at the bottom of the Spacing section), click the drop-down arrow and choose from the list (Single, 1.5, Double, At Least, Exactly, or Multiple).

When you need to set an increment that is different from any of the options listed in the Indents and Spacing dialog box, you will need to think in point sizes rather than in whole numbers. Choose Exactly or At Least from the Line Spacing list. Then type in the number for the point size or click the increase/decrease arrows next to the At option until you have the desired point size increment (72 points equal 1inch; double spacing is 24 points.)

Use Multiple when you want to increase or decrease line spacing by a percentage. For example, to increase line spacing by 10 percent, enter 1.1 in the At option. To decrease line spacing by 10 percent, enter .9.

TIP   When you create your own custom toolbar (see Chapter 12), you can add a spacing button to the toolbar, which will give you a third method for changing the spacing in a document.

Setting the Spacing between Paragraphs

Spacing between paragraphs stays constant and does not change when a typeface's point size changes. You can also use different paragraph spacing increments for different areas within the same document (for example, body text spacing can be different from header spacing, which can be different from footer spacing).

To specify no paragraph spacing or to set new paragraph spacing, select multiple paragraphs or click in a single paragraph. Choose Format ➤ Paragraph. Increase or decrease the points in the Before and After options in the Spacing section. Single spacing is approximately 12 points if you are using the default 10-point font size; if you are using a 12-point font size, a 14-point setting here is single spacing. Enter 0 points for the Spacing Before and After options to allow for no extra spacing between paragraphs.

Because a paragraph, according to Word's definition, can be any amount of text that ends in a return, single lines that have a return at the end are considered paragraphs. When there are spacing problems between lines with returns at the end of each one, you may wonder whether to fix the problem with line spacing or paragraph spacing. This is a paragraph spacing issue. Sometimes when mailing labels are typed, there is too much space between the lines. Use the paragraph spacing option to fix such problems.

Controlling Where Word Wrap Breaks Words

Although spacing between words is considered a normal part of business typing, and word wrap is considered a normal word processing feature, you may sometimes want the software to keep multiple words together, regardless of whether they are at the end of a line and should be word wrapped. You may need some words to word wrap together. For example, dates (May 15, 1997) or proper names (Mr. John Coltrane) should stay together; their multiple parts should not be separated, even though there is a legitimate space between the words.

You must use the keyboard combination of Shift+Ctrl+spacebar to space between words that you want to word wrap together. This type of space is called a *nonbreaking space*.

Like a regular space character, a nonbreaking space allows for a space to appear in the text on screen and in the printout. However, the nonbreaking space prevents a word wrap that would separate the words. Figure 7.15 shows a paragraph where the first example shows the date breaking up because of a regular space between the date elements. The second example shows the entire date has wrapped together to the next line by using a nonbreaking space.

The second paragraph in the figure was formatted by deleting the space after the word *May* and inserting a nonbreaking space with Shift+Ctrl+spacebar. After the 15, we substituted another nonbreaking space. That way, the 15 will always stay with the 1997. This date will never break up into separate words on multiple lines because of the use of the nonbreaking space.

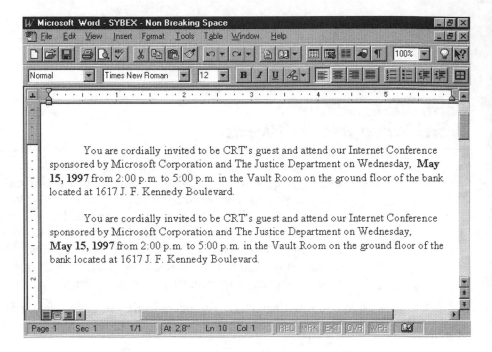

Figure 7.15   **The nonbreaking space is used to allow words to wrap together**

This chapter has just touched the surface of the formatting capabilities provided by Word. In the next chapter, we will continue with the options available for page views and formats.

Chapter 8

Page Views and Page Formats

Featuring

I n Word, you have the ability to work with your documents in various views. A *view* is a particular perspective on your document. Word offers six unique views: Normal, Page Layout, Outline, Print Preview, Master Document, and Full Screen. Each view has different advantages.

Page formats are formats that control entire document pages, not just characters or paragraphs. For example, headers and footers are page formats. When you create a header or footer, it sits at the top or bottom of the page and appears on every page that you designate. Page numbering is another format that affects the pages in your document. Page formats also include margins, page orientation, and paper size.

Let's look at the multiple views first, and then move on to examine the page format options.

Changing Your View

Four of the views are represented on the screen with toolbar buttons.  Normal, Page Layout, and Outline view have icons on the horizontal scroll bar near the bottom of the screen, in the Status bar area.

 The Print Preview button is located next to the printer button on the Standard toolbar.

You can also use menu commands to change to another view. The Print Preview option is listed on the File menu. All of the other views, plus the Master Document and Full Screen commands, are options on the View drop-down menu.

Normal View: An All-Purpose Typing View

Normal view, the default, allows you to type, format, and edit your work. In this view, you can see all character formats (such as bolded text and font size changes) and all paragraph formats (such as indents, tabs, and alignments). Tables (discussed in Chapter 10) are visible and print as shown. Columns (also covered in Chapter 10), however, display as a single strip of text until you switch to Page Layout view or Print Preview.

One of the advantages of Normal view is that the screen scrolls faster than it does in other views. This can be important when you work with longer documents with various formats and graphics. Page Layout view, although more graphical in its display, scrolls slower than Normal view. Figure 8.1 shows a document in Normal view and in Page Layout view.

To switch to Normal view, use one of these methods:

▶ Choose View ➤ Normal from the menu.

▶ Click the Normal view button to the left of the horizontal scroll bar.

▶ Use the keyboard shortcut, Alt+Ctrl+N.

Page Layout View: A Graphical View

Page Layout view is preferred as a "wysiwyg" (what you see is what you get) view of margins, page breaks, headers, footers, and graphics. Although the screen scrolls slower than it does in Normal view, if you're fortunate enough to have a fast computer, you won't see a big difference between the screen scrolling in these views.

The advantage of Page Layout view is that you can see your pages in whole page magnifications. Especially helpful is the ability to change the

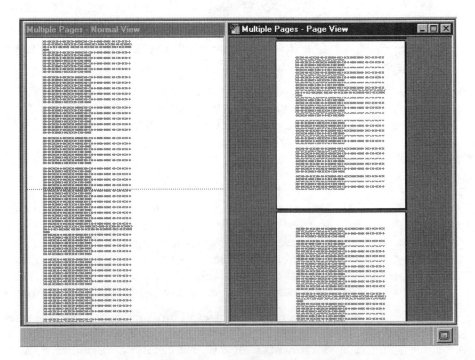

Figure 8.1   *Normal view versus Page view of a multiple-page document*

magnification (zoom control) to 10% or 15% and view up to 18 to 21 pages at a time. This is an excellent method for finding blank pages, seeing where graphics will fall, investigating hanging lines, and checking for other problems. Figure 8.2 shows a multiple-page document in Page Layout view.

To switch to Page Layout view, use one of these methods:

▶ Choose View ➤ Page Layout.

▶ Click the Page Layout view button on the horizontal scroll bar.

▶ Use the keyboard shortcut, Alt+Ctrl+P.

Outline View: An Organizational Tool

Outline view allows you to organize and collapse your document into up to eight levels of headings and subheadings. This view makes it easy to reorganize documents by copying and moving lines or paragraphs of text. Outline view gives you the ability to indent and outdent (demote and promote) lines of text.

Part
2

Communicating
with Word

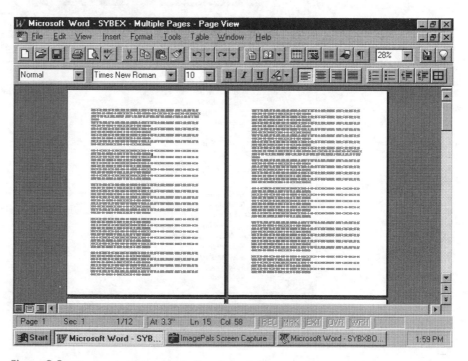

Figure 8.2 *Viewing multiple pages in Page Layout view*

To switch to Outline view, use one of these methods:

▶ Choose View ➤ Outline.

▶ Click the Outline view button on the horizontal scroll bar.

▶ Use the keyboard shortcut, Alt+Ctrl+O.

NOTE   Documents created in Outline view using Word's default style headings are already in a format that can be used as the basis for creating slides in PowerPoint.

After you have outlined a document with the default roman numeral numbering style, you can change to another numbering style, including a custom style you've defined. Use the Format ➤ Heading Numbering command to try out other numbering styles on an existing outlined document. Figure 8.3 shows an Outline view with a different numbering scheme.

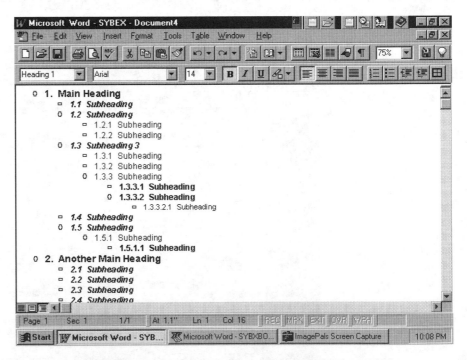

Figure 8.3   *Outline view using a numbering style common in the legal community*

Print Preview: A View of the Printed Document

Print Preview gives you an accurate picture of how your document will print to the printer. It is similar to Page Layout view. An advantage is that Print Preview has its own toolbar, and it's easy to see multiple pages and change the magnification of the screen. You can also edit your document in Print Preview mode. Figure 8.4 shows a document in this view.

Use one of these methods to switch to Print Preview:

▶ Choose File ➤ Print Preview.

▶ Use the keyboard shortcut, Ctrl+F2.

▶ Click the Print Preview button on the Standard toolbar.

While in Print Preview, you can perform many of the same actions that are available to you in Page Layout or Normal view. You can change the zoom control, the document's margins, and the headers and footers. You can also edit, move, and copy text. An option that is unique to Print Preview is the ability to shrink a document to fit to a single page.

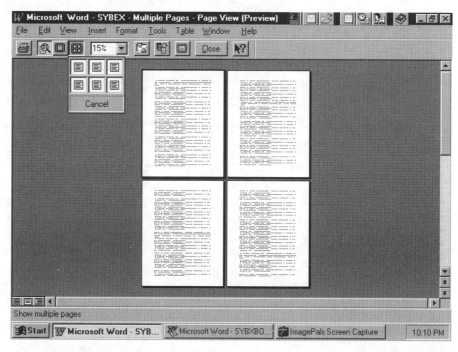

Figure 8.4   Print Preview shows multiple pages of your document and allows you to edit them.

Part 2

Communicating with Word

Using the Print Preview Toolbar

Many of the Print Preview options are available through its own toolbar. When you click the print button, Word immediately prints one copy of your entire document.

Your entire document is printed with the default options. The print button on the Print Preview toolbar doesn't display the Print dialog box for you to enter how many copies or specific pages to print. Press Ctrl+P or choose File ➤ Print to make choices in the Print dialog box.

When the magnifier button is depressed, the mouse toggles between small page and 100% magnification.

When you first start Print Preview, your document is shown in full page view (approximately 30% magnification on monitors with 640 × 480 pixel concentration; 55% on 1024 × 768 monitors). Hover the mouse over the page of text, and the mouse pointer turns into a magnifying glass with a plus sign, which means you can increase the magnification. Click the mouse button once, and the magnification increases to 100%. The magnifying glass shows a minus sign, which means you can decrease the magnification.

The one page button shows a single page at a time.

You will see whatever page your pointer was on in Normal or Page Layout view. Use the vertical scroll bar or press the PgUp and PgDn keys to move backward and forward through the pages of your document, one page at a time.

The multiple pages button allows you to decide how many pages you wish to see at one time (reduced magnification, of course).

The maximum number of pages you can view depends on the resolution of your monitor. On computers with SVGA (Super Video Graphic Adapter), sometimes known as high-resolution, monitors, you can see up to 21 pages at a time. VGA monitors let you see a minimum of 12 pages. Click the multiple pages button, and drag the mouse down and over the number of pages to be shown at one time. When you release the mouse button, you will see a display of miniature pages.

The zoom control on this toolbar functions the same in Print Preview as it does in the other views. You can click the drop-down list arrow on the right side of the zoom control box and choose from the different zoom percentages, or you can type in a zoom percentage of your own choice.

 The view ruler button allows you to toggle the display of the horizontal and vertical rulers on and off, so you can see margin and tab stop settings.

You can also turn the ruler on and off by choosing View ➤ Ruler.

 If the last page of your document has only a few lines of text, you can click the shrink to fit button. This tells Word to try to shrink everything so that the lines of text stuck on a page by themselves fit on the previous page.

Note that sometimes you can do a better job yourself by changing the left and right margins to fit more text on a line or by changing the font size of your type.

 Full screen is a toggle button that switches between a screen with or without the menu bar and the ruler (if you have the ruler turned on).

The Print Preview buttons always remain on the screen. Be careful about closing the Print Preview while in Full Screen view, because you will also be in Full Screen view when you return to your document typing view and will not see the menu bar or the toolbars.

To return to the view you were in before you chose Print Preview, click the Close button on the Print Preview toolbar. You can also click one of the view buttons at the bottom of the screen to change to Normal, Page Layout, or Outline view. If you choose File ➤ Close, you will close your document, not just exit Print Preview.

 When you click the Help button, the mouse pointer turns into a question mark.

Point to any text, and the paragraph and font formatting information box will appear, telling you which formats have been placed on the text. If you click on any screen element, such as the horizontal ruler, you will see help information explaining that element.

Editing in Print Preview

You can type in Print Preview at any time. The typing will appear where your pointer was positioned in the document before you switched to Print Preview.

Part
2

Communicating
with Word

To actually see where the blinking insertion point is positioned, make sure you are viewing in 100% magnification. Click the magnifier button on the Print Preview toolbar again (so that it does not appear pushed down). The mouse turns into an I-beam. Click anywhere on your document screen, and you will now see the insertion point, where you can type additional text or edit the text on the page. Now that you are in full edit mode, you may want to use your Standard and Formatting toolbars. Right-click in the toolbar area and select the Standard toolbar from the pop-up menu. Right-click again and select the Formatting toolbar. Click the magnifier button again to return the mouse pointer to a magnifying glass that toggles between magnifications.

You can also change the page margins in Print Preview. Display the ruler (by clicking on the button in the toolbar or by choosing View ➤ Ruler). To change the top or bottom margin, drag the gray sections of the ruler on the left side of your document screen. Figure 8.5 shows an example of how the top margin of a document can be adjusted in Print Preview.

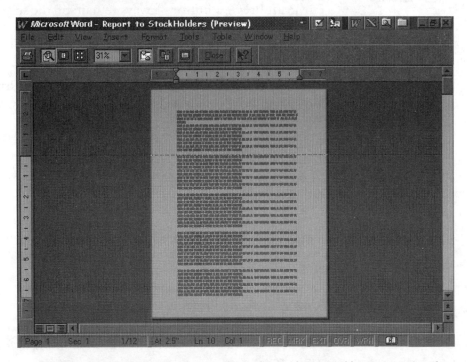

Figure 8.5   **You can use the Print Preview ruler to change the top and bottom margins of your document.**

To change the left or right margin, hover the mouse on the gray part of the top ruler above the bottom indent marker. When the mouse pointer turns into a two-headed arrow, you can drag the left or right margin toward the left or right. Do not drag the actual indent markers. Figure 8.6 shows an example of changing the right margin of a document in Print Preview.

Full Screen: A View without Obstructions

You can remove the menu bar, toolbars, rulers, and other screen elements by choosing the Full Screen command (View ➤ Full Screen). Word will show you a screen with only your text lines. This view is useful when you want to concentrate on the text on the screen, such as when you want to proofread it.

In the lower-right corner of the screen, you'll see a small toolbar with one button of a tiny monitor. When you click the button, all the screen elements will return. The View ➤ Full Screen command is a toggle; select it again to turn Full Screen view off.

Part 2

Communicating with Word

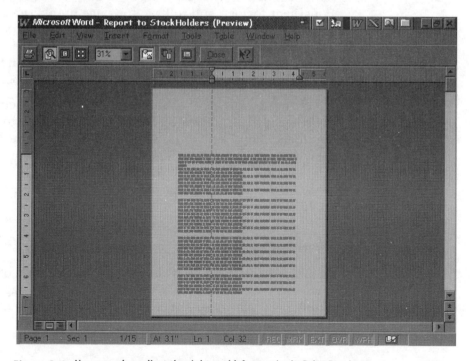

Figure 8.6 *You can also adjust the right and left margins in Print Preview.*

WARNING   Sometimes the Full Screen button does not seem to return the screen elements. If this occurs, press the Esc key. This should bring back all of the toolbars, rulers, and other screen elements.

Because you cannot access the menubar or toolbars in Full Screen view, you'll need to issue commands in other ways. You can right-click to use the shortcut menus or use the keyboard shortcut keys (such as Ctrl+B for bold, and Ctrl+E for centering text). To display the Standard or Formatting toolbar in Print Preview, point to the Print Preview toolbar text area, right-click to see the Toolbar pop-up menu, and select the toolbar.

Master Document View: Keeping Track of Subdocuments

Word's Master Document feature helps you organize long documents by separating them into separate document parts, or *subdocuments*. Each subdocument is saved in its own file. Use this feature to create a consistent format, and to have the page numbering, index, cross references, and table of contents apply across all the subdocuments. For example, if you're writing a book or report, you can create separate files for the chapters, and let the Master Document feature maintain the page numbering and other information about the subdocuments for you.

To change to this view, choose View ➤ Master Document. The Master Document view, shown in Figure 8.7, is similar to the Outline view. Outlining, however, works with a single document; Master Document view lets you compile different files and view them in an outline form. Just like in Outline view, you can easily move subdocuments up and down in the outline. A Master Document can be a maximum total size of 32 megabytes with all of its subdocuments.

Magnification: Zoom Control in Any View

In all Word views, you can change the magnification of the screen from as large as a 200% magnification to as small as 10% magnification. Click the drop-down arrow on the 100% zoom control button at the end of the Standard toolbar to change the magnification.

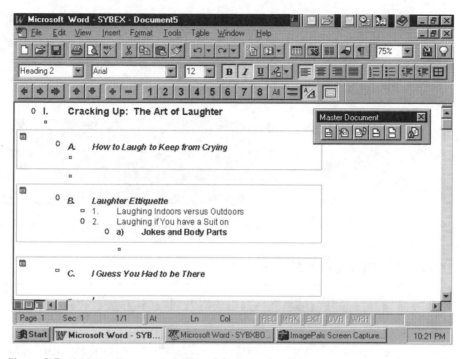

Figure 8.7   A Master Document with its subdocument headings

The Print Preview and Page Layout views allow for reduced magnifications to display small and multiple pages on the same screen (commonly called *thumbnails*).

The View menu also contains the Zoom option, which displays the dialog box shown in Figure 8.8. You can change to multiple-page zooming by choosing View ➤ Zoom and clicking the Many Pages radio button. Click on the PC pushbutton just below the Many Pages option and drag across and down to display multiple pages.

Remember, the zoom control magnifications are different from view to view. Normal view cannot display whole pages as can Page Layout view. Print Preview has all of the magnification and zoom options on its own toolbar.

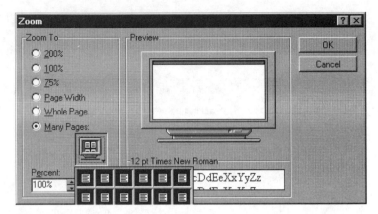

Figure 8.8   *The Zoom dialog box includes a Many Pages option for multiple-page zooming.*

Formatting the Page

Formatting pages can mean changing the margins, paper size, or orientation (landscape or portrait). You may need to center text vertically on a page, insert new pages, number existing pages, or use headers and footers to contain the same information on multiple pages. You may need to have different page numbers in different sections. All of these formats involve the entire page rather than just characters or paragraphs of text.

Word's page-formatting commands are plentiful and can be applied before or after you have created your document. The following sections focus on the most frequently used page formats.

Setting Margins

Setting the margins for your documents is a fundamental feature of any word processing program. In Word, this is one of the easiest tasks to perform.

Word sets default margins: 1-inch top and bottom margins and 1.25-inch left and right margins. You can change any of these margins to suit your documents.

Part
2

> **TIP** If you print on letterhead paper, its logo placement determines what types of margin widths you need. With a ruler, measure from the top of the paper to where the text should begin. Measure from the left edge how many inches your text needs to "come in" on the left. Use these measurements when setting the margins in Word. If you will print to this paper most of the time, you can make these margins the new default settings.

If you want to make margin changes from a certain page forward in the document, position the pointer at the top of the page on which you want the new margins to take effect. Otherwise, Word will start new margins on a new page and move the text after the I-beam cursor to that new page. Then choose File ➤ Page Setup ➤ Margins tab. Figure 8.9 shows the Margins page in the Page Setup dialog box. You can change the margins to the dimensions you need for your work.

Notice the Apply To option at the bottom of the dialog box. You can set the margin change for This Point Forward, Whole Document, or This Section. The This Section option is available if you have text selected in the document. You can select multiple pages of text and give different margin settings to these pages. Word will create multiple section breaks before and after these pages so that it knows that the margin settings are different for these pages. (In Normal view, you can see the section break lines.)

You cannot set different margins on the same page. Use the left and right indent options in the Format ➤ Paragraph dialog box to create temporary

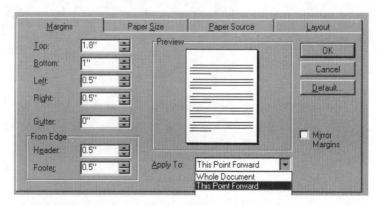

Figure 8.9 Change the dimensions of the margins and see the results immediately in the Preview box on the Margins page.

Communicating
with Word

left and right margins at different locations on the same page, as described in Chapter 7.

Printing in Landscape or Portrait Orientation

Your printer controls whether a document image can be rotated to print landscape (sideways). For example, for LaserJet and inkjet printers, you can easily change the size and orientation of your paper. Dot-matrix printers may require that you place the paper in sideways before printing a page that has a landscape orientation.

To change the paper orientation, position the pointer at the top of the page on which you wish the change to take effect. Choose File ➤ Page Setup ➤ Paper Size tab. Figure 8.10 shows this page in the Page Setup dialog box.

In the Orientation section at the bottom of the dialog box, the capital *A* shows the current orientation setting. You can also see this in the Preview section of the dialog box. To change the orientation, click the radio button to the right of the capital *A*. The Preview changes to reflect a different orientation.

The Apply To option lets you choose whether the Whole Document or only from This Point Forward will have the different orientation. (A This Section choice is also available if you have selected text in the document, as described in the next section.) Click OK to close the Page Setup dialog box.

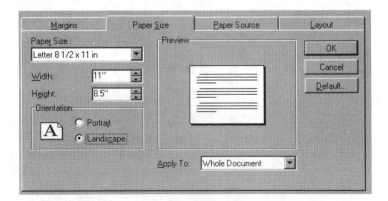

Figure 8.10   *Change the page orientation in the Paper Size page of the Page Setup dialog box.*

Multiple Orientations in a Document

You can mix and match orientations in a document, with some pages in portrait and others in landscape orientation. Word will insert section breaks above and below the pages that have a different orientation.

If you have already typed your text and discover you need multiple orientations in the same document (for example, pages 1 through 3 are portrait, pages 4 through 6 should be landscape, and then pages 7 and 8 are portrait), you can select the multiple pages and change the orientation for those pages. Here are the steps for setting multiple page orientation:

1. Switch to Page Layout view and set the zoom control to approximately 20% so you can see miniature pages. Figure 8.11 shows how multiple orientations in the same document appear in Page Layout view.

2. Select the multiple pages to receive the different orientation.

3. Choose File ➤ Page Setup ➤ Paper Size tab. In the dialog box, click on the A in the Orientation section to change to Landscape.

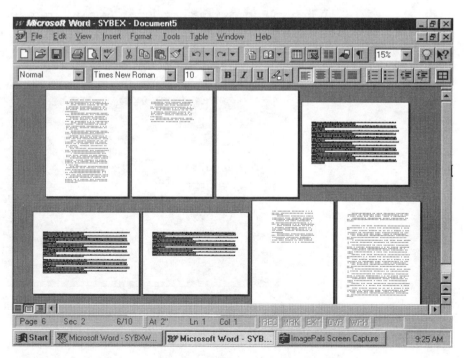

Figure 8.11   Select the multiple pages and choose a different orientation for these pages.

4. Make sure the Apply To option is set to either Selected Text or Selected Sections, and then click OK.

    If you do not get the results you desire, immediately click the Undo button on the Standard toolbar or press Ctrl+Z. Try again.

Setting Paper Size

Your printer also determines the paper sizes you can print. To change the paper size, choose File ➤ Page Setup ➤ Paper Size tab. The Paper Size option defaults to Letter $8^1/_2 \times 11$ in (see Figure 8.9, in the previous section).

Word provides preset paper sizes other than $8^1/_2 \times 11$ and $8^1/_2 \times 14$ (legal paper). For example, the $9^1/_2 \times 4^1/_8$ size is popular for printing letter envelopes. You can choose other page sizes as well as specify your own custom page sizes.

Setting Up, Creating, and Printing Envelopes

When you choose the Envelope paper size from the File ➤ Page Setup ➤ Paper Size tab, the orientation for the envelope is still portrait. You must choose landscape to have the envelope rotate its orientation. Figure 8.12 shows the settings for envelope printing.

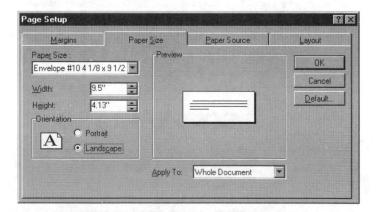

Figure 8.12   **The Paper Size page with an envelope size and landscape orientation**

Setting Envelope Margins

You may also want to change the margins of the envelope so that your text will appear on the envelope at the proper locations. Envelopes that already have a return address printed on them need only the delivery address. In general, business envelopes have a top margin of 2 inches and a left margin of 4 inches. The bottom and left margins are .25 inch.

To change the margins on an envelope, choose File ➤ Page Setup ➤ Margins tab (or if you are already in the Page Setup dialog box, click on the Margins tab) and change the margins to suit the envelope format.

Creating Envelope Text

When you return to the view you were working in after you set up the envelope page format, the insertion point will be at the proper location for you to begin typing. To see a graphical representation of the envelope paper size, switch to Page Layout view (View ➤ Page Layout) and change the 100% zoom control to Whole Page.

An easier way to create an envelope is to let Word do it for you. Word will create an envelope for you automatically using the inside address that you typed on a letter as the address on the envelope. Follow these steps to have Word quickly create an envelope from pretyped information:

1. Type a letter with the inside address of the person to whom the letter is going.

2. When you have finished typing the letter, select the inside address.

3. Choose Tools ➤ Envelopes and Labels. The Envelopes and Labels dialog box appears with the address from the letter selected in the Delivery Address text area, as shown in Figure 8.13.

4. If you do not wish to use the Return Address shown at the bottom of the dialog box (perhaps because the envelope already has a preprinted return address), click the Omit checkbox above the Return Address area. You can also delete the Return Address shown and type a new one.

5. If you need to change the address, first click the mouse on the line where you wish to make a change. Note that if you start typing on the address line, the entire address will be overwritten because it is selected. Remember to click the mouse first before typing on the address line, unless you want to replace the entire address.

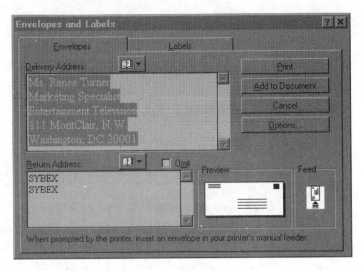

Figure 8.13   Word can quickly create an envelope from address information in your letter.

6. Once everything looks correct, click the Print button on the right side of the dialog box to signal to Word to print only the envelope. Make sure that you feed the envelope according to the small Feed diagram shown in the lower-right corner of the dialog box.

7. If you would like to add the envelope to your document to save it, click the Add to Document button on the right side of the dialog box.

Centering Text on a Page

Centering words *on a line* (between the left and right margins) takes one click of the mouse or the keypress Ctrl+E (think "Even" between the margins). However, when you need to have text centered between the top and bottom margins, such as for a title page or report cover page, there are a few more actions involved. Figure 8.14 shows an example of a page with text centered between the top and bottom margins.

The traditional method for centering has been to add returns (press the Enter key) in order to "shove" the text down. Usually, part of the text disappears onto the next page, and then you must delete the extra returns.

Figure 8.14   *Titles that are centered between the top and bottom margins on a page.*

Word has a feature called Vertical Alignment, which centers text on a page between the top and bottom margins. Use the following steps to apply this feature:

1. Type your text normally near the top of the page. Use the normal command to center the text between the left and right margins (Ctrl-E, the Formatting toolbar button, or the Format ➤ Paragraph command).

2. Position the pointer at the top of the page containing the text to be centered on the page.

3. Choose File ➤ Page Setup ➤ Layout tab. This page is shown in Figure 8.15. Notice the Vertical Alignment section near the bottom-left side of the dialog box. The default setting is Top (text begins at the top of the page normally).

4. Click the drop-down arrow to the right of the current alignment and choose Center.

5. Make sure the Apply To option says Selected Text.

6. Click OK. Your selection of text will be centered between the top and bottom margins on a new page.

Part 2

Communicating with Word

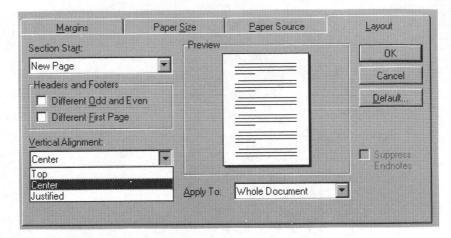

Figure 8.15 *Use the Vertical Alignment setting in the File ➤ Page Setup ➤ Layout page to center text on a page vertically.*

Numbering Pages

For multiple-page documents, Word provides a page numbering feature so you don't need to type in the page numbers yourself. Word has a myriad of page numbering options that allow you to choose different positions and formats.

If you have a typed document that only has one section, it does not matter where you position the insertion point to start the page numbering. The page numbering always starts on the first page (although you can tell Word to not show the number on that page).

To place page numbers on all pages of a document with a single section (Sec 1) layout, first switch to Page Layout view (View ➤ Page Layout). Then choose Insert ➤ Page Numbers. Figure 8.16 shows the Page Numbers dialog box. For the Position, choose whether you want the numbering at the top or bottom of the page. For the Alignment, select whether you want the numbering on the left side, center, right side, inside, or outside. In Figure 8.16, the page numbering is set for the upper-right corner of the page.

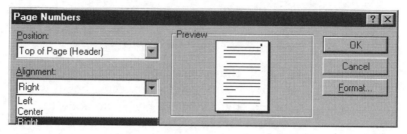

Figure 8.16   *Page numbers can be inserted at the top or bottom of pages, with left, right, centered, inside, or outside alignment.*

Adjusting Page Numbering

If you do not want the page number to appear on the first page, but the second page should start with the number 2, uncheck Show Number on First Page in the Page Numbers dialog box. Click the Format button on the right side of the dialog box to see the Page Number Format dialog box, shown in Figure 8.17. Make sure that the number for the Start At

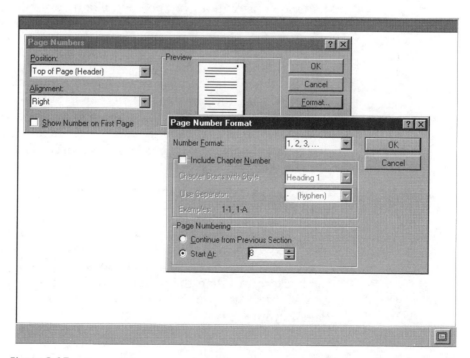

Figure 8.17   *You can suppress the page numbers on the first page and start the numbering with any number.*

Part
2

Communicating
with Word

option is 1. The 1 will not show on the first page—because you turned that option off—but the page number on the second page will pick up with the next number after the Start At value.

You can change the Start At value in the Page Number Format dialog box to have the page numbering begin with whatever number you like. For example, you probably would not want numbering to begin on the title page of your report, nor would you want the page after the title page to start with the number 2. To set up this numbering, uncheck Show Number on First Page in the Page Numbers dialog box. Then click the Format button and make sure that the number for the Start At option in the Page Number Format dialog box is 0. The 0 will not show on the title page, but a page number will show on the second page, and it will be 1.

Deleting Page Numbering

Once you have turned on page numbering, it seems difficult to remove the numbering. Remember that the Undo button is ideal in a situation where you want to reverse the action you have just performed. However, the Undo button does you no good if you have inherited someone else's document or you decide down the road that there should be page numbering in another position (top instead of bottom, for example). Then you need to delete the current numbering.

You can delete the numbering and start again, but it will require that you work with the Header and Footer features of Word. If your page number is at the bottom of the page, it is in the footer. If it is at the top of the page, it is placed in a header. The next section goes into more depth about working with headers and footers. For now, let's just get rid of the page numbers:

1. Change to Page Layout View (View ➤ Page Layout) if you are not already in this view.

2. Find the page showing the first occurrence of your page numbering (you may need to go to the bottom of the page if you asked for page numbers at the bottom). The number will appear in gray and seem to be more in the background than the foreground of your document typing. This is how Word shows you that you have numbering in a header or footer in Page Layout view.

3. Double-click on the grayed-out page number or choose View ➤ Header and Footer from the menu bar. An outlined box, labeled Header or Footer, will appear. The page number will appear within this box.

4. Drag the mouse I-beam over the number so that a framed gray box appears around the number and the number inside of the box is selected and in gray. To delete page numbering throughout all sections of a document, press Ctrl+A or choose Edit ➤ Select All to select everything in the header or footer, including the page number.

5. Press the Delete key to delete the number. It will disappear from all pages within that section of the document, or throughout all sections of the document if you used Select All to select the page number.

WARNING When you use Select All in a header or footer and then use a deletion command (for example, press the Delete key), *all* of the information in all the document's headers or footers will be deleted.

Repeating Information in Headers and Footers

Headers and footers are word processing holding areas for repetitive information that must appear either in the top margin (header) or in the bottom margin (footer) of every page of your document. You can format and align text, add page numbers, insert the current date or time, and show graphics, clip art, or lines within the boundaries of headers and footers.

Word also gives you the ability to have different headers and footers for different sections of your document. You must insert a section break to designate different headers and footers for the new section. Headers and footers can also be different for odd and even pages.

TIP You can create WordArt, change the color to gray, and place the art (or clip-art pictures) in headers to act as a background impression behind your text. This feature is called a *watermark*.

When you choose headers and footers (View ➤ Headers and Footers), Word switches to Page Layout view automatically. The insertion point is placed in the dashed outlined area of the header. A special Header and Footer toolbar appears:

Creating a Header or Footer

As an example, suppose that you want to create a header that repeats the name of a corporation and the page number on every page of the document except for the first page. The corporate name is on the left side of the header, the words *Draft Report* are centered, and the page number is right-aligned. The page numbering begins at 100 (implying that there are previous sections being done by other individuals). Although we are putting this information in a header, you can follow the same procedure for a footer.

1. Choose View ➤ Header and Footer. If you are in Normal view, you will be switched to Page Layout view. The insertion point is on the left side of the Header box. (If you wish to create a footer instead of a header, click the first button on the toolbar to move to the Footer box.)

2. Type **ABC Corporation**.

3. Press the Tab key. The insertion pointer jumps to the center of the header.

4. Type **Draft Report**. The text centers as you type.

5. Press the Tab key. The insertion pointer jumps to the right side of the header.

6. Type the word **Page** and press the spacebar.

7. Click the page number button on the Header and Footer toolbar or press the Alt+Shift+P key combination. The page number will appear. Don't worry that it shows as page 1. We will change this to the number 100. Leave the insertion point right where it is.

8. Choose Insert ➤ Page Numbers. The Page Numbers dialog box appears.

9. Click the Format option on the right side of the dialog box.

10. In the Page Number Format dialog box, click the Start At radio button and type the number **100**.

11. Click OK twice.

12. Click the page setup button on the Header and Footer toolbar. You will be taken to the Page Setup dialog box.

13. Click the Layout tab. In the Headers and Footers section, click Different First Page (see Figure 8.15, shown earlier in the chapter).

14. Click the OK button. When you return to the document, your header text will seem to have disappeared, but notice the name of the header: First Page Header. We just told Word that we did not want a header on the first page. So there is an empty header on this page.

15. Click the show next button on the Header and Footer toolbar. Your header is visible. The page number is 101. Once you have viewed the header, click the Close button.

After you return to the typing area, you will not see the header on the first page. When you move to subsequent pages, you will see the header with the appropriate page numbers. Switch to Page Layout view if you do not see your header. Also notice the page number on the Status bar at the bottom of the screen. It shows the number 100 or 101, depending on which page you are observing:

Editing and Deleting Headers

To change an existing header or footer, choose View ➤ Header and Footer. If you don't see your header or footer, click the show next button to move to the next header or footer, or click on the button to switch between the header and footer. You can edit the header or footer text to make your changes. To delete the header or footer, select the lines of text and press the Delete key.

To delete headers or footers in all sections, position the insertion point in the header or footer and press Ctrl+A or select Edit ➤ Select All. Press the Delete key. All the headers or footers will be deleted throughout the document.

When you're finished, click the Close button on the toolbar.

Inserting and Deleting Pages in a Document

When you wish to end one page and start another, it is not necessary to press the Enter key repeatedly in order to force the automatic break to end a page. You can insert a page break at any place on the page to end that page and start another.

Choose Insert ➤ Break ➤ Page Break. Click OK. When you return to the document, the previous page will have ended, and you will be on a new blank page. You can also use a keyboard shortcut that all experienced Word users choose to manually break the page: Ctrl+Enter.

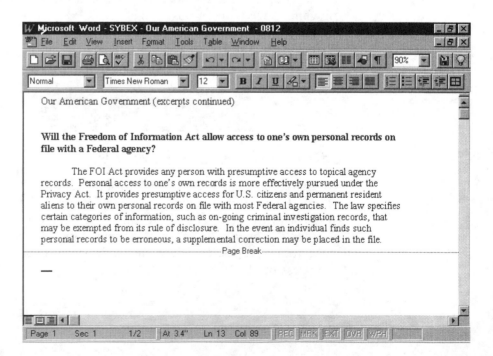

Figure 8.18 The page break indicator in Normal view

If you are in Normal view, you will see a line shoot across the screen and the words *Page Break* appear at the spot where you issued the new page command, as shown in Figure 8.18. If you are in Page Layout view, the graphical representation of a page break appears in gray, showing the separation between the pages.

The easiest way to delete blank pages is to remove the page break indicator in the document. If you are in Normal view, double-click on the line labeled Page Break that heads the blank page. If you are in Page Layout view, click the show/hide paragraph button at the end of the Standard toolbar (or press Ctrl+Shift+*) to show the nonprinting characters of the document. Then double-click on the page break line and press the Delete key to remove the indicator and the blank page.

This chapter has covered Word's page view and page formatting capabilities. The next chapter deals with managing your Word files and printing.

Chapter 9

Managing and Printing Your Files from Word

FEATURING

This chapter describes how to use the file and print features of Word. File and print operations are essential components of any document management process.

Basic file operations include saving, closing, opening, finding, deleting, renaming, and copying files. Advanced file operations include inserting (combining) multiple files, setting the AutoSave intervals, and making automatic backups.

Word's printing features include options for printing selected pages and multiple copies, and for managing multiple paper bins.

Starting a New File in Word

When you first launch Word, a fresh document has been started for you. From this point, you can begin working with a new document or choose File ➤ Open to load a previously saved document.

To start a new document (file) with either the standard defaults or any of the preformatted document templates, choose File ➤ New from the menu bar. Figure 9.1 shows the tabbed dialog box, with the categories of documents.

Starting a "Normal" Document

To start a new document with default settings, click on the General tab and double-click the Blank Document icon. This document will have the following default settings:

▶ Left and right margins of 1.25 inches

▶ Top and bottom margins of 1 inch

▶ Tab stops set every .5 inch

▶ Paper size of $8\frac{1}{2} \times 11$ inches

▶ Portrait orientation

▶ Times New Roman typeface (depends on your default printer settings)

▶ Font size of 10 points

When you start a new document with Word's normal defaults, you are actually using something called the Normal template. You can, however,

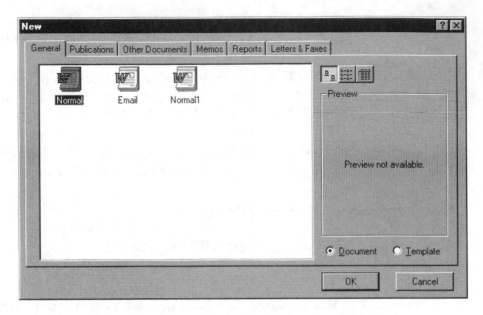

Figure 9.1   The File ➤ New command displays the template categories in Word.

base your document on other kinds of templates, as described in the next section.

If you know that you want to use the default Normal template, you can save yourself a few steps by clicking the first button on the Standard toolbar:

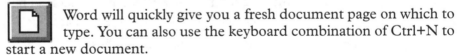 Word will quickly give you a fresh document page on which to type. You can also use the keyboard combination of Ctrl+N to start a new document.

Starting a Document Using a Template Wizard

In addition to the Normal template, Word supplies a number of other templates, including a special type of template called a Template Wizard. The Template Wizard helps you to develop your document by following a series of steps and questions.

There are six categories of Word templates:

▶ General

▶ Publications

▶ Other Documents

▶ Memos

▶ Reports

▶ Letters & Faxes

The General category contains the Blank Document template, with the default settings described in the previous section. The Publications and Other Documents categories include some interesting templates, which are listed with a brief description in Tables 9.1 and 9.2.

Template	Description
Brochure	Steps to create a tri-fold brochure
Contemporary Press Release	Steps to create a stylish, two-page press release
Directory	Steps to create an eye-catching, two-page directory
Elegant Press Release Wizard	Sample of a one-page press release layout
Manual	Sample eight-page manual and steps for creating it
Newsletter	Dramatic, three-page newsletter with a mailer on the back
Newsletter Wizard	Steps to create a multiple-page, multiple-column newsletter, complete with graphics
Professional Press Release	Steps to create an attractive, one-page press release
Thesis	A ten-page layout displaying sections needed for a university dissertation

Table 9.1 **Word's Publications Templates**

Template	Description
Agenda Wizard	Steps to create an agenda for meetings
Award Wizard	Steps to create a certificate or an award
Calendar Wizard	Steps to create different calendar styles (you cannot write into calendar blocks)
Contemporary Resume	Professional, one-page resume layout
Elegant Resume	Fancy, one-page resume layout
Invoice	Detailed invoice form
Pleading Wizard	Steps to create a legal pleading paper
Professional Resume	Solid, one-page resume layout
Purchase Order	Detailed purchase order form
Resume Wizard	Steps for creating four different types of resumes
Table Wizard	Steps to develop professional-looking tables (includes AutoFormat feature)
Weekly Time Sheet	Detailed time sheet (autocalculates fields to total weekly hours)

Table 9.2 **Word's Other Documents Templates**

NOTE You can create your own templates, by saving documents as templates (see Chapter 11) or by modifying one of Word's templates (see Chapter 12).

If you are not familiar with business letter layouts or are just curious about Template Wizards, follow these steps to create a new letter using the Letter Wizard:

1. Choose File ➤ New from the menu bar.

2. Click the Letter & Faxes tab. This page lists a number of templates, and also includes two template buttons with a large letter "W" and a magic wand.

3. Double-click the Letter Wizard icon.

4. On the Letter Wizard screen, shown in Figure 9.2, the first question is "What would you like to do?" The option Select a Prewritten Business Letter is already selected. Click the Next button at the bottom of the dialog box.

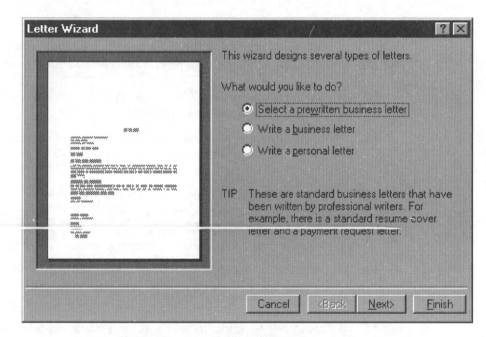

Figure 9.2   **The Letter Wizard prompts you through the steps of creating a letter.**

5. You now see a list of pretyped letters. It is unlikely that you will want to use one of the specific letters among these already typed documents. Click the Back button to return to the previous screen.

6. Click the second selection on the first page, Write a Business Letter.

7. Click the Next button at the bottom of the dialog box. Notice that Word already has the page numbers and date options checked, because it assumes you will want to include these items in your letter. You can check or uncheck any of the items.

8. Click the Next button. Specify whether you have letterhead or plain paper. If you have letterhead paper, Word needs to know where the letterhead logo is on the page and how many inches of space that logo

requires. You may need to get a piece of your letterhead paper and take these measurements.

9. Click the Next button. Type the name and address of the person who is receiving the letter. Delete the generic categories in the box by dragging the mouse over them and pressing the Delete key. Type a return address for yourself if it is not already on the letterhead.

 NOTE Use Tools ➤ Options ➤ User Info to set the Mailing Address you want to appear as the return address whenever you use the envelope feature.

10. Click the Next button. Choose a style: Professional, Contemporary, or Elegant. (You are almost finished.)

11. Your last choice, when you see the checkered Finish Flag, is to decide whether or not you want an envelope or mailing label to go along with the letter.

12. Click the Finish button. In a couple of seconds, depending on your choice in the previous step, Word will either lay out your letter or show you the Envelope and Labels dialog box. If you asked for an envelope, choose Add to Document on the right side of the dialog box.

13. In your letter, notice the areas in which Word has designated for you to fill in the body of the letter. If you asked for additional items, such as enclosures or CCs, you will see the areas designed for this information.

14. Click at the location in the letter where Word tells you to "Click here and start typing the letter." When you begin to type, the message will disappear, and you can create your letter.

15. Go ahead and type your letter. When you're finished, save your work (File ➤ Save).

Saving Your Work

It is necessary to tell Word to save a copy of your document onto a more permanent medium (hard disk, floppy disk, network drive, or tape drive). The document you see when you are typing is a reflection of what is in the computer's memory. If you turn off the computer or experience electrical problems while you are creating your document (and you have not told Word to save your work), you will lose the valuable effort you have made, because the computer's memory will be cleared.

One way to ensure that you keep a copy of your work is to frequently save to disk what you have done so far. Another way to protect yourself from electrical problems is to request an automatic save every couple of minutes. If your computer shuts down before you have saved your file, you can "recover" the last document on which you were working.

Naming and Saving Files to Disk

At any point while you are typing or editing, you can save your work by choosing File ➤ Save from the menu bar. You should save your work frequently.

When you save your work the first time, you must name the document. The name of your document can be up to 255 characters long and can contain spaces and periods. However, if you think that you might be sharing documents with other individuals who are using previous versions of Word, you should restrict your name to eight characters only, without spaces or periods.

To save and name your document the first time, follow these steps:

1. Your pointer can be anywhere in the document. Choose File ➤ Save from the menu bar. The File ➤ Save As dialog box will appear. At the bottom of the dialog box is a text area designated for the file name.

2. Click in the File Name area and type the name for your document. As noted, you can enter up to 255 characters and can include spaces and periods. Figure 9.3 shows a completed Save As dialog box.

3. After you have typed the name of your document, click the Save button on the right side of the dialog box.

When you return to your document, the name you assigned to it will appear in the document's title bar at the top of the Word screen.

WARNING   Be careful not to use the same name as another document when saving a new document, unless you want to replace the existing file with the new one. Word will write over any previous document with that name. Fortunately, Word will prompt you to confirm the replacement.

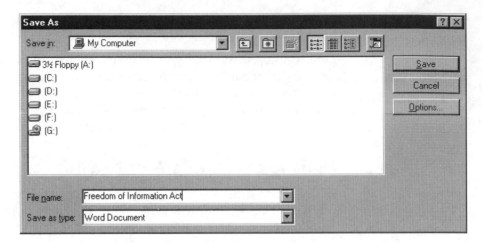

Figure 9.3   Word allows file names up to 255 characters with spaces and periods in the name.

After you have named and saved your document the first time, you do not need to designate the name again for subsequent saves. It is recommended that you save your work again and again as you are creating and editing your document. Saving frequently serves two purposes:

▶ You have a stored copy of your latest changes if there is any electrical problem (or human error) in your office and the computer's power is turned off. You can restart the computer and open the document you were working on with its most recent edits, because you were saving every few minutes.

▶ You have a stored copy on disk in case you "mess up" the copy of the same document on the screen. You can always close the copy of the document on the screen—without saving—and use File ➤ Open to go back to the last saved copy.

NOTE   You will never see multiple saved copies of the same document within the same folder. Because Word replaces your last saved file with the most recently saved file, you will see only one copy of your document (with the same name) in a folder.

Word provides a toolbar button to allow you to quickly perform saves. Click on the button with the image of a diskette on the Standard toolbar (third button in from the left):

If you have already named and saved your work, Word will simply replace your old saved version with the new version on the screen. There is no message on the screen to tell you that the save was completed. You can, however, look down at the Status bar at the bottom of the screen, where you should see the horizontal blue box, showing the saving action "thermometer-style." If your document is short, the action is very quick.

You can also use the keyboard combination of Ctrl+S to save your work. Again, you will see the horizontal blue box with the thermometer-style saving indicator at the bottom of the screen.

Making Quick Copies of Files with Save As

Each time you choose File ➤ Save (or use the toolbar button or keyboard shortcut, Ctrl+S) after you've named a file, Word remembers the name and immediately saves over your old version with the latest version of your document.

To make a copy of your document and work on the copy, use the File ➤ Save As command or the shortcut key, F12. In the Save As dialog box, enter a new name for your document. You will have two documents: one under the old name and one under the new name.

When you return to the document, you will see the new name in the title bar. This is the copy you are working on. The original file is still on the disk. You can open that file by choosing File ➤ Open and selecting the original file name.

Saving Your Work Automatically

The AutoSave command tells Word to automatically save your work at specific intervals. You can set the automatic save interval (number of minutes) by choosing Tools ➤ Options ➤ Save tab. Keeping an automatic save interval set is good protection for your work. The default setting for AutoSave is every 10 minutes.

AutoSave does not make a copy of your file that you can see on the disk. Rather, at regular intervals, Word automatically saves a special copy to be used in case of an emergency. This is a precautionary measure that Word takes in case your computer locks up or there is an electrical problem and you are unable to save your work.

When you reboot (start the computer again) and launch Word, the document that was automatically saved will appear on the screen as a "recovered" document. It will reflect the last save that was automatically performed. For example, if you have set the AutoSave for every 30 minutes, the document reflects your work up to that time. You will not have a saved copy of any of the changes you made in the 30 minutes between automatic saves.

To set a different interval for the automatic save, follow these steps:

1. Choose Tools ➤ Options ➤ Save tab. You'll see the page shown in Figure 9.4. Notice the Automatic Save Every checkbox at the bottom of the list of Save Options.

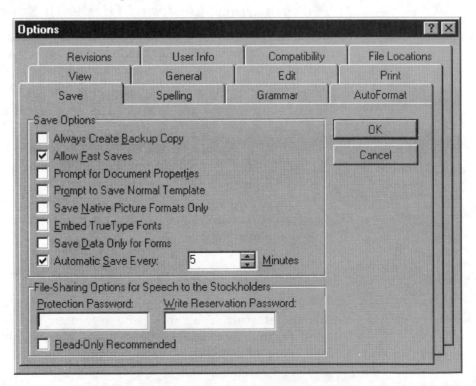

Figure 9.4 **Setting an AutoSave interval is important for those times when the computer shuts down or locks up and you must restart Word and cannot save your document.**

2. Click the spinner buttons (up and down buttons) next to the current interval to increase or decrease the number of minutes between automatic saves. If you think you need more protection than the default of every 10 minutes, set a more frequent interval. On the other hand, for large documents, frequent AutoSave interruptions can be time-consuming, so you may want to set a less frequent interval.

3. Click OK to close the Options dialog box and save your changes.

Part
2

Recovering an Automatically Saved File

If you set an interval for the automatic save, Word has been saving your document for you according to this interval. If your computer shuts down, you can recover the AutoSave version.

When you restart your computer and start a new Word session, it will immediately "recover" the last automatically saved version. There is no special command to issue. When Word loads, the special AutoSave version of your document appears. Take a look at it and see how current you think it is.

You, of course, should have been saving all along (with File ➤ Save, the save button on the toolbar, or Ctrl+S), and your own saved version should be very current. If you think that your own saved version is more current than Word's automatic saved version, then choose File ➤ Save As to save Word's "recovered" file under another name (to keep it just in case), and then use File ➤ Open to choose your file from the file list. You will see the last saved version of the file you, yourself, saved.

 WARNING If you exit Word normally or close your file and *you* forget to save your document, you cannot recover the automatically saved version. Word keeps this special saved version only if you must reboot or restart the computer and you are not able to exit Word using the normal method of File ➤ Exit. If you exited or closed normally, Word throws away the automatically saved version.

Communicating with Word

Closing a File

When you are finished working with your document and want to remove it from the screen, you can close the document by selecting File ➤ Close. If you have not performed a recent save, Word will ask you if you wish to save your work:

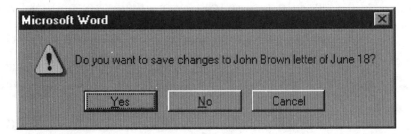

This prompt is a built-in safeguard, which allows you to perform a last-minute save before closing the document.

> **WARNING**   If you use a floppy disk to save your work, after you save and close a document residing on the floppy, make sure that you allow Word to fully close the document before pulling the diskette from the floppy disk drive. Files can become corrupted and unreadable if Word does not fully close the document before the diskette is removed.

Opening Saved Files

You can open a saved file in Word directly from the Desktop or from within Word. You can also tell Word what information to display in the list of saved files.

Word's shortcuts let you open your most recently used files from the File menu or store frequently used files in a Favorites folder. You can easily open multiple documents at once and switch between them.

Opening a Saved File from the Desktop

Word does not need to be launched first in order for you to open a Word document. Windows 95 has a Documents folder, activated from the Start menu. This folder lists the last 15 documents you saved.

TIP The list in the Windows 95 Documents folder can include saved file names from all of your programs: Excel, PowerPoint, Access, and so on, as well as Word. When you click on a file in this list, the program that was used to create that document launches with the document in tow.

If Word is already launched, you can still use the Start menu's Document option to open your files. If you work fairly exclusively with Word, you will see the last 15 files you were working on listed there (Word's File menu lists the last 9 files, by default).

Follow these steps to open a document from the Desktop:

1. Click the Start button on the Taskbar.

2. Choose the Documents option on the Start menu. The last 15 documents that you created, saved or just opened will be listed.

3. Click once on the document file you wish to be loaded into memory.

Note that you cannot load multiple files at the same time. However, you can click on the Start button and choose the Documents option again to continue to load more document files into memory.

Opening a Saved File within Word

Within Word, the File ➤ Open command, or the Ctrl+O shortcut, allows you to see a list of your files on disk and select the files you wish to load into memory (display on the screen). When you choose File ➤ Open or press Ctrl+O, Word shows you the names of files you have stored, listed in alphabetical order, as shown in Figure 9.5. Word documents have a green-blue letter *W* icon next to them.

By default, the file list shows only the Word files, but you can select to see files of a different type. At the bottom of the File ➤ Open dialog box, click the drop-down arrow next to the Files of Type box and choose another file type from the list that appears:

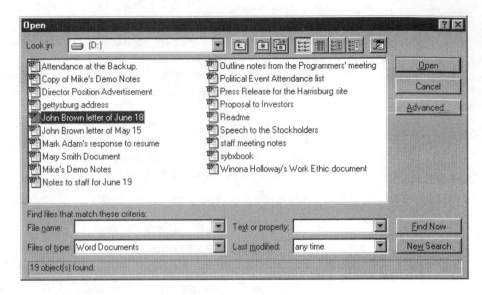

Figure 9.5   **The list of files in the File ➤ Open dialog box**

The All Files (*.*) option shows every file in your folder, even if the file is a proprietary one that only Word understands. After you select a different file type, the file list will show the files of this type.

In the File ➤ Open dialog box, double-click on the name of the file you wish to open. Alternatively, click once on the file name and then click on the Open button on the right side of the dialog box. Word will open the file and place you in the Word typing area on the first page of the document. Press Shift+F5 to return to the last location where you were editing or typing when you saved the file.

Displaying and Sorting File Details

You can tell Word to show details about the files in your file list and rearrange their sort order. For example, in addition to the full name of the file, you may want to see when a file was created or how large a file is in size. You may also want to sort your file list by date from the oldest files to the most recent, or vice versa.

At the top-right of the File ➤ Open dialog box, you'll see a number of buttons. Some of these buttons control how the files in the list will be displayed. Hover the mouse over the buttons and read the tips until you find the button called Details:

 Click on the Details button. The file list area will change to display columns with the headings Name, Size, Type, and Modified, as shown in Figure 9.6.

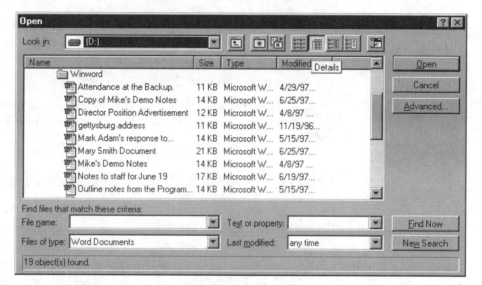

Figure 9.6 You can see and sort important details about your documents. Choose the Details button in the File ➤ Open dialog box, and then click on the column headings to sort the list of files by different categories.

 TIP To widen a column, hover the mouse at the top of the column at the divider line between the column heading names. When the mouse turns into a small black cross, double-click. The column will automatically adjust to fit the widest entry.

You can choose a sorting order for your file list as follows:

▶ Click the Name column heading to sort by file names.

▶ Click the Size column heading to sort by file sizes.

▶ Click the Type column heading to sort by file types.

▶ Click the Modified column heading to sort files by the dates the files were modified.

You can toggle between ascending and descending order for each sort category by clicking on the column heading again.

To display the files again as a simple list of names, click the List button at the top of the File ➤ Open dialog box:

 The list will return to the default columnar list style. In this style, you can see the entire file name but none of the details.

Selecting from the List of Recently Used Files

At the bottom of the File menu, Word displays, by default, the names of the last four files that were opened:

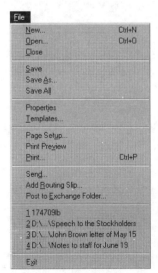

You can increase or decrease the number of documents listed on the File menu by choosing Tools ➤ Options ➤ General tab. Click the spinner button next to the Recently Used File List number to change the number of files you wish to be shown on the File menu's list. You can choose to display up to nine recently used file names.

Finding Files

When you cannot remember the exact name of a file, but you remember a few words that may be in the file name, use the Find Now button in the File ➤ Open dialog box. This allows you to have Word search through the list of files for your particular file.

One of the best aspects of the Find Now command is that you can enter any amount of characters from the file name that you want to find. For example, you can type the letters *att* to find a file that has a full name of Political Event Attendance List. Word will locate this file, even though the letters you entered are in the word *Att*endance, which is the third word in the file name.

Use these steps to find files:

1. Choose File ➤ Open to see a list of your files.

2. In the File Name text box at the bottom of the screen, type in any amount of characters you remember in the name. You can type uppercase or lowercase characters (the search is not case-sensitive).

3. Press the Enter key, or select the Find Now button in the lower-right corner of the dialog box. Word will display a list of files matching the characters you typed (if any matches were found), as shown in Figure 9.7.

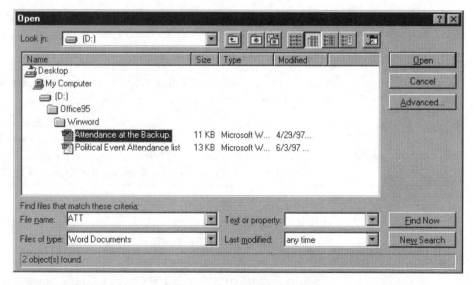

Figure 9.7   You can use partial file name characters to have Word search for all files that have those characters in it.

4. Once you have located your file, double-click the file name or click once and then click the Open button.

5.   To clear the list, click the New Search button below the Find Now button in the Open dialog box. The dialog box will list all the files again.

Word remembers the searches that you perform in the File ➤ Open dialog box. When you want to perform the same search again, instead of typing in your file name characters, click the drop-down list arrow next to File Name text box and select the search you performed previously.

Working with Favorites

You can place shortcuts to documents that you use over and over into a Favorites folder. The Favorites folder eliminates the chore of searching among hundreds of files for your most frequently used Word documents. This folder is set up by using the new shortcuts feature in Windows 95.

The Favorites buttons are at the top of the File ➤ Open dialog box. You can add selected files to the Favorites folder, or you can request to see what is in the Favorites folder.

Word allows you to select folders or individual document files and place them in the Favorites folder. In other words, if you have a folder called Johnston where you store all of the documents for your client named Johnston, you can add the name of this folder to your Favorites folder. Then you won't need to look all around the hard disk or the network for your client's folder.

TIP   If you want to place multiple folders in your Favorites folder, you can select them all at once by Shift-clicking. Then click Add to Favorites, and all of the folder shortcuts will be listed in the Favorites folder.

You will want to store the names of files you use frequently. For example, this is the place to keep monthly minutes that are revised each month or weekly reports in which only a few items change from one week to another.

To add documents to the Favorites folder, follow these steps:

1.   Choose File ➤ Open.

2.   Select the files you wish to place in your Favorites folder. To select multiple, noncontiguous files, hold down the Ctrl key and then click on each file name. To select a contiguous group of files, click once on the first file, hold down the Shift key, and click once on the last file.

3. Click the Add to Favorites button at the top of the dialog box:

4. When the submenu appears, click the second option, Add Selected Items to Favorites.

5. Click the Look in Favorites button (to the left of the Add to Favorites button). You will see your file names in the Favorites folder, as shown in the example in Figure 9.8.

Figure 9.8   The Favorites folder includes shortcuts to your documents and other folders.

Look at the Word icon to the left of the name of one of the files you placed in your Favorites folder. You will see that the Word icon has a tiny, curved arrow at the lower-left bottom. This arrow means that you have created a shortcut to your original document. This "proxy" for your document in the Favorites folder is merely a "pointer" to your original file.

What does that mean? Well, you can still open the original document in your regular File ➤ Open dialog box. If you make changes and save them, the changes will be there the next time you open the file, whether you pull the file up from the Favorites folder, from the regular Winword folder, or from the My Documents folder. You are not working with two different copies of the same file.

> **NOTE   Of course, you can set up your own folders to organize your Word documents. To learn how to create your own folders, see Chapter 3.**

From the list of the Favorites folder files, you can click the Look in Favorites button again to toggle back to the folder you were working in, with all of your original documents.

Deleting a Favorite Shortcut

When one of the files in your Favorites folder is no longer a "favorite," you can remove its shortcut. Choose File ➤ Open and click the Look in Favorites button at the top of the dialog box. Click on the shortcut associated with your file name, and press the Delete key on the keyboard. Word will ask if you are sure that you want to remove this shortcut. Notice that the deleted shortcut file will be sent to the Recycle Bin. This means you can still retrieve it, as explained later in this chapter.

When you delete a shortcut associated with a file name, it does not delete your original file. Click on the Look in Favorites button again to toggle back to your normal file list, and you will still see the name of your file.

If you delete the original file in your regular documents folder but leave the shortcut in the Favorites folder, the shortcut will no longer have a correct pointer to the original file. If you choose to open a shortcut file that points to a deleted or moved original file, Word searches but comes up "empty handed," telling you that it was unable to locate the file.

Opening Multiple Files

You can open multiple files into memory one at a time, by continuing to choose File ➤ Open and double-clicking on a different file name each time. However, there is another, easier way to select multiple files to open.

When you choose File ➤ Open, you can select contiguous (all together) and noncontiguous (in any order) file groups to open at the same time, as follows:

▶ To select a contiguous group of files, click once on the first file, hold down the Shift key, and click once on the last file name in the group.

▶ To select noncontiguous groups, hold down the Ctrl key and click once (don't double-click) on each file you wish to open.

When you have selected the multiple files, click the Open button on the right side of the File ➤ Open dialog box. Figure 9.9 shows an example of multiple files selected in the Open dialog box.

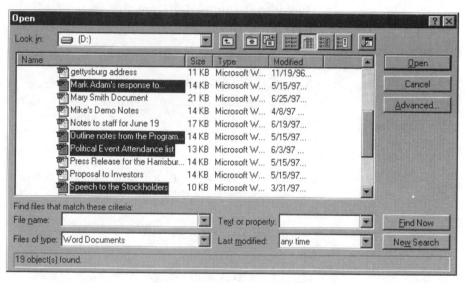

Figure 9.9   *You can select multiple files and open them all at once.*

All of the files will open at one time. Click on the Window command on the menu bar to see a list of the different files open in memory.

The amount of memory your computer has available is your only limitation on how many files you can have open at the same time. Each program and document file open in memory takes up a different amount of memory. Word will alert you when it has run out of memory and ask you to close some of your files.

Switching between Multiple Open Files

If you have several files open at the same time, you will want to switch between them so that you can edit or read their contents. You can select a window from the Window menu's list of the files currently open in memory. Press the number associated with the file, or just click on it, to make it the active window.

Part
2

Communicating with
Word

A quicker way to cycle through each of your open files is to use the shortcut keyboard combination, Ctrl+F6.

> **TIP**   When you have multiple files open in memory, you can easily copy text from one open document to another. Switch to the document that has the information you want to copy. Select the text to be copied and press Ctrl+C. Switch to the other document that should receive the copy. Position the insertion point where the copy should be inserted and choose Ctrl+V.

Closing Multiple Files

When you have a number of files open in memory, it can become tedious to close each one separately with the File ➤ Close option. Word has a hidden shortcut that you can use to close all files open in memory. Just like with the regular File ➤ Close command, Word will ask you if you need to save any files that you may have forgotten to save.

This hidden shortcut requires that you use the mouse. It does not work with the keyboard method of closing files. Follow these steps to close all open files:

1.   Hold down the Shift key.

2.   With the Shift key still down, click the mouse on the File menu in the menu bar. The Close option is no longer listed. Instead, a new option, Close All, is displayed:

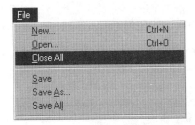

3.   Choose Close All, and Word will automatically close the files. If any file has been changed but not saved when you issue this command, Word will give you a chance to save it before closing that file.

When all the files are closed, you will see the blank Word screen. From there, you can open a new or existing file or exit Word.

Renaming a File

If you do not like the name you designated for a document and have come up with a better name for it, you can rename the file without making a copy of the document.

Choose File ➤ Open to see the list of file names in the dialog box. Click once on the name of the file you wish to rename to select it. Then click once again. This requires two separate clicks, not a rapid double-click, which would open the file into memory. To rename the file you must perform two single clicks, with a pause between one click and the next.

After you have clicked twice, an outline box will appear around the entire filename. The name will be selected. You can type over the entire selected name with a new name or select individual characters or words and change them to something new. For example, Figure 9.10 shows a file being renamed. In this example, the word *Document* is selected, indicating that this one word can be typed over.

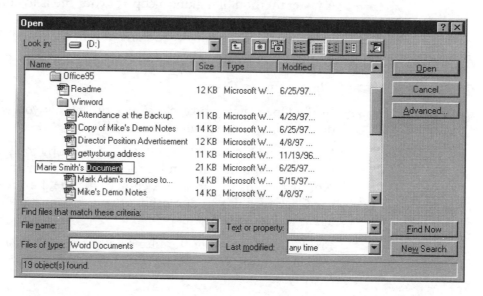

Figure 9.10　*Word makes it easy to rename a file. In the File ➤ Open dialog box, click twice on the file name, pausing between clicks. An outline box appears around the file name to let you change the name.*

Press the Enter key after you have renamed the document. The screen will flash and redisplay with the new name. If you do not want to open the file, you can click the Cancel button. The file will maintain its new name.

 TIP   You can also rename a file by right clicking the mouse on the file name and choosing Rename from the pop-up, shortcut menu.

Copying Files in the File List

You can always copy a file by opening the file and then choosing File ➤ Save As to make a copy of your document file under a new name. You will then have two documents, one under one name and the second under a new name. This feature is very helpful when you want to base a new document, such as a letter or report, on a previous one. You can make a copy of the original file and then make your changes to the copy without harming the original.

A faster method of making a copy of your file is to copy it directly in the file list, without bothering to open the original file. You can copy a file immediately while you are looking at it in the list of files.

Follow these steps to copy a file directly within the file list:

1. Choose File ➤ Open.

2. In the Open dialog box, click once on the file you wish to copy (don't double-click, or you will open the file).

3. Use the keyboard combination Ctrl+C to copy the file into memory (or right-click on the file and choose Copy from the shortcut menu). Nothing seems to happen! A copy of the file, however, was placed into the Clipboard. If you don't think that the copy registered, press Ctrl+C again to make another copy.

4. Press Ctrl+V to paste the file. The screen will flash for a minute and rewrite the list. Your original file now appears twice, but the copy says *Copy of* ....

5. To rename the copy, while the copied file is still selected, click once on the file to get the outline of the rename box.

6. Type the new name over the copy's name. Remember, you can have up to 255 characters in a name, and you can include periods and spaces in the name. Figure 9.11 shows a file and its copy being renamed.

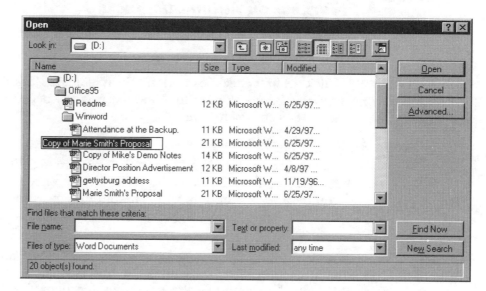

Figure 9.11 *Copies of files can be made directly from the File ➤ Open dialog box and easily renamed.*

Making Backup Copies Automatically

You can customize Word so that you get an automatic backup of every document you create. Every time you save your work (not each time Word performs an automatic save), Word will make another copy of your document (the extension on the file is WBK—an extension you may or may not see in the default view of the file list depending on your Windows 95 settings. The automatic backup feature is the ultimate in word processing insurance, but it is also very costly in disk space.

For every document you create and save, there will now be another copy: a backup copy. Your hard disk storage space will fill up more quickly when you request that there be two of everything. Use the backup feature judiciously. If you know that you are working on an extremely important document and you must protect yourself at all costs, turn on the automatic backup feature. When you working with less critical documents, make sure automatic backup is turned off. Remember, you must continuously save your document as you are working on it if you want the automatic backup to reflect the most current edits.

Turning on Automatic Backup

Follow these steps to set the automatic backup feature:

1. Choose Tools ➤ Options ➤ Save tab.

2. Click the first checkbox option: Always Create Backup Copy. Word will remove the check next to Allow Fast Saves, because the backup save requires a complete save.

3. Click OK. You will be returned to your document area.

4. You must close Word and restart the program to activate the new setting for the automatic backup option. If you don't need a backup right after you have set the option, you can continue to work in Word. The next time you start the Word program, the automatic backup option will be on.

With the backup option set, whenever you create and save any document, another copy of your work will be made with a prefix word of *Backup*. For example, the copy of a file named REPORT97 will be named Backup of REPORT97. As long as the backup option is set, Word will duplicate each of the documents you save.

Opening a Backup Copy

After you have turned on the automatic backup feature as described in the previous section, you can open (retrieve) the backup copies Word has made of your documents. To see these files in the Open dialog box, follow these steps:

1. Choose File ➤ Open.

2. At the bottom of the Open dialog box, type the word **backup** in the File Name text area.

3. Click on the next text line, labeled Files of Type (it currently says Word documents). Click the drop-down arrow and choose All Files. Word will now list the names of all of your backup files, as shown in Figure 9.12. Notice how Word precedes each of the backup copy names with the word *Backup*. Also notice the special icon to the left of the file name designating that this is a backup copy of the original file.

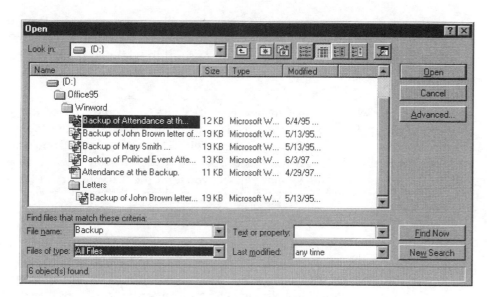

Figure 9.12   All backup copy files names are preceded with the words Backup of.

 TIP   You can also see the backup files without changing to the All Files type. Let the Files of Type option remain Word Documents. In the File Name text area, type *.WBK and press Enter. Word will show you all of the backup files.

Deleting Files

Files that have served their purpose and no longer need to be stored should be deleted so that you can maintain adequate disk space. Extraneous files obscure the list of current and relevant files.

To delete a file from the File ➤ Open dialog box file list, click once on the file to be deleted. Press the Delete key on your keyboard, or click the right mouse button and choose the Delete command from the shortcut menu (you can click on the word Delete with either mouse button). You will see the Confirm File Delete message box:

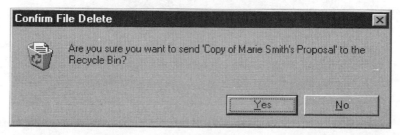

As noted in this message, files are sent to the Recycle Bin. This allows you to recover a file you deleted if you realize later that you need the file. Click the Yes button to send the deleted file to the Recycle Bin. The file will be removed from your list of files.

TIP If you are absolutely sure that you will never need a file again, you can bypass the Recycle Bin option when you delete a file from the File ➤ Open list. When you select a file(s) to be deleted, hold down the Shift key and then press the Delete key. Word will ask you if you truly want to delete the file(s)—not whether you want the file(s) sent to the Recycle Bin.

Deleting Multiple Files

You can select multiple files for deletion using the Windows Shift-click or Ctrl-click techniques. As when you choose multiple files to open, the Shift-click method selects contiguous file groups (multiple files in a row), and Ctrl-clicking selects noncontiguous file groups (multiple files not in a row). To unselect individual files in the noncontiguous list, hold down Ctrl and click the file name again.

After you have selected the multiple files, press the Delete key on the keyboard or hover the mouse over any selected file and right-click. Choose the Delete command from the shortcut menu. Figure 9.13

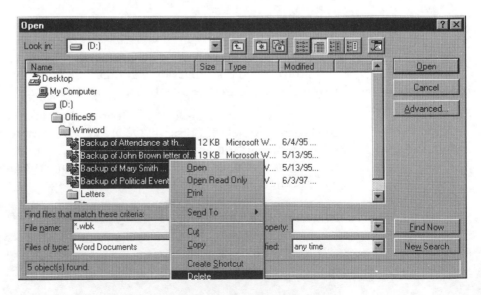

Figure 9.13 *You can select multiple, contiguous files to be deleted.*

shows this action in progress. After you choose Delete, the Confirm File Delete message box appears, just as it does for single files.

Restoring Deleted Files

If you wish to restore a file that was deleted and sent to the Recycle Bin, you must activate the Recycle Bin. After you have chosen to restore files in the Recycle Bin window, the restored files will again be listed in the File ➤ Open dialog box.

Follow these steps to restore deleted files:

1. Find a blank area on the Taskbar at the bottom of the screen and right-click to see the shortcut menu.

2. Choose Minimize All Windows from the shortcut menu. You will be returned to your Desktop.

3. Double-click the Recycle Bin icon on the Desktop to open the Recycle Bin window. This window lists the names of the files that were sent to the Recycle Bin.

4. To rearrange this list, click the column headings by which you wish to sort the files (Name, Original Location, Date Deleted, or Type).

5. Click the name of the file to be restored and choose File ➤ Restore. You can also right-click on the file name and choose Restore from the shortcut menu, as shown in Figure 9.14. The name will disappear from the Recycle Bin list (it is back in your file list in Word).

6. Repeat step 5 for each file you want to restore.

7. Close the Recycle Bin window. The restored files will once again be listed in Word's File ➤ Open dialog box.

8. Right-click on a blank section of the Taskbar and select Undo Minimize All to return to where you were.

NOTE The Recycle Bin retains all of the files you have deleted in each application, even after you turn off the computer. You must occasionally empty (clean out) the Recycle Bin, because the deleted files are taking up hard disk space. Sometimes Windows 95 will discover that you are running out of disk space and will prompt you to empty files from the Recycle Bin.

Part
2

Communicating with
Word

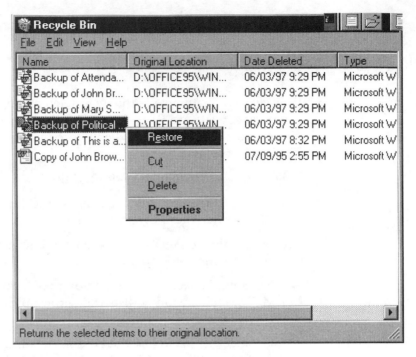

Figure 9.14   *The Recycle Bin shows the list of deleted files. Use the Restore command to "undelete" files.*

Combining Files Using the Insert Command

You can combine files by inserting one into another. For example, you may have a set of paragraphs that you usually need to insert into the middle of a monthly report. If you have typed these paragraphs and saved them by themselves in a separate file, you can insert this file into your report. You may also need to combine files when others have worked independently on sections of a report and now you need to combine their sections with yours.

When you use the Insert ➤ File command to combine multiple files, the inserted file is actually a copy of the file's contents. You are not removing any files from the disk.

You can also use the Insert ➤ File command to insert just a part of another Word document or Excel file. First you must select the part and gave it a bookmark name in Word (Edit ➤ Bookmark) or a range name in an Excel file (Insert ➤ Name ➤ Define).

Follow these steps to combine files:

1. Make sure you have the original document on the screen. This will be the main document into which other documents will be inserted.

2. Position the insertion point at the exact location where you want the other file to be inserted.

3. Choose Insert ➤ File. The Insert File dialog box appears.

4. At the bottom of the dialog box, click into the File Name text area to specify a file. The Range text area is used to designate a part of another Word document or of an Excel spreadsheet. You can type in a bookmark or range name to insert the text specified by the bookmark or range name.

5. Type the name of the file to be inserted or double-click on the file name that you see in the list of files. The new file is inserted into the document.

6. Tap the PgUp key to see all of the inserted information.

 TIP The AutoText feature in Word allows you to store frequently used paragraphs, pages, tables, graphics, and clip-art. If you need to insert the same text on a routine basis, consider using this feature, which is described in Chapter 11.

Printing Your Documents

Word lets you see on screen how your printed document will look. When you're ready to print to the printer, you can display the Print dialog box and choose a different printer, select specific pages to print, and print multiple copies. If necessary, you can usually cancel a print job that is in progress.

Printing to the Screen

Before printing your document to the printer, you may want to preview it with Word's Print Preview feature. Choose File ➤ Print Preview or click the Print Preview button on the Standard toolbar (the button to the right of the printer button) to see a representation of how your document will print. Print Preview is another view within Word, just like the Page Layout, Normal, and Outline views.

Although you are not required to view your document in Print Preview before actually printing your work, it can be a time and paper saver. You can see how the document will print before you expend time, effort, and paper on a print job that turns out to have problems, such as blank pages or too much spacing between some paragraphs. You can edit the document or print it directly from the Print Preview screen, or return to another view before printing. See Chapter 8 for more information about working in Print Preview.

Printing to the Printer

The successful printing of your document to the printer requires that your printer(s) are correctly installed by Windows 95.

> **NOTE**   If you are going to give your file to someone else to print on a printer that is not attached to your computer, have Windows 95 install that particular printer for your computer. Then the correct fonts and printer information will be used in your document. When you transfer the document to the other printer, you will not have any problems printing it.

To print to the printer, use one of these methods:

▶ Choose File ➤ Print.

▶ Click the print button on the Standard toolbar.

▶ Press the keyboard shortcut Ctrl+P.

Both the menu (File ➤ Print) and the shortcut (Ctrl+P) bring up the Print dialog box, shown in Figure 9.15. Here you can specify the number of copies and tell Word that you want to print just specific pages. Clicking the Print button on the Standard toolbar, however, sends one copy of your entire document to the printer immediately, according to the default settings, without showing the Print dialog box.

> **WARNING**   Although the Print dialog box has a Properties button that shows options to change the paper to landscape orientation, you shouldn't change the orientation this way. Use the File ➤ Page Setup ➤ Paper Size option to set the paper size and landscape orientation, as explained in Chapter 8.

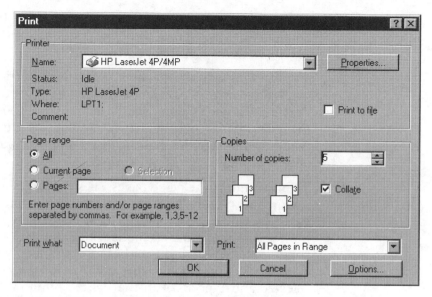

Figure 9.15 *The Print dialog box allows you to specify printing parameters.*

Selecting a Different Printer

If you use only one printer, it is not necessary to choose a printer each time you start Word. But if you can use multiple printers (such as different network printers), you must first select your printer from the Print dialog box. Click the drop-down list arrow next to the Name text box and choose the name of another printer. When you click OK, the document will print to the selected printer.

Printing All Pages

The default page range setting is to print All pages in the document. This option is immediately activated when you click the print button on the Standard toolbar. When you choose File ➤ Print or press Ctrl+P, the Print dialog box allows you to see the actual setting and change it to current page or multiple pages.

Printing Selected Pages

You may need to reprint one page or print a range of pages rather than the whole document. Word gives you the ability to print multiple pages, single pages, a range of pages, or pages you have selected with the mouse.

Part
2

Communicating with
Word

In the Page Range section of the Print dialog box, All is selected by default. Word will print all of the pages of your document unless you specify one of the other options.

To print the current page, make sure your insertion point is on the page you want to print. For example, if you only want to reprint page 16, click the mouse anywhere on page 16 before you choose File ➤ Print. In the Print dialog box, click the radio button next to Current Page to tell Word that only the page that has the insertion point should be printed. Then click OK. Only page 16 will be printed.

To print multiple selected pages, click the radio button next to the Pages option and type in noncontiguous pages separated by a comma. For example, to print pages 4, 11, 13, and 16, type in all of these page numbers and separate each one with a comma (4,11,13,16). A range of pages is separated with a dash. For example, if you want to print pages 8 through 14, make sure the radio button next to the Pages option is selected and type 8-14 in the Pages option. You can mix and match multiple pages with a range of pages. For example, you can specify that Word print pages 5, 8, 12-16.

Sometimes, you may want to print a selection, such as text that starts in the middle of page 5 and continues three-quarters of the way through page 7. Drag the mouse and select these pages and then choose File ➤ Print. Click the radio button next to the Selection option (across from the Current Page option). Click OK to print just your selection.

Printing and Collating Multiple Copies

To the right of the Page Range option in the Print dialog box is an option for printing multiple copies of your documents. There is no limit to the number of printed copies that can be produced. You can use this option whether you are printing all pages, selected pages, or page ranges.

The default setting for the Collate option is on. This option tells Word to print all the pages in one copy of a document before printing the pages in the next copy. For example, if you choose to print three copies of a five-page report, Word prints all five pages, then prints all five pages again, and then prints all five pages of the final copy. If the Collate option is not on, Word would print three copies of page one and then three copies of page two, and so on.

Part
2

Communicating with
Word

Printing to a File

Instead of printing to a printer, you can print a document to a file on the disk. You can then take the file to another computer and print from there (using the printer you specified when you printed the file to disk).

To print to a file, choose File ➤ Print. Check the Print To File box under the Properties button. In the Name box, choose the printer that you want to use for printing. For example, to print a text-only (ASCII) document file, choose Generic/Text as the Name. Click OK. Immediately close the file so that Word can complete the printing of the file to disk.

Printing from Multiple Trays

If you have a printer that supports dual printing trays, such as a Hewlett-Packard 4si, Word has options that allow you to specify which tray to use for printing letterhead and second sheets. Follow these steps to designate your printing trays:

1. Make sure that the printer Name in the Print dialog box is set to the printer that supports dual trays.

2. Choose File ➤ Page Setup ➤ Paper Source tab to see the page shown in Figure 9.16. This page lists options for the sources of First Page and Other Pages.

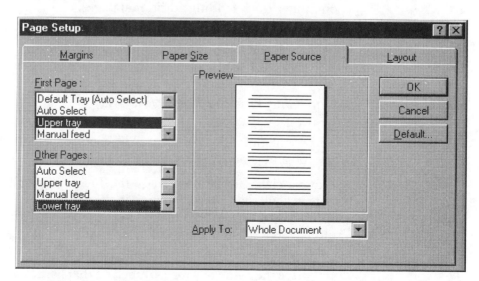

Figure 9.16   *Word allows you to use printers with multiple paper trays for letterhead and second sheets.*

3. Select which tray will hold your First Page letterhead.

4. For Other Pages, select the appropriate tray (usually Lower Tray).

5. Click OK.

When you print your document, Word will now "pull" from the correct tray for your first page and for the following pages.

Stopping the Printer

There will be occasions when you may need to stop a print run before it is completed. If the print run is between one and five pages, don't bother trying to stop the printer, particularly if it is a laser printer. By the time you got to the option that tells the computer to stop sending the pages to the printer, the entire print job will already have been sent.

Stopping the printer requires that you stop the computer from sending the data to the printer. When you issue a print job, Word begins to send the pages of your document to the printer's buffer (memory area). On the right side of the Status bar, you can see a small printer icon flashing the pages that are being sent. Immediately begin double-clicking this printer icon to cancel the current print job. The printer may continue to print a few more pages, but you will have effectively stopped the computer from sending additional pages.

It is not a good idea to turn off the printer in the middle of printing because it can cause paper jams. You also may not be physically near a printer to turn it off, such as when you are in an network environment.

Canceling Printing from Windows

When the printer is printing, you will see a printer icon on the Taskbar, next to the time (not flashing). This icon represents that the printer has the job and is now getting ready to print.

Double-click the printer icon on the Taskbar, and the Print window will appear, with the name of your job in the window, as shown in Figure 9.17. If your document job name does not appear, it means that the printer has already sent the entire document through its memory to the printer. You cannot cancel the job.

If you see the name of your job, click on that name and choose Document ➤ Cancel Printing from the menu bar. In a few seconds, the printer will

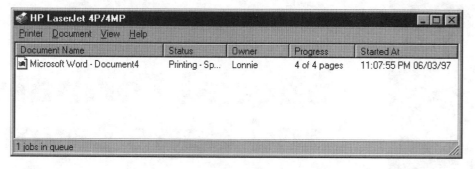

Figure 9.17   *For longer print jobs, you can use the Print window to cancel the job.*

begin deleting the print job (a few pages left in the print buffer will still print).

This chapter has covered the information you need to manage your files in Word and to print those files. The next chapter describes Word's special formats, such as borders and shading, bullets and numbering.

Part
2

Communicating with Word

Chapter 10

Special Formats and Page Layouts

Featuring

Enhancing Documents with Borders and Shading

Creating Bulleted and Numbered Lists

Quick and Easy Formatting with Autoformat

When word processing software first started to become widely available, users were limited to basic fonts, which could not be scaled to various sizes and could only represent basic alphanumeric characters. Even the simplest desktop publishing work needed to be sent out to a printer for the professionals to handle from start to finish.

Today, with Microsoft Word, you can generate most of your desktop publishing originals right from your desktop. Although most users do not need the full arsenal of Word publishing tools, you will find some special formatting layouts and tools extremely helpful.

WARNING When you're using the formatting features or Word, it is very easy to get carried away with all of the options. Try to remember while you are formatting your document that more is not always better; definitely use the tools, just not all at one time.

Adding Borders and Shading

One basic yet effective formatting option in Word is the ability to apply borders and shading to parts of your document. Borders and shading are generally used in conjunction with either paragraphs or tables. Other objects in Word, such as frames and pictures, can also have formatted borders.

Like most of Word's formatting features, applying borders and shading is a *select* and then *apply* process. You select the area or object that you want to format, and then you apply borders or shading. To apply this formatting to the selection, choose Format ➤ Borders and Shading from the menu bar. The dialog box shown in Figure 10.1 will appear. This dialog box has two tabs: one for its Borders page and the other for the Shading options. We'll describe the border options first.

Types of Borders

Word supplies some preset border options. These border options depend on what you selected before accessing the Borders and Shading dialog box. If you selected a paragraph of text or a single cell in a table, the border options that appear in the Presets section of the dialog box will be None, Box, and Shadow.

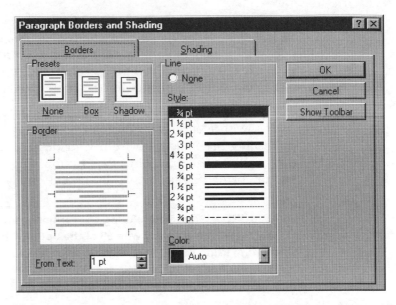

Figure 10.1   *The Borders and Shading dialog box is displayed by the Format ➤ Borders and Shading command.*

Figure 10.2 shows both a paragraph and a table formatted with the Box option. The Shadow option applies a similar border, except that the border has a three-dimensional, or shadowed, look to it.

If you selected multiple cells within a table, the Shadow option is replaced with a Grid option, which formats the outside and grid borders of the selected table. Figure 10.3 shows the same table in Figure 10.2 formatted with the Grid option.

PLEASE NOTE: The information provided above is for internal use only. Any correspondence regarding the procedures detailed in this manual should be considered CONFIDENTIAL and distributed only within our organization. Amendments to these policies must be approved by the board and all employees affected by the changes will be notified 30 days prior to them being instituted.

		Schedule	Of	Events		
SESSION	Monday	Tuesday	Wednesday	Thursday	Friday	Saturday
Morning	Part 1 of 2-Leadership Workshop	Part 2 of 2-Leadership Workshop	NSC Mgmt Lecture	Part 1 of 2 -TQM Group Workshop	Part 2 of 2 -TQM Group Workshop	Corporate Outings
Afternoon	Part 1-Time Mgmt Luncheon	Part 2-Time Mgmt Luncheon	Free Afternoon	Part 3-Time Mgmt Luncheon	Part 4-Time Mgmt Luncheon	Corporate Outings
Evening	Evening Roundup	Evening Roundup	Free Evening	Evening Roundup	Card Exchge Cocktail Party	Corporate Outings

Figure 10.2   *A paragraph and table formatted with the Box border*

		Schedule	Of	Events		
SESSION	**Monday**	**Tuesday**	**Wednesday**	**Thursday**	**Friday**	**Saturday**
Morning	Part 1 of 2- Leadership Workshop	Part 2 of 2- Leadership Workshop	NSC Mgmt Lecture	Part 1 of 2 - TQM Group Workshop	Part 2 of 2 - TQM Group Workshop	Corporate Outings
Afternoon	Part 1- Time Mgmt Luncheon	Part 2- Time Mgmt Luncheon	Free Afternoon	Part 3- Time Mgmt Luncheon	Part 4 Time Mgmt Luncheon	Corporate Outings
Evening	Evening Roundup	Evening Roundup	Free Evening	Evening Roundup	Card Exchge Cocktail Party	Corporate Outings

Figure 10.3 **A table formatted with the Grid option**

When you're formatting borders, however, you do not need to restrict yourself to the preset border styles. Below the preset options is a Border preview that allows you to control how your border will appear. The easiest way to use the Border preview area is to select the closest preset option, and then select or deselect the appropriate border lines to achieve the format you want to apply.

As an example, we will go through the steps to format the table shown in Figure 10.3 with a grid, but without the horizontal grid lines so that the table borders are only for the columns. (This example demonstrates how borders can be used to enhance a table; creating tables in Word is discussed later in this chapter.)

1. Insert a table into your document by selecting Table ➤ Insert Table.

2. Change the Number of Columns to 5 and the Number of Rows to 3. Then choose OK.

3. Click into your table and select Table ➤ Select Table.

4. Select Format ➤ Borders and Shading.

5. Choose the Grid option.

6. In the Borders preview section of the Borders and Shading dialog box, click twice on the thin, horizontal line. It should disappear. You need to click twice because the first time switches the line to the point size selected. When the point size selected is the same size as the line's current size, you only need to click once to remove the line in the preview.

7. Choose OK.

8. Click somewhere outside the table to deselect it. Your table should look like the one shown in Figure 10.4.

		Schedule	Of	Events		
SESSION	Monday	Tuesday	Wednesday	Thursday	Friday	Saturday
Morning	Part 1 of 2- Leadership Workshop	Part 2 of 2- Leadership Workshop	NSC Mgmt Lecture	Part 1 of 2 - TQM Group Workshop	Part 2 of 2 - TQM Group Workshop	Corporate Outings
Afternoon	Part 1- Time Mgmt Luncheon	Part 2- Time Mgmt Luncheon	Free Afternoon	Part 3- Time Mgmt Luncheon	Part 4 Time Mgmt Luncheon	Corporate Outings
Evening	Evening Roundup	Evening Roundup	Free Evening	Evening Roundup	Card Exchge Cocktail Party	Corporate Outings

Figure 10.4   **A table formatted with the horizontal line of the grid removed**

> **TIP**   Formatting the borders of tables is a great way to reproduce the appearance of paper forms in Word. By selecting various groups of cells within a table and applying different borders, you can achieve quite effective results.

Shading Paragraphs

Another effective method of bringing attention to sections of your document is to format the interior of paragraph or table selections with shading. Used in the right places, shading can help turn a bland document into a polished piece.

Select the paragraph or table cells you want to shade, and then choose Format ➤ Borders and Shading ➤ Shading tab to see the options. The Shading page of this dialog box is shown in Figure 10.5.

You can pick from the available Custom Shading options, which range from clear to 90% shaded or 100% solid. A few options at the bottom of the list box offer varying line patterns.

If you want to have the effect of reverse printing (white text on black background), select the Solid shading option. This is a helpful technique for bringing crucial text to the attention of a reader. Shading percents over 75% all result in this reversed print. Figure 10.6 shows examples of shading, including the Solid and 20% options and a table with shading and borders.

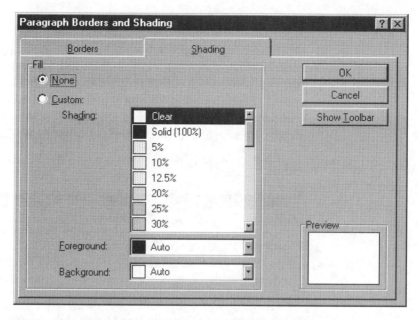

Figure 10.5   **The Shading page of the Borders and Shading dialog box**

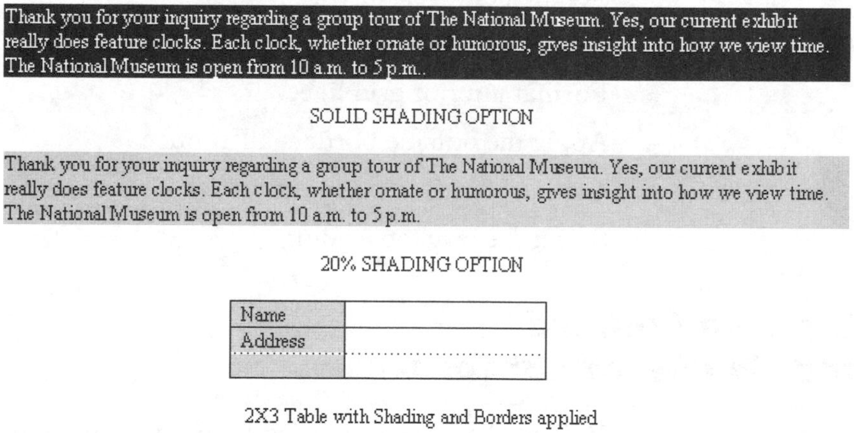

Thank you for your inquiry regarding a group tour of The National Museum. Yes, our current exhibit really does feature clocks. Each clock, whether ornate or humorous, gives insight into how we view time. The National Museum is open from 10 a.m. to 5 p.m..

SOLID SHADING OPTION

Thank you for your inquiry regarding a group tour of The National Museum. Yes, our current exhibit really does feature clocks. Each clock, whether ornate or humorous, gives insight into how we view time. The National Museum is open from 10 a.m. to 5 p.m.

20% SHADING OPTION

Name	
Address	

2X3 Table with Shading and Borders applied

Figure 10.6   **A few examples of Word's shading formats**

Using the Borders Toolbar

Working with a document that has multiple border and shading formats could require many trips through the menu and dialog box to get to your formatting options. An alternative is to use Word's Borders toolbar. Like the other toolbars, the Borders toolbar is available through the View ➤ Toolbars dialog box. It is also available through a button on the Formatting toolbar (the one that looks like a window pane).

This button is a toggle to turn on or off the display of the Borders toolbar:

Using the Borders toolbar, you can access just about all of the options in the Borders and Shading dialog box. The exceptions are shadowed borders, the distance your borders are from the text, and the optional shading color.

From left to right on your Borders toolbar, you can perform the following formatting:

▶ Set the point size of your borders

▶ Turn on and off the top, bottom, left, and right borders individually

▶ Format interior grid lines

▶ Apply the outside borders all at once

▶ Clear all border options at once

▶ Select the level of shading

Applying Bulleted and Numbered List Formats

Bulleted lists are often used to bring main points to a reader's attention. With Word, creating bulleted lists has become as easy as clicking a toolbar button. Word's automatic numbering and bulleting features allow you to create a bulleted or numbered list as you type it into your document. You can also apply a format after the list has been entered.

Numbering a List As You Go

When you are ready to begin typing a list, you can choose to have that list either bulleted or numbered. On the Formatting toolbar, the list buttons are the fourth and fifth buttons from the right. The button with 1, 2, and 3 on it will begin a numbered list format. The button with the picture of the bullets on it will begin a list formatted with bullets.

Here is the procedure for applying either a numbered or bulleted list format:

1. Position your insertion point on the line that you want to begin your list.

2. Click the numbering or bullets button on the Formatting toolbar. You will see either a number 1 or a bullet.

3. Type the first line of your list and press Enter. A number 2 or another bullet will appear, ready for you to type your second line.

4. Type your second line, and press Enter. Repeat step 3 for each item in your list.

5. Press Enter on the last line of your list.

6. To end the numbering or bulleted style, press Enter without entering text on the new line.

> **TIP** If you want to move to a second line for the same number in your list, and you need to stop typing before the text wraps at the end of the line, press Shift+Enter to end the line but not the whole numbered paragraph.

Formatting Existing Text as a List

Forethought is a wonderful thing. The problem is that many of us simply don't have it when we are rushing to get a document ready. Fortunately, as with most Word formatting options, you can apply a numbered or bulleted list format after the fact. Here's a simple example to demonstrate:

1. Type the following four words into your document, pressing Enter after each one: **Top**, **Bottom**, **Left**, **Right**.

2. Select the four lines.

3. Click the bullets button on the Formatting toolbar. Your list should now be bulleted and look like this:

    - Top
    - Bottom
    - Left
    - Right

Stopping and Resuming a List Format

When you are using a bulleted or numbered format in your document, you may want to have your list stop for supporting text or graphics and then start again. The problem is that if you try to add lines in the middle of a list, they will also be numbered or bulleted. The solution is to insert the line, which is really a paragraph, and remove the numbered or bulleted format from that line.

If you are inserting a break as you type a list, you need to press the spacebar and Enter key on the line from which you want to remove the format. This way, another line can be added to carry on the list, with the correct numbering, after you change the formatting of the blank line. The new line below the line you are removing the format from will automatically be renumbered.

If the list is already formatted and you want to add a space to insert a chart, diagram, or other information, position your insertion point at the end of the numbered or bulleted line right before the space you want to add and hit Enter. A blank numbered line will appear. Leave your insertion point on the new line and click the numbering or bullets button on the Formatting toolbar to remove the format. The number on the blank line will be removed, and the other items in the list will return to the way they were before you inserted the line.

Note that even when you remove the numbering or bulleting format from a line, the indentation of the line will remain so that you will have a forced .25-inch indent. If you try to remove the indent, the numbering of the bottom portion of your list after the list will reset to start at 1. To modify the numbering of the bottom list so that it begins at the desired number, place your insertion point in the list, select Format ➤ Bullets and Numbering, and click the Modify button.

Changing Bullet Styles

Naturally, you will want to know if you can change the style of the bullet Word adds to your bulleted lists. The answer is yes.

As with most detailed options in Word, to modify a bullet, you must go through the dialog box. Select Format ➤ Bullets and Numbering ➤ Bulleted tab from the menu bar, or right-click in a bulleted list and select Bullets and Numbering from the shortcut menu, to see the dialog box shown in Figure 10.7.

The Bulleted page offers six preset bullet options. If one of these will do the job, all you need to do is click on its preview and then click OK. If you want even more choices of bullet types to choose from or need to modify one of the preselected bullets, click the Modify button. You will see the Modify Bulleted List dialog box, shown in Figure 10.8.

This dialog box lets you change the bullet character, as well as its point size, color, and position. You can even turn off the hanging-indent format for a list by clicking on the Hanging Indent checkbox to remove the check.

You can follow these steps to begin a list with a custom bullet:

1. Place your insertion point on a blank line and select Format ➤ Bullets and Numbering.

2. Be sure that you are on the Bulleted tab and click the Modify button.

Part 2

Communicating with Word

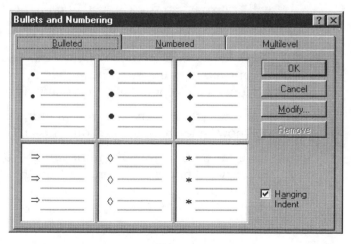

Figure 10.7   The Bullets and Numbering dialog box

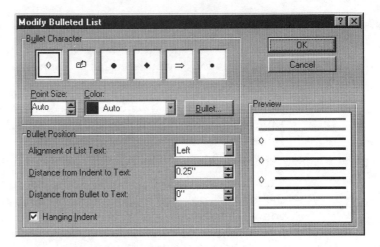

*Figure 10.8 **The Modify Bulleted List dialog box lets you modify preselected bullets or choose from all available symbols.***

3. Click on the Bullet button in the dialog box. The Symbol dialog box will open. The combo box at the top tells you which font your bullet is in.

4. Click on the drop-down arrow of the Symbols From combo box and choose the font from which you want to select a bullet symbol. For example, you might select Wingdings, which should be toward the bottom of the list.

5. Click on the different pictures in the grid of the dialog box. The picture will "pop out" so you can get a better view of it.

6. When you find the bullet you want, click OK.

7. You will be returned to the original dialog box where you can now either accept the new bullet with its default properties or modify the other options, such as point size, color, and alignment.

8. Once everything is the way you want it, click OK. The line you were on will now be formatted with your chosen bullet.

9. Type the lines of your list until you get to the last line, and then press Enter twice; once for the line and another time to get rid of the leftover bullet.

Here's an example of a list with a custom bullet:

☺**Think Happy Thoughts**

☺**Be Kind to Others**

☺**Smile, Smile, SMILE!**

> **NOTE** You can use basically the same steps as above to modify the bullets in an existing list. Select the list first (the bullets will not appear to be selected, but they are) and work through the dialog boxes as described in this section.

Changing Your Numbering Scheme

In some cases, 1, 2, 3 does not make the grade as a numbering style. You might prefer a lettering style (A, B, C) or roman numerals for your list. You can choose a different numbering style in much the same way that you can select different bullet styles.

To change a numbering scheme, choose Format ➤ Bullets and Numbering ➤ Numbered tab. The Numbered page allows you to choose from six preselected numbering options. The Modify button on this page will take you to the Modify Numbered List dialog box, shown in Figure 10.9. The options here let you specify text before and after the number, various numbering schemes, which number to start at, and the number's position.

As an example, we will create a numbered list format with the word *PHASE* before the numbers and the characters ---> after the numbers. Follow these steps:

1. Place your insertion point on a blank line and select Format ➤ Bullets and Numbering ➤ Numbered tab.

2. Click the Modify button.

3. In the Text Before box, type **PHASE** (replace any existing text in this box).

4. In the Text After box, type **--->** (replace any existing text in this box).

5. Click OK. The line you were on will now have PHASE 1---> on it.

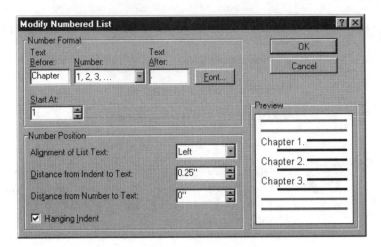

Figure 10.9 *The Modify Numbered List dialog box lets you customize your numbered list format.*

6. Type the lines of your list until you get to the last line, and then press Enter twice; once to start a new line and another time to get rid of the leftover number.

Here's an example of a numbered list formatted as described in the steps above:

```
PHASE1--->Database Design
PHASE2--->Non-Functional GUI designed
PHASE3--->Customer authorization to proceed
PHASE4--->Functionality put behind GUI
PHASE5--->In house Testing
PHASE6--->Beta Testing
PHASE7--->Installation
PHASE8--->Support
```

When You Need More Details—Multilevel Lists

It would be nice if everything remained at one general level and specifics were not important, but in the real world, that is just not the case. There will be times that you need to include a multiple-level list in your documents in order to provide more details about what you are trying to say. When you need to show levels of details in your lists, use Word's improved multilevel list formatting features.

To see your options, choose Format ➤ Bullets and Numbering ➤ Multilevel tab. This page of the Bullets and Numbering dialog box, shown in Figure 10.10, offers six preset formats, along with a Modify button that allows you to specify a custom multilevel list format.

After you select one of the multilevel formats, your list will be formatted so that each time you press the Tab key at the beginning of a line, it will be demoted one level. To promote a line, press the Backspace key or Shift+Tab.

Follow these steps to get a feel for creating multilevel lists and modifying the preselected options:

1. Place your insertion point on a blank line and select Format ➤ Bullets and Numbering ➤ Multilevel tab or right-click and select Bullets and Numbering from the shortcut menu.

2. Click on the second multilevel option in the top row, then click OK.

3. Type **Chapter** and press Enter.

4. Press Tab, type **Section**, and press Enter.

5. Type **Section** and press Enter.

6. Hold down the Shift key and press Tab.

7. Type **Chapter** and press Enter.

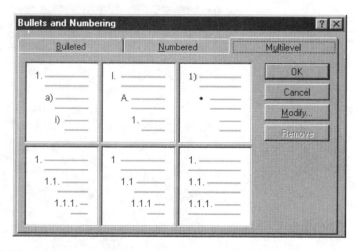

Figure 10.10   *The Multilevel page of the Format ➤ Bullets and Numbering dialog box formats your list to allow for multiple levels.*

Part
2

Communicating
with Word

8. Press Tab, type **Section**, and press Enter.

9. Press Tab, type **SideBar**, and press Enter twice. Your multilevel list should look like this:

```
I.    Chapter
      A.    Section
      B.    Section
II.   Chapter
      A.    Section
            1.    SideBar
```

10. To modify this format, select the lines that make up the list.

11. Select Format ➤ Bullets and Numbering ➤ Multilevel tab.

12. Click the Modify button to see the Modify Multilevel List dialog box, shown in Figure 10.11.

13. In the Level 1 section on the right side of the dialog box, click once on the down arrow, and it will change to Level 2.

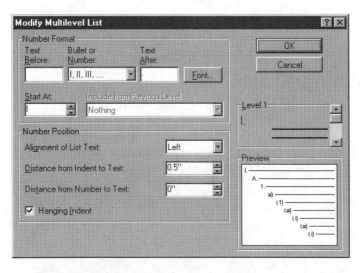

Figure 10.11   *The Modify Multilevel List dialog box lets you customize your list format.*

14. Click on the drop-down arrow of the Include from Previous Level box and select Numbers.

15. Choose OK. Your modified list should look like this:

```
I.      Chapter
        I.A.    Section
        I.B.    Section
II.     Chapter
        II.A.   Section
                1.       SideBar
```

Leaving the Formatting to Word with AutoFormat

When you are creating documents, you may have some formatting chores that will always need to be done. These tasks may be small, simple things, such as replacing a typed-out fraction with a true fraction character (1/2 with $\frac{1}{2}$). Or you may want Word to take over the whole job of formatting any part of the document (when time is of the essence and that is one thing that you don't have). Word helps you along in both cases with its AutoFormat features.

You can have Word apply the AutoFormat feature automatically as you type your document, all at once after your typing is completed, or a combination of the two. To get an overview of what AutoFormat can do, select Tools ➤ Options ➤ AutoFormat tab. This page of the Options dialog box is shown in Figure 10.12.

Clicking on either of the two radio buttons at the top of the dialog box will take you to a different view of the page. The views the buttons show are the two main categories of AutoFormat: options applied when requested (by selecting Format ➤ AutoFormat from the menu bar) and options that can be applied directly as you type your document. The options are virtually identical; it is your decision when it is best to apply Word's AutoFormat.

The AutoFormat options consist of formats that can be applied and items that can be replaced. To see how this works, we'll create a new document and let Word format it automatically. This example uses the

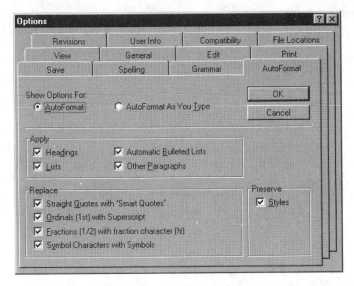

Figure 10.12   The AutoFormat page in the Options dialog box shows the ways that Word can format for you.

AutoFormat options that are selected by default when Word is installed. Follow these steps:

1. Click the new document button on the Standard toolbar (it is the first one on the toolbar and its picture looks like a white piece of paper).

2. Press Enter four times.

3. Type in the following address, pressing Enter after each line:

    John Smith

    1212 Long Lane

    Somewhere, PA 81091

4. Press Enter two times.

5. Type **Dear John:** and press Enter.

6. Press Enter twice.

7. Type the following text for the letter:

    Please be advised that I am writing you to attempt to get a few points about formatting across to you. Please review these points.

8. Press Enter twice.

9. Type an asterisk (*), and press Tab.

10. Type the following and press Enter:

    Lists with asterisks can be automatically converted to a list with bullets.

11. At the newly inserted bullet, type the following and press Enter:

    Normal straight quotes can be changed to "Smart Quotes."

12. Press Enter on the next blank line. The bullet should disappear.

13. Type the following and press Enter:

    I also have these points I would like you to examine.

14. Press Enter again, type **1.**, and press Tab.

15. Type the following and press Enter:

    Lists can be numbered automatically.

16. On the line with the 2 inserted, type the following and press Enter:

    Ordinals like 1st can be converted to superscripts.

17. On the line with the 3 inserted, type the following and press Enter:

    Fractions like 1/2 are changed from basic text.

18. On the line with the 4 inserted, type the following and press Enter:

    Special symbols like (C), (TM), (R), and :) can be inserted easily.

19. On the line with the 5 inserted, press Enter twice to stop the numbering and insert a blank line.

20. Type the final line of the letter and press Enter:

    Thank you for taking time to review these issues. I will be in touch soon.

21. Press Enter twice.

22. Type **Sincerely,** and press Enter three times.

23. Type **Gary Stevens** and press Enter.

24. Hold down the Ctrl key and press Home to go to the beginning of the document.

25. Select Format ➤ AutoFormat from the menu bar.

26. Click OK in the AutoFormat dialog box. When Word has finished reviewing the document, the dialog box will give you a chance to accept or reject all changes, review individual changes, or choose a different style from the Style Gallery.

27. Click the Review Changes button in the AutoFormat dialog box.

28. Click the Find button until you reach the end of your document to see the changes made after your document was created.

29. When you are finished reviewing the changes, choose Cancel.

30. Decide whether you want to accept the changes or reject them and click the appropriate button.

If you accept Word's changes, the print preview of your document will look like Figure 10.13. Even with the minor AutoFormat changes in this example, the document looks a lot more polished with a lot less effort.

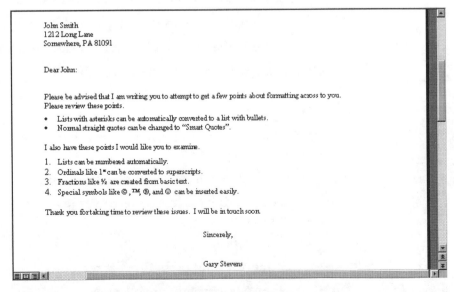

Figure 10.13   *A document with AutoFormats applied, both as you typed and after you were finished with Format ➤ AutoFormat*

Adding Formatting with Styles

When you are working with documents, especially long documents, formatting your text with multiple levels of headings and various formats for different parts of your body text can become tedious. Word assists in making formatting text in your documents more efficient by providing built-in styles and allowing you to create custom styles of your own.

In Word, a *style* is a collection of formatting options labeled with one name. Styles define all aspects of formatting—from the font and point size of the text to paragraph formatting, such as alignment, line spacing, borders, and tab stops.

Word's Built-in Styles

Even if you are not aware of it, you are always working with styles in Word. The Normal style is the default, and it is the style that all other styles are based upon.

The first item on your Formatting toolbar is a combo box that identifies the current style that you are using. If you do nothing with styles, the combo box will show that you are using the Normal style.

The Normal style comes with the default font of 10-point Times New Roman, single-spacing, left-aligned paragraphs, and other default format settings that you can view in the Modify Style dialog box. To see this dialog box, select Format ➤ Style and click the Modify button. In the Modify Style dialog box, click the Format button to see the different categories of formats that a style contains. Figure 10.14 shows the Modify Style dialog box with the Format list for the Normal style.

In addition to the Normal style, Word comes with a number of other built-in styles that help you format your document. One group of these styles is the nine levels of heading styles provided by Word. Starting with Heading 1 at the highest level down to Heading 9 at the lowest level, these styles provide a set of formats that visually identify the different levels of headings.

Here is a quick example to give you an idea of how styles in general, and the heading styles in particular, format your documents:

1. Start a new document in Word.

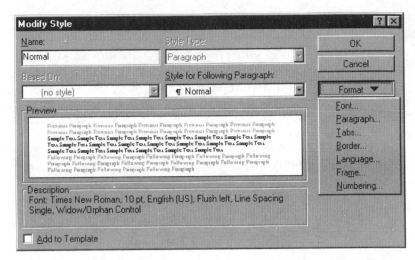

Figure 10.14 *The Modify Style dialog box shows the settings for the style in effect (in this case, the Normal style).*

2. Click on the Style combo box on the Formatting toolbar and select Heading 1 or press Ctrl+Alt+1.

3. Type **Heading 1** and press Enter.

4. Click on the Style combo box on the Formatting toolbar and select Heading 2 or press Ctrl+Alt+2.

5. Type **Heading 2** and press Enter.

6. Click on the Style combo box on the Formatting toolbar and select Heading 3 or press Ctrl+Alt+3.

7. Type **Heading 3** and press Enter.

Although you can only see three heading styles when you click on the Style combo box on the Formatting toolbar, six other heading levels are available. A quick way to access the other heading styles, and all the other built-in styles as well, is by holding down the Shift key while clicking on the Style combo box.

> **TIP** Word provides an entire view that allows you to focus on your heading styles. In Outline view (select View ➤ Outline or click on the Outline view icon on the Status bar), you can work with your document in the context of an outline. This makes it easy to promote and demote levels and move chunks of your document around at one time. To switch back to Normal view, select View ➤ Normal or click on its icon in the Status bar.

Defining Your Own Styles

One of the biggest benefits of Windows and programs like Word is that they are customizable; no two people need to use them in the same way. The styles that come with Word are by no means meant to be the "be all to end all" in styles. You can create you own styles to fit your needs.

For example, suppose that you need a heading style that has a 20-point Bold Arial font, is centered, and always has a border around it. You could create it by following this process:

1. Start a new document in Word.

2. Select Format ➤ Style.

3. In the Style dialog box, click the New button to open the New Style dialog box.

4. In the Name text box, type **MY STYLE** (do *not* press Enter).

5. Click the Format button and select Font from the list.

6. In the Font dialog box, choose Arial for Font, Bold for Font Style, and 20 for Size. Leave the other options as they are and click OK.

7. Click the Format button and choose Paragraph from the list.

8. Click on the Alignment combo box in the bottom-right corner of the Paragraph dialog box.

9. Select Centered from the list, and then click OK.

10. Click the Format button and choose Border from the list.

11. Select the Box preset option in the Borders dialog box and click OK.

12. Click OK in the New Style dialog box.

13. Click the Close button in the Style dialog box. Your style is now available to this document.

14. Type **This is MY STYLE** on the first line (do not press Enter).

15. Click on the Style combo box on the Formatting toolbar to see your style.

16. Select your style. Your screen should look like the one shown in Figure 10.15.

If you now press Enter, you will see that the style is carried forward to the next paragraph. If you want to go back to the Normal style or another style, you can select it from the combo box on the Formatting toolbar. If you know that there will never be two paragraphs in the style you created following each other in your document, you can specify the style for the following paragraph as part of your style. Choose Format ➤ Style,

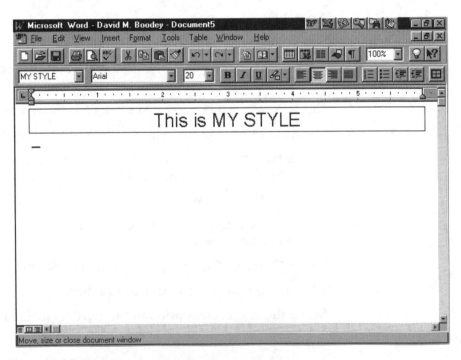

Figure 10.15   **Your new style applied to the first paragraph**

select your style and click the Modify button. In the Modify Style dialog box, change the setting for the Style for Following Paragraph option.

At this point, MY STYLE will be available only in the current document. If you want to make the style available in all of your documents, click the Add to Template checkbox in the bottom-left corner of the Modify Style dialog box for MY STYLE.

If you no longer need a style you created, you can delete it. However, you cannot delete Word's built-in styles. To delete a style such as MY STYLE, select Format ➤ Style, select your style, and click the Delete button. Close the Style dialog box when you're finished.

Creating Styles by Example

Instead of using the dialog boxes to create a style, you can create a style by example. To create a style by example, format a paragraph in your document the way you want the paragraph to look and select the paragraph. Then click in the text box portion of the Style combo box on the Formatting toolbar. Type the name of the new style over the name that appears in the text box and press Enter. Your new style is now available in your document.

> **TIP** If you have a set of formats that you want to use a couple of times but do not want to go through the process of setting up a style, you can use the Format Painter button (the one with a paintbrush) on the Standard toolbar. The Format Painter allows you to take all of the formatting from one paragraph and apply the format to another paragraph. See Chapter 7 for details.

Seeing Styles in a Document

If you wish to view all of the styles being used in your document without placing your insertion point in different paragraphs, select Tools ➤ Options ➤ View tab. In the dialog box, increase the size of the Style Area Width to 1" and click OK. Your style names will be listed along the left side of your screen, similar to Figure 10.16.

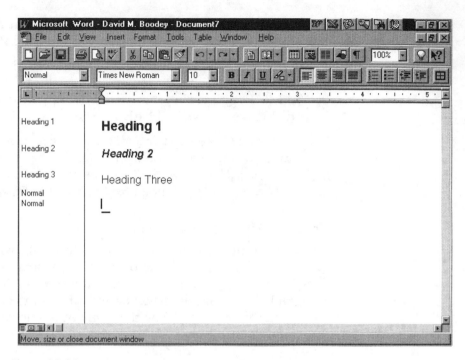

Figure 10.16   **When you set a size for Style Area Width on the View page of the Options dialog**

Wrapping Up

This chapter has described Word's special formatting and layout options that help you produce professional-looking documents. The next chapter covers some more of Word's time-saving features, including Find and Replace, AutoCorrect, AutoText, and Mail Merge.

Chapter 11

Word's Reusability Features—Never Type Again

FEATURING

Word has wonderful tools that you can use to reduce or eliminate the retyping of words, phrases, or even whole documents. Which tool is the best one to use depends on what you are trying to accomplish. The tools we are going to explore in this chapter are Find and Replace, AutoCorrect (for more than just fixing spelling errors), AutoText, Bookmarks, Word's renowned templates, and finally Mail Merge.

Each feature provides a different way in which you can avoid the rekeying of text. Each tool comes with its own set of rules and methods.

The Find and Replace function has Word search through a document looking for specific characters, and if requested, replace them with the other characters you specified. You can search for special characters (such as page breaks and paragraph symbols) and for formatting, as well as for words and phrases.

The AutoCorrect and AutoText tools actually allow you to store frequently used text within your template instead of requiring you to retrieve the text from the disk.

The Bookmark feature allows you to use a field name instead of real words. Later, you can tell Word to substitute real words for those field names. This is a great feature for letters or legal documents that are used again and again, with only a name change each time you reuse the document.

Word bases all documents on templates. Templates are predesigned and preformatted documents that you can use for your work. When you choose a new, blank document screen, Word has served you up the Normal template. There are many other templates, such as the Letter Wizard template and Fax templates, which you can access by choosing File ➤ New from the menu bar. But you can also design your own templates and use them again and again.

Mail merge has long been a word processing tool used to automate periodic mailings, such as letters, invitations, or newsletters, to many individuals. You don't need to rekey the address and personalized information from mailing to mailing.

Let's get started and see how these features actually work in practice. Once you know about these features, you will never retype text without first considering using one of them to do the work for you.

Finding and Replacing Text and Formats

As with most quality word processing programs, Word gives you the ability to find specific words or phrases in your document (Edit ➤ Find). The Find feature is extended through the Replace command (Edit ➤ Replace) so that you can both find and replace text. (This feature is sometimes called Search and Replace in other word processing programs.)

The Find command is a higher-level function than the Goto command (Ctrl+G), which jumps to specific pages or sections. Find allows you to specify the particular word or phrase without knowing the page number(s) on which this text resides.

As an example of using the Find and Replace feature, suppose that you typed a name at least four to five times in a document, and then you discovered that the name is spelled differently. You may have typed Mr. John W. Smith only to find that the man's name is Mr. John W. Smythe. You could locate the word, *Smith*, delete it, and then rekey it four to five times. But it's easier to use the Find and Replace feature to find every occurrence of the name *Smith* and replace it with *Smythe*. Using Find and Replace also eliminates typos that can occur when you manually rekey multiple changes.

It is always a good idea to first save your document before you perform a Find and Replace, because the results may not be what you expected. If you save the document immediately before you perform the Find and Replace, you can always call up the previously saved version if things go wrong. The Undo button is also handy when you see a Find and Replace that has gone haywire.

Imagine finding and replacing all occurrences of the word *men* with the word *chaps*. If you do not specify that Word should Find Whole Words Only (one of the options you can set in the Replace dialog box), Word will find the letters within any word in the document and replace them with the characters you specified. You can end up with the word *women* becoming *wochaps* and *increment* becoming *increchapst*. Thank goodness for the Undo button.

Specifying Search Criteria

The previous section described a Find and Replace requirement that could have come up with unexpected results if the Find Whole Words search criteria had not been used. Search criteria allow you to narrow your search and to find and replace information that is represented by symbols or special characters, such as page breaks and paragraph endings.

The search criteria in Word allow for tremendous flexibility when finding and replacing text and special characters. The checkboxes in the dialog box offer the following options:

▶ **Match Case:** Finds only the characters that are the same case as the ones in the Find What box and replaces them with the same case as in the Replace With box.

▶ **Find Whole Words Only:** Finds the whole word rather than the specific characters. For example, if you enter the Find text *men* and specify Find Whole Words Only, Word will locate only those characters as a word by themselves, and not words with the characters within them, such as incre*men*t.

▶ **Use Pattern Matching:** Allows you to specify wildcard symbols in your Find text. Using wildcards is described a little later in the chapter.

▶ **Sounds Like:** Finds different spellings of words that sound similar. For example, the Find text *Here* will find *hear, hair, hare,* and *heir.*

▶ **Find All Word Forms:** Finds all grammatical forms of a word. If you search for s*it*, Word will find *sat* and *sitting.* This is an added feature in Word's Find and Replace function that is not common to other programs. (This new capability is the result of Microsoft's Intellisense Technology—a bonus to all Office 95 users.)

The three buttons at the bottom of the dialog box provide more ways to specify the type of Find and Replace operation:

▶ **Formatting:** You can find different formats (fonts, styles, paragraph alignments, and so on) and replace them with other formats.

▶ **No Formatting:** If you specified formatting with the Formatting button, this option removes it.

▶ **Special:** You can find and replace special characters, such as page breaks, paragraph marks, and tab symbols. If Pattern Matching is checked, clicking the Special button displays a list of symbols for complex search criteria.

The Basics of Finding and Replacing Characters

The general steps for finding and replacing text in Word are as follows:

1. Choose Edit ➤ Replace or press Ctrl+H.

2. In the Find What text box, specify the text or special characters you are looking for in the document.

3. Optionally, check one of the search criteria options (such as Match Case or Find Whole Words Only).

4. If you are looking for special formats or characters, select the Format or Special button at the bottom of the dialog box.

5. In the Replace With text box, specify the text or special characters you are substituting.

6. In the Search box, specify the direction of the search. Click the drop-down arrow to see your choices: Down, Up, or All. The search will be conducted in the direction you specify, beginning where the insertion point is placed.

7. When you are ready to start the operation, click the Replace or Replace All button. The Replace button will first stop at each occurrence and wait for you to click the Replace button or Find Next button, giving you the opportunity to accept or reject each change. The Replace All button goes through the document rapidly, replacing everything at once. It does not ask you first before making the replacements.

8. When it is finished, Word will display a dialog box showing the number of replacements made in the document.

WARNING Be careful about choosing Replace All. If you think that there may be occurrences that should not be replaced, use the Replace button instead of the Replace All button.

Finding with Wildcards

When searching for words, you may want to use *wildcards* instead of typing out the entire phrase. Wildcards are special symbols that can be substituted for text. Used correctly, they can help you search for every variation of a word.

To use wildcards, first check the Use Pattern Matching checkbox, and then click the Special button at the bottom of the dialog box. You will see the list of complex search criteria symbols. Once you know what a symbol looks like, the next time you are using a wildcard, you can type that symbol directly into the Find What box without choosing it from the Special list. Whenever you are using a wildcard, you must check Use Pattern Matching.

A simple example of using pattern matching is to find *Smith, Smythe,* and any other variations of this spelling. You could search for all occurrences of any word that begins with *S*, may have multiple characters after the *S*, and also includes an *H* in the word. You can use the asterisk wildcard to represent multiple characters: *S*h*. Figure 11.1 shows the Find dialog box filled in for a wildcard search that will find *Smith, Smythe, Smithsonian,* and any other words that begin with *S* and include an *H*. Note that the Use Pattern Matching option must be checked to allow the wildcard search.

NOTE   Using Find and Replace with wildcard characters can be a little tricky. Remember, if your Replace operation does not give you the results you wanted, immediately click the Undo button to reverse the last action.

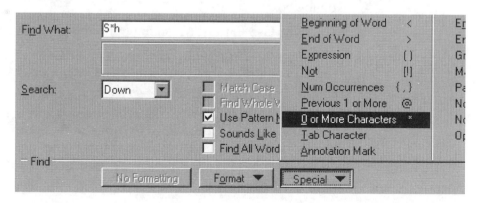

Figure 11.1 *You can use wildcards (pattern matching) in your Find text.*

Let's go through the actual steps to take care of two variations of a company name that should be replaced with one, standard nomenclature. The sample letter contains two variations of a company called Community Concern #13, Inc. In the letter, the name of the company is referenced with CC13 and also CC#13, Inc. Figure 11.2 shows part of the letter before the Replace operation has been performed.

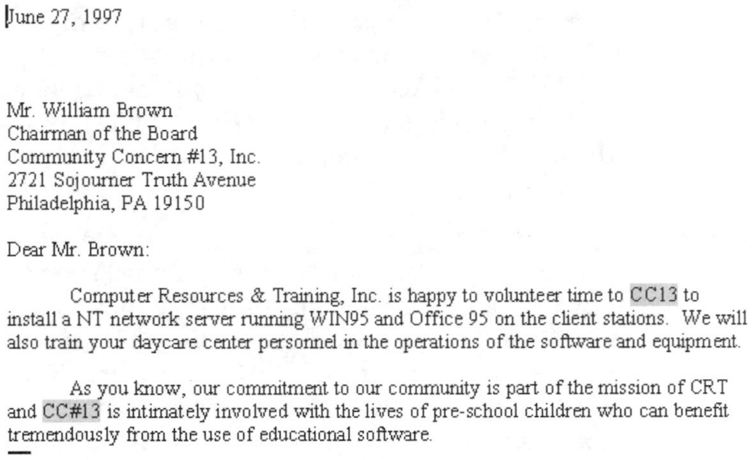

June 27, 1997

Mr. William Brown
Chairman of the Board
Community Concern #13, Inc.
2721 Sojourner Truth Avenue
Philadelphia, PA 19150

Dear Mr. Brown:

Computer Resources & Training, Inc. is happy to volunteer time to CC13 to install a NT network server running WIN95 and Office 95 on the client stations. We will also train your daycare center personnel in the operations of the software and equipment.

As you know, our commitment to our community is part of the mission of CRT and CC#13 is intimately involved with the lives of pre-school children who can benefit tremendously from the use of educational software.

Figure 11.2 **A letter that needs the characters CC13 and CC#13 replaced**

Here are the steps for performing the Find and Replace operation on the sample document:

1. Position the insertion point at the top of the document and choose Edit ► Replace from the menu bar or press Ctrl+H to open the Replace dialog box.

2. Click the Use Pattern Matching option to put a check in its checkbox.

3. Click into the Find What text box and type **CC★13**. The asterisk symbol represents any characters between the last C and the 13. This covers both variations, CC13 and CC#13.

4. Press the Tab key to move the insertion point to the Replace With text box area. Type in **Community Concern #13, Inc.** Figure 11.3 shows the Replace dialog box for this operation.

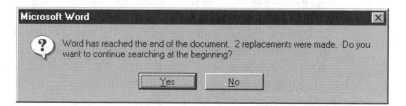

Figure 11.3 *Use Pattern Matching must be checked when you are using wildcard symbols in your Find and Replace operation.*

5. Click the Replace All button on the right side of the dialog box. Word will go through the entire document replacing each occurrence automatically. When Word is finished, you will see an information box indicating the number of replacements that have been made:

6. Click OK, and then click the Close button to close the Replace dialog box. Figure 11.4 shows our sample document with the changes.

NOTE If you did not start at the beginning of the document, Word will make replacements to the end of the document, and then ask if you wish to start searching again at the beginning.

Part 2

Communicating with Word

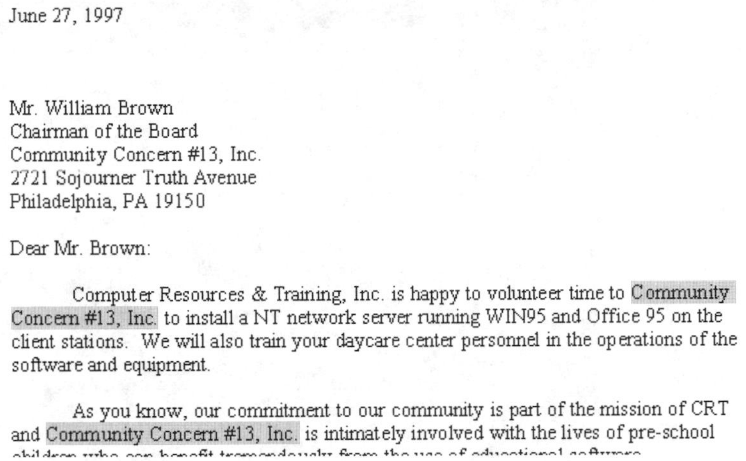

June 27, 1997

Mr. William Brown
Chairman of the Board
Community Concern #13, Inc.
2721 Sojourner Truth Avenue
Philadelphia, PA 19150

Dear Mr. Brown:

Computer Resources & Training, Inc. is happy to volunteer time to Community Concern #13, Inc. to install a NT network server running WIN95 and Office 95 on the client stations. We will also train your daycare center personnel in the operations of the software and equipment.

As you know, our commitment to our community is part of the mission of CRT and Community Concern #13, Inc. is intimately involved with the lives of pre-school children who can benefit tremendously from the use of educational software.

Figure 11.4 **Word replaced the abbreviated company names with the correct, spelled-out version.**

Formatting with Find and Replace

The Find and Replace feature also allows you to find and change character formats and some paragraph formats. For example, suppose that you are typing a long proposal and have referred to a company name several times. Then you discover that the name is always in bold and italics as part of its company logo copyright. You can use the Find and Replace feature to find the company name and replace it with the same name, but in the bold and italics type styles. Click the bold and italics buttons on the Formatting toolbar (or press Ctrl+B and Ctrl+I) before you type the name of the company in the Replace With text box. You can also set these formats by clicking the Format button at the bottom of the dialog box and choosing the Font option.

Note that the next time you use the Find and Replace dialog box, the previous information will be shown. You can take off the formatting in the Replace With text box by clicking in this area and selecting the No Formatting button at the bottom of the dialog box.

Word also lets you find and replace special characters, such as tabs, page breaks, and paragraph symbols. Envision a multiple-page report in which each paragraph has the first line tabbed in to indent the paragraphs. For the final draft, however, someone decides to have all the paragraphs flush left. You could go through the entire document, manually moving to each paragraph (Ctrl+↓) and deleting each tab character. An easier way is to use Find and Replace.

To change from tab-indented to left-aligned paragraphs, specify the special character for a tab (^t) in the Find What box (by typing it in directly or by selecting it from the list displayed by the Special drop-down button at the bottom of the dialog box). Leave the Replace With box blank—to replace the tab with nothing. After you finish the Find and Replace operation, each paragraph's tab character will be removed, and the text would align along the left margin.

 TIP For a complete list of complex search criteria and their meanings, choose Help ➤ Microsoft WordHelp Topics. When the Help Topics dialog box appears, click the Index tab and type in *Finding*. The Finding and Replacing topic will appear. Double-click Search Criteria. In the Topics Found dialog box, double-click Complex Search Criteria. When the list of different wildcard search criteria appears, click the Options button at the top of the dialog box, and print the page so you can use it as a reference.

Using AutoCorrect to Substitute Characters

Word automatically corrects some typos as you type them. This automatic correction is different from the spelling check function, which displays a wavy red line underneath the word that is misspelled. If you are not watching carefully, you will not realize that Word is helping you out by automatically correcting some of your words.

To test this, type the phrase **You adn me** and press the spacebar. You cannot make this happen, because Word is watching in the background and has been preprogrammed to change the typo *adn* to the correct word.

AutoCorrect entries are activated by typing the entry name and pressing the spacebar, the Enter key, or the Tab key. The Tools ➤ AutoCorrect command displays a dialog box that includes the list of common typing errors that Word is programmed to change. You can remove entries from this list or add your own errors to correct automatically.

If you do not want Word to automatically correct any errors at all, you can turn off the AutoCorrect feature. Choose Tools ➤ AutoCorrect and remove the check in the Replace Text As You Type checkbox. The other checkboxes in the AutoCorrect dialog box let you disable AutoCorrect's rules for its corrections.

Defining AutoCorrect Exceptions

When AutoCorrect is on, Word will try to do you a favor by capitalizing the first letter of any word that follows a period. The program thinks that a word that follows a period must be the beginning of a sentence. Word will happily uppercase the first letter of the word.

Word's AutoCorrect feature maintains a list of exceptions to its rules for capitalizing the first letter. If Word keeps annoying you by capitalizing a term you use often, you might want to select Tools ➤ AutoCorrect and remove the check next to the Capitalize First Letter of Sentences checkbox to turn off this rule. An alternative is to leave the rule checked, but add this particular term to the Exceptions list; thereafter, Word will leave it as you typed it.

Choose Tools ➤ AutoCorrect and click the Exceptions button to see the AutoCorrect Exceptions dialog box. Click on the First Letter tab. The dialog box lists the words that end in a period but should not begin with a capital letter, as shown in Figure 11.5. Add any special words you want to this list by clicking the Add button. Delete words from the list by

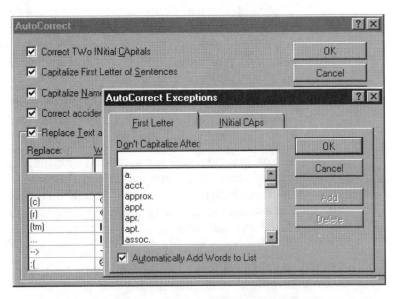

Figure 11.5　You can add or remove terms that are exceptions to AutoCorrect's rules.

clicking once on the word and clicking the Delete button. You can follow the same procedure to add or remove exceptions to the rule about not allowing two capitalized letters followed by lowercase ones. Click on the INitial CAps tab to move to those exceptions.

> **TIP** The Automatically Add Words to List checkbox in the AutoCorrect Exceptions dialog box allows you to add words to the list of exceptions "on the fly." When Word automatically corrects a word that you don't want it to change, press Backspace and type over the correction. Word will then add that word to the AutoCorrect Exceptions list. The next time you use that word, Word will not correct it.

AutoCorrect as a Reusability Tool

If Word's AutoCorrect feature can recognize a series of characters and then substitute other characters, this means that you can use this capability for all types of reusability needs. Think of AutoCorrect as a shorthand-expansion program—you type the shorthand word, and AutoCorrect will interpret it as the longer version.

But the AutoCorrect feature can stretch a lot further. You can store tables, graphics, text, and fields. Imagine typing the letters LTR1 and Word substituting a three-page form letter or a twenty-page report. This is also possible with the AutoCorrect feature.

In addition to adding typos to the AutoCorrect list during a Spell Check operation, Word allows you to select any amount of already typed text and store it as formatted text. The Unformatted Text option stores up to 255 characters of selected text as an AutoCorrect entry (you can only go up to 195 characters if you type it in yourself). However, AutoCorrect also has an extended capability to use preselected text as the substituted text.

You can select any amount of text and then choose Tools ➤ AutoCorrect and assign a short name to represent the text. Click the Formatted text radio button, then the Add button, and then the OK button in the dialog box. Back in your document, when you type the short name you assigned and press the spacebar or Enter key, Word will "explode" the text that you stored. This feature has been used by Word aficionados for letter closings, paragraphs that must be substituted at certain places, and anywhere else repetitious text can be recycled.

Naming AutoCorrect Entries

Your AutoCorrect entry name can be a maximum of 31 characters and cannot contain spaces in the name. The number of AutoCorrect entries you can have seems to be unlimited; one user was up to 800 entries and still adding. One AutoCorrect entry was a formatted, 200-page proposal. Word's AutoCorrect happily stored it without a problem.

Note that Word's AutoCorrect feature for the abbreviated name is case-specific. When you create an AutoCorrect entry name (abbreviation), enter it in lowercase. When you are ready to use the name in a document, type the name in either uppercase or lowercase. Word will recognize both cases and expand the abbreviated name. If you create the name in uppercase, Word will only expand the AutoCorrect entry name if you type it into the document in uppercase.

Be careful which words you use for AutoCorrect entry names. Don't use an actual word that you might type normally in a document. Whenever Word sees that word, it will substitute your AutoCorrect entry. One convention you can use to avoid this problem is to precede the Auto-Correct entry name with an *x*. For example, *xletter* might expand into a four-page letter, but you can still type the word *letter* in a document without activating the AutoCorrect version.

Another technique for generating unique AutoCorrect entry names is one that power users employ. Place a right parenthesis after a normal word, as in *Bob)*. The advantage of this method, in addition to making the name unique, is that the right parenthesis immediately expands any AutoCorrect entry name, so you don't need to press the spacebar, Enter key, or Tab key to activate the entry substitution.

Creating an AutoCorrect Entry

As an example, let's go through the steps for creating two different letter closings: one with a full, formal name and another with an informal name. (You can use your own closing and AutoCorrect entry name instead of those given in the example.)

1. On a blank screen, type the following letter closing:

   Very Truly Yours,

   (blank line)

   (blank line)

   Robert M. Dawkins

   Sales Manager

   (blank line)

   Enclosure

2. Select the entire closing (drag the mouse over the text to select it).

3. Choose Tools ➤ AutoCorrect.

4. In the Replace text area of the AutoCorrect dialog box, type **RMD1,** click the Add button, and then click OK. The formal closing is added as the entry RMD1.

> **NOTE** If you made a mistake and typed in the wrong entry name, choose Tools ➤ AutoCorrect again and find the incorrect entry. Click on it and type a correct name for the entry. Delete the incorrect entry name.

5. In the closing you typed, change the name from *Robert* to *Bob*.

6. Select the entire text of the closing again and choose Tools ➤ AutoCorrect.

7. In the Replace text area, type **RMD2**. Click the Add button and then click the OK button.

8. Choose File ➤ Close. Click No to indicate that you do not wish to save the document (of course, if you typed this text into a document you want to keep, you should save it).

9. Start a new document to test your closings.

10. Type the letters **RMD1** and press the Enter key or the spacebar. You should see the formal closing for your letter expand into multiple lines.

11. Try the **RMD2** closing to make sure that works correctly.

    Remember, you should activate the AutoCorrect entry at the exact spot you needed to have the text appear in the document. We expanded the text on a blank screen to see how this feature works. In practice, you should type the AutoCorrect name in the correct position to place the text at the end of a letter, where you would expect to see a closing.

If you want to delete these test AutoCorrect entries, choose Tools ➤ AutoCorrect. Find the RMD1 entry, click on it, and click the Delete button. Repeat this procedure for the RMD2 entry.

Changing AutoCorrect Entries

You may need to add or delete text from one of your AutoCorrect entries. To change an AutoCorrect entry, you actually replace that entry with a new one that has the same name.

Select the new text (with the additions or deletions), and then choose Tools ➤ AutoCorrect. Type the same entry name that you used before. When Word sees the same name being used again, it substitutes the Replace button for the Add button. Click the Replace button. Word will ask you to confirm that you wish to replace the entry name with the new text. Figure 11.6 shows the AutoCorrect dialog box with the Replace option and message.

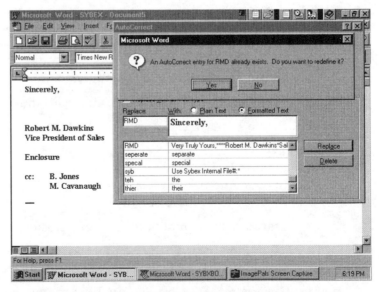

Figure 11.6   *It is simple to redefine an AutoCorrect entry. Select the text and when you choose Tools ➤ AutoCorrect, use the same name. Click Replace.*

AutoText for Storing Entries in the Normal Template

Unlike the AutoCorrect feature, AutoText does not automatically correct as you type. But AutoText can store any amount of text, graphics, tables, and other items, just as AutoCorrect can. AutoText entries are stored with the Normal.dot template. This is in contrast to the AutoCorrect entries, which are globally available, regardless of which template you are using.

An advantage of using AutoText over AutoCorrect is that you can print the list of AutoText entries that you have stored. Word gives you the option in the Print dialog box to print the document or choose other printing options such as the AutoText entries, as shown in Figure 11.7.

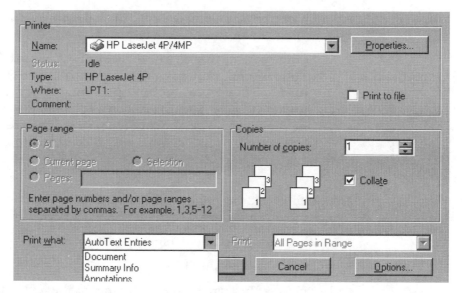

Figure 11.7   *One of the advantages of using AutoText is that you can print the list of entries that are stored.*

Another advantage of using AutoText is that you can create your own custom button from an AutoText entry and place it on a toolbar. To insert the entry, you can just click your AutoText button.

Part 2

Communicating with Word

Storing an AutoText Entry

To store an AutoText item, select (drag the mouse over) the paragraph lines, pages, graphics, or tables you wish to store. Choose Edit ➤ AutoText and type in a shorter name than what Word recommends. You can store your entries under names containing any words and including spaces. Thus an entry name of *Briefing Paragraph* is acceptable. The recommendation, however, is to keep the name short so that you do not need to type a long name to activate your AutoText entry.

Suppose that there is a paragraph that you use often during document production. You want to store this paragraph as an AutoText entry, rather than as an AutoCorrect one, because you want to make your own custom toolbar button for this paragraph (we'll do this a bit later in the chapter). The following steps demonstrate the process:

1. In a blank document area, type the following paragraph. You can indent the first line or type it flush left.

   Once again, thank you for inquiring about Dalton Industries. You are cordially invited to attend our weekly Wednesday free tour of the manufacturing plant. Tours of the plant begin promptly at 10:00 a.m. and end at 12:00. We ask that you register no later than Tuesday at 3:00 p.m. to insure that there is room for your group. Please call Kia Darling at 612-111-1111 to register your attendees.

2. Spell check the paragraph (press F7 or click the ABC button on the Standard toolbar) and correct any typing errors.

3. Select the text of the paragraph (drag the mouse over the lines of text).

4. Choose Edit ➤ AutoText.

5. Type over the suggested entry name for the text with the word **Tour**, as shown in Figure 11.8.

6. Click the Add button on the right side of the dialog box. You will be returned to the document.

7. Click below the selected text and press the Enter key a couple of times so that there are a few blank lines between the previous paragraph and the insertion point.

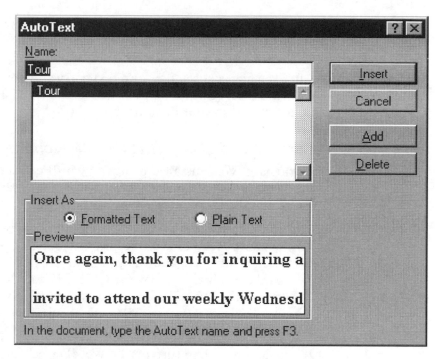

Figure 11.8 Highlight any repetitive text and choose Edit ➤ AutoText. Enter a short name to identify the stored text. Click the Add button.

8. To test the AutoText entry, type **tour** in the document and press the F3 key. The entry name expands to display the entire paragraph.

Retrieving AutoText Entries

As you just learned, to retrieve (expand) a stored AutoText entry, type the name of the entry where you wish for the text to be inserted in the document and press the F3 key. You can also retrieve a stored AutoText entry by choosing the Edit ➤ AutoText menu command.

If you choose AutoText from the Edit menu, you will see a dialog box with the names of your entries. Click on the name of the entry that you want to insert.

If you want the text to be inserted with the same formats it had when you stored it, make sure the Insert As radio button for Formatted Text is selected. With this option, whatever fonts and point sizes that the original text had when you stored it will be retained. If you want the paragraph to pick up the formats of the document into which it is being inserted, select the radio button for Plain Text. The entry will have the fonts, point sizes, and styles of the document into which it is coming.

After you have chosen the AutoText entry and how it should be inserted, click the Insert button on the right side of the dialog box. The text will be inserted into your document.

AutoText and WordPerfect Help Key Conflict

If you have Word installed using the WordPerfect Help key, F3 activates the WordPerfect Help dialog box; it does not expand the AutoText entry name into the stored item.

You can turn off the WordPerfect Help option by clicking the Options button in the Help for WordPerfect Users dialog box. Uncheck Help for WP users and Navigation keys if you do not want any WordPerfect keyboard combinations to work. Click OK and then Close. Another way to turn off the WordPerfect Help is through the Options dialog box. Choose Tools ➤ Options ➤ General tab and deselect the Help for WordPerfect Users and Navigation Keys for WordPerfect Users options.

If you do not wish to turn off the WordPerfect functions, just remember not to use F3 to expand an AutoText entry. Choose Edit ➤ AutoText, click on the name of the entry, and click the Insert button to expand it.

Changing or Deleting an AutoText Entry

To change an AutoText entry, you redefine it by replacing that entry with a new one that has the same name. Expand the AutoText entry that you want to change (type the name and press F3 or use Edit ➤ AutoText) on a blank document screen. Make your changes. Select the text again and choose Edit ➤ AutoText. Use the same name you had before and click the Add button on the right side of the dialog box. Word will recognize that this name was used previously and will ask whether you wish to redefine the entry:

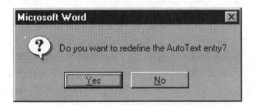

To permanently delete an AutoText entry from storage, choose Edit ➤ AutoText. In the dialog box, click on the entry you wish to delete, and then click the Delete button on the right side of the dialog box. Unfortunately, you will not be asked to confirm the deletion. Word swiftly removes the entry and only offers the Close button, not a Cancel button. (Of course, if you inadvertently delete an AutoText entry, you can find the text in another document and store it again.)

Creating a Custom AutoText Button

Once you have stored an AutoText entry, you can make your own custom button that can appear on any of Word's toolbars with the other buttons. Chapter 12 provides details on creating your own toolbars. Here we will add a button to one of the existing toolbars.

Follow these steps to create your own button for an AutoText entry:

1. Choose View ➤ Toolbars.

2. Click the Customize button on the right side of the Toolbars dialog box to open the Customize dialog box.

3. Scroll down through the Categories list box until you see the category called AutoText. Click onto this category. In the AutoText list box, you will see the names of the AutoText entries you have stored, as shown in Figure 11.9.

4. Click on the AutoText entry if it is not already selected.

5. Here is where it gets tricky: Drag the name of the AutoText entry up towards one of the toolbars. You will see the gray outline of a small button appear as you drag the name up.

6. Drag the button outline to the spot on the toolbar where you want the button to appear. Lift your finger and drop the button onto that spot. The Custom Button dialog box appears.

7. Choose from button designs offered in the dialog box. You can have the button show the name of the AutoText entry by using the first suggested button on the list, Text Button, or you can select a "happy face," or any other custom button to represent your AutoText entry. Click on the button and click the Assign button on the right.

8. If you want to assign other AutoText entries to toolbar buttons, repeat steps 4 through 7 for each one.

Part
2

Communicating with
Word

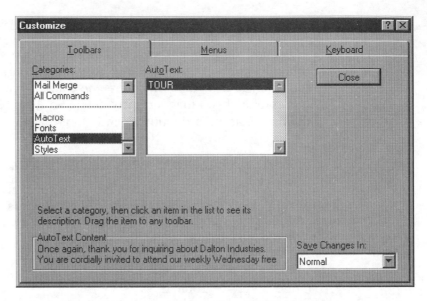

Figure 11.9 **You can make your own buttons from stored AutoText entries.**

9. When you're finished, click the Close button in the Customize dialog box.

Now whenever you wish to have the AutoText entry inserted into your document, all you need to do is position the insertion point at the correct place in the document and click the toolbar button assigned to the AutoText entry.

 TIP To move the custom button from the toolbar, hold down the Alt key and drag the button to the right or left, or up or down, to another toolbar. To remove the button, hold down the Alt key and drag the button completely off the toolbar. See Chapter 12 for details on customizing your toolbars.

Using Bookmarks

The Bookmark feature found on the Edit menu can be used in both a simple and an advanced manner. At its simplest, a bookmark is a marker name you can give to a specific part of your document so that you can go directly to the marked spot by using the Go To command (Ctrl+G). Readers who are Lotus or Excel users can think of a bookmark as you would a range name.

Word's Bookmark feature is more powerful, however. You can use a bookmark name like a programming variable name, substituting specific data "into" the name. For example, you can create a field name called PERSON and then use this PERSON field name throughout your document instead of typing a real name. When you are finished, the real name can be selected or typed once and then referenced as the bookmark called PERSON. Word will go through your document and substitute the name at each location it finds the field name of PERSON.

Creating a Bookmark

To create a simple bookmark, select a word in the text of the section you want marked. Choose Edit ➤ Bookmark from the menu bar. Type in the name for your bookmark. The name can be a maximum of 40 characters, without any spaces or symbol characters. Click the Add button to create the bookmark. Figure 11.10 shows the Bookmark dialog box.

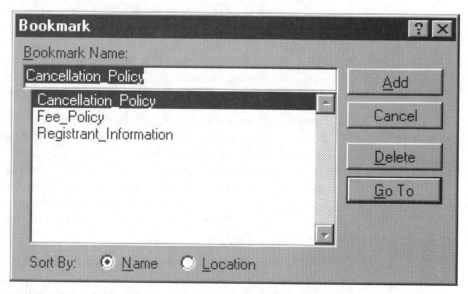

Figure 11.10   *Create a bookmark to mark the text area you want to return to.*

To go to the document area marked by the bookmark, choose Edit ➤ Go To or press Ctrl-G. Figure 11.11 shows the Go To dialog box when Bookmark is selected in the Go to What list box and the names of the different bookmarks are available.

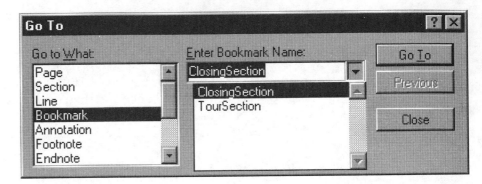

Figure 11.11 You can go directly to marked locations in your document using the Bookmark and Go To feature.

Bookmarks as a Reusability Tool

Suppose you have a document in which only the names included in the text change for each printing. For example, in legal documents, such as leases, agreements, and wills, once the party or parties are named in the document, the names are then repeated throughout the standard document. It would be very convenient if you could type the names of the parties once, and in two keystrokes, their names appeared in all of the bookmark locations you specified in the document form.

In our next example, we'll use a prenuptial agreement as the standard document form. We will refer to the names of the parties one time at the opening of the document. We will select these names and create bookmarks for each one. The bookmark for the man will be named TheGuy, and the bookmark for the woman will be named TheGirl. In the document itself, every time there is a reference to the man or the woman, we will enter a field symbol by pressing Ctrl+F9, and then type either TheGuy or TheGirl.

When we have finished, we will save the form, select the entire document (Ctrl+A), update the fields (F9), and then tap the Shift+F9 key combination to display the bookmark names. Word will convert the bookmarks into the names we selected in the first paragraph.

Ready to go? Here are the steps:

1. Type the information as it appears in Figure 11.12.

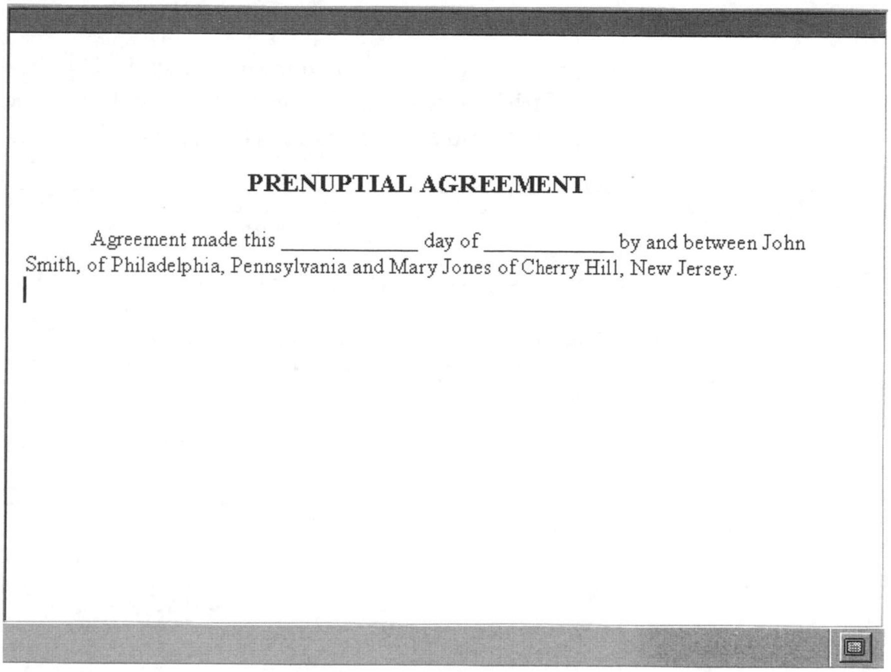

PRENUPTIAL AGREEMENT

Agreement made this _____ day of _____ by and between John Smith, of Philadelphia, Pennsylvania and Mary Jones of Cherry Hill, New Jersey.

Figure 11.12   The beginning of our legal document

2. Select (drag the mouse over) John Smith's name only. Do not include the comma.

3. Choose Edit ➤ Bookmark, type the bookmark name **TheGuy** (no spaces), and then click the Add button.

4. Select Mary Jones' name only.

5. Choose Edit ➤ Bookmark, type the bookmark name **TheGirl** (no spaces), and then click the Add button.

6. Start a new paragraph and type **WHEREAS**, and then press Ctrl+F9 to insert a bookmark field. The open and close curly braces will appear, with a gray area in between the braces.

7. In the gray area between the braces, type the name of the bookmark that is appropriate in the sample prenuptial agreement: **TheGuy**. Remember

to type the bookmark exactly as you defined it in the Bookmark dialog box. There are no spaces between the two words.

8. Press the right arrow key twice to move the insertion point outside the curly braces so that you can continue to type.

9. Type the rest of the document as shown in Figure 11.13. Make sure you press Ctrl+F9 and do not type the curly braces yourself. You can copy and paste if you do not wish to type in each field and bookmark reference.

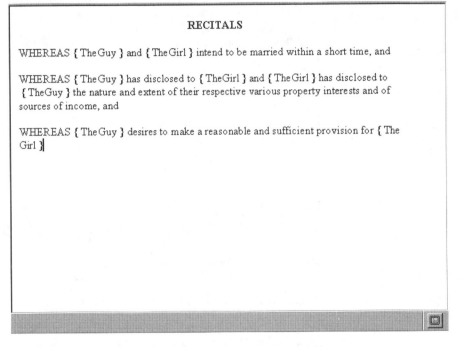

Figure 11.13   **The rest of the prenuptial agreement**

10. When you are finished, select the entire document by pressing Ctrl+A.

11. Press the F9 key. This will alert Word to update the fields and substitute the specific names you designated in the first paragraph into each bookmark. You will see a blue bar at the bottom with the message "Word is updating the fields in your document."

12. After the fields are updated, you will still only see the bookmark reference. Press Shift+F9, and you will see the names John Smith and Mary Jones substituted for the bookmark references.

13. Press the Shift+F9 key again, and you will see the bookmark references.

    Each time you create another Bookmark field using Ctrl+F9 and typing in the name of a bookmark associated with text, you must repeat the keystrokes in steps 10 and 11. Word must have the fields selected (Ctrl+A) and then the fields updated (F9). The Shift+F9 key toggles between displaying the bookmark reference and the substituted bookmark value.

    Now test the document with other names to see if Word will substitute any two individuals' names that have bookmark names of TheGuy and TheGirl.

14. Select and delete the names John Smith and Mary Jones in the first paragraph.

15. Type two new names to replace the original ones.

16. Select the man's name and give the appropriate bookmark name of TheGuy, but this time press Shift+Ctrl+F5 instead of Edit ➤ Bookmark. This shortcut provides a convenient way to name bookmarks. Click the Add button.

17. Repeat step 16 for the woman's name and give her selected name the bookmark name of TheGirl. Make sure you use the same names that you laboriously produced in the bookmark fields of the document form.

18. To see if Word recognizes your bookmark name, go to the top of the document and press Ctrl+G or F5 to activate the Go To dialog box.

19. In the Category list, choose Bookmark to see the list of bookmarks. Click on TheGirl, and then click Go To on the right side of the dialog box. Word will show you what text it thinks is marked with that name, as shown in Figure 11.14.

20. Repeat steps 10 through 12 to select and update the fields. Figure 11.15 shows the finished product. Now you could continue and make bookmarks to replace the city and state for each guy and girl.

    If your updated fields produce bookmark errors, go back through the Edit ➤ Bookmark dialog box and make sure that the names are defined and associated with the correct text in your document. When you create a name, make sure that you click the Add button.

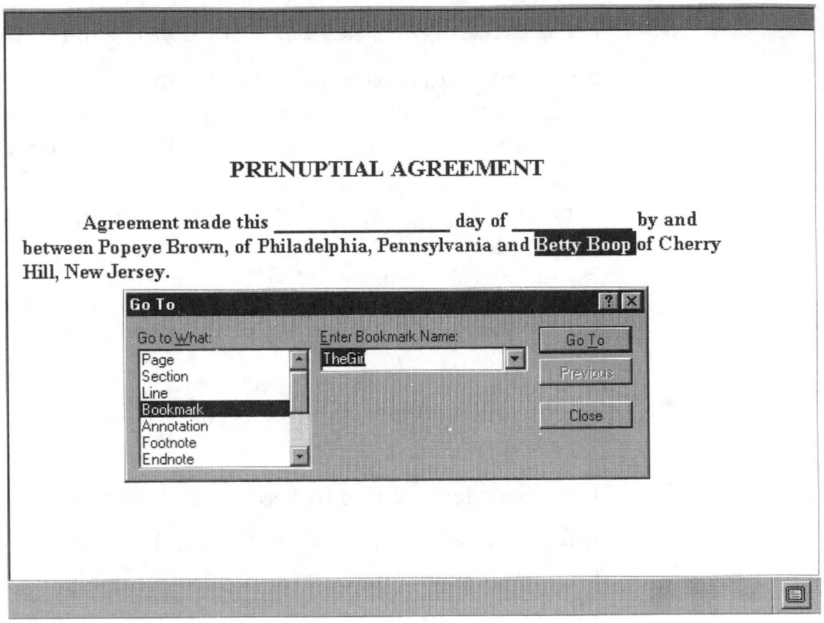

Figure 11.14   The Go To dialog box allows you to go to a bookmark reference.

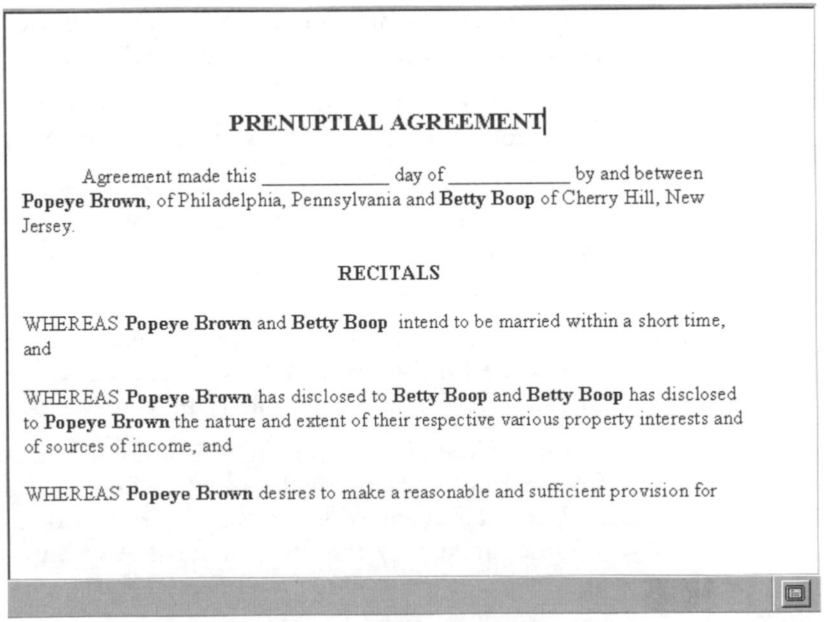

Figure 11.15   Bookmark fields are sophisticated reusability tools.

Creating Templates from Documents

The ultimate in reusability of text is to create a template that can form the basis of new documents. You already know about templates. Whenever you choose File ➤ New from the main menu, the Normal template is presented to you as the basis of your next document.

Even though the Normal template does not include text, it does contain certain margin settings, font and typeface defaults, styles, macros, and toolbars. Word saves you time and effort when you create a new document by allowing you to base new documents on templates.

Word provides a number of templates for common types of documents: memos, reports, letters, newsletters, and manuals. You can use Word's templates without modification, or you can change them to more closely mirror your business needs. At the simplest level, think of a Word template as a form document. You may have a special memo form that your company prefers. If you create a memo template and store it for continued use, you will no longer need to retype the information that stays the same from memo to memo.

Although it may seem just as easy to open a previously saved document and make changes to it, the danger is that you will overwrite that document or that you will not be able to locate the file containing the previous version of a customized agreement.

When you create a template from the existing document, you can ensure that the document settings are appropriate and the text is correct. Word will store the template in a special subdirectory with its other templates. This avoids the possibility of overwriting or losing the data, because the template is served to you as a copy of the original for you to modify as you wish.

Creating a Template from a Document

The option to create a template from a document is in the File ➤ Save As dialog box. First, open the document you wish to use as the basis for a template. Make it as generic as possible and perfect the fonts, margin settings, and other formatting.

When the document is ready, choose File ➤ Save As. At the bottom of the Save As dialog box is a Save As Type text box. Click the drop-down arrow and choose Document Template (*.dot). You will be switched to the Templates subdirectory, which is the area of the disk where Word likes to store templates; usually, it's above the Winword subdirectory. You can double-click on one of the Templates subdirectories and save your template into a special category, such as Letters & Faxes or Memos. Type a name for the document template in the File Name text area, as shown in the example in Figure 11.16. Finally, click the Save button on the right side of the dialog box.

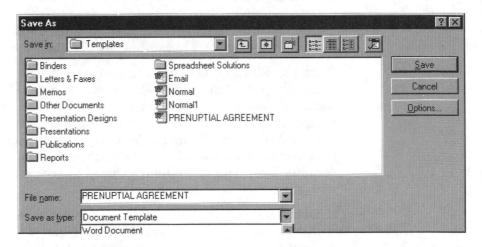

Figure 11.16   You can create a custom template by saving an existing document as a template.

Basing a New Document on a Template

To start a new document based on a document template, choose File ➤ New. Go to the page that has icons for the category in which you saved your document template and double-click on the template name.

When you choose a template, a *new* document is created. At the top of the screen in the title bar area, you will see the generic document number. Customize or change the document and save it under a different name.

Producing Form Documents with Mail Merge

A common word processing task is to produce periodic mailings to a group of individuals. The documents must be customized with the individual's address information and usually other types of personal information, such as a spouse's name or the name of an item the individual purchased.

To produce these types of form documents, you can use Word's Mail Merge feature. Mail Merge requires three types of documents:

▶ The personalized document or envelope or mailing label, known as the *main document.*

▶ A list of individuals and their addresses or other specific pieces of information, called the *data source.*

▶ The result of merging the main document with the data source produces a third document, called the *merge* document. The merge document can be merged to the screen or directly to a printer.

To make the job simple, Word supplies a "Helper" to assist you through the steps of a merge. The Mail Merge Helper helps you to identify the documents for the merge and guides you through the options available to you during each step of the merge process.

Creating the Main Document

The main document is the form into which the data information (for example, addresses or billing information) will be merged. The main document is most often a form letter. However, it can also be a mailing label, a postcard, an envelope, a name card, or any other type of document that can fit the categories of your data (such as name, address, account balance, date of appointment, and so on).

Create a simple letter. Insert the date (Insert ➤ Date and Time) at the top of the letter and then tap the Enter key approximately eight times so that you are ready to type the body of the letter. Do **not** type the inside address. The inside address will come from the categories contained within your data source, which you will create in the next section. Figure 11.17 shows an example of a main document for Mail Merge.

Using the Mail Merge Helper

Now that you have created a main document (letter), you can let the Mail Merge Helper guide you through the steps of what to do with the letter, how to create the data source, and then how to merge the two documents to produce the final merged document.

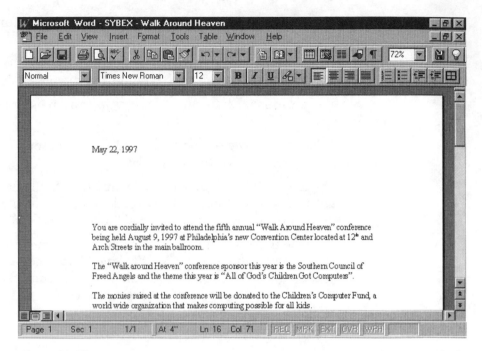

Figure 11.17   *A main document to use with the Mail Merge feature. Notice that the inside address is not typed in.*

1. With the letter you are using as the main document on the screen, choose Tools ➤ Mail Merge.

2. In the Mail Merge Helper dialog box, step 1, marked Main Document, has the Create button available. Click the Create button.

3. Choose Form Letters from the drop-down list of suggestions. Click the Active Window button since your main document is already open on the screen. Figure 11.18 shows the Mail Merge Helper screen after finishing step 1.

Creating a Data Source

If you do not have an existing database of information, you must create your own data source of the categories (fields) of information that will be inserted into the letter. For example, a Mail Merge letter might require that you have the following categories (fields): Title, First Name, Last Name, Job Title, Company, Address1, Address2, City, State, Zip, and Salutation. If one of your addressees does not have information for

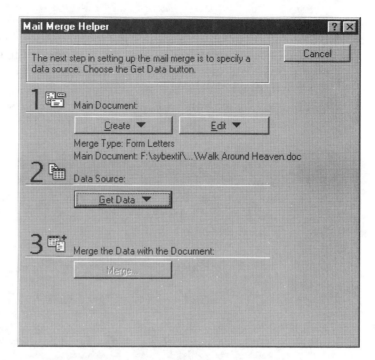

Figure 11.18 The Mail Merge Helper display after setting the main document, step 1 of the Mail Merge process

a title or a company, Word will merge only the categories that have information and close up the blank categories.

In the previous section, we left the Mail Merge Helper ready for step 2, specifying the data source. You can proceed as follows:

1. In the Mail Merge Helper dialog box, after specifying the main document in step 1, click the Get Data button next to step 2.

2. Choose Create Data Source. The Create Data Source dialog box appears.

NOTE To use an existing data source instead of creating a new one, choose Open Data Source instead of Create Data Source in the Mail Merge Helper dialog box. You can use files in Word, Access, and Excel formats. You can also use the Personal Address book you created in Schedule+ or Microsoft Exchange Server. WordPerfect 5.*x* files can be used if the correct converter was installed.

Word has anticipated that you will need certain fields (categories) in the letter, and it has supplied the most commonly used fields for form letters. These fields are listed on the right side of the Create Data Source dialog box. For our example, we need to add one field that has not been supplied, Salutation, and remove three fields that we don't need: Country, HomePhone, and WorkPhone. Of course, if you actually need these fields in your own form letters, you wouldn't remove them. You can also add any other fields that you may need for this form letter, such as Account Balance or Spouse Name.

3. In the Create Data Source dialog box, click on the field named Country, then click the Remove Field Name button on the left side of the dialog box. Figure 11.19 shows the Create Data Source dialog box with the field ready to be removed.

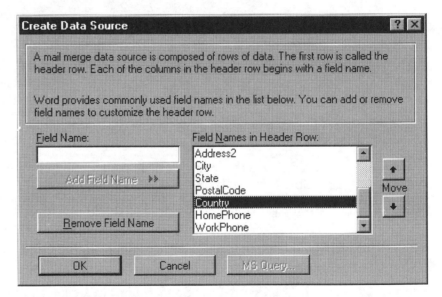

Figure 11.19 **You can add and delete categories in the Create Data Source dialog box.**

4. Repeat step 3 to remove the HomePhone and WorkPhone fields.

5. To add the Salutation field, type the name of the field in the Field Name text box on the left side of the Create Data Source dialog box (type over any existing data that may be there). Then click the Add Field Name button. Figure 11.20 shows the Create Data Source dialog box with the Salutation field being added.

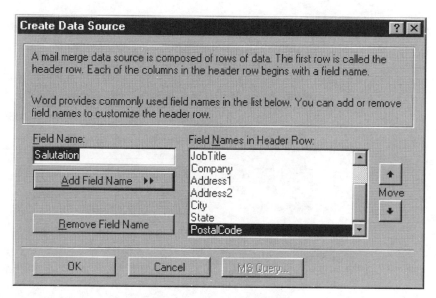

Figure 11.20 *You can add your own categories (fields) in the Create Data Source dialog box if Word does not have a category that you need for your Mail Merge.*

6. When you are finished, click the OK button. The Save As dialog box appears. Word wants you to immediately save the categories you decided should be in your form letter.

7. In the Save As dialog box, type in a name for the data source file that contains these categories. For example, you might name your data source **Invitation List for Conference**.

8. Click the Save button. The next dialog box wants to know if you want to edit the data source, because this file does not contain any data (names and addresses) yet:

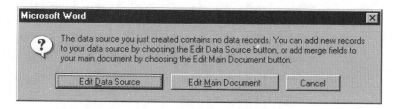

9.   To add data to the file, click the Edit Data Source button. A data form appears with the fields that you designated, as shown in Figure 11.21. You are now ready to add information to the data source form.

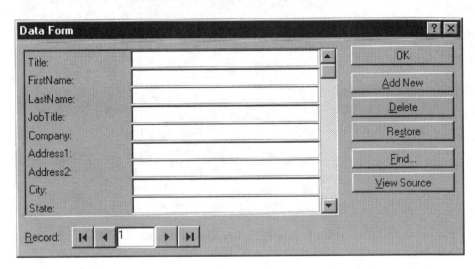

Figure 11.21   Word has one of the most attractive data forms for entering database-type information into a word processing program.

Type one piece of information per field on your data form. Press the Enter key or the Tab key to move from field to field. The Shift+Tab key combination moves back field by field. You can also click the vertical scroll arrows to move up and down to see more fields. Once you have completed the field information for each category, the entire group of fields is called a *record*. If you do not have information for a particular field, just leave that field blank. Word will make sure that a blank line does not print for the blank field.

10. Fill in the fields for the first person's record, and then click the Add New button on the right side of the dialog box. You will be presented with a new blank form. You can also press the Enter key after typing the last field's information, and a new blank form will appear automatically.

NOTE If you inadvertently click the data form's OK button prematurely before you have finished adding your records, you will see the merge letter on which the fields will be placed. Choose Tools ➤ Mail Merge to reactivate the Mail Merge Helper. Click on step 2's Edit Data Source button. You will be returned to the data form. Also, if you press the View Source button and see your data in the form of a Word table, follow this same procedure to get back to your data form.

11. Continue entering the names and addresses of individuals to whom this letter is going.

12. When you are finished, click the OK button. You will be returned to the merge letter.

After you've created a data source this way, you can always use this list again. The next time you create another merge letter, you can open any existing data source that has the fields you need for your main document (and in the proper format) by choosing Open Data Source instead of Create Data Source in step 2 of the Mail Merge Helper dialog box.

Placing Data Source Fields into the Merge Letter

After you've created your data source, you are ready to place the categories of your data source into the appropriate places within the letter. Although you now have the data source, the merge letter does not have any connection to the data source yet. You must place these fields into the letter where you wish for the information in the fields to appear when the merge has been completed.

Word will automatically produce a separate letter for each record in your data source file. This is handled during the merging in step 3 of the Mail Merge Helper.

You must have completed steps 1 and 2 and created both a basic letter and a group of records in a data form. If you have been following along with this example, you have just completed step 2 of the Mail Merge Helper and entered records into the data form. You are now looking at the merge letter and ready to insert the fields of the data source into the appropriate places on the letter. Follow these steps for placing the appropriate fields into the letter:

1. Click two lines below the date of the letter. This is the line where the inside address fields will be inserted so that Word knows where to display this field information.

2. A new toolbar appears at the top of the screen. If you do not see this toolbar, click View ➤ Toolbars and put a check in the Mail Merge checkbox, as shown in Figure 11.22.

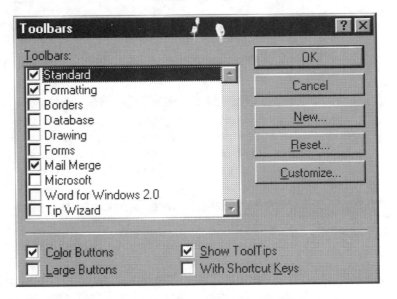

Figure 11.22 *The Toolbars dialog box lets you turn on the Mail Merge toolbar.*

3. Click the Insert Merge Field button on the Mail Merge toolbar to see a list of the fields available. Figure 11.23 shows the list of fields from the data source form we created earlier.

4. Click the Title field. Word inserts the field called Title within double right and left arrows. This field name will be replaced with the real title of the individual from your data source. Press the spacebar after the inserted field to insert a space after the title (you don't want the letter to say something like *Mr.JohnBrown*).

5. Click the Insert Merge Field button again and click on the field called FirstName. Press the spacebar to separate this field from the next one.

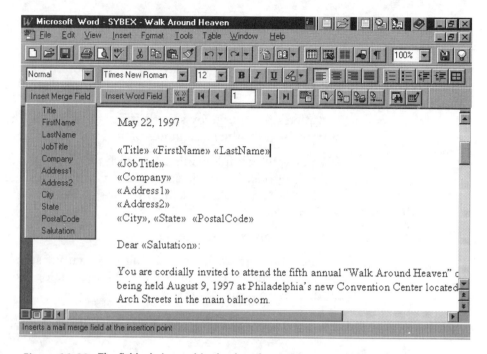

Figure 11.23 *The fields designated in the data form are now available for insertion into the main document merge letter.*

6. Click the Insert Merge Field button again and click on the field called LastName. Press the Enter key to move to the next line.

7. Continue to place the fields. Press the Delete key to remove the extra blank lines until your document looks like the sample shown in Figure 11.23. You must enter all punctuation (spaces, commas, colons, and so on), such as the comma after the City field.

8. After you have entered all of the fields where you wish them to be displayed, save the file again. (You should have already had the file saved before; if you have not saved previously, create a name for your file.) You are now ready to merge.

NOTE If you add a field that you do not want on your merge letter, drag the mouse over the field and press the Delete key on the keyboard. The field will be removed from the merge letter, but not from the fields contained on the Insert Merge Field list.

Part 2

Communicating with Word

Merging a Letter with a Data Source

You have completed steps 1 and 2 of the Mail Merge Helper's merge process. You created and saved a main document form letter. Then you created a data source form and entered records that will be merged into the letter. Step 3, the last step within the Mail Merge Helper system, completes the merge by substituting the actual information in the data source form for the field names placed within the main document letter.

If you have been following along with this example, the main document letter is currently on the screen and you have finished inserting merge field names and saving the file. Follow these steps to merge the document and the data:

1. Choose Tools ➤ Mail Merge.

2. In the Mail Merge Helper dialog box, within step 3, click the Merge button. Figure 11.24 shows the Merge dialog box with the default settings for a mail merge.

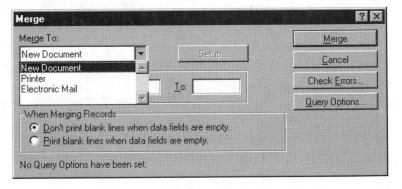

Figure 11.24 **Word's Merge dialog box includes a setting that prevents blank lines from printing for empty data fields.**

The results of your merge can be directed to a printer or to a new document (on-screen copy). You can even merge to electronic-mail or fax addresses. To merge to electronic mail, your system must have an MAPI-compatible electronic-mail or fax application (such as Microsoft Exchange or Microsoft Mail), and one of the fields in your data source must contain the electronic-mail addresses or fax numbers.

The default is to direct the merge to a new document so that you can look at the results before printing them. No sense in you finding out that there are mistakes in the merge after you have wasted your letterhead and printed a number of these letters.

3. Click the Merge button on the right side of the dialog box to begin the final merge process.

Inspecting a Merged Document before Printing

When the final merge step is completed (with the default of merging to a new document on the screen), you will see a new document, called FormLetters1, at the top of the screen (it may say a different number if you have already merged documents).

As you tap the PgDn key and view the completed form letters, you will notice that each record's information from the fields in the data source is in a separate letter (page) and that there is a page break between the letters.

If all looks good, you can click the print button on the Standard toolbar to print the merged letters. If you see problems, however, you can go back through the Mail Merge Helper and edit the files in which the problem lies (either the main document or the data source). If you find that there are mistakes in the letter, you should make corrections on the main document form letter. If you find that there are mistakes in the personal data, such as a typo in someone's name, you should make corrections in the data source form.

Do not make corrections on the FormLetters1 file. This is the result of the merge of two other files: the main document and the data source document. If you correct the result, the original problem will show up again the next time you merge. You must correct the source of the errors or problems by using Tools ➤ Mail Merge and selecting the step and document in which you think the problem occurred.

You do not need to save the results of the merge file once you have merged. If the merge results look good, then you can print them. If not, make corrections and discard the FormLetters1 file. You have the two original files from which the merge was created. Close the FormLetters1 file without saving and merge again to produce a new merge result. Word will call the next merge result FormLetters2.

Changing the Data Source File without Merging

You may want to add to or update records in your data source file without having those changes be involved in a current merge process. The next merge may require that additional names be used, or you may need to make corrections to certain addresses because you received returned mail from the post office.

When you are not involved in an actual merge process, Word does not make step 2 active in the Mail Merge Helper dialog box (Tools ► Mail Merge). The Helper forces you to create or open a main document before you can use step 2, which allows you to open a previously created data source. You can, however, open the data source file directly and still get to the data form view.

Viewing Your Data in a Word Table

Close any active files that may currently be in memory (make sure that important files are saved). Now open the data source file through the File ► Open dialog box and not through the Tools ► Mail Merge option. The file that appears looks like a Word table, with the fields of your data source listed on the first row of the table as the headings. The actual data that you typed into the data source appears in each subsequent row, but word wraps in the small widths of the columns. This is how Word stores a data source. When you go through the Mail Merge process, this information merges correctly.

You can add new records right here in the table by clicking into the last column, last row of the table and pressing the Tab key to start a new row. Make sure you type the correct information in the proper field, as designated by each column heading. Figure 11.25 shows data being added to a data source table.

You can also delete a record by deleting a row in the table. Click on the row of the record to be deleted and choose Table ► Select Row from the menu bar. Click the cut button on the Standard toolbar. The row is immediately deleted. If you make a mistake, click the Undo button to reverse the action.

Title	FirstName	LastName	JobTitle	Company	Address1	Address2	City	State	PostalCode
Mr.	John	Brown	President	ABC Products	123 Mary Lane	Suite 400	Philadelphia	PA	19103
Dr.	Laura	Peters	Chief of Surgery	Einstein North	1850 N. Broad Street		Any Town	NJ	08003
Dr.	Thomas	Powell	Chief of Surgery	Holy Health Hospital	4218 Pennsylvania Avenue		Philadelphia	PA	19133
Father	Michael	Val	Pastor	St. Mary's Church	118 Denmark Road		Cherry Hill	NJ	08002

Figure 11.25   You can open a data source file directly and add records and make changes to existing records, because the data source file is stored as a Word table.

Viewing Your Data in the Data Form

Working with the data source as a Word table gives you tremendous control and allows you to see a number of records at the same time. But you can still use the data form to add, edit, delete, and find records. The convenient form keeps your data organized and provides a database-type interface.

To place the data form on top of the table, you must first activate Word's Database toolbar. Follow these steps to activate the data form from the Database toolbar:

1. Open the data source file if you do not already have the file active on the screen. The data source file appears as a Word table when opened through the File ➤ Open command.

2. Choose View ➤ Toolbars from the menu bar. Put a check in the checkbox next to Database (see Figure 11.22, shown earlier), and then click the OK button. The Database toolbar will appear below the Formatting toolbar at the top of the screen.

3. Click the first button—the data form button—on the Database toolbar. The data form is superimposed on top of the table, and you can see the information in the table through the data form.

4. Make whatever additions, deletions, or changes you wish. The VCR-type buttons at the bottom of the form move you record-by-record through the database. Use the Edit ➤ Find command to locate a specific piece of information in a field.

5. Click the View Source button on the right side of the data form, and you will be returned to the table point of view.

Using the Database Toolbar

The Database toolbar remains on your screen, even when you are looking at the data in a Word table. You can quickly add and delete records while in the table by choosing the Add New Record or Delete Record buttons. You can perform quick sorts on any column by clicking the mouse into the column on which you want to sort the records and clicking the A to Z button on the Database toolbar to sort in ascending (alphabetical) order. Table 11.1 describes the functions of the buttons on the Database toolbar.

Printing the Data
Source File as a Directory of Names

To print the data source as a directory of names, you must use the Mail Merge feature. Fortunately, Word makes this quick and easy to set up. Word has preprogrammed a mailing label form that can be used for two-across labels. You can view the records in the Word table and sort the data by any of the columns by clicking on the appropriate sort button on the Database toolbar, as described in the previous section.

Once the names are sorted and then merged into the mailing label form, you can print them on regular paper instead of mailing label stock to produce a columnar directory from the names in your data source file. Here are the steps to produce a directory of names:

1. Choose File ➤ Open and bring the data source file to the screen, if it is not there already. The data source file will appear as a Word table. (If the data form is superimposed on the table, click the View Source button on the right side of the data form so that you can see your data source file as a Word table.)

2. If the Database toolbar is not on the screen, choose View ➤ Tools and select Database.

Button	Name	Purpose
	Data Form	Creates a data entry form
	Manage Fields	Add and Remove Fields from the database form
	Add New Record	Adds a blank row to a data source Word table to insert new records.
	Delete Record	Deletes the row on which the insertion point is placed.
	Sort Ascending	Sorts in low to high order by the column in which the insertion point is placed.
	Sort Descending	Sorts in high to low order by the column in which the insertion point is placed.
	Insert Database	Inserts information from databases outside Word
	Update Fields	Updates and displays the results of selected fields
	Find Record	Searches for information that may be contained within any field of your database
	Mail Merge Main Document	Switches to a main document set up through the Mail Merge Helper

Table 11.1　**The Database Toolbar Buttons**

Part
2

Communicating with
Word

3. Click into the column by which you wish to sort your data (for example, LastName, Account Balance, JobTitle, or PostalCode for bulk mailings).

4. Click the A to Z button on the Database toolbar to sort in ascending order (low to high, or alphabetically) or the Z to A button for descending order (high to low).

5. Once the data in the Word table is in the sort order you need for the directory, choose Tools ➤ Mail Merge.

6. Click the Create button in step 1 to create a main document that will hold the data records. Choose Mailing Labels, not Catalog. When the confirmation dialog box appears, choose New Main Document (not Active Window), so that Word will create the mailing labels in a new document.

7. Click on step 2's Get Data button and choose Open Data Source. Browse the hard disk until you find your data source (even though it is currently in memory, Mail Merge likes to get the file itself). Select the file and click Open.

8. Word will alert you that you need to set up the main document for labels. Click the Set up Main Document button. The Labels Option dialog box appears, as shown in Figure 11.26.

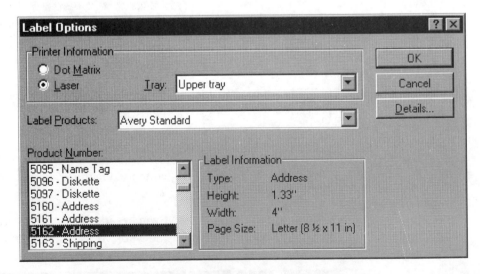

Figure 11.26 **The Mailing Label main document is an excellent form to create a directory of names.**

9. For Label Products, choose Avery Standard. In the Product Number list box, click 5162–Address. Then click OK.

10. The Create Labels dialog box appears. Insert the fields exactly as you would for an inside address. Then click OK. Figure 11.27 shows a sample label with the data source fields.

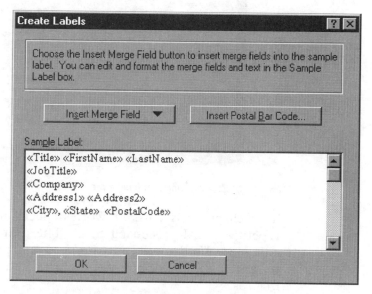

Figure 11.27   You insert the fields that you want to see in the directory.

11. You are ready to merge the data source records into the mailing label form. Click step 3's Merge button. The Merge dialog box appears.

12. Click the Merge button on the right side of the Merge dialog box. Word will begin merging the information into the mailing label. Figure 11.28 shows the finished product merged to the screen.

13. Save the file and click the Print button on the Standard toolbar to print the mailing label pages.
    If you need to correct either the main document (mailing label form) or the data source after completing a merge, click on the Window command in the menu bar and find the name of the main document. If the main document is what you wish to edit, it now appears on the screen. If you wish to edit the data source, however, choose Tools ➤ Mail Merge and select Step 2.

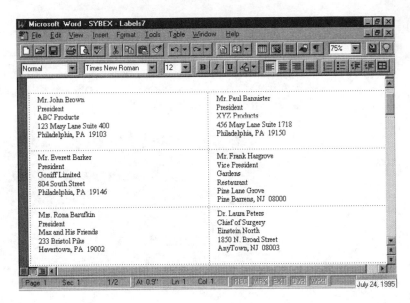

Figure 11.28 **Merging to a label form**

This chapter has covered Word's special tools for automating many repetitive word processing tasks. The next chapter describes how to customize Word to suit your own needs and preferences. You'll learn how to customize Word's options, toolbars, and templates, and how to use macros.

Chapter 12

Customizing Word with Options, Toolbars, Templates, and Macros

FEATURING

A great deal of the power of Word comes from the amount of customization that Microsoft has built into it. Changing even a few of Word's options from their default values can dramatically change the way a user interacts with the program.

With the options available in Word, the user—not the program—becomes the one in charge. While the basic functionality of Word will always remain the same, a user with the knowledge of the available options can make Word a more personal and powerful tool.

Customizing Word's Options

Most of the customization options available in Word can be accessed by choosing Tools ➤ Options from the menu bar, which opens the Options dialog box. The Options dialog box, shown in Figure 12.1, has 12 tabs at the top, each representing a different page of options.

The following sections provide an overview of the choices available on the pages of the Options dialog box. Some of these settings will not be useful for your situation, but there are quite a few that you will appreciate knowing about.

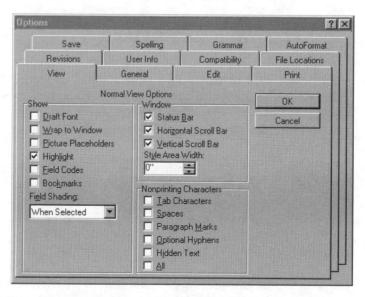

Figure 12.1   Word's Options dialog box, accessed by choosing Tools ➤ Options

Setting View Options

The first page of interest to most users will be the View page, shown in Figure 12.1. The options on the View page control how Word documents appear on the screen.

The checkboxes and drop-down list box in the Show section turn on and off the screen display of the features listed. For example, when Highlight is checked, you see the highlights created with the Highlight tool; when it's unchecked, the highlights don't appear on the screen (although they are still stored with the document).

The checkboxes in the Window section control whether or not you see three of Word's major window components: the Status bar, horizontal scroll bar, and vertical scroll bar. The Style Area Width option is set by default to 0". If you increase the width of the style area, you can see all of the styles that you are using in your document. The style area runs along the left side of the window.

The checkboxes in the Nonprinting Characters section of the View page turn on and off the display of special characters, including tabs, spaces, paragraph marks, optional hyphens, and hidden text. The last checkbox, All, provides a quick way to toggle on an off the display of all of these nonprinting characters.

Setting Save Options

The Save page of the Options dialog box is another area that you may want to visit. As you learned in Chapter 9, this page contains the setting for the AutoSave feature, which is the Automatic Save Every *n* Minutes option. The other options you may find useful here are Allow Fast Saves and the File Sharing password settings.

> **NOTE** Remember, when you set the Automatic Save option, Word is saving a copy and not the original document. If you have AutoSave set for every 15 or 20 minutes, there is a good chance that you have saved a more recent version than what is in the recovered document. See Chapter 9 for more details.

The Allow Fast Saves option tells Word whether you want to save just the changes to your document when you select Save (a "fast save") or if you want the entire document saved. Fast saves are quicker than normal saves because they save only the changes made to the document since the last time you saved it.

The down side to fast saves is that they take more disk space than normal saves. Microsoft does suggest that if you plan on performing a memory-hungry operation, such as searching for text or compiling an index, you should use a full save. You should also think about performing a full save once you have completely finished a document or before you convert a document into another file format.

Fast saves cannot be performed across a network. Also, if you choose Always Create Backup Copy on the Save page, Word will disable Allow Fast Saves, because it needs to perform full saves for backups. When the Always Create Backup Copy option is checked, Word automatically creates a backup copy of your file each time you save it. See Chapter 9 for more information about automatic backups.

The File Sharing Options section of the Save page includes a Protection Password, a Write Reservation Password, and a Read-Only Recommended checkbox. The Protection Password restricts any access to a file without the specified password. The Write Reservation Password requires that a user enter the designated password before being allowed to save changes to the original file. If you check the Read-Only Recommended option, Word suggests to users that they open a file read-only (disallowing any changes). It does not, however, restrict them to opening the file in this mode; it only suggests.

Setting User Info Options

At first glance, there does not seem to be much to the User Info page of the Options dialog box. What it does provide, however, will make your work much easier and fluid.

The User Info page contains the user name, initials, and mailing address. Word uses this information throughout its operation. The user name is used to define the Author property of documents that you create. The Author property and the user initials are used with Word's Revisions feature. The Author property identifies the original author who owns a document, and the user initials are included with comments inserted during revisions, by the author or by another reviewer. The mailing address information in used as the default return address for labels and envelopes.

If you take the time to verify (and modify if necessary) the information here, you will not be surprised when Word uses the information.

Setting Spelling Options

The Spelling page of Word's Options dialog box has many very useful options regarding the way that Word spell checks your document. Figure 12.2 shows the Spelling page with the default options selected.

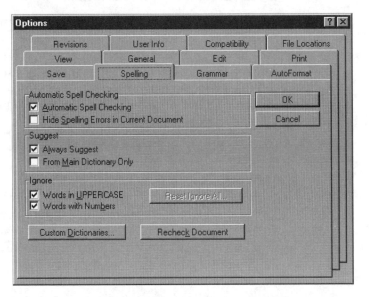

Figure 12.2   **The Spelling page of Word's Options dialog box (Tools ➤ Options)**

The Automatic Spell Checking section offers two options. The first checkbox turns on and off the new feature in Word that spell checks your document as you type. When Word finds a misspelled word, it places a wavy red line under it. If you don't want this spell checking as you go along, uncheck the Automatic Spell Checking checkbox. If you simply don't want to see the red lines until you are ready, check the Hide Spelling Errors in Current Document option. Once you are finished with your document, and you are ready to see your spelling errors, you can uncheck the option to see the work done by the automatic spelling checker.

The Suggest section includes an option to control whether on not the Spelling dialog box includes suggestions for correcting an error (Always

Suggest) and an option that restricts where the suggestions come from (From Main Dictionary Only).

The first checkbox in the Ignore section allows you to instruct the spelling checker to ignore any words that are in all uppercase. This can be a useful feature, as long as you spell everything that is all capitals correctly. You can also change the spelling checker behavior to ignore words with numbers in them. This is a little more on the dangerous side, because a slip-up here is more common, such as when you type a number 0 instead of a letter O.

At the very bottom of the dialog box there are two buttons:

▶ Custom Dictionaries takes you to a dialog box that allows you to manipulate your custom dictionaries, including opening the dictionaries and editing them.

▶ Recheck Document allows you to force a refresh of the automatic spelling check of the current document.

WARNING When you click the Custom Dictionaries button and then proceed to edit an existing document, the Automatic Spell Checking feature is turned off. Be sure to check the option when you want to have Automatic Spell Checking on again.

Setting General Options

The options on the General page of the Options dialog box are, as the name suggests, general—they cover a variety of areas that do not necessarily fit on any of the other pages. Figure 12.3 shows this page of the Options dialog box.

The second and third options in the dialog box, Help for WordPerfect Users and Navigation Keys for WordPerfect Users, provide help for users who are switching from WordPerfect to Word. While these options are helpful for WordPerfect users in the beginning, even the most diehard WordPerfect user will eventually get tired of the constant migration assistance from Word.

Further down on the list of options is the one to increase the number of your most recently used files listed on the File menu. As described in Chapter 9, the number of file names you can set to appear on the menu range from 0 to 9.

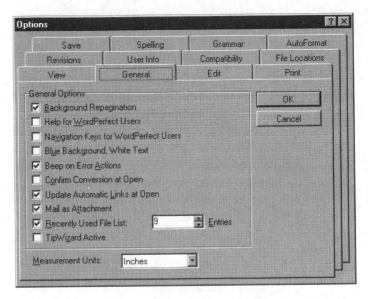

Figure 12.3   The General page of Word's Options dialog box (Tools ➤ Options)

If you do not like inches being used for measurements, use the last option on the General page. Measurement Units gives you a choice of units to choose from, including centimeters, points, and picas. The Measurement Units setting affects the numbers on the horizontal ruler and measurements you type in any dialog boxes.

Setting Grammar Options

The Grammar page provides options for customizing the way Word checks grammar. On this page, you can choose from six levels of grammar checking, three predefined and three customizable. Figure 12.4 shows this page of the dialog box.

Choose one of Word's built-in sets of rules or click the Customize Settings button and define your own. You can also specify whether you want the spelling check to be run before the grammar check and whether you want readability statistics to show at the end of the grammar check.

Setting File Locations

The File Locations page specifies the default path for various file types. Knowing where Word retrieves information and places files can be

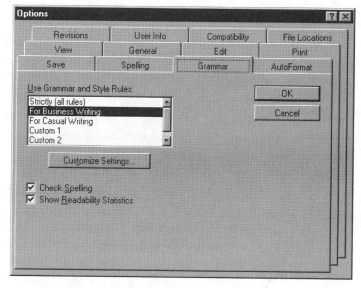

Figure 12.4   *The Grammar page of the Options dialog box (Tools ➤ Options)*

helpful. Figure 12.5 shows the File Locations page with all of the specified paths.

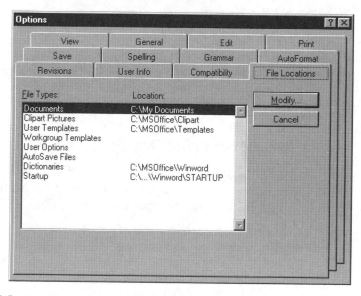

Figure 12.5   *The File Locations page of the Options dialog box*

The first file type location is the default setting for documents saved and opened in Word. When Word is installed, a folder called My Documents is created and is used as the default location for your documents. If you want to modify this or any other file location, select the location, click the Modify button, and set the new path and folder.

When you insert a picture into your document, Word uses, by default, the Microsoft Office Clip Art collection. The path specified for clip-art pictures in the File Locations page points to this folder.

Two really important file locations are those for user and workgroup templates. These two paths tell you where Word retrieves the available templates from when you choose File ➤ New from the menu bar. If Word is installed on a machine that does not reside on a network, chances are that the Workgroup Templates path is blank. If only User Templates has a path, that is where Word gets all of the templates. If you are on a network, templates that everyone has access to are located in the Workgroup Templates path, and templates that are meant just for you (or that you create on your own) are stored in the User Templates path.

If you see a path that is blank, such as the location for AutoSave Files, it means that the files, if they exist, reside in the default location, which is the main Word folder, generally \MSOFFICE\WINWORD. The AutoSave Files path specifies where you want Word's temporary AutoSave documents stored while you are editing you main document.

The Startup path specifies files to start when you start Word. If you store documents in the specified folder, Word will open these documents or templates immediately after you launch the program. This is a nice feature if you consistently open certain documents or templates in Word.

Setting Print Options

The Print page of the Options dialog box contains numerous options that will give you more flexibility in printing your documents. Figure 12.6 shows this page of the Options dialog box.

Checking the Draft Output option causes your printer to print you document in draft mode with minimal formatting (if your printer supports this mode). This is ideal when all you need is a hard copy of a document to look at its contents.

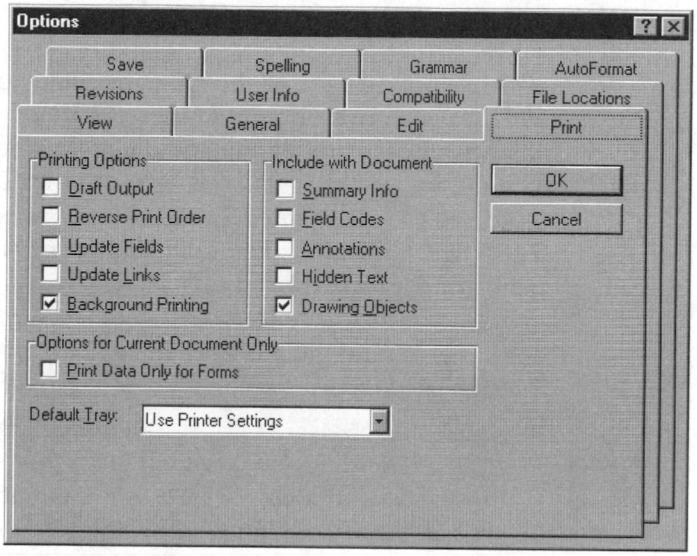

Figure 12.6 **The Print page of the Options dialog box (Tools ➤ Options)**

The Reverse Print Order option causes your document to print last page first, first page last. Do not select this option if an envelope will be printed, because it will not work correctly.

The Update Fields and Update Links options determine whether your fields and links will be updated right before the document is printed. If you check these options, you won't need to remember to use the Update command to get the most up-to-date information. If you are trying to quickly print a draft with a great number of links and/or fields and the accuracy of the information is not imperative, be sure to have these options unchecked, because updating of fields, and especially links, takes some time.

Background Printing, if checked, will allow you to return to Word for editing while your document is printing in the background. This requires more memory and is not as quick as printing in the foreground. If memory or speed is important, you can deselect Background Printing.

The Include with Document group on the Print page allows you to choose what will print. The most notable option is Drawing Objects, which lets you turn on or off the printing of drawing objects created in Word. Turning off Drawing Objects in Word while printing will speed up the printing of a document.

Setting Other Options

The Revisions page of the Options dialog box includes options that are used to customize how revisions are made to documents. The first two groups of options set the method of marking (bold, underline, italics, double-underline, strikethrough, or hidden) insertions and deletions made to a documented protected for revisions. In addition, the color used for changes can be set to different colors for different reviewers. The third group of options allows you to choose whether you want revised lines to have Outside, Left, or Right outlines and what color to make the outline. Changing the Highlight color used is also an option on this page.

NOTE Choose Tools ➤ Revisions to see the Revisions dialog box. This dialog box contains options for turning on and off revision marking, reviewing revisions, and accepting or rejecting revisions.

The Edit page of the Options dialog box lets you refine the editing functions of Word. One interesting option is Typing Replaces Selection, which you can turn off to prevent accidental deletion of selections with extraneous keystrokes. For example, if you have a paragraph selected in order to cut or copy it, and accidentally hit the spacebar, the selection will be replaced by a single space, unless this option on the Edit page is unchecked.

Another option on the Edit page that you might find useful is Automatic Word Selection. When checked, this option causes entire words to be selected when the mouse is used to click and drag selections of text. When the option is not checked, you can click and drag to select parts of words.

The Compatibility page of the Options dialog box is relevant when you are using Word to work with documents created in other file formats. Once you have the file open, you can select the file format you are working with on the Compatibility page and select your conversion options from the Options list box.

The AutoFormat page is where you can customize Word's AutoFormat feature. The AutoFormat feature and the options on this page are discussed in Chapter 10.

NOTE To see an explanation of any of the options in the Tools ➤ Options dialog box, click the Help question mark in the top-right corner of the window and then click the option of interest.

Modifying Toolbars

Another area that you can customize in Word is its toolbars. You can do everything from changing the placement of the basic toolbars to creating new toolbars with your own custom buttons.

Moving Toolbars

When Word is first installed, two toolbars appear at the top of the screen: the Standard toolbar and the Formatting toolbar. The first level of customization is the ability to move these toolbars from their default location.

Moving a toolbar is a simple dragging operation. Try moving the Formatting toolbar to see how this works. With your mouse, point to a place on the Formatting toolbar that is not a button or a combo box. For example, point to the space between the point size combo box and the bold button. Click and hold your left mouse button as you drag down into the center of the current document. Once you have an outline of the toolbar, let go of the mouse button. Your toolbar should now be floating, as shown in Figure 12.7.

Next, try and grab the same spot on the toolbar and drag it to the right side of the screen. When the outline turns into a vertical shape, let go of the left mouse button. You will now see the toolbar docked along the right side of the window. You can use the same technique to move the toolbar to the bottom or left side of the screen. This same technique works with all of Word's toolbars.

 NOTE When toolbars are docked on the left or right side of the screen, combo box options are replaced with pushbuttons that open dialog boxes that provide access to the option available from the corresponding combo box.

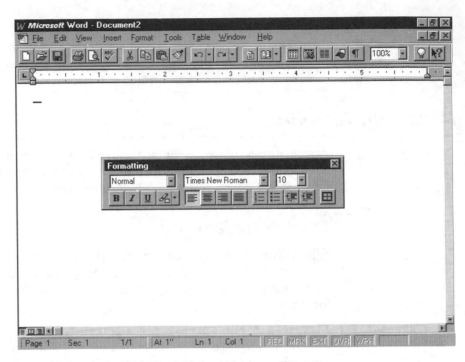

Figure 12.7   The formatting toolbar floating in the middle of the screen

Creating Your Own Toolbars

Word comes with nine built-in toolbars. As you've learned in previous chapters, you can turn on and off the display of these toolbars by selecting View ➤ Toolbars from the menu bar. The Toolbars dialog box lists all of the toolbars currently available. If a toolbar has a checkmark next to it, it means that it is currently visible.

If you want to create your own toolbar, click the New button on the right side of the Toolbars dialog box. This opens the New Toolbar dialog box:

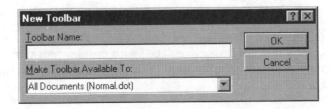

Type a name for your toolbar and click OK. Your new toolbar, which currently has no buttons on it, and the Customize dialog box appear. Whenever you have the Customize dialog box in view, your toolbars are not active. In order to populate your toolbar, or any of the other visible toolbars, click and drag the buttons from the Toolbars page of the Customize dialog box onto your toolbar.

The Customize dialog box, shown in Figure 12.8, can also be opened by selecting Tools ➤ Customize from the menu bar. When you pick a category of commands from the Categories list box, the buttons in the selected category will appear on the right. If you want to know what a particular button will do, click the button and view the description at the bottom of the dialog box.

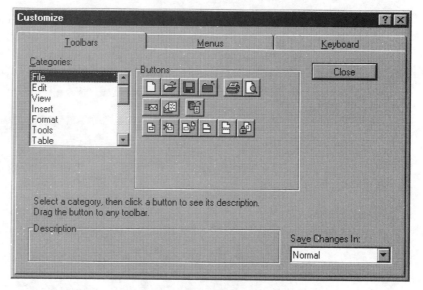

Figure 12.8   You can open the Customize dialog box through either the Tools ➤ Customize dialog box or by clicking the New button in the View ➤ Toolbars dialog box, entering a toolbar name, and clicking OK.

The other tabs of the Customize dialog box give you the ability to perform the same type of customization for menu bar items and keyboard shortcuts.

When you drag new buttons onto your toolbars, drag the buttons on top of an existing button, and that button will shift to the right to make room for your button. If you want to remove a button from a toolbar, you can click and drag the button off the toolbar.

> **TIP** If you want to drag a button off of a visible toolbar, you do not need to open the Customize dialog box. Hold down the Alt key, and then click and drag the button you no longer need off the toolbar into your document area.

Modifying Existing Toolbars

Before you can modify a toolbar that comes with Word, the toolbar must be visible. Select View ➤ Toolbars, check the toolbars that you want to see, and click the Customize button. You'll see the Customize dialog box (Figure 12.8).

Assigning Word commands to toolbars is an excellent way to customize your working environment within Word. An extension of this ability is adding toolbar buttons that give you direct access to AutoText, fonts, macros, and styles. Figure 12.9 shows the Customize dialog box with these special categories visible in the Categories list.

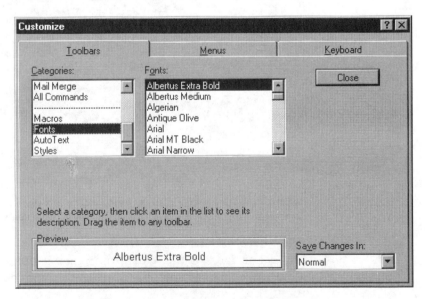

Figure 12.9   Customize dialog box with the AutoText, Macros, Fonts, and Styles categories in view

When you select any of the four categories, the available entries will appear in the list box to the right. Once you have found an item in one of the four categories you want to add, click and drag it to the toolbar you want it to be on.

As when you create your own toolbars, drag the new button on top of an existing button, and that button will shift to the right to make room for the new one. To remove a button from a toolbar, click and drag the button off the toolbar.

Customizing Templates

Templates allow you to have basic text and page formatting available when you want to create new documents. In addition to providing you with the boilerplate text and page formatting, the template can store document-specific styles, AutoText, toolbars, and macros. This way, you avoid filling up your global template (Normal.dot) with items you will only need with certain documents.

Word comes with a number of predesigned templates, which help you with the creation of basic documents (memos, letters, fax cover sheets, calendars, and so on). Some of the templates are actually "Wizards," which take you through the creation of these documents, step by step. These templates store most of the text and all of the AutoText, macros, toolbars, and styles you will need to create the specific document.

Word's built-in templates are definitely useful, but there is no way that the available templates could cover all of the needs of everyone. For this reason, Word allows you to design your own templates to reduce the time necessary to create your specific documents. Chapter 11 described how to create a template from an existing document. The following sections describe how to set up a new template from scratch and how to modify one of Word's predefined templates.

Designing Your Own Template

A Word template is virtually identical to a Word document. The process of creating a fresh new template is also similar to creating a new document.

As an example, we will go through the steps to create a template for memos. We will base this new template on the Normal template (a blank, portrait-orientation page, with 1-inch top and bottom margins and 1.25-inch left and right margins). Follow these steps:

1. Select File ➤ New from the menu bar.

2. On the General page of the New dialog box, select Blank Document.

3. Click on the Create New Template button in the bottom-right corner of the dialog box.

4. When your New dialog box looks like the one shown in Figure 12.10, click OK.

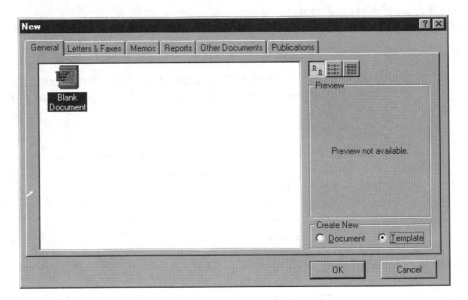

Figure 12.10   *The New dialog box set to open a new template*

After you click OK, Word opens your new template, which will look like Figure 12.11. Note that the title bar reads *Template1*, not *Document1*. You can now proceed to create your new template with any text, macros, AutoText, styles, and toolbars specific to your template.

5. Change the font size of your text to 14 by clicking on the point size combo box on the Formatting toolbar.

6. Type the word **Memo**. Center the text by clicking the center alignment button on the Formatting toolbar.

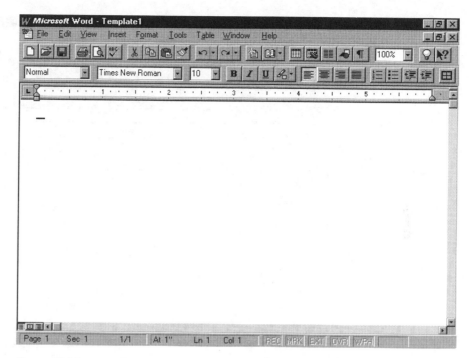

Figure 12.11 *A blank template created by clicking the Create New Template button in the File ➤ New dialog box*

7. Change the point size to 12 and press Enter twice. Click the left alignment button on the Formatting toolbar.

8. Type **TO:** and press Enter twice.

9. Type **FROM:** and press Enter twice.

10. Type **SUBJECT:** and press Enter twice.

11. Type **DATE:** and press Enter twice. Your template should look like the one shown in Figure 12.12.

It would be much more efficient if you did not need to go through these steps every time you want to create a new memo. Basing any new memos on this new memo template will save you from these rote steps. Before you can use the template, however, you must save it.

12. To save the template, select File ➤ Save. The Save As dialog box will appear, as shown in Figure 12.13. Because it is a template, Word has

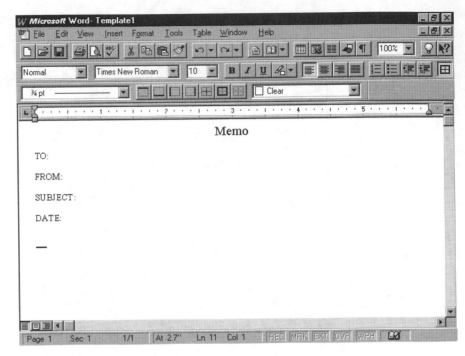

Figure 12.12   Creating a memo template

taken you into the Templates folder and disabled the ability to change the document type.

> **WARNING**   Remember that the Templates folder that Word opens is specified on the File Locations page of the Tools ➤ Options dialog box. Be certain that when you save a template, you save it in the folder Word opens for you (or in one of the folders contained within that folder). If you do not, Word will not be able to find the template when you select File ➤ New from the menu bar.

13.   Change the name of the template in the Save As dialog box to **My Memo** and click the Save button. The title bar of your template should now read *My Memo*.

14.   Close your template by selecting File ➤ Close from the menu bar.

To create a new document based on your template, choose File ➤ New. You will see My Memo as a template option on the General page of the New dialog box, as shown in Figure 12.14. Click on the My Memo

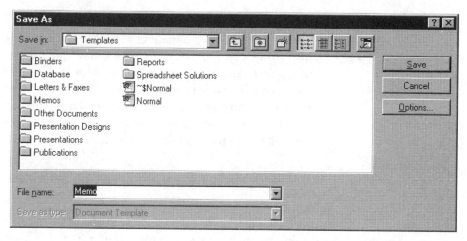

Figure 12.13 The Save As dialog box appears when you choose to save a template for the first time.

choice and choose OK. Do not change the Create New option from Document to Template, because you do not want to create another template; you want to create a new document based on the template you have already created. When you click OK, a new document will open with the text that you had in your My Memo template.

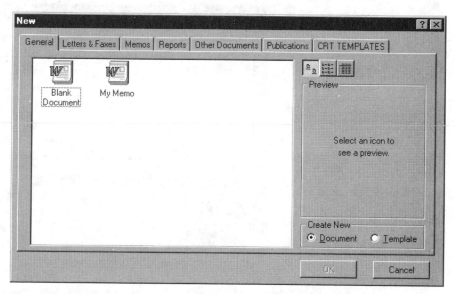

Figure 12.14 The New dialog box now contains your new template as an option.

TIP If you will have a number of custom templates that you want to put into a logical group, you can create a new folder under the main Templates folder and store all of your new templates in that folder. When you choose to create a new document, your new folder will appear as a new tab in the New dialog box, as long as it has at least one Word template in it. The more folders you have, the smaller and harder to read the tabs in the New dialog box will be, so try to avoid adding too many of them.

Storing Special Elements in Templates

Keep in mind that you are not restricted to storing just text in your templates. When you create new AutoText, macros, styles, or toolbars, you will be prompted for a template in which you want to store the new item.

If your template is open when you are creating one of these elements, you will have the option to store the element for documents based on your template. Figure 12.15 shows an example in which a new AutoText item is being added to a template. The default option is All Documents (Normal.dot).

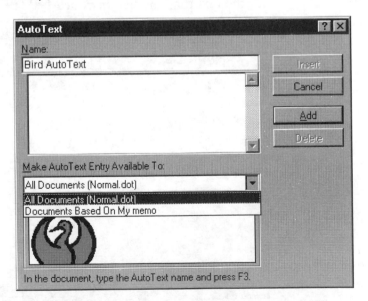

Figure 12.15 *Storing an AutoText item in a template other than Normal.dot*

Once you store one of the items in a template, it will be available whenever a document based on that template is open. Storing items in specific templates will help you to keep the size of your Normal template as small as possible. This ensures that documents that do not need certain AutoText, macros, toolbars, or styles will not be larger in size for no reason.

Changing Word Templates

You can work with the templates that come with Word in two ways: create new templates based on the ones provided with Word and then modify the new template, or open the original template and make the changes you need.

Creating a New Template Based on an Existing Template

Creating a new template based on an existing one is the safest way to modify existing templates. It's safer than modifying the original template, because you will still have the original as it was before you started modifying it. If you make a mistake, you can always return to the original.

To create a new template based on any existing template, select File ➤ New from the menu bar. In the New dialog box, select the template you want to make a copy of, select the Create New Template option button, and then click OK. The resulting template will be an exact replica of the original, but the modifications to the new template will not affect the original.

Opening an Existing Template

When you begin to modify the templates themselves, be careful, especially when you are working with the predesigned templates provided with Word. Be careful, because when you modify a template, you are working with the original. Changes you make to the template once you save them are permanent. You won't have a copy of the original template with which to start fresh.

If you do need to make changes to the original, open it as a template by selecting File ➤ Open and changing the Files of Type option to Document Templates. When you find the folder that has the template you want to open, select the template and click Open. (If you are not sure where your templates are stored, look on the File Locations page of the Tools ➤ Options dialog box, described earlier in this chapter.)

Once the template is open, the changes you make will affect how all new documents based on the template will look.

Taking Advantage of Macros

Word's macro language is Word Basic. With Word Basic, you can automate many of the procedures you perform in Word on a regular basis. To create Word macros, you can record the steps with the Macro Recorder or edit the macro directly in a code window.

In practice, you will usually combine the techniques of recording and editing of macros. Some commands that you want to use in your macros will be easier to record than write from scratch. You may not be able to record other commands, so you will need to edit your macro code.

The point that most people start needing to code their macros is when they need to get user input. While recording a macro, there is no way to pause for user input. For instance, you may record a macro that inserts specific text and then formats it. When you create the macro, it records the specific text that you typed. When you run the macro, it will always insert the same text. However, you may want to improve the macro by having it prompt the user for the text to insert. To do this, you need to edit the macro to add code. We will use this scenario for our example in the following sections.

Creating Macros

The majority of macros that you will be creating will be recorded, at least at the start. To begin recording a macro, select Tools ➤ Macro from the menu bar. You will see the Macro dialog box, shown in Figure 12.16. Any existing macros will be listed in the list box on the left side of the dialog box. Buttons with the various operations you can perform with macros are on the right. Depending on whether you have selected a macro and which one it is, specific buttons will either be enabled or disabled.

To record a new macro, enter the name you want to give to the macro in the Macro Name text box and click the Record button. The Record Macro dialog box appears, as shown in Figure 12.17. You can enter a

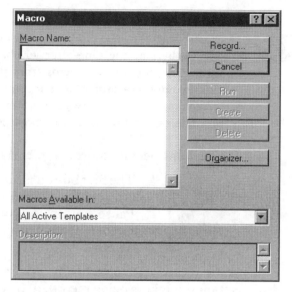

Figure 12.16 *The Tools ➤ Macro dialog box allows you to work with macros.*

description of the macro, specify a specific template in which you want to store the macro and, by using one of three corresponding buttons, assign the macro to a toolbar, the menu bar, or a shortcut key combination. When you are finished detailing the macro with the Record Macro dialog box, click OK.

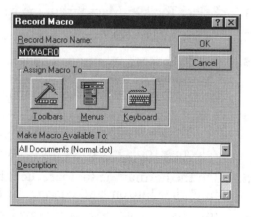

Figure 12.17 *The Record Macro dialog box lets you set up your new macro.*

NOTE Macros can be assigned to the menu bar, shortcut key combinations, and toolbars at any time after you have recorded them. Select Tools ➤ Customize and choose Macros from the category list. Concentrating on making a good recording of your steps should be your primary concern. It is recommended that you wait until after you have successfully recorded your macro to assign it to any of the shortcut options.

When Word begins recording, the Macro Recorder toolbar appears:

The first button is Stop, and the second is Pause. (There are very few occasions where you will need to use the Pause button, so you can think of this as the STOP toolbar, for when you are finished the steps of your macro.)

After you have turned on the Macro Recorder, remember that every action you take is being recorded. If you make a mistake and then fix the mistake while the recorder is running, every time you run your macro, Word will make the mistake and then fix it. If you are working on a complicated macro, you may want to run through the steps once before you turn on the recorder.

Follow these steps to create a very simple macro that we will modify in the next section:

1. Select Tools ➤ Macro from the menu bar.

2. In the Macro Name text box, type **MYMACRO**.

3. Click the Record button. The Record Macro dialog box will open. Note the option to store the macro in a specific template and the three buttons that you can use to assign the macro to various shortcuts.

4. Leave the template option as All Documents and click OK without assigning the macro to any shortcuts (this can always be done later by selecting Tools ➤ Customize). The Macro Recorder toolbar will appear.

5. On the Formatting toolbar, click the bold button, the italics button, the underline button, and change the font size to 24.

6. Type the words **FORMATTED TEXT**.

7. On the Formatting toolbar, click the bold button, the italics button, the underline button, and change the font size back to 10.

8. Click the Stop button on the Macro Recorder toolbar.

You have created your first macro. When you run this macro, it will insert the words FORMATTED TEXT in a 24-point, bold, italics, and underlined font, and then switch to plain 10-point text.

Executing Macros

To run a macro that you have created, select Tools ➤ Macro. You should see your macro in the list box on the left side of the Macro dialog box. Select your macro from the list, and several of the buttons in the dialog box become enabled. Click the Run button and watch your macro run.

You can assign your macro to run from the toolbar, menu bar, or a shortcut key by using the Customize dialog box. The basic steps to using the Customize dialog box are:

1. Select Tools ➤ Customize.

2. Select the appropriate tab for where you want to assign the macro: Toolbars, Menus, or Keyboard.

3. Select Macros from the Category list.

4. If you are assigning a macro to a toolbar, click and drag the macro name from the Macros list to the toolbar. For the Menus and Keyboard pages, fill in the appropriate text boxes.

5. When you're finished assigning your macro to a shortcut, click the Close button on any of the pages.

Editing Macros

The simple macro we created is sufficient if we will always want to enter the same text to be formatted. However, with only a few more steps, we can edit this macro so that it pauses and asks the user for the text to enter.

Part
2

Communicating with Word

To edit the macro, follow these steps:

1. Select Tools ➤ Macro, select MYMACRO (the one we recorded earlier in this chapter), and click Edit. Your screen should resemble Figure 12.18.

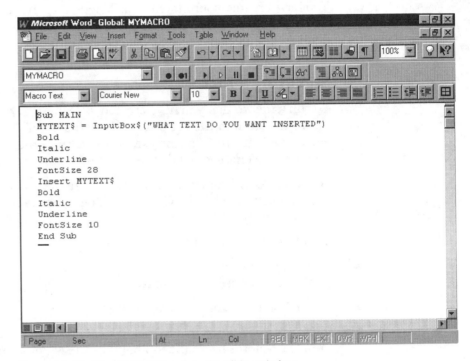

Figure 12.18 *The MYMACRO code in the editing window.*

Notice that Word Basic code is not that difficult to understand if you are looking at it after the recorder has created it. Even if you have never seen a line of Word Basic before, you can pick out the specific lines that bold, underline, change point size, and insert text.

The line that reads Insert "FORMATTED TEXT" is the line that types the text when you run the macro. If you simply modify this line and add one more line of code, you can have the macro ask the user for the text to type instead of typing the same text over and over.

2. Your insertion point should be blinking on the line the reads *Sub MAIN*.

3. Press the End key to go to the end of the line.

4. Press the Enter key to add a new line.

5. Type the following on the new line and press Enter:

   MYTEXT\$ = InputBox\$("WHAT TEXT DO YOU WANT INSERTED")

6. Change the line that reads *Insert "FORMATTED TEXT"* to **Insert MYTEXT\$.**

7. Select File ➤ Close from the menu bar. Click Yes when asked if you want to save the changes.

   Try running your macro now. Select Tools ➤ Macro, choose MY-MACRO from the list, and click Run. You should now be prompted with an input box:

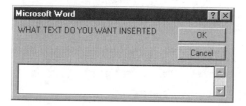

   Enter the text you want inserted and click OK. The text you typed should be inserted into the document from which you ran the macro.

   Note that with very little effort, we made a macro much more powerful than it was before, simply by braving the code and making a couple of modifications. A good amount of editing you may do will be as simple as changing the point size stored in the code of a macro to a different size, thereby saving you from rerecording the entire macro for one change.

   If you want to learn more about Word Basic, refer to Word's on-line help and the Answer Wizard. Look up the information about syntax (how you need to write the commands) and study examples of code. You can copy and paste these examples right into your own macro. An interesting place to start would be to look up InputBox\$ in the help text to get more information about the command we added to the MYMACRO macro to get user input.

   This chapter described how to customize some of Word's features to make it more personalized and efficient in your user environment. The next chapter, the last one in this part, shows you how you can integrate your work in Word with the other Microsoft Office applications.

Chapter 13

Office Connections—Pulling a Proposal Together

FEATURING

Understanding fully the features and capabilities of one of the Microsoft Office programs is the first step to integrating your work in all of the programs. Unfortunately, the real-world demands of the job do not follow the sequential pages of a book.

In this chapter, we will use the information we have already covered and also skip ahead to use features that we haven't explored yet. The example in this chapter demonstrates how a proposal written by several people can be brought together using three Microsoft Office programs: Word, Excel, and PowerPoint.

Here is our scenario. Shawn is the technical assistant for a New Jersey consulting firm that specializes in installing networks for banks in the area. Her job is to understand the scope of work for any bank installation project and to create professional, eye-catching proposals and presentations to communicate her company's installation plans and costs for the network.

Shawn uses Word, Excel, and PowerPoint to create each proposal. She combines Excel data and graphs and embeds network flow charts and diagrams from PowerPoint into sections of the proposal she has written in Word. For the cover pages of some of her proposals, she uses PowerPoint slides used in preliminary presentations.

Under Shawn's direction, other staff members also use Word to work on specific sections of the proposal. When these sections are ready, Shawn links them into the master proposal. To perform these tasks, she must have a knowledge of Word, Excel, and PowerPoint and a clear understanding of how to link data from multiple Office programs.

An Overview of Inserting and Linking in Office Applications

When you have multiple files that must be combined or linked together into one file, you can take a couple of approaches. We'll refer to the files that will be inserted as *subfiles*, and the main document into which the other files will go as the *main file* (not to be confused with Word's Master Document feature).

One approach is to insert the files at their appropriate locations in the master file using the Insert ➤ File command on the menu bar. The Insert

➤ File option inserts an entire document, or you can specify specific ranges (bookmark sections).

The Insert ➤ File command also offers a Link to File option. This option allows you to *link* the multiple files into a master file. You can link an entire file or specific sections.

The Insert ➤ File approach without the Link To File option checked inserts only *copies* of the other Word files. If the authors of the inserted files make changes, these changes will not be reflected in your copies of their work. You will need to reinsert their files on a regular basis to make sure you have the latest changes. If you are sure that no more changes will be made to those files, you may only need a copy inserted with the Insert ➤ File command.

If you select the Link To File option in the Insert File dialog box, the subfile will have a link to the original file. With linked inserted files, other authors can make last-minute changes to their documents. These changes will be reflected in the master file, without requiring you to reinsert their files. To update the files and show the latest changes, you can use the Edit ➤ Links command, or you can use the Edit ➤ Select All command (Ctrl+A) and press F9 to update linked field information. You can also break a link connection through the Edit ➤ Links command.

Another approach to linking files is to select and copy data from one program file into another and choose Edit ➤ Paste Special. In the Paste Special dialog box, choose the Paste Link radio button. We'll use this method to link Excel data to a Word document.

If you simply want to copy (or move) data from one application to another, you can use the standard copy and paste through the Clipboard technique. But you can also employ a one-step method: dragging and dropping. We will use this method to design a PowerPoint slide with text created in Word.

Linking in Word

In our example, five files are involved: one master file and four subfiles created by four different authors. These are called MasterFile, Sub-FileOne, SubFileTwo, SubFileThree, and SubFileFour.

> **NOTE** The generic names we are using in our example are not necessary in order to perform linking operations. Use any normal file name (maximum of 255 characters, with spaces and periods allowed).

To link these files, open MasterFile and position the insertion point at the location where you wish to place the text from SubFileOne. Then choose Insert ➤ File and select the file in the list box. Click the Link To File checkbox on the right side of the dialog box. Figure 13.1 shows the Insert File dialog box with the Link To File option checked.

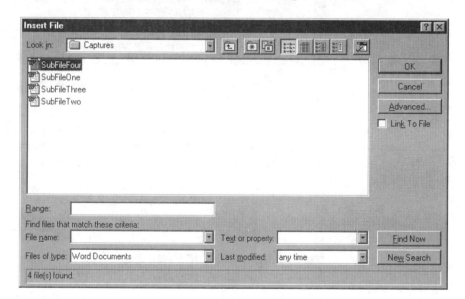

Figure 13.1 *While working in Word, it is easy to link multiple Word documents. Use the Insert ➤ File command and check the Link To File option.*

When the linked file is inserted, there is no immediate indication that you have a linked file within another file. Click in the section of information that has been inserted, and you will see that section appear in gray. Figure 13.2 shows the linked file within the master file. Although it appears that you can edit the linked information, the next time you update the file link, your edits will be replaced by the original's author's changes.

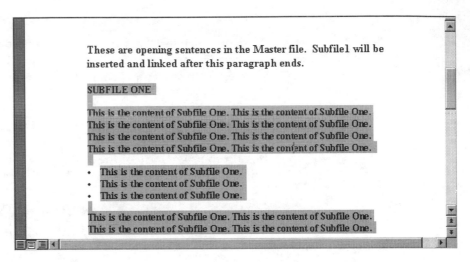

Figure 13.2   *When you click into a linked subfile's text area, it displays in gray within the Master File.*

For each of the other files to be inserted and linked to the master file—SubFileTwo, SubFileThree, and SubFileFour in our example—choose Insert ➤ File, select the file, and check the Link To File option.

TIP   A master file with multiple links can also be a linked file within another master file.

Inserting and Linking Selected Areas within a Word File

You may not want an entire subfile to be inserted into your master file. You just need to insert different sections within the subfile. This can be done through the Insert File dialog box, as long as the bookmark (or range name in an Excel file) has already been created in the linked subfile.

The first step is to have the authors of the subfiles select and give a bookmark name to the subsections that will be inserted and linked. Each author will select the paragraphs, choose Edit ➤ Bookmark, type the name for the subsection (no spaces in the name; maximum of 40 characters), and click the Add button to add the bookmark. This procedure needs to be repeated for each subsection you wish to insert.

When the sections are marked, you can open the master file and choose Insert ➤ File. Click once on the name of the file. Click the Link To File option on the right side of the dialog box. In the Range text box below the file list, type in the name of the bookmark section. Figure 13.3 shows the Insert File dialog box with a Range bookmark name specified. You will need to insert each bookmark section separately.

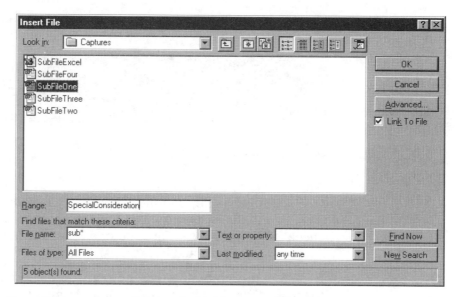

Figure 13.3 *You can insert and link a section of another file if the section has been given a bookmark name. Enter the bookmark name in the Range text box.*

Updating Word Links

As each author of a subfile continues to make changes, you will want to update the links so that the latest changes are reflected in the master file.

To manage your Word links, choose Edit ➤ Links from the menu bar. In the Links dialog box, click on the name of the file for which you wish to update links, and then click the Update Now button on the right side of the dialog box. Figure 13.4 shows the Links dialog box.

If you want to remove the link between the subfile and the master file, click the Break Link button in this dialog box. If you need to change the name of a linked file or the location of the file, click the Change Source button and enter the new file name or location.

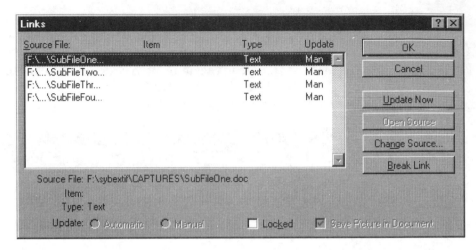

Figure 13.4   **Use the Update Now button in the Edit ➤ Links dialog box to update the files so that they reflect the latest changes.**

Another way to update your links is to let Word do it for you automatically when you open the master file. Choose Tools ➤ Options ➤ General tab. This page contains a setting for Update Automatic Links at Open. If you check this option, each time you open the file, any new changes in the subfiles will be reflected in the master file.

In Word, the linked file can be considered to be just a field within the master file. Another method for updating the links is to click into the linked subfile text to be updated (the text that appears in gray), and then press the F9 key to update the field. With the insertion point still in the field, you can press Shift+F9 to toggle between the display of the actual field definition, which includes the file name and path, and the text for the linked subfiles that you want to see in the finished document. Figure 13.5 shows the subfiles with the field formats.

TIP   Press Ctrl+A to Select All and then press F9 to update fields. This is an easy way to update all of the linked subfiles at once. If you want to toggle the field codes for all of the linked subfiles and other fields in your document at one time, press Alt+F9.

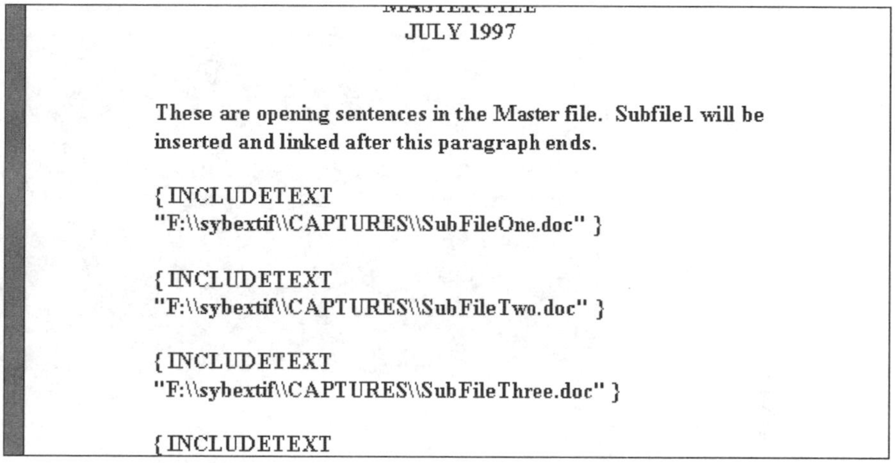

```
                          MASTER FILE
                          JULY 1997


      These are opening sentences in the Master file.  Subfile1 will be
      inserted and linked after this paragraph ends.

      { INCLUDETEXT
      "F:\\sybextif\\CAPTURES\\SubFileOne.doc" }

      { INCLUDETEXT
      "F:\\sybextif\\CAPTURES\\SubFileTwo.doc" }

      { INCLUDETEXT
      "F:\\sybextif\\CAPTURES\\SubFileThree.doc" }

      { INCLUDETEXT
```

Figure 13.5   *Linked files can be displayed as fields or text by toggling back and forth with the Shift+F9 keyboard combination.*

Linking Excel Data and Charts

For Excel data, the Paste Special method of inserting from a file is more efficient than using Word's Insert ➤ File command. In our example, we will use this method for the spreadsheet section that must be linked into our master file.

Creating the Excel Link

To create the Excel link, follow these steps:

1. Open the Excel workbook that contains the data that should be linked into the master file.

2. Open the Word MasterFile document.

3. Choose Excel from the Taskbar at the bottom of the screen or hold down the Alt key and press Tab to cycle through the open applications until you find the Excel program in memory.

4. Select the range of data to be inserted and linked, and then click the copy button on the Standard toolbar or press Ctrl+C to copy the data into the Clipboard. Figure 13.6 shows the Excel data being copied.

5. After the Excel data is copied to the Clipboard, click the Word program button on the Taskbar to make the master file active.

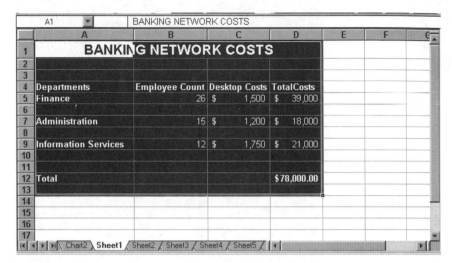

Figure 13.6 *In your Excel workbook, select the range of cells to be inserted and linked into another file.*

6. Click the insertion point at the location where you wish to insert the Excel data.

7. Choose Edit ➤ Paste Special from the menu bar.

8. In the Paste Special dialog box, click the Paste Link option and choose Microsoft Excel Worksheet Object in the drop-down list, as shown in Figure 13.7. Click OK, and the data appears in the master file.

9. From the Borders toolbar, choose a double-line, outline border style to place around the Excel object. Figure 13.8 shows the pasted, linked worksheet data, outlined with a border.

Your Excel data is now inserted into the Word main file. If you double-click on the Excel object, you will be returned to the Excel program so that you can make changes. Any changes you make are immediately reflected in the Word master file when you switch back to that file.

 TIP Rose, the financial manager for a large nonprofit service organization in Philadelphia, provides this tip regarding copying and linking with Paste Special. If the Excel spreadsheet being pasted and linked is longer than one page, do not select to paste it as a Microsoft Excel Worksheet Object, because the object will not cross a page boundary. Instead, Paste Link it as Formatted Text (RTF).

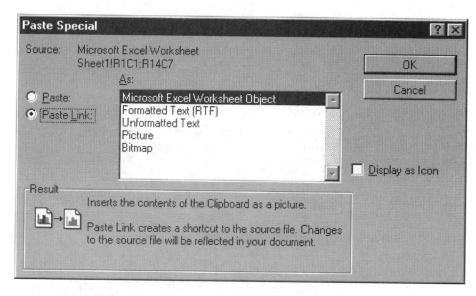

Figure 13.7 *To link an Excel Worksheet Object, use the Edit ➤ Paste Special command and select the Paste Link option.*

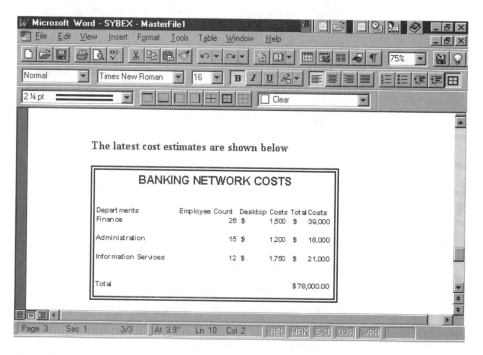

Figure 13.8 *You can place a border around the inserted Excel object.*

Creating and Linking an Excel Chart

You can easily create a basic chart in Excel using Excel's Chart Wizard. The Chart Wizard walks you through the process of creating a 3-D bar chart.

Here are the steps for creating the chart:

1. In Excel, select the labels, and then hold down the Ctrl key and select the data series. Figure 13.9 shows the labels and data series selected for the chart.

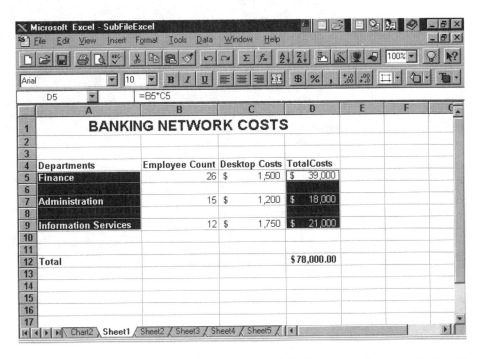

Figure 13.9   An Excel chart is easy to create. Select labels (X axis) and the data series (Y axis) and choose Insert ➤ Chart ➤ On This Sheet.

2. Choose Insert ➤ Chart ➤ On This Sheet from the Excel menu bar.

3. Click the mouse and drag the outline onto an area where your chart can spread out without overlaying your data. The Chart Wizard appears, displaying the ranges that you selected.

4. Click the Next button.

5. At Step 2, choose the 3-D Column chart, as shown in Figure 13.10. Then click the Next button.

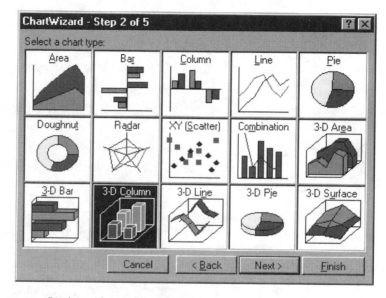

Figure 13.10 **Excel provides 15 different chart types.**

6. At Step 3, choose the number 4 format for the chart: gridlines behind the bar charts. Then click the Next button.

7. At Step 4, click the Next button.

8. At Step 5, type a chart title. Then click the Finish button. The chart appears on the worksheet.

After the chart is in the worksheet in Excel, you can enlarge or shrink it by dragging the chart's sizing handles.

Linking the Chart in Word

You use the same procedure to link an Excel chart as you do to link an Excel spreadsheet. The contents of the linked chart depend on the numbers in the Excel worksheet. When the numbers change in the worksheet, the chart is updated in Excel, and the linked chart in Word reflects the update.

Follow these steps to link the chart into Word:

1. Click on the chart to be linked. The sizing handles appear around the chart object.

2. Choose Edit ➤ Copy from the menu or click the copy button on the Standard toolbar.

3. Switch to Word. Position the insertion point in the master file where the chart should be located.

4. Choose Edit ➤ Paste Special from the menu bar. The Paste Special dialog box appears.

5. Click the Paste Link radio button. The Microsoft Excel Chart Object is the source. Figure 13.11 shows the dialog box at this point. Click OK. The chart is inserted and linked into the Word master file.

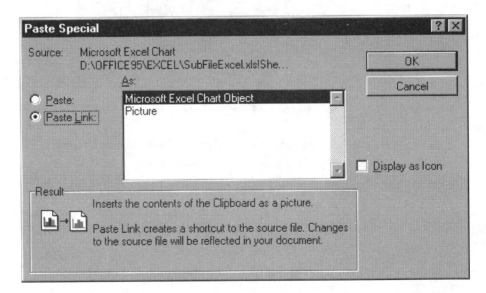

Figure 13.11   The Paste Special dialog box shows the type of data that has been copied into memory.

You can size the chart object while it is in Word using the standard techniques. When you double-click on the chart in the Word document, you are launched directly into the Excel worksheet that contains the original chart.

Using a PowerPoint Slide as a Cover Page

In our scenario, during the initial presentation to the bank, the company executives were shown a PowerPoint slide show demonstrating our approach to the network installation. Shawn wants to create a new slide as the basis for the cover page of the actual proposal. The template design for the slide, however, should be the same as the one used in the original presentation.

Shawn also wants the PowerPoint slide to use a copy of text that was originally in a Word proposal designed for another client. This is a simple process of dragging and dropping. The slide will then be ready to be inserted in the master file for its cover page.

In the following sections, we will create a simple PowerPoint slide, give it a template design, and then drag-and-drop text from Word to Power-Point. Finally, we will insert and link the PowerPoint slide into the Word proposal as the cover page.

Designing a PowerPoint Slide

We first need to create the PowerPoint slide to use as a cover page. Follow these steps:

1. Launch PowerPoint using the Start button on the Taskbar.

2. When the Tip of the Day appears, click the OK button.

3. When the PowerPoint dialog box appears, click the Blank Presentation radio button, and then click OK.

4. In the New Slide dialog box, click the first slide format, Title Slide. Then click OK. You will see a window with a blank PowerPoint slide, as shown in Figure 13.12. We now need a template design so that the slide isn't so bare.

5. To use a template design, either apply one from a previously created presentation or apply a predesigned template sample supplied by Microsoft.

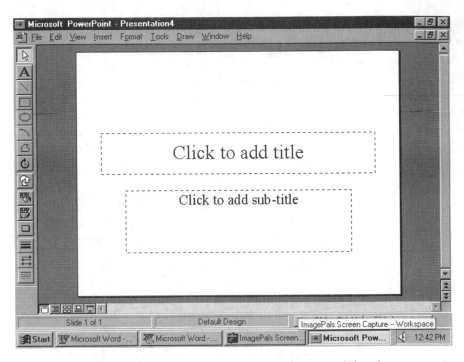

Figure 13.12 **A blank title slide shows the areas into which you can click and type your text.**

- To apply a template design from an existing presentation, choose Format ➤ Apply Design Template from the menu bar. Select the name of the existing presentation and click the Apply button on the right side of the dialog box. PowerPoint will copy the template design of the existing presentation to your new slide.

- To choose a predefined template design, choose Format ➤ Apply Design Template from the menu bar. If the Presentations folder is not opened automatically, look for it under the MSOFFICE\Templates folder. You can preview the different types of template designs available. When you find the template design you want to use, select it and click the Apply button on the right side of the dialog box.

6. Click into the add title text area and type a title for the slide.

7. Click into the add subtitle text area to select the text box. This is the area into which you are going to drag-and-drop text from the Word program. Leave the insertion point here at this spot.

Dragging and Dropping Text from Word to PowerPoint

Our goal is to copy the text from Word into the PowerPoint slide to create the text for the new slide. As you've learned, there are various methods for copying and pasting items from one application to another, such as copying and pasting text through the Clipboard. Dragging and dropping text, data, or objects is another method of transferring items into another application. And it has the advantage of being a one-step process.

1. Start the Word program and open the document that contains the text that is to be dragged and dropped into PowerPoint.

2. PowerPoint and Word should be the only windows open (or not minimized). Right-click on an empty area of the Taskbar and choose Tile Vertically from the shortcut menu. The PowerPoint and Word windows should now be side by side, taking up equal amounts of screen real estate.

3. Click the title bar of the Word document to make it the active window.

4. Select the text in Word that you want to copy.

5. Hold down the Ctrl key while you drag the selected text across the window boundary onto the PowerPoint slide. Drop the text into the subtitle text box area. Holding the Ctrl key makes the drag-and-drop a copy operation, leaving the original text instead of cutting it out. Figure 13.13 shows the Word text copied to the PowerPoint slide.

NOTE   If you cannot get the drag-and-drop operation to work correctly, use the traditional copy and paste method. Select the text in Word, and then press Ctrl+C or click the copy button on Word's Standard toolbar. Switch to PowerPoint by clicking on its title bar. Click into the text area to receive the Word text. Press Ctrl+V or click the paste button on the PowerPoint Standard toolbar.

6. The PowerPoint window is now the active window. Choose File ➤ Save from the menu bar and type a new name for the presentation. We will insert and link this file into the Word master file.

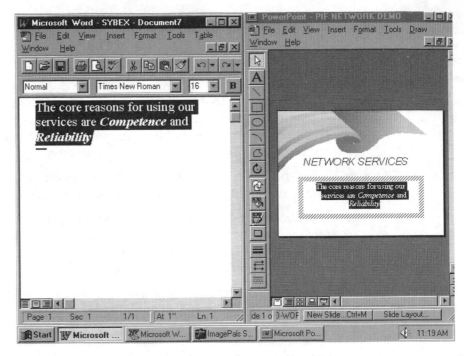

Figure 13.13 *You can easily restore and size the different applications so that dragging and dropping between applications is seamless.*

Inserting and Linking a PowerPoint Presentation into Word

You can insert and link an entire PowerPoint presentation as an object in a Word document. If you insert and link an entire presentation, the PowerPoint Viewer becomes part of the inserted presentation so you can view the entire presentation.

To link a PowerPoint presentation, follow these steps:

1. Open the MasterFile example or any other Word document.

2. Choose Insert ➤ Object from Word's menu bar.

3. Click the Create from File tab at the top of the dialog box.

4. Click the Link to File checkbox on the right side of the dialog box.

5. Type in the name of the file or click the Browse button to look for the file. Once you find the PowerPoint file, click on it, and then click the OK button. You will be returned to the Object dialog box.

6. In the Object dialog box, the name of the PowerPoint file will appear. Click the OK button. It will take a couple of seconds for the presentation to be inserted and linked into the Word document, with the first slide in the presentation showing.

Because the file is linked, you can make changes to the slide in Power-Point, and the changes will be updated and reflected in your Word document. If you double-click on the PowerPoint slide, the actual PowerPoint presentation begins. Microsoft uses the PowerPoint Viewer to make it possible to view an actual slide show while you are in a different program.

NOTE   The method described here shows the first slide in a presentation in your document. If you want a slide other than the first one to appear in your Word document, switch to Slide Sorter view in PowerPoint, click on the slide that you want to link, and select Edit ➤ Copy. When you switch to Word, select Edit ➤ Paste Special and choose to Paste Link the Slide object. Double-clicking on an individual slide linked this way does not start the PowerPoint Viewer; instead, it opens the presentation file that holds the slide and allows you to edit it.

The proposal is now complete. The cover page is a PowerPoint slide, and the proposal sections are inserted and linked Word files from multiple authors. Excel worksheet data and an Excel chart are also linked as objects. Shawn can now work on the original copies of each of the inserted files, and the master proposal file will always reflect the current changes.

Adding headers with identifying information and footers with page numbers completes the proposal design. Figure 13.14 shows the proposal in Word's Print Preview screen.

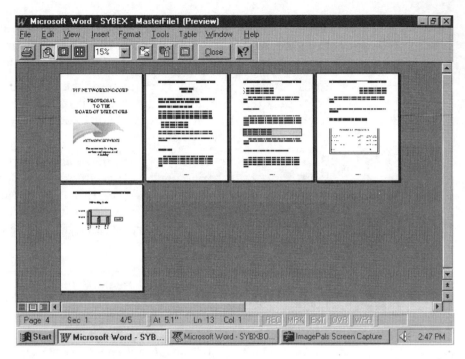

Figure 13.14   The Print Preview's multiple-page view allows you to see the layout of our proposal.

In this final chapter in the Word section, we created a proposal by inserting and linking files created in three different Microsoft Office applications: Word, Excel, and PowerPoint. In the next chapters, we move on to explore the features of Excel.

Business Processing: Analyzing with Excel

This part delves into the creation of Excel financial workbooks,

which allow you to use mathematical expressions and formulas to

generate answers from raw data. Also explored are the

analyzing, charting, and mapping of your numbers. Other

chapters in this part teach you how to use Excel's powerful list

and database features to sort, subtotal, and filter the data.

The integration chapter of this part takes a growing Word table,

imports it into Excel for list management, and uses forms and

reports while linking the information to Access.

Chapter 14
The Road Map

FEATURING

I f you are eager to get a feel for what Excel can do for you, this is the chapter for you. For in-depth coverage of specific Excel features, check out the subsequent Excel chapters.

Overview of Excel

Imagine you have a large workbook on your desk, stacked full of accounting spreadsheets. In Microsoft Excel you have this workbook in electronic form. The stack arrangement gives you the advantage of a 3-D work area. For example, in addition to adding numbers across or down a worksheet, you can "drill down" through a stack of worksheets to work with their numbers as well.

In addition to supplying you with the functions and tools that make moving your numbers to the computer a pleasure, Excel also supplies tools you can use to store, analyze, and manipulate entire *databases* of information. If the databases that you are storing grow beyond the capacity of Excel, tools are available in Excel to convert your data into a Microsoft Access database. (Access is a full-fledged database management program that is part of the Professional version of Microsoft Office. It is the subject of Part Six in this book.)

No matter how much of its functionality you plan to exploit, Excel will prove to be an invaluable member of your Office team.

Jump-Start into Excel

This jump-start chapter will allow you to get started with some of Excel's basic functions. If you just want to get your feet wet, this is the way to go. If you find a feature here you find of particular interest, turn to the following chapters for more information.

Starting Excel

To start Excel, you can use the Start button on the Task Bar.

1. Click the Start button on the Windows 95 Taskbar at the bottom of the screen.

2. Highlight the Programs item. The Program menu will open.

3. Select Excel from the list of programs, as shown in Figure 14.1.

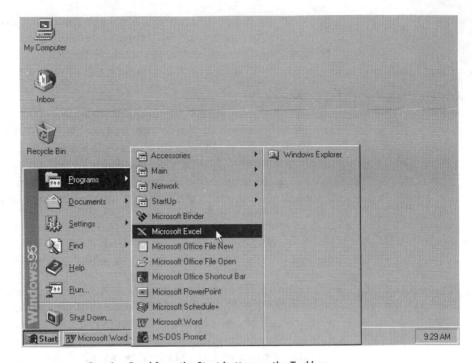

Figure 14.1 **Starting Excel from the Start button on the Taskbar**

Starting a New Workbook

Excel opens with an unused workbook entitled **Book 1**. The view is of Sheet 1 with the cell A1 active and ready to receive your entry. (See Figure 14.2)

If you are already in Excel, you can select File ➤ New to start a new workbook.

▶ The workbook opens by default with a stack of 16 worksheets. The sheet name tabs are visible at the bottom edge of the Excel window. Though you can't see them all in one screen, each worksheet consists of 256 columns listed in alphabetical order and 16,384 rows listed by number.

▶ It is a good idea to browse the areas of this window to get a feel for those buttons along the top of your screen. Although the pictures on the buttons are helpful, it isn't always easy to grasp a button's purpose by its picture alone. If you move your pointer to any button on a toolbar and simply let it rest there, the name of the button will appear (Figure 14.3).

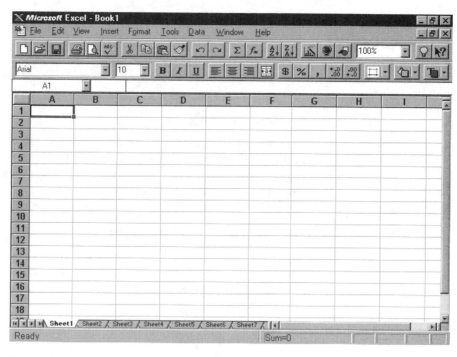

Figure 14.2 **The opening view of Excel**

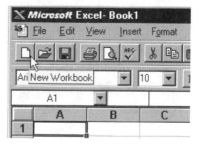

Figure 14.3 **As with the other Office programs, holding your pointer over a toolbar button will cause the name of the button to appear alongside it.**

Saving Your Workbook

Even though you have a brand new workbook open, it is a good idea to go ahead and save it. Save your work regularly! This falls under the "better safe than sorry" rule. It is very frustrating to lose your most recent work due to sudden power failures or system shutdowns. To guard

Part
3

Analyzing with Excel

against the most heinous of disasters it is a good idea to get in the habit of saving your work often.

▶ To save your work, select File ➤ Save from the Excel menu bar. The Save As dialog box (Figure 14.4) will open.

▶ Type a name for your workbook. The name can be a maximum of 255 characters (including spaces).

▶ Don't expect to be prompted for a name every time you save a workbook. Excel only asks for the name of a workbook the first time you save it. To change the name (or any of the other options it was initially saved with) you need to select File ➤ Save As.

Entering and Editing Data

In Excel, you have to press the Enter key on your keyboard to accept the data before you do anything with it (such as format the data or perform a calculation). You can click on the Confirm button (the checkmark button) on the formula bar to accept your entry as well. Should you choose not to accept your entry, you can click on the Cancel button (the ×) in the formula bar (Figure 14.5).

Listed below are some methods of editing your cell entries.

▶ To correct your typos as you make them, use the **Backspace** key. Each press of the Backspace key will erase the character to the immediate left of the cursor.

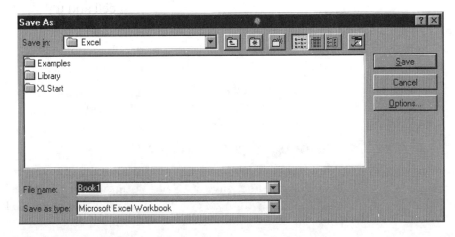

Figure 14.4   The File ➤ Save As dialog box

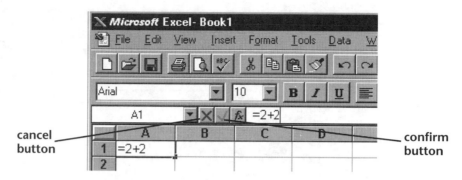

cancel button

confirm button

Figure 14.5 *The formula bar, showing the Cancel and Confirm buttons*

▶ To clear a cell already containing an entry, click on the cell you wish to clear, and then press the **Delete** key or the **Backspace** key and the active cell will clear.

▶ You can replace a cell entry by selecting the cell and simply typing in your new information to be located there. If you accept the new information, by pressing **Enter** or clicking on the Confirm button (Figure 14.5), the new entry replaces the original entry. If you reject the new information, by pressing the **Esc** key or clicking on the Cancel button (×) on the formula bar, the original entry remains.

To delete entries in a range of cells, use the following steps.

1. Click on the top left hand cell of the range you want to delete. Move your pointer to the center of that cell and it will change into a large white plus sign.

2. Click on the cell and, while holding down the primary mouse button, drag it across to highlight the entire range you wish to delete, as illustrated in Figure 14.6.

3. Once highlighted, release the mouse and press the **Delete** button.

Formulas

To do any type of calculation in Excel you need to provide a formula. You can enter the formula on the formula bar or within the active cell itself. Basic editing rules still apply. Formulas require that the entry begin with an equals sign (=) so Excel will know that an expression that needs

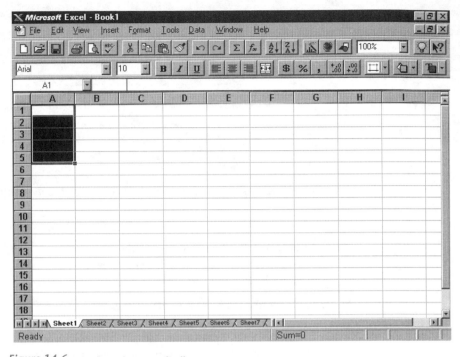

Figure 14.6   *A selected range of cells*

to be *evaluated* is about to be entered. To get you started let's try an example that introduces the AutoSum button.

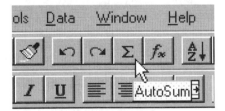

1. In cells A1 through A4 (represented as **A1:A4**), enter numbers **1** through **4** (that is, **1** in A1, **2** in A2, **3** in A3, and **4** in A4).

2. Select cell A5.

3. Click on the AutoSum button, on the Standard toolbar.

4. Notice that the formula in Figure 14.7 appears. The formula that is automatically entered when you clicked on the AutoSum button uses

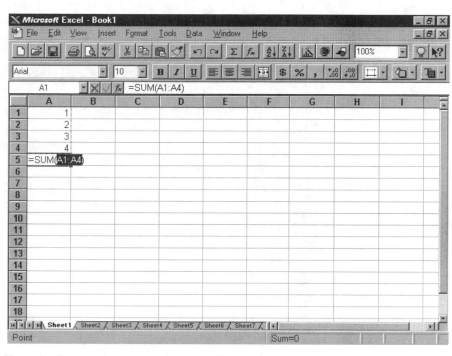

Figure 14.7 *A SUM formula appears in the formula bar when you click on the AutoSum button.*

the Excel's SUM function to total the values from all the cells above the current one (cell A5).

5. Press Enter to accept the proposed action. The sum of values in the cell range A1:A4 will appear in cell A5, as it does in Figure 14.8.

Should you need assistance in choosing a function for your formula, click on the Function Wizard button, directly to the right of the Confirm and Cancel buttons on the Standard toolbar. It will take you through the steps of creating a formula while showing you the proper syntax as well as the resulting value for your active cell.

If you have a long series of values that you would like to quickly sum, simply highlight the range and, by default, the sum appears automatically in the *AutoCalculate area* of the Status bar at the bottom of the Excel screen, as shown in Figure 14.9.

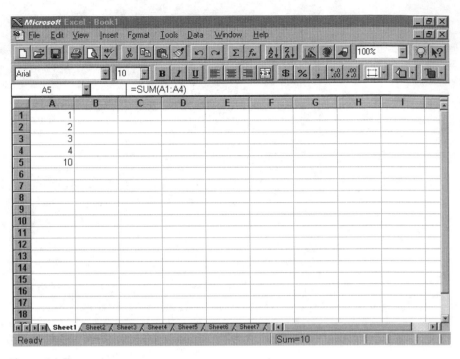

Figure 14.8   *The resulting entry appears in the selected cell (A5) when you press Enter.*

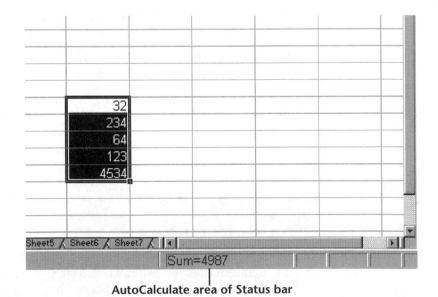

AutoCalculate area of Status bar

Figure 14.9   *By default, the AutoCalculate area of Excel's Status bar shows the sum of any range you highlight.*

You can change the default operation carried out by this automatic calculating feature by clicking in the AutoCalculate area with your right mouse button (leaving the range of data highlighted) and choosing the function you want from the AutoCalculate shortcut menu that pops up. From that time onward, whenever you highlight a range Excel automatically calculates and displays the result.

Formatting Your Work

After you have edited your data, you will want to *format* it—by arranging it consistently or by otherwise changing its looks. For example, throughout your worksheet, you can group cell entries that are of similar types by formatting them similarly. You may also want to add descriptive titles for certain rows or columns or even for individual cells. To quickly introduce you to Excel's formatting capabilities, we will first look at the formatting options on the Formatting toolbar. If this toolbar is not on your screen, go to the menu bar and select View ➤ Toolbars. Verify that the checkbox next to Formatting in the Toolbars dialog box is checked, and then click on OK.

 NOTE To format the contents of a cell, first activate the cell by moving your pointer to that cell and clicking on it.

▶ Reading from left to right, the first two items on the Formatting toolbar are drop-down combo boxes. They display the name of the current font and font size, respectively, and allow you to change them by clicking on the down-arrow buttons next to them to drop down a list of choices.

▶ The next group of buttons are the Bold, Italicize, and Underline buttons.

▶ They are followed by a group of four buttons for aligning the cell's data entries. In order, these are the buttons for Left Alignment, Center Alignment, Right Alignment, and Center Across Columns. The Center Across Columns button is a handy tool for making a title or heading that spans multiple columns. Figure 14.10 shows an example of centering text across columns.

▶ The next group of buttons are number style buttons. These are buttons for setting the Currency, Percent, and Comma Styles. The Increase Decimal and Decrease Decimal buttons are also available for formatting the decimal precision of your numbers. Figure 14.11 gives an example of the Currency setting.

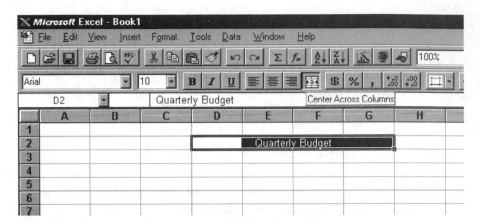

Figure 14.10   *A title in row 2 centered across columns D through G.*

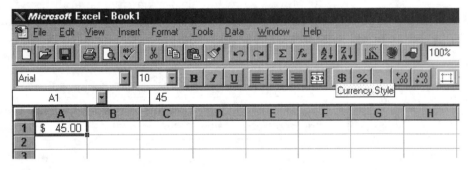

Figure 14.11   *The Currency style applied to the value in cell A1*

▶ The last three buttons on the Formatting toolbar, combining a regular picture-face button with a drop-down list button, are called tear-off palettes. These buttons are the Borders button, the Color button, and the Font Color button. When you click on the picture portion of the button the format shown in that picture will be applied to the contents of the cell selected. You can change the picture displayed on the button by dropping down the tear-off palette. To do this, simply click on the down-arrow button alongside the picture-face button and a sample palette will drop down for you to choose from.

TIP To have a tear-off palette remain displayed for ready availability, activate the palette by clicking on the down arrow portion of the appropriate button. Next click with your pointer on any area within the palette and drag it away from the toolbar, letting go wherever you want it on your worksheet. Now the palette samples are handy for you to quickly redesign your efforts as you create your worksheet.

Copying Formatting from One Cell to Another After you have formatted a cell to your liking and would like to duplicate the formatting without having to repeat all of the steps, you could use the Format Painter button on the Standard toolbar. Using it is quite simple. Select the cell that has the format you want to copy, click on the Format Painter button, and then click on the cell to which you want to copy the format.

Formatting Your Worksheet

To quickly format your worksheet to look like or serve as a table of information, you can use the AutoFormat feature. First highlight the range of data that you want arranged in a tabular format. Next select Format ➤ AutoFormat from Excel's menu bar. A dialog box will open with many tabular formats to choose from and apply.

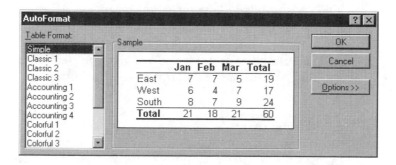

If you enter too many digits to be displayed in a cell, Excel displays the number in scientific notation, or, if even that is too many characters, uses pound signs (number signs, hash marks, tic-tac-toes, whatever you're used to calling them) to signify that there's a wide entry there.

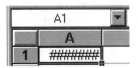

You can widen the column to fit your entry. The following steps show you how to adjust the column quickly.

1. Place your pointer at the top of the worksheet on the right border of the column you wish to adjust (the pointer should be in the same row as the column letter). Your pointer should change to a double-headed arrow.

2. Double-click the mouse, and the column to the left of it will automatically adjust to fit the largest entry in the column. This procedure is called AutoFit.

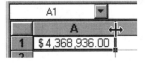

TIP   If you want to adjust the column yourself (to make it even wider or perhaps a little narrower), follow the first step above, but in the second step, instead of double-clicking, click and drag the border to the width you desire.

The double-headed arrow can also quickly adjust row height by following an analogous procedure. Simply place the pointer at the left side of the worksheet, on the bottom border of the row you would like to adjust, and double-click or click and drag to the desired height. (The pointer should be in the same column as the row letters.)

Sorting Your Data

On the Standard toolbar, there are Sort Ascending and Sort Descending buttons for sorting a column of data in your worksheet in ascending or descending order. The Sort tool sorts alphabetically, numerically, and by date.

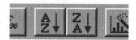

Zoom Control

The Zoom Control on the Standard toolbar is a drop-down box that allows you to adjust the magnification of your work area. To decrease the magnification, and therefore increase the overall view of your worksheet,  you can zoom out to 50% or 25%. To increase the magnification level to make it easier to see and/or view a particular section, you can zoom in at 100% or 200% or move your pointer to the Selection option. You can also type a magnification level directly into the Zoom Control box, up to 400%.

Charting Your Data

It pays to use every means available to you to analyze your data. A graphic representation allows you to quickly perceive an overview of your data more easily than a lot of worksheet numbers allows. One of the best ways of visually representing your worksheet's data is by means of *charts*. To get a jump-start on charting your data you can use the Chart Wizard button on the Standard toolbar. The steps for creating an embedded chart are very simple.

1. Select the range you intend to chart.

2. Click on the Chart Wizard button on the Standard toolbar.

3. The Chart Wizard pointer appears, as shown in Figure 14.12. Move it to an area of the worksheet where you would like to position the chart, and click and drag to create a rectangle signifying the chart's eventual location.

4. When you release the mouse button, the Chart Wizard appears to lead you through the steps to create a variety of charts. In each Step dialog

box, make your choices from the options and instructions, and click on the Next button to proceed to the next Step.

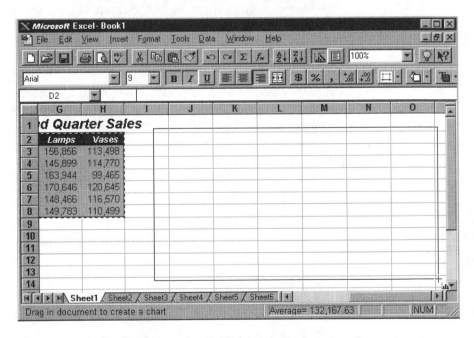

Figure 14.12   Top: The Chart Wizard pointer lets you choose a place to put your chart before formatting it. Bottom: Click and drag to create a rectangle that indicates where the chart will appear

After your chart is embedded you can activate it for editing by double-clicking on it. (An example is shown in Figure 14.13.) Within the activated chart, you can highlight any of the objects to edit. For example, you can delete a series by selecting it and pressing the Delete key on your keyboard. If you want to include a new series of data from your worksheet, you can simply select the data and drag it into the chart.

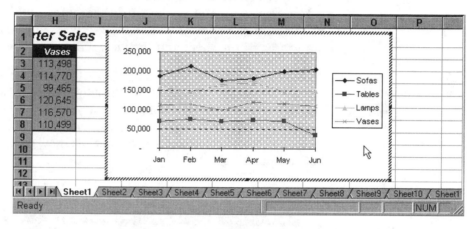

Figure 14.13 **Double-click to activate a chart for editing.**

Previewing and Printing Your Work

Spreadsheets can be tricky to print; therefore, previewing your work is very important. You can make the necessary changes using the Print Preview feature before you send your work to the printer. A little time put into preparing the worksheet for printing saves a lot of paper, not to mention the time it takes to wait for the printer to spit out your creation.

1. Click the Print Preview button on the Standard toolbar.

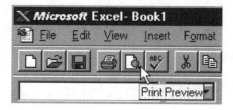

2. Your current worksheet will appear, but not all 16,000-plus rows of it! Excel infers that the area you want to print is the area where you have actually entered data, and will print only that portion of your worksheet. For example, the Print Preview window shown in Figure 14.14 is what Excel displays after selecting Print Preview in the worksheet we dealt with in the preceding discussion.

3. You can see more detail within the Print Preview window by zooming in. Move your pointer to the worksheet page within the Print Preview window, and the pointer will change to a small magnifying glass. Click on any area in the sheet and the view will zoom in on that area.

NOTE When you've zoomed into the Print Preview window and some cells display pound signs, this indicates that you need to widen the columns before printing. Be sure to return to your worksheet and adjust your column widths before printing, or your printout will show the number signs instead of your numbers.

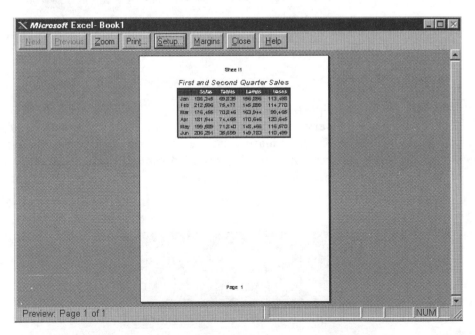

Figure 14.14   *The Print Preview window shows how your worksheet will look on the printed*

4. Within the Print Preview window you can click on the Print button to print your worksheet, or you can click on the Close button to return to your worksheet and make any further modifications.

    If you click on the Setup button in the Print Preview window, you can modify certain aspects of your worksheet page. Should you elect to print your work in Landscape, or horizontal, orientation (see Figure 14.15) instead of the Portrait, vertical, arrangement, select the Page tab in the Page Setup dialog box, and select the Landscape option in the Orientation group box.

    The appearance of the worksheet in Print Preview is a true representation of what will print out. It's a view that may be different from what you see in the Excel application window. This is because Print Preview shows you what your printout will look like when it takes your system's printing specifications into consideration. Small adjustments may be made by Excel to make your worksheet fit proportionally on standard $8\frac{1}{2}''x11''$ paper. These adjustments could compromise the look you intended for your spreadsheet, so be sure to check out Print Preview before printing.

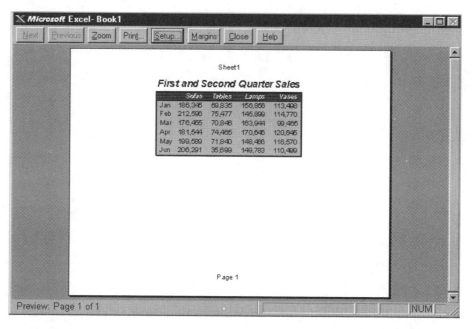

Figure 14.15 *Landscape orientation arranges the worksheet on the page horizontally.*

More Possibilities

The amount of time Excel can save you is immense. There are many enhancements to the latest version that make it a lot easier to keep track of data and calculations. Excel allows you to perform "what if" analysis with ease. Excel can plot trends in your charts as well as in your worksheet. Exploring the following chapters will help you to learn more about how Excel can work for you.

Chapter 15

Data Entry Tips and Tricks

FEATURING

The more comfortable you are with the layout of the workbook and the methods available for data entry, the easier it will be for you to learn the more sophisticated features provided by Excel. This chapter focuses on shoring up your skills in the fundamental areas of data entry and navigation so that the techniques to come in later chapters will come to you rather easily.

The Worksheet

Excel's worksheet is made up of little rectangles, called *cells*. The cells are arranged in columns and rows. The columns are labeled alphabetically; there are 256 of them (A through Z, then AA through AZ, then BA through BZ, then CA through CZ, all the way to IV—almost 10 alphabets' worth of columns). Usually, if the document is zoomed to 100%, you can only see columns A through I at first view. We say "usually" here because it actually depends on your monitor's display type and resolution. Similarly, you can usually see only rows 1 through 16 to begin with, but there are far more than 16 rows in a worksheet. Each worksheet in Excel contains 16,384 rows, numbered 1 through, you guessed it, 16,384.

In referring to the cells in the worksheet, you must identify the letter of the column header plus the number of the row header. This combination of letter and number is called the *cell reference*, or *cell address*. You can view the cell reference for a selected cell or cells in the name box to the left of the formula bar (identified in Figure 15.1).

Selecting Cells and Ranges

To enter data into your worksheet you must first have a cell or range selected. Once you open an Excel worksheet cell A1 is already *active*. Only an activated cell can receive entries, so it is important to learn how to select and thus activate cells and ranges.

Selecting with a Mouse

The simplest way to select a cell is with your mouse pointer. You simply move your mouse to the desired cell and click with your primary mouse button (usually the left button). Figure 15.2 shows cell C4 being selected.

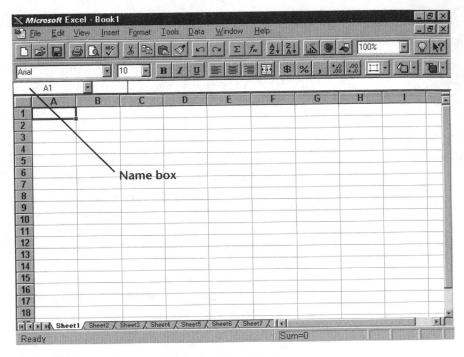

Figure 15.1   *Identifying the selected, or active, cell*

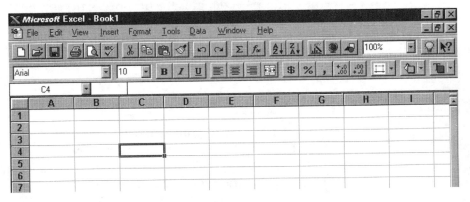

Figure 15.2   *Select a cell by clicking on it with your pointer.*

To select multiple but adjacent cells, click with your mouse on the first cell in the range and hold down the Shift key while you drag the mouse to select the last cell in the range, as in Figure 15.3.

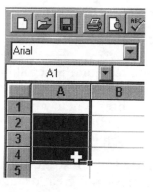

Figure 15.3 *Select a range of cells by holding down the Shift key while you click and drag from the first cell in the range to the last.*

To select multiple *non*-adjacent, or noncontiguous, cells, click with your mouse on the first cell, then hold down the Ctrl key as you select the other cells. Figure 15.4 shows noncontiguous cells being selected.

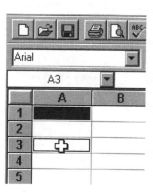

Figure 15.4 *Select non-adjacent cells by holding down the Ctrl key as you click on the cells.*

Navigating with the Keyboard

To move around the worksheet area with your keyboard, you can use the arrow keys and the PgUp and PgDn keys, as well as various key combinations.

Moving around the Worksheet with the Scroll Bars

If you click on the scroll bars, you can advance through your worksheet by rows, with the vertical scroll bar, or by columns, with the horizontal scroll bar. When you click on the scroll bar, a tool tip will appear alongside the bar identifying the row or column your view is advancing to, as is shown in Figure 15.5.

Figure 15.6 illustrates that if you hold down the Shift key as you scroll, you can scroll great distances through your worksheet.

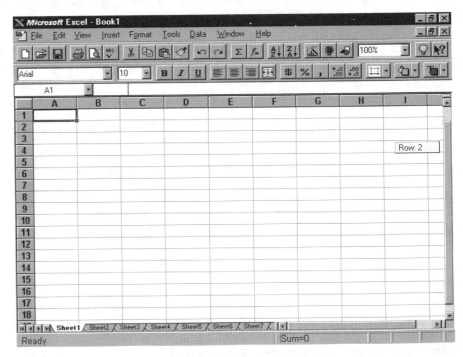

Figure 15.5   Advancing a row at a time by clicking on the scroll bar

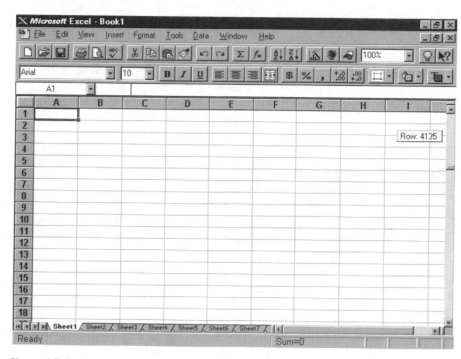

Figure 15.6 Scroll through thousands of rows quickly by holding down the Shift key as you click on the scroll bar.

Data Entry

When a cell is activated, its cell address or cell reference is seen in the name box. The active cell, also called the *current* cell, is highlighted with a border surrounding it. By double-clicking on the cell, the formula bar becomes visible, with a cursor blinking. Although you may be entering characters directly into the cell, your actions are displayed in the formula bar simultaneously.

The buttons in Figure 15.7 appear on the formula bar when any activity is taking place there. The first button is a red ×, which is the reject or *Cancel* button. Clicking it rejects whatever has been entered into the activated cell or range. The second is the accept or *Confirm* button, a green checkmark. Clicking the green checkmark accepts, confirms, or enters whatever is in the formula bar. The last button is the *Function Wizard*—clicking on this button invokes a series of dialog boxes that step you through the process of building a formula.

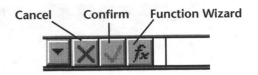

Figure 15.7 *The buttons that appear in an active formula bar*

Entering Numbers

Your numeric entries can be from the entire range of numeric values: whole numbers, decimals, and scientific notation. Excel displays scientific notation automatically if you enter a number that is too long to be viewed in its entirety in a cell. You may also see number signs (######) when a cell entry is too long. If you see number signs, widen the column that contains the cell with number signs to be able to read the number.

Text

You can use numbers, letters, or symbols when you enter text into a cell. Although the text that you enter into a cell may consist of both numbers and other characters, Excel will always consider as text anything it does not recognize as a pure number or date. If you have numbers that you want to be interpreted as text, for example a product ID number, simply begin the number with an apostrophe. This alerts Excel that the entry should be treated as text—or, more to the point, that it shouldn't treat it as a number, which it might automatically add, multiply, divide, or otherwise use in a calculation.

Date and Time Entries

When you enter dates and times, Excel converts these entries into serial numbers. The serial numbers are a numeric breakdown of the passage of time since the beginning of the century. Using serial numbers allows Excel to perform calculations with dates and times. The serial numbers are kept in the background however, with Excel displaying the dates and times on the worksheet in whatever format you have selected. For instructions on the various time and date formats within Excel, consult the sections on formatting.

TIP If you are unsure whether Excel accepted your entry as text or numeric, it might help to remember that numbers and dates are by default right-justified within the cell and text is justified to the left. Of course, if you want to change this, you can always change the alignment format of the cell or cells.

Entering Series

When working in Excel, there will be times when you need to enter a series of data. A series may be numbers, dates, or text. You can enter series quickly in Excel with the assistance of the AutoFill handle. Below are examples of the various types of series you can quickly enter with AutoFill.

Filling a Text Series with AutoFill

Follow these steps to use AutoFill to fill in the months of the year across a row:

1. Select cell A1.

2. Type **January**.

3. Move the mouse pointer to the AutoFill handle, the tiny square located at the lower right corner of the cell's border. The pointer turns into a cross hair, as shown in Figure 15.8.

4. Using your mouse with the cross-hair pointer, click and drag the AutoFill handle across the next 11 columns, to column L.

5. Let go of the mouse button. Notice that Excel has entered all the months of the year, as shown in Figure 15.9.

Excel also recognizes abbreviated monthly names, days of the week and their abbreviations, and quarterly names and abbreviations as well, and follows your cue when AutoFilling the rest of the range. For example, if you enter **Qtr 1** and use AutoFill, Excel will enter Qtr 2, Qtr 3, Qtr 4. This series repeats itself in sequence throughout the range you selected. Because this is a common sequence, you can enter **Qtr 2** and drag the AutoFill handle for three more columns and AutoFill will enter Qtr 3, Qtr 4, Qtr 1.

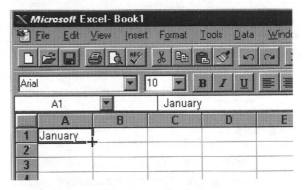

Figure 15.8   *The pointer changes into a cross hair when positioned on the AutoFill handle, located in the lower right corner of the active cell.*

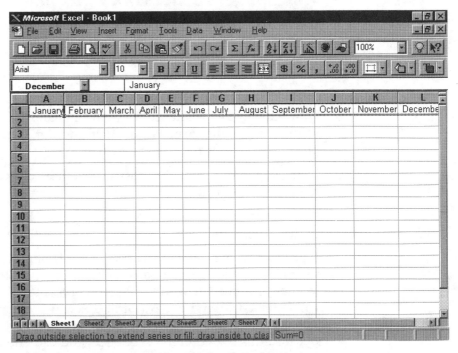

Figure 15.9   *Drag the handle over the range to input the series.*

Filling a Number Series

Excel makes it easy to enter a series of numbers that increment by a specific amount. Below are the steps to enter a number series with a specific increment.

1. Select the first cell in your range and enter the number **5**.

2. In the next cell enter the second number in the series; try **10**.

3. Select the two cells containing the numbers.

4. Click and drag the AutoFill handle at the lower right corner of your selection across a range of cells, as is being done in Figure 15.10 (in the figure, we're extending the range downward).

5. Release the mouse button. Notice how the numbers increase by 5 across the range.

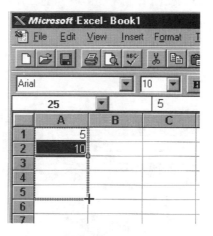

Figure 15.10   Autofill with 5 and 10. AutoFill recognizes this as an increment of 5, and will increment each cell in the rest of the range by 5.

Series of Dates

You can also increment dates across a range just as you incremented numbers. Here is an example.

1. Enter a date in the first cell of the range. Try **1/7/95**.

2. In the second cell enter the second date. Try **1/14/95**.

3. Select the two cells.

4. Click on the AutoFill handle and drag it down two rows.

5. Release the mouse button to get the results in Figure 15.11.

Series: Edit ➤ Fill

For more options to control your series than Autofill allows for, you can use the Edit ➤ Fill ➤ Series command from the menu bar. Edit ➤ Fill has the features of Step Value and Stop Value (Step is the increment amount, and Stop is the value for Excel to stop at), as well as a Trend option that provides best fit lines for linear growth, and geometric curves for growth series. You also have Type options of Linear, Growth, and Date, as well as AutoFill. The steps for using Edit ➤ Fill ➤ Series are as follows:

1. In the first cell of your range, enter your starting value.

2. Select Edit ➤ Fill ➤ Series from the menu bar. The Series dialog box in Figure 15.12 will open.

3. Click on or enter the options for your series.

4. Click on OK to close the dialog box.

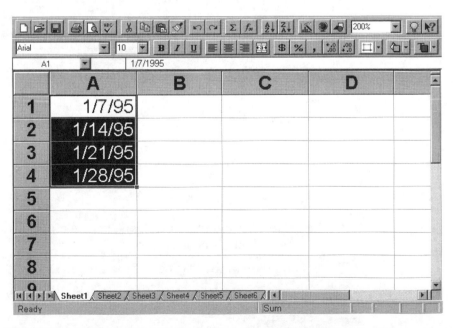

Figure 15.11   *Example of AutoFill date series in one-week increments*

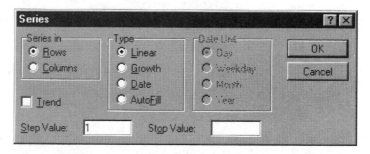

Figure 15.12   The Edit ➤ Fill ➤ Series dialog box

AutoComplete

When Excel's AutoComplete feature is active, Excel automatically completes the letters of any name you type into more than one cell in the same column. All you have to do is enter the first two letters of an entry you typed earlier in the column, and AutoComplete recognizes the entry and finishes entering it for you. Look for more information about AutoComplete in the section on Custom Lists.

Editing Data

Editing your Excel worksheet data is very easy. You can edit your entries in either the formula bar or the cell itself.

To edit a cell, double-click on the cell to activate it for editing. The insertion point will appear in the cell and in the formula bar. The Reject, Confirm, and Function Wizard buttons, as well as the contents of the cell, will appear in the formula bar. You can position the cursor anywhere in the contents of the cell or the formula bar and begin editing the cell contents. Here are two of the simplest ways to edit a cell:

1. If the insertion point cursor does not appear in the cell you want to edit, double-click on the cell.

2. Backspace over characters you want to change—Backspace erases the character to the left of the cursor.

   or

   With your mouse, click and drag within a cell to highlight only the characters you want to change. When you release the mouse button, anything you type will replace the entire highlight.

Clearing the Entire Contents of a Cell

1. Click on the cell you want to clear.

2. Press the Delete key once or the Backspace key once and the cell will clear.

3. Press Enter to accept this action.

    To clear the contents without using the keyboard, try the following.

1. Click with your *secondary* mouse button, usually the right one, on the cell you want to clear. This brings up the shortcut menu for cells.

2. From this shortcut menu, click on Clear Contents. It is not necessary to press Enter or otherwise confirm this action; it's carried out immediately.

Replacing the Contents of a Cell

1. Click on the cell and type your new entry.

2. Press Enter or click on the Confirm button (the green checkmark button on the formula bar) to accept your new entry.

    or

1. Click on the Cancel or Reject button (the red × button on the formula bar) to keep the original entry.

Deleting the Contents of a Range of Cells

1. Click on the first cell of what will be your range.

2. Move your pointer to the center of the cell and it will change into a solid white plus sign.

3. Click again on the cell and, without releasing the mouse button, drag the mouse across the range to highlight all the cells whose contents you want to delete; then release the mouse button.

4. Press the Delete key to delete the contents.

Rearranging Worksheet Data

Excel gives you many tools to copy the data in your work area. The quickest way to copy within a worksheet is with drag-and-drop. For complex copying or copying between worksheets, you will probably need to use the Edit ➤ Copy commands. (However, you can use drag-and-drop to copy between worksheets if both worksheets are open.)

Copying Data with Drag-and-Drop

Drag-and-Drop is the fastest way to copy data in your worksheet.

1. Select a cell to copy.

2. Move your mouse to the border of this cell. It changes to an arrow pointer.

3. Click your left mouse button and hold down the Ctrl key to let Excel know you are copying and not moving. A tiny plus sign will appear next to your pointer letting you know Excel is copying and not moving. Continue holding the Ctrl key for the next step.

4. Drag the pointer across the worksheet to the location you would like to paste the cell contents. Notice in Figure 15.13 that the pointer is dragging an outline that represents the cell you are pasting.

5. Let go of your mouse button and a copy of the cell's contents are pasted to the location you have dropped them into.

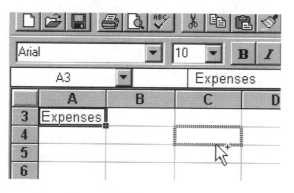

Figure 15.13 **The outline of the copied cell range travels with the pointer while you are dragging-and-dropping.**

Part
3

Analyzing with Excel

Edit ➤ Copy

There are numerous ways to invoke the Edit ➤ Copy command in Excel. The steps below will show you how.

1. Select the cell or cells you want to copy.

2. Select Edit ➤ Copy from the menu bar. Notice the blinking marquee surrounding your copied selection.

    You can also click the Copy button on the Standard toolbar (Figure 15.14),

    or

    Click with your secondary mouse button and, from the shortcut menu it pops up, choose Copy.

3. Select the new cell to paste your copy into.

4. Select Edit ➤ Paste. You can also click on the Paste button on the Standard toolbar, or click with your secondary mouse button and select Paste from the shortcut menu that pops up.

When you use the Edit ➤ Copy command, the information you copy is stored on the Clipboard, and you can paste it as many times as you want—that is, until you press the Enter or Esc key, at which point the marquee disappears from the selection being copied and it can no longer be pasted.

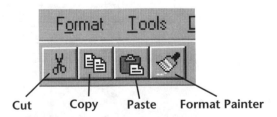

Figure 15.14   **The Editing buttons on the Standard toolbar**

Copying Formatting from One Cell to Another

Among the choices offered in the right-click shortcut menu when you have a cell selected is Format Cells.

1. Click to select a cell that is in a format you would like to use elsewhere.

2. With the cell selected, click on the Format Painter button. Your pointer will show the Format Painter paintbrush alongside it.

3. Click on the cell (or click and drag to select a range of cells)that you want to share the same formatting as the cell you selected in step 1, and release your mouse button.

> **TIP** If you double-click on the Format Painter button in step 2 (that is, after you select the cell whose format you want to copy), you can paste the format several times. If you single-click on the Format Painter button, you can only paste the format once.

Moving Worksheet Data

The steps for moving your data are very similar to those for copying your data. The methods are principally drag-and-drop and the Edit menu.

Moving with Drag-and-Drop

1. Select a cell or range to move.

2. Move your mouse to the border of this cell. It changes to an arrow pointer.

3. Drag the pointer across the worksheet to the location you would like to move the cell's contents. The pointer will drag an outline representing the cell you are pasting.

4. Let go of your mouse button. The cell's contents are pasted to the location you have dropped them into.

Whether you are copying or moving with drag-and-drop you are not limited to pasting within the same worksheet. You can also drag-and-drop into another sheet, as follows.

▶ If the other sheet is in the same workbook, follow the steps above, but in step 3 hold down the Alt key while you drag the pointer to the desired sheet's tab at the bottom of the worksheet (this makes that worksheet the top sheet), then release the Alt key but keep holding the mouse button, so you can continue to drag-and-drop your data anywhere within the intended sheet.

▶ If you have more than one workbook window open *and visible*, you can simply drag-and-drop the data from one window to the other.

Moving with Edit ➤ Cut

1. Select the cell or cells you want to move.

2. Select Edit ➤ Cut from the menu bar. Notice the blinking marquee surrounding your copied selection.

    You can also click the Cut button on the Standard toolbar (Figure 15.15),

    or

    Click with your secondary mouse button and, from the shortcut menu it pops up, choose Cut.

3. Select the new cell to move your data to.

4. Select Edit ➤ Paste. You can also click on the Paste button on the Standard toolbar, or click with your secondary mouse button and select Paste from the shortcut menu that pops up.

    • As far as this last step is concerned, if you selected the Edit ➤ Cut command in step 2, it is not necessary to use Edit ➤ Paste or to click on the Paste button—you can simply select the first cell of the new location and press Enter.

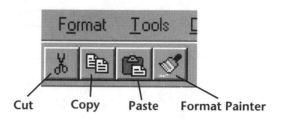

Cut   Copy   Paste   Format Painter

Figure 15.15 *Editing buttons on the Standard toolbar*

Transposing Your Data

You do not always have to paste cells to the same arrangement. You can quickly switch data that is in rows to data in columns by using Excel's transposing feature.

1. Select the range you want to transpose.

2. Copy the range.

3. Select the first cell of the paste area.

4. Click the right mouse button to bring up the shortcut menu.

5. Choose Paste Special from the shortcut menu to open the Paste Special dialog box (Figure 15.16).

6. Select the Transpose checkbox.

7. Click on OK. The row values will transpose to column values. See Figure 15.17 for the final result.

Spell-Checking

Spell-checking allows you to check for spelling errors in your worksheet. To use the spelling checker, select Tools ➤ Spelling from the menu bar, or click on the Spelling button on the Standard toolbar. Excel will check the entire worksheet. If you only want to spell-check a specific range, select that range first and run the spelling checker.

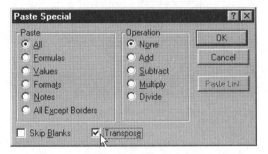

Figure 15.16   Top: Select the first cell for the new range and click the right mouse button, then choose Paste ➤ Special to bring up the Paste ➤ Special dialog box, bottom.

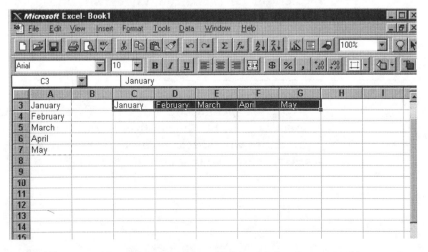

Figure 15.17   The column of cells from Figure 15.16, copied and transposed into a row of cells

Don't worry about the spelling checker performing the corrections in the background, without letting you know; it will prompt you before it makes a change, using a dialog box similar to the one shown in Figure 15.18. The Spelling dialog box gives you the option to change or ignore the spelling error. You may also elect to add it to the dictionary.

Part
3

Analyzing with Excel

Figure 15.18 **The Spelling dialog box**

AutoCorrect

Excel has a new feature for correcting your work, called AutoCorrect. Select Tools ➤ AutoCorrect from the menu bar to see the options available. For more information on AutoCorrect see Chapter 22.

Undo and Redo

The Undo and Repeat buttons allow you to undo and redo your last action.

Finding Data in a Worksheet

Edit ➤ Find allows you to search through your data to find a character or characters entered on your worksheet. Select Edit ➤ Find from the menu bar and the Find dialog box (Figure 15.19) appears. You can specify what you are searching for and elect to replace it or not. You can also search within formulas instead of in values.

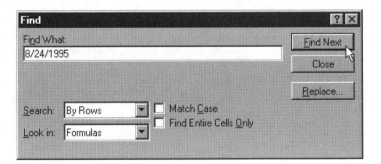

Figure 15.19   **The Find dialog box**

File Close

To close the workbook you are working on, you can select File ➤ Close from the menu bar. You can also close it with the window's close button.

Chapter 16

Crowd Pleasing Worksheets— Formatting

FEATURING

Figure 15.11

You can make your worksheets more exciting in Excel with some of the very features that are available to you in other Office applications.

Formatting Data

In Excel, you can make many different font and format changes. Let's have a look at the Formatting toolbar to see what we can do with it.

Fonts

The first item on the Formatting toolbar is the Font combo box. When you use this box to select a font, by clicking on the box's drop-down arrow, you will see a list of available fonts. If there is a small graphic to the left of the font name on this list, you can get an idea of how well the font will print. If the graphic shows a TT, the font is a TrueType font, which means the font prints with the same appearance it has on the screen, and can easily be scaled larger and smaller. If the graphic shows a printer, the font is a scalable printer-resident font, which means the font on screen might not match the printout's font. If there is no graphic, the font will print with the closest available match.

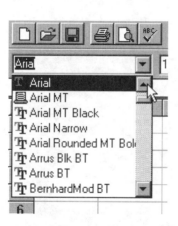

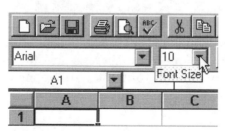

The Font Size box will allow you to change your point size (a measure of the size of your font). The row height automatically adjusts to accommodate your chosen font size.

The Font Style Buttons

Excel allows you to Bold, Italicize, and/or Underline your cell entries. You can apply these formats by following these steps.

1. Select the cell or cell range you want to format.

2. Click on the Bold, Italic, or Underline button on the Formatting toolbar. You can click on more than one button to impose a combination of the chosen formatting.

For even more formatting options you can use the Format Cells dialog box.

1. After selecting the cell or cells that you want formatted, select Format ➤ Cells ➤ Font from the menu bar (or click the secondary mouse button anywhere on your worksheet and select Format Cells).

2. The Format Cells dialog box opens. Click on the Font tab.

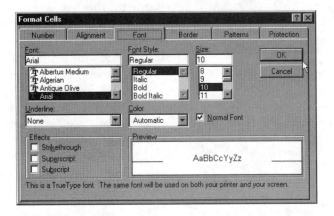

Here you can choose many font changes at once and view the result in the preview window. Notice that there is an Effects option group box that allows you to change your data to Superscript, Subscript, or Strikethrough.

Aligning Data

The next four buttons on the Formatting toolbar are for aligning your entries. By default, number entries are right-aligned in the cell and text entries are left-aligned. To change the alignment of a cell's entries, follow these steps.

1. Select the cell or cell range you want to realign.

2. Click on either of the first three buttons that will align all entries of the cell range according to the chosen button. The entries will all align regardless of whether they are text or numeric.

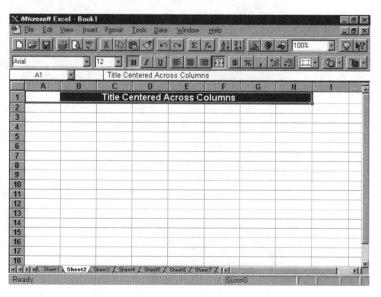

3. To reverse the action, click on the button again and it will return to the default.

    The last of the alignment buttons is the Center Across Columns button. If you are placing a title across a section of your spreadsheet, the Center Across Columns button is a quick way to apply one.

1. In the leftmost cell of the range where you would like your title to appear, type the entire title.

2. Select the range across which you would like the title to appear (starting with the cell into which you placed the title).

3. Click on the Center Across Columns button and you should get a result similar to Figure 16.1.

Part
3

Analyzing with Excel

Figure 16.1 *A title centered across columns.*

In appearance, the entry is entered across several columns. In actuality, the entry is entered in the first cell only, as you can see by looking at the formula bar and the cell address box. To edit the entry, select the first cell of the range and edit either within the formula bar or the first cell itself.

The Alignment dialog box offers you more options than the alignment buttons on the Formatting toolbar. For example, you can format text wrapping in this dialog box. The steps will format the selected cell(s) so that the text inside will wrap to multiple lines if needed.

1.   Select a cell and enter text that is too long to fit in it.

2.   Select Format ➤ Cells from the menu bar and click on the Alignment tab to see the alignment tab page.

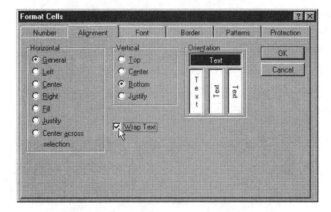

3.   Check the Wrap Text box and click on OK. Your text should now wrap like the text in Figure 16.2.

Number Style Format

The next group of buttons on the Formatting toolbar is used to format numbers. Select the range you would like to format and click on one of the following buttons to apply that style to the numbers.

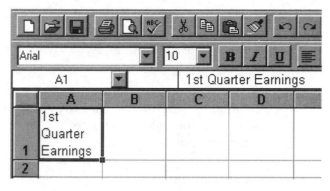

Figure 16.2 **The Wrapped Text option lets the text in this cell wrap to three lines instead of being truncated.**

Button	Purpose
Currency Style	The number will receive a dollar sign, a comma, and a decimal point followed by two number places.
Percentage Style	The number will be formatted as a percentage.
Comma Style	The number will be formatted with a thousands separator and two decimal places.
Increase Decimal	Increases the number of places to the right of the decimal point by one.
Decrease Decimal	Decreases the number of places to the right of the decimal point by one.

Border and Color

The last three buttons on the Formatting toolbar are for adding borders, cell shading, and font color. These buttons are actually *tear-off palettes*. When you click on the picture portion of the button, the format of the picture displayed will be applied to the contents of the cell(s) you have selected in the worksheet. You can change the picture displayed on the button by clicking on the button's small drop-down arrow to see the

Part
3

Analyzing with Excel

palette of samples from which to choose. Once you choose a particular format from the palette, the choice is immediately applied to the selection, the palette box closes, and your most recent choice takes its place as your button's picture.

To have the palette remain open so you can make fast selections of the formats as you work, activate the palette as mentioned before. Next, click and drag the palette away from the toolbar and drop it wherever you want on your worksheet.

Border Styles

The first of the palette buttons is the Borders button. If the border you desire is on the face of the button, simply select the cell range you want to add a border to and click on the Borders button. If you need a different border follow these steps.

1. Click on the drop-down arrow to the right of the Borders button.

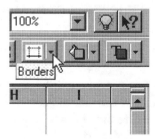

2. The Border palette opens.

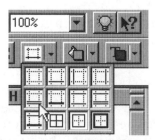

3. Format your selection by clicking on the style of borders you would like. The palette will close and the style you selected will be the picture on the Borders button.

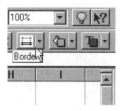

If you prefer to keep the palette open and available as you work, follow these steps.

1. Click on the drop-down arrow to the right of the border picture on the Borders button.

2. The Border palette opens.

3. Instead of selecting a border, in this step click and hold your pointer within the area of the palette and drag it onto your worksheet.

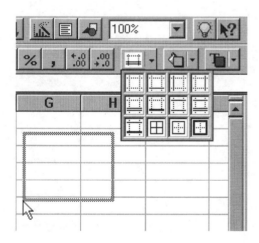

4. The Border palette is now open and available for repeated use. To close the Border palette, click on the Close Window button (Control box).

This same palette opening technique applies to the Color and the Font Color buttons.

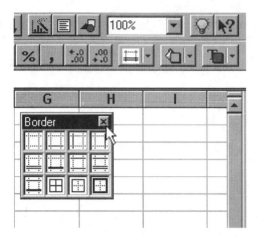

The Border tab of the Format Cells dialog box (select Format ➤ Cells from the menu bar) offers more of a selection for formatting borders, as you can see in Figure 16.3.

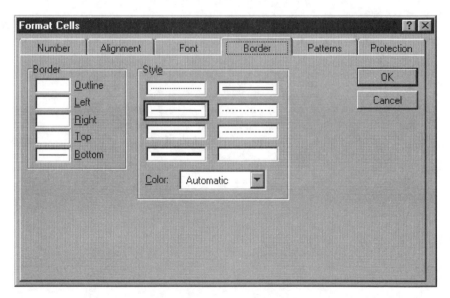

Figure 16.3   *The Border page of the Format Cells dialog box offers more options than the Borders button on the Formatting toolbar.*

Cell Color Shading

The cell shading or Color button is the next button on your Formatting toolbar. It is applied in the same way as the Borders button.

Here is the Color palette you get by clicking on the drop-down arrow.

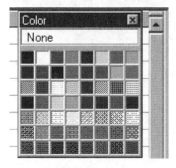

The Format Cells dialog box (select Format ➤ Cells from the menu bar) uses the Patterns tab for cell shading colors as well as for cell shading patterns.

To enhance a cell range with shading and/or patterns using the Format Cells dialog box, follow these steps:

1. Select a range to format.

2. Select Format ➤ Cells from the menu bar. (You can also click the right mouse button and choose Format Cells.) From the Format Cells dialog box, select the Patterns tab, shown in Figure 16.4.

3. Choose a color from the Cell shading box. The Sample box will show an example of your chosen color.

4. Click on the drop-down arrow from the Pattern box and select a pattern. The Sample box will now show the selected pattern in the chosen color.

5. Click on OK.

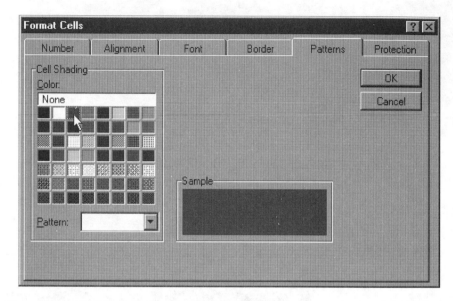

Figure 16.4   *The Patterns page of the Format Cells dialog box lets you choose cell shading colors as well as patterns.*

Font Color

Use the same steps above to use the Font Color button or the Font Color palette.

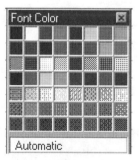

The Font tab of the Format Cells dialog box allows you to select the font color using the color drop-down list box seen in Figure 16.5.

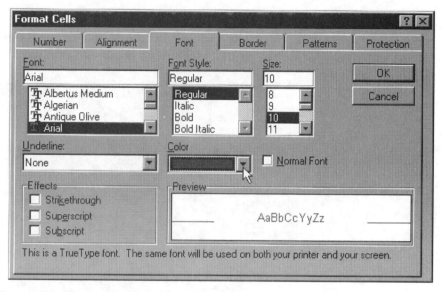

Figure 16.5 *The Font tab of the Format Cells dialog box lets you choose a cell shading color via the Color drop-down list box.*

AutoFormat

To quickly format a table, you can use what is called AutoFormat.

1. First highlight the range of data.

2. Select Format ➤ AutoFormat from the menu bar.

3. The dialog box in Figure 16.6 will open with many tabular formats to choose from and apply.

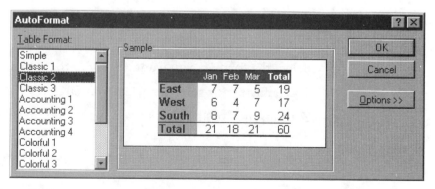

Figure 16.6 *The AutoFormat dialog box*

If you like one of the formats but do not want to apply every aspect of it, click on the Options button to pick the different aspects that you do or don't want to apply to your table (as shown in Figure 16.7).

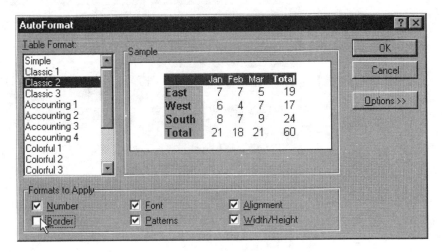

Figure 16.7   The Options button displays different aspects of the format that you can choose to use or not use.

Format Style

Styles allow you to store all of a cell's formatting definitions so that if you want to have a very complicated format available for use in other cells, you can apply it all in one step. If you want to define your own format style:

1. Select a range you want to format.

2. Select Format ➤ Style from the menu bar.

3. Click on Modify.

4. Select the formats you want on any of the tabs in the dialog box.

5. To confirm your selections, click on OK.

6. You can click on the checkboxes to select or deselect the styles they offer to apply.

7. Enter a name for the style in the Style Name box.

8. Click on OK to apply the new style format to the selected range. Clicking on Add and then on Close allows you to define the new style while not applying it immediately.

Formatting Workbooks

The Excel workbook contains 16 worksheets by default. The sheet name tabs are at the bottom of the Excel window. You can view only a few sheet tabs at a time. You can adjust this view by placing your pointer on the tab split bar. When it is positioned exactly on the bar the pointer becomes a double-headed arrow, as shown in Figure 16.8. Drag it to the left or right to view fewer or more sheet tabs. To undo your adjustment, double-click on the tab split bar.

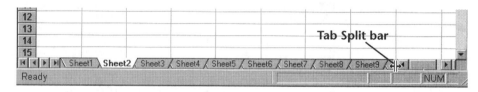

Figure 16.8 Drag the tab split bar to view more sheet tabs.

Arranging Multiple Workbooks or Multiple Windows

If the sheets you need to work on are in different workbooks, follow these steps to see them all.

1. Open the workbooks you need.

2. Once your workbooks are open, select Window ➤ Arrange from the menu bar to open the Arrange Windows dialog box.

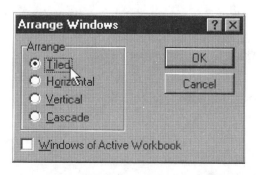

3. Select one of the option buttons in the top part of the dialog box and click on OK. In Figure 16.9, the windows show the result of the Tiled arrangement.

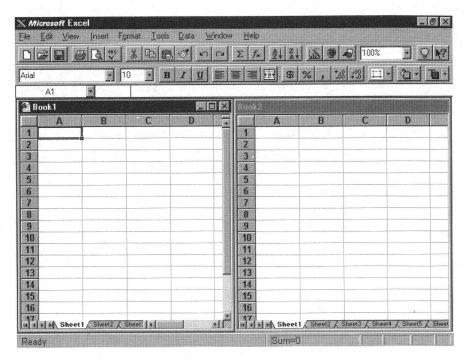

Figure 16.9 **Tiled windows**

To view multiple sheets within the *same* workbook:

1. Select Window ➤ New Window from the menu bar. This opens a new window with the same worksheet in it.

2. Switch to the new window and click on a sheet you want to view.

3. Repeat steps 1 and 2 for each sheet you want to view.

4. Once you have all of the windows opened that you will need, select Window ➤ Arrange from the menu bar.

5. Click on the Windows of Active Workbook checkbox at the bottom of the dialog box and click on OK.

To restore a worksheet or workbook window to full size, click on the Maximize button at the upper right corner of the workbook window (where the pointer is located in Figure 16.9).

Hiding and Unhiding Workbooks, Worksheets, Rows, and Columns

You can hide workbooks, worksheet, rows, and columns to make your view easier to read and to help prevent unwanted changes. For example, you can hide sheets containing macros or critical data. The hidden workbook or sheet remains open, and all sheets in the workbook are available to be referenced from other documents.

To hide a column, follow these steps:

1. Select the column you want to hide by clicking on its column header, as in Figure 16.10.

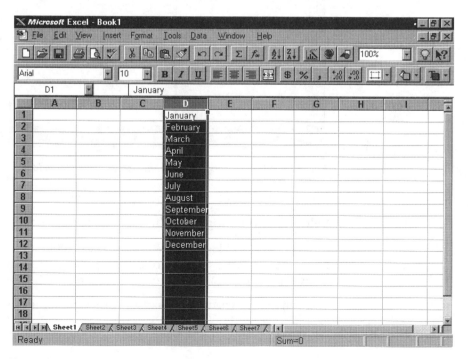

Figure 16.10 *A selected column*

2. Select Format ➤ Column ➤ Hide from the menu bar (or click within the selected column(s) with your secondary mouse button and choose Hide from the shortcut menu that pops up). The column should be hidden, as in Figure 16.11.

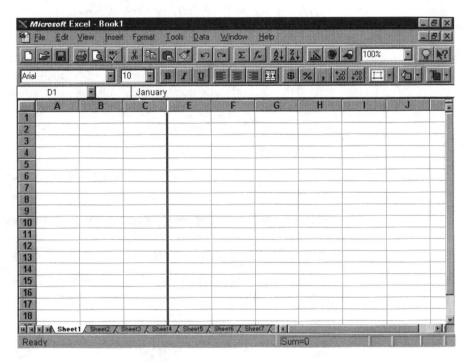

Figure 16.11 **After choosing Hide, the selected column is hidden.**

To unhide the column follow these steps:

1. Select a visible range of columns that includes the hidden column.

2. Select Format ➤ Columns ➤ Unhide from the menu bar (or click within the selection with your secondary mouse button and click on Unhide, as in Figure 16.12). The hidden column should now reappear.

You can follow basically the same procedures for hiding and unhiding rows.

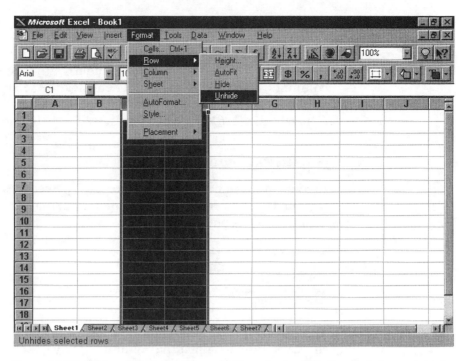

Figure 16.12   Click on Unhide to bring any hidden columns within the selected range into view.

TIP   If you want to unhide all rows or columns on a worksheet, select the whole worksheet by clicking the block at the top left intersection of the row and column headings—in other words, the corner block: just to the left of the column heading for column A and above the header for row 1. Once everything is selected, follow the directions above for unhiding columns and rows.

To hide an active workbook you do not need to select anything, simply select Window ➤ Hide from the menu bar to hide it and Window ➤ Unhide to unhide it.

NOTE   If the workbook window that you hid was the last open window, the Window menu item disappears from the menu bar. The Unhide command will still be available, however; it's on the File menu whenever the Window menu is gone.

Inserting Columns and Rows

To insert a column or row, click on a column or row header to highlight the column to the right or the row underneath where you want the new column(s) or row(s) to appear. Then click the secondary mouse button within the selected area to bring up the shortcut menu, and select Insert. (Or, select Insert ➤ Columns or Rows from the menu bar).

Adjusting Widths

If you enter a number too large to be displayed in a cell, Excel displays the number in scientific notation, or, if even that is too wide to be shown, simply displays pound signs.

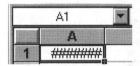

You can widen the column to show all of your entry. The following steps show you how to adjust the column quickly.

1. Place your pointer at the top right border of the column header of the column you wish to adjust. In this area your pointer changes to a double-headed arrow.

2. Double-click your pointer, and the column to the left of it will automatically adjust to fit the data entries within it. This procedure is called AutoFit.

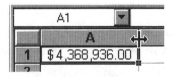

If you want to adjust the column quickly without using AutoFit, follow the first step above, and instead of double-clicking in the second step, click and drag the border to the new width you desire.

The double-headed arrow can also adjust row height quickly, by following the same procedures listed above for adjusting column widths. The only difference is that you place the pointer on the bottom border of the row you would like to adjust.

You can also adjust columns and rows very precisely with the Format command on the menu bar. To adjust column widths:

1. Make sure that you have activated a cell or a range in the column you want to adjust.

2. Select Format ➤ Column ➤ Width from the menu bar.

3. Type a width, measured in characters, in the Column Width box and click on OK. The range is 1 to 255 characters.

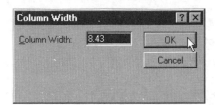

Copying and Moving Sheets

The easiest and quickest way to move or copy a worksheet is to use the sheet's shortcut menu, by following these steps.

1. Activate the sheet to copy by clicking on its sheet tab.

2. Click with your mouse's secondary button on the sheet tab to reveal the sheet's shortcut menu.

3. Choose Move or Copy from the shortcut menu.

4. In the Move or Copy dialog box, select a destination. The *To Book* drop-down box has the names of workbook destinations for the sheet to be moved or copied to.

5. When you select the workbook destination, the sheets of that book are displayed in the *Before Sheet* list box. This confusing title merely means, "The sheet has to go somewhere in the destination workbook; where do you want it? That is, in front of which sheet?" Select where you want to place the sheet.

6. If you're *copying* the worksheet, select the Create a Copy checkbox, and click on OK. Otherwise, if you're *moving* the worksheet, just click on OK.

To move or copy sheets using the menu bar, select Edit ➤ Move or Copy from the menu bar. This brings up the same dialog box you opened by right-clicking on the sheet tab.

TIP Another way to copy a sheet quickly is to hold down the Ctrl key while you click and drag the sheet tab to another location in your workbook. This is useful only when you can see the destination location to begin with, but don't forget that you can have multiple windows open for this very purpose.

Inserting Worksheets

Inserting is different from copying or moving an existing sheet: inserting means inserting a brand new sheet. When you insert a sheet, it is placed before the current active sheet. Here's how it's done:

1. Select Insert ➤ Worksheet from the menu bar, or select Insert from the sheet's shortcut menu (brought up by right-clicking on the sheet's tab).

2. If you used the shortcut menu, the Insert dialog box in Figure 16.13 appears. If the General tab page isn't displayed, click on it to bring it forward. Then click on the Worksheet item in the icons box, and click on OK.

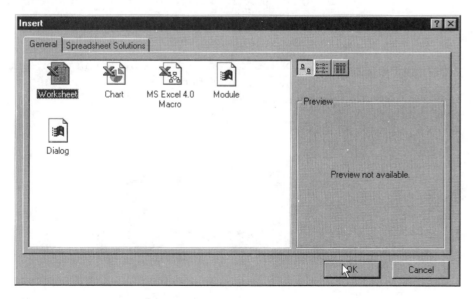

Figure 16.13 *The Insert dialog box lets you choose from a variety of objects to insert.*

Deleting Sheets from a Workbook

Worksheets may need to be deleted if the information on the sheet is no longer needed or is erroneous enough to warrant starting over on a new sheet. You may also simply want to remove unused worksheets that were added by default when you created the workbook.

To delete a sheet, select the sheet(s) you want to delete and select Edit ► Delete Sheet from the menu bar.

To delete a sheet with the sheet's shortcut menu, click on the sheet tab with the secondary button and select the Delete command, then click on OK.

Renaming Sheets

Probably the most important thing you can do to immediately make your worksheets useful, beyond naming your rows and columns, is to name your worksheets. (Of course, if you'd rather, you can keep the default names of Sheet1, Sheet2, Sheet3, etc.) To rename the sheet tabs:

1. Double-click on the sheet tab with your primary mouse button. The Rename Sheet dialog box.

2. In the Name text box, type the name you want, up to 31 characters and choose OK. Remember, you can't use the following characters in the worksheet name:

/ \ ? : and *

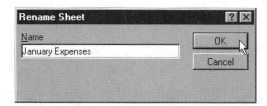

3. After clicking on OK you should have a renamed sheet tab like the one shown here:

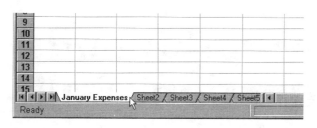

Chapter 17

Formulas and Functions Built to Last

FEATURING

The real power in using a spreadsheet lies in specifying the mathematical relationship between the numbers in various cells. You do this by means of a *formula*. In Excel you literally type in these relationships, or point out to Excel the relationships necessary to formulate an answer. An example of a simple formula would be "Hours Worked" multiplied by "Rate of Pay" equals "Dollar Compensation" or "Check" to be paid to workers. The exact values would vary depending upon the situation, but the formula would be the same for calculating base pay for any hourly workers.

Creating a Simple Formula

Suppose you are making $40,000 a year in salary and in a company announcement you have just heard that there will be a 10% increase across the board, for all employees. You would certainly want to know how that 10% translated into dollars. If you were handed a calculator, you would carry out the calculation in seconds if not in milliseconds, because you're probably able to do the mathematics for this one in your head. The answer is, of course, $4,000. How was this derived? All of us have learned the business math formula of multiplying a base salary by the percentage of increase in order to obtain the dollar amount of the increase. Therefore, the formula would be represented in words as: **Base Salary * Percentage of Increase**. (The asterisk represents the multiplication operation on computers.)

To represent such a formula in Excel you would first type an equals sign and then reference the cell address of the Base Salary, type the asterisk to represent multiplication, and then reference the cell address of the Percentage of Increase. Follow these steps:

1. Type **40,000**, the amount of the base salary, in cell A5.

2. In cell B5, type **10%**, the percentage amount of the increase.

3. In cell C5 click on the pointer so that Excel will know that the answer should appear in this cell. Begin the formula with a special signal: an equals sign (=). By using this sign you are telling Excel that you are starting a formula and not a simple calculation. You are now ready to represent the business formula stated above by showing (referencing) the locations (cells) that contain the numbers and typing the mathematical operators.

4. After typing the equals sign, click on the cell that contains the 40,000 base salary.

5. Press the asterisk key on the keyboard to declare that multiplication is the mathematical operator.

6. Click on the cell that contains the 10%, the percent of increase. The formula bar at the top of the screen displays the cell references and the asterisk.

7. Click on the green checkmark next to the formula bar or press the Enter key on the keyboard. The cell displays the answer to this simple business formula and the formula bar displays the cell references and mathematics that were involved in producing the answer.

	A	B	C	D
			=A5*B5	
1				
2				
3				
4				
5	$40,000.00	10%	$4,000.00	
6				
7				
8				
9				
10				
11				
12				
13				
14				

Once you have entered a formula, you can change, delete, type over, format, align, copy, move, protect, print, find, name, "goto," or place a note on the formula.

NOTE If you are a Lotus user and are used to beginning all formulas with a plus sign, you can continue to use the plus sign to start a formula. Excel will translate the plus sign to an equals sign. But Lotus users must always remember to start even simple calculations with either a plus sign or an equals sign. Excel needs the sign for all calculations, not just formulas.

Mathematical Operators

An *operator* is a special symbol that tells a program what action to take on a series of numbers. The mathematical operators to Add, Subtract, Multiply, and Divide are the cornerstones of our most basic means of quantifying information. We learn these operators early, as children.

All computer programs use a common set of symbols to represent these four mathematical operators. Table 17.1 lists the four basic mathematical operators.

Operator Symbol	Meaning
+ (Plus sign)	Addition
– (Minus sign or hyphen)	Subtraction
* (Asterisk)	Multiplication
/ (Slash)	Division

Table 17.1   *Mathematic Operators and Their Meanings*

TIP   To enter numbers and operators, get in the habit of using the keys on the numeric keypad to the far right side of the keyboard—it will greatly increase your data entry speed. (Laptop and notebook computers may not have this extra keypad, though it can be purchased as optional equipment for many models.)

TIP   To quickly sum a column or row of numbers, click in a cell below (for a column) or to the right (for a row) of the numbers, then double-click on the AutoSum button on Excel's Standard toolbar.

Exponentiation and Percentage Operators

Although the mathematical operators of Add, Subtract, Multiply, and Divide are the most common operators, there are other operators represented by special symbols.

Part
3

Analyzing with Excel

The exponentiation symbol is the ^ (caret or circumflex) character, the character above the number 6 on the standard keyboard. When Excel encounters this symbol, it is programmed to multiply the number to the left of the exponentiation symbol by the power indicated to the right of the symbol. For example, 2^3 means 2 raised to the 3rd power, which is the same as entering 2*2*2.

Which Operator Takes Precedence over Another?

In Excel you can enter up to 255 characters in a single cell. This amount will allow for multiple operators and numbers to be used in a calculation or a formula. The calculation capabilities of Excel are like those of a physical calculator. Begin with an equals sign and enter up to 255 numbers and operators. When you press the Enter key, there will be one answer.

The *order* in which you enter your mathematical operators, however, will produce different answers even while using identical numbers and operators. All spreadsheet programs perform mathematical operations in a specific order. This order of operations is called *precedence*. Excel gives precedence to certain operations over others.

When Excel encounters more than one operator in a formula or calculation, the rule that is applied is this: Perform any Exponentiation first, then Multiply and Divide numbers before Adding and Subtracting the numbers (the MDAS system). Because the four core mathematical operators are the most common, let's create an example of precedence using only mathematical operators without exponentiation. Look at the graphic below and try to determine the correct answer before reading further.

The correct answer according to the precedence rules used by Excel is −2. When Excel encounters more than one mathematical operator in a formula or calculation in a cell, multiplication and division are performed before addition and subtraction. In our small example, Excel skipped right past the subtraction and went straight for the multiplication, multiplying 2*4. The answer to that part of the formula is 8. Then it went back and performed the subtraction operation: 6−8=−2. If Excel had not followed this order of precedence, it would have come up with a different answer, 16, by performing the subtraction first (6−2=4) and then multiplying that by the following number (4*4=16).

Changing the Order of Operations

To change the natural order of operations, use parentheses. In the example in the previous paragraph, to force an answer of 16 for the calculation of =6−2*4 you must change the default order of operations. Surround with parentheses the particular mathematical relationship that you want performed first. Excel will change its order of operations to perform the math within the parentheses. If you must use multiple sets of parentheses, Excel calculates the innermost pair first, then moves out through each subsequent set.

Look again at the graphic with its new answer now that parentheses have been placed around the subtraction relationship (next page).

	A	B	C	D	E	F
1						
2						
3						
4		=(6-2)*4				
5						
6		16				
7						
8						
9						
10						
11						
12						
13						

Logical or Comparison Operators

Comparison operators are used to compare one value to the other. The reason why these operators are also called *logical* operators is that the resultant answer in the cell is either the word TRUE or the word FALSE. If you use the following calculation using the comparison operator of > (Greater Than) the resultant answer will be FALSE: =4>5. The comparison operator has posed a question to Excel: "Is 4 greater than 5?". The answer from Excel is FALSE, or NO. Change the comparison operator to < (Less Than) and the answer from Excel is TRUE, or YES: =4<5. When any of the comparison operators are used in a mathematical expression, Excel can give only one of two answers: TRUE or FALSE.

Using the Comparison Operators in an IF Function

Comparison operators are used extensively within the **=IF** function, which we will explore in more depth in a section later in this chapter. A *function* is a calculation engine that internally performs complex or large calculations on values placed within the function's parentheses. Functions reduce the amount of time it would take to manually calculate a complex answer. Look at the following =IF function:

```
=IF(B2>1000,"Overbudget","OK")
```

The **=IF** function tells Excel to evaluate a number or expression as TRUE or FALSE by comparing it to another number or expression. In this example, Excel must evaluate the number in cell A2. Whatever number is currently in A2 should be compared to the value of 1000 to see if it is greater than 1000. Once the evaluation has been performed, instead of printing the word TRUE or the word FALSE, Excel is to print **Overbudget** if the answer is TRUE or **OK** if it's FALSE. The accompanying graphic shows the result of using an =IF function similar to the one above, comparing the value of cell A2 against the value of 1000. Refer to Table 17.2 for the comparison/logical operators you can use in Excel.

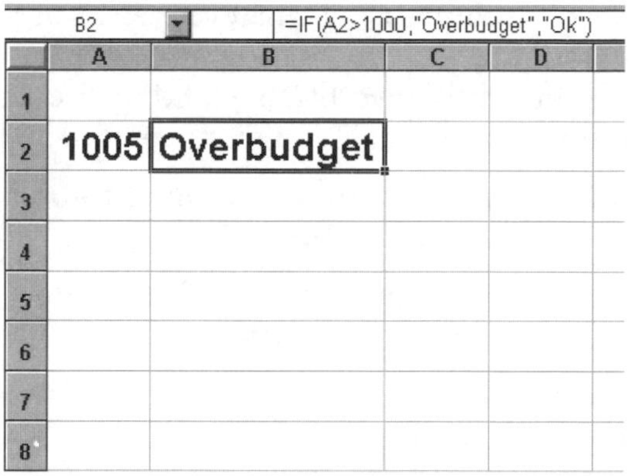

Operator Symbol	Comparison Meaning
=	Equal to
>	Greater than
>=	Greater than or Equal to
<	Less than
<=	Less than or Equal to
<>	Not equal to

Table 17.2 Comparison Operators and Their Meanings

Creating and Changing Formulas

Now that you have a basic understanding of the components involved with Excel formulas, let's create a few example formulas so that you can see how easy it is to have Excel calculate the answer.

The beauty of a formula is that once the mathematical relationship has been established between various numbers and expressions, you can substitute different numbers while keeping the same mathematical relationships. Or, to say it another way, the formula is the same regardless of whether you change the specific numbers. To calculate the gross check amount for hourly workers, you need to relate Hours and Rate. It does not matter what specific hours are entered or what specific rates are used, once you have set up the formula, Excel will automatically recalculate the gross check amount using whatever values are in the cell containing the hours and the cell containing the rate. Create a formula that calculates Hours multiplied by Rate and then change the numbers and view the automatic recalculation that is performed.

1. Click on cell A1, and type the following headings in cells A1 through D1: **Name, Rate, Hours, Check**.

2. Click on cell A2, and type the following names in A2 through A5: **JONES, BROWN, SMITH, DAVIS**.

3. Click in cell B2 and type the following rates of pay in B2 through B5: **12.5, 13, 14.75, 13.5**.

4. Click in cell C2 and type the following hours worked in C2 through C5: **40, 40, 38.5, 39**.

5. Select B2 through C5. Click once on the Increase Decimal Place button on the Formatting toolbar to format both the Rate and the Hours columns for two decimal places.

6. Click in cell D2 to begin typing the first formula to calculate the check amount, as presented in the following exercise.

	B2	▼		12.5		
	A	**B**	**C**	**D**	**E**	
1	NAME	RATE	HOURS	CHECK		
2	JONES	12.50	40.00			
3	BROWN	13.00	40.00			
4	SMITH	14.75	38.50			
5	DAVIS	13.50	39.00			
6						
7						
8						
9						
10						
11						

Using the Mouse to Create Formulas

The formula to calculate the check amount for the hourly worker model is: RATE ⋆ HOURS or HOURS ⋆ RATE. You can establish the formula by pointing out the cell locations of the values involved in the formula.

1. With the cursor in cell D2, type the equals sign to signal the start of a formula.

2. Click the mouse on Mr. Jones' rate of 12.50. The address of this cell (B2) shows up in the formula bar. Notice the moving marquee around the cell being referenced.

3. Type the asterisk (the multiplication symbol).

4. Finally, click on the cell with Mr. Jones' hours worked. The address of this cell (C2) shows up in the formula bar.

5. Click on the green checkmark up on the formula bar, or press the Enter key. The formula calculates the check amount using the data in the cells specified, and the result (500) is shown in the originally selected cell (D2). Look in the formula bar at the formula itself (versus the result, 500, in the cell).

D2	▼	=B2*C2			
	A	**B**	**C**	**D**	**E**
1	NAME	RATE	HOURS	CHECK	
2	JONES	12.50	40.00	500	
3	BROWN	13.00	40.00		
4	SMITH	14.75	38.50		
5	DAVIS	13.50	39.00		
6					
7					
8					
9					
10					
11					

6. Change Mr. Jones' hours worked to **45**. That is, click on cell C2 and type over the 40 hours with 45 and press the Enter key. The check amount is automatically recalculated to 562.5, because the mathematical formula has been set to multiply B2*C2 regardless of the specific values in those cells. Change Mr. Jones' hours back to **40** and press Enter.

Part 3

Analyzing with Excel

Changing and Deleting Formulas

There are a number of methods for changing or deleting formulas. Click on the cell whose formula you want to delete or change, and then use one of the following techniques to begin editing:

▶ Press the Delete key and start creating the formula again.

▶ *Or* press the F2 (Edit) key and perform cell editing as described below.

▶ *Or* click in the formula bar and perform cell editing as described below.

▶ *Or* double-click on the cell to perform cell editing as described below.

Once you are in the cell editing mode, you can use the following techniques:

▶ Use the left or right arrows to reposition the cursor in the formula.

▶ Use the Backspace key to back over particular references in the formula.

▶ Double-click on one of the cell references within the formula and then click the mouse on the correct cell. This enters the address of that cell as the new reference in the formula.(For example, suppose the formula to calculate Mr. Jones' check amount reads =A2*C2 but you want to change it to =B2*C2. After you've activated the cell editing mode, you can double-click on **A2** within the formula and then click on cell B2. Excel will change A2 in the formula to the correct reference of B2.)

	A	B	C	D	E
				=A2*C2	
1	NAME	RATE	HOURS	CHECK	
2	JONES	12.50	40.00	=A2*C2	
3	BROWN	13.00	40.00	520.00	
4	SMITH	14.75	38.50	567.88	
5	DAVIS	13.50	39.00	526.50	
6					
7					
8					
9					
10					
11					

Copying Formulas

When the same formula is needed in multiple cells, there is a good chance that you can copy the original formula to the other cells that need the formula. In the example being used here of Hourly Workers, Mr. Jones' check amount was calculated using the formula of Rate * Hours. The other workers will need the same formula. Instead of manually entering each formula for every worker on your worksheet, Excel not only allows you to copy the existing formula, it will automatically change the row numbers involved in the formula's original location to reflect the appropriate rows needed for each new location. For example, the original formula you created was =B2*C2, to calculate the check amount for Mr. Jones. The formula that will calculate Mr. Brown's check amount, on the other hand, will be =B3*C3. Notice that the same relationship exists between the column references of the values (columns B and C in both instances), but the row reference is different (row 2 in Mr. Jones' case, row 3 in Mr. Brown's).

The Copy command will change each copy of the original formula to reflect the correct row of the new formula. This property of the Copy command is called *relative referencing*: Excel takes the original formula being copied and makes each copy relate to the new row.

1. Click on cell D2 where the original formula produced the first check amount. The Copy command is not going to copy the value (500). It will copy the formula (=B2*C2).

2. Click on the Copy button on the Standard toolbar, or right-click on selected cell area and select Copy from the shortcut menu.

3. Select rows D3 through D5 (drag the mouse over these rows to select the destination for the copy).

4. Click on the Paste button on the Standard toolbar (the button is next to the Copy button—a clipboard button), or choose Paste on the shortcut menu, or merely press the Enter key.

5. Excel copies the formula into the designated cells, but each copy uses the row number for the row on which it resides. The fact that the values calculated in each cell are different is an indication that the formula is using different values in each location.

	A	B	C	D	E	
1	NAME	RATE	HOURS	CHECK		
2	JONES	12.50	40.00	500		
3	BROWN	13.00	40.00	520		
4	SMITH	14.75	38.50	567.875		
5	DAVIS	13.50	39.00	526.5		

D3 ▾ =B3*C3

6. Make the decimal places the same for each of the check amounts by clicking and dragging to select all four check amounts (D2 through D5) and clicking twice on the Increase Decimal Place button on the Formatting toolbar.

Copy Tips and Tricks

Excel has a number of copy and paste methods available.

▶ The Edit menu contains Copy and Paste commands.

▶ The Standard toolbar contains the Copy and Paste buttons.

▶ There are shortcut keys: Ctrl+C to copy and Ctrl+V to paste.

▶ The Shortcut menu (right-click the mouse) contains Copy and Paste commands.

In addition, for each of these approaches, Excel allows you to press the Enter key instead of using the Paste command.

The next sections describe alternatives to the four ways of using the two-step Copy and Paste/Enter method.

Using the Fill Command to Copy

When copying into a stack of cells, you can use Excel's Fill ▶ Down operation that copies and pastes data or formulas vertically in one step. Select the original data or formula and the destination cells as one long selection. Press Ctrl+D. Excel will copy the formula down into the destination locations.

For copies across columns, select the original data or formula and the destination cells in one long horizontal selection. Press Ctrl+R to copy to the right. To copy up or to copy left, select the source and the destination and then choose Edit ➤ Fill and then Up or Left. (These operations do not have shortcut keys as do the Down and Right operations.) Figure 17.1 displays the Edit ➤ Fill submenu items.

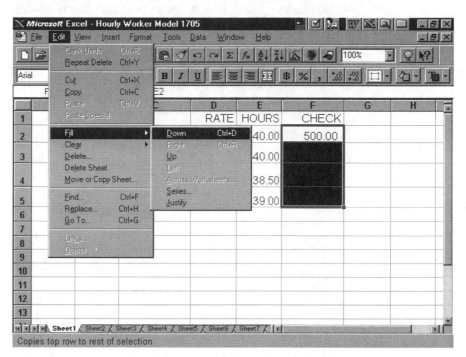

Figure 17.1 **There are multiple copying methods available with the Fill command.**

Using AutoFill to Copy

The AutoFill command allows you to automatically fill in dates, days of the week, names of the months, or series of incremental values, and is very useful as a fast copy command in Excel. AutoFill is activated when you drag the *fill handle* that resides at the lower right corner of a cell or a selected range. Follow these steps to copy the Check Amount formula for the Hourly Workers model we have been using.

1. Delete the formulas in cells D3 through D5. Leave your original check formula intact in cell D2. This will be the original source for the copy using AutoFill.

2. Click on cell D2 which contains the original formula.

3. Position the mouse at the lower right-hand corner of cell D2. Notice that a small gray button appears in this corner. The mouse pointer turns into a small black cross.

4. Drag the small black cross pointer down to cell D5 and release the mouse. Excel will copy the formula to D5.

This technique of dragging the fill handle of the cell containing the source formula through the destination cells also works for copying and filling horizontally across columns.

	A	B	C	D	E	
				=B2*C2		
1	NAME	RATE	HOURS	CHECK		
2	JONES	12.50	40.00	500.00		
3	BROWN	13.00	40.00			
4	SMITH	14.75	38.50			
5	DAVIS	13.50	39.00			
6						
7						
8						
9						
10						
11						

A Step-Saving Trick Using the Fill Handle

In the previous section you learned to copy by dragging the fill handle of the source cell through the destination cells. There is an added trick you can use when copying with the fill handle. This trick, however, works only with vertical destinations, and requires that there be a column of data (any kind) to either the left or the right of the source cell. In addition, the column of data must already comprise the number of cells you expect the copy to occupy. In other words, if you must copy data or a formula into twenty rows, the column of data to the left or right must already extend twenty rows.

In our Hourly Worker model, the column of data is to the left of the formula. This column contains the hours worked. When we use the fill handle trick, Excel will calculate how far down to take the copy by analyzing the distance of the previous column (down to row 5). Here are the steps:

1. Click on the formula in cell D2. Make sure that there are no copies in the rest of the cells between D3 and D5.

2. Locate the small gray box of the fill handle in the lower right-hand corner of the selected cell. The mouse pointer turns into a small black cross.

3. When the mouse is positioned over the fill handle and has turned into a small black cross, double-click the mouse and Excel will automatically copy the formula down to row 5 (which is the length of the column of data to the left of the formula). To see that again, delete the copies of the formula but keep the original in cell D2. Repeat steps 2 and 3.

Copying While Entering a Formula

Our final copy trick (although not the last copy trick that Excel has up its sleeve) is to make Excel copy the formula as you create and enter the formula or data. Use the Hourly Worker model again. This time delete the original formula in cell D2 and all of the formulas you have copied to the other workers' rows. We are starting again in order to demonstrate this trick.

1. Click on cell D2 and select from D2 through D5. There should be no information in D2 through D5—just an empty selection.

2. Create the formula to calculate the check amount for Mr. Jones. Type = and click the mouse at B2, the rate of pay. Type the asterisk to specify multiplication, and then click on C2, the hours worked. Do not press the Enter key.

3. Hold down the Ctrl key and, while still holding Ctrl, press the Enter key. The Ctrl key combined with the Enter key tells Excel to enter and copy into all of the selected cells the information you are entering into the first cell of the selected range.

   You can perform this operation horizontally also. Simply select a horizontal range for the copy instead of a vertical range in step 1.

Part 3

Analyzing with Excel

Copying Data and Formulas to Other Worksheets

Copying your data and formulas to other worksheets is a three-step process:

Step 1: Select the range of data or formulas to be copied, and click on the Copy button on the Standard toolbar, or choose Copy from the right-click shortcut menu.

Step 2: Select the worksheet where the copy will be placed (click on the worksheet number or name on the bottom of the screen).

Step 3: Press the Enter key or click on the Paste button. Remember you can click on the Undo button if the copy does not perform correctly.

Viewing the Formula Instead of the Result

Excel has a great shortcut to allow you to quickly toggle back and forth between the text of your formula and the value of the result. Hold down the Ctrl key and tap the backward apostrophe ('). On most keyboards the backward apostrophe is located on the same key as the tilde (~), below the Esc key. Pressing this key combination repeatedly turns on and off the ability to view the text of the formulas.

Converting Formulas and Functions to their Values

By default, the worksheet area of the Excel window displays the results of your formulas and functions, and the formula bar shows the actual formula and/or function. There may be times when you want to use the number from a formula or a function as the basis of another set of calculations but need the actual *value*, not the formula or function that produced the value.

Excel has a variation on the Copy command that copies a formula but, when pasted, converts the formula or function to the actual value. Here are the general steps to convert a formula's result to an actual value:

1. Select the cells containing the formulas or function results.

2. Click on the Copy button on the Standard toolbar.

3. Click on the new location where the copy will be placed.

4. Choose Edit ➤ Paste Special and click on the Values radio button.

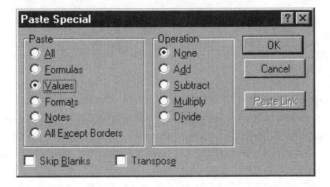

Part
3

Analyzing with Excel

5. The result of the formula appears. When you look in the formula bar, the actual value shows, not the formula references.

Relative Referencing

When you copy formulas containing row or column references, the copies of the formulas will change to reflect the row or column to which they are being copied. This capability of Excel is known as *relative referencing*. The formula copies are copied relative to their original source. If in cell D1 there is a formula such as **=C2+B1,** copies of this formula to cells D10, D12, and D14 will copy relative to the original. Figure 17.2 shows the relative referencing involved with copying.

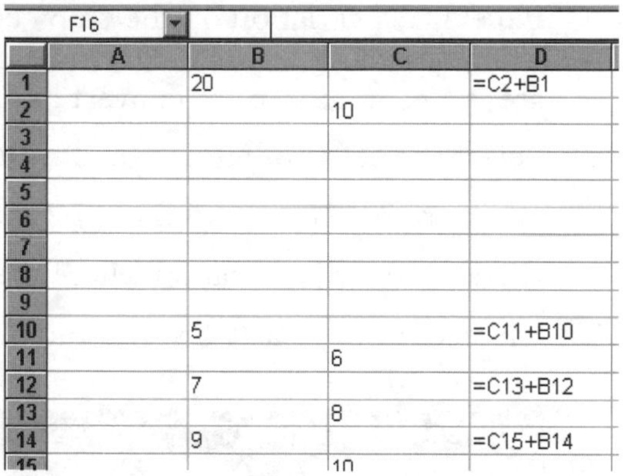

	A	B	C	D
1		20		=C2+B1
2			10	
3				
4				
5				
6				
7				
8				
9				
10		5		=C11+B10
11			6	
12		7		=C13+B12
13			8	
14		9		=C15+B14
15			10	

Figure 17.2   *When formulas are copied, their original row and column references are changed to reflect their new position.*

Absolute Referencing

There will be times when you want to copy a formula but you do not want Excel to perform relative referencing; that is, you do not want it to change the row or column coordinates of the copies. You need the capability to make a cell reference stay constant and not change to reflect the row or column to which it is being copied.

Figure 17.3 shows the result of a simple Percentage of the Total formula that calculates what percentage of the total sales each sales representative produced. When the original formula was copied, the resultant copies produced a series of errors.

Excel took the original formula =C2/C8 (Southern Sales divided by Total Sales = Percent of Sales) and made the copies maintain their relative positioning. What this means is that location C8 was copied and became C9, C10, etc. The problem is that Total Sales is only at location C8 and not at the other locations. Excel displays a spreadsheet error of #DIV/0!, the Division by Zero error. To avoid this error, you need a way to tell Excel not to change the row 8 reference.

Excel offers an *absolute reference* feature, which involves placing a dollar sign ($) in front of the column or the row that should stay constant when it is copied. Thus, if you type a dollar sign in front of the row 8 reference in the original formula, then when the copies are made each copy knows not to change the row 8 reference. The left side of the formula is relative

D2	▼	=C2/C8		
	A	**B**	**C**	**D**	**E**
1	Sales Rep	Territory	Sales	% of Total	
2	Powell, Tracey	Southern	29,900	17%	
3	Spezzano, Frank	Western	32800	#DIV/0!	
4	Morgan, Jan	Eastern	41700	#DIV/0!	
5	Barton, Doug	Northern	38000	#DIV/0!	
6	Sloan, Chris	MidWest	33500	#DIV/0!	
7					
8	Total		175,900	#DIV/0!	
9					
10					
11					
12					
13					
14					
15					

F15	▼			
	A	**B**	**C**	**D**
1	Sales Rep	Territory	Sales	% of Total
2	Powell, Tracey	Southern	29900	=C2/C8
3	Spezzano, Frank	Western	32800	=C3/C9
4	Morgan, Jan	Eastern	41700	=C4/C10
5	Barton, Doug	Northern	38000	=C5/C11
6	Sloan, Chris	MidWest	33500	=C6/C12
7				
8	Total		=SUM(C2:C7)	=SUM(D2:D7)
9				
10				
11				
12				
13				
14				
15				

Figure 17.3 **Top:** *The copies of the formula produced a Division by Zero error because absolute referencing was needed in the formula. When you look at the formula text* (bottom), *you can see that the location for the Sum of Sales is being referenced relatively, causing the error.*

but the right side of the formula is absolute. Figure 17.4 shows the absolute referenced formula results (top image) and the formula text (bottom image) showing where the absolute reference symbol was placed into the formula before being copied.

TIP If you know that you are going to need an absolute reference symbol in the formula when you create the formula, start the formula normally—using the equals sign and then clicking on the cell references of the formula. When you click on the cell reference that should be absolute, however, press the F4 key. Excel will automatically place dollar signs into the cell references.

Part 3

Analyzing with Excel

	A	B	C	D
1	Sales Rep	Territory	Sales	% of Total
2	Powell, Tracey	Southern	29,900	17%
3	Spezzano, Fra	Western	32800	19%
4	Morgan, Jan	Eastern	41700	24%
5	Barton, Doug	Northern	38000	22%
6	Sloan, Chris	MidWest	33500	19%
7				
8	Total		175,900	100%
9				
10				
11				
12				
13				
14				

	A	B	C	D
1	Sales Rep	Territory	Sales	% of Total
2	Powell, Tracey	Southern	29900	=C2/C$8
3	Spezzano, Frank	Western	32800	=C3/C$8
4	Morgan, Jan	Eastern	41700	=C4/C$8
5	Barton, Doug	Northern	38000	=C5/C$8
6	Sloan, Chris	MidWest	33500	=C6/C$8
7				
8	Total		=SUM(C2:C7)	=SUM(D2:D7)
9				
10				
11				
12				
13				
14				

Figure 17.4 **Top:** *When the absolute reference symbol of the dollar sign was used in the formula, the results are the correct percentages.* **Bottom:** *The dollar sign placed in a formula before a column reference or row reference (or both) dictates that that reference remain constant during a copy.*

Formula Error Messaging

As you saw in the previous section on absolute referencing, a problem occurred when relative-reference copying of a formula produced a #DIV/0! (division by zero) error. There are a number of error messages that can occur when creating formulas. Although these are Excel's attempts to be helpful in explaining the error, the messages are rather cryptic. Table 17.3 lists the error messages that occur and their meanings.

Error Message	Meaning
#DIV/0!	A division by zero has occurred in the formula.
#N/A	A value is not available to the formula.
#NAME?	An unrecognizable range name is used in the formula.
#NULL!	A reference in the formula specifies an invalid intersection of cells.
#NUM!	An incorrect number is used in the formula.
#REF!	An invalid cell is referenced in the formula.
#VALUE!	An incorrect argument or operator is used in the formula.

Table 17.3 **Error Messages for Errors in Formulas**

Formula Auditing

As you gain experience with creating spreadsheets, you may be required to explain the basis of a formula or function or to teach another person the mathematical expression being used in a formula. Excel's *Auditing* feature can display all of the locations involved in a formula. You trace the *precedents* of a formula and you trace the *dependents* of a value. Excel creates visual tracing arrows to show the various locations involved in a formula or function, as shown in Figure 17.5.

Using our Sales Territory model, we'll trace the precedents for the absolute-reference formula that calculated percentage of Total Sales.

1. Click on cell D4.

2. Choose Tools ➤ Auditing ➤ Trace Precedents from the menu bar. Blue arrows appear indicating the cells involved in the formula. Remember you can also use the Ctrl+' key combination (Ctrl plus the backward apostrophe, which is on the ~ key, below the Esc key), which toggles between displaying the formula text versus the formula answer.

The Precedents command only works on formulas or functions. If you position the pointer on a cell containing only a value and not a formula, you can use the Tools ➤ Auditing ➤ Trace Dependents command. To remove the auditing arrows, choose Tools ➤ Auditing ➤ Remove All Arrows.

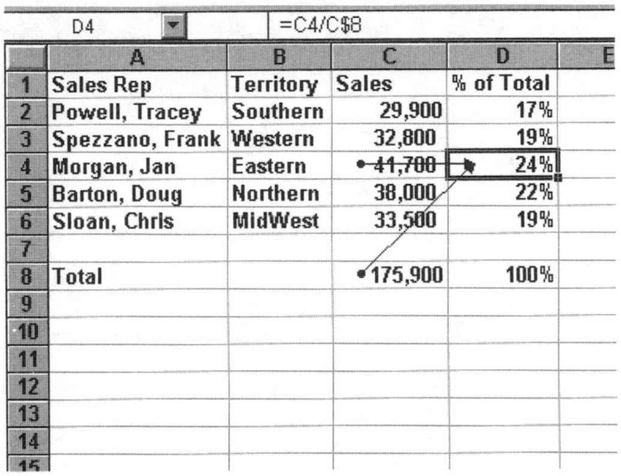

Figure 17.5 Auditing arrows displayed for a formula

Functions

Functions are predefined formulas. They have also been called calculation engines, because functions deliver their results quickly by internally calculating multiple and sometimes complex sets of mathematical expressions.

The syntax of a function consists of the following:

▶ The equals sign

▶ The name of the function

▶ An opening, left parenthesis

▶ The arguments or ranges needed

▶ A closing, right parenthesis

The SUM function is the most common function used in all spreadsheet programs. This function saves you the time of adding each individual cell of data involved in the summation. To illustrate this as simply as possible, look at the difference between entering the operations on your own for a range of data and using the SUM function for the same range. If you were to add up ten numbers starting at B1, your calculation would look like the following:

    =B1+B2+B3+B4+B5+B6+B7+B8+B9+B10

The SUM function could produce the same answer using the following expression:

```
=SUM(B1:B10)
```

The SUM function requires that a range of cells be specified. The range is specified by means of its start location, then a colon to represent the word "through," and then the stop location for the range. Said simply, using the SUM function, it would be just as easy to add 500 rows as it is to add 10 rows.

Excel has over 250 functions, which perform a variety of calculations. The functions fall into ten categories:

- Financial
- Date and Time
- Math & Trig
- Statistical
- Lookup & Reference
- Database
- Text
- Logical
- Information
- User Defined

The most commonly used functions are in the categories Math & Trig, Statistical, and Financial. The SUM function falls within the Math & Trig category. If you want to find Excel Help for a function, it is useful, though not necessary, to remember the category a function falls into. The AVERAGE function, for example, falls within the Statistical category, and the PMT (Payment function) falls within the Financial category.

When you activate the Function Wizard, a two-step dialog box helps you enter information necessary to the function. The Wizard lists all the functions, their uses and meanings, and what arguments are needed by each. Click on Insert ➤ Function to activate the Function Wizard, or click on the Function Wizard button on the Standard toolbar. Figure 17.6 displays the Function Wizard with the Financial category and PMT (Payment) function selected.

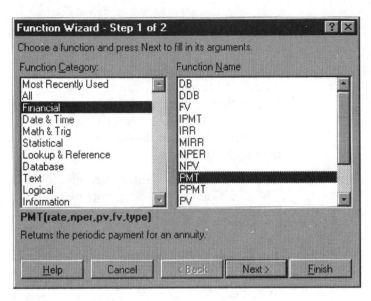

Figure 17.6 **The Function Wizard can be invaluable when searching for a particular function.**

Summing Data

Because adding columns and rows of numbers is involved in all spreadsheet models, Excel provides an AutoSum button on the Standard toolbar so that you can quickly add your numbers. If your numbers are listed vertically, select a cell immediately under the last number in the column—or, if you wish, skip a cell after the last number and select the next cell down, to make the total stand out from the rest of the column. Click on the AutoSum button once. Excel will surround the column of numbers with a moving marquee, and the bottom cell will display the =SUM function with the start and stop locations of the range of numbers, as shown in Figure 17.7. Click on the AutoSum button a second time, and Excel enters the function and displays the result.

To sum numbers at the end of a row, click on the cell to the right of the last number in the row and click on the AutoSum button twice. Figure 17.8 shows AutoSum being used on a row of numbers.

TIP You can press the AutoSum shortcut key of ALT+= (Alt plus the equals sign) instead of clicking on the AutoSum button on the Standard toolbar.

| C1 | ▼ | ✕ | ✓ | *fx* | =SUM(C1:C13) |

	A	B	C	D	E
1		item 1	104		
2		item 2	212		
3		item 3	784		
4		item 4	331		
5		item 5	27		
6		item 6	508		
7		item 7	288		
8		item 8	184		
9		item 9	472		
10		item 10	108		
11		item 11	487		
12		item 12	111		
13					
14			=SUM(C1:C13)		
15					

Figure 17.7   *The =SUM function is the most commonly used spreadsheet function.*

| B2 | ▼ | ✕ | ✓ | *fx* | =SUM(B2:D2) |

	A	B	C	D	E
1	EXPENSES	JAN	FEB	MAR	QTR 1
2	item 1	104	114.4	125.84	=SUM(B2:D2)
3	item 2	212	233.2	256.52	
4	item 3	784	862.4	948.64	
5	item 4	331	364.1	400.51	
6	item 5	27	29.7	32.67	
7	item 6	508	558.8	614.68	
8	item 7	288	316.8	348.48	
9	item 8	184	202.4	222.64	
10	item 9	472	519.2	571.12	
11	item 10	108	118.8	130.68	
12	item 11	487	535.7	589.27	
13	item 12	111	122.1	134.31	
14					
15		3616	3977.6	4375.36	

Figure 17.8   *You can use the AutoSum button to add vertically (as in the previous figure) or horizontally (as shown here).*

NOTE   **When you want to quickly view the sum of a column or row of numbers, you can simply select the series of numbers to be summed and look at the Status bar. Excel automatically displays the sum of the selected cells. (If the Status bar is not visible, choose View ➤ Status Bar.)**

Averaging Data

Sometimes it is easier to enter a simple function directly without using the Function Wizard. The AVERAGE function's arguments are identical to the SUM function's. Unlike the SUM function, there is no equivalent button on the toolbar to click on, but you can enter the name of the function and quickly select the range to be averaged.

1. Click on a blank cell below or to the right of the numbers to be averaged.

2. Type an equals sign.

3. Type the word **AVERAGE** (upper or lower case; it doesn't matter).

4. Type a left parenthesis.

5. Click and drag the mouse over the range of numbers to be averaged (see Figure 17.9).

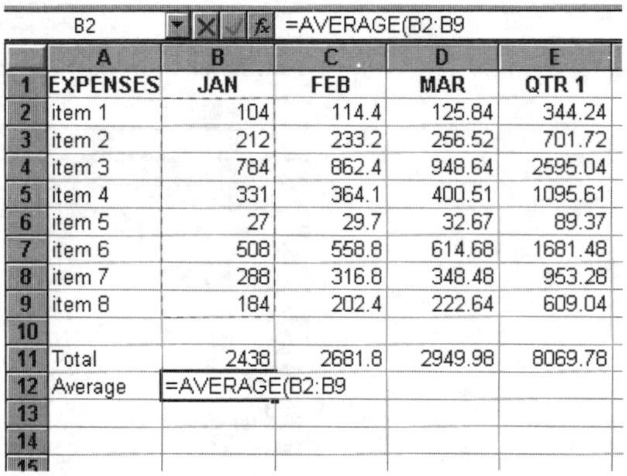

	A	B	C	D	E
	B2 ▼ ☒ ✓ *fx* =AVERAGE(B2:B9				
	A	**B**	**C**	**D**	**E**
1	EXPENSES	JAN	FEB	MAR	QTR 1
2	item 1	104	114.4	125.84	344.24
3	item 2	212	233.2	256.52	701.72
4	item 3	784	862.4	948.64	2595.04
5	item 4	331	364.1	400.51	1095.61
6	item 5	27	29.7	32.67	89.37
7	item 6	508	558.8	614.68	1681.48
8	item 7	288	316.8	348.48	953.28
9	item 8	184	202.4	222.64	609.04
10					
11	Total	2438	2681.8	2949.98	8069.78
12	Average	=AVERAGE(B2:B9			
13					
14					
15					

Figure 17.9   The AVERAGE function is easily entered without using the Function Wizard.

6. You do not have to enter the right parenthesis. Click on the green checkmark on the formula bar or press the Enter key.

The COUNTIF Function

The COUNTIF function is similar to the AVERAGE and the SUM functions. You specify the range you wish included and Excel counts only the number of values contained in the range. The COUNTIF function allows you to use criteria to focus in on the specific values you want to be counted. The syntax of the COUNTIF function is in the following form:

```
=COUNTIF(range, criteria)
```

where *range* is the location of all the values the COUNTIF is to choose from and *criteria* are the expressions, text, or values that define which cells will be counted.

For example you can find the number of Expense items that are over $100 for each month of the quarter with the formula:

```
=COUNTIF(B2:B9, ">100")
```

In this formula the range B2:B9 is the range of Expense costs, and the criterion is specified in quotes using the comparison operator (see Figure 17.10).

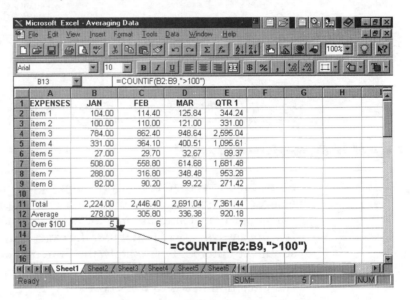

Figure 17.10 The COUNTIF function allows you to use criteria by which Excel should count the number of values in a range.

Using the SUMIF Function

Like the COUNTIF function, the SUMIF function can be supplied a set of criteria by which it controls what data gets summed. A simple use of the SUMIF function would be to sum values greater than a specific value. As with COUNTIF, you must provide the function with the range of values to be summed and the criteria to be used.

```
=SUMIF(C2:C6, ">35,000")
```

In this formula the range C2:C6 is the range of sales figures and the criterion specified in quotes focuses the sum only on values over 35,000. (See Figure 17.11.)

	C11	▼	=SUMIF(C2:C6,">35,000")
	A	**B**	**C**
1	Sales Rep	Territory	Sales
2	Powell, Tracey	Southern	29900
3	Spezzano, Frank	Western	32800
4	Morgan, Jan	Eastern	41700
5	Barton, Doug	Northern	38000
6	Sloan, Chris	MidWest	33500
7			
8	Total		=SUM(C2:C7)
9	Highest Sale		=MAX(C2:C6)
10	Lowest Sale		=MIN(C2:C6)
11	Sales Over $35,000		=SUMIF(C2:C6,">35,000")
12			
13			
14			
15			

Figure 17.11　The SUMIF function is a powerful tool for focusing on specific values to include or exclude when summing the values in a range.

Using the Function Wizard

Some functions require that you supply information other than a range. Many of the Financial functions require multiple arguments, such as the current principal amount *and* how long an amount will be invested, etc. It is not always easy to remember the exact order in which the arguments should be entered. Fortunately, the Function Wizard walks you through the steps of creating a function, and lists the exact requirements that each function needs to work correctly.

Figure 17.12 displays a Payment model where the monthly payment for an automobile is being calculated by the PMT function. The PMT function, part of the Financial function group, requires specific arguments in a specific order. Furthermore, you can mathematically modify one of these arguments by multiplying or dividing. Let's use the Function Wizard to figure out the monthly payment.

1. Create the model shown in Figure 17.12.

2. Position the pointer at D9.

3. Click on the Function Wizard button on the Standard toolbar (the button next to the AutoSum button).

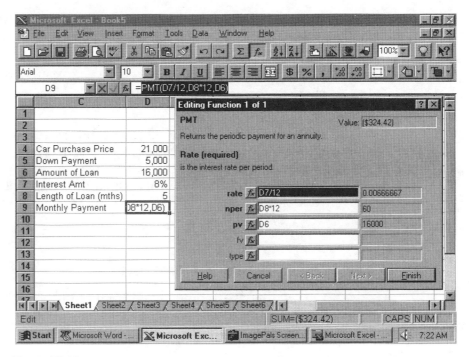

Figure 17.12 *The Function Wizard helps you remember the arguments required for a sophisticated function.*

4. When the Function Wizard dialog box appears, it might be covering the data you need to see. Move the Function Wizard dialog box out of the way by clicking and dragging its title bar, and click on the Financial category on the left side of the dialog box.

5. Click on the PMT function on the right side of the dialog box, then click on the Next button.

6. Three arguments are required for the PMT function: Interest rate, the number of periods over which the loan will be paid back, and the loan amount. At the Interest Rate text box, click on the interest rate at cell D7. Divide this (yes, the location D7) by 12 to produce the following interest rate reference: D7/12. The interest rate will be calculated more accurately if it is divided by the 12 months of the year, since a monthly payment should be calculated by the monthly, not the annual, interest rate.

7. Click on the Nper text box to specify the number of periods. Click on D8 and multiply this reference by 12 to produce the following reference

to the number of periods: D8*12. We're multiplying the number of periods by 12 so that the number of years is reflected as the number of monthly payments.

8. Finally, click on the PV text box (Present Value) and then click on D6 where the principal amount of the loan is located. Click on the Finish button.

Excel shows the monthly payment, but in red to indicate a negative number. It's negative because Excel considers it to be money out of your pocket each month. To reverse the negative to a positive, if you wish, double-click on the payment located at D9 and place a minus sign in front of the function name:

```
=-PMT(D7/12, D8*12,D6)
```

Changing Your Functions

You can change your functions as you would any other formula in Excel. There are three different ways to activate the Edit mode.

▶ Double-click on the cell you wish to edit.

▶ Press F2.

▶ Click on the formula bar.

You can also use the Function Wizard, so that you can see the descriptions of the arguments. This method offers the advantage of letting you see if you are changing the correct arguments.

1. Click on the cell that has the function you wish to edit. In the Payment example we have been using, we'll use cell D9.

2. Click on the Function Wizard button on the Standard toolbar or choose Insert ▶ Function from the menu bar.

3. When the Editing Function dialog box appears, click on the argument whose reference you wish to change. When you have finished, click on the Finish button.

Importance of Names in Formulas and Functions

An invaluable feature within Excel is the ability to assign a name in plain English to a cell or to a range of cells. Instead of reading a function and trying to recall what the cell references mean, you could assign a real name to each of the cells referenced in the formula or function. A function that reads:

```
=PMT(D7/12,D8*12,D6)
```

could be made easier to understand by changing its cell references to more descriptive terms:

```
=PMT(Interest_Amt/12,Years*12,Loan_Amount)
```

The ability to give a range a name allows for instant documentation and clarity of meaning in formulas and functions.

Defining a Cell or Range Name

You can give a cell or a range of cells a name by selecting the cell or the range and then using a menu command or shortcut, both of which are presented in this section. In the following steps, we'll use our example of the Car Purchase Loan model to define a name for a single cell:

1. Select the cell or cells to be named. For this example, click on cell D7.

2. Choose Insert ➤ Name ➤ Define from the menu bar, as shown in Figure 17.13.

3. The Define Name dialog box appears. Note that Excel has already created a name for you within this dialog box—it has assumed that **Interest Amt**, the text label to the left of the selected cell, might already serve a labeling function. Keep this choice by clicking on the Add button, or change it to what you want first and then click on the Add button.

Part 3

Analyzing with Excel

4. Click on OK. When you return to the worksheet, the pointer is still on cell D7, but now the name of the cell appears in the Name box (to the left of the formula bar).

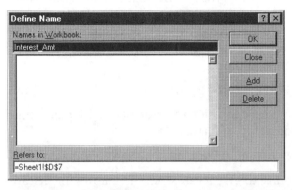

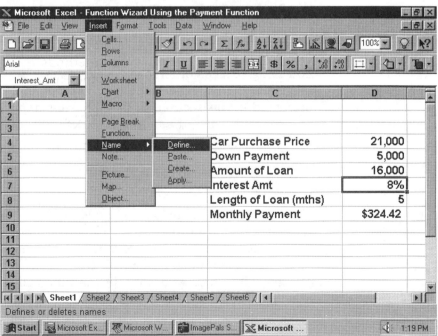

Figure 17.13   Car Loan model using range names

The next name you are going to define uses a shortcut for quickly defining a cell name.

1. Click on cell D8.

2. Click on the Name box's drop-down-list arrow.

3. Type the name **Years** in the text box area, then press the Enter key. You have defined another cell name.

Years			5	
Interest_Amt		C	D	E
Years				
2				
3				
4	Car Purchase Price		21,000	
5	Down Payment		5,000	
6	Amount of Loan		16,000	
7	Interest Amt		8%	
8	Length of Loan (mths)		5	
9	Monthly Payment		$324.42	
10				
11				
12				
13				

For practice, use either of the methods above to create a label for cell D6. Accept the suggested name **Amount of Loan**, and return to the worksheet.

You have defined three cell names. You can now use these names when creating your formulas or functions.

Inserting Cell or Range Names

The Name box is a handy and quick method for inserting names into your formula as you are creating the formula. To use the cell names defined above in the PMT function, delete the existing PMT function answer and start again so that you can view the process from the beginning:

1. Click on cell D9, where the PAYMENT function will be entered.

2. Start the function normally with **=PMT(**

3. Click on the drop-down arrow next to the Name box, to the left of the formula bar.

4. Select Interest_Amt from the Name list. The name is inserted into the function.

Interest_Amt	▼ X ✓ ƒₓ	=-PMT(Interest_Amt		
Amount_of_Loan	C		D	E
Interest_Amt				
Years				
2				
3				
4	Car Purchase Price		21,000	
5	Down Payment		5,000	
6	Amount of Loan		16,000	
7	Interest Amt		8%	
8	Length of Loan (mths)		5	
9	Monthly Payment		=-PMT(Interest_Amt	
10				
11				
12				
13				

5. Divide the Interest_Amt by 12 months and type a comma:

    `(=PMT(Interest_Amt/12,`

6. Select Years from the Name box's drop-down list. The name is inserted into the function.

7. Multiply the Years by 12 months and type a comma.

8. Select Amount_of_Loan from the list of cell names from the Name box. The name is inserted into the function. Press the Enter key. The right parenthesis will be inserted automatically. (If you wish to see a positive number instead of a red, negative number, edit the formula and place a minus sign in front of the function name: **=-PMT.**

> **TIP** You can define cell and range names on different worksheets as long as the names you use on each sheet are unique for that sheet. You can quickly position at any name regardless of what sheet it resides on. Select the name from the Name box. The pointer will jump to the cell or range indicated by that name. (If you have named an entire selection, the pointer goes to the top or left of the range.)

Deleting Names

To delete names, choose Insert ➤ Name ➤ Define and the Define Name dialog box appears. Click on the name you wish to delete and click on the Delete button on the right side of the dialog box. Click on the OK button to close the dialog box.

Chapter 18

Charting and Mapping Your Data

FEATURING

Data is just data until you've organized it usefully. When you can present your data informatively, you're providing far more than just data; you're offering *information*. One of the best ways of conveying information is by means of pictures. Excel offers various charting and mapping features to help you present your data most effectively.

Charting Your Data

Charting your data allows you to represent your worksheet's information visually. It is good to use every means available to you to analyze your data. A graphic representation allows you to get a big-picture view of your data much easier than looking at a lot of worksheet numbers.

Inserting a Chart

To create a chart of your worksheet data on its own sheet, select Insert ➤ Chart ➤ As New Sheet from the menu bar.

To embed a chart on your current sheet, follow these steps.

1. Select the range of data you want to chart.

2. Click on the Chart Wizard button on the Standard toolbar. The range of data you selected will activate.

    The Chart Wizard pointer appears (it can be seen in Figure 18.1). It is ready for you to select an area on your worksheet where you want your chart to be embedded.

3. Click and drag the Chart Wizard pointer across the worksheet area of your choice, as in Figure 18.2.

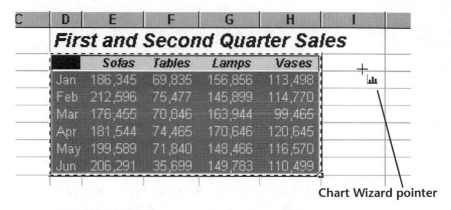

First and Second Quarter Sales

	Sofas	Tables	Lamps	Vases
Jan	186,345	69,835	156,856	113,498
Feb	212,596	75,477	145,899	114,770
Mar	176,455	70,846	163,944	99,465
Apr	181,544	74,465	170,646	120,645
May	199,589	71,840	148,466	116,570
Jun	206,291	35,699	149,783	110,499

Chart Wizard pointer

Figure 18.1   **Chart Wizard pointer**

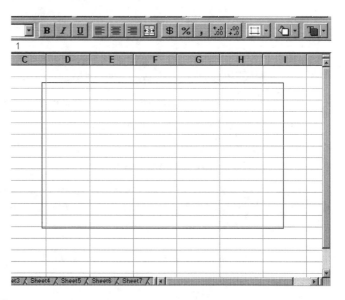

Figure 18.2   **Drag to draw an area in which to embed your chart.**

The Chart Wizard appears to lead you through the five steps to creating your chart.

1. The first step suggests the range of data to be used for the chart. To accept the suggested range click on Next.

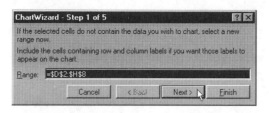

2. Step 2 prompts you to select a chart type. The Column chart type is displayed by default. If you prefer a different chart type, click on it and select Next to accept your choice.

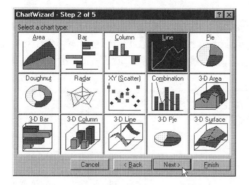

3. Step 3 prompts you to select a format of your chart type. Choose the variation of your chart type that you prefer and click on Next.

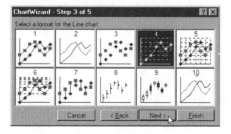

4. Step 4 previews your chart and suggests the location of the data series, category titles, and legend text. Click on Next to accept the suggestions, or modify them as you see fit.

Part 3

Analyzing with Excel

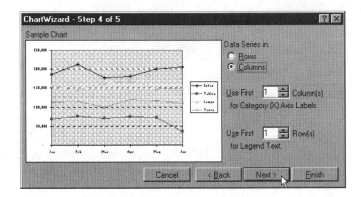

5. Step 5 again previews your chart and gives you the option of keeping a legend, adding a chart title, and adding axis titles. Click on Finish to close the Chart Wizard and generate your chart.

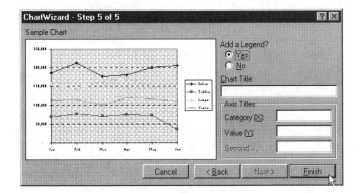

After your chart is embedded you can still make changes to its appearance and even to its content. To edit the chart, activate it by double-clicking on it. Once the chart displays its selection marquee (the highlighting box, as shown in Figure 18.3), you can select an object within the chart area by double-clicking on the object.

For example, you can delete a series by double-clicking on it and then pressing the Delete key on your keyboard. If you want to include a new series of data from your worksheet, you can select the data, drag it into the chart area, and drop it into your chart. We'll discuss chart editing techniques later in this chapter.

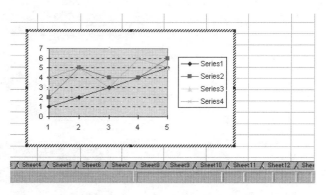

Figure 18.3 **You can activate your chart by double-clicking on it.**

Chart Types

On the one hand, you shouldn't let yourself feel overwhelmed by the numerous chart types available in Excel. On the other hand, don't get stuck in a rut using the same chart type over and over. This section will introduce you to the various chart types you can choose in Excel.

Remember, you can select from a whole palette of chart types in Step 2 of the Chart Wizard. There's also another way to choose chart types: you can select them from the Chart Types tear-off palette on the Chart toolbar. If the Chart toolbar isn't open, open it by selecting View ➤ Toolbars from the menu bar and click on Chart, or click on any toolbar with your secondary button to pop up the shortcut menu and then click on Chart.

The Chart toolbar appears, as shown in Figure 18.4. Click on the down-arrow on the Chart Types button to drop down the tear-off palette.

Following is a brief overview of some of the chart types represented on this and the Chart Wizard's palette.

Area Charts

Area charts show the relative contributions over time that each data series makes to the whole picture. The smaller the area a data series takes up, the smaller its contribution to the whole. This type is good for

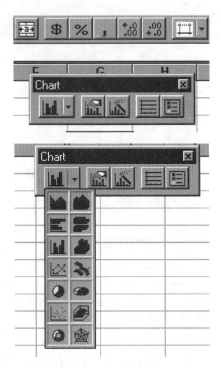

Figure 18.4 **Top:** *The Chart toolbar. Click on the down-arrow next to the leftmost button to display* **(bottom)** *the Chart Type palette.*

individual expense categories, sales regions, and production costs. (See Figure 18.5.)

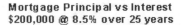
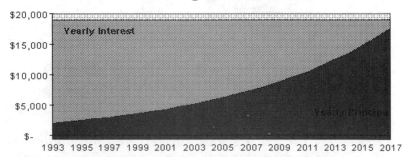

Figure 18.5 *An area chart*

Bar Charts

Bar charts compare distinct items or show single items at distinct intervals. Use bar charts to show the results of sales contests, or any competitive activity. (See Figure 18.6.)

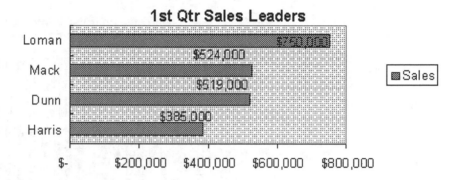

Figure 18.6 **A bar chart**

Column Charts

Column charts are similar to bar charts in that they compare distinct items. However, the 2-D column chart's value axis is vertical, with its category axis horizontal. These charts are best suited for comparing items over a time period. It is important to keep the number of series in a column chart to a minimum. Too many series cause the column to narrow and become difficult to analyze. (See Figure 18.7.)

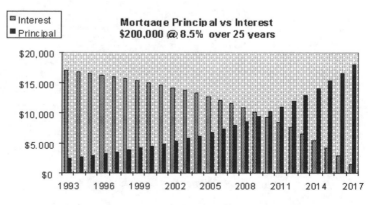

Figure 18.7 **A column chart**

Stacked Column Chart

Stacked column charts, selected by choosing a column chart that has a stacked style, combine the power of area charts and column charts. Series values are stacked, to show the relative contribution of each series, and then reflected at discrete intervals. (See Figure 18.8.)

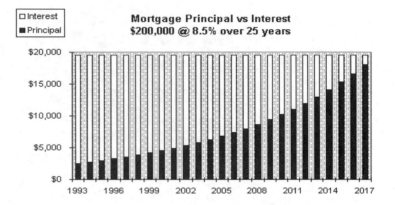

Figure 18.8   A stacked column chart

Line Charts

Line charts reflect the changes in a series over time. Use when you are concerned more with the trend of a data series than with the actual data series' values. (See Figure 18.9.)

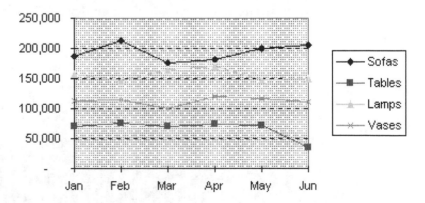

Figure 18.9   A line chart

There are several line chart formats, including the High, Low, Close line chart, which is good for plotting stock market prices. (See Figure 18.10.)

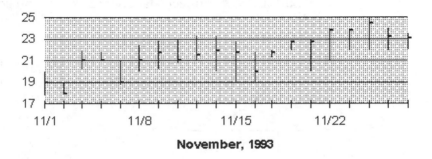

B&C co. Stock Market Price

Figure 18.10   A High, Low, Close line chart

Pie Charts

Pie charts are good for showing the proportion each value represents to the whole of a singe data series. Pie charts are good for showing proportional sales figures as well as population data. (See Figure 18.11.)

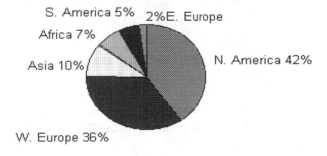

XYZ SALES 1990

Figure 18.11   The pie chart

Radar Charts

Radar charts make comparisons between data series relative to a center point. They are designed much as an air traffic controller's radar screen, and are viewed the same way, as if you the viewer are the center point and you have radar emitting a beam (the value axis) away from you in all directions. When it makes contact with something a blip appears on the screen. In your chart the blip is the data point shown with a data marker. In addition, Excel automatically draws lines from one data point to the next (that is, it connects data points that are on adjacent axes), forming polygons that make it easy to keep track of different sets of data on the same screen.

In Figure 18.12, two products are rated on a scale of 1 to 10. The polygon covering the most area represents the product ranking highest in more categories.

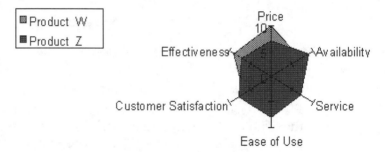

Figure 18.12   *Radar charts are good for comparisons between products.*

X-Y (Scatter) Charts

X-Y charts show the relationship between numeric values in two different data series. They also plot a series of data pairs using X and Y coordinates. An X-Y chart is a variation on the line chart, in that the category axis is replaced by a second value axis. This makes it excellent for plotting survey and experiment results. (See Figure 18.13.)

Doughnut Charts

Doughnut charts are similar to pie charts. Like a pie chart, the doughnut chart shows the proportion of the whole that is contributed by each value in a series. Unlike a pie chart, however, you can use more than one series with a doughnut chart, because the chart can arrange a number of doughnuts concentrically. (See Figure 18.14.)

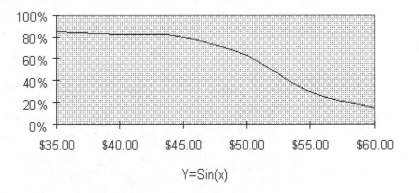

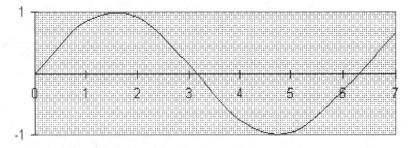

Figure 18.13   **Top:** *X-Y charts are good for plotting items such as survey data and experiment results.* **Bottom:** *They are also good at plotting mathematical functions. In the bottom chart, the X-axis values in the bottom chart are independent variables and the Y values are dependent variables.*

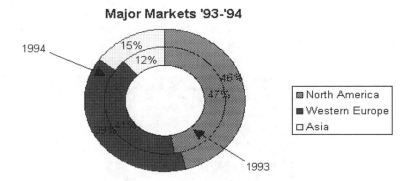

Figure 18.14   *A doughnut chart*

Picture Charts

By using small pictures as the units for the data series, this type of chart is great for presentations and is easy to create. We'll discuss the pictures available for these charts later in the chapter, under "Adding Clip Art to Your Charts." (See Figure 18.15.)

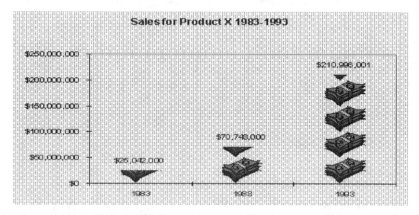

Figure 18.15   *A picture chart*

Modifying Charts

The quickest way to modify your chart is to double-click on an object within an activated chart to open the formatting dialog box for that type of object. Figure 18.16 shows the Format Data Series dialog box opened by double-clicking on one of the data series (one of the bars) in a bar chart.

If you want to add new objects into your chart after you have created it, you can select Insert from the menu bar and choose one of the available items. The dialog box below was opened by selecting Insert ➤ Gridlines from the menu bar.

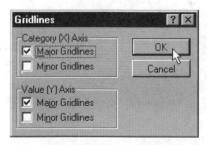

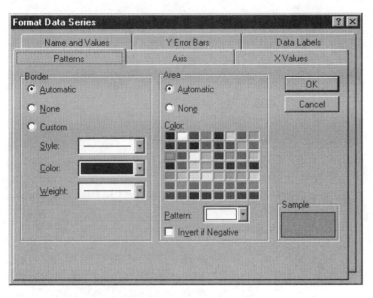

Figure 18.16 **Format Data Series dialog box**

Advanced Charting Formats

Let's create a simple column chart and then format it using a couple of formatting tips. You will need to type in some data for use with our chart and then create a basic chart.

1. In cells A1:A6 enter **NY**, **NJ**, **PA**, **MD**, **DE**, and **VA**.

2. In cells B1:B6 enter **76**, **77**, **66**, **55**, **88**, and **44**.

3. Select your data by clicking and dragging over cells A1:B6.

4. Click on the Chart Wizard button on the toolbar.

5. Outline the area on your worksheet where you want to insert your chart, by clicking and dragging with the Chart Wizard pointer.

6. When Step 1 of the Chart Wizard opens specifying the data range, click on Next.

7. In Step 2, select the Column chart type and click on Next.

8. In Step 3, select the first layout, and click on Next.

9. Click on Next when the next Chart Wizard dialog box appears.

10. Under *Add a Legend?* choose the No radio button. Enter the title **Atlantic Region**, and click on Finish.

Now that we have created a simple column chart in Excel, we'll format it a couple of different ways to make it more interesting and create a better impact.

Exploding Pie Charts

First, let's create an exploding pie chart—a pie chart with a slice removed from the pie and set aside. This can be very useful if you want to point out a specific piece of the pie that is considered more important than the others, such as one department's budget in your organization or the profits of one fiscal quarter.

1. Double-click on the chart we created above.

2. With the mouse pointer anywhere on the chart, click on the right mouse button and choose Chart Type from the menu.

3. Click on the 3-D radio button, then select the 3-D Pie chart type and click on OK.

4. Click on the pie. Then click on one slice so that it alone is highlighted.

5. Click and hold down the left mouse button and drag the slice away from the center. Release the mouse button.

6. The result should resemble Figure 18.17.

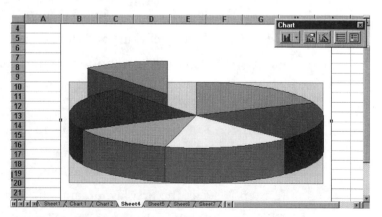

Figure 18.17 *Exploding Pie chart*

Using Clip Art in Your Chart

A little-known function of Excel is the ability to paste a clip art picture onto a chart, and use the picture as the units in the columns.

To use this feature, make sure that you have clip art installed on your computer. If you have previously selected to do a full installation of the Office, the clip art that comes with PowerPoint and Word should already be installed.

1. Double-click anywhere on the chart we used above or on another one you may have created.

2. Change the chart type to a 2-D Column chart by right-clicking and choosing Chart Type from the shortcut menu.

3. Click on one of the bars in the chart. They should all activate at once.

4. Select Insert ➤ Picture from the toolbar.

5. Find the location of your clip art (the default folder would be under Msoffice/Clipart). Select the bullmrkt.wmf clip art, or another of your choice, and click on OK.

6. Click on the right mouse button and select Format Data Series.

7. Click on the Stack radio button under the Patterns tab and click on OK.

8. Your final chart will look similar to Figure 18.18.

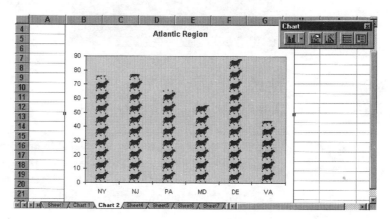

Figure 18.18   **2-D Column chart with clip art used as units of measure**

Part
3

Analyzing with Excel

NOTE Pasting a picture onto a chart will only work with a 2-D chart that is based on the radar, scatter, line, column, or bar layouts. It will not work with 3-D or other charts, like the pie chart or doughnut chart.

Mapping Your Data

Charts are not the only graphics you can generate from your data. Excel's mapping feature allows you to make geographic maps of your data as well.

In order to take advantage of the mapping features in Excel, you will need to create a range of data that will be appropriate to map.

1. Select the range A1:B7.

2. Enter the following information, pressing Enter after each entry: **State, KS, ND, NE, OK, SD, TX, Sales Totals, 60, 40, 20, 40, 30,** and **50.**

	A	B	C
1	State	Sales Totals	
2	KS	60	
3	ND	40	
4	NE	20	
5	OK	40	
6	SD	30	
7	TX	50	

Using standard abbreviations for states makes it easier for Excel's mapping tool. Each row will be represented by one region of the map.

Once the map program recognizes the data, it produces a map automatically.

1. Select the range A1:B7

2. Click on the Map button on the toolbar.

NOTE If the map button is not available on your toolbar, it may mean that you did not select to install this feature with Excel during the installation of Office. To perform mapping with Excel, rerun the Setup program, making sure that the Mapping feature is selected.

3. The pointer changes to a cross hairs. Drag the pointer across the range C1:H10 to draw a rectangle in which to embed the map.

4. The Multiple Maps Available dialog box appears. From the list, select *United States (AK&HI Inset)* in *US with AK & HI Insets*.

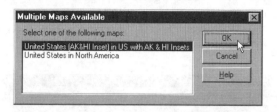

5. Click on OK. The map appears with the data entered and a Data Map Control dialog box for you to make changes. (See Figure 18.19.)

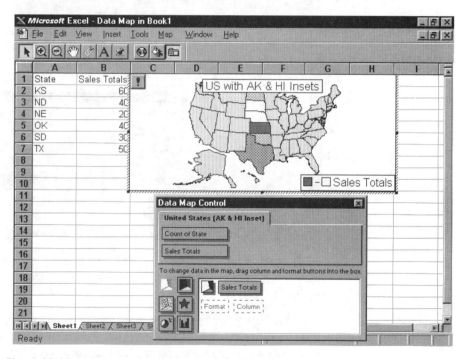

Figure 18.19 *The Data Map Control dialog box appears when you select the type of map you want to display.*

In the editing area in the bottom half of this dialog box, you can see the icon indicating the current map type being used. In our example, the icon for the Value Shading map appears alongside the Sales Totals column. You can change the map type by dragging a different type symbol from the bottom left of the dialog box into the editing area to the right of the symbols.

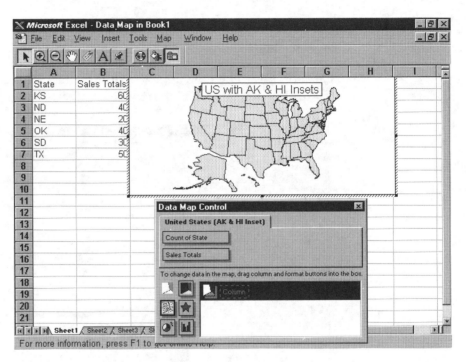

By dragging the icon for the Dot Density map type into the editing area, we switch the map type from Value Shading to Dot Density. (See Figure 18.20.)

You can edit your map objects directly in the map when you are in the map window. To deactivate the map window and return to your worksheet, click anywhere outside the map but on your worksheet.

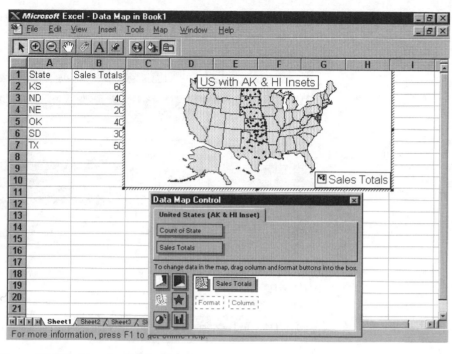

Figure 18.20   Map showing Dot Density

Adding Drawings to Your Charts

You can use the tools available through the Drawing toolbar to add drawings to your charts. To view the Drawing toolbar, click on the Drawing button on your Standard toolbar.

The drawing tools in this toolbar (Figure 18.21) can be used on your charts and worksheets. They allow you to add graphics that enhance your work.

To clear some space to make it easier to work on your drawing, you can drag the Drawing toolbar, or any other toolbar, anywhere it fits in your Excel window, by clicking on an open area (a nonbutton area) of the toolbar and dragging it to where you want it.

With the Arrow drawing tool you can add an arrow to your chart for special emphasis. Click on the Arrow drawing tool, then click and drag from where you want the line of the arrow to begin to the item that you want the arrow to point out.

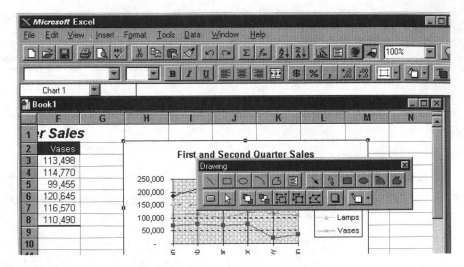

Figure 18.21   **The Drawing toolbar provides tools for enhancing your charts and your worksheet.**

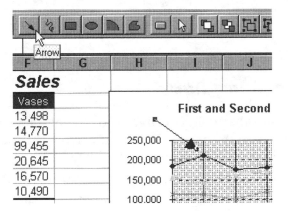

To format the Arrow object, for instance, to make it show up in a different color, or with a different arrowhead for higher visibility, double-click on the arrow to bring up the Format Object dialog box, or click on it with the right mouse button and, from the shortcut menu, click on Format Object. Select from any of the Pattern options and click on OK to activate the new arrow style.

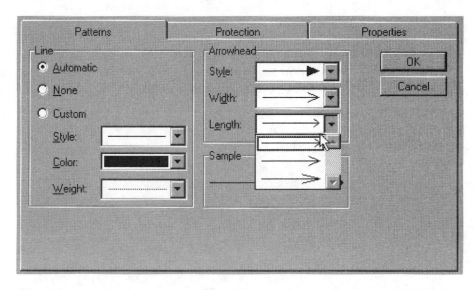

To make your arrow most useful, add a text box to the back end. Click on the Text Box button on the Drawing toolbar to add a text description to the arrow, as shown in Figure 18.22, by moving the cross-hair pointer to a place near the arrow and dragging it to create a box of the size you want. Then type in the text and press Enter.

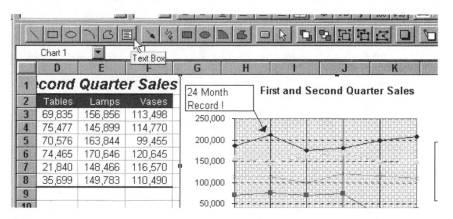

Figure 18.22 **Text Box object added**

While the Arrow and the Text Box are the tools that you are most likely to need on the toolbar for charts and maps, you might want to experiment with the other buttons as well. Among them are buttons that can be used to create the shapes indicated on the button, buttons that are used to group or ungroup the shapes that you create, and buttons to help you specify which shapes should be in the foreground and which should be in the background. The next-to-the-last button can be used to apply a shadow to any selected object on your worksheet, and the last button is used to apply a pattern to a selected drawing object.

Chapter 19

Linking Worksheets and Workbooks

FEATURING

Spreadsheet programs proved early on that they were a powerful and indispensable tool. As powerful as they were, power users who needed to push them to their limits quickly found that a traditional spreadsheet model, with 256 columns and 8,192 rows, simply was not enough to do the job. Not only was there the restriction on the number of records that could be kept (due to the limited number of rows), but if a user wanted to keep monthly, quarterly, or yearly information, they would either have to divide the sheet into the appropriate number of sections or move to multiple spreadsheet files.

For instance, if someone wanted to track the detail of quarterly sales figures and then consolidate that information, they would more than likely need five separate files—one for each quarter and an additional one for the consolidation. In addition to the inconvenience of keeping track of all these separate files, information from the quarterly sheets would have to be manually entered into the consolidation sheets every time any of the figures changed.

With Excel, not only does a user have twice as many rows per worksheet, for a total of 16,384, but a single file, called a *workbook*, can contain hundreds of worksheets. By default, a workbook is set to contain a maximum (depending on the amount of memory available) of 255 worksheets, but you can change this to a much higher number if you have a lot of memory to work with. With workbooks, you no longer need to use separate files to record large amounts of information. Instead, you can logically group your worksheets into workbooks.

In addition, your worksheets are no longer isolated containers of cells and numbers:

▶ If you have four quarterly sheets and one consolidation sheet in a workbook, you can have the totals from the quarterly sheets linked to the consolidation sheet so that no manual updating is necessary.

▶ If multiple people have workbooks that they work on separately, but from which the data needs to be collected into one source, you can link the data stored in the multiple workbooks into one workbook, or between the multiple books.

A Short Review on Selecting Cells

Becoming adept at the various methods for entering cell references and ranges will go a long way in helping you with linking cells from worksheet to worksheet and workbook to workbook. The techniques we'll review in this part of the chapter, on working with cell references and ranges on a single sheet, can be applied in the later sections when we link between sheets and workbooks.

Entering Cell References and Ranges Directly

The most direct way to enter cell references and ranges is to type them right into the formulas of your cells. If you have gotten as far as needing to link sheets or workbooks, you have surely experienced entering cell references into your formulas with your keyboard, so we will only quickly review this technique here. For more information on entering cell references using the keyboard, refer to the first chapters of this part.

Let's enter some data into a couple of cells on a worksheet and then use those values in the formula of another cell.

1. On a blank worksheet, enter **100** in cell A1, **200** in cell A2, and **300** in cell A3.

2. In cell A5, type the formula **=A1** and press Enter.

3. Change the value of cell A1 to **500**. Notice how cell A5 is linked to cell A1 and changes as you change A1.

4. In cell A6 type **=SUM(A1:A3)** and press Enter to reference the sum of the range of cells A1, A2, and A3.

5. Change the value of cell A2 to **600**. Note how the value of your sum formula changes when you change the value of a cell it uses in the formula.

6. When you want to use Excel's functions, like SUM, COUNT, AVERAGE, MAX, and MIN, to calculate the ranges of cells that are not contiguous (next to each other), you can separate the cell or ranges with commas. For example, in cell A7 type **=SUM(A1:A3,A5:A6)** to reference the sum of the range of cells A1, A2, A3, A5, and A6.

7. Your worksheet should now look similar to Figure 19.1.

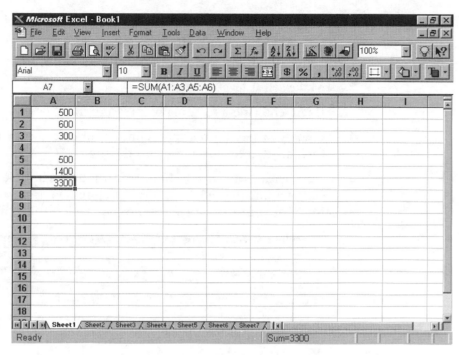

Figure 19.1   Worksheet with cell ranges typed directly into formulas

Entering Cell References and Ranges with the Mouse

In explaining something to one another, the instinct to point to something we can both see, and to say "That one" instead of going into a description of it, whatever it is, is a trait that we all fall back on at one time or another. When working with worksheets, this can actually be a more accurate and reliable way to refer to cell ranges than entering them manually. With the mouse, you can click and drag over the ranges you are referring to, a technique that ensures accuracy in that you are not only seeing and "touching" the exact range that you want to include in a formula, but you are reducing the risk of typos, since Excel is handling the inputting of the range. When you move into working with multiple worksheets, selecting ranges with your mouse may well prove to be "the only way" in your mind to refer to ranges on other worksheets and workbooks.

Select a blank worksheet and try the following exercise that demonstrates the use of the mouse to select ranges:

1.   Enter **100** in cell A1, **200** in cell A2, **300** in cell A3, and **.05** in cell A4.

2.   Make cell C1 your active cell.

3.   Begin entering a formula by pressing the = key.

4.   Once you begin an expression, Excel can accept cell ranges into the formula that are selected with the mouse. Click on cell A1.

5.   The border of cell A1 should turn into what looks like marching ants surrounding the cell. Your formula should look like =A1. See Figure 19.2 for what your worksheet should look like at this point.

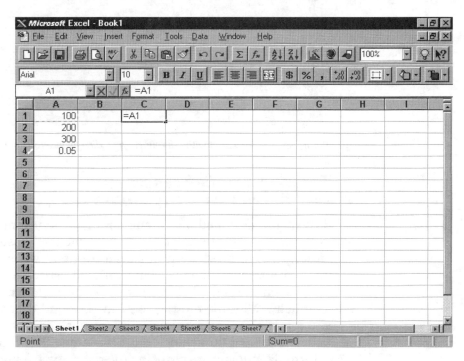

Figure 19.2   Using the mouse to enter cell references

6.   Click on cell A2. You may notice that your formula has changed, because Excel thinks that you are still searching for the cell or range of cells that you want to refer to. Click on cell A1 again.

7. Press the + key on your keyboard. Once you use a mathematical operator in your formula, Excel anchors the previous cell or range reference.

8. Click on Cell A2. Notice that because you used the plus sign, Excel now thinks that you want to add another cell reference. Your formula should read =A1+A2

9. Press Enter. The value in cell C1 becomes 300.

    You can also use the mouse to enter ranges into formulas instead of just single cells.

1. Using the worksheet above, click on cell A6.

2. Type **=SUM(** into the cell.

3. Using your mouse, click and drag from cell A1 to A3. Your worksheet should look like Figure 19.3.

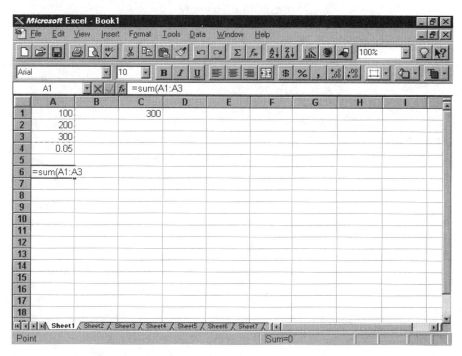

Figure 19.3 *Selecting a range of cells with Excel.*

4. Notice how Excel enters the notation A1:A3 into the formula. Type the closing parentheses for the Sum function and press Enter.

TIP If you are entering a function or using only the one set of parentheses in a formula, you do not need to close the parentheses; Excel will do it for you. Simply press Enter when everything but the closing parenthesis has been entered. (Excel will *not* close any sets of parentheses if you have more than one set in the formula, even if all but one set are closed.)

Entering noncontiguous ranges with the mouse is as easy as selecting the first range and then holding down the Ctrl key while selecting the remaining ranges in the noncontiguous range. The next few steps illustrate this.

1. Using the worksheet we created above, click on cell A9.

2. In cell A9 type **=SUM(**

3. Select the cell range A1 through A4.

4. Hold down the Ctrl key and click on cell A6. Notice that Excel places a comma and then the reference to cell A6 in your formula, as in Figure 19.4.

5. Press Enter.

Entering Cell References and Ranges with the Arrow Keys

In Excel, you can enter cells into a formula using the arrow keys on your keyboard just as easily as you can with the mouse.

1. Select a blank worksheet.

2. In cell A1, type **100**, in cell A2 type **200**, and in cell A3 type **300**.

3. In cell A4 type **=SUM(**

4. Press the up arrow on your keyboard until cell A1 has a dotted border or "marching ants" around it.

5. Holding down the Shift key, press the down arrow key until the dotted border surrounds cells A1:A3.

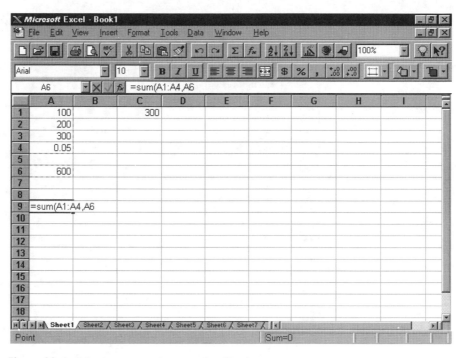

Figure 19.4   Selecting noncontiguous cells using the mouse

6. The formula in cell A4 should now read =SUM(A1:A3 like in Figure 19.5.

7. Press Enter.

    You can also use your arrow keys to enter noncontiguous cells into a cell formula. To do this, type a comma between each range that you want included. Let's go through the steps necessary to total two separate ranges that are noncontiguous:

1. Using the same worksheet used in the previous exercise, select cell C1.

2. In cell C1, type **200**, in cell C2 type **400**, and in cell C3 type **800**.

3. Type **=SUM(** in cell C4 and move to cell A1 using your arrow keys.

4. Hold down the Shift key while clicking on the down arrow key until you arrive at cell A3. Type a comma.

5. Use the arrow keys to move to cell C1.

6. Hold down the Shift key while using the arrow keys to move to cell C3.

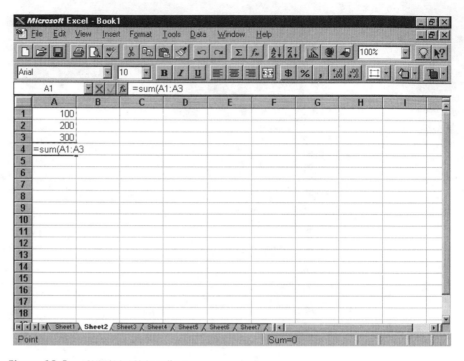

Figure 19.5   =SUM(A1:A3) in cell A4

7. The formula in cell C4 should now read:

    =SUM(A1:A3,C1:C3

    and your screen should resemble Figure 19.6. Press Enter.

Working with Worksheets

Using workbooks, you can organize your data according to separate categories, assigning each category its own sheet(s). For instance, if your workbook is the financial data for 1995, you might want to store the data in 4 sheets (one for each quarter), or even 12 (one for each month). You may also want to add one more sheet to use for the consolidation of information.

Excel opens a new workbook with the default of 16 worksheets. You can add, move, delete, or copy any of the worksheets in the workbook. You can also format multiple sheets simultaneously by selecting the sheets and then entering the data on one of the selected sheets. You can also

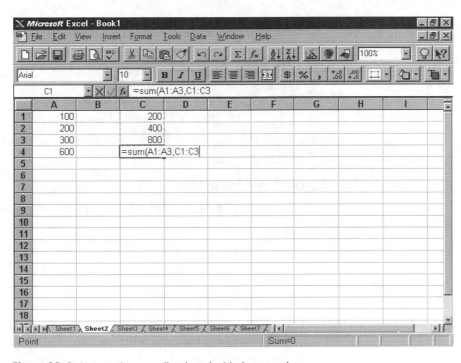

Figure 19.6 Noncontiguous cells selected with the arrow keys

customize the names of each of your sheets, so you can refer to sheets by using a name like January or First Quarter instead of Sheet1 or Sheet2.

Naming Worksheets

Excel automatically creates the names Sheet1, Sheet2, and so on for each sheet in the workbook. Of course, it's much easier to comprehend the contents of a worksheet if it has meaningful names in the tab of each worksheet. Perhaps you have organized your data into months, and you would now like the name of each month—"January," "February," etc.—to appear on the appropriate worksheet tabs.

You can easily edit the name of a worksheet in Excel. To change the name of a worksheet, double-click on the worksheet tab and enter the new name for the worksheet, as follows:

1.   Double-click on the worksheet tab you wish to rename.

2.   Type the new name of the worksheet in the Rename Sheet dialog box.

3. Click on OK or press Enter to apply the new name to the sheet.

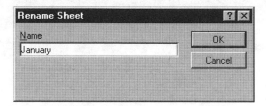

Forbidden Characters

You cannot use the following characters in the name of your sheet:

: (colon)

/ (forward slash)

\ (back slash)

? (question mark)

* (asterisk)

In addition to these forbidden characters, you cannot use the following characters as the first or last character in the name of your sheet:

' (accent grave or backwards apostrophe)

[(opening bracket)

] (closing bracket—you *can* use this as the last character, however)

> **TIP** When you have many worksheets, it becomes tedious searching for the names of worksheets that are further down in the tab sequence. You can see a list of all worksheet names at one time by right-clicking the mouse on the VCR-type directional "Go To" arrows at the beginning of the sheet tabs, as shown in Figure 19.7.

Moving Worksheets

Moving worksheets is just as easy as renaming them. In many cases it is truly a matter of pointing and clicking with the mouse. You may create a worksheet, name it, and enter data into it, and later discover you need to move the worksheet to a more logical position in your workbook. To

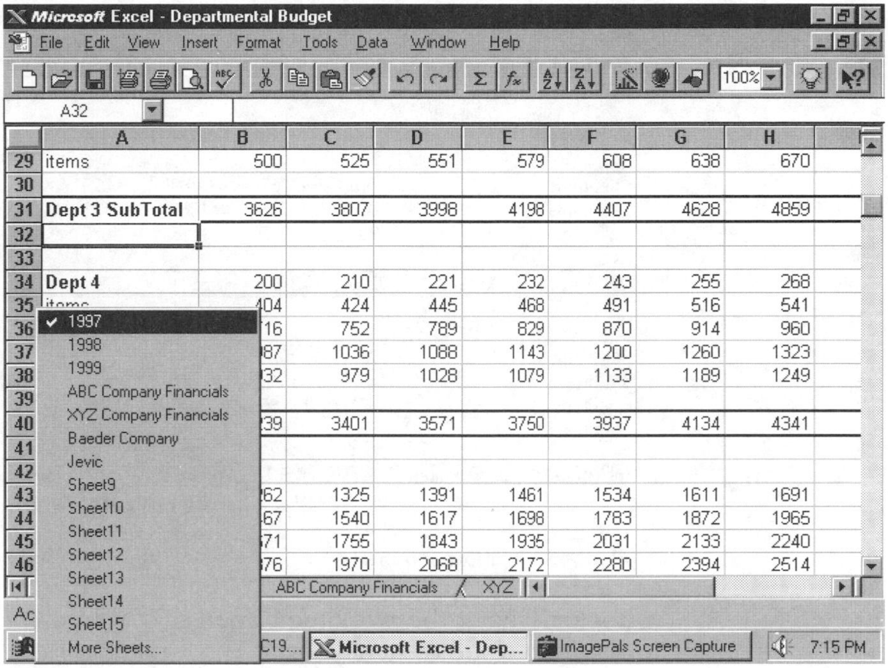

Figure 19.7 *Finding multiple sheet names with the sheet list*

accomplish this, click and hold the sheet tab while dragging it to its new position. Let's walk through these steps briefly.

1. Click on the tab of the worksheet you wish to move and hold down the mouse button. A document icon should appear near the mouse pointer, along with a small black arrow indicating the current sheet position.

2. While holding the left mouse button, drag the sheet to its new position indicated by the black arrow as in Figure 19.8.

3. Release the mouse button to complete the move.

The method above works best when you can see your destination to begin with. You can even click and drag worksheets from one workbook to another if the windows of both books are visible. Before attempting this, refer to the section later in this chapter that discusses viewing multiple worksheets and workbooks.

You may also use the Move or Copy dialog box to move and copy your worksheets. This method is frequently used to copy worksheets from one book to another. To run through the steps of this exercise, you should

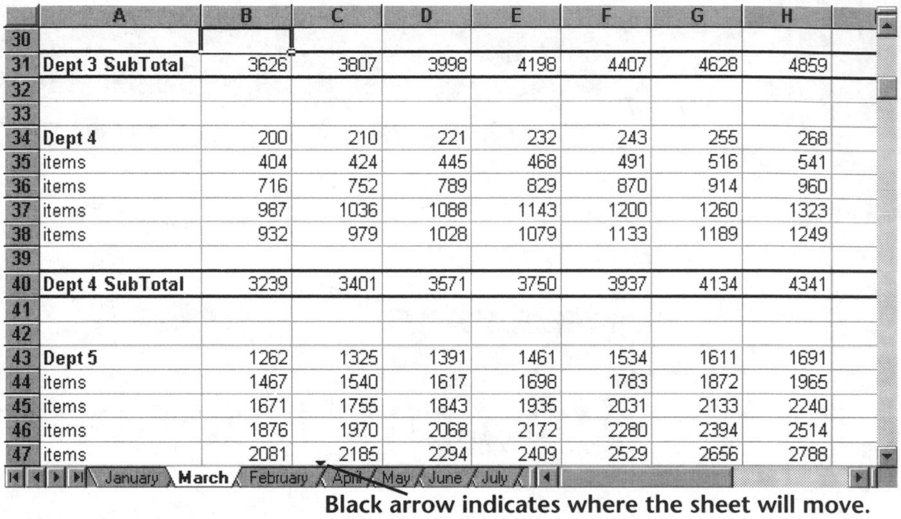

	A	B	C	D	E	F	G	H	
30									
31	Dept 3 SubTotal	3626	3807	3998	4198	4407	4628	4859	
32									
33									
34	Dept 4	200	210	221	232	243	255	268	
35	items	404	424	445	468	491	516	541	
36	items	716	752	789	829	870	914	960	
37	items	987	1036	1088	1143	1200	1260	1323	
38	items	932	979	1028	1079	1133	1189	1249	
39									
40	Dept 4 SubTotal	3239	3401	3571	3750	3937	4134	4341	
41									
42									
43	Dept 5	1262	1325	1391	1461	1534	1611	1691	
44	items	1467	1540	1617	1698	1783	1872	1965	
45	items	1671	1755	1843	1935	2031	2133	2240	
46	items	1876	1970	2068	2172	2280	2394	2514	
47	items	2081	2185	2294	2409	2529	2656	2788	

January \ **March** / February / April / May / June / July /

Black arrow indicates where the sheet will move.

Figure 19.8 Moving a sheet

not only have the workbook open that we have been using but also a blank workbook where you can move your worksheet temporarily. If you do not have a blank workbook open, create a new workbook by choosing File ➤ New and base the workbook on a blank workbook. (Of course, the blank workbook is just for this example. You could use any workbook you want.) Click on OK.

1. If you are not in your original workbook, switch to that workbook by selecting it from the Window menu.

2. Click on the tab of the worksheet you have been using before.

3. Click your right mouse button on the tab of the sheet that you want to move and click on Move or Copy.

4. Under *To Book:* in the Move or Copy dialog box (Figure 19.9), select the new workbook you have created.

5. Under *Before Sheet:* select Sheet3.

6. Click on OK to move your sheet.

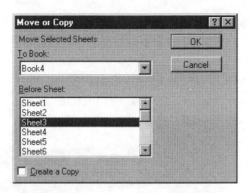

Figure 19.9   Move or Copy dialog box

Copying Worksheets

If you want to create a copy of a worksheet to use elsewhere in the same workbook or in another workbook, you can use the same techniques presented above, with only slight variations:

▶ Using the mouse: Hold down the Ctrl key while you click and drag a sheet. The sheet will be *copied* to its new location instead of being moved.

▶ Using the Move or Copy dialog box: Select the Create a Copy checkbox to activate the copy function.

Inserting and Deleting Worksheets

You can also insert blank worksheets into your workbook when needed.

1. Select the tab of the worksheet where you want a new sheet to be added.

2. Select Insert ➤ Worksheet from the menu bar. Alternatively, click your right mouse button on the selected sheet to get the shortcut menu and choose Insert, then click on OK.

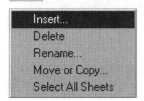

3. The worksheet you selected will be shifted to the right. Excel will insert a new worksheet to the left of the selected sheet.

To delete a worksheet, you need only select the sheet and then either select Edit ➤ Delete Sheet or right-click on the sheet for the shortcut menu and choose Delete. You will be prompted with a dialog box to confirm your deletion.

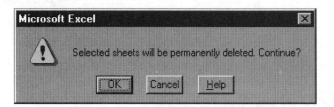

Selecting and Editing Multiple Worksheets

Sometimes you'll need to create a workbook with several worksheets that are copies of each other. For instance, if you have four fiscal quarters, and four regions in your organization, you might want five worksheets that are exact copies of each other: one for each quarter, and a fifth that totals all the quarters together. To accomplish this, you could create each worksheet separately, entering the row and column titles on each worksheet. You could also create one worksheet, format it, and then copy the sheet four times. However, there is an easier way. In Microsoft Excel, you can select multiple sheets and edit them all at the same time.

In this situation, you would select your five blank sheets that you want to format alike, and then edit any one of the sheets. Any data you enter or formatting that you apply to one of the selected sheets will show up on the other four sheets selected. Let's work through how to select and edit multiple worksheets:

1. Open a new workbook.

2. Click on the first sheet tab that you wish to edit.

3. Hold down the Shift key and click on the tab of the last sheet in the series you wish to edit.

4. Release the Shift key to finish your selection. Your series is now grouped as appears in Figure 19.10. The grouped sheet tabs all appear in white.

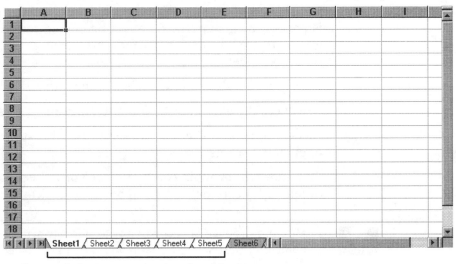

Grouped sheet names appear in white.

Figure 19.10   Grouped worksheets

NOTE   You can also edit noncontiguous worksheets by using the Ctrl key instead of the Shift key to select the various worksheets.

You can now edit all of the selected sheets simultaneously by entering data or applying formatting on one of the sheets:

1. Select the first worksheet in the group and choose Cell A2 and type **North** and press Enter.

2. Type **South** in cell A3.

3. Type **East** in cell A4.

4. Type **West** in cell A5.

After you finish editing the data, click on the tab of another worksheet in your group. You should see an exact copy of your data from the first worksheet in the other selected sheets.

Part 3

Analyzing with Excel

It doesn't matter onto which sheet you enter data. As long as that sheet is part of the group, the data will be copied to the other sheets in that group. To see how this works, let's walk through editing some of the data on a worksheet.

1. Select the last sheet in the series by clicking on the worksheet tab.

2. Select cell A2 and change North to **Northeast** and press Enter.

3. Switch to the first sheet in the series. Northeast now appears in cell A2 of all of the sheets.

To remove the grouping of sheets, click on a sheet that is not in the group of selected sheets, or hold down Shift and click on the first grouped sheet.

> **TIP**   Use grouped sheets when widening the same column throughout a number of sheets. The columns will widen simultaneously in all the sheets that are grouped.

Linking Sheet to Sheet

You can reference the data on one sheet from another within the same workbook. This is very useful, because you don't have to enter data twice, and if data in the first sheet is changed, that change is automatically updated in the second.

Linking sheet to sheet works just like linking cell to cell. You can either enter cell references manually in formulas, or you can use the mouse. You could also use the arrow key method demonstrated earlier in this chapter, but it is a little more tricky.

Linking with the Mouse

If you do not have a blank workbook open, create a new, blank workbook to work with for these exercises. For this first exercise, we will look at how you would sum together three worksheets onto one, consolidation worksheet.

First we need to enter some data in our worksheet. Follow these steps to enter data in your workbook.

1. Click on the tab for Sheet2 and enter the value **250** in cell A1. Press Enter.

2. Click on the tab for Sheet3 and enter the value **500** in cell A1. Press Enter.

3. Click on the tab for Sheet4 and enter the value **1000** in cell A1. Press Enter.

    We will now move to Sheet1 and sum the values we placed on the other sheets.

1. Click on Sheet1 and click on cell A1.

2. Type **=** and then click on the Sheet2 tab. Click on A1 and the formula bar indicates the following:

    ```
    =Sheet2!A1
    ```

3. Press the **+** key. Notice that the cell is no longer activated. Click on the tab for Sheet3.

4. Click on cell A1. Notice that the cell is now activated and the formula bar indicates the following:

    ```
    =Sheet2!A1+Sheet3!A1
    ```

5. Press the **+** key, and click on the tab for Sheet4.

6. Click on cell A1 and press Enter to complete the formula.

7. The formula for cell A1 now reads:

    ```
    =Sheet2!A1+Sheet3!A1+Sheet4!A1
    ```

    The value in cell A1 on Sheet1 should read 1750.

Referencing Syntax

When Excel references one cell from another on the same worksheet, it simply refers to the cell by its address, such as A1 or C3. When Excel references another sheet, it also needs to reference the sheet's name as well as the cell's address.

For one-word sheet names, Excel simply places a **!** (exclamation point) between the sheet name and the cell address, for example Sheet1!A1.

However, if the sheet name contains a space, then Excel encloses the name in apostrophes, such as 'Fall 1995'!A1.

Linking Workbook to Workbook

Linking between workbooks is similar to linking between worksheets. As with the additional references created when linking cells between sheets, one more reference is added by Excel when you link sheets between workbooks.

> **TIP**   Use File ➤ Open and click on the first workbook you want, then hold down Ctrl while you select multiple workbooks to open. Once multiple workbooks are open, repeatedly press Ctrl+Tab to move among the open workbooks in memory.

> **TIP**   To switch from one worksheet to another in the same workbook, hold down Ctrl and press PgUp or PgDn. Release all keys when you are at the worksheet you would like to use.

Linking with the Mouse

Just like linking between worksheets in the same workbook, you can use the mouse to link between sheets in separate workbooks. In order to use the mouse, you need to have all referenced workbooks open in Excel at the time of linking. (If you manually enter the names of the workbooks in the formula bar without using the mouse, you do not need to have the workbooks open.)

To do the following exercise, you should have two workbooks open. It will be easiest with two fresh, blank workbooks.

First we need to add some data to the workbooks so we can see Excel at work linking workbooks:

1. If you have not opened two new workbooks, do so now.

2. Activate the first sheet of one of the workbooks and enter **200** in cell A1.

3. Activate the second sheet of the same workbook and enter **300** in the cell A1.

4. Activate the third sheet of the same workbook and enter **500** in cell A1.

5. Save the workbook as **MYBOOK**.

   Now we need to link the workbooks together.

1. Switch to the blank workbook by selecting Window from the menu bar and choosing the workbook from the list.

2. Activate the first worksheet and click on cell A2. Type **=**

3. Select Window ➤ MYBOOK from the menu bar.

4. Click on the first worksheet tab and click on cell A1. Type **+**

5. Click on the tab of the second worksheet and click on cell A1. Type **+**

6. Click on the tab of the third worksheet and click on cell A1. Press Enter to complete the formula.

7. Click on cell A2 on the first worksheet. The formula should read as follows, (though all on one line in the formula bar; it's only broken here to fit the margins of this book):

```
[MYBOOK.XlS]Sheet1!$A$1+ [MYBOOK.XLS]Sheet2!$A$1+ [MY-
BOOK.XLS]Sheet3!$A$1
```

Referencing Syntax

Examine the formula in cell A2 and see how MYBOOK is referenced in the formula bar. To see how Excel changes the syntax when the linked workbook is closed, close the MYBOOK workbook, then look at the formula bar for cell A2 of the other workbook.

From this you can see that the complete syntax for referencing ranges in other workbooks is:

```
'PATH\[workbook name]Sheet Name'!Cell Reference
```

Because Excel can specify the path for linked workbooks, a linked workbook does not need to be open for another workbook to get information from it. If a linked workbook is not open when you open a workbook that references it, Excel will ask you if you want to re-establish links.

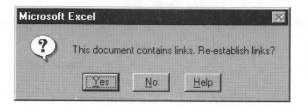

Viewing Links

To view or change the location for the links within a worksheet, choose Edit ➤ Links. The Links dialog box (Figure 19.11) appears with the name of the Linked file, the type of Link and the status flag of Automatic Update. You can open the source file or change its location by selecting the options on the right side of the dialog box.

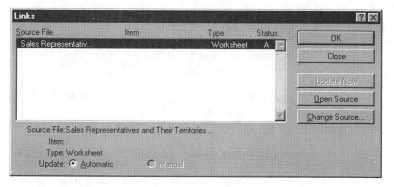

Figure 19.11   Link dialog box

Working with Multiple Windows

Now that you have seen how you link worksheets and workbooks together, it would be useful to be able to see both the referencing and referenced sheets or books at the same time on the same screen in Excel.

Viewing Multiple Worksheets at the Same Time

To view multiple sheets from the same workbook at the same time, you need to create a new window for your workbook by selecting Window ➤ New Window from the menu bar.

Now that you have a second view of the same workbook, you need to arrange the windows so more than one is visible. To arrange multiple windows, follow these instructions.

1. Select Window ➤ Arrange from the menu bar to open the Arrange Windows dialog box.

2. Click on the Tiled radio button and click on the OK button.

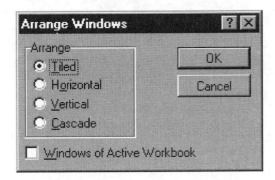

Viewing multiple windows of the same workbook allows you to select a different sheet in each window and immediately view how changing a value on one sheet affects the cells of another sheet that may be linked.

1. Open a new workbook and make sure you are on Sheet1. Type **200** in cell A1 and **200** in cell A2.

2. Switch to Sheet 2. In cell A1, type **=**

3. Click on Sheet1, select A1 and press **+**

4. Select A2 and press Enter.

5. Select Window ➤ New Window from the menu bar. Select Window ➤ Arrange, click on the Tiled button, and click on OK.

6. In your first window, highlight cell A1 on the first sheet.

7. In the second window, highlight cell A1 on the second sheet.

8. Watch the first window while changing the value of cell A1 in the second window from 200 to **2000** and pressing Enter. The first cell in the first window should automatically update itself accordingly. Your screen should look like Figure 19.12.

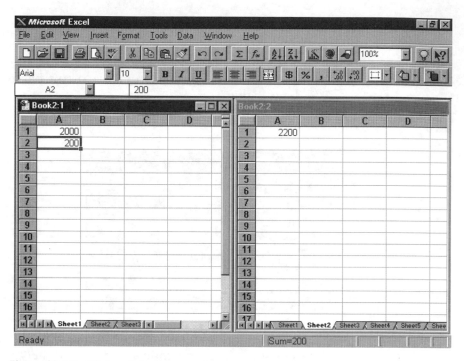

Figure 19.12   Tiled worksheets

 NOTE   When you select Window ➤ New Window from the menu bar, the window that you create is merely another view of a workbook file that you already have open. (The title bar indicates that multiple views are open by following the workbook name with a colon and the view number, for example, Book1:2.) Because both windows are looking at the same workbook, when you change the value in either of the windows, Excel automatically updates both of them—they are both still views of the same workbook.

Viewing Multiple Workbooks at the Same Time

To view multiple workbooks at one time, you simply need to open each workbook you wish to work with and then arrange the windows as you did with worksheets by selecting Windows ➤ Arrange from the menu bar. However, to view separate workbooks at the same time, make sure that the Windows of Active Workbook checkbox is not checked.

Workspaces

It is possible to save your arrangement of worksheet and workbook windows so that the next time you need to work with these specific workbooks and views, you only need to open one file. Choose File ➤ Save Workspace to save the arrangement of worksheet and workbook windows. For a in-depth discussion about saving workbooks together, refer to Chapter 20 for a discussion of saving *workspaces*.

Closing Multiple Views

You close the different views of a workbook the same way that you would close a single view, by selecting File ➤ Close from the menu bar. As you close the views of a workbook the numerals signifying the other view numbers will decrease in number until only one view is left, at which point the colon and view number is no longer a part of the title bar.

Chapter 20

File and Print Operations

FEATURING

Filing and printing are the two core operations that you will perform using computer software. You must be able to store (save) and retrieve (open) the work you create, and produce finished printed copies of this work. Each Office application has a File menu that holds commands for creating new files, saving and opening files, and previewing and printing. Figure 20.1 displays the File menu in Excel.

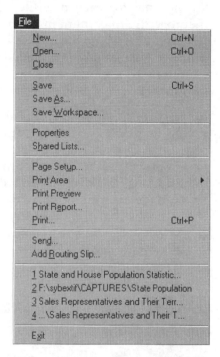

Figure 20.1   *The File menu contains the core commands needed by Office 95 applications.*

Because of the variety of financial and database layouts that are possible, Excel offers more file and print features than some of the other Office applications. For example, Excel has a command in the file menu for saving a *workspace*. This is a new concept—the ability to save how the overall Excel screen looked at a particular moment. Excel also provides extensive printing capabilities allowing you to print data across multiple sheets; to store preformatted data as views, and to print them in a single report. Excel's header and footer capabilities are the best in their class.

In these following sections, you will become well-versed in these fundamental tools needed to expertly use the Office applications.

Creating a New Workbook

When you launch Excel for the first time, a new worksheet appears with a generic Book# name in the title bar at the top of the screen. Excel designates a file as a book. By default, each book is capable of containing up to 255 multiple sheets, although only 16 of these sheet tabs are visible at one time for each new file. (Actually, depending on your system's memory, the maximum number of multiple sheets can be increased. At last count we were able to insert over 1000.) If you wish to increase the number of sheet tabs in a file, choose Tools ➤ Options and click on the General tab, then increase the number in the *Sheets in New Workbook* option.

To start another new file, choose File ➤ New from the menu bar. Click on OK in the New dialog box and a new file will be created with the next sequential Book#. If there is an existing book (file) on the screen, each new book will "slide" in front of the existing file. You can start as many new book files as you wish. Excel will keep track of these files in memory. Look at the bottom of the Window menu on the menu bar to see a list of the books that you currently have in memory. When you pull down the Window menu, you can click on one of the files in this list to make it active on the screen. An alternative is to press Ctrl+Tab to toggle back and forth between files or books opened.

Each time you create a new file, Excel will provide a new generic Book# name and increase the number. If you exit the Excel program and start again, the generic book numbering starts again at 1. This generic name will change once you formally save your work with a more descriptive name (using File ➤ Save).

Saving Your Workbook

Both while you are creating and after you have finished creating your Excel workbook, you will want to save your work to disk. Saving your work to disk allows for a permanent copy of your data to be stored.

When you save a workbook, you are required to provide a name. The name can be up to 255 characters and may contain spaces and periods. Until you save your work, the name listed for the worksheet is the generic Book# name. You may save your work using this name, but, as it is little more than a number, it is not very descriptive. Whatever name you decide, the new name appears at the top of the screen in the title bar.

1. Choose File ➤ Save from the menu bar, or click on the Save button on the Standard toolbar, or press the shortcut key of Ctrl+S, to save your worksheets.

2. In the File Name text box, type over the generic Book# name with the name you want for the file. Click on the Save button on the right side of the dialog box to complete the Save operation (see Figure 20.2).

3. The name of the file appears in the title bar of the worksheet.

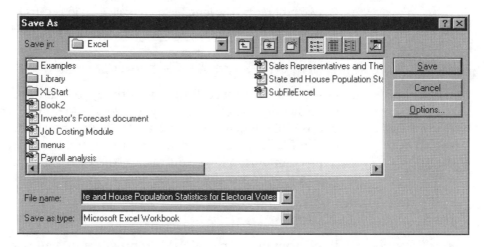

Figure 20.2 **The names of files can be up to 255 characters with spaces and periods allowed in the name.**

NOTE   Although Windows 95 allows for file names that can be as much as 255 characters, you can still use these files with programs running under the previous version of Windows 3.1. When you are running these other programs in DOS or under other operating systems, however, the long file names will appear truncated and numbered with an eight-character file name: the truncated name consists of the first six characters of the long name, a tilde, and a number. For example: A long file name such as State and House Population Statistics for Electoral Votes appears as STATEA~1.XLS when viewed on the disk or from other programs.

Once you have named and saved your file, any subsequent saves will automatically update the file on your hard drive or floppy disk. You will not see the Save As dialog box again or be prompted to rekey the file name. Make sure that you save often. Click on the Save button on the Standard toolbar for quick saves. It only takes a second. You are insuring that your current work is safely stored on disk.

TIP   You can share Excel 95 files with individuals who have Excel 5.0. The file formats are the same and there is no conversion needed between the two programs. The long file names allowed in Excel 95 are actually stored in a truncated, eight-dot-three traditional DOS file name (see previous Note).

Using the Save As Command

Once you have saved for the first time, you can use the File ➤ Save As command to make a copy of your work under another name. When you choose File ➤ Save As, the Save As dialog box shows the current name of the file. Type a new name, and you will have two copies of the file. This command allows you to save the changes made to an opened file with a new name, thus preserving the original file.

Using AutoSave

Excel contains a special Add-In program that allows for automatic saves to your worksheet. You can set the increment for the automatic save, and Excel will save the file every *x* minutes. Setting a 10-minute AutoSave can be a tremendous safeguard against unexpected power failures or machine lockups.

You must first "add-in" the additional program and then activate its setting. To do this, choose Tools ➤ Add-Ins from the menu bar. The Add-Ins dialog box appears. Check the AutoSave option and click on OK. Now when you choose Tools from the menu bar you will see that there is an AutoSave option on the menu list. Click on it to bring up the AutoSave dialog box. You can use this box to change the minutes increment for saving the file. You can also specify that Excel prompt you at the time for the AutoSave so that you can decide at the time whether to save or not. If you have multiple books opened, you can have AutoSave save their information in addition to the information in the active workbook.

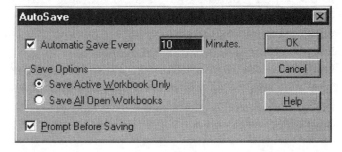

File Management

The following sections provide some helpful hints and instructions for many common file-management operations you will be performing as you create more worksheets and workbooks in Excel.

Closing a Workbook File

To clear the screen of files choose File ➤ Close. If you have not performed a recent save and have made changes to your worksheet, Excel will prompt you to save your work, as shown here:

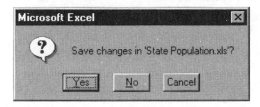

> **TIP**   Instead of closing one file at a time, you can close all the files in memory at the same time. Hold down the Shift key and, with the mouse, click on the File menu. You will see the command Close All rather than the regular Close. Choose Close All and all of the files in memory will close. If any of the files needs saving first, each one that needs to be saved will prompt you as to whether you wish to save it before closing.

Opening a Workbook File

Once you have saved and closed a file, you can then open it by choosing File ➤ Open from the menu bar, or pressing Ctrl+O, or clicking on the Open button on the Standard toolbar. Excel also lists the last four most recently used files at the end of the File menu. You can choose a file from here. The Open dialog box will list all of the previously saved Excel files residing in the current folder as shown in Figure 20.3.

To open a particular file, double-click on the file name, or click once on the file name and then click on the Open button on the right side of the dialog box.

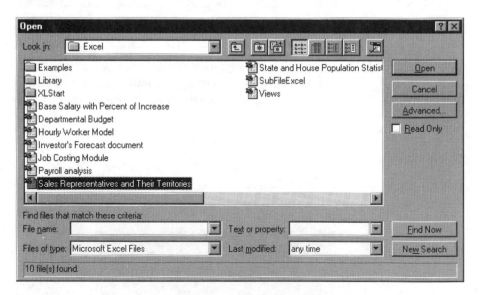

Figure 20.3   You can see a list of Excel files when you choose File ➤ Open.

Previewing a File before Opening

In the Open dialog box (File ➤ Open) there are a number of buttons at the top right side. These buttons control the list display and property information. You can change the way your files are listed. The Details button allows you to see file information as to when the file was created and its size. The Preview button allows for a display that shows the file name on the left and a small preview of the file to the right. Figure 20.4 displays the Open dialog box with a file preview of the selected file.

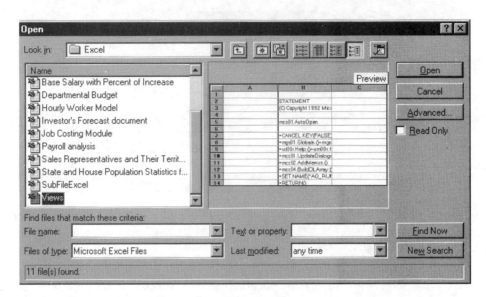

Figure 20.4   *You can preview a file before opening.*

Opening Multiple Workbook Files

Excel allows you to select and open multiple files. Using the Windows techniques of contiguous or noncontiguous selecting, click once to select the first file to be opened (do not double-click). For noncontiguous file selection, hold down the Ctrl key and click on any of the other files you wish to open.

If the files you want to open are all in sequence (i.e., they are contiguous), click once on the first file to select it and hold down the Shift key, then click on the last file in the list to be selected. All of the files between the first and the last will be selected. Click on the Open button on the right side of the Open dialog box (see Figure 20.5). Excel will open all of the files at once. Use the Window command on the menu bar to see the list of open files in memory. Select any file from the Window list to make it the active file.

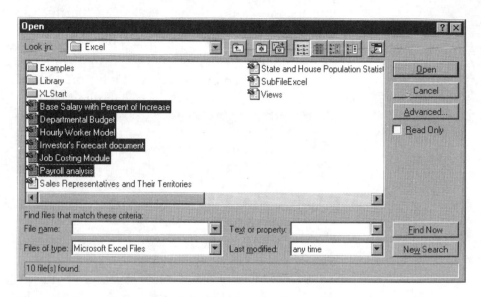

Figure 20.5 *You can open multiple files in Excel by using the Shift or the Ctrl key to select contiguous and noncontiguous file names.*

Finding Files Containing Specific Information

You can search for files containing specific words or values in the file. Choose File ➤ Open from the menu bar. On the right side of the Open dialog box, in the *Text or property* area, type in the text or property you wish to find. Click on the Find Now button and Excel will look through each file, searching for the text or property you specified. When found, the file is displayed in the list window. Excel "remembers" each find that you conduct and lists the Find criteria in the drop-down *Text or property* list box.

Opening Lotus and Other Spreadsheet File Types

You can open or "import" existing Lotus files by simply choosing File ➤ Open from the menu bar and, at the bottom of the Open dialog box, clicking on the drop-down arrow next to *Files of type*, and choosing Lotus 1-2-3 Files from the list. Excel will display any existing Lotus 1-2-3 files, and you can double-click on the name of the file you wish to open.

Lotus files are opened directly into Excel with Lotus macros being preserved. You can activate one of the Lotus macros by pressing Ctrl plus the letter name of the macro. You cannot create a new Lotus macro in Excel, but you can create the macro using Lotus and once again open the file in Excel. When it is time to save your Lotus file, you can decide whether to save as a Lotus or Excel file. Before saving it as an Excel file, consider carefully whether you or others will still need to be able to use Lotus to open your new version of the file.

Opening or importing an ASCII-delimited text file is performed in the same manner as other file types. Choose Text Files from the *Files of type* list at the bottom of the Open dialog box in order to see the list of text files you have on the specified disk. Once the file is opened, each long string of text must then be "parsed"—separated into the appropriate columns of information. Choose the Data ➤ Text to Columns command to parse delimited files into separate columns of values and labels.

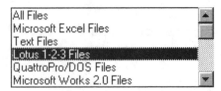

Opening QuattroPro for DOS and Windows

Excel can open and read files that were created in QuattroPro for DOS or for Windows. If you have problems reading the files, contact the person who created the spreadsheets and ask if they can convert them to another format. Even though you cannot save to the QuattroPro format, you can read the files. If you need to save the file, choose a format that both Excel and QuattroPro can read and save to.

NOTE   If a file is already open in memory and you open the file again, Excel does not list the file twice in the Window command list.

Renaming a Workbook File

Once you have named and saved a file, you may discover that the name is not as descriptive as you would like. You can easily rename the file. Follow these steps:

1. Choose File ➤ Open to see the list of Excel file names.

2. Click once on the name of the file you wish to rename. This selects it. Then click once again. (Do not perform a rapid double-click on the file name or the file will be opened into memory.)

3. Once you have clicked twice, the name of the file will appear in an outline box around the entire file name. The name will be selected.

4. Now you have two choices:

   • You could simply start typing at this point, but the selected file name will instantly disappear as you start typing; thus you must type an entire replacement file name.

   • *Or* you could select just the part of the selected file name that you want to change and then start typing to replace those parts.

WARNING   If the filename extension was showing as part of the name, you must make sure that your new file name also includes the extension. See the next section for the importance of the extension.

---

5. Press the Enter key after you have finished renaming. The screen will flash and redisplay with the new name.

6. If you do not want to open the file at this time, you can click on the Cancel button. The file will maintain its new name.

More on Saving: Choosing a File Type

There are several different formats in which you can save your files other than as an Excel file. Depending on what you want to do, you can choose the file type that matches or most closely resembles the destination program type. For example, if you are sharing files with Lotus 1-2-3 users, you will need to save your work as a Lotus 1-2-3 workbook.

In the Save As dialog box (Figure 20.6), click on the drop-down arrow next to the Save As Type text box. Excel lists the different file types

available. There are a number of Lotus 1-2-3 file formats. The WK?
names are all Lotus type files. If your Excel file has multiple worksheets,
you will want to save as a Lotus file type that supports multiple worksheets. (WK4, WK3 files are multiple-worksheet Lotus formats.)

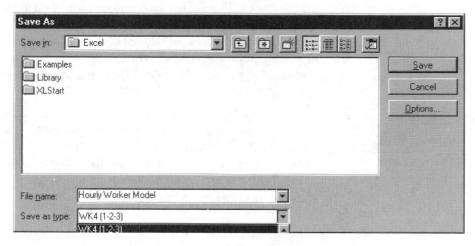

Figure 20.6 *Excel allows you to save in a number of different file formats.*

Saving in Lotus File Formats

Excel permits you to save your file in one of several different Lotus
formats. You should refer to your documentation for Lotus, or ask the
Lotus user who will be accessing your spreadsheet what file extension
corresponds most closely to the version of Lotus to be used. Some
versions of Lotus, such as Lotus Release 3.x and Lotus for Windows,
permit you to use multiple-sheet workbooks. Be sure to get that information before creating your workbook. In addition, Excel macros will
convert into Lotus macros; however, you should be aware that not all
commands are available in both programs. If you are converting a
workbook to Lotus, it is best to let the receiving program create a macro
so that nothing will be lost in the conversion.

WARNING   The most important thing to remember is that if you are saving your Excel workbook as anything other than a Microsoft Excel Workbook (for Version 5 or 7—that is, for Version 5 or for Office 95) or as a Microsoft Excel 4.0 Workbook, chances are you will lose some data in the conversion. Some spreadsheet programs do not support multiple-worksheet workbooks or workspaces. Other programs do not have very good macro languages, or have extremely limited worksheet sizes. Experiment by saving in different formats and opening the converted Excel file in the other program.

 TIP   When you save in a different file format, the extension on the file name is usually different than that used by Excel. However, you will have two copies of the file: one in Excel's format and the other in the converted file type. Always keep the Excel copy of the file so that you can bring it up in Excel if the other user has questions.

Saving as Text-Delimited

A file saved in the text-delimited ASCII format permits that file to be read by a database program, or even a computer language. Basically, there are three types of delimited text files:

▶ Space-delimited

▶ Tab-delimited

▶ Comma-delimited

In each case, a character is placed between fields in the file. Where that character occurs, a new field begins. For most purposes, you probably will use a tab-delimited or comma-delimited text format. Using the space format with text can cause problems. You should have a systems support person work with you to learn more about how to convert your Excel worksheet properly for use in non-spreadsheet programs. Opening a text-delimited file requires that you "parse" the information coming into Excel. Choose Data ➤ Text to Columns to parse delimited files.

Saving a Workspace

As you know, you can open multiple workbooks. Each workbook is stored in memory and can be viewed by choosing the Window command on the menu bar or by pressing Ctrl+Tab. It may be necessary for you

Part
3

Analyzing with Excel

to work with several workbooks at the same time as part of an analysis procedure. For instance, if you have two workbooks that are updated separately by two departments, such as Payroll and Accounts Payable, but you want to use the information in both workbooks for your own workbook, you would need to have all the books open in front of you for reference.

Once you have closed all of the files, the next time you are ready to open them, you must manually open each one or select the files with either the Ctrl key or the Shift key. The Workspace command eliminates reopening a specific group of files. The Workspace command allows you to save the names of all open files under one file name. Thus, you only need to remember one workspace name. When you open the workspace file, Excel will "point" to the names of the specific files contained in the workspace and open them all at once.

Follow these steps to save a workspace file:

1. Open two or three files onto the screen. (The Window menu will show the names of the multiple files.)

2. Choose File ➤ Save Workspace. In the Save Workspace dialog box, Excel suggests the generic name of *Resume*. This is a reminder that the Workspace file lets you resume where you left off.

3. Type a more descriptive name and click on the Save button or press Enter. Figure 20.7 displays the Save Workspace dialog box.

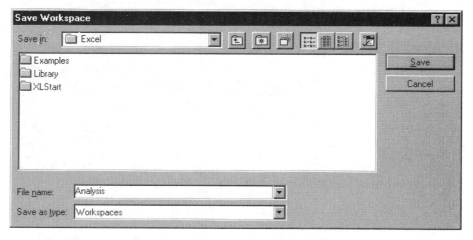

Figure 20.7 *The Save Workspace dialog box.*

4. To close all of the files, hold down the Shift key and click on File ➤ Close All. If needed, save your work when prompted.

5. To open the workspace file, choose File ➤ Open. You will see the name of your workspace file appearing in the same list as your Excel workbook files. When the workspace file is opened, Excel points to and opens the actual files involved in the workspace.

TIP   Whereas files have a filename extension of .xls, workspace files have the extension .xlw.

If you have the screen split into multiple windows, Excel's workspace file will even remember the saved split screen arrangement and open the files into the same arrangement. When you open multiple files, you can split their arrangement on the screen. Choose Window ➤ Arrange, then click on Tiled radio button. Figure 20.8 displays four workbooks open in memory with the tiled arrangement.

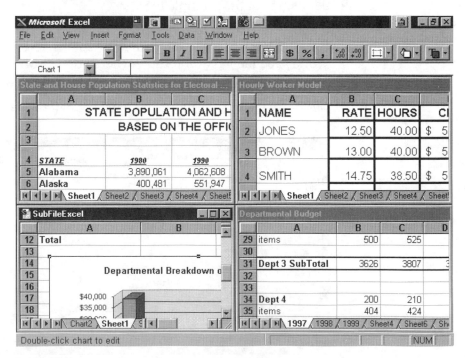

Figure 20.8   *Multiple opened files in a tiled arrangement can be saved as a workspace.*

Shared Lists

A new workgroup feature that has been designed for Excel 95 is the Shared Lists feature, accessed from the File menu. With this feature active, multiple users in a network environment can work on the same Excel list. To make an Excel workbook file shareable, open the file and choose File ➤ Shared Lists from the menu. When the Shared Lists dialog box appears, click on the checkbox to Allow Multi-User Editing (see Figure 20.9). You can also find out which other users currently have this workbook open by clicking on the Status tab. When you click on OK, Excel will prompt you to save the file.

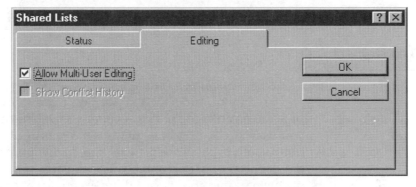

Figure 20.9   The Shared Lists command allows multiple users to update Excel lists of information, and to see who else has the list open.

File Properties

When you have a file open in Excel, you can view important information about the file such as creation and modification dates, file size, worksheets and file summary information. Open a file and choose File ➤ Properties from the menu bar. Click on the General tab to see file information (see Figure 20.10). If you have multiple files open, the active file will be the one whose properties are available.

Part
3

Analyzing with Excel

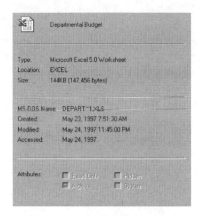

Figure 20.10 **The Properties command displays multiple tabs of information about the file.**

Printing in Excel

Printing your data can sometimes be the most exhausting part of creating and producing worksheets. You may encounter columns that fall off the paper and move to the next page, page breaks that will not occur where you want them, headings that insist on printing only the first page but not the other pages, and a cadre of hardware problems occurring with the printer itself. Fortunately, Excel offers solutions to 90% of printing problems—just about everything except for changing the toner or ribbon cartridge for your printer.

This section describes the methods for previewing before printing, printing single and multiple worksheets, defining the page setup and layout, naming and printing multiple ranges of data, naming and assigning views, and printing reports.

Print Particulars

Excel allows you to print an entire workbook, a selected sheet, or selected sheets within the workbook, selected ranges with single sheets, and selected ranges across multiple sheets. The default setting is to print the selected worksheet: the worksheet that is active at the time of printing.

When you click on the Printer icon on the Standard toolbar, Excel immediately prints the active worksheet and applies the name of the worksheet as the header, and the page number as the footer. If you print using the menu options of File ➤ Print or if you press Ctrl+P, the Print dialog box appears, allowing you to specify your specific printer, multiple copies, and page ranges. The default settings for printing are listed below. Figure 20.11 shows the Margins page of the Page Setup dialog box.

Setting	Defaults
Page Orientation	Portrait
Scaling	100%
Paper Size	8.5" × 11"
Top Margin	1"
Bottom Margin	1"
Left Margin	.75"
Right Margin	.75"
Header	The Sheet Name
Footer	The Page Number
Sheet	No Gridlines

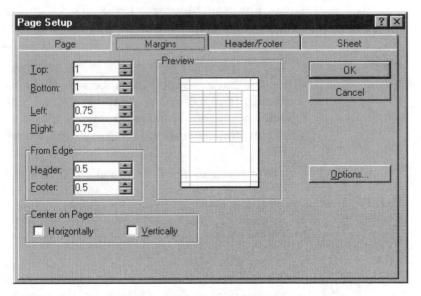

Figure 20.11   *The default settings for printing are located on the Page Setup dialog box tabs.*

Part
3

Analyzing with Excel

Printing an Entire Workbook

To print an entire workbook (including all of the sheets in the workbook), choose File ➤ Print from the menu bar. Click on the Entire Workbook radio button. All pages in all sheets will print. The page numbering will be sequential across all sheets in the workbook; they will not start over again for each new sheet being printed. The Header containing the sheet name will change as each separate sheet is printed. If you wish to print multiple copies, type or click on the spinner buttons in the Copies option group to specify the number of copies to print.

To reprint random pages, specify the pages to print in the Page Range section of the dialog box.

Printing Multiple Sheets

You can always click on each individual sheet and then click on the Print button on the Standard toolbar. But to print multiple sheets at the same time, group the multiple sheets you wish to print. To group noncontiguous sheets, hold down the Ctrl key and click on the sheet names for each sheet. For contiguous groups of sheets, click on the first sheet in the group. Hold down the Shift key and click on the last sheet in the group. Grouped sheet names appear in white in the sheet tab area at the bottom of the screen.

Once you have grouped the sheets to be printed, choose File ➤ Print from the menu bar or press Ctrl+P. In the Print dialog box the Selected Sheets option should be on. If it isn't, click on it to activate it. Click on the Print Preview button to see exactly what will print.

NOTE If you are not seeing Sheet tabs at the bottom of your screen, turn on this option by choosing Tools ➤ Options, clicking on the View tab, and, at the end of the middle set of Window options, checking the Sheet tabs option.

WARNING If you can only view a partial spreadsheet, you may have a previous print area that has been set. Ungroup the sheets by holding down Shift and clicking on one of the sheet tabs. Then choose File ➤ Print Area ➤ Clear Print Area for each sheet so that your entire sheet area is available for printing.

Previewing before Printing

With spreadsheet printing, it is always recommended that you preview before you print, as there are layout factors that can be known ahead of time (before wasting your good paper on, for example, a misaligned print job). With Print Preview you will be able to see if the last column of one page has moved to a second page. You can then reformat the data so that the column remains on the page with other text.

To preview a worksheet, select the worksheet(s) with the data to be printed and choose File ➤ Print Preview from the menu bar, or click on the Print Preview icon on the Standard toolbar. Excel will compose a graphical representation of your worksheet in full-page view. Click on the Zoom button at the top to increase the Zoom setting. You can also click on whatever portion of the worksheet you wish to zoom in on.

The Print Preview toolbar lists the actions that are possible in Print Preview. The Next button is enabled if there is more than one page that will print. When there are no additional pages (i.e., you're on the last page), only the Previous button is enabled. Figure 20.12 displays the second page of a printout.

Inserting Manual Page Breaks

If you do not like where Excel automatically breaks the page, you can insert your own page break so that the end of a page is exactly where you wish. In Figure 20.13 you can see that a new section will be starting at the bottom of the page instead of on the next page, as it should. Because Excel uses a mathematical formula to figure out the page length and subtracts the margin settings from this page length, you cannot always know where the break is going to occur. Being able to manually insert and remove your own breaks can make a report more readable.

Both the automatic and manual page breaks can be seen in the worksheet. You will be able to see the gray dashed lines of the page breaks as you scroll through the spreadsheet.

NOTE If you do not see the automatic or manual page breaks in the worksheet, turn on this option by choosing Tools ➤ Options, clicking on the View tab, and, in the top section of Window Options, click on the Automatic Page Breaks checkbox.

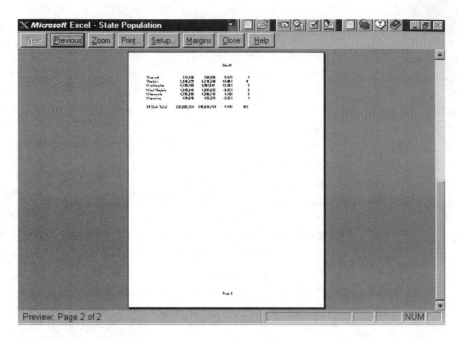

Figure 20.12 Print Preview helps you to correct problems before printing the worksheet.

17 items	500	525	551	579	608	638
18 items	608	638	670	704	739	776
19 items	716	752	789	829	870	914
20 items	824	865	908	954	1002	1052
21 items	932	979	1028	1079	1133	1189
22						
23 Dept 2 SubTotal	3580	3759	3947	4144	4352	4569
24						
25 Dept 3	714	750	787	827	868	911
26 items	688	722	759	796	836	878
27 items	900	945	992	1042	1094	1149
28 items	824	865	908	954	1002	1052
29 items	500	525	551	579	608	638
30						
31 Dept 3 SubTotal	3626	3807	3998	4198	4407	4628
32						
33						
34 Dept 4	200	210	221	232	243	255
35 items	404	424	445	468	491	516
36 items	716	752	789	829	870	914

Figure 20.13 Excel will not always break the page where you want in a long worksheet printout.

To insert your own page break into a worksheet, follow these steps:

1. Position the pointer on the row line that should start the new page. (Alternatively, you can think about it as positioning the pointer below the last line of text that should appear on the current page.)

2. Choose Insert ➤ Page Break from the menu bar. If there is only a Remove Page Break option, then you already have an inserted page break at that spot. Check in the Print Preview view to see where the page breaks. Decide if this is where you want the page to break. If it isn't, choose Insert ➤ Remove Page Break and insert the break at another line.

3. The page break shows up as a gray dashed line. The manual page break's dashes are a little longer than the automatic page break's. (You can barely tell the difference in appearance, however, unless you highlight cells that include the page breaks.)

4. Click on the Print Preview button again to see if the page break is now where you wish for it to occur (see Figure 20.14). Repeat this process as needed if you want to manually control the page breaks for each page.

    To delete a page break, position the pointer on the line where you broke the page and choose Insert ➤ Remove Page Break from the menu bar. The change in the wording of the menu from Insert Page Break to Remove Page Break is how Excel shows that a manual page break has already occurred and therefore can only be removed.

WARNING You cannot remove the automatic page break directly. The automatic break gets removed when you insert your own page break above the automatic break. Always insert your own break above the automatic break, if you wish to convert the automatic break to your own manual break. If you insert a page break below the automatic page break, Excel will both keep its own automatic break and give you another page break. You may end up with a page that has only two or three lines on it.

TIP If you have multiple sheets that need the Page Break at the same spot in all of the sheets, group the sheets before inserting the page breaks (hold down Shift and click on the last sheet in the group).

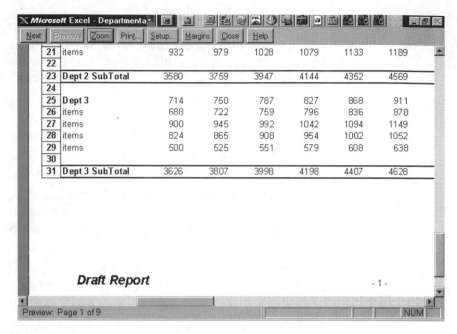

Figure 20.14   The automatic page breaks in Excel may not be to your liking. You can insert your own break.

Fitting to One Page

Worksheets that break onto two pages can sometimes be adjusted so that the entire worksheet prints on one page. If you have more than two pages, Excel will attempt to adjust the sizing so that all the pages squeeze onto one page—but the font size becomes too small to read. Generally, $1\frac{1}{2}$ to 2 pages can be adjusted to print onto a single page with the print remaining readable.

To adjust a worksheet to fit on one page follow these steps:

1.   Open the worksheet to be adjusted.

2.   Click on the Print Preview button or choose File ➤ Print Preview to see how many pages there will be for the worksheet. If there are more than two pages, do not attempt to adjust to one page.

3.   While in Print Preview, choose the Setup button on the toolbar. Click on the Page tab on the Page Setup dialog box.

4. In the Scaling section of the dialog box click on the *Fit to 1 page* radio button. Click on the OK button to see another preview.

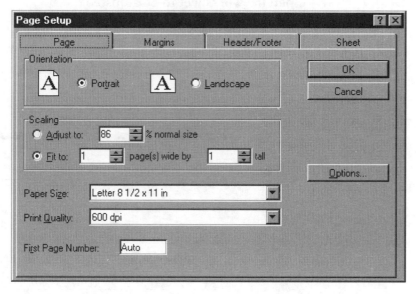

Figure 20.15 You can manually change the amount of compression that Excel performs on a worksheet to squeeze it all onto one page.

5. Excel has adjusted the worksheet to fit onto one page. Click on the Setup button again at the top of the Print Preview screen to return to the Page Setup dialog box. Notice the percentage of compression that was needed in order to squeeze the worksheet onto one page. Figure 20.15 shows the Page Setup dialog box with the Page tab selected and the adjustment percentage displayed.

Printing Landscape

Another method for handling worksheets that do not fit onto a page is to change the orientation from portrait to landscape. With a landscape orientation you can fit more columns on the page but fewer rows. You may still need to use Excel's adjustment scaling of the document to force the sheet to print on one page. The landscape orientation, however, is a tremendous help for multicolumn worksheets.

Landscape printing is very straightforward and we will once again perform the operation from the Print Preview screen. Follow these steps:

1. Open the worksheet to be adjusted.

2. Click on the Print Preview button or choose File ➤ Print Preview to view the layout of your pages, as shown in Figure 20.16.

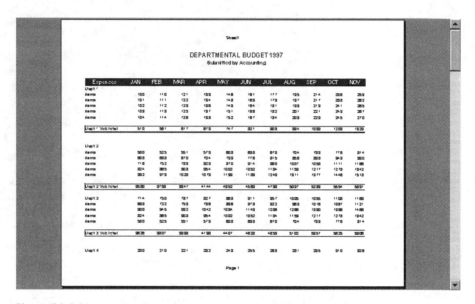

Figure 20.16   **A multicolumn worksheet that doesn't all fit on one page**

3. Click on the Setup button on the toolbar at the top of the Print Preview screen.

4. Make sure the Page tab is selected, then click on the Landscape radio button. Click on OK to return the Print Preview screen.

5. If the landscape orientation is still not sufficient to fit all of the columns across a single page, choose Setup again and repeatedly decrease the scaling until all of the columns fit on a single page. Changing the percentage of scaling compression might allow all the columns to be squeezed onto one page, as shown in Figure 20.17.

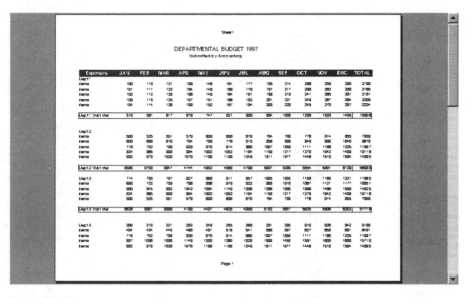

Figure 20.17   The entire worksheet is printable on one page.

TIP   To set all sheets in a workbook to a landscape orientation, group the sheets by Ctrl-clicking on each name to group noncontiguous sheet names or Shift-clicking at the end of a contiguous range of sheet names. The grouped sheet names will be in white. Choose File ➤ Page Setup, and on the Page tab click on the Landscape radio button. Click on the Print Preview button on the right side of the dialog box. All of the selected sheets will be in landscape orientation.

Changing Margins

There may be times when it is not feasible to change the scaling, as Excel simply prints in smaller font sizes in order to produce smaller scaling. Changing the default margins has always been one method for increasing the amount of data that can fit onto one page. Figure 20.18 displays the Print Preview with the Margin button selected. Notice the vertical and horizontal lines of the current margin settings. To change the margins, you can click the Margin button on and off to graphically display where the margin lines reside. Click and drag the horizontal and/or vertical margin lines to change the margins on screen. Print Preview updates instantly so that you can immediately see the implications of changing

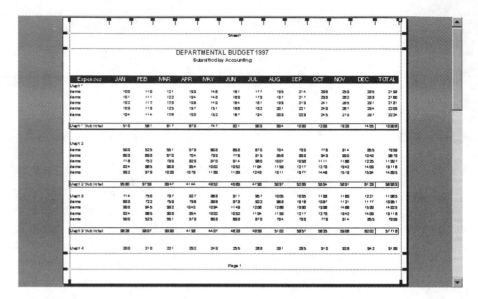

Figure 20.18   You can change the margins in Print Preview by clicking on the Margin button and dragging the vertical or horizontal lines.

the margin. You can also choose the Margin tab page of the Page Setup dialog box and type in specific margin settings. These settings are saved when you save the file.

> **WARNING**   Most laserjets won't print text if the text is too close to the edge of the piece of paper. Therefore, don't decrease your margins to less than .20 inches.

Centering the Worksheet on a Page

Excel prints all worksheets starting from the upper left corner of the page. When you have small worksheets that do not take up the full width and height of a printed page, you may want them to print centered between the margins of the page. Excel has an option that you can check so that worksheets print centered horizontally and vertically on a page. Figure 20.19 shows a small worksheet printing in its default position: the upper left corner.

Choose File ➤ Page Setup and click on the Margin tab in the Page Setup dialog box. If you are already in Print Preview, click on the Setup button on the toolbar and, in the Page Setup dialog box, click on the Margin tab.

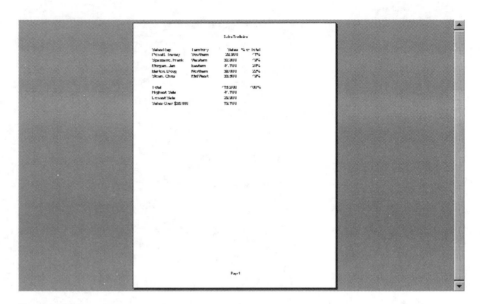

Figure 20.19   *Print Preview shows the default position for printing: the upper left corner of the page.*

Mark both the horizontal and vertical checkboxes in the Center on Page section. (If you only wish the spreadsheet to be centered between the left and right margins, then choose Horizontally.) Click on the OK button. Figure 20.20 displays the Center on Page section of the Margin tab page in the Page Setup dialog box. If you wish to see the effect, make sure you're in Print Preview.

Printing Selected Ranges

You can select a range of data and have Excel print only the selection you specify. The quickest method to print a selected range of data is as follows:

▶ Select the range to be printed.

▶ Choose File ➤ Print from the menu bar or press Ctrl+P to activate the Print dialog box.

▶ When the Print dialog box appears, click on the Selection button on the left side of the box. Then click on OK. Excel prints the selected range (see Figure 20.21).

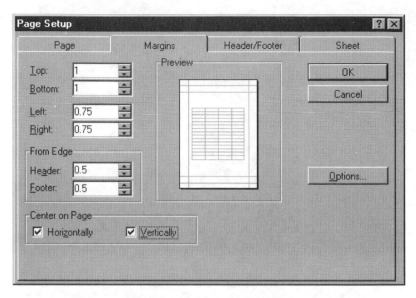

Figure 20.20   You can center a worksheet between the margins using the Center on Page section of the Margin tab page in the Page Setup dialog box.

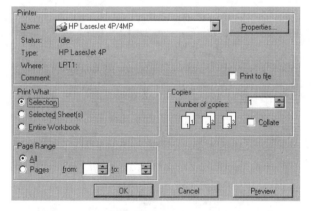

Figure 20.21   To print a range, select the area, choose File ➤ Print, and click on the Selection button.

Another method of printing only the selection you specify is to select the range to be printed, then choose File ➤ Print Area ➤ Set Print Area. Then print.

TIP Once you have printed a selected range, you can repeatedly click on the Printer icon on the Standard toolbar and Excel will reprint the same range without you selecting again. To clear the range from Excel's printing memory, choose File ➤ Print Area ➤ Clear Print Area from the menu bar.

Printing Multiple Ranges from the Same Sheet

When you wish to print multiple ranges residing on the same sheet, select the first range and then hold down the Ctrl key and select the other ranges. Click on File ➤ Print from the menu bar. Choose Selection from the Print dialog box. Click on the Preview button at the lower right side of the dialog box to view your choices. The ranges will each print on a separate page.

 TIP You cannot make multiple ranges print on the same page, but you can hide columns or rows that may lie between the multiple print ranges. Select the column letters or the row numbers, then right-click the mouse and choose Hide from the shortcut menu. When you print your worksheet, the hidden columns will not appear in the printout.

Printing the Same Range Across Multiple Sheets

You can select the same range across multiple sheets by first grouping the multiple sheets containing the range to be printed. Hold down the Ctrl key (noncontiguous ranges) or the Shift key (contiguous ranges) and click at the bottom of the screen on the names of the individual sheet tabs. The grouped sheets will display the tabbed sheet names in white. You must "group" the sheets first before making your across-sheet selection.

With the sheets grouped, drag the mouse over the range of data to be printed. On all the selected sheets, this same range is being selected. Choose File ➤ Print or press Ctrl+P to get the Print dialog box. Click on the Selection radio button to designate that you have a range to print. Click on the Preview button at the bottom right of the Print dialog box to verify that the specific ranges across the multiple sheets will be printing. Choose the Next button on the Print Preview screen to see each page that will print.

To ungroup the sheets, click on a sheet tab not already involved with the grouping, or hold down the Shift key and click on one of the grouped sheets.

WARNING When you group sheets and select a range, this same range will print across multiple sheets. Make sure, however, that you choose File ➤ Print ➤ Selection. Do not choose Selected Sheets even though Selected Sheets would be the logical choice. Excel considers a selected range across multiple sheets still a range.

Printing Different Ranges on Different Sheets

To print different ranges on different sheets within the same workbook, select the sheet and select the range to be printed on the first sheet. Choose File ➤ Print Area ➤ Set Print Area. Select the other sheets and other ranges. Note: You can select multiple, noncontiguous ranges on the same sheet by using the Ctrl key to click on the ranges. You can then select a different sheet and again specify multiple, noncontiguous ranges. Excel is extremely flexible in allowing you to specify different ranges on different sheets. Make sure that you choose File ➤ Print Area ➤ Set Print Area for each of the ranges you select on each of the sheets.

Once all of the Print Areas for all of the ranges have been set, the important step is to choose File ➤ Print from the menu bar or press Ctrl+P. In the Print dialog box, select the Entire Workbook radio button. Choose the Preview button in the lower right corner so that you can see the print ranges on the different pages. When you are in Print Preview, choose the Next button to move from page to page displaying the selected ranges.

Setting a Permanent Print Range

If there is a print range area of the worksheet that you always print, you can designate this range area in the Print Area text box on the Sheet tab page of the Page Setup dialog box. All future printings can then be done by clicking on the Print button on the Standard toolbar. Excel will automatically print the data that falls in this range.

Naming Print Ranges

You can assign names to different print ranges. The name can then be referenced in the Print Area text box of the Sheet tab page on the Page Setup dialog box or as the Selection option on the Print dialog box. Follow these steps to assign a name to a range:

1. Select the print range to be named.

2. Choose Insert ➤ Name ➤ Define from the menu bar. Type in a name for the range and click on the Add button on the right side of the dialog box. Click on OK.

NOTE Your name cannot include spaces. Use an underscore to represent a separation in the name. For example, Year_To_Date.

3. Repeat Step 2 for each range to be assigned a name. Alternatively, note that you can also assign a name using the Name box that appears below the Font name on the Formatting toolbar (see Figure 20.22). Select range to be assigned a name. Click the mouse in the Name box and type the range name and press Enter. To delete a name choose Insert ➤ Name ➤ Define from the menu bar. Select the Range name to be deleted and click on the Delete button on the right. Click on OK.

Jan_Mar ▼		JAN			
Apr_Jun		B	C	D	E
Jan_Mar					
Jul_Sep					**DEPAI**
Oct_Nov					
Print_Area					
Print_Titles					
4					
5	**Expenses**	**JAN**	**FEB**	**MAR**	**APR**
6	Dept 1				
7	items	736	810	891	9€
8	items	482	530	583	6,
9	items	852	937	1031	11:
10	items	487	536	589	6,
11	items	100	110	121	1:
12					
13	Dept 1 SubTotal	2657	2923	3215	35:

Figure 20.22   Range names can be easily assigned by selecting the range and using the Name box to assign a name.

Designating Named Ranges to Print

When you are ready to print the data in a named area, click on the drop-down arrow of the Name box and choose the range name. The named area will be immediately selected for you to see. Choose File ➤ Print and click on the Selection radio button in the Print dialog box. (Alternatively, you can press the F5 Go To key and select the name listed in the dialog box and click on OK, or double-click on the range name. The named area will be selected. Then choose File ➤ Print and click on the Selection radio button from the Print dialog box.)

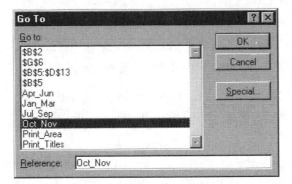

If you wish for a particular range name to be the default print range, type the name into the Print Area text box on the Sheet tab page of the Page Setup dialog box. You cannot choose the name from a list, but you can type in the range name in the Print Area text box. This will be the default print area until you change or delete the range name.

NOTE   Once you close the Page Setup dialog box and reopen it, the range name you typed in the Print Area text box will have been converted to its row/column worksheet range address.

Managing Headers and Footers

By default Excel prints a *header* and a *footer* on each page of the worksheet printout. These can be deleted, customized, realigned, and shortened.

Excel allots half an inch for the header area and the same for the footer area. You may want this space shortened in order to fit a worksheet onto one page. You may also want the header to print but not the footer. In the following sections you'll learn how to make these changes and more.

Deleting a Header or Footer

The procedure for deleting a header or footer is the same as for removing a header or footer. Choose File ➤ Page Setup from the menu bar and select the Header/Footer tab; or while in Print Preview, click on the Setup button and choose the Header/Footer tab.

Click on the drop-down arrow to the right of the current header and scroll up until you find the [none] option. Choose None. In the Header Preview you will no longer see a sample for the header.

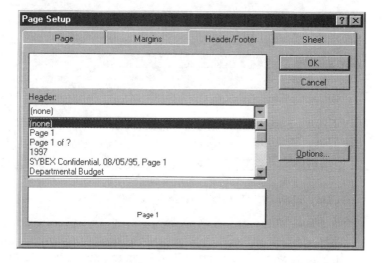

Eliminating the Space Allotted for the Header/Footer

Once you have removed a header or footer, you may want to recover the half inch that Excel allots for it. Chose File ➤ Page Setup or click on the Setup button on the Print Preview toolbar. Choose the Margins tab. The half inch allotment for the header and footer appears in the lower left corner of the dialog box in the From Edge section. Reduce to zero the amount of space Excel is holding for a header or footer to print.

Using Excel's Header/Footer Options

You can choose from Excel's Header/Footer options before deciding to design your own. A very popular option is to print both the current page number and the total number of pages in the footer. For example: **Page 1 of 10**. In the Footer section of the Header/Footer tab page, click on the drop-down arrow and choose *Page 1 of ?*, and Excel will include this information in the footer.

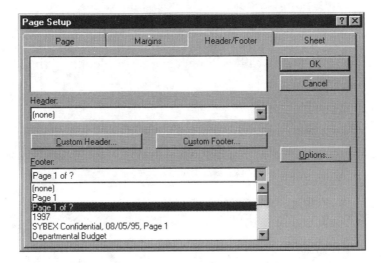

Customizing a Header/Footer

Suppose you wanted the footer to print total pages but you did not want this option centered. You preferred that the footer print this information in the lower left corner of each page. You can customize a header or a footer to type the words you desire or the realignment you need. To customize a header or footer follow these steps:

1.   Choose File ➤ Page Setup and click on the Header/Footer tab, or, from the Print Preview screen, click on the Setup button and choose the Header/Footer tab.

2.   Choose the Custom Header or the Custom Footer button in the middle of the dialog box. This example is going to use a customized footer.

3.   The Footer dialog box appears. There are a number of buttons you can choose to assign different options. Right-click the mouse on any of the buttons to see a description of what the button will offer. Figure 20.23 shows the Footer box options.

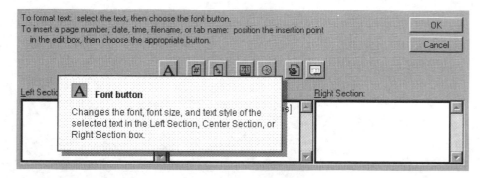

Figure 20.23   When you customize a header or a footer, you can change the font typeface and size as well as other options.

4. We are going to change the font size and style for text that will appear at the lower left-hand corner of each printed page. Start by clicking the mouse in the Left Section text box and then click on the Font button, designated by the capital A. Choose a Bold and Italic font, 14 pt size, for the footer text that will appear on the left. Type the words **Draft Report**.

5. Click on the Custom Footer box. Click in the Right Section area of the Footer dialog box and click on the Date button (button with the tiny calendar on it). Notice the ampersand symbol (&) that prefaces the Date. This symbol is used to specify *linked text*. If you wish to use the ampersand as part of your text, as, for example, in the name *Computer Resources & Training, Inc.*, you need to specify two ampersands next to each other so that Excel would know to not interpret the first ampersand as a special linking symbol. ...If you print a single ampersand or two ampersands with a space between them, Excel does not show any ampersands at all. Figure 20.24 displays a Customized Footer dialog box. Figure 20.25 shows a completed Print Preview of a page with a customized footer.

Printing Repeating Row and Column Data on Multiple Pages

When long worksheets print across multiple pages, the headings that you typed in the beginning rows of the spreadsheet, which print on page 1, do not print on the subsequent pages without you specifying that they should do so. This is also the case with multiple-column documents. When there are too many columns to fit on one page, the trailing columns will print to the next pages. The data is now printing without any

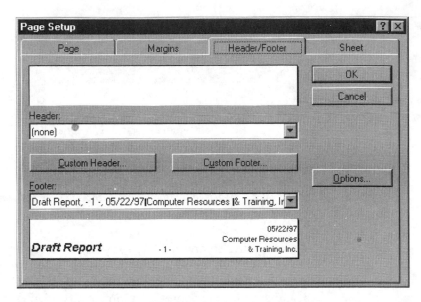

Figure 20.24   *When an ampersand must be used in your custom footer, type two adjacent ampersands and the second one will display.*

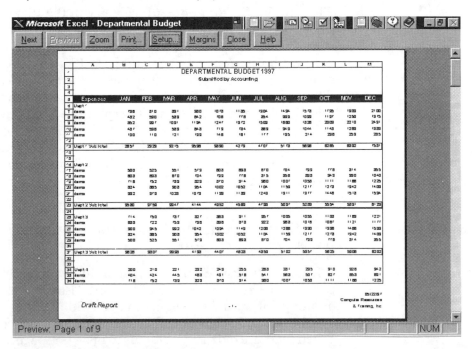

Figure 20.25   *Customizing the Footer or the Header can add needed description to each page of your printout.*

reference to what categories the data belongs to. You will need to specify that a specific category column always print at the left side of the page on all subsequent pages.

Called the Print Borders feature in Lotus 1-2-3, Excel uses the term Print Titles to describe the option that allows you to print the same column and row headings across multiple pages of a worksheet printout. Follow these steps to set a Print Title border of rows:

1. Open the workbook with the multi-page sheet that has a column that you would like printed across all pages.

2. Choose File ➤ Page Setup from the menu bar.

3. Click on the Sheet tab from the Page Setup dialog box.

4. Click the mouse in the section called *Print Titles Rows to Repeat at Top*. Move the dialog out of the way by dragging its title bar down or to the right so that you can see the rows you wish to be repeated at the top of each page.

5. Drag the mouse over the rows you wish to be repeated at the top of each page. Excel enters the row specifications into the dialog box (as shown in Figure 20.26).

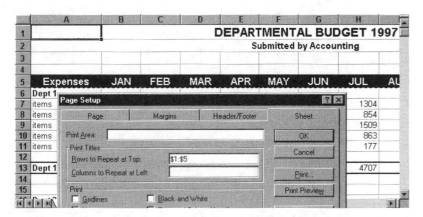

Figure 20.26   Rows that must repeat on each page of the printout are specified in the Rows to Repeat text box here. Drag the mouse over the rows to repeat.

Part
3

Analyzing with Excel

6. Click in the *Columns to Repeat at Left* text box.

7. Select the Columns that should be repeated at the left on every page.

8. Click on the Print Preview button on the right side of the dialog box so that you can view the repeating information before printing.

Printing Extras

With Excel you can print notes in a cell, or switch back and forth from printing formula text versus the result of formulas. You can also print column letter and row number borders. You can print gridlines, and you can direct Excel to printing directly from disk. These are all features that are grouped into Excel's Print Extras category.

Printing Cell Notes

Excel notes are a great form of documentation for cell information (Insert ➤ Note, type in the Text Note text box, then click on OK). When you hover your mouse over a cell that has a note, Excel displays the entire content of the note, as shown in Figure 20.27. (Note that a cell with a note in it has a little red square in the upper right corner.)

You may want to print the content of all of the notes in a worksheet instead of viewing the notes individually on the screen. Follow these steps:

1. Choose File ➤ Page Setup and click on the Sheet tab in the Page Setup dialog box. Do not use the Setup button in the Print Preview screen to access the Page Setup dialog box. The printing of notes is only available if you start through the File ➤ Page Setup command.

2. Click on the Notes checkbox. Simply checking this option will allow the notes of a worksheet to print on a separate page, but the cell references for the note will not print. There is one additional step to make the cell reference for the note to print:

3. Across from the Notes checkbox there is the *Row and Column Headings* checkbox. Select this checkbox and click on the Print Preview button on the right side of the dialog box.

4. You will, of course, see your entire worksheet also. Continue to click on the Next button until you see the page that has the notes and their cell

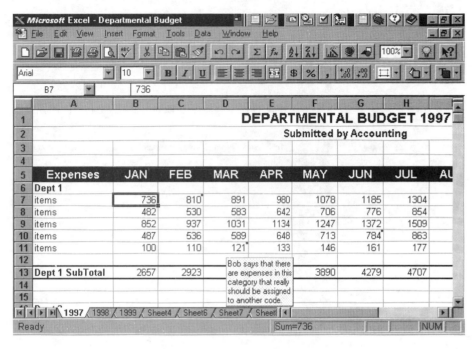

Figure 20.27   *Spreadsheet with the mouse hovering over a note*

references, as shown in Figure 20.28. Note the page number at the bottom of the screen so that you can print this page only. Click on the Close button.

5.   To print this one or two pages with the notes, press Ctrl+P or choose File ➤ Print from the menu bar. When the Print dialog box appears, click on the Pages option in the Print Range section at the bottom left. Type or click on the spinner button to insert the page number in the From: and To: text boxes. Click on OK and Excel will print only the pages specified.

Printing Formulas

You can view the formula text versus the formula result by using the shortcut key of Ctrl+' (Ctrl plus the backwards apostrophe—located below the Esc key). This is a toggle key; use it to alternate between showing the formula text and the formula results.

To print your document with the formula text displayed, use this shortcut key to display formula text. Choose File ➤ Page Setup from

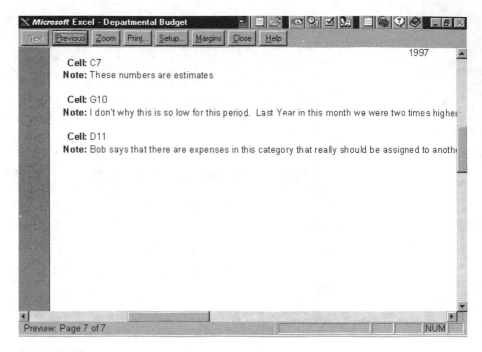

Figure 20.28 **Print Preview of how Notes print in Excel**

the menu bar and click on the Sheet tab. Check the Row and Column Headings option in the middle of the Sheet tab page. Click on the Print Preview button so that you can see the printout before committing to paper. Figure 20.29 shows how the printout will look.

Printing Gridlines

Excel does not print gridlines unless you explicitly ask for this setting to be on. Follow these keystrokes to add and remove gridlines to and from your printed copy.

1.   Choose File ➤ Page Setup from the menu bar, or, if you are in Print Preview, click on the Setup button on the toolbar at the top of Print Preview.

2.   Choose the Sheet tab.

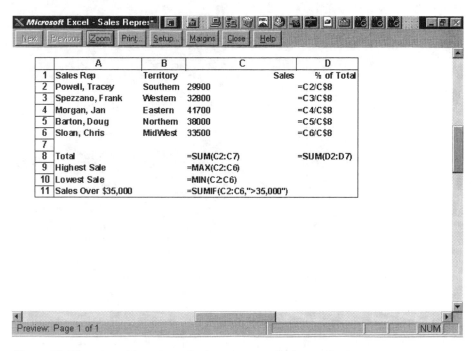

Figure 20.29 Being able to print the formulas and the row and column headings can help someone analyze a spreadsheet more quickly than they could do if they could only refer to them on the screen.

3. Click on the Gridlines option box to turn on gridlines. Click on the Print Preview button or on OK to see how the worksheet will look with gridlines (see Figure 20.30).

4. If you like the effect, click on the Print button on the toolbar at the top of the Print Preview screen.

TIP If you only want gridlines around a few cells but not others, don't use the gridlines options. Instead, select the range of cells that should be bordered with lines and choose Format ➤ Cells from the menu bar. Click on the Border tab on the Format Cells dialog box. Choose where you wish the line (Outline, Left, Right, Top, or Bottom) and then choose a style for the line (dashed, thick, dotted, etc.). Click on the OK button when finished. Alternatively, you can use the selections in the Borders button's drop-down palette on the Formatting toolbar.

Part
3

Analyzing with Excel

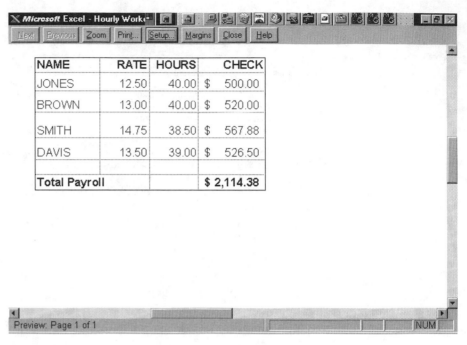

Figure 20.30   *Gridlines don't print unless you specify the setting in the Sheet page of the Page Setup dialog box.*

Printing from the Disk

To print a workbook file from disk, choose File ➤ Open from the menu and select the workbook to be printed—do not double-click. Click the right mouse button to activate the shortcut menu. Choose Print from the shortcut menu. Excel will quickly open the file, print the sheet that was the active sheet when the file was saved and then quickly close the file before you can change any print settings. Make sure that the file already has the correct print settings (margins, orientation, etc.) before choosing to print from the disk. Figure 20.31 shows the shortcut menu with the Print option selected.

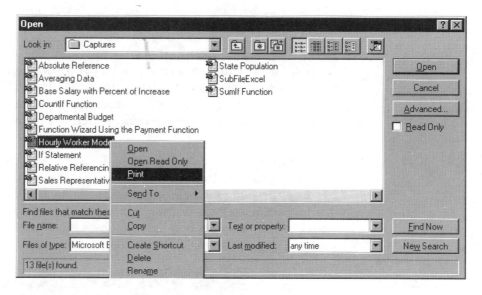

Figure 20.31 *You can print a selected workbook from disk. When you right-click the mouse, you can choose the Print option from the shortcut menu.*

Views and Reports

To fully appreciate the View Manager and Report Manager's possibilities, it is best that you become comfortable with the range of Excel's printing capabilities, as presented throughout the preceding sections of this chapter. Once you have some familiarity with what is available, you'll see the true value of these two managers. The View Manager allows you to define different print and page settings under unique view names and then, in a report, designate which views should print and in which order.

Your multiple settings might include a requirement that data needs to print with the formula text as well as with the formula results. Instead of toggling to see the formula text and changing the row and column headings to display, and then changing back to normal (take off the Row and Column Heading setting, etc.), you can name each view and Excel will automatically remember the setting that went along with the view. You can print different headers and footers with the same printout and have one view with a certain header and footer and the same worksheet print with another header and footer but named as a different view.

Creating Views

The example we are going to use to demonstrate the View Manager's possibilities is to have a printout with formula text as well as formula results. The Formula text view will be in portrait mode and have header and footer settings; the normal worksheet that displays the formula's results will have a landscape orientation and different headers and footers. Here are the general steps needed to create views and to report on them.

1. The first step is to make sure that the View Manager and the Report Manager program have been added into Excel. The View and Report Managers are actually extra programs that come with Excel. Choose Tools ➤ Add-Ins from the menu bar. Make sure that the View Manager and Report Manager options are checked. Click on the OK button. Figure 20.32 shows the Add-Ins dialog box.

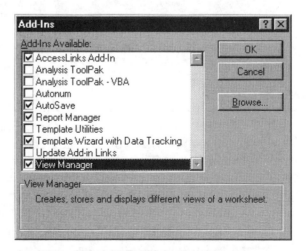

Figure 20.32 *Additional programs available in Excel can be added in through the Tools ➤ Add-Ins command.*

2. Apply some print settings to your worksheet (e.g., Landscape orientation, a specific Header or Footer, shaded headings, etc.)

3. Select the range of cells that will be printed, and choose View ➤ View Manager from the menu bar. Click on the Add button on the right side of the View Manager dialog box.

4. Type a unique name for your view.

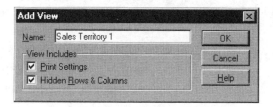

5. Make another view: Change the formatting or the orientation, add a different header or footer, etc.

6. Repeat Step 3 and 4 to select and name the cells to be designated by another unique view name.

7. Using our example here, there will be two unique view names listed in the View Manager box.

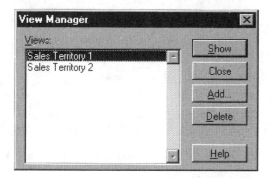

Creating a Report from the Views

Your views can now be placed into a report and printed in a specific order. You will be able to name your report, and future printings will not require the changing of settings, since they will have been performed ahead of time and stored in a View. Here are the steps to attach your views to a report:

1. Choose File ► Print Report and click on the Add button on the right side of the dialog box to add in the views to print.

2. Type a name for the report in the Report Name text box.

3. In the View text box area, click on the drop-down arrow and choose the name of the first view to print. Click on the Add button. The first view name appears at the bottom of the Sections area in this Report part of the dialog box.

4. Choose the second view in the same manner and click on the Add button. Both views are displayed in the Sections area, shown in Figure 20.33. Click on the OK button to close the Add Report dialog box.

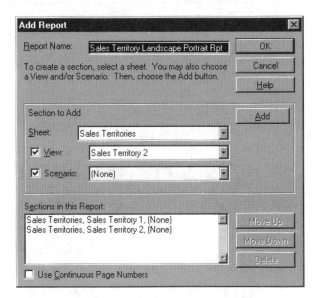

Figure 20.33 *You can create various reports by combining different Views under different report names.*

5. To print the report, click on the Print button on the Report Manager dialog box. Specify the number of copies that should print. Click on OK. Excel will save both the views and the report information, and both views will print under the single report name. Notice how each view prints with the settings you specified.

To edit the report and add or delete a view, or to print with continuous page numbers, choose File ➤ Print Report and click on Edit. To print continuous page numbers check the box at the bottom of the Edit Report dialog box.

The View Manager and Report Manager, although not frequently used, can save a tremendous amount of time, and virtually eliminates setting up different page options like Portrait versus Landscape. Data that resides on the same sheet can be formatted differently and printed as a complete report.

Chapter 21

Ask Excel—Data Handling

FEATURING

Excel's data handling capabilities are the best in the spreadsheet industry. List-management operations that previously required knowledge and use of a full-blown database programs such as dBASE, Access, Paradox, FoxPro, or Approach can now be handled directly in the workbook. Data can also be brought in from one of these databases into an Excel worksheet so that you can use the powerful but easy-to-use features of the worksheet and not have to learn the commands of the particular database program.

Similarly, Excel's data commands allow some very sophisticated data handling. You can use the *Quick Sort By Single Column* feature or the *Data Sort* feature to sort by multiple columns. You can generate Excel's *Quick Form* so that data entry is easier to control. Excel's *AutoFilter* command allows you to filter (exclude) items on the list so that you see only the records that are relevant. Filtered lists can then be subtotaled by any of the column categories you designate. And finally, you can create sophisticated summary reports by using the *PivotTable* command.

Lists in Excel

You can easily manage your data by creating *lists*. Lists encompass information that is organized plainly into column headings and rows. The columns are considered *fields* and the rows are considered *records*.

Creating the List

In previous sections you learned to enter data and words into columns and rows. Creating a list will require no more knowledge than the general methods for entering information.

The spreadsheet list is the most recognizable data model. Figure 21.1 shows a simple list of sales data. Each column heading is considered the field name or category name for the data that is in the column. The row information is considered a record; each record contains related field values.

Entering Information into the List

A rule of thumb: *You should not have any blank columns or rows between your data.* To enter information for your list, type your column headings.

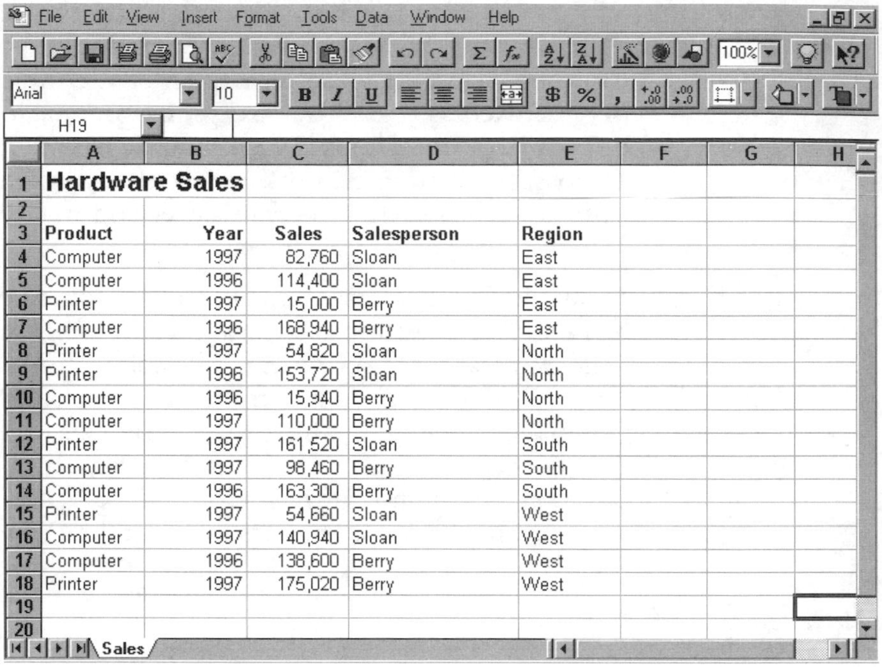

	A	B	C	D	E
1	Hardware Sales				
2					
3	Product	Year	Sales	Salesperson	Region
4	Computer	1997	82,760	Sloan	East
5	Computer	1996	114,400	Sloan	East
6	Printer	1997	15,000	Berry	East
7	Computer	1996	168,940	Berry	East
8	Printer	1997	54,820	Sloan	North
9	Printer	1996	153,720	Sloan	North
10	Computer	1996	15,940	Berry	North
11	Computer	1997	110,000	Berry	North
12	Printer	1997	161,520	Sloan	South
13	Computer	1997	98,460	Berry	South
14	Computer	1996	163,300	Berry	South
15	Printer	1997	54,660	Sloan	West
16	Computer	1997	140,940	Sloan	West
17	Computer	1996	138,600	Berry	West
18	Printer	1997	175,020	Berry	West

Figure 21.1 ***Column headings designate the specific categories of your list. Records are the rows of values for each heading.***

Do not create blank columns between your headings. Your headings can have multiple words but must be typed on a single row—no double row headings. Try to have only one category per column. If you are going to enter employees' names, for example, create a First Name and Last Name column, not just an Employee Name column. As your list grows, you may want to use the list for a mail merge with Word or for a formatted report in Access. You will be glad later that you made specific categories for each type of information you are tracking.

You can format the headings if you desire with bold or with a different font or point size. This single row of column headings is considered a header row by Excel. The row of words on the header row is used by Excel to break out the data below the column headings. For example, Excel will know to never inadvertently sort the column headings into the data when you perform a sort. If you put a blank row between your headings and the first row of data, Excel will confuse your first row of data as the header row because of the blank row between. So, keep blanks out.

On each row, type a value for each heading. These are values that related to one record. Do not create blank rows between your data. Keep the list tight so that Excel can sense its boundaries (the white space around it). If you do not have a specific value for a column, you can leave that *cell* blank, but do not leave a whole record (row) that is blank. Each record must have at least one value. You can continue to add fields and records at any time. Excel will always know where the header row is and where the last record resides.

Generating a Data Form to Add Records Easily

Adding records to your list is as easy as clicking below the last row of data and beginning a new row of information per each column heading. When entering your list information in this manner, you are moving horizontally across the worksheet. If you have more columns than can be seen at one time on the screen, you may notice you have a problem: The data entry becomes tedious as you try to remember what is in the first columns or you double-check yourself by constantly scrolling back and forth.

Excel has a data form feature that allows you to quickly generate a basic data-entry form from the column headings in your list. The form allows you to enter your information vertically into the form, field by field. Excel will then horizontally place the field values into the next blank. Figure 21.2 shows the Excel-generated data form.

The steps to create the form are simplicity itself:

1. With a list already started (that is, with a header row and at least one record already entered), click the pointer on any cell within your list area.

2. Choose Data ➤ Form from the menu bar.

3. A form will be immediately generated from the header row of column text. Each field is displayed vertically, with the first record's information appearing already in the form. Notice that the sheet name appears as the name on the Form dialog box. The current record of the pointer and the total number of records appears in the upper right side of the dialog box.

4. Click on the New button on the right side of the dialog box to generate a blank form. Excel will go to the bottom of the list. Fill in another record of information.

Part
3

Analyzing with Excel

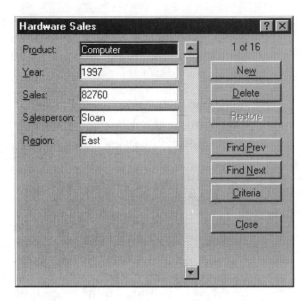

Figure 21.2   *The data form is quickly generated through the Data* ➤ *Form menu.*

Make sure you press the Tab key, not the Enter key, to move from field to field. If you press the Enter key, Excel will give you a new blank form. If this happens, click on the Find Prev button to return to the last record you were entering or editing.

Looking through Records

To look through the records one at a time, click on the Find Prev or Find Next buttons, or use the vertical scroll arrows. The down and up arrows on the keyboard are like the Find Prev and Find Next buttons on the dialog box. They position one record at a time. To move to the first record in the list, press Ctrl+PgUp, or Ctrl+↑. To move to the last record in the list, press Ctrl+PgDn, or Ctrl+↓, and then press the up arrow key once or click on Find Prev.

Editing and Deleting Records

As you move through the list of records, you may see some that need to be edited. Click on the field that you are going to edit. The Home key and the End key move you to the beginning and end of the information in the field. Left and right arrows move the pointer horizontally along the value characters in the field.

To delete a record, click on the Delete button on the right side of the dialog box. Excel will prompt you to confirm the deletion. Note that records that are deleted using the Data Entry form cannot be undone using the Undo feature.

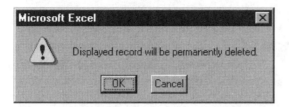

Finding Records Using Criteria

If you want to view records that match a particular set of criteria, you can use the data entry form to perform queries on your list of data.

1. Click on the Criteria button on the right side of the form dialog box.

2. A blank form appears that you can use to specify your criteria. In this example we are going to specify that Excel display only records where the year is 1997 and the sales are equal to or more than 100,000. The graphic shown below shows the data entry form with the criteria information entered.

3. After you enter your criteria, press the Enter key. Excel will jump to the first record that matches the criteria. To find each matching record, press the Find Next button. When there are no more records matching the criteria, Excel beeps to let you know to start looking in the other direction. Click on the Find Prev record to go back through the matching records.

4. To clear the criteria, click on Criteria and then click on the Clear button on the right side of the dialog box. Excel will clear out the cells that contained your criteria. Click on the Find Prev or Find Next buttons to continue moving through all of the records.

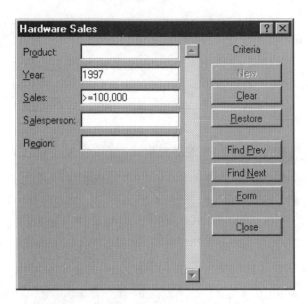

Sorting and Sifting through Data

Organizing your data has always been a capability of spreadsheet programs. The primary tool for organization has been a *sort* feature. Excel's sort feature is extremely easy to use. When your information is organized in manner of an Excel list, you can use the Quick Sort buttons on the Standard toolbar to perform a sort on any particular field (column). Excel will not include the items in your header row as part of the sort as long as your column headings are the first row of your list. For more powerful sorts, Excel has the Sort command which allows multiple sort keys at once.

In addition to sorting as a way of organizing your information, Excel adds an additional tool, the AutoFilter. The AutoFilter allows you to sift through your data and isolate those records that equal specific values. For example, to see only the sales for the Western region, you would use the AutoFilter. Excel would exclude any records that did not match your filter criteria. You can combine sorting with the AutoFilter so that, after you have isolated the records you want, you can then sort them in any fashion.

Let's perform a quick sort and a full blown, multiple-key sort to get an understanding of how to use the sort. Then we will go on to the AutoFilter commands.

Quick Sorts

To perform a sort on a column, click the pointer in the column and then click on one of the Sort buttons on the Standard toolbar. The Sort Ascending button sorts in alphabetical order (or, for numbers, low value to high value). Use the Sort Descending button to sort in backwards-alphabetical order (highest value to lowest value). Excel knows the boundaries of your list and quickly selects the range of the list. The first row is the header row and is not included with the sort.

> **WARNING** Do not select (highlight) a range of cells within the list before sorting. If you do, Excel will only sort the selected range and leave the other values where they were. You can undo this action with Ctrl+Z or by clicking on the Undo button.

Multiple Sort Keys

The quick sort is great for sorting one or two columns, but when you need to control the sort and assign a sort order (specifying what will sort first and then within that sort a secondary or tertiary sort, etc.), use the Data ➤ Sort option to sort your list of information. Using the previous Sales model example, suppose you needed a sort first by Region, then by Sales, then by Salesperson. The quick sort is not powerful enough to handle this. The Data ➤ Sort can perform it easily. Follow these steps:

1. Click on any cell of your list area and choose Data ➤ Sort from the menu bar.

2. The Sort dialog box appears with three sort key options.

3. At the bottom of the dialog box, the Header Row radio button should already be selected. Make sure that it is. This option prevents the column headings from being sorted in with the rest of the data in your list.

4. The name of one of the column headings may appear in the first Sort By text area. You can change this to whatever field you desire. For this example, click on the drop-down arrow of the Sort By text box and choose Region.

5. Make sure the Ascending button is checked. This will tell Excel to sort the Region column in alphabetical order (low value to high value).

6. Click on the first Then By text area's drop-down arrow and choose Sales from the list. Click on the Descending button so that the Sales will sort from the highest sale amount to the lowest sale amount.

7. Click on the last Then By button and choose Salesperson. Click on the Ascending button so that the Salespersons' names will sort in alphabetical order. Figure 21.3 shows the Sort dialog box with the columns designated.

Figure 21.3   **You can have multiple sort keys.**

8. Click on the OK button to perform the Sort.

TIP   You can sort by more than three sort fields if you do it in multiple passes. Suppose you need six sorts. Sort the last three first and then sort by the first three. That is, start from the least important sort fields to the most important. The sort order will be fields 6, 5, 4, 3, 2, 1 with Field 1 ending up as the column that is listed in the Sort By field of the Sort dialog box.

Custom Sort Orders

You may need a sort order for text that is not alphabetical in nature but adheres to other conventions. For example, when you sort month names, Excel sorts the months of the year in the alphabetical order of Apr, Aug, Dec, Feb, Jan, Jul, Jun, Mar, May, Nov, Oct, and Sep. The program is performing the sort correctly according to what it knows about the data. You know, of course, that the month order in a calendar is very specific, and is not alphabetical. Until now, those of us who wanted to sort by the words of the months had to use a month number instead of the month name in order to produce the Jan through Dec order needed. Excel, however, has a Custom sort order option that uses the data of the Custom List items. Excel can be told to sort in the order that the Custom list displays the data. This is an invaluable feature.

Creating a Custom Sort Order List

Looking at the data example being used in this chapter, suppose you needed the regions to sort in an order of North, South, East, and West instead of the default alphabetical order of East, North, South, and West. If your Custom list contains the items North, South, East, and West, we can assign a custom sort order by using this list.

Create the list of regional items in the order of North, South, East and West. Choose Tools ➤ Options and click on the Custom List tab. Click on the right side of the dialog box in the List Entries box and type the four regional items. Press the Enter key after each entry. Click on the Add button when finished and then click on the OK button. Figure 21.4 shows the custom list items with the order of the regions specified.

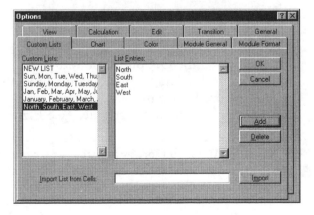

Figure 21.4 *You can produce a custom sort order by adding items in their desired sort order in the Custom List text box.*

Using the Custom Sort Order List

To specify a custom sort order, follow these steps:

1. Click on any cell of your data list so that you are within the area of your list.

2. Choose Data ➤ Sort from the menu bar.

3. In the Sort By text area, select the Region field.

4. Click on the Options button on the right side of the Sort dialog box. The Sort Options dialog box appears.

5. Click on the drop-down arrow for the First Key Sort Order text box list. Choose the region names that were added to the Custom List as shown in graphic below.

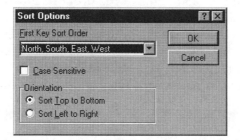

6. Click on the OK button to return to the Sort dialog box. Click on OK to sort the data by the Region name but in the order designated by the Custom List items. The data is sorted in alphabetical order by Region but in the custom sort order (see Figure 21.5).

 NOTE If you sort by a custom order but in descending order, Excel will use the custom list but will simply sort in the opposite order of the custom list.

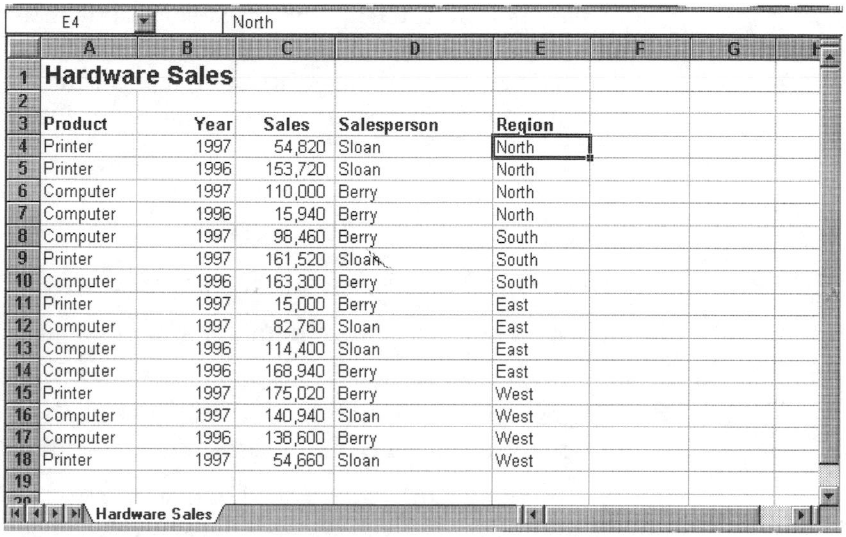

Figure 21.5   Using a custom sort order enables you to sort according to your own conventions for the order of data.

Seeing What You Want to See—Using Filters

Excel's unique AutoFilter feature allows you to display only those records that match particular criteria values. Once records are filtered you can edit or copy them to another sheet or workbook; subtotal them using the Subtotal feature (see next section) or sort the records. As with the Sort command, the powerful AutoFilter ability is extremely easy and intuitive to use.

The AutoFilter displays the records that match your criteria and temporarily hides the records that are not matching. Excel places drop-down arrows next to each column heading and, when you select the list, you see one occurrence of each of the values contained in that column. You can select one of the values and Excel will hide the records that do not match this value.

You can also design a custom filter when looking for values that fall in a range. For example, you would not pick the number 19,810 as a specific value to be used as a criterion but you might want Excel to find all records with values between 15,000 and 20,000. The custom filter allows you to designate criteria that involve a range.

Part 3

Analyzing with Excel

A new item in the AutoFilter list selections is the inclusion of a Top 10 criterion. Excel will display the top ten values in a field. Excel will even let you customize this feature so that you can specify that the AutoFilter display up to the top or bottom 500 values in a field. This is a potent command.

Setting Up the AutoFilter

To use the AutoFilter feature, follow these steps:

1. Click on any cell of your data list so that you are within the area of your list.

2. Choose Data ➤ Filter ➤ AutoFilter from the menu bar. Excel places drop-down arrows next to each column heading in the list.

3. Select the AutoFilter drop-down arrow next to the Region column heading. Excel displays the unique occurrences of each of the region names including the All, Top 10, Custom, and Blank options.

4. Choose North from the selection list (see Figure 21.6).

Excel immediately filters out any records that do not match the value of North in the column. Repeat step 3 for each field criteria you desire per column, then choose the region you want filtered out.

You can readily discern which column fields are involved with the AutoFilter, as the drop-down arrow next to the columns appear in the color of blue and the row numbers are also displayed in blue. This is your indication that AutoFilter is on. The Status bar at the bottom of the screen tells you how many records are involved in the Filter and the total number of records in the whole list. Once the records are filtered, you can continue to sort these records using the quick sort keys on the Standard Toolbar. Excel will use the displayed records as the source of the list.

To display all records again, click on the drop-down arrow next to the fields that are displayed in blue and choose the All option. You may need to use the PgUp key or click on the vertical scroll box to see all the way to the top of the selections in order to find the All option. You can also choose Data ➤ Filter ➤ Show All from the menu bar.

You can turn off the AutoFilter feature by choosing the same commands used to start the Filter: Data ➤ Filter ➤ AutoFilter. The drop-down list arrows disappear when you turn off the feature from the menu bar.

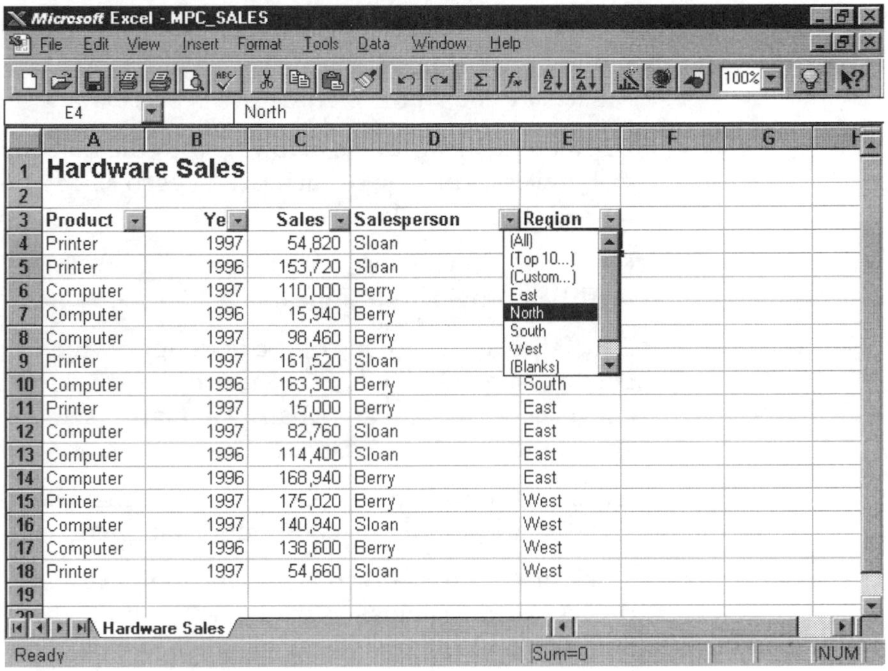

Figure 21.6 Excel's AutoFilter feature is an intuitive database query operation available in an easy worksheet format.

Part
3

Analyzing with Excel

> **TIP** You can use the AutoSum button to add columns even though the data is in a filter. Click on a blank row below the data to be summed and click on the AutoSum button. Excel displays a subtotal function instead of the normal Sum function. Click on the button again, or press Enter to enter the subtotal. Whenever you change to another filter, the AutoSum will automatically recalculate a new sum.

Defining a Custom Filter

As was stated before, your criteria may be that you want to see records that fall within a range of values and not one specific value. This is especially true when you are filtering for numeric data. It is rare that you want to see records that match an exact value such as $486.32. Rather, seeing records that fall into a range, for example, records with values >=200 and <=500 would be more meaningful. The custom filter option allows you to further refine the filter on the column.

Using our example again, we are going to filter for records that fall between sales values of 100,000 and 150,000.

1. Make sure the AutoFilter feature is on (Data ➤ Filter ➤ AutoFilter).

2. Click on the drop-down arrow next to the Sales column heading. Excel displays each unique occurrence of each sales number. Not very useful for selecting records.

3. Click on the Custom option in the drop-down list and the Custom AutoFilter dialog box appears.

4. Excel displays the name of the field upon which you are performing the custom AutoFilter. Click on the drop-down arrow next to the equal sign and click on the greater-than-or-equal-to symbol (>=). Press the Tab key to move to the next text area.

5. Type in **100,000** in the text area. Make sure the And radio button is selected, as you want a compound statement.

6. Click on the drop-down arrow for the next logical expression. Choose the less-than-or-equal-to symbol (<=). Press the Tab key to move to the next text area.

7. Type in 150,000 in the text area.

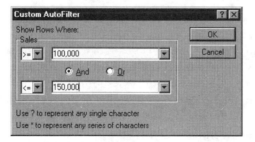

You have defined a custom filter that requests to see records whose sales are greater than or equal to 100,000 and less than or equal to 150,000. In other words, between 100,000 and 150,000 inclusive. Click on the OK button to perform the filtering. Excel displays the records that match (see Figure 21.7).

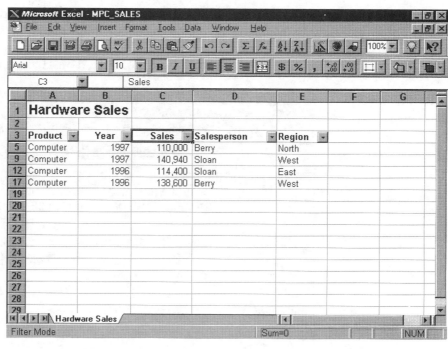

Figure 21.7   Defining Custom Filters allow you to find records that fall within a range of values.

NOTE   You can also use wildcards in your Custom filter criteria. If you need to find all values that start with the letter C and have any other characters following the letter, use the * character (the asterisk) to designate all the rest of the characters. The question mark is the wildcard for a single character. For example, C* finds any word that begins with the letter C. C?t would find Cat, Cut, and Cot, but not Cart or Count.

Filtering for the Top 10 Records

Top 10 is a new option in the AutoFilter drop-down list. The Top 10 option displays the ten highest values or percentages in a particular field range. Excel takes this option further, however, by allowing you to change the number of top units from 10 to as low as 1 or as high as 500. You can find the Top 20 or Top 100 or Top 5. You can also find the Bottom as well as the Top. No sorting is involved. Once the records are displayed, however, you can perform sorts to achieve a different organization for your data.

Part
3

Analyzing with Excel

Using a political example of the number of Congressional House seats per state based on the 1990 census, we are going to find the top ten states with the most amount of House seat apportionments. Figure 21.8 displays the data with the AutoFilter, Top 10 option selected.

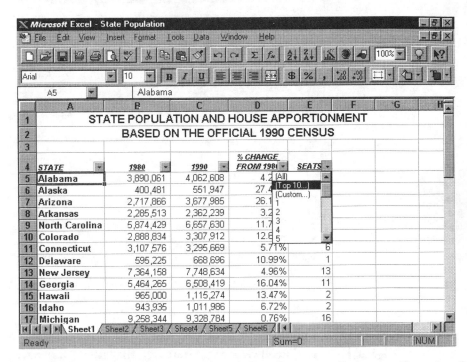

Figure 21.8 *The new Top 10 option in the AutoFilter allows you to display a specific number of high or low values.*

Once you select the Top 10 option, the Top 10 AutoFilter dialog box appears for you to specify your settings.

Creating Subtotals

The Subtotal feature allows you to mathematically summarize data by a particular field. If you want to see the total sales per region, you would request a subtotal on the Region field. At the row where the Region value changes from one region to the next, Excel displays a subtotal on that field that contains numeric data (for example, Sales). The mathematical summary can be any of the following: sum, average, count, maximum, minimum, product, standard deviation, and variance.

The main trick to using the subtotal feature is to make sure that you sort on the column field that will be used in the subtotal. Excel must have a contiguous group of the same items in order to give you an accurate subtotal for all of these items. In other words, all of the records that have the same regions must be sorted so that the North records are together, the South records are together, etc. Follow these steps to use the subtotal feature:

1. Click on the field column by which you want to subtotal. For example, click on Product or Region or Salesperson's name.

2. Click on the Sort Ascending or Sort Descending button. If you need a multiple sort as in this example, use the Data ➤ Sort menu to define multiple sort keys. In this example, the data is first sorted by Region (which is the field by which we are subtotaling) and then by Salesperson so that the Salespersons' last names are sorted within the Region.

   Sorting is an important step needed by the Subtotal feature. Make sure that the column you are subtotaling on is sorted before using the Subtotal feature. Figure 21.9 shows a sort ascending by Region and then by Salesperson. Note, if you want to sort according to a custom sort order as indicated in the graphic below, see the previous section on Creating a Custom Sort Order List. This feature in the Data ➤ Sort ➤ Options dialog box allows you to use the order of data that was defined in the Custom Lists command as the basis of your sort.

3. Choose Data ➤ Subtotals from the menu bar. The Subtotals dialog box appears for you to define the settings.

4. In the *At Each Change in:* text box, click on the drop-down arrow so that you can select the Region field (even though Excel suggests the first column in your list). Remember you sorted on Region because you wanted a subtotal each time that the region changed from North, South, East, and West.

5. At the *Use Function:* text box, click on the drop-down arrow so that you can select the Sum function. You want Excel to add the values of the Sales for each region.

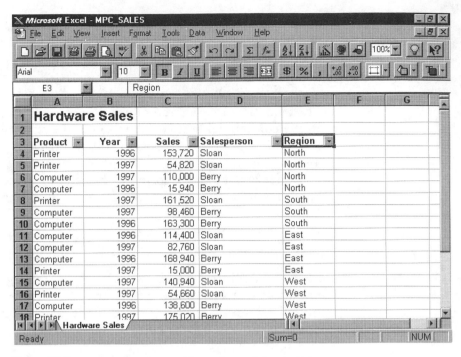

Figure 21.9   **The Sales model sorted by Region and then by Salesperson**

6. At the *Add Subtotal to:* check box options, make sure you check the Sales (numeric data) field. Uncheck any field that is not numeric—Excel cannot sum words. It can only sum the Sales numbers, which are the only numeric values in this model that should be mathematically manipulated.

7. At the bottom of the Subtotal dialog box, the additional options define what will happen each time you run the subtotal feature and where the subtotal information should appear. Leave these settings in place for right now. Once all of your settings are correct, click on the OK button. The graphic below shows the settings for the Subtotal.

> **TIP**   If you have multiple numeric fields for which you want to show subtotal summaries, add them to the field list in the *Add Subtotal to:* text box. For example, you may have a Sales field, a Sales Commission field, and a Units Sold field. You can check all three fields so that when each Region changes, you will have subtotal information for each of these fields of information.

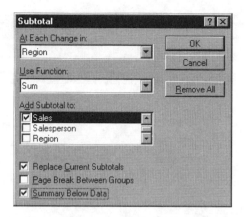

Using the Subtotal Outline View

When the Subtotal feature is active, the defined subtotals are usually displayed below the field (if you kept the setting Summary Below Data in the Subtotals dialog box). Whenever the sorted column changes grouping, the subtotals appear. At the same time, the area to the left of the Subtotaled list changes automatically to provide tools for showing or hiding the level of detail shown in the columns.

The area to the left shows by means of outlining tools the levels of detail possible within the subtotal. At the top of the outline area, as shown in Figure 21.10, there are three outline-level buttons designated by small numbers (1, 2, and 3). By default you are seeing the total amount of detail for this particular subtotal—which is level 3 detail. Each level number expands and contracts the amount of records that are viewable. At level 3 you are seeing all of the detail records that made up the subtotal sum.

To see different outline levels, click on the tiny number buttons at the top of the outline area. Level 2 detail shows only the subtotal records that were added to your list. This is an extremely powerful capability, as you may need to report only the subtotals and their grouping label of North, South, East, and West. Level 1 detail shows the Grand Total. You can immediately print any of these outline views. Although it is difficult to chart this data as Excel wants to display all of the values instead of the outlined values, when we use PivotTables in the next section, you

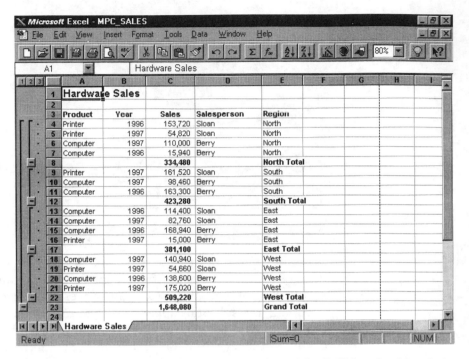

Figure 21.10   Subtotals can display multiple levels of record detail. Click on the plus and minus signs to expand and contract the detail.

can achieve the same results and easily graph the data. Figure 21.11 shows a Level 2 detail with only the subtotals displayed.

Combining AutoFilter and Subtotals

You can request subtotals on a filtered list. Apply the AutoFilter first (Data ➤ Filter ➤ AutoFilter) and then define the subtotal (Data ➤ Subtotals). For example, suppose you want to see subtotals but for only one Salesperson. You can AutoFilter to display the records for the specific Salesperson and then define a subtotal on the filtered records. Figure 21.12 shows a filtered and subtotaled list.

Removing Subtotals from the List

At any time you can remove the subtotals and return the data list to its simple column and row format. When you have finished viewing or printing the subtotaled data, click on any cell of the subtotal data;

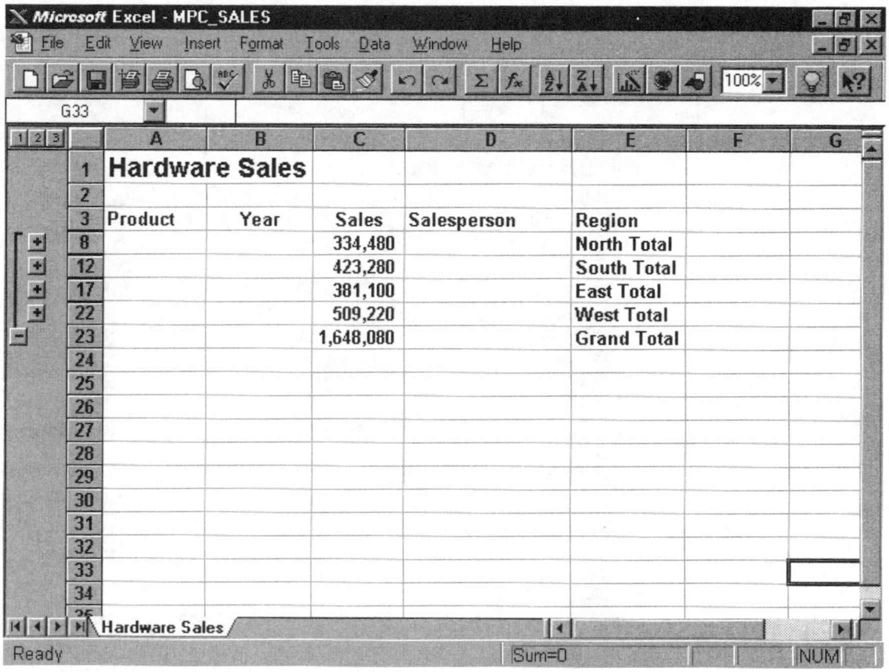

Figure 21.11   Level 2 detail on the Subtotal model

otherwise Excel will not be able to locate the data list. Then choose Data ➤ Subtotals, and click on the Remove All button on the right side of the Subtotal dialog box. Your list is returned to its original format.

Using PivotTables to Summarize and Organize

Excel's list capabilities are extended with the PivotTable feature. Similar to the CrossTab feature in other spreadsheet programs, the PivotTable is a CrossTab superhero. A simple Excel list can be instantly summarized and grouped, allowing you to see your data from points of view that would not have been obvious looking at the raw data. The PivotTable is interactive. You can literally "pivot" the data by quickly switching the results.

Even with the power of the Subtotal feature, you are still looking at a two-dimensional view of your data. Suppose in the model that we have been working in that, instead of the list arrangement you currently

Figure 21.12 **You can apply multiple filters and then subtotal the filtered records.**

have of the data, you are asked to show the Years field across the worksheet in columns and the names of the Salespersons along the left, going down in rows. In the intersection of each Year and Salesperson, you must show the sum of Sales and then a grand total for each year (column-wise) and a grand total for each salesperson (row-wise). This would be a tall order if you were to manually rearrange and copy the list data to fit these specifications. Particularly difficult if you were told that you had only five seconds to do it—but Excel's PivotTable feature can accomplish this easily. Immediately after viewing the data with the Years along the columns, you may decide to switch the Salespersons' names to the columns and the Years to the rows. While you're at it, by the way, add another variable: the Product. Not to worry: this is a normal capability of Excel's unique PivotTable feature. Heralded for its innovation and ease of use, the PivotTable brings a new dimension to data analysis. This is a tool that enables you to see the big picture of your data. The more data fields you have the more you can appreciate the Pivot-Table's power.

Creating a Simple PivotTable

As with your other data list operations, make sure that you have a simple list with column headings (fields) and row values (records). There should be no blank rows between the columns or the row. Remove any Subtotals or AutoFilters from the data. The first PivotTable example will generate a Sales summary that displays the Years across the columns and the Salespersons' names along the rows. The Regions will be placed as Page filters. Follow these steps to create the first PivotTable:

1. Click the pointer on some cell of your data list. If the pointer is outside the list, Excel cannot determine the boundaries of the list.

2. Choose Data ➤ PivotTable from the menu bar. Step 1 of the PivotTable Wizard appears (see Figure 21.13).

Part
3

Analyzing with Excel

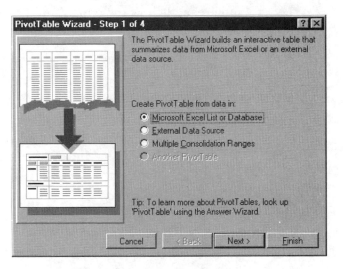

Figure 21.13 **You can use different types of data to generate a PivotTable.**

3. Make sure the Microsoft Excel List or Database radio button is selected. Click on the Next button on the PivotTable Wizard dialog box to move to the Wizard's Step 2.

4. Step 2 of the Wizard requests that you define the range of your list. The correct range should be displayed if your pointer was already within the boundaries of your worksheet data list when you started the PivotTable option. If the range is not correct, select the range while Step 2 is on the

screen. The graphic below displays the range of the example we are using. Click on the Next button to move to the Wizard's Step 3 dialog box.

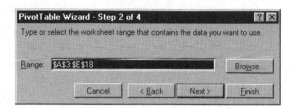

5. Step 3 of the Wizard is the heart of the PivotTable's power. The layout allows you to define which fields will be displayed in the table. On the right side of the Step 3 dialog box are the different field names of your data. You will drag the field names to the different positions on the layout to define exactly how the table should appear. Figure 21.14 displays the finished layout.

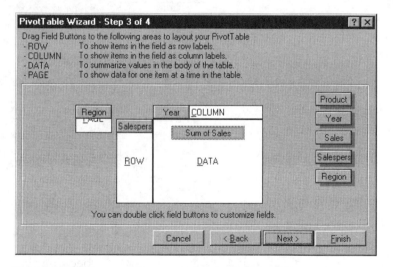

Figure 21.14   *You drag and drop field names to the different layout areas.*

a. Drag the Region field to the Page area.
b. Drag the Year field to the Column area.
c. Drag the Salesperson field to the Row area.
d. Drag the Sales field to the middle Data area.
e. Do not use the Product field yet.

6. Click on the Next button to move to the Wizard's Step 4 dialog box.

7. At the Wizard's Step 4 dialog box you are going to specify where you want the PivotTable to start on the worksheet. Designate a cell that is within a range that does not contain current data. Leave this option blank so that Excel will create a new sheet. Click on the Finish button at the bottom of the dialog box.

> **TIP** You can have multiple fields on the columns and rows of the PivotTable layout. Whichever field is first determines the primary grouping.

The new PivotTable is displayed on a new sheet. Notice the generic sheet name at the bottom of the screen on the sheet tab. If you wish, you can double-click on the name and create a more descriptive name for this sheet containing the PivotTable. Excel also activates the *Query and Pivot* toolbar that will now be handy when working with this PivotTable. If you do not see the Query and Pivot toolbar floating on the screen, look up near your other toolbars. You may need to force a view of this toolbar. Choose View ➤ Toolbars, look to see that the Query and Pivot toolbar is checked, then click on OK to return to the PivotTable worksheet area.

Viewing PivotTable Data

Once you generate a PivotTable, as in the short exercise above, the fun begins. The layout of the PivotTable adheres to the field arrangement you created during the PivotTable Wizard steps. You can now see the summary of the list data with the Year fields along the columns and the Salesperson fields along the rows. The Sum of Sales is contained in the intersection of the other fields. The Region field at the top of the table acts like a filter (see Figure 21.15). You can select a Region and the summaries will reflect the sales for that region. When the Southern Region is selected, it suddenly becomes clear that no sales occurred in 1996 for Sloan. This is information that is not obvious in the flat data

Part 3

Analyzing with Excel

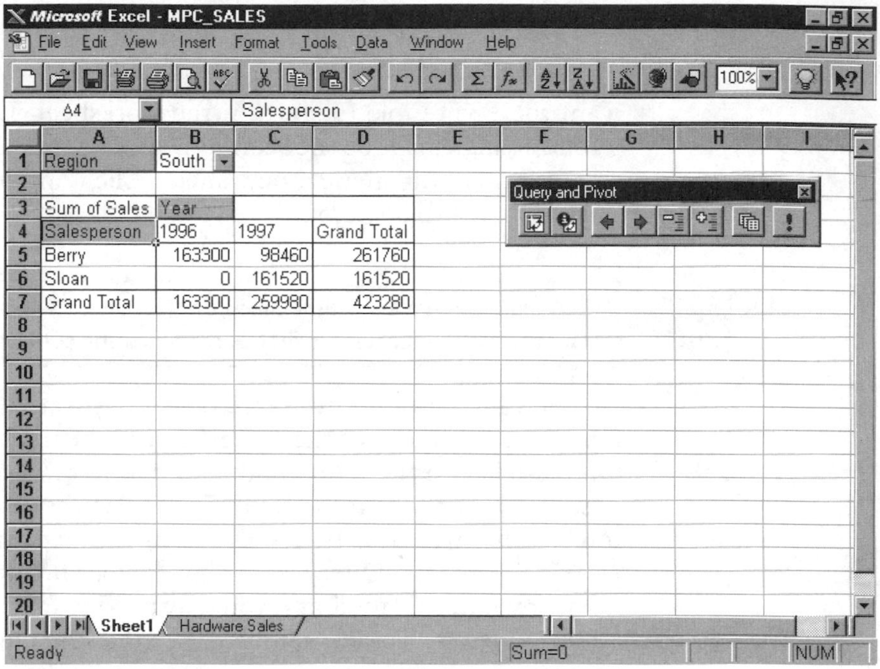

Figure 21.15   **The PivotTable quickly summarized the Sales by Region, Year, and Salesperson.**

list. You can print and chart the PivotTable data (an example is shown in Figure 21.16).

Changing the Default PivotTable Sum Function

The default calculation for a numeric field that is dragged to the Data section (center) of the PivotTable layout screen is the Sum function. If you drag a text field to the center, the default calculation is the Count function, since Excel cannot "add" words. The summary functions available for the PivotTable are Sum, Count, Average, Max, Min, Product, Count Nums, StdDev, StdDevp, Var, and Varp.

To change the type of function that Excel uses, follow these steps:

1. Click on a cell in the PivotTable that contains numeric data.

2. Choose Data ➤ PivotTable Field from the menu bar or click the right mouse button and choose PivotTable Field from the shortcut menu. You can also click on the first button on the Query and PivotTable toolbar

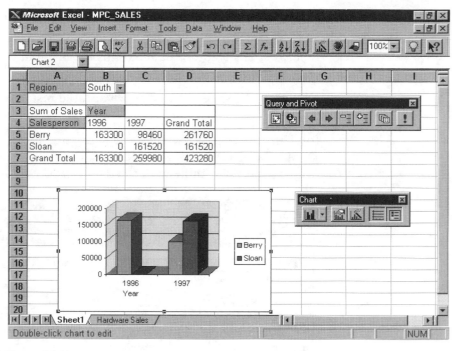

Figure 21.16 *You can print and chart the results of a PivotTable.*

and redisplay the PivotTable Layout screen (Step 3 of the PivotTable Wizard). Double-click on the Sum of Sales field in the middle of the layout. The PivotTable Field dialog box appears.

3. In the *Summarize by:* list box, select another function you want to use to summarize the data. (If you choose Average and you get a Division by Zero error, it's because there is a zero value in the PivotTable. For this exercise, choose the Max function instead.)

4. Choose OK or press Enter.

Refreshing PivotTable Data

Don't make direct changes to the data in the PivotTable; rather, make changes to the original data and then *refresh* the PivotTable's data. For example, suppose in 1997 another Salesperson was responsible for the majority of sales in that year. On the original data list change the name of the Salesperson from Berry to Smith. When you view the PivotTable, however, the PivotTable still reflects the old data. You must issue the

Refresh command to tell Excel to regenerate the table. Here are the basic steps to refresh data in the PivotTable:

1. Click on the sheet tab that contains the original data list, and correct or change the data.

2. Return to the sheet where the PivotTable resides.

3. Click on the exclamation point (last button) on the Query and Pivot toolbar. (Alternatively, right-click on the mouse and select Refresh Data.) Excel refreshes the data and displays a message. Figure 21.17 displays the PivotTable with the data refreshed.

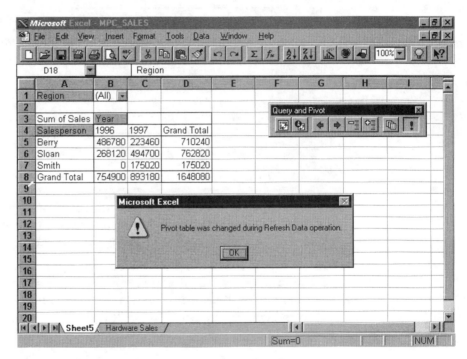

Figure 21.17   *If you've changed the original data, you must refresh the PivotTable. You can do this by using the Refresh Data button on the Query and Pivot toolbar.*

Pivoting the PivotTable

Once the PivotTable is generated, you can rearrange or "pivot" the fields in the table. In our example, the reason for rearranging the data would be to see the Salespersons' names across the columns and the Years on the rows (as shown in Figure 21.18). You have two methods for arranging: 1) Call up the PivotTable layout dialog box or 2) drag fields interactively. We will work with both methods.

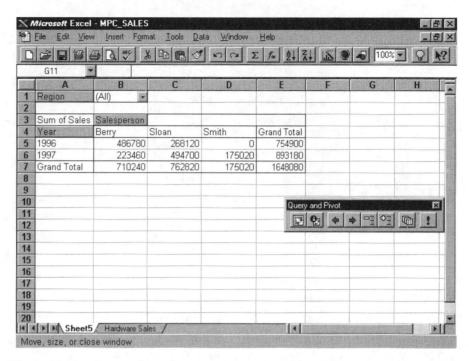

Figure 21.18 *You can rearrange the fields by selecting the first button on the Query and Pivot toolbar.*

Rearranging Using the PivotTable Layout Screen

Click on any cell of the current PivotTable and click on the first button on the Query and PivotTable toolbar. Step 3 of the PivotTable Wizard appears on the screen. Drag the Salesperson field to the Column area and drag the Year field to the Row area. Click on the Finish button.

Rearranging Interactively

You can also drag the fields of your PivotTable interactively while you are viewing the PivotTable. Click on the sheet tab that contains your PivotTable. Drag the field(s) that lie on the column to the row position. Notice that the small icon which represents the field name switches its direction. Figure 21.19 shows a PivotTable that has no column field, only two row fields. You can cluster fields on one axis. The first field in the cluster determines the primary grouping.

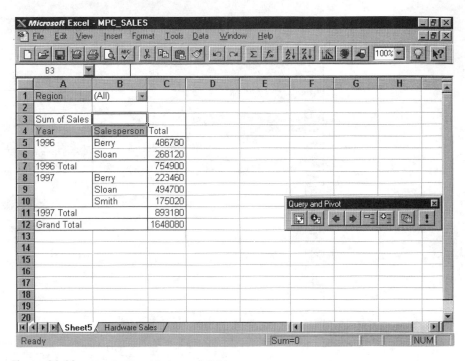

Figure 21.19   PivotTable with two row fields

Adding, Removing and Renaming Fields from the PivotTable

Once you see the capabilities of the PivotTable, you will want to add fields to the layout so that you can perform more in-depth analysis of your data. To add fields, activate the PivotTable layout form by clicking within the range and then clicking on the first button on the Query and Pivot toolbar. The PivotTable Wizard's Step 3 dialog box appears. Drag additional fields to the columns or the rows. You can reposition existing fields. You can also add fields by right-clicking on an existing field in the worksheet's PivotTable. (see Figure 21.20).

To quickly remove a field from the layout, drag the field outside the white layout area onto the gray background of the Query and Pivot dialog box. You can also drag fields back to the list of fields displayed on the right side of the dialog box.

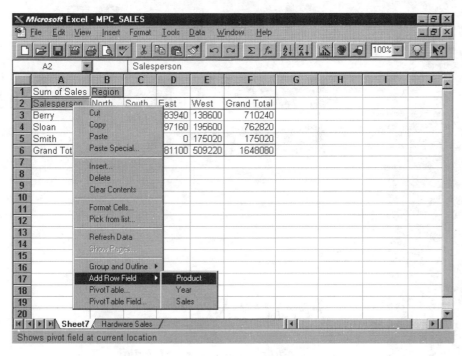

Figure 21.20 The PivotTable can accommodate multiple fields on the columns and rows.

To rename a field, double-click on the field name on the PivotTable's Layout screen. The PivotTable Field dialog box appears. Type over the existing name to change it to something more descriptive. You can also change the numeric format of a numeric field by clicking on the Number option on the PivotTable Field dialog box. Choose from among the various numeric formats.

To change the appearance of the PivotTable, click on a cell of the PivotTable and choose Format ➤ AutoFormat from the menu bar, then choose from among the suggested table layouts.

Chapter 22

Excel's Reusability Features

FEATURING

Advanced and beginner users alike will be able to take advantage of the reusability features in Excel. The features available range from customized lists to workbook templates.

A new reusability feature implemented in Word, AutoCorrect, is now available in Excel as well. Any AutoCorrect entries that you make in Excel are available in Word and PowerPoint, and vice versa. The spelling dictionary used by Word can be shared by Excel, PowerPoint, and Word to eliminate the tedious reentry of specialized words.

Excel's AutoComplete feature provides a way for you to reuse entries typed in a column. You will save time and avoid typos when you do not need to rekey the same data that already occurs in the column.

The Custom Lists feature forms the basis of the AutoFill (pretyped months, days, dates) and the Custom Sort Order features. You can add entries to the Custom Lists page of the Tools ➤ Options dialog box and use them to automatically fill in cells.

The final feature we will discuss in this chapter is Excel's templates. Excel allows you to format spreadsheets and then reuse their layouts and formulas. No longer do you need to open, copy, and clean out an old spreadsheet. You can use Excel's predefined templates (a cadre of built-in templates for home and business use now accompany Excel), modify the AutoTemplate (the one used every time you choose to create a new workbook), and create and save your own custom templates.

Working with AutoCorrect

Some of the most common English words are also the ones most people have difficulty spelling. Words like *accommodate*, *balance*, and *occasion* give even the most confident spellers just a slight pause of uncertainty. And the simplest words are the ones that we mistype again and again. How many times have you accidentally transposed the letters in the words *the*, *and*, and *but*?

The Excel AutoCorrect feature looks for common letter patterns and replaces them with the correct spelling of the word. In fact, you can even tell the program to look for patterns that you know you have difficulty with—including personal nouns. AutoCorrect also looks for two initial capitals at the beginning of a word, automatically reduces the second letter to lowercase, and will always capitalize the names of days.

To access the AutoCorrect feature, choose Tools ➤ AutoCorrect from the menu bar. A dialog box like the one in Figure 22.1 will appear.

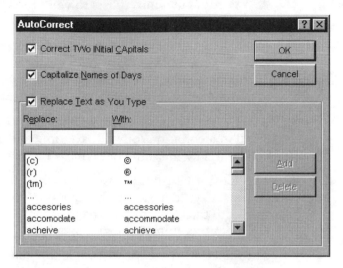

Figure 22.1 **AutoCorrect dialog box with checks in all three boxes.**

The AutoCorrect options work as follows:

▶ **Correct Two Initial Capitals:** A checkmark here tells AutoCorrect to look for two initial capitals (a common typographical error) and change the second capital letter to lowercase.

> **NOTE** AutoCorrect's initial capitals feature only works with words containing three or more letters (two capital letters together will not be changed). AutoCorrect is unable to distinguish intended usage of capitalization, so it will merely follow the rule. For example, if you are typing USA and accidentally capitalize the first two letters (the *U* and *S*) but not the third (*a*), AutoCorrect will change the second letter to lowercase, resulting in *Usa*.

▶ **Capitalize Names of Days:** When checked, this option will automatically capitalize the first letter of day names.

▶ **Replace Text as You Type:** When checked, this option allows you to add your own replacement text as you type. Under this checkbox are boxes labeled Replace and With, The Replace list shows common symbol shorthand and spelling and typing mistakes, and the With list shows the correct symbols and spellings. Excel will automatically replace the listed errors with the correct versions as you type.

If you would prefer Excel not to automatically correct the types of mistakes represented by an AutoCorrect checkbox, click once to remove its checkmark.

Using the scroll bar to the right of these entries, scroll through to see the large number of entries that come with Excel. There are 350 predefined AutoCorrect entries. You may also add your own—as many as you wish. You can add words to the Replace and With lists to replace any characters you type with any new characters.

Adding AutoCorrect Entries

The capability to add your own AutoCorrect entries can save you lots of typing. For example, suppose your company name is extremely long and you want to use an abbreviation instead of typing in the long company name. You can add the shorthand name to the Replace list and the full name in the With list (you can use capitalization and spaces), and then Excel will make the change automatically. Your formal name is another good AutoCorrect candidate. Your initials can be used as the shorthand, and AutoCorrect will replace these initials with the full name.

To see how this works, let's step through a simple example:

1. Choose Tools ➤ AutoCorrect.

2. Click inside the empty text box area under the word Replace.

3. Type your initials. If the three characters of your initials spell a real word, use only two letters of your initials. You don't want Excel to replace a real word that has the same characters as your initials.

4. Click inside the empty text box under With or press the Tab key.

5. Type your full name. As soon as you began typing in the With box, the Add button becomes enabled.

6. When you have finished typing your entry, click the Add button. The entry will now appear alphabetically in the list below. Figure 22.2 shows an example of an entry added to the AutoCorrect list.

Part
3

Analyzing with Excel

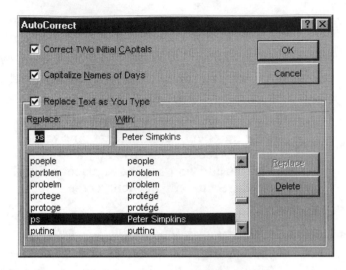

Figure 22.2 **Adding an entry in the AutoCorrect dialog box**

7. Click the OK button to close the dialog box and return to your spreadsheet.

8. Place your cursor in cell A1 and type your initials. When you have finished, press the spacebar, Enter, Tab, or any of the arrow keys. Your full name should now appear.

Deleting AutoCorrect Entries

You may find it necessary to delete certain word patterns in the AutoCorrect list because they conflict with what you want to do. For example, if your name is Carl Nathaniel Adams and you want Excel to replace your initials (*cna*) with your name, you would need to delete the AutoCorrect entry that already exists for that word pattern or choose another abbreviation. Otherwise, each time you type your initials, the word *can* will appear, not your name, because Excel "corrects" this typo.

To delete an AutoCorrect entry, select Tools ➤ AutoCorrect and click once on that letter pattern. Once you have highlighted the entry, it will appear in the Replace and With text boxes. Click on the Delete button on the right side of the dialog box. The selection will be deleted from your list. Keep in mind that if you delete an AutoCorrect entry in Excel, it will be deleted from Word and PowerPoint as well.

TIP Instead of scrolling through the long list of AutoCorrect entries, you can jump to an entry. Click once on any entry name in the list. Press the first letter of the entry you are seeking, and Excel will jump to the first entry that begins with that letter (only the first letter works, however).

Filling in Cells with AutoComplete

The AutoComplete feature performs two functions: it keeps track of the items of a list you are typing in a column, and it attempts to fill in following cells with repetitive list items as it begins to recognize the word pattern. The feature can be disabled and enabled.

There are three basic things to remember about AutoComplete:

▶ The function works in columns, not rows.

▶ Skipping an entirely blank row will cause AutoComplete to reset.

▶ AutoComplete completes only entries that contain words or words combined with numbers. Entries that contain only numbers, dates, or times are not captured for completion.

Using AutoComplete

To see how AutoComplete works, start a new worksheet and follow these steps:

1. Type the name **David** in cell A1. Press Enter. (Cell A2 should now be your active cell.)

2. Type the letter **D**. Do **not** press the Enter key. AutoComplete attempts to fill in the remainder of the cell with the name David. Complete the name Denise and press the Enter key. (Cell A3 should now be your active cell.)

3. Type the letter **D**. AutoComplete has not completed the word since it has more than 1 entry that begins with **D**.

4. Type the letter **a**. AutoComplete attempts to fill in the name David since it now recognizes a unique word pattern. Complete the name **Daniel** and press the Enter key. (Cell A4 should now be your active cell.)

Part 3

Analyzing with Excel

5. Type the letter **D**. Now hold down the Alt key while pressing the down arrow key. A drop-down list of all the entries found in the prior cells will appear:

	A
1	David
2	Denise
3	Daniel
4	D
5	Daniel
6	David
7	Denise

6. Choose the name David from the list and press the Enter key. (You can also right-click the mouse and choose Pick from List to display the list of AutoComplete entries.)

7. Activate cell A6. Type the letters **De**. AutoComplete cannot fill in the name because there is a blank row between the current active cell and the original list. When there is a break in the line, AutoComplete resets its list of values.

Disabling and Enabling AutoComplete

In some cases, you may not want Excel's "help" in filling in your list. You can disable or enable AutoComplete through Excel's Options dialog box.

To turn on or off AutoComplete, select Tools ➤ Options from the menu bar. Click on the Edit tab. The last checkbox on this page of the dialog box is for AutoComplete. A checkmark here enables the option.

Filling In Cells with Custom Lists

Excel's Custom Lists feature can help you avoid the repetitive typing of items commonly listed in worksheets, such as month names. When you type any word in a defined list of words, Excel recognizes the name as being part of a custom list. Then you can use Excel's AutoFill feature to automatically complete the rest of the list.

If the number of cells you selected is more than the number of items in the custom list, Excel will repeat the list until all the selected cells are filled. You do not need to use the first name in the list for Excel to recognize it as belonging to the group; you can start anywhere.

Using Custom Lists

Excel has predefined the text of the twelve months of the year and the seven days of the week in custom lists of common repetitive items. To see how this works, start a new sheet and follow these steps:

1. Click on cell A1. Type the word **Sunday** and press Enter.

2. Click again on cell A1.

3. Drag the AutoFill's fill handle across the cells in row 1 to column I. To drag this handle, place your mouse pointer over the bottom-right corner of cell A1, where a small gray box appears. The pointer turns from the white cross shape to a small black cross. With the black cross pointer, drag the gray box to the right across the row. Release the mouse at column I. Excel will fill in the cells with the day names, as shown in Figure 22.3.

   Notice that after AutoFill completed the cycle, it began again. You can leave your list selected and format it (bold, centered, and so on).

Creating Your Own Custom Lists

You can create your own custom lists for use with the AutoFill feature. For example, you might define lists with the names of people, departments, or complex labeling systems. Then you will only need to type them once for use in all your workbooks, old and new. Through the Custom Lists page of the Options dialog box, you can either type in your own lists or import existing text for your custom lists.

Typing In a Custom List

To add your own custom list by typing in its items, follow these steps:

1. Select Tools ➤ Options ➤ Custom Lists tab.

2. In the Custom Lists list box, highlight NEW LIST. A cursor will appear in the List Entries list box.

3. Type your list in this box, pressing Enter after each entry.

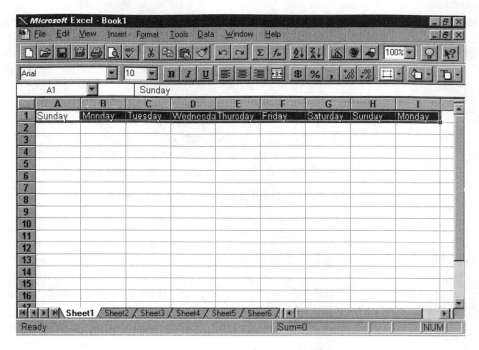

Figure 22.3 Excel can automatically fill in items of a custom list.

4. When you have finished typing your list, click the Add button. Your list will now appear in the Custom Lists box on the left. To add another list, simply repeat these steps.

5. Click OK to save your custom list(s) and close the dialog box.

Importing Text into a Custom List

If a workbook already contains a list of entries that you would like to make into a custom list, follow these steps:

1. Highlight the cells that contain the list you wish to import.

2. Select Tools ➤ Options ➤ Custom Lists tab.

3. Check that the Import List from Cells text box at the bottom of the dialog box shows the correct cell range (the cells you selected). If it does not, type in the cell range where the list resides on the worksheet.

4.   Click the Import button in the lower-right corner. Your list should now appear in the Custom Lists box. Click Add if you would like to import another list.

5.   Click OK to save your custom list(s) and close the dialog box.

Setting Up with Custom Lists

Now try this example to create and use two custom lists:

1.   In cell A1 of a new sheet, type **Marketing**.

2.   In cell A2, type **Sales**.

3.   In cell A3, type **Client Services**.

4.   Select Tools ➤ Options ➤ Custom Lists tab.

5.   Click once on NEW LIST in the Custom Lists box.

6.   In the List Entries box, enter the following names, pressing Enter after each one: **Stephen Nicholas, Alexandra Florence,** and **Deborah Schockley.** Click the Add button so that the names will be listed in the Custom Lists text area on the left side.

7.   In the Import List from Cells box, type **A1:A3**.

8.   Click the Import button. Both of your new lists should now appear in the Custom Lists box, as shown in Figure 22.4.

9.   Click OK to return to your worksheet.

10. In cell A5, type the word **Sales**.

11. Grab the fill handle and drag across to cell C5. Widen the columns if necessary.

12. In cell A6, type the name **Stephen Nicholas**.

13. Grab the fill handle and drag across to cell C6. The names flow from the list.

As the example demonstrates, custom lists can save you hours of typing and reduce your typographical error rate dramatically. Now you only need to worry about the numbers, not the text. What a relief for spreadsheet users!

Part
3

Analyzing with Excel

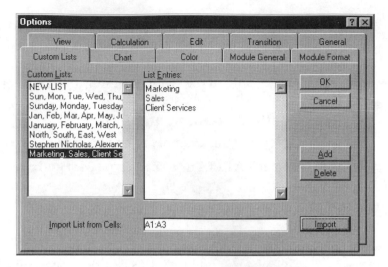

Figure 22.4   You can either type a custom list into the List Entries area or import a list of typed items from the worksheet.

TIP You can also tell Excel to use a custom list as the basis of a sort. For example, you might want to sort in calendar month order instead of alphabetical order if you must sort months of the year. See Chapter 21 for more information about using the Custom Sort Order List feature.

About Templates

You've done all the work. The report looks exactly as you want it. The formatting is attractive and easy to read, the columns perfectly spaced, the cell references finally where you want them, and the macros are debugged. Your workbook should look just like this every time you create this report. It can, if you save the workbook as a template and use the template as the basis of your next report.

Templates serve as patterns for creating new workbooks, sheets, charts, modules, and dialog boxes. They can save you a lot of time and hard work and add consistency to your workbooks. Templates can also give you a jump start on worksheets that use complex calculations by storing them for repeated use. Just as you can create Word templates for form letters, you can create Excel templates for "form worksheets."

In addition to creating custom templates, you can also alter Excel's default template, the AutoTemplate. For example, you can change the font size, column widths, page orientation, and headers that will be the defaults for every new workbook.

You may also find that Excel has anticipated your needs. Excel comes with 12 predefined templates for you to use.

In the following sections, you will learn to create a new AutoTemplate and set up your own custom templates. Then you will take a tour of Excel's predefined custom templates.

Creating a Workbook AutoTemplate

Excel uses a default workbook AutoTemplate every time you click the new workbook button on the Standard toolbar or choose the Workbook icon on the General page of the File ➤ New dialog box. The default workbook AutoTemplate contains the column widths, styles, formatting, page setup, and other settings for the new workbook.

You can change these default settings by customizing any blank workbook and saving it as the new default AutoTemplate. The name of the template must be Book. It must be saved as a template in a specific folder under the Excel folder called XLStart.

As an example, suppose you want every new workbook to have a 14-point font, column widths of 15, a currency format (with two decimal places), and the current date in the first cell at A1. You can create a workbook that has these formats, column widths, and a date formula and save it as the new AutoTemplate. Follow these steps:

1. Create a workbook with the following settings.

    - Choose a 14-point font using the Formatting toolbar.

    - Select the entire workbook by clicking on the empty button to the left of the column A letter and above row 1:

    - Click the currency format button.

- Choose Format ➤ Column ➤ Width. Type in **15** and click OK.

- Click in cell A1, type the function **=NOW()**, and press the Enter key.

- With cell A1 selected, choose Format ➤ Cells, select the Date format, choose a date style, and click OK.

- If you want to modify the page setup, choose File ➤ Page Setup and make changes (such as landscape versus portrait or remove the header).

2. Once the workbook has been formatted, choose File ➤ Save or Save As.

3. In the File Name text box, type the name **Book**. You must use this name if you want the new template to be the AutoTemplate.

4. In the Save As Type text box, click the drop-down arrow and change the type from Microsoft Excel Workbook to Template. Immediately, Excel switches to the Templates folder.

5. In the Save In text box at the top of the dialog box, find and click the XLStart folder within the Microsoft Excel folder, as shown in Figure 22.5

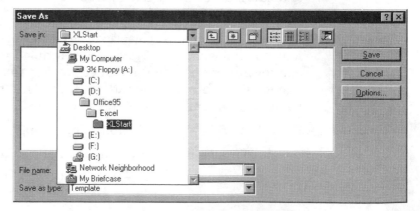

Figure 22.5 *Excel allows you to customize the default workbook AutoTemplate.*

6. Click the Save button on the right side of the dialog box. Your file is saved with an XLT (template) extension instead of the usual XLS (sheet) extension.

7. Close the file (File ➤ Close) so that there are no open workbooks.

8. Click the new worksheet button on the Standard toolbar or choose File ➤ New ➤ General tab and click OK. The new workbook now contains all of the defaults you defined and saved. The NOW function produces the current date in the first cell.

If you want to change or enhance your new default AutoTemplate, make the changes on any new workbook and then repeat steps 2 through 6 to save it as the new default worksheet template.

When you want to use the AutoTemplate for the workbook, click the new worksheet button on the Standard toolbar or choose the Workbook icon from the General page of the File ➤ New dialog box.

Creating Other AutoTemplates

Excel uses a number of AutoTemplates to manage the defaults for new sheets, charts, dialog boxes, and programming modules. All the AutoTemplates must be stored in the XLStart folder, and they must have specific names, as follows:

Sheet Type	Default AutoTemplate Name
Workbook	BOOK.XLT
Worksheet	SHEET.XLT
Module	MODULE.XLT
Chart	CHART.XLT
Dialog	DIALOG.XLT

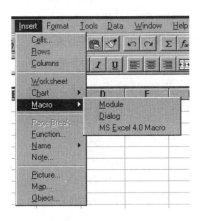

Set up the AutoTemplate by creating a workbook with the sheet names and text, chart settings, or programming code that you wish to insert automatically. Save the workbook under the identifying AutoTemplate name, choosing to save it as a template in the XLStart folder. Make sure that the active sheet is the one you want to use as the template when you save the workbook.

When you want to use your new sheet, chart, module or dialog box in a workbook, choose the item from the Insert menu on the menu bar.

Creating Custom Templates

When you have set up a worksheet with formatting and other items that you will use again in certain worksheets, you can create a custom template. Begin by setting up the existing workbook just as you want it to look for the template. For example, if you are setting up a periodic report, you may want to erase the numbers that change from report period to report period—but not formulas.

To create a template from an existing workbook on the screen, choose File ➤ Save As from the menu bar. Type any name for the workbook. Change the Save As Type setting from Microsoft Excel Workbook to Template. Templates are saved in a default folder called Templates. You can have as many custom templates as you desire.

Once your template is saved, you can choose it from the list of templates in the File ➤ New dialog box. The workbook that appears on the screen will be a copy of the template, not the original. Your custom template name, followed by the number *1* appears in the title bar (like the AutoTemplate Book1 name).

As an example, here are the steps to create a simple custom template:

1. Select a new workbook.

2. In cell A1, type **Summit Bank Monthly Analysis Report**.

3. In cell H1, type **=NOW()** so that the default system date will appear each time you use the template.

4. Press Ctrl+1 to activate the Format ➤ Cells dialog box. Choose the Date category and select a date format type.

5. Choose File ➤ Save As.

6. Type the filename **Summit Bank**.

7. For Save As Type, choose Template from the drop-down list.

8. Click the Save button

9. Close the workbook.

10. Choose File ➤ New. You will see an icon for your template on the General page of the dialog box, as shown in Figure 22.6.

11. Select the Summit Bank icon to open the template.

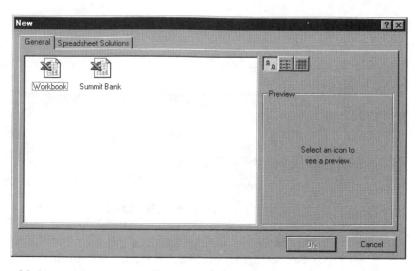

Figure 22.6 *When you create a custom template, it is listed on the General page of the File ➤ New dialog box.*

Your new sheet will already have the name Summit Bank Monthly Analysis Report in cell A1 and the current date in cell H1. Any other information you saved as part of your workbook template will also be included.

Editing or Deleting a Custom Template

To edit an existing template, choose File ➤ Open from the main menu or click on the open button on the Standard toolbar. Enter the name of

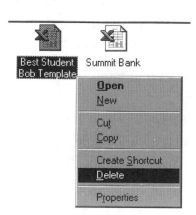

the template as the filename. For Files of Type, choose Template. Excel will switch you to the Templates folder. Once you have located the file, choose Open.

Make your changes directly to the open template file. When you have completed your edits, simply save the file with the changes, and then close it.

You can delete templates in the same way that you delete other files, Select the file directly from the Excel file list screen (File ➤ Open or File ➤ Save) and click the right mouse button to access the shortcut menu. Choose Delete from the shortcut menu.

As when you delete other files, Excel will ask for confirmation:

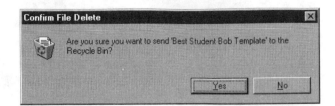

Remember, the deleted file has been sent to the Recycle Bin. If you delete the wrong file, return to the Desktop (right-click on the Taskbar and minimize your applications). Then double-click the Recycle Bin icon, select the file to be restored, and choose File ➤ Restore to restore the deleted file. The file will be returned to the proper folder.

Creating a Custom Template Folder

If you have created a number of custom templates, you may want to group them in their own categories in the File ➤ New dialog box. To create your own pages with tabs within the New dialog box, create a folder within the Templates folder under Office 95. You can use the Explorer to find the Templates directory and create the folder there, or you can create a new folder using Excel.

The following steps guide you through creating a new folder using Excel and placing your custom template within this new folder.

1. Choose File ➤ Open and open the custom template used in the previous example or one of your own custom templates. Remember, change the Files of Type option at the bottom of the dialog box to Templates and locate the Templates folder under Office 95 using the Look In text box at the top of the dialog box, as shown in Figure 22.7.

2. Open the custom template, and then choose File ➤ Save As.

3. In the Save As dialog box, click the create new folder button (the third yellow folder button at the top of the dialog box). The New Folder dialog box appears, as shown in Figure 22.8.

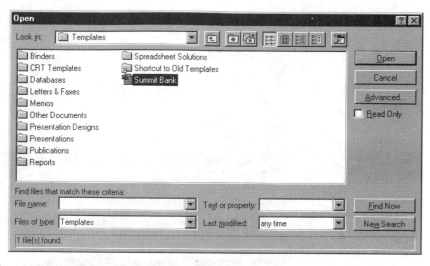

Figure 22.7 *You can open a template you designed by looking for it in the Templates folder under Office95.*

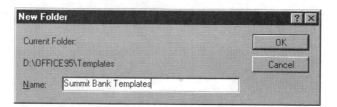

Figure 22.8 *Creating a new folder in Excel*

4. In the New Folder dialog box, type the name for the folder that you want to appear on the tab, and then click the OK button.

The new template folder is listed with the other template folders. Figure 22.9 shows an example of a new folder in with the other templates. Our next steps are to save the custom template into this new folder.

5. With the Save As dialog box still on the screen, double-click on the name of the new template folder you just created. The folder will be empty, as shown in Figure 22.10.

6. Because your custom template is still on the screen behind the dialog box, you can save the template into this new folder. You will delete the extra copy of the template that is the General folder in a later step.

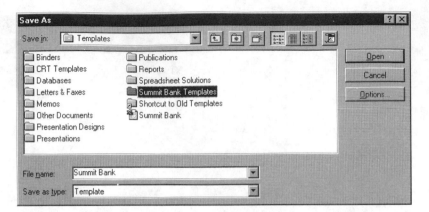

Figure 22.9   *You can create new folders within the Templates folder by using the File ➤ Save As command and selecting the new folder button.*

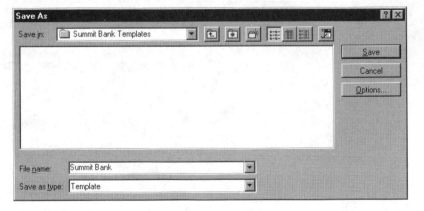

Figure 22.10   *An empty folder waiting for a template to be saved there*

7. Click the Save button on the right side of the Save As dialog box. You will be returned to your custom template workbook.

8. Close the workbook and choose File ➤ New from the menu bar to see your new tab in the dialog box. Click on the new tab to see the saved contents of your custom folder, as shown in Figure 22.11.

9. To remove the extra copy of the custom template from the General page, choose the General page and select the template.

10. Right-click the mouse to access the shortcut menu; but hold down the Shift key before you click on the Delete option. The Shift key combined with the Delete option tells Excel not to send the deleted object to the

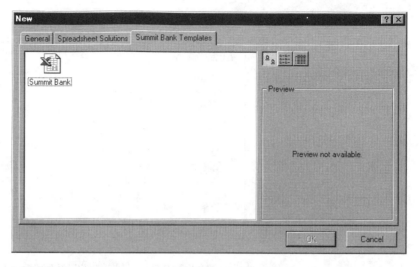

Figure 22.11 *You can add your custom template to a new folder within the Templates folder.*

Recycle Bin. Since you already have a copy of the template in the correct folder, there is no need to have an emergency copy in the Recycle Bin. Excel asks you to confirm your choice.

11. Click Yes to remove the extra copy of the template.

Using Excel's Predefined Templates

You can select from among Excel's predefined templates when you choose File ➤ New. Excel has placed 12 business and personal templates in the Spreadsheet Solutions folder, as shown in Figure 22.12. Double-click on any of these templates to examine their formats and formulas to see if any of them can be of use to you. For example, the Budget template, shown in Figure 22.13, includes multiple sheets for tracking different budget categories, such as entertainment, credit card expenses, and so on.

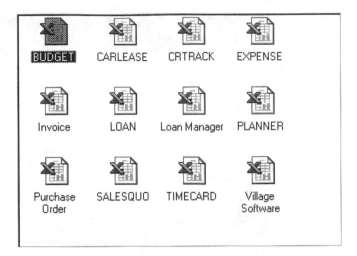

Figure 22.12   Excel has a number of templates created for your business or personal use.

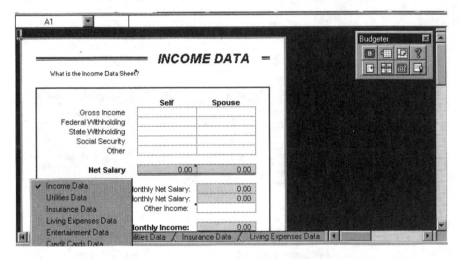

Figure 22.13   Excel's predefined Budget is a tremendous time saver and has an attractive design.

When you choose File ➤ New and select an Excel predefined template, you are given a copy of the template to serve as the basis for a new workbook. You can make whatever changes you wish, and then save the file either as a workbook or as a new template with a different name.

As you learned in this chapter, Excel provides many reusability features that save you time and make your work more accurate. The next chapter describes how you can customize Excel toolbars and use macros to maximize your efficiency.

Chapter 23

Customizing Excel with Toolbars and Macros

FEATURING

The toolbars within all of the Office 95 programs can be customized with different buttons to suit your needs and preferences. Each button on a toolbar is really a small macro that automates a process.

The default toolbars reflect only some of the button commands that are available to you. Excel provides buttons for almost every command. For example, you may want to add buttons for inserting and deleting rows or columns, or for the equals sign and the four mathematical operations (add, subtract, multiply, and divide).

Of course, not every command you want to automate is currently a part of the Excel program. For example, Excel does not automatically know your company name and address. If this is information that you need to appear on your worksheets, you may want to create a macro that types your company name and address whenever it is activated.

In this chapter, we'll begin with the ways that you can customize Excel's toolbars. Then we'll discuss the basics of macro design and creation.

Viewing and Customizing Toolbars

Excel places the Standard and Formatting toolbars on the screen when you launch the program. Some of the toolbars, such as Chart and Query and Pivot, are automatically shown during certain operations. You can show Excel's other toolbars at any time.

If you do not see a toolbar that you need, choose View ➤ Toolbars from the menu bar, to see the Toolbars dialog box, shown in Figure 23.1. Check the toolbars you wish to see. You can make the buttons larger by selecting the Large Buttons option at the bottom of the Toolbars dialog box.

You can also use the shortcut menu: Point to any button on any toolbar and click the right mouse button.

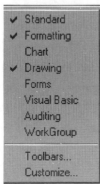

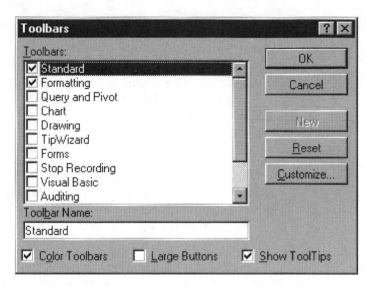

Figure 23.1 *There are a number of toolbars that Excel uses in addition to the Standard and Formatting toolbars that appear when you launch the program.*

Adding Buttons to the Toolbars

To add a button to any toolbar, select the Customize option from the View ► Toolbars dialog box or the Toolbars shortcut menu. Figure 23.2 shows the Customize dialog box.

The list box on the left side of the Customize dialog box shows the categories of button commands. The button pictures to the right of the selected category reflect the predefined commands available. In Figure 23.2, you can see that some of the buttons in the File category are already on the Standard toolbar. You can view the meaning of each button by clicking on it and looking at the description at the bottom of the Customize dialog box.

As an example, let's add the insert column button to the toolbar. This can be handy for Excel users because it lets you quickly insert a column where the pointer resides. Follow these steps:

1. Choose View ► Toolbars ► Customize or point to any button on a toolbar, right-click the mouse, and select Customize.

2. In the Customize dialog box, click on the Edit category (the second category in the list).

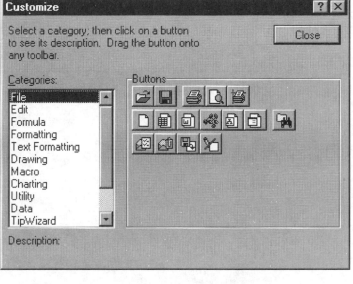

Figure 23.2 You can add and remove buttons by customizing the toolbars.

3. When the Edit buttons appear, find the insert column button (third row, third in from the left).

4. Click on the button and drag it onto the Standard or Formatting toolbar. A copy of the button is dragged onto the toolbar.

5. Drop the button where you want it to appear on the toolbar. You can move it by dragging directionally across the toolbar.

6. Close the Customize dialog box.

    To test your button's capabilities, click into a column of text and then click the new button. Figure 23.3 shows the new button and the column it inserted.

Removing Buttons from the Toolbar

Another way to customize a toolbar is to remove buttons from it. To get rid of a button you do not need, select View ➤ Toolbars ➤ Customize, or point to any button on a toolbar, right-click, and select Customize from the shortcut menu.

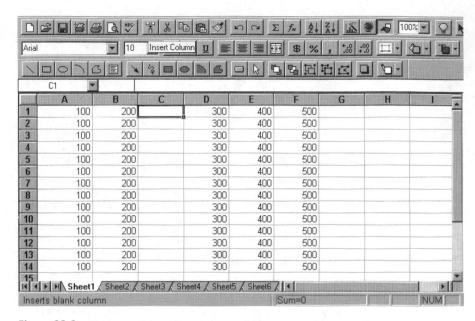

Figure 23.3 **The Insert Column button is a useful button to add to a toolbar.**

When the Customize dialog box is visible, point to the button to be removed, click and hold down the mouse button, and drag the button off the toolbar on top of the Customize dialog box.

WARNING You cannot undo the removal of a button from a toolbar. You will need to manually drag the button back onto the toolbar to reinstate it.

Floating and Docking Toolbars

When you add buttons to an existing toolbar, the toolbar cannot display all of its buttons. Each additional button pushes down the other buttons. Eventually, you will not be able to see the buttons on the furthest right side of the toolbar.

Excel allows you to float and dock the toolbars. When you *float* a toolbar, you can place it in any position on the screen. You can then shape the toolbar so that you can see all of the buttons.

Floating a toolbar does not require the Customize dialog box to be active. Find a small gap between one button and another on the toolbar and click into this space. Drag the toolbar down into the middle of the screen.

You can then drag the sides to narrow or widen the toolbar to put the buttons in multiple rows so that you can see all of them. Figure 23.4 shows an example of a floating Standard toolbar with its buttons on two rows.

To dock the toolbar to another position or back to its original position, first float the toolbar, and then drag the blue title bar that contains the toolbar's name to either the top or the bottom of the screen. If you double-click the title bar, the toolbar will dock to its last position. Figure 23.5 shows an example of a toolbar docked at the bottom of the screen.

Creating New Toolbars

You may want to create your own toolbar that contains only the custom buttons you need in order to efficiently perform your worksheet operations. The Formula category in the Customize dialog box is a favorite because of the buttons relating to creating worksheet formulas—equals sign, mathematical operators, and so on. As an example, we will first

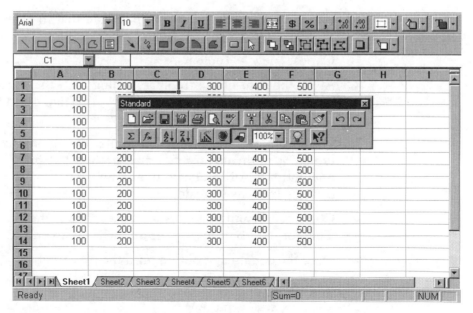

Figure 23.4 *When you float a toolbar, you can position it anywhere on the screen and arrange the buttons in rows.*

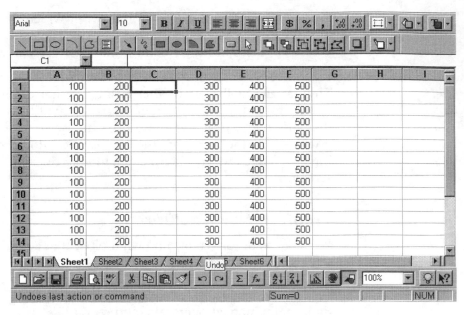

Figure 23.5 *A toolbar docked at the bottom of the screen*

create a new toolbar and then populate that toolbar with buttons from the Formula category. Follow these steps:

1. Choose View ➤ Toolbars.

2. At the bottom of the Toolbars dialog box, the name of the Standard toolbar appears. Drag the mouse over this name and type a new toolbar name. The New button becomes available.

3. Click the New button. The Customize dialog box appears, and the new toolbar is in the upper-left corner of the worksheet. It is only the size of one button until you begin to add buttons. It will stretch to accommodate the buttons you add.

4. Click the Formula category on the left side of the Customize dialog box. The Formula buttons appear on the right, as shown in Figure 23.6.

5. Drag the equals sign button onto the new toolbar.

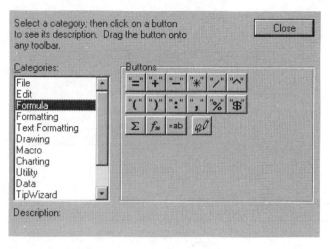

Figure 23.6   **The Customize dialog box with the Formula category buttons**

6. Continue to drag each Formula button you want to appear on your new toolbar. (You may need to drag the Customize dialog box out of the way by dragging its title bar.) Your toolbar will look something like this:

7. Click the Close button when you are finished adding buttons.

   Your new toolbar can now be docked. Double-click the blue title bar with the name of your new toolbar, and the toolbar will dock itself at the top of the screen. You can also click on the toolbar's title bar and drag it where you want it to appear on the screen. When you right-click the mouse while pointing to any button on any toolbar, you will see the name of your new toolbar(s) listed with the others:

   To delete one of your own toolbars, choose View ➤ Toolbars from the menu and select the name of your toolbar from the Toolbars dialog box. When you click on the name of your toolbar, the Delete button becomes available. Click Delete, and Excel will ask you to confirm the deletion:

Understanding Macros

Excel provides a number of shortcut methods for commands. The buttons on the toolbars are like "instant macros." The keyboard short-cuts, such as Ctrl+S for Save or Ctrl+P for Print (the File and Edit menus list some of the shortcut key combinations) are also like instant macros. By creating your own templates (discussed in Chapter 22), you can have formatting and formulas automatically in place when you start a work-book. So, before you decide that you need a full-blown macro, first consider if what you need to automate can be done by adding buttons to the toolbar, by using a predefined shortcut key, or by creating your own template.

However, you may find that Excel does not provide instant macros for some specific commands that you use often. For example, the following functions may be candidates for your own macros:

▶ Printing specific sections of a report

▶ Exporting or importing data

▶ Typing your company name and address

▶ Applying particular formats to different ranges

▶ Changing printer settings and print ranges

Whenever you find yourself repeating particular workbook processes, these processes are generally good candidates for macro instructions. Repetitive keystrokes and mouse movements can be directly typed or recorded as instructions. A single name is given to each set of instructions. Thus the origins of the name macro—one "big" overall name that represents multiple, small "micro" steps.

When you are recording your keystrokes and mouse movements, Excel writes down these movements as a series of instructions. The macro instructions are stored as a list and appear in a special language called Visual Basic for Applications (VBA) on the last sheet in your workbook. You can then run these instructions by activating the macro.

Recording Macros

Once you begin to record a macro, you do not want to type any characters or perform any actions that are not part of the macro recording. Although you can edit your macros (as described later in the chapter), it is best to plan your steps before you begin recording.

As an example, we will record a simple macro that types a company name and address. Follow these steps:

1. Click on a blank area of the worksheet.

2. Choose Tools ➤ Record Macro ➤ Use Relative References. This option tells Excel that you want to be able to play back your macro from any cell in the worksheet. Otherwise, Excel will always try to play back the macro at the exact cell in which you recorded the macro.

3. To start the actual recording, choose Tools ➤ Record Macro ➤ Record New Macro. The Record New Macro dialog box appears, as shown in Figure 23.7.

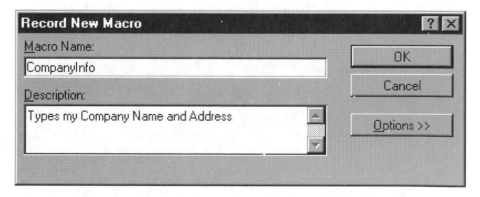

Figure 23.7 *When recording a macro, you should always add a brief description for the macro.*

4. Type a name for the macro in the Macro Name text box. Your name can be up to 255 characters and must begin with a letter. You can have numbers and underscores in the name, but it cannot include spaces or other punctuation marks.

5. Type a description for the macro in the Description area of the dialog box. Although this is an optional feature, it is recommended that you enter some type of short description of what the macro does.

6. Click the OK button. If you included spaces or other punctuation in the name, you will see an invalid name error message box.

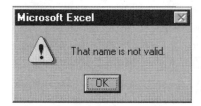

If you see this message, click OK (or press Esc) and make the appropriate changes to the macro name. Click OK after making the changes.

When the recording starts, Excel displays a stop macro recording button in its own toolbar in the upper-right corner of the worksheet, and the word *Recording* appears on the Status bar at the bottom of the screen.

7. With the Macro Recorder on, type your company address information. Use a separate row for each part of the address.

8. Drag the mouse over the rows of information and click the bold button. Click on the next blank cell below the company name. Your screen should look similar to the example in Figure 23.8.

9. Click the stop macro recording button, or choose Tools ➤ Record Macro ➤ Stop Recording.

Running Macros

After recording a macro, you will want to test your keystrokes immediately to see if they perform correctly. If you recorded the macro on a worksheet that you want to keep, save your file before running the macro in case something goes wrong. You can always open the last saved copy.

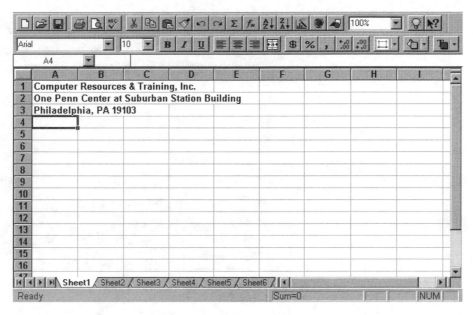

Figure 23.8 When recording a macro, perform only the exact keystrokes that you planned.

Follow these steps to run the macro we recorded in the previous section:

1. Position the pointer in a blank area of the worksheet and choose Tools ➤ Macro.

2. In the Macro dialog box, select the name of your macro, as shown in the example in Figure 23.9.

3. Click the Run button. Excel plays back the keystrokes and bolds the company name and address information.

4. Click into another empty cell and run your macro again. Your screen might look something like Figure 23.10.

 TIP An easy way of repeating a macro that has just been run is to select Edit ➤ Repeat Macro or simply press Ctrl+Y.

Notice that no matter what cell the pointer is in, when you run the macro, the company information appears. This is why you chose the Relative References option before you began the actual recording of the macro. If you had not, the macro would only run in the cell in which you began the recording, regardless of where you positioned the pointer.

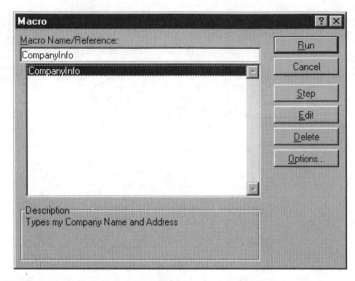

Figure 23.9   After you record a macro, its name is listed in the Macro dialog box.

	A	B	C	D	E	F	G	H	I
1	Computer Resources & Training, Inc.								
2	One Penn Center - Suburban Station Building								
3	Philadelphia, PA 19103								
4									
5									
6					Computer Resources & Training, Inc.				
7					One Penn Center - Suburban Station Building				
8					Philadelphia, PA 19103				
9									
10									
11									
12									
13		Computer Resources & Training, Inc.							
14		One Penn Center - Suburban Station Building							
15		Philadelphia, PA 19103							
16									

B16

Sheet1 / Sheet2 / Sheet3 / Sheet4 / Sheet5 / Sheet6 /

Figure 23.10   Run your macro a couple of times to test it.

The sample macro that you recorded only works on the current workbook. If you close the file containing this macro, no other workbook will be able to access the macro. Later in this chapter, you'll learn how to make a macro global to all workbooks.

When you want to run a macro, you can always use the formal method of choosing the macro name from the Tools ➤ Macro menu and clicking the Run button. But you probably want a quicker way to run your macro. Excel lets you assign your macros to keyboard combinations, the Tools menu, toolbar buttons, or custom worksheet buttons. These alternatives are discussed in the following sections.

Creating a Macro Shortcut Key

You can assign your macro to a keyboard combination. Then, when you want to run the macro, you can press these keys instead of going the long way through the menus. Here are the steps for assigning a macro to a shortcut key:

1. Open the workbook that contains your macro and choose Tools ➤ Macro.

2. Select the name of your macro. The buttons on the right side of the Macro dialog box become available.

3. Click the Options button. Another dialog box, Macro Options, appears. Here is where you can assign a keyboard shortcut.

4. Check the Shortcut Key checkbox and click into the Ctrl+ text box area.

5. Press the keys that you want to use in combination with the Ctrl key as the shortcut for your macro. For example, to assign the keyboard combination Ctrl+Shift+N (N=Name) to the sample macro we created, hold down the Shift key and tap the letter N. (The Ctrl key is already set.) The keys you pressed will appear as the shortcut key, as shown in Figure 23.11.

6. Click OK in the Macro Options dialog box.

7. Click the Close button in the Macro dialog box.

8. Once you return to the worksheet, click into a blank cell and press your shortcut key combination (such as Shift+Ctrl+N) to activate your macro.

Assigning a Macro to the Tools Menu

If you have many macros, it can be difficult to remember all the different shortcut key combinations you assigned to them. You may just want to

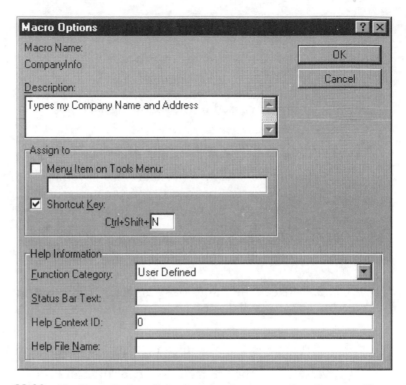

Figure 23.11   The Macro Options dialog box contains many options that you will want to use while working with macros, including one to assign a keyboard shortcut.

be able to choose the macro name from a menu. Excel lets you add the macro to the bottom of the Tools menu.

When you assign a macro to the Tools menu, it is not necessary to use the same name on the menu as you used for the macro name. Unlike the name you specify when you create the macro, the name you assign to the macro on a menu can include spaces. Another advantage of assigning a macro to the menu is that you can add a description of the macro to appear on the Status bar (at the bottom of the screen) when you highlight the macro name on the menu.

Follow these steps to assign a macro to the Tools menu:

1. Open the workbook that contains your macro and choose Tools ➤ Macro.

2. Select the name of your macro.

3. In the Macro dialog box, click the Options button.

4. In the Macro Options dialog box, check the Menu Item on Tools Menu checkbox and click into the text area below the option.

5. Type the name that you wish to see on the menu. The name on the menu can be up to 255 characters and include spaces. Keep the name fairly short, however, because the drop-down Tools menu will enlarge to fit the size of your name. For example, you might name our sample macro CRT Company (for the company name it types, Computer Resources & Training).

6. Click into the Status Bar Text box in the Help Information section at the bottom of the dialog box. Type in information that will help you or other users know what this menu item does. For example, you might describe our sample macro with the text "Bolds and Types the Company Name and Address." This is the text that will appear on the Status bar when the macro is highlighted on the menu.

7. Click OK and then click Close in the Macro dialog box to return to the worksheet.

8. Choose Tools from the menu bar. At the bottom of the menu, your macro name appears.

9. Select the name, and the macro will run in the worksheet.

Part
3

Analyzing with Excel

You can change the macro name that appears on the Tools menu by repeating the same steps you followed to create the name (Tools ➤ Macro ➤ Options).

To remove the name from the menu, return to the Macro Options dialog box and remove the check from the Menu Item on Tools menu checkbox.

Assigning a Macro to a Toolbar Button

You can also assign your macro to its own button on a toolbar. You may want to assign all of your macros to a new, custom toolbar instead of placing them on existing toolbars (customizing toolbars was described earlier in this chapter).

Follow these steps to assign a macro to a toolbar:

1. Choose View ➤ Toolbars and click the Customize button, or point to any button on a toolbar, right-click, and select Customize from the shortcut menu.

2. Scroll down through all the categories until you get to the end of the list. Choose the category called Custom. When you select Custom, you will see 28 custom buttons appear in the dialog box.

> **NOTE** Do not choose the category called Macro, even though you are assigning a macro to the new button. The buttons in the Macro category are for recording, running, and stopping macros, not for assigning macros to these buttons.

3. Drag one of the buttons to a toolbar. When you release the mouse, Excel displays the Assign Macro dialog box.

4. Select the name of your macro and click the OK button. Click the Close button on the Customize dialog box. Your macro can now be activated by clicking its new button on the toolbar.

You can use buttons from categories other than the Custom category. While the Customize dialog box is on the screen (View ➤ Toolbars ➤ Customize), drag a button from another category to a toolbar. While the button is still selected, choose Tools from the menu bar. The Tools menu will drop down, even though the Customize dialog box is on the screen. Choose Assign Macro, as shown in Figure 23.12. Select the name of

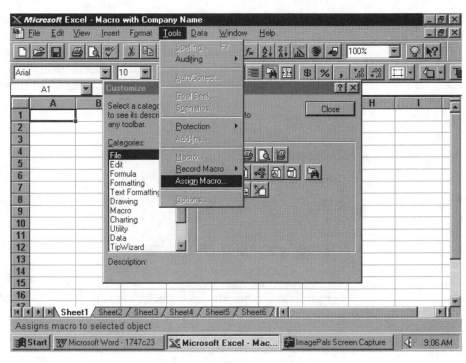

Figure 23.12   *You can assign macros to any button available in Excel.*

your macro and click OK. Click the Close button to close the Customize dialog box. You can now activate your macro by clicking the assigned button on the toolbar.

WARNING   When you assign macros to buttons that are not in the Custom category, the original ToolTip and Status bar text for the button stay the same, even though you have assigned a personal macro.

As mentioned earlier, the sample macro that we have been working with only works for the current workbook. When you close this workbook and try to access that macro in a new workbook, it is not available through the Tools ➤ Macro dialog box. If you assigned the macro to the Tools menu or to a shortcut key, it would not be available in other workbooks—only the original one in which it was created.

The one exception is when you have assigned the macro to a button on a toolbar, and then click that toolbar button while in a new workbook.

Excel loads the workbook that contained the macro and then activates the macro on the new workbook. In other words, you now have two workbooks in memory: the workbook on the screen and the workbook that contains the macro. Choose Window from the menu bar to see the name of your other workbook that contains the macro:

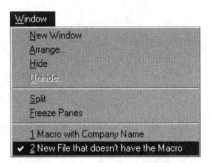

Advanced macro users will sometimes use this technique for making a macro available all the time. However, there is an "official global macro method" that does not cause the original macro's workbook to load into memory. Later in this chapter, you will learn how to create a Personal (global) Macro workbook. Macros contained in this workbook can be activated at any time in different workbooks.

Creating Worksheet Buttons for Macros

There is yet another method for assigning a shortcut to a macro. You can create your own custom command button objects that appear directly on the worksheet instead of on a toolbar. The button objects on the sheet can use real names (unlike the toolbar button names). Follow these steps to assign a macro to a worksheet button:

1. Display the Drawing toolbar by clicking on the drawing button on the Standard toolbar (this button contains a yellow square and a green circle). You can also choose View ➤ Toolbars and check the Drawing option, or point to any button on a toolbar, right-click, and select Drawing.

2. On the Drawing toolbar, click the create button icon (to the left of the button with the white arrow).

3. Position the mouse pointer where you want the button to appear on your worksheet. Click and drag a box across one column and down three rows.

When you release the mouse button, Excel displays the Assign Macro dialog box. Your screen should look similar to the one shown in Figure 23.13.

4. When the Assign Macro dialog box appears, select the name of your macro from the list or begin recording a new macro by clicking on the Record button on the right side of the dialog box. If you are assigning an existing macro, click OK after selecting the macro name. The button is on the worksheet, and it is selected, as you can tell by the sizing handles around the button. The generic name Button 1 appears.

5. Drag across the generic name and type a more appropriate name for the button. (Don't press the Enter key while you're typing the name, unless you want two lines of text on the button.)

6. Click on another part of the worksheet to move away from the button.

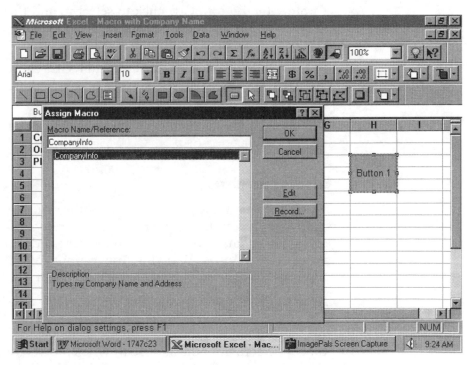

Figure 23.13 You can assign a macro to a button on the worksheet by using the Drawing toolbar's create button choice.

7. Test the button by clicking on an empty cell and clicking the button. Notice that the mouse pointer changes to a tiny pointing finger. When you click the button, the macro runs.

    After you've created a worksheet button, you can change it, but you need to select it first. You cannot just click the button, because that activates the macro. Hold down the Ctrl key while you click the button, and you will be in edit mode for the button. You can change the button in the following ways:

▶ To change the name that you gave the worksheet button, Ctrl-click to select it, and then click again on the name. Delete it, and then type a new name.

▶ To resize the button, Ctrl-click to select it, and then pull on the small, gray boxes that surround the button.

▶ To move the button, Ctrl-click to select it, and then point to any edge of the button (in between the sizing handles). The pointer changes to a white arrow. Drag the button to another location.

▶ To reassign another macro to the button, Ctrl-click to select it, and then choose Tools ➤ Assign Macro. Choose another macro name and click OK.

When you're finished making changes to the worksheet button, click on a blank cell or press Esc.

Editing Macros

If you discover a mistake in one of your macros (such as a typo in our sample company name macro), you can rerecord the entire series of keystrokes again, or you can edit the macro code directly. The macro is written in the Visual Basic for Applications (VBA) programming language and resides on the last sheet (after Sheet 16) of the workbook.

To see and edit your macro, click the last VCR-type button on the sheet tab (the arrow pointing to the right with a vertical line). Click on the Module1 sheet tab. You can also get to the Module sheet by choosing Tools ➤ Macro from the menu bar. When the Macro dialog box appears, select the name of your macro and click the Edit button on the right side. The Module sheet will be activated. Figure 23.14 shows the sample macro we recorded earlier in the chapter on the Module1 sheet.

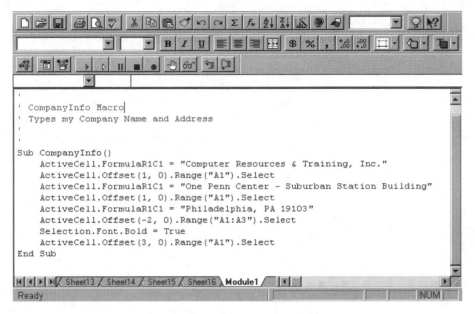

Figure 23.14 *You can view and edit a macro. The macro is written in the VBA programming language.*

The words that you typed while recording the macro are within quotation marks. If you see a typo in one of the words, click on the word and make changes just as you normally make changes to text in the worksheet. Delete the incorrect characters and type the correct ones. Do not press the Enter key; use the mouse to move to another line if you need to make changes there.

When you are finished editing, select the first sheet again (Sheet 1) or whatever sheet you were working on. Your changes will be saved when you save the workbook.

WARNING Unless you know the Visual Basic for Applications programming language, do not make any changes to the macro code. Just edit the text that you typed for the macro, such as your own company information. For more information about working with Visual Basic for Applications, see the programming documentation that comes with Excel.

Storing Global Macros

Excel gives you the ability to record and store global macros. You can create your own macro library full of commonly used macros. These macros can work on all workbooks. Global macros are stored in a Personal Macro workbook. The first time you create a global, personal macro, Excel creates this hidden workbook. It is stored in the XLStart folder. The workbook actually stays in memory but is hidden.

Creating a Global Macro

Our sample company name macro cannot become a global, personal macro after the fact. You must select the option to make the macro global before you begin recording it. In the following steps, we will rerecord another version of our company name macro as a global, personal macro.

1. Start a new workbook or select a blank cell range on the workbook that is currently on the screen.

2. Make sure that the option Use Relative References is checked and choose Tools ➤ Record Macro ➤ Record New Macro.

3. In the Macro dialog box, type a name for the new macro (don't use exactly the same name as you used for the earlier sample macro, because we want to keep the original macro for now). Then type a description for the macro.

4. Click the Options button.

5. In the Record New Macro dialog box, click the Personal Macro Workbook radio button in the Store In section at the bottom of the dialog box, as shown in Figure 23.15. Also make sure that the Visual Basic radio button in the Language section is checked.

6. Click the OK button. In the worksheet, you will see that the Macro Recorder is on. The stop macro recording button is in the upper-right corner of the worksheet and the word *Recording* appears on the Status bar.

7. Type your company name and address. Select the lines and bold them. Then click on the blank row below the company name.

Record New Macro

Macro Name:
Global_CompanyInfo

Description:
Company named is typed and bolded. This macro works across all workbooks

Assign to
☐ Menu Item on Tools Menu:

☐ Shortcut Key:
Ctrl+ e

Store in
◉ Personal Macro Workbook
○ This Workbook
○ New Workbook

Language
◉ Visual Basic
○ MS Excel 4.0 Macro

OK

Cancel

Options >>

Figure 23.15   To create a global macro while recording, click the Options button before you choose OK so that you can choose the Personal Macro Workbook option.

8. Click the stop recording button or choose Tools ➤ Record Macro ➤ Stop Recording.

9. To run this macro, choose Tools ➤ Macro from the menu bar. The name of the global, personal macro is listed.

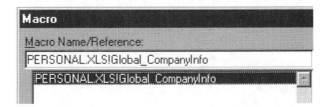

Macro

Macro Name/Reference:
PERSONAL.XLS!Global_CompanyInfo

PERSONAL.XLS!Global_CompanyInfo

10. Select the macro and click the Run button.

Assigning and Editing Global Macros

You can assign a global, personal macro to the bottom of the Tools menu, a shortcut key, a toolbar button, or to a worksheet button in the same

Part 3

Analyzing with Excel

way that you assign shortcuts for local workbook macros (as described earlier in this chapter).

To edit the global macro, however, you must first unhide its workbook. Choose Window ➤ Unhide from the menu bar. When the Unhide dialog box appears, you will see the name Personal workbook, as shown in Figure 23.16. Click the OK button to unhide the workbook with your global macro.

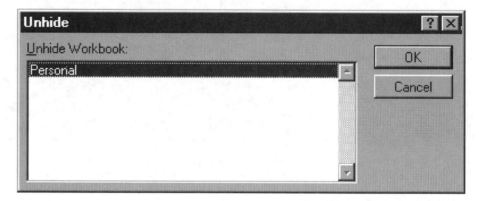

Figure 23.16　*Choose Window ➤ Unhide, then click OK to unhide the Personal Macro workbook with your global macro.*

Once the Personal Macro workbook is unhidden, Excel immediately displays the macro programming code. You will notice that there are no other sheet names at the bottom of this workbook; it contains only the Module sheet. Make your changes to the global macro and save the workbook (click the save button on the Standard toolbar, choose File ➤ Save, or press Ctrl+S).

Rehide the Personal Macro workbook by choosing Window ➤ Hide from the menu bar. The workbook is immediately hidden back into memory.

NOTE　You can hide any workbook that is active on the screen by choosing Window ➤ Hide from the menu bar. Be careful, because you might forget that you hid your workbook, and you may find yourself looking around under your desk for it. Use Window ➤ Unhide to make any of your hidden workbooks visible.

If you created an AutoTemplate for a module of programming code, you can insert this module into the Personal Macro workbook. While the Personal Macro workbook is in edit mode, choose Insert ➤ Macro ➤ Module from the menu bar. Your AutoTemplate macro module will be inserted into the global workbook. Your additional lines of code will be available to all workbooks. See Chapter 22 for more information about Excel's AutoTemplates.

Creating Print Macros Using VBA

One of the most common requests for macros in a spreadsheet program is to print various ranges of data. The actual values may change weekly or monthly, but the area of the spreadsheet where the data resides does not change. In other spreadsheet programs, you can create names for these print ranges and design a quick macro that prints a specific range. It is just as easy to do similar tasks in Excel, but the use of the VBA programming language is necessary.

So far in this chapter, you have learned how to record macros and view the code on the Module sheets. In this next example, you will write the code from the beginning, without recording the macro first, and then assign the macros to worksheet buttons. We won't go into details about the VBA language. See the programming documentation that comes with the Excel program for more information about VBA.

Writing the Macros

This VBA print macro example requires that you have three print ranges defined with range names. Follow these steps to define the ranges and write the macros:

1. In the workbook that contains the various print ranges, select (highlight) the first print range and click the Name box above the A column. Type a name (no spaces are allowed). You can also select Insert ➤ Name ➤ Define, type a name for the range, and click OK. Figure 23.17 shows an example of the name Dept1 being defined for a print range.

2. Repeat the process described in step 1 to define two more print range names. (The range names Dept2 and Dept3 are used in this example.)

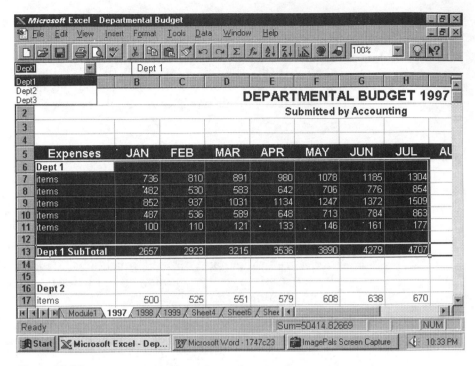

Figure 23.17   Defining a range name for a print area

 NOTE   To delete a range name, choose Insert ➤ Name ➤ Define. Select the name, click the Delete button, and click OK.

3. To insert a programming module sheet on which to write your Visual Basic routines, select Insert ➤ Macro ➤ Module. Don't worry that the Module sheet is inserted at the beginning of your other sheets; you can move it later.

4. Type the following lines at the top of the sheet:

    ```
    ' Print Macro Example
    ' Prints Three Ranges to the Print Preview Screen
    ' June 1997
    ```

    These are remarks (or documentation) about what the macro will be doing. Programming remarks or documentation are preceded with backward apostrophes on each line. Excel knows that is should not perform the keystrokes that are on the lines preceded with the backward apostrophe. The lines of documentation appear in green for quick viewing. In your own macros, you should include your name and the date of creation as remarks. This information can be important for future reference.

You are now ready to write your lines of code. A subroutine reference must precede the name of each macro. Each macro must have a unique name. The name must be followed by parentheses.

5. As the name of the first macro, type the line:

```
Sub Dept1()
```

> **NOTE**   You can use any name you like for your macro—RossPerot if you like. We are using the name of the range so that it is easier to distinguish which macro prints which range.

6. On the line below the subroutine reference is the actual line of code that prints the range. Type the following:

```
Range("Dept1").PrintOut Preview:=True
```

This line says "On the Range defined as 'Dept1,' perform a PrintOut method of action." The range name is in quotation marks because quotation marks represent literal text that is typed. The macro name is not in quotation marks. The optional parameter of Preview is set to True so that the printout will appear on the screen before it is printed to the printer. You will remove this optional parameter after you test the macros.

7. Type the last line of the macro:

```
End Sub
```

This tells Excel that the macro is over and to end the subroutine. Both the Sub and the End Sub lines are in blue to let you know that these key words are typed correctly. When there is a severe problem with a line of programming, the problem line will appear in red. You must then find your mistake in that line and correct it.

8. Repeat steps 5 through 7, substituting the name of the other print ranges to create the two other macros. Figure 23.18 shows the three macros on the Module sheet.

9. Save the file.

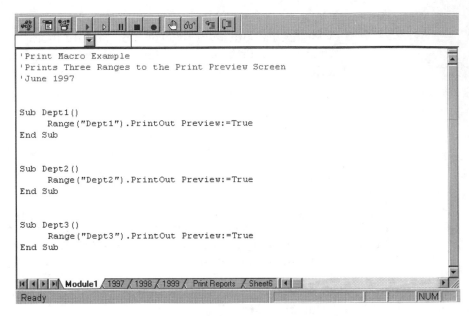

Figure 23.18 *The print macros print three different print ranges. These macros can be assigned to buttons on the worksheet or on the toolbar.*

10. Choose Tools ➤ Macro. Alternatively, you can click the run macro button (the one with a green right arrow) on the Module sheet's Visual Basic toolbar. You will see your new macros listed in the Macro dialog box, as shown in Figure 23.19.

11. Select the name of the print macro you wish to preview and click the Run button.

12. Repeat step 11 to test each of the macros.

13. After you have tested the macros and are sure they work as you intended, remove the Preview:=True statement from each macro so that the macro prints directly to a printer. To edit the macro to remove the statement, choose Tools ➤ Macro, select the name of the macro, and click the Edit button. You can also select the Module sheet containing the macro.

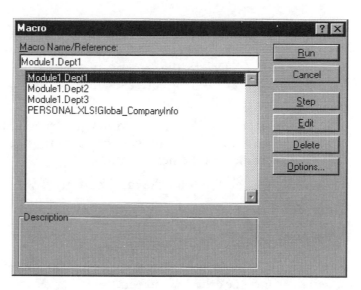

Figure 23.19 *The Macro dialog box displays the names of each of your subroutines, just as if you had recorded the macros.*

 WARNING If you delete a macro using the Macro dialog box, the macro instantly disappears from the Module sheet. Use Undo (press Ctrl+Z, click the Undo button, or choose Edit ➤ Undo Delete) immediately to reverse the deletion if you want to keep the macro.

Assigning Your Print Macros to Sheet Buttons

Now that you have created and debugged your macros, you can assign each one to a worksheet button for easy access. Follow these steps:

1. In cell A3 of an empty worksheet, type **Click Here to Print the Dept1 Report.** Change the point size to 14 and bold the words.

2. Copy the text to cells A7 and A11. Change the number of *Dept* for each copy (*Dept2* and *Dept3*).

3. Display the Drawing toolbar and click the create button icon. Draw a rectangle that stretches from column G through H and covers row 3.

4. When you are finished drawing the rectangle, the Assign Macro dialog box appears with the names of the macros you have created. Click on the Dept1 macro and click OK. The Dept1 macro has been assigned to this first button.

Part 3

Analyzing with Excel

5. To change the name on the button, hold down the Ctrl key and click the button to select it. Click again on the button, and you will be in text edit mode. Delete the generic button name and type the name **Dept 1 Report**. When you are finished, click outside the button on an empty cell.

6. To copy the button, hold down Ctrl and click the button. Continue to hold down Ctrl while you drag the gray edge of the button (not the sizing handles) to the next location.

7. Repeat step 6 for the third button.

8. Select the second button. (Remember to hold down the Ctrl key before clicking on the button or you will activate the macro that has been assigned to the macro.)

9. Choose Tools ➤ Assign Macro from the menu. Select the Dept2 macro and click the OK button.

10. Repeat step 9 for the third button and assign the Dept3 macro.

11. Double-click on the sheet name at the bottom of the screen and name the sheet **Print Reports**. Your worksheet should look like the one shown in Figure 23.20.

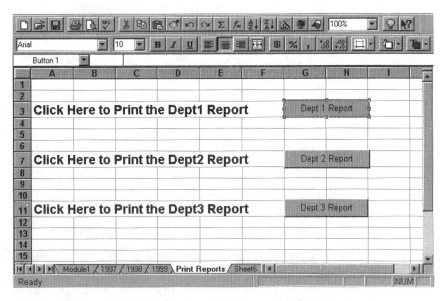

Figure 23.20   You can create worksheets with buttons that can be clicked to activate your custom macros.

12. Test your worksheet buttons by clicking each one to print each range.

   You can also assign the macros to the end of the Tools menu, as described earlier in the chapter.

   This chapter has described how to customize toolbars and automate your work with macros. The next chapter is about integrating your work in Excel with other Office 95 applications.

Chapter 24

Office Connections— Handling a Table that Keeps on Growing

FEATURING

Office 95 is known for its enhanced ability to integrate data from multiple applications. In the Office Connections chapter at the end of the Word 95 section, our real-world person focused on linking files between Word and Excel and Word and PowerPoint.

The example in this chapter demonstrates how you can integrate a "simple" project that starts in Word, expands to Excel, and finally finds a true home in Access. You'll learn more about Access and its query and reporting features in Part Six.

The Project's Route through the Office

Here is our scenario. Renee is a marketing specialist for a Washington-based Entertainment Television show. One of her projects involved developing a table that lists the participants who attended different focus groups. Participants were asked questions about what they liked and didn't like on the Entertainment Television. She needed to track the dates that the different groups attended the focus group, the questions asked, and their names and demographics (age, sex, income, marital status, and so on).

Renee initially created that table in Word. She used Word's Database toolbar and buttons to create a database form. Then she used the sort button on the toolbar to quickly organize the data.

As the table grew, individuals in her department began to depend more and more on the information it contained. The table continued to grow as columns were added. It became obvious that Renee would need to move the table to another program that allowed her to more easily add categories of information. She decided to move the table to Excel.

Once in Excel, the table grew more. Renee learned how to use Excel's Access form to help with the data entry. Eventually, the table became too unwieldy to keep in Excel. Renee's colleagues were asking more questions about the data than Excel could answer with its current tools. It was obvious that the query and reporting features of Access were needed by the department members. Renee exported the table to Access, and has been happy ever since.

Many times a process "evolves." At the start of a project, it is hard to know how the project will grow over time. Renee's information eventually had to be organized differently and her single table divided into multiple related tables. Mass mailings are now conducted on the data using Word form letters. The process comes full circle. Let's get started and follow Renee's route around the Office.

Creating a Database in Word

Word's Table feature is ideal for managing columnar and row information. A Word table is used as the data source for the mail merge feature because it can organize information in database-type fields and records.

Here are the steps for creating a Word database:

1. Create a new file in Word.

2. To change the page orientation to landscape (to allow for ten columns of information), choose File ➤ Page Setup ➤ Paper Size tab and select the Landscape option.

3. To change the margins to $\frac{1}{2}$-inch on all sides, click the Margins tab in the Page Setup dialog box and set all four margins to .5", as shown in Figure 24.1. Click OK in the Page Setup dialog box.

4. To create the table, choose Table ➤ Insert Table. In the dialog box, click the up spinner buttons and change the settings to 10 columns and 10 rows, as shown in Figure 24.2. Click OK.

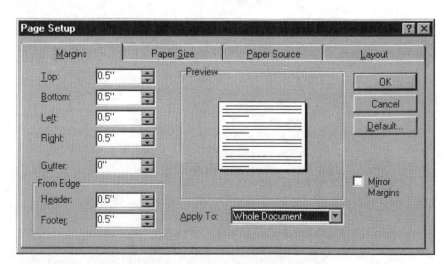

Figure 24.1   *Setting the margins for a table with landscape orientation*

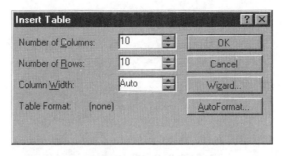

Figure 24.2 *Inserting a table with ten columns and ten rows*

5. Enter the following column headings into the first row, using the Tab key to move from column to column (use Shift+Tab to move backward from right to left):

> **Focus Group Name➥Date of Group➥Last Name➥First Name➥
> Gender➥Date of Birth➥Marital Status ➥Income➥ Race➥
> Address**

6. Click on the row of column headings, and then choose Table ➤ Select Row. Click the bold and the center buttons on the Formatting toolbar.

7. Click into the second row of the first column below your first heading, choose View ➤ Toolbars, and click the Database toolbar.

8. Click the first button on the Database toolbar, the data form button. A data form appears, as shown in Figure 24.3.

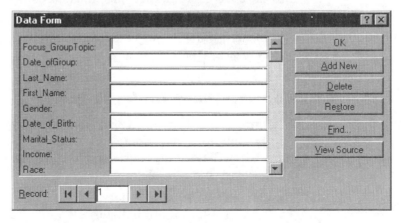

Figure 24.3 *Word allows any table to be used as a simple database. Click the data form button on the Database toolbar to create a data-entry form.*

9. Enter some sample records to represent Renee's data.

   Diana Ross comeback tour➼8/1/96➼Frierson➼Mary➼F➼
   8/23/35➼S➼37,000➼B➼Stover Ave., DC

10. Click the Add New button or press the Enter key when you have typed
    the information into the last field of the data form.

> **NOTE** If you use the table and not the form to type the information, press
> the Tab key on the last column and last row to add a new, blank row. To move
> from the data form to the table, click the View Source button in the Data
> Form dialog box. To return to the form, click the first button on the Database
> toolbar.

Sorting a Word Database

Once the data is in a Word table, separated in columns and rows, you
can use the Database toolbar's sort buttons to organize the data. If this
toolbar is not on your screen, choose View ➤ Toolbars and check the
Database option.

If you are in the Data Form, click View Source to return to the table. Click
into the Last Name column of the table. Make sure that you do not select
the entire table. Just position the insertion point in the column by which
you are going to sort. Then click the ascending sort button (A to Z). Click
into the Date column, then click the descending sort button (Z to A).

You can also use the Sort dialog box, shown in Figure 24.4, to sort by
different columns at once. Use the Table ➤ Sort command to get to this
dialog box.

Copying Word Tables to Excel

When the table outgrew Word, Renee transferred it to Excel. This is a
simple copy-and-paste operation. The table does not need to be linked,
because it will no longer be managed in Word. Here are the steps to copy
and paste the Word table:

1. To select the Word table, click in any cell of the table and choose Table
   ➤ Select Table, or hold down Alt and press the number 5 on the
   calculator pad at the right side of the keyboard.

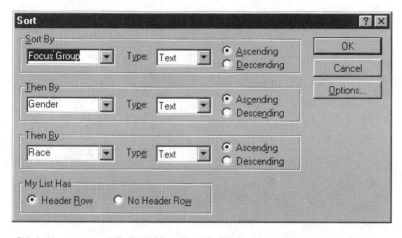

Figure 24.4 **You can use Word's Table ➤ Sort dialog box to sort by multiple fields.**

2. Copy the table information into the Clipboard (click the Copy button on the Standard toolbar or press Ctrl+C).

3. If Excel has not been launched, click the Start button on the Taskbar and choose Programs. Click the Excel program menu item to launch the program. Click back on the Word program that is listed on the Taskbar.

4. Make sure the pointer is in cell A1 on a blank worksheet in Excel. Click the Paste button on the Standard toolbar or choose Edit ➤ Paste from the menu. The Word table flows into the columns and rows. Widen the columns as needed. Figure 24.5 shows the Word table copied into Excel.

	A	B	C	D	E	F
1	Focus GroupTopic	Date ofGroup	Last Name	First Name	Gender	Date of Birth
2	Diana Ross comeback tour	08/01/96	Frierson	Mary	F	08/23/35
3	Diana Ross comeback tour	08/01/96	Carter	Steven	M	05/08/61
4	Gangster Rap and its effects	05/01/96	Baron	Rona	F	04/20/57
5	Gangster Rap and its effects	05/01/96	Coutant	Scott	M	07/01/65
6	Gangster Rap and its effects	05/01/96	Luber	Harvey	M	08/15/55
7	I am not a role model - discuss	07/01/96	Cooper	Melissa	F	05/22/58
8	I am not a role model - discuss	07/01/96	Corbin	Norman	M	08/13/57
9	I am not a role model - discuss	07/01/96	Jones	Victor	M	12/05/59
10	I am not a role model - discuss	07/01/96	Kincus	Larry	M	12/15/61
11	Music Video themes	06/01/96	Jackson	Tileen	F	11/23/61
12	Music Video themes	06/01/96	Flamer	Yvonne	F	09/18/59
13	Music Video themes	06/01/96	Still	Linda	F	01/12/62
14	Social Engineering through entertainment	09/01/96	Watson	Dee	F	05/01/44
15	Social Engineering through entertainment	09/01/96	Harris	Michael	M	05/01/44
16	Social Engineering through entertainment	09/01/96	Garcia	Eduardo	M	09/15/67

Figure 24.5 **Word table copied to Excel**

5. Before continuing, save the Excel file under the name Focus Group Data (choose File ➤ Save or press Ctrl+S).

Using Access Wizards in Excel

As new columns are added to a table, it becomes more difficult to fill in the data horizontally across the wide rows. An Access data-entry form makes it easier to enter more records. From Excel, you can access the Access Form Wizard and set up your form in a few steps. Another Access Wizard available from Excel lets you design sophisticated reports from your Excel data.

Using the Access Form Wizard

The Access Wizards are options on Excel's Data menu. Follow these steps to create the Access data-entry form:

1. With the pointer in any cell of the Focus Group Data file, choose Data ➤ Access Form from the menu:

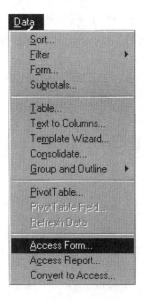

If you did not save your Excel file before choosing to create an Access form, Excel will remind you:

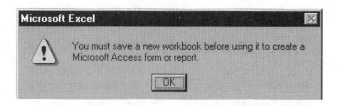

2. In the Create Microsoft Access Form dialog box, click the New Database button. Make sure the Header Row button at the bottom of the dialog box is selected. The first row of column headings is considered the header row, and these headings will be the field names used on the Access form. Figure 24.6 shows the dialog box with these settings. Click OK to begin designing the form.

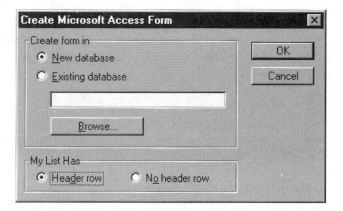

Figure 24.6   *Select to create the form in a new database and specify that your list has a header row.*

WARNING   You may need to wait a minute (or more) for your Access connections from Excel.

3.   Access welcomes you to the Access Form Wizard and allows you to select particular fields to be used for data entry. Because you need all of the fields on the form, click the double right arrow button to copy all of the fields to the Selected Fields box on the right, as shown in Figure 24.7.

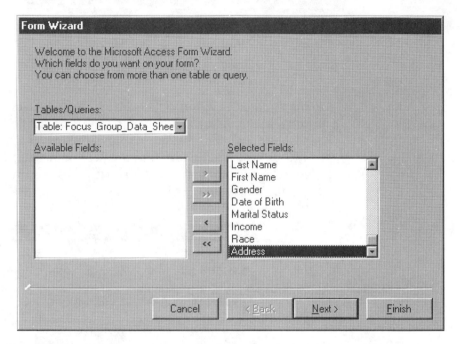

Figure 24.7   *The fields you choose for the form appear in the Selected Fields list.*

4.   The Access Form Wizard asks you to choose a layout for your form. Choose Columnar, as shown in Figure 24.8. (You can click the other layout choices and see a preview of each before you make your final selection.) Then click Next to continue.

5.   The Access Form Wizard asks you to choose the style you prefer for your data form. Choose International, as shown in Figure 24.9. In this style, the fields of your Excel sheet will appear against a background of a world map. Click the Next button to go to the next screen.

6.   The Access Form Wizard's final choices appear, as shown in Figure 24.10. Type a name for your data-entry form and select the Open the Form to View or Enter Information option. Then click the Finish button.

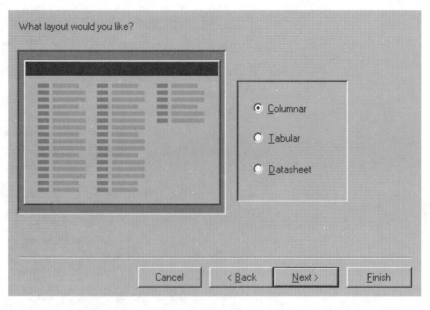

Figure 24.8 *The Access Form Wizard asks you to choose the type of layout you prefer.*

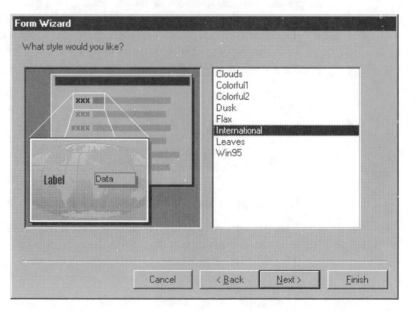

Figure 24.9 *You can choose from a variety of attractive background styles for your data-entry form.*

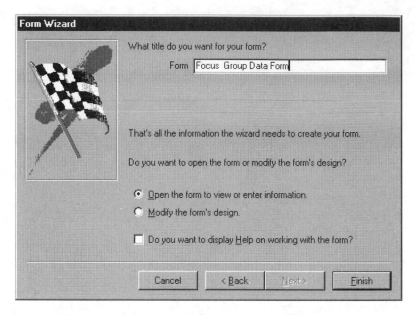

Figure 24.10   The Access Form Wizard allows you to name this particular data-entry form. You can have multiple forms for the same data.

The finished form, shown in Figure 24.11, is attractive and easy to use. Use the Access toolbar buttons to sort and filter your data. See Part Six for information about using the Access program.

When you are finished viewing or entering data in your Access form, choose File ➤ Close and return to Excel. After the last column of data in the Excel file, you will see an Access form button. Whenever you want to use your data-entry form, click the Access form button to launch the form you just designed.

Using the Access Report Wizard

In addition to creating an Access data-entry form, you can use the Access Report Wizard to design a sophisticated report from your Excel data. The Wizard guides you through the process of designing the report. Here are the general steps for using the Report Wizard:

1. Save your Excel data and make sure your pointer is within the data area.

2. Choose Data ➤ Access Report from the menu bar.

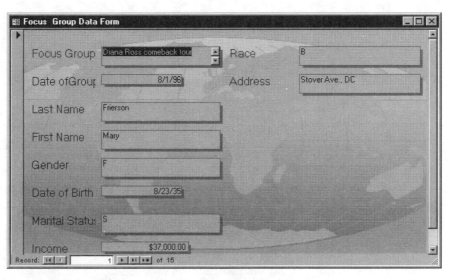

Figure 24.11 *It is easy to enter records into an Excel worksheet using an Access data-entry form.*

3. In the Access Report Wizard dialog box, choose the fields you want on the report. Figure 24.12 shows the fields selected for this example. Click Next to move to the next screen.

4. The Access Report Wizard asks if you would like to have the data on the report grouped by a particular field. For this example, choose Gender as the field for grouping, as shown in Figure 24.13.

5. The Access Report Wizard asks you to choose a sort order. Click the drop-down arrow next to item 1 and choose the Focus Group Topic field, as shown in Figure 24.14. The report will be grouped by the Gender field, and within that field, the names will be sorted by the topics. You can have up to four sort fields in the report. Click Next to continue.

6. The Access Report Wizard asks you to choose a layout for your report. Choose the Outline1 layout, as shown in Figure 24.15. Then click Next.

7. Your next step is to specify a typeface and font style for the report. For this example, choose the Compact style, as shown in Figure 24.16. (You can select each of the style types and see a preview before making your final selection.) Click Next after you make your selection.

8. When you are at the "Finish" line, the Access Wizard asks for a name for the report, as shown in Figure 24.17. Type in a descriptive name and click the Finish button.

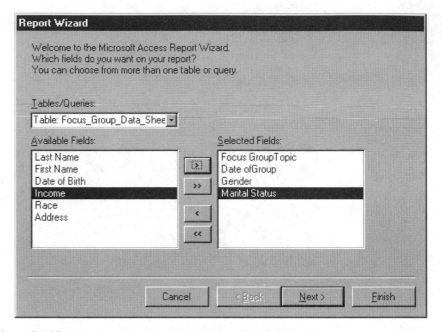

Figure 24.12   The Access Report Wizard lets you select the Excel fields to include in the report.

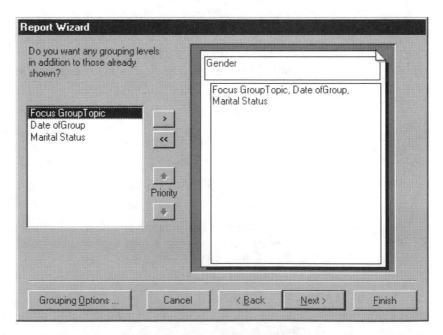

Figure 24.13   You can group Excel Reports by any of the fields in the worksheet.

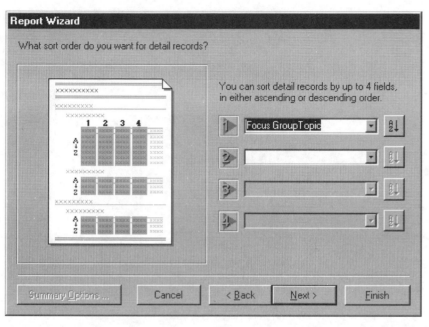

Figure 24.14   *The Access Report Wizard allows you to sort your data before running the report.*

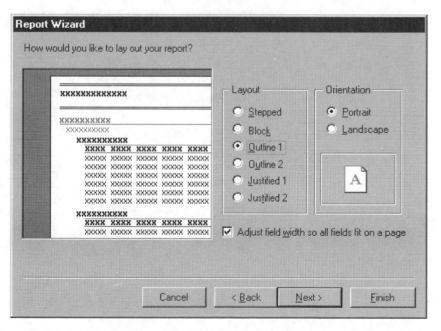

Figure 24.15   *The Access Report Wizard lets you choose from a variety of report layouts.*

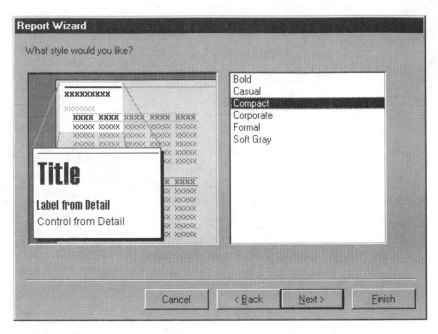

Figure 24.16   *You can choose from various typeface styles for your Excel reports.*

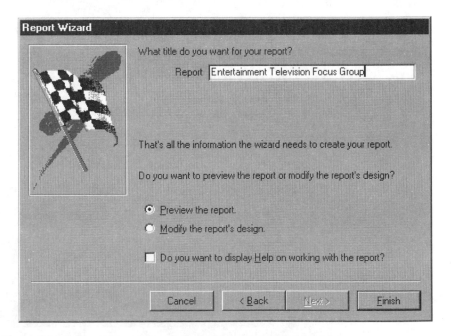

Figure 24.17   *You can create multiple reports for your spreadsheet data.*

Excel to Access—The Final Transition

These connections to Access while you are working in an Excel file are certainly helpful, but the connections are also slow. After Renee, our marketing specialist became comfortable with the Access data-entry form and the Access report, it made sense to move the entire table to Access. The powerful tools provided by Access are appreciated by everyone in the department who uses the focus group table. Renee saved Access queries and reports so that users can run them simply by clicking on the objects she created. Access's powerful relational database capabilities allowed Renee to divide her data into smaller, more manageable tables as she began to reinterview the same people during different focus groups.

Converting Excel data to an Access database is a quick and straightforward process. Here are the steps:

1. Save your worksheet data. Then choose Data ➤ Convert to Access from the menu bar.

2. In the Convert to Microsoft Access dialog box, select the New Database option, as shown in Figure 24.18. Then click the OK button.

3. Select the Include Field Names on First Row option to let Access know that the column headings are to be used as the field names for the database. Figure 24.19 shows the column headings becoming field names in Access.

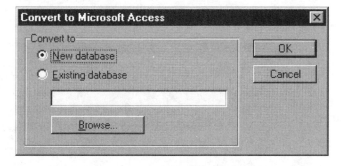

Figure 24.18 **You can easily convert all the Excel worksheet data to an Access database.**

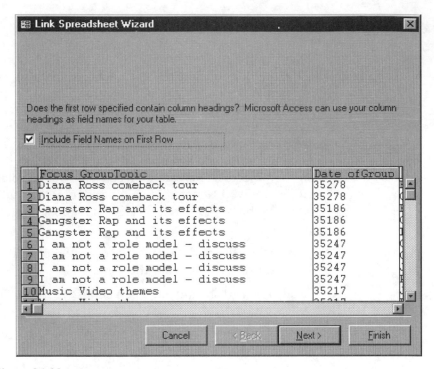

Figure 24.19 *The Excel column headings are quickly converted to fields for the Access database.*

4. This is all the information that Access needs to convert your data. When you are prompted for the table name, accept the default name or type a more descriptive name. Then click the Finish button. You will be alerted that the conversion link was completed.

5. Click the OK button to continue.

6. Double-click on the name you gave to the table, and your Access table will appear. Figure 24.20 shows the Excel data transformed into an Access table.

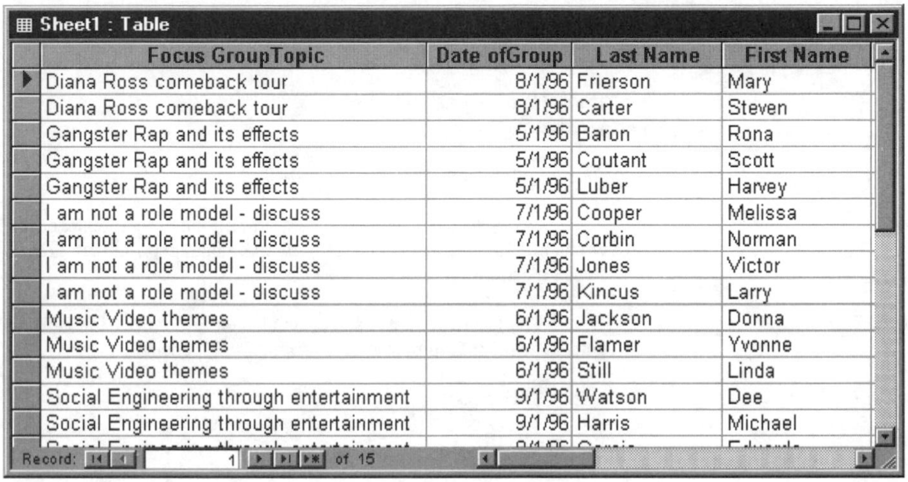

Focus GroupTopic	Date ofGroup	Last Name	First Name
Diana Ross comeback tour	8/1/96	Frierson	Mary
Diana Ross comeback tour	8/1/96	Carter	Steven
Gangster Rap and its effects	5/1/96	Baron	Rona
Gangster Rap and its effects	5/1/96	Coutant	Scott
Gangster Rap and its effects	5/1/96	Luber	Harvey
I am not a role model - discuss	7/1/96	Cooper	Melissa
I am not a role model - discuss	7/1/96	Corbin	Norman
I am not a role model - discuss	7/1/96	Jones	Victor
I am not a role model - discuss	7/1/96	Kincus	Larry
Music Video themes	6/1/96	Jackson	Donna
Music Video themes	6/1/96	Flamer	Yvonne
Music Video themes	6/1/96	Still	Linda
Social Engineering through entertainment	9/1/96	Watson	Dee
Social Engineering through entertainment	9/1/96	Harris	Michael

Figure 24.20 ***The conversion process from an Excel worksheet to an Access database is easy. Use the Data ➤ Convert to Access option from within Excel.***

After the data has been converted, you can begin using Access commands to query and report on the data. See Part Six for more information.

Mail Merging with Access Data

It is the start of a new year, and Renee wants to invite the participants from last year's focus groups to participate in a new round of discussions. Letters must be sent to all of the participants. Once again, the focus group data is being managed through Word, but at another level of operation. Renee now uses Word to design form letters to send to the focus group members. The data resides in Access, however, not in Word or Excel.

Word allows Renee to design and format the letter to be printed on snappy, special marketing letterhead. Word's Mail Merge Helper guides her through the process of merging the names of the focus group participants with the letter.

In Step 1 of the Mail Merge Helper (Tools ➤ Mail Merge), Renee designed the letter, as shown in Figure 24.21. In Step 2, she choose to open the Access focus group database as her data source, as shown in Figure 24.22.

January 2, 1997

«First_Name» «Last_Name»
«Address»

Dear «First_Name»:

Last year you were a participant in a focus group on «Focus_GroupTopic». We would like to invite you again to participate in Entertainment Television's 1997 Focus Group meetings.

The following dates and topics have been chosen for 1997. Please let us know if you are again able to provide the same valuable feedback that you gave us last year.

Listing of Events

Figure 24.21   **The form letter for merging**

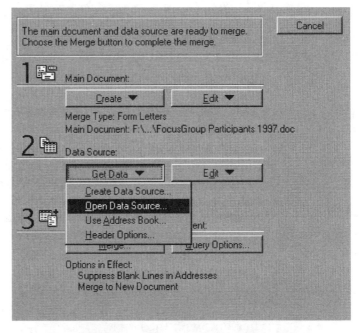

Figure 24.22   **Selecting an existing data source with the Mail Merge Helper.**

As you have seen in the example in this chapter, Office 95's flexibility and power allow for productivity gains. Small applications can grow and move into more sophisticated tools as your knowledge of the Office suite grows.

Business Processing: Presenting with PowerPoint

This part covers the fundamentals needed for creating colorful and effective slide presentations using PowerPoint. Features explored include everything from the use of Wizards and templates for quickly getting presentations ready to the new animation and multimedia effects that will make your presentations stand out.

The integration chapter of this part follows the process of a user who needs to create a presentation that incorporates data and charts from Word and Excel.

Chapter 25

Road Map/
Jump Start

Featuring

Before presentation software became available, public presentations relied heavily on printers and graphics designers to outline, edit, and create graphical representations for visual aids. Often it took several weeks between original concept and final design to take all the necessary steps, which cost hundreds or even thousands of dollars. Most large organizations established their own graphics design departments for in-house manufacturing of presentations. Not only did this offer employees a great convenience, it helped keep confidential information from having to leave the premises.

Today with PowerPoint, anyone can create a complete slide show presentation. Instead of taking weeks to complete a presentation, you can organize an entire conference within a few hours. No longer is security an issue, since one person can design and implement the entire presentation from one computer without any need for outside organizations.

Main Points of PowerPoint

To maximize your presentation potential with PowerPoint, you must first be familiar with the parts that make up the PowerPoint whole. The next few sections provide the information you need.

Slides

Anyone who has taken a class or attended a meeting where an overhead projector was used or has sat through a friend's vacation slides is familiar with slides. The term *slides* in the context of PowerPoint refers to the individual pages of your presentation. You can use the pages, or slides, once created, for on-screen presentations that take advantage of animation features or to print to transparencies or slides. Figure 25.1 shows a basic PowerPoint slide.

Speaker Notes

Speaker Notes are designed to assist the speaker in the presentation. Anyone who has spent time sifting through note cards knows the anxiety that can occur without organization. PowerPoint handles the organizing for you. With each slide, you can create a complete set of notes, as

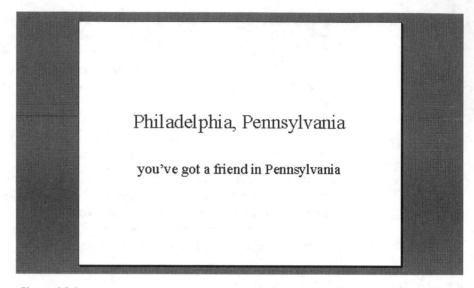

Figure 25.1   *A Sample slide as it appears in PowerPoint*

detailed or basic as you like, and you can create a complete script or just a general outline. The audience does not see the notes, but they are printed for the speaker's use. Accessing Speaker Notes is as easy as this:

1. Select View ➤ Notes Pages from the menu bar.

2. Use the bottom block to type any notes you will need for your presentation.

   Figure 25.2 shows the Speaker Notes for the slide in Figure 25.1.

   To return to the Slide view of your presentation, select View ➤ Slides from the menu bar.

TIP   The view items on the menu bar correspond with the view buttons at the bottom left of the PowerPoint window. If you want to switch quickly to one of the views, you can click on the buttons instead of going through the menu bar.

Organization Charts

You can use organization charts in a presentation to visually display the hierarchical structure of a company, an organization, or even a conceptual design. In the past, special programs were needed to create organizational charts, but with PowerPoint, you can easily create these charts and incorporate them into slides or export them to other applications in Office 95. Figure 25.3 shows an example of an organizational chart.

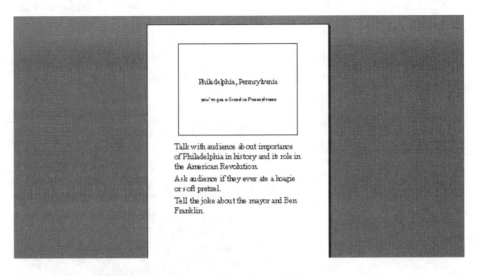

Figure 25.2   Set of Speaker Notes for the slide in Figure 25.1

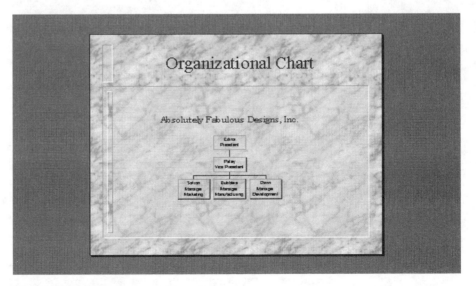

Figure 25.3   An Organization Chart in a slide

Media Clips

The term *media clips* includes the sound, animation, and now, even video clips you may want to insert into your presentation. Once you have inserted a media clip into a slide, you can activate it with a simple click while viewing your presentation. Whether you want to play a message from the chairman in a company meeting or take a tour of your state-of-the-art facility in a sales demo, media clips can really pump up your presentation. Figure 25.4 shows a media clip waiting to be activated.

Figure 25.4   **A media clip waiting to be activated in a presentation.**

Graphs

Nothing shows sales trends better than a graph. You can insert graphs into your slides to add visual punch to the numbers you want to get across to your audience. PowerPoint uses Microsoft Graph and all its available formats, including those in 3-D (see Figure 25.5).

Clip Art

Whether you use the collection of clip art that comes with PowerPoint or decide to supplement your library with one or more of the innumerable libraries available through third parties, clip art is a nice way to add descriptive visuals to your presentations. If you don't overuse it, clip art helps you emphasize the points you are trying to make. When appropriate, many of the clip art selections can also add a bit of levity to your presentation. Figure 25.6 shows a slide that uses clip art from PowerPoint.

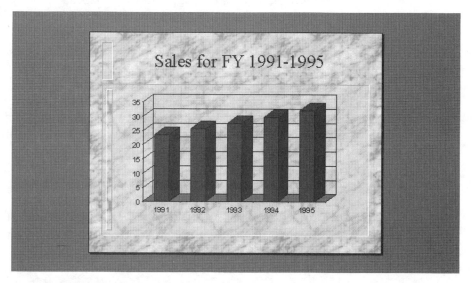

Figure 25.5 **3-D graph showing the increase in sales over five years**

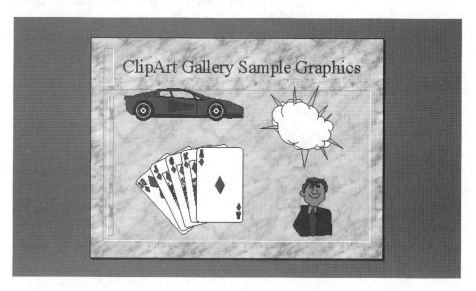

Figure 25.6 **Slide filled with a number of samples from PowerPoint's clip art collection**

Part 4

Presenting with PowerPoint

Views in PowerPoint

PowerPoint consists of multiple views to help you in the creation, presentation, and maintenance of your presentations. The various views, which you access through View on the menu bar or the View buttons at the bottom left of the PowerPoint window, are described in the following sections.

Slide

Slide view is the default view when you open PowerPoint. You can think of the Slide view as a picture of your slide as it will appear when printed or in the slide show. Only one slide is visible at a time in Slide view (see Figure 25.7).

Outline

Outline view provides an organized way to view your slides in the order in which they will appear in your presentation. Using Outline view, you can step back and look at the big picture of the message you will be trying to get across. Figure 25.8 shows a slide presentation in Outline view.

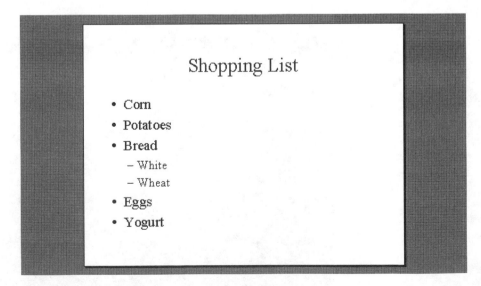

Figure 25.7   A slide on the computer screen in Slide view

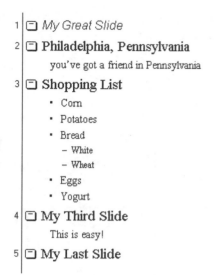

Figure 25.8 **Sample outline for the sample slide**

Notice the number that appears next to the vertical line on the left-hand side of the screen. This number represents the number of the slide in the presentation. The small Slide icon next to the number represents a slide.

TIP Double-clicking on a slide listed in Outline view allows you to jump back quickly to Slide view.

Slide Sorter

Slide Sorter provides a more detailed view than Outline, which shows only the text and titles of slides. Slide Sorter shows the completed slides as they will appear in the presentation. The number at the lower left of each slide indicates the order in which it will appear.

In addition to showing slides in their completed form, in Slide Sorter you can change the presentation order. For instance, moving Slide 1 after Slide 2 in Slide Sorter reverses the order in which they will appear.

Slide Sorter not only allows for changes in slide order, it permits you to create effects for the slide show. For instance, you can build the slide itself from several blocks on the screen, and you can slide in the text for the slide from the left. Figure 25.9 shows the example presentation in

Slide Sorter view. You can also add sound to a slide in Slide Sorter view, enhancing your presentation.

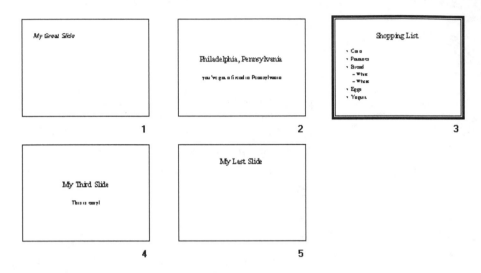

Figure 25.9 **Slide presentation in Slide Sorter view**

Notes Pages

Notes Pages view allows you to see both your notes and the slide that will be viewed during a presentation at the same time. Figure 25.10 shows a slide with its notes in Notes Pages view.

Slide Show

Slide Show view for your presentations is equivalent to Print Preview in Word for documents. When in Slide Show view, you are completely out of design mode; you see the slide as your audience will. In fact, if you want to take advantage of the animation effects of PowerPoint, you will need to use Slide Show view instead of the PowerPoint Viewer to give your on-screen presentations.

Figure 25.10 **Slide with its notes in Notes Pages view**

Design Tips for PowerPoint

While PowerPoint provides you with some very powerful tools to give top-notch presentations, making the wrong design choices can defeat all your efforts. Making the right decisions is not hard. By following the guidelines below and taking time to step back and look at your slides with a critical eye, you will be on your way to bringing your audiences to their feet.

▶ Pick fonts your audience can read easily. Fancy fonts are fine if they are readable and you use them mainly for emphasis.

▶ Use clear, easy-to-understand language in your slides. Remember to keep it simple and to the point.

▶ Choose font and screen colors that will contrast enough to be viewed at a distance and in low light.

▶ If you use symbols, graphics, or sound effects, make sure they are appropriate and easy to identify.

▶ Remember, less is more. Don't overburden your audience with many slides when just a few are needed.

Launching PowerPoint

As with any Office 95 application, click on the PowerPoint icon in the Office Manager shortcut bar to start, or choose Start ➤ Programs ➤ Microsoft PowerPoint. Remember, you can always create a shortcut icon on your desktop to launch PowerPoint directly. Refer to Chapter 2 for the specifics of how to do this.

Starting with a Blank Presentation

When you begin PowerPoint, you see the Tip of the Day dialog box. You can choose either the Next Tip or More Tips button for more useful information that will make your work with PowerPoint more effective, efficient, and enjoyable. To begin PowerPoint, click on the OK button.

 TIP   You can always uncheck the Show Tips at Startup checkbox to prevent this dialog box from appearing in the future. If you later choose to see the Tip of the Day each time you start PowerPoint, you can select Help ➤ Tip of the Day from the menu bar and recheck the box.

After the Tip of the Day dialog box, you see a dialog box that asks whether you want to open an existing presentation or use the AutoContent Wizard, a template, or a blank presentation, as shown in Figure 25.11. To start a new presentation from scratch, choose Blank Presentation.

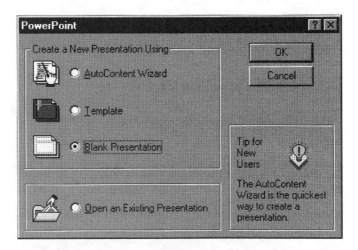

Figure 25.11   **Startup dialog box for PowerPoint**

When you start PowerPoint, the default is Template. All the options are listed here:

AutoContent Wizard—Select this option to take advantage of the Wizards in PowerPoint; you'll get help at every step along the way in creating a new presentation.

Template—If you want to create a new presentation by taking advantage of one of the several presentation templates that are included with PowerPoint or, perhaps, use a template of your own, choose Template on startup. This choice is ideal for those who get writer's block when looking at a blank piece of paper.

Blank Presentation—Just as the name implies, there are no templates, master slides, notes, or slides included in a blank presentation. You might want to use this option if you have a new approach to a presentation or if none of the templates suit your needs.

Open an Existing Presentation—Make this choice if you want to work with an existing presentation—for instance, if someone gives you a presentation file to edit or if you have already set up a presentation and want to continue working with it.

TIP If you are a new PowerPoint user, the AutoContent Wizard is a helpful starting point. Many people like to work for a while with a Wizard, until they have gained experience, and then work from templates or blank presentations.

To choose a blank presentation, click once on the radio button next to Blank Presentation and click on the OK button. When you select Blank Presentation, you will have a new presentation with no slides, notes, templates, or outlines.

If you wish to skip the Startup dialog box every time you open Power-Point, you can change your startup option by following these steps:

1. Select Tools ➤ Options from the menu bar.

2. Click once on the Show New Slide Dialog checkbox under the General tab of the dialog box shown in Figure 25.12. The check should disappear from the checkbox.

3. Click on the OK button.

Your changes have now been saved into PowerPoint. From this point forward, each time you start PowerPoint, you will not be asked to open an

Part 4

Presenting with PowerPoint

Figure 25.12   **General tab of the Options dialog box**

existing presentation or select one of the other forms for a new presentation. Instead, PowerPoint will automatically default to a blank presentation.

Adding a New Slide

Once you have chosen a blank form for your new presentation, the New Slide dialog box appears on the screen. Again, PowerPoint helps you each step of the way. In this dialog box, shown in Figure 25.13, you are asked to choose how you want the first slide of your presentation to appear.

There are 24 different slide layouts from which to choose. Each choice, described below, dictates how your completed slides will appear.

Title Slide—This option is useful for beginning a presentation or a major section of a presentation; use this slide if you want to include subtitles or smaller text underneath a title.

Bulleted List—Anytime you need to make a list of things that fall underneath a general subject, choose this layout.

2 Column Text—This is a useful option for doing pro/con lists.

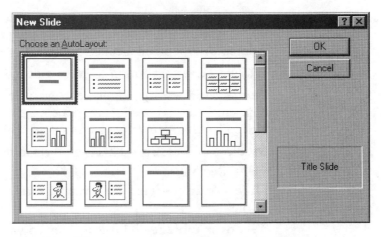

Figure 25.13 PowerPoint prompts you for a format for your first slide.

Table—This option is perfect for organizing and classifying things.

Text & Graph—This option is good for showing a graph or chart with explanatory text.

Graph & Text—This is a reversed variation of the Text & Graph layout.

Organization Chart—This is a great option for corporate hierarchical structures or flows of command.

Graph—Use this layout if you want to include a graph or chart.

Text & Clip Art—Use this layout to show a graphic with text.

Clip Art & Text—This is a reversed variation of the Text & Clip Art layout.

Title Only—This option is great for the beginning of a presentation; no subtitles are included in this layout.

Blank—Use this layout if you want a blank slide formatted according to the Master Slide.

Text & Object—If you want to include text with a linked object, such as a spreadsheet, graph, or database, choose this layout; it's the perfect choice to take advantage of OLE.

Object over Text—This is a variation of Text & Object layout, with the text above the object.

Part
4

Presenting with
PowerPoint

Large Object—This new layout for Office 95 allows a large object to be linked to the slide without any text; this format is ideal for workbooks or spreadsheets from Excel.

Object—Use this option to place a title over one linked object.

Text & Media Clip—This new layout for Office 95 uses media clips embedded in a slide; media clips can be animation, sound, or video files that you want to embed in a presentation.

Media & Text Clip—This is a reversed variation of the Text & Media Clip layout.

Object & Text—This is a reversed variation of the Text & Object layout.

Text over Object—This is a reversed variation of the Objects over Text layout.

Text & 2 Objects—This is a variation of the Text & Object layout, but with two embedded objects.

Objects over Text—This option is a combination of the Object over Text and Text & 2 Objects layouts.

2 Object & Text—This is a reversed variation of Text & 2 Objects layout.

4 Objects—This is a very useful layout if you need to include multiple objects from one or more applications.

If a slide *almost* meets your needs, you can always use it as the foundation for your new slide and then modify it as you see fit.

Possibilities

PowerPoint can bring your presentations alive. Use PowerPoint to graphically present data from a spreadsheet or database. You can create graphs to show sales reports in a more colorful form.

With the multimedia tools, not only can you create a slide show with quotations, you can now embed an actual video movie. Just imagine a presentation in which the CEO of a company not only outlines sales plans for the coming year in text but *talks* to the audience from the company headquarters.

The Pack and Go Wizard lets you save all the files you'll need for your presentation on a disk to take on the road. You can even include a Viewer so you can give your presentation on a computer without PowerPoint.

What's Next

This is only the beginning. You'll see how powerful PowerPoint is in the remaining chapters in this part of the book. Don't be afraid to experiment. As you walk through PowerPoint, if you wonder what will happen if you click on a button or choose a layout or template, go ahead and try it. PowerPoint has a multiple-level undo feature, which you access by clicking the Undo button on your toolbar, that will keep you from making permanent errors. And most important, have fun!

Chapter 26

Text Tips and Formats

Featuring

N **ow** that you understand the process of creating a presentation, you'll need to know how to work with the text in the presentation. Being able to give a presentation doesn't mean much if there are spelling errors, problems with the text format, and incorrect slides or misplaced text. With PowerPoint, you can be sure that whatever text you create for a presentation, you can always change or enhance it later. No one wants to hear snickering from the audience or be embarrassed because of a spelling error or out-of-date information. Now, there's no reason your presentation can't be perfect.

Text and Text Objects

Before we jump into the subject of working with text, you need to understand a few concepts. PowerPoint holds text in text *objects*. All the text contained in a text object is affected by the formatting of the object. Because of this, you can change the way all the text will appear by selecting and formatting the object, or you can select just a few words to change.

If you click on the text in a text object, an *insertion point* (blinking vertical line) appears. However, you can select a text object without getting an insertion point. As shown in Figure 26.1, if you hold down the Shift key as you click on the text, you select the entire object, not just a word or two.

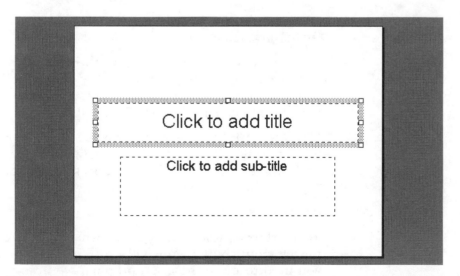

Figure 26.1   *Holding down the Shift key selects the whole text object.*

> **TIP**   You can always toggle between the text contained in an object and the object itself. To do this, just press F2 after you have selected the text or object.

Editing Text

Editing text in PowerPoint is just a matter of pointing and clicking. As long as you have an insertion point, you can work with the text you have typed or add new text to your slide.

> **TIP**   When opening a new slide with text in the layout, you don't have to select the text object to add text. Just begin typing when the slide appears on the screen, and PowerPoint automatically adds the text to the title text object.

Selecting Text

To select any text in an object, move your mouse to the text you want to select and click the left mouse button. A single click of the mouse button creates an insertion point for inserting text. A double-click selects an entire word. A triple click selects an entire paragraph. To select all the text in an object *without* selecting the object itself, press Ctrl+A after clicking inside the text object to get an insertion point.

Deleting Text

Once you have selected the text you wish to delete from your slide, you can delete it by pressing the Delete key on your keyboard. If you choose, you can use the Cut button on the toolbar or even select Edit ➤ Cut from the menu bar. Use Ctrl+X as a shortcut to delete text.

If you select Edit ➤ Clear or press the Delete key, you will not be able to paste your deleted text. But remember, if you make a mistake, just click on the Undo button to bring back your text.

Inserting Text

To insert text, position your mouse where you need to add text and click the left mouse button. You will see an insertion point at that location. If you need to move the insertion point, you can use the arrow keys on your keyboard to move the point left, right, up, or down. Once you have placed your insertion point where you want it, type the text you want to insert. If you just need a space between two words, press the spacebar. To add a blank line, press the Enter key. Any text you insert into a text object will have the same formatting as the text directly to the left of the insertion point.

Although PowerPoint will automatically size a text object for you to fit your text, it cannot become any larger than the slide. If you type too much or if your text is too large, PowerPoint will not enlarge your text object to a size greater than the slide to fit the added text. PowerPoint, unlike Word, cannot create a new slide for you, and the text that doesn't fit on your slide will be cropped, or cut, from the slide, and your audience will not see it. Be careful!

If you have too much text for the object but it will fit on the slide, you can enlarge the text object to fit the text.

Copying Text

Not only can you delete text, you can copy it. To copy, first select the text and then press Ctrl+C. This procedure saves a copy of the text to the clipboard. Then move your mouse to the location where you want to copy the text. You can copy text to another place in a text object, to a different text object on the same slide, or to another slide in an open presentation. You can also use the Copy button on the toolbar or Edit ➤ Copy from the menu bar.

Moving Text

You can move text in PowerPoint from one place to another on a single slide or between slides and presentations. If you have a lot of text to move or feel "lost" between your slides, you can use Outline view to move your text between slides. If you have more than one presentation open and need to copy between them, you can select Window from the menu bar to switch between open presentations.

To move text, follow these steps:

1. Select the text you want to move.

2. Cut the text by selecting Edit ➤ Cut from the menu bar.

3. If you are moving the text to another slide, move to that slide using the slide bar at the right of the screen.

4. Click on the text object at the point where you want to insert the text.

5. Select Edit ➤ Paste from the menu bar.

TIP If you are moving text to a new location on the same slide, you can highlight the text, hold down the left mouse button, and drag-and-drop it at the new location.

Formatting Text

At times you may want to make a word or sentence stand out from other text. For instance, if you want to indicate a new term used in a presentation, you can choose to make it italic or bold. You can underline words to indicate stress or change the font or color to make the word stand out even more.

Remember, when you are creating a presentation, to be careful about the size and color of your text. If you want to create 35mm slides, you should use a font that is at least 18 points in size.

NOTE Because color choice is critical when creating a presentation, Power-Point has virtually eliminated the guesswork. PowerPoint has chosen colors that work well together, but be careful. If your text and background are too close in color, the text could be invisible during the presentation. It's best to use the actual projection equipment or test print slides before your presentation to make sure the colors will look right.

Italics, Bold, Underline, and Shadow

To italicize text, select the text you want and click on the Italic button on the toolbar. You can also press Ctrl+I to make the text italic.

In the same way, you can create bold text by selecting the text and then clicking the Bold button on the toolbar. You can also use a shortcut key to bold text: press Ctrl+B.

To underline text, select your text and then click on the Underline button on the toolbar or press Ctrl+U.

TIP If you are unsure how your text is formatted, you can select the text and check the toolbar. If the text is bold, italic, or underlined, the associated button appears depressed or "gray" on the toolbar.

To use shadow, just select the text you want to shadow and click on the Shadow button on the toolbar. There is no shortcut for this format.

Text Color

You might want to change the color of the text on your slide so it stands out against the background. If you choose to change the color of text, be sure it doesn't conflict with the background.

To change the color of your text:

1. Select the text you want to color.

2. Click on the Text Color button on the toolbar.

3. Select the color from the palette that drops down.

   When choosing a different color for your text, you are not limited to the colors listed in the drop-down palette. If you want to pick another color, follow these steps:

1. Select your text.

2. Click on the Text Color button on the toolbar.

3. Click on Other Color to see the Colors dialog box shown in Figure 26.2.

4. Select the color you want from the hexagon of colors.

   If you don't see a color you like on the hexagon of colors, you can select a specific color from the Custom color tab of the Colors dialog box, as shown in Figure 26.3. This option is useful if you have a specific color in mind or if your company uses a particular color scheme. When using custom colors, you can create almost any color in the rainbow. To create a custom color, follow these steps:

1. Select the text you want to color.

2. Click on the Text Color button on the toolbar.

3. Click on Other Color.

4. Click on the Custom tab.

Part 4

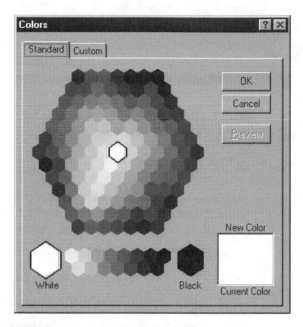

Figure 26.2   The Standard tab in the Colors dialog box provides a lot of colors from which to choose for text.

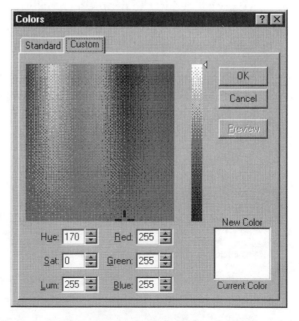

Figure 26.3   You can select almost any color from the Custom tab in PowerPoint.

5. Move the cross hairs until you find the right color.

6. Click on OK.

Embossing

You can emboss your text, although you should use this option with caution. It may look impressive on the screen, but it may not print or present as you think it will. Again, test any changes you make to your text before giving your presentation.

To emboss your text:

1. Select the text you want to emboss.

2. Select Format ➤ Font from the menu bar.

3. Click on the Emboss checkbox in the Font dialog box shown in Figure 26.4.

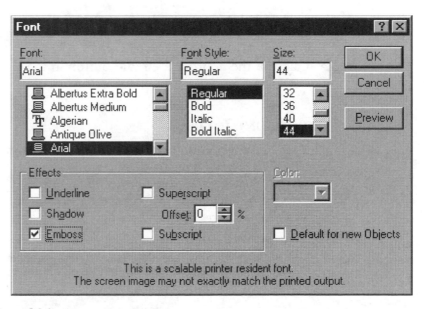

Figure 26.4   *From the Font dialog box, you can change font attributes such as embossing.*

> **TIP** You can change your default font style by clicking on the Default for New Objects checkbox in the Formatting dialog box. Simply choose a font, size, and style, and then click on the checkbox to set this as the default font for new text. If you do this, all the text on your new slides will be formatted accordingly.

Changing Case

If you type your text in a hurry, you might make capitalization mistakes. In PowerPoint you can easily change the case of any selected text. However, you should use this option only for small selections of text. PowerPoint has a more powerful tool called Style Checker, explored later in this chapter, that can scan your entire presentation to make sure your text is formatted properly.

To change case for a small selection of text, follow these steps:

1. Select the text you wish to change.

2. Select Format ➤ Change Case from the menu bar.

3. Click on the appropriate radio button in the Change Case dialog box, shown in Figure 26.5.

Aligning Text

You can align your text any way you want in PowerPoint. You can left-align, right-align, or center the text or use full justification. Full justification expands the text to fill an entire line. If you are creating a presentation with a large font, avoid using this option; your text will look awkward and the lines and paragraphs will appear "empty."

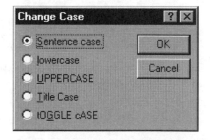

Figure 26.5 *You can change the case of your text to suit your needs.*

To align your text, follow these steps:

1. Click on the text you wish to align. You can place your insertion point anywhere within the paragraph you want to align; you don't need to highlight it.

2. Select Format ➤ Alignment from the menu bar.

3. Select the appropriate alignment from the submenu.

Line and Paragraph Spacing

You can change the line spacing and spacing between paragraphs in PowerPoint. Line spacing is the space between lines in the same paragraph, and paragraph spacing is the space between separate paragraphs. Remember, PowerPoint starts a new paragraph each time you press Enter while entering text. Since it works just like Word, you will recognize the look and feel immediately. Let's briefly walk through changing line and paragraph spacing:

1. Select the text you want to format for spacing.

2. Select Format ➤ Line Spacing from the menu bar.

3. Choose the line and paragraph spacing appropriate for your text.

Text Objects

PowerPoint holds all of your text in text objects for easy editing. You can format text objects to add colors, lines, and even shadows.

Text Anchor

It's important to understand the difference between using text alignment and using a text anchor. Aligning text affects how it will appear on the screen. When you use Text Anchor, you affect how the text in the object will appear relative to the text object. To change how the text will anchor itself to the text object:

1. Select the text object you wish to edit by holding down Shift and clicking on the object.

2. Select Format ➤ Text Anchor from the menu bar.

3. Select the proper anchor point from the Text Anchor dialog box, shown in Figure 26.6.

You can select whether you want PowerPoint to automatically change the size of the text object to fit your text by clicking on the appropriate checkbox. You can also choose word wrap in this dialog box. But remember, even if you ask PowerPoint to enlarge the text object to fit your text, if the object is too large for the slide, only part of it will appear in your presentation.

TIP   If you want to change all the text objects on your slide, you can press Ctrl+A to select all the objects. Only the objects on the current slide will be selected. To select objects on another slide, move to that slide and hold down the Ctrl key as you click on the objects.

Textures

You can think of textures as pictures of surfaces, such as wood and stone. You can experiment with different textures to see how they will appear on your presentation. If you are using older projection equipment or an older computer with an EGA or monochrome screen, you might want to shy away from this option; the textures may appear grainy or distorted.

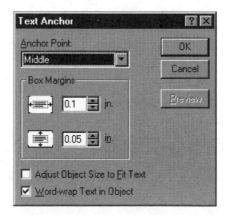

Figure 26.6   In the Text Anchor dialog box, you can change how your text will appear relative to the object.

To add texture to an object:

1. Select the text object you wish to fill with a texture.

2. Select Format Colors and Lines from the menu bar.

3. Select Fill from the dialog box.

4. Choose Texture from the drop-down menu.

5. Select a texture from the menu shown in Figure 26.7 by clicking on the texture and choosing OK.

6. Click on OK again.

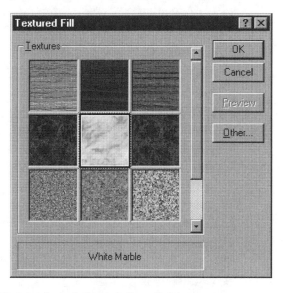

Figure 26.7 **Fill textures for text objects in PowerPoint.**

Using Tables in PowerPoint

If you have ever had to create a list or define terms, you know how unreliable it is to use the spacebar to align text in columns. You work for hours, pushing the spacebar to get your text to look just right, only to print it out and discover it looks like a crowd at the Super Bowl doing the Wave. You might have heard about table options but were a little shy about using them. Word provides table options, and perhaps you have used them. When working with tables in PowerPoint, such as the one shown in Figure 26.8, you are actually using Word tables embedded into PowerPoint.

You have two options for inserting a table onto a slide in PowerPoint. Although you can create a table by clicking on Insert on the menu bar or by clicking on the Insert Microsoft Word Table button on the toolbar, it is easier to create a new slide and change the slide layout for a table. The reason is that the table will overlay anything you have on your slide, and if you have not chosen a blank layout, you could accidentally end up with a table lying on top of a title or text object. Let's examine both ways to create a table, and you can decide the best way for you.

Tables from the Toolbar

To create a table from the toolbar, you can use the Table button. When you click on the Table button, PowerPoint opens up a Table tool that uses the same commands as the Table tool in Word. You may find it works a little slowly, but it is well worth the wait. This versatile tool provides the ability to create borders and shading just as in Word and to change column widths and numbers. You will soon wonder how you ever lived without it.

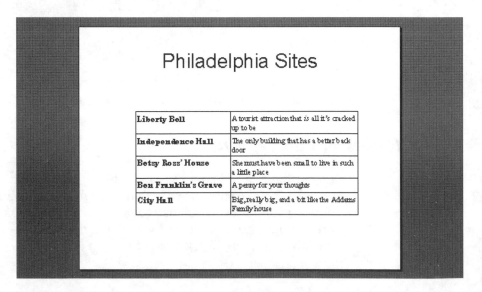

Figure 26.8   *Tables are ideal for definitions or terminology.*

Let's walk through the steps of creating a table from the toolbar:

1. Choose the slide into which you want to insert your table.

2. Using the Insert Microsoft Word Table button on the toolbar, choose the number of columns and rows you want in your table.

3. Type your text and press Tab to move to the next column.

4. Repeat step 3 for each cell in your table.

5. Press Esc when you are in the last cell.

6. Press Esc to release the mark on table entries.

Creating a Table from a New Slide

Let's take a look at the steps for creating a table with a new slide. You will probably find that creating a new slide based on the Table layout is easier than inserting a table into an existing slide.

1. Click on the New Slide button on the status bar. If you don't see the New Slide dialog box to choose a layout, click the Slide Layout button on the status bar.

2. Choose the Table layout and click on OK.

3. Once you see your new slide, double-click on the Table icon.

4. Choose the number of columns and rows and click OK.

5. Enter your text just as you would in any table.

6. Press Esc to return to Slide view.

7. Press Esc to release the mark on table entries.

TIP If you press Tab in the last cell of your table, a new row is created. If you don't want a new row, you can click on the Undo button on the toolbar or choose Edit ➤ Undo from the menu bar.

NOTE For more information about inserting objects onto a slide in Power-Point, see Chapter 31, which deals with linking and embedding objects.

Part
4

Presenting with
PowerPoint

Using Tools in PowerPoint

PowerPoint provides some very useful tools to help you work with your text. You can find and change text throughout your presentation. You can check your style and spelling. You can even replace one font with another in your presentation. Some of the tools work just like those in Word, but two are unique to PowerPoint. Let's take a look at those that Word and PowerPoint have in common and then look more closely at those only found in PowerPoint.

Finding Text

You can use the same tool that Word provides to find any text you want in your presentation. Let's take a look at how you accomplish this:

1. Select Edit ➤ Find from the menu bar.
2. Type the text you want to find in the Find What text object.
3. Click on Find Next.
4. When you are finished finding your text, click on Close.

Replacing Text

You can replace text just as easily as in Word, using the same dialog boxes:

1. Select Edit ➤ Replace from the menu bar.
2. Type the text you want to find and what you want to replace it with.
3. Click Replace or Replace All and click on OK.
4. When you are finished replacing text, click on Close.

TIP   If you mistakenly replace any text, you can use Undo to restore your text to its original form.

Spelling

The Spell Checker in PowerPoint works exactly like the one in Word. To check the spelling of your presentation, just press F7 or select Tools ➤ Spelling from the menu bar. You will see the same dialog box Word provides to help you with suggestions for your spelling errors.

AutoCorrect

PowerPoint now has the same AutoCorrect option that Word does. To access AutoCorrect, just follow the same steps as in Word. You can always add text to AutoCorrect to change any errors you frequently make when typing. You can also choose to turn off AutoCorrect or delete any changes you don't want PowerPoint to make. To use the AutoCorrect option, follow these steps:

1. Select Tools ➤ AutoCorrect from the menu bar.

2. In the AutoCorrect dialog box shown in Figure 26.9, add and delete any items you wish, or change the options in the dialog box.

3. Click on OK to accept the changes or on Cancel to keep your old settings.

Replacing Fonts

This tool is unique to PowerPoint. If you find that you have used a font in your presentation that does not work well on your slides, you can

Part 4

Presenting with PowerPoint

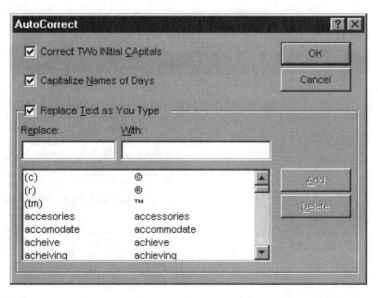

Figure 26.9   You can change your AutoCorrect options in the AutoCorrect dialog box.

always change that font to another font more suited to your presentation's formatting and colors. To do so, follow these steps:

1. Select Tools ➤ Replace Fonts from the menu bar.

2. In the Replace Font dialog box shown in Figure 26.10, select from the font list the font that needs to be replaced.

3. From the font list, select the font that will replace the current font.

4. Click on Replace.

5. Repeat steps 3 and 4 if you need to replace other fonts.

6. Click on Close when you are done.

Style Checker

Finally, after you have created your presentation, are happy with the fonts, and are pleased with the layout, you can let PowerPoint perform a final check for you, to make sure there are no inconsistencies. Although this tool may take some time to run, it is so valuable it is worth the wait. You can always help yourself to another cup of coffee or take a break if it seems as though it's taking too long. This tool is only found in PowerPoint.

You can set the options for Style Checker. You can choose what Power-Point will check and report on in your presentation. For instance, if you have already performed a spell check, you can open the Style Checker dialog box by choosing Tools ➤ Style Checker and uncheck the appropriate box.

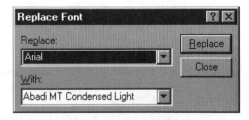

Figure 26.10   *In the Replace Font dialog box, you can replace a font for your entire presentation.*

Take a look at the steps for changing the options in Style Checker to see whether they are appropriate for your presentation:

1. Select Tools ➤ Style Checker from the menu bar.

2. In the Style Checker dialog box shown in Figure 26.11, click on the Options button to see what Style Checker uses as benchmarks.

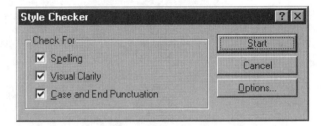

Figure 26.11   **Style Checker dialog box**

3. Make any changes you deem necessary while under the Case and End Punctuation tab, as shown in Figure 26.12.

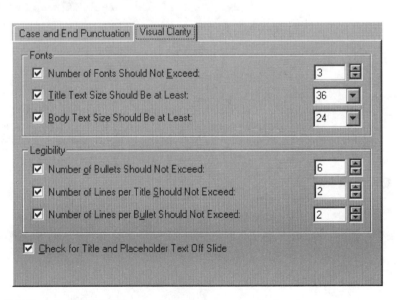

Figure 26.12   **Case and End Punctuation tab**

4. Click on the Visual Clarity tab to see the dialog box shown in Figure 26.13, and make changes to the way Style Checker will check your slides for clarity and visibility.

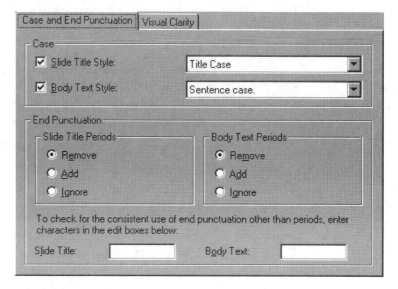

Figure 26.13   **Visual Clarity tab**

5. Click on OK when you are satisfied with the options.

6. Click on Start to begin Style Checker.

7. After PowerPoint is finished checking your presentation, the Style Checker Summary dialog box appears. When you are finished reviewing the errors, click on OK to return to your slide.

What's Next?

In this chapter you have seen how to edit and format the text in your presentation. In the next chapter we will look at adding clip art and media clips to give your presentation a life of its own.

Chapter 27

Animation, Art, and Sound

Featuring

Because of the explosion in multimedia applications, more and more computers are being sold as "multimedia" or "family" machines. Where once the word *family* implied "general use" or "suitable for children," in the world of computers, *family* means entertainment. A family is no longer limited to using a personal computer to balance budgets and write letters. Today, more and more individuals and families are buying full-blown entertainment boxes with sound, video, and CD capabilities. Where once only the handful in Hollywood could edit movies digitally, now, with only a small investment, anyone can buy such a machine.

What Is Multimedia?

You can think of multimedia as taking any picture from your photo album, any song from your favorite singer, or any scene from a great action flick and digitizing it. When you digitize something, all you are doing is reducing its form to something a computer can read and reproduce: 0's and 1's.

PowerPoint and Multimedia

PowerPoint takes such advantage of multimedia that it's almost like having a producer, director, and a small cast working with you to create your slide show. You can play sounds, show video clips, use clip art, animate text and slides, and have PowerPoint run other programs from a slide show. Just imagine the possibilities. You could communicate a record sales quarter by inserting a slide into your presentation that shows a graph of regional sales, alongside a media clip that plays a rocket launching, all introduced by the sound of an audience clapping.

Adding Art to Your Presentation

First, let's take a look at creating a new slide with art. You do not have to be a Picasso or Rembrandt, because PowerPoint has included both the tools you'll need and sample clips for creating a very impressive slide with art. You can also use other vendors as a source for art.

WordArt

WordArt gives you the ability to morph your text into various shapes and designs. The important thing to remember for our purposes in PowerPoint is that WordArt is *not* plain text. It is an object and therefore behaves like an object. This means that if you make a spelling error using WordArt, the Spell Checker will not alert you to your mistake. You must edit the WordArt object by double-clicking on it.

Creating WordArt

Let's walk through the steps of creating WordArt in PowerPoint. If you have used WordArt before in Word, this procedure will seem familiar. However, you must perform some extra steps to ensure that the object embeds properly. First, you need to have a presentation open. If you don't have a presentation open, go ahead and open either one of the presentations you have worked with before or a blank one. Then follow these steps:

1. Click on the Insert New Slide button on the toolbar or use the New Slide button on the status bar at the bottom of the screen.

2. Select a layout that is based on an object—for example, the Large Object layout. Figure 27.1 shows a slide with WordArt based on this layout.

3. Click on the Apply button.

4. Double-click on the Object icon to add an object.

5. Select Microsoft WordArt 2.0 from the Object Type list box.

6. Type your text in the Enter Your Text Here text box, and select a shape from the drop-down combo box on the toolbar. The box will display plain text. From the toolbar, you can add to the text any other properties you like.

7. When you are finished creating the WordArt, press Esc twice to return to your slide.

TIP Instead of creating a new object, you can always select an object you created earlier by clicking on the Create from File radio button. You can browse your drive(s) or floppy for the proper file.

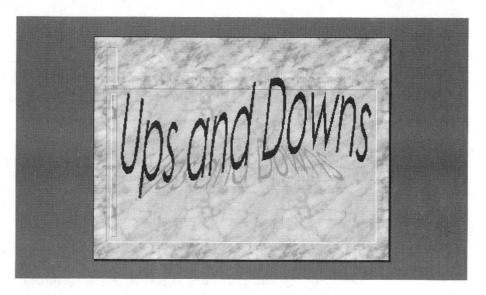

Figure 27.1   A slide with WordArt based on Large Object AutoLayout

As mentioned earlier, if you don't see an AutoLayout you want in the New Slide dialog box, you can embed an object on a blank slide. You can also choose a slide layout that is close to the one you want and delete, copy, or edit object sizes to suit your needs.

Clip Art versus Drawing

Working with clip art is basically the same as working with WordArt. Although you can create your own art, you may want to find clip art that fits your needs instead. If you are not familiar with the Paintbrush program or another drawing program or you have minimal artistic abilities, sticking to clip art instead of trying to draw pictures on your own may be your safest bet in making a nice-looking presentation. You can spend a lot of time creating a picture, but in the end it may not be very effective if it is not as good-looking as a similar picture already in clip art.

Creating Images from Scratch

To create images from scratch, follow these steps:

1.   Click on the New Slide button on the button bar.

2. Choose a layout that contains an object.

3. Click on Apply.

4. Double-click on the Object icon to create the picture.

5. From the Object Type list box, choose either Bitmap Image or Paint-brush Picture.

6. Draw a picture using the Paintbrush tools.

7. Press Esc twice to return to PowerPoint and your slide.

Figure 27.2 shows the result of a time-consuming effort in Paintbrush.

Clip Art

Now that you have created your own picture, let's try to insert an image already created by PowerPoint. This should prove to be simpler and will probably be more attractive than anything most of us could create with Paintbrush.

The next slide, shown in Figure 27.3, is based on the Text & Clip Art layout from the New Slide dialog box. After inserting the art, you select

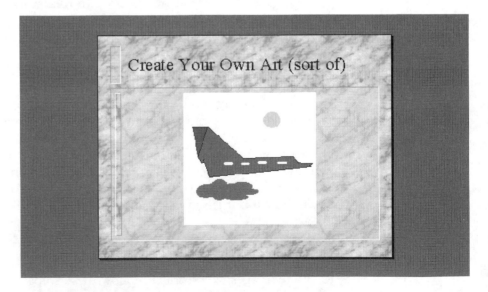

Figure 27.2 A plane created in Paintbrush

Figure 27.3 *A clip art airplane*

the text object and delete it by pressing the Delete key. You then reposition the clip art object on the slide.

Here are the steps:

1. Create a new slide from the toolbar or status bar.

2. Select either the Text & Clip Art or Clip Art & Text layout.

3. Click on Apply.

4. Double-click on the clip art object.

5. When the Clip Art Gallery dialog box opens, select one of the categories listed on the left and then, on the right, select a piece of clip art under that category.

6. Click on Insert.

7. Move or resize the object as desired.

8. Press Esc twice to return to PowerPoint or the slide.

TIP   If you don't like the way your clip art appears on your slide, you can always replace it with another piece of clip art by double-clicking on the object and inserting a different piece of art.

AutoShapes

AutoShapes are probably the easiest objects to add to a slide in Power-Point. You can see an example in Figure 27.4. There are several shapes from which to choose, so feel free to select whichever one you like.

To add an AutoShape, follow these steps:

1. Click on the AutoShape button on the Drawing toolbar, which is normally to the left of your screen.

2. Choose the shape you like.

3. Place and size the shape on your slide by holding down the left mouse button and dragging.

4. Type the text you want in the AutoShape.

5. Press Esc when you are done.

Figure 27.4   Don't forget what you learn about AutoShapes in PowerPoint!

Graphs

You can easily add a graph to your slide. You can also insert an Excel spreadsheet or graph, but this section focuses on creating a graph from scratch. (For more information about embedding a graph in and linking it to a spreadsheet, see Chapter 31, which discusses integrating Power-Point with other Office programs.)

Let's run through the process of creating a graph from scratch and then placing it onto a slide:

1. Create a new slide by clicking on the New Slide button.

2. Select the Graph layout.

3. Click on Apply.

4. Double-click on the Graph icon to create the graph.

5. If there is already data in the datasheet, delete it by clicking and dragging to select the cells and pressing Delete.

6. Type your data in the datasheet.

7. Choose a form for the graph using the toolbar button at the top of the screen that shows a picture of a chart and a drop-down arrow.

8. Close the datasheet by clicking on the *X* in its upper right-hand corner.

9. To leave Graph mode, press Esc twice.

Figure 27.5 shows a datasheet being edited.

Organization Charts

If you have ever tried to create an organization chart from a table in Word or from lines in an Excel spreadsheet, you probably have spent hours creating your perfect chart, only to later discover that you left out a level or you weren't basing your chart on your company's new organization structure.

Microsoft has included, with the suite, an Organization Chart utility to use with the Office programs. Let's take a brief look at using this tool:

1. Create a new slide by clicking on the New Slide button.

2. Choose Organization Chart from the New Slide dialog box.

Part
4

Presenting with
PowerPoint

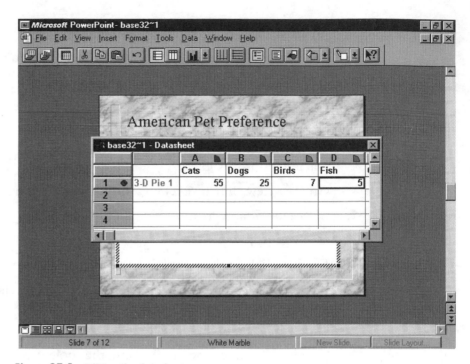

Figure 27.5   Editing the datasheet

3. Click on Apply.

4. Double-click on the Organization Chart icon to add the chart. Your screen should look similar to the one in Figure 27.6.

   To edit a position in the organization chart, click on it and fill in the name, title, and any other information associated with the position. When you are finished with a position, just choose another, and the box will automatically resize itself to fit the text.

   You can add positions by clicking on one of the position buttons on the organization chart toolbar and, with the position now attached to your mouse pointer, click within the box where you want the new position to be attached, as shown in Figure 27.7.

WARNING If you delete positions, your organization chart will automatically shift all the subordinate positions to fit the chart style. Be careful—you can completely change your organization chart by deleting one position.

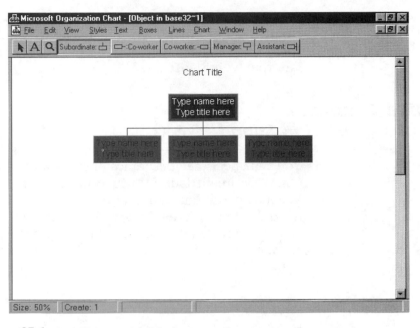

Figure 27.6 **Attaching a new position to an org chart**

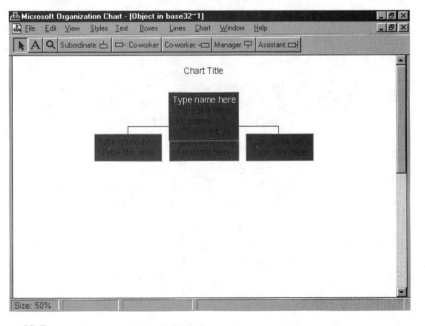

Figure 27.7 **Creating an organization chart**

When you are finished creating your chart, select File ➤ Close and Return from the menu bar. You are asked whether you want to update your slide. Click on Yes if you want to include the chart. If you click on No, your work is discarded.

Slide Transition, Animation, and Sound Effects

You can affect the appearance of slides and objects in your slide show. One slide might fade in, while the following slide might open like a Venetian blind. You can have text appear to fly into position, word by word or letter by letter. You can have bulleted lists materialize one level at a time. You can even give sound to your slides, either by using a sound effect already in PowerPoint or by choosing another sound file you have available.

Slide Transition

Transition controls the way each slide will appear as it opens on the slide show screen. You have a long list of effects from which to choose, and since a picture is worth a thousand words, this would be a good time to see how using this option will affect the slides' appearance in the show. Changing the Slide Transition effects alters only the current slide.

TIP   If you want to change settings for multiple slides, switch to Outline view. Then select multiple continuous slides by clicking on the first slide, holding down the Shift key, and choosing the last slide of your selection. You can then change the slide transition for multiple slides.

To open the Slide Transition dialog box shown in Figure 27.8, choose Tools ➤ Slide Transition from the menu bar. You can change the picture on the sample slide in the dialog box by clicking on it.

If you want to see how each transition will affect the way your slide appears in the slide show, click on the down arrow next to the effect listed and use your arrow keys to scroll through the list. As you scroll, each transition effect is demonstrated for you.

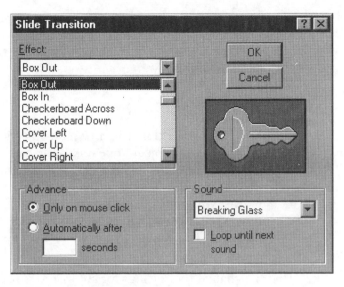

Figure 27.8   *Slide Transition dialog box*

 TIP The Random Transition effect at the end of the list randomly chooses an effect for use in the presentation. If you are preparing a slide show you plan to use a lot, picking this transition effect will add variety to your show.

In the Slide Transition dialog box, you can also set slide advancement to occur after a certain number of seconds. This is a useful feature for either self-running demos or presentations you have timed well enough that you can let the computer handle the slide advancement, freeing you to move around.

If you want a sound to play at the transition of a slide, you can choose from the sounds listed in the Sound combo box in the bottom right-hand corner of the Slide Transition dialog box. You can also select another sound by choosing Other Sound at the bottom of the combo box list and selecting the sound you want to use. Clicking the Loop until Next Sound checkbox determines whether the sound you choose will continue until another sound is activated or just play once. If you choose to loop your sound, you should view the slide show to see whether the sound is effective or distracting. A typewriter sound may be a good effect, re-creating the teletype sounds that television news once used. On the other hand, a cash register sound played in a loop may become distracting.

Once you have made your selections, just click on the OK button to save your settings for that slide. Remember, in Slide view only this slide is affected by these settings. You will have to create new settings for each slide in your show.

Animation

You can change the order in which objects enter the slide and the manner in which each object appears on the slide. You can also attribute sound to individual objects on a slide. The animation settings made for each object on a slide are independent of the Slide Transition settings. In other words, you could have the slide appear in a checkerboard pattern with a typewriter sound effect, but you could also have the objects fly in from the left. The dialog box in Figure 27.9 shows the animation options for a text object.

To change the settings for an object, simply select the object and choose Tools ➤ Animation Settings. Remember, you can choose multiple objects on the same slide by clicking on each object while holding down the Shift key. If you select more than one object type, you will be able to modify only the properties the objects have in common.

If you have selected a text object, you have three Build options: Don't Build, All at Once, and By Paragraph Level. If you have a bulleted list, you can choose which level will form first by enabling or disabling the Reverse Order option.

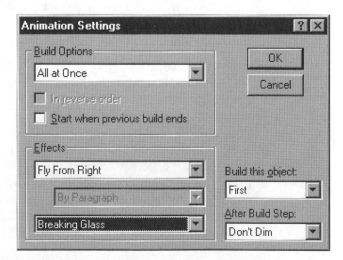

Figure 27.9 *Animation settings for a text object*

If you build your text all at once, all your text will appear at one time, as a block, using the effect you have chosen. If you build your text by paragraph level, you can choose to have the entire paragraph appear word by word or one letter at a time. If you have a long list or paragraph, choose to have the text build by word or by paragraph; building by letter may take too much time.

Additionally, you can associate a sound effect with each individual object, just as you did for slide transition. Again, you have the option of associating your own sounds with the objects.

If, on the active slide, you have several objects that use animation, you can choose the order in which they appear. If you change the order of one object, the others will change order automatically.

If you have a chart or other object (other than text), you can choose from several Play options, as you can see in Figure 27.10. If you choose to play, you actually open, during the slide show, the program that produced the object, such as the graph program. If you choose Edit, you can edit the data in the graph. This might be useful if you want to interactively change a graph or spreadsheet on a slide during a presentation.

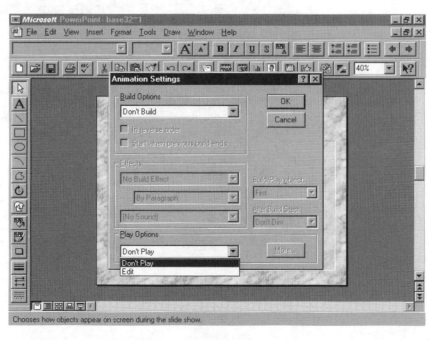

Figure 27.10 *Animation settings for a nontext object*

Part
4

Presenting with
PowerPoint

If you have clip art, you are given two choices, Don't Play and Replace, as you can see in Figure 27.11. If you choose Replace, you can dynamically replace the clip art during the presentation from the list of clip art available to you on the presentation computer.

Finally, you can have your Power Point objects change color after you build them. Under After Build Step, you can choose to hide the object or text, change the color, or, by choosing Don't Dim, not change it.

Interactive Settings

You can add another setting to an object on a slide by using the Interactive Settings dialog box shown in Figure 27.12. Interactive settings affect how an object will react when you click on it in Slide Show view. You have four options from which to choose: None, Go to, Run Program, and Object Action.

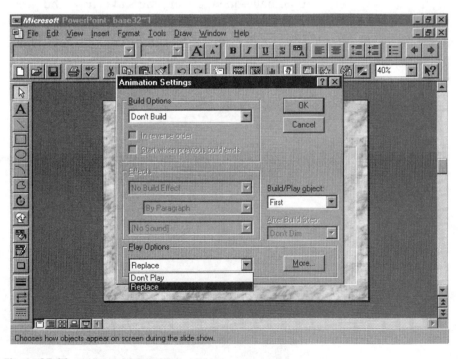

Figure 27.11   **Animation settings for clip art**

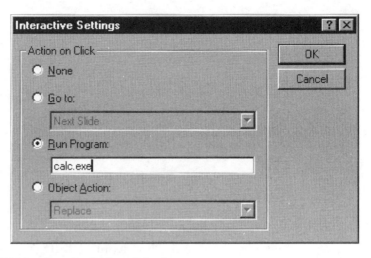

Figure 27.12   *Interactive Settings dialog box*

If you want an object to go to another slide in a slide show, you can pick any slide in your show. When you click on the object during the presentation, PowerPoint moves you to the slide you have selected. For example, you may want to reference numbers previously mentioned in another slide if audience members have questions; being able to jump back to your justification without fumbling around is very impressive.

TIP   If you move to another slide, PowerPoint continues the presentation from that slide and does not return you to the calling slide. If you know you will be jumping from one slide to another, be sure you have an interactive way to jump back to the original slide.

You can change the object action for an object as long as it isn't a text object. The actions from which you choose are the same as the options under the Play in Animation settings. During your slide show, you can edit a graph, change the data, and have the graph change to reflect your new data.

Finally, you can choose to run a program from the Interactive Settings dialog box. If you select the Run Program radio button, you simply type the name of the program you want to run when you click on the object. PowerPoint opens the application on top of your slide during the slide show.

Part
4

Presenting with
PowerPoint

TIP A very good use of the Run Program option is to run Calculator when showing numbers in a presentation. If you are presenting a graph during a slide show, you can run Calculator and quickly do calculations to show the audience confirmation of what you are stating.

Media Clips

Finally, you can insert multimedia clips into a slide in PowerPoint. The ability to add media clips is an area where PowerPoint really shines. If you plan on using sound, just make sure you have a sound card installed in your machine.

To insert a media clip, open a new slide based on the Media Clip & Text or Text & Media Clip layout. Although you can insert an object using Insert ➤ Object from the menu bar, we'll walk through the process of creating a new slide to get our media clip onto the slide. (In Chapter 31 we will discuss linking objects; at that time you will see the advantages and disadvantages of inserting objects into a slide.)

1. Create a new slide by clicking on the New Slide button.

2. Choose either the Media Clip & Text or Text & Media Clip layout.

3. Click on Apply.

4. Double-click on the Media Clip icon.

5. Select Insert Clip from the menu bar and select a type from the list shown.

6. Choose the particular clip you want and click on Open to see a screen similar to the one in Figure 27.13.

7. Select Edit ➤ Selection from the menu bar to edit the playback length, as shown in Figure 27.14.

8. Select Edit ➤ Options from the menu bar to further modify media clip options, as shown in Figure 27.15.

9. Click elsewhere on the slide to insert the media clip.

If you choose to use media clips, be aware that these files can be extremely large, making your presentation much bigger each time you include one. Also, media clips behave poorly on slower computers. Experiment with different types and lengths of media clips to see how

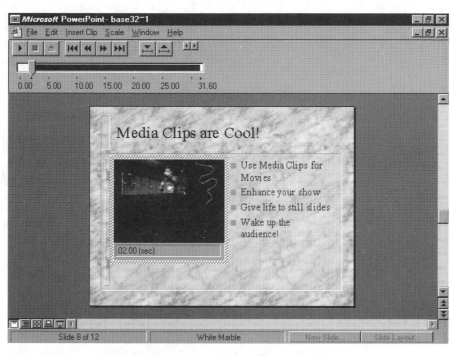

Figure 27.13 **Editing a media clip**

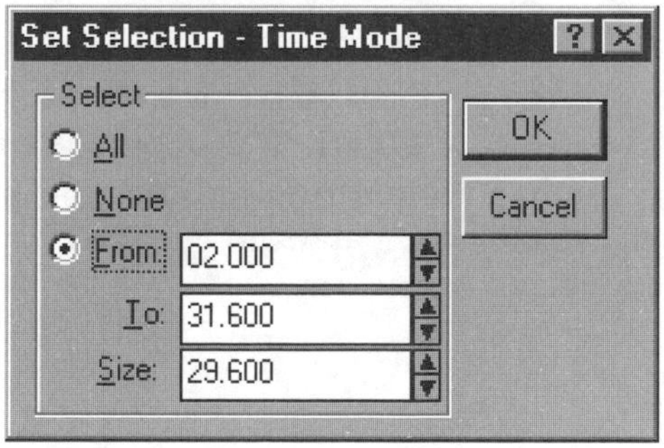

Figure 27.14 **Set Selection dialog box**

each will work on your system. Some video boards are designed specifically to work with multimedia. You can greatly enhance your media clip performance by working on a system that has such a board, although it is not necessary.

Figure 27.15   **Options dialog box**

What's Next?

In Chapter 31 we will look at how you can insert these objects from existing files, how you can link your presentation to those individual files, how that will affect your slide show, and how to resolve any errors you might encounter.

In the next chapter, however, you will see how all the objects and their settings will work in the completed presentation. You'll see the different tools at your disposal, and you'll learn about creating handouts and printing your notes to get the most out of your slide show.

Chapter 28
Making the Presentation

Featuring

Now that you have learned how to create your own presentation, you're ready for the moment when all the hard work pays off: when you finally give your presentation before an audience that is glued to your every slide.

PowerPoint offers you several effective tools for giving power to your presentation: Meeting Minder, Write-Up, Slide Meter, Pointer, and Presentation Conference.

Meeting Minder: Keeping Track

With Meeting Minder, you finally have a powerful way to keep track of all the slides in your presentation, any notes you have attached to the slides, and any items that will require action later. Meeting Minder contains three major components: Notes Pages, Meeting Minutes, and Action Items. Not only can you keep track of all these items, you can create a Microsoft Word document based on these components. You can then print this document so you have a handy script to help guide you through your presentation.

You can access Meeting Minder during the creation or editing of a presentation and while viewing it in Slide Show view. To access Meeting Minder while editing your presentation, select Tools ➤ Meeting Minder from the menu bar. To access Meeting Minder during the slide show, click your right mouse button and choose Meeting Minder from the shortcut menu. In either case, you will see the screen shown in Figure 28.1.

Notes Pages

You can attach notes to each slide in your presentation. You can use Notes Pages to write a script for each slide or to make notes you can refer to during a slide show. Each slide has its own individual set of Notes Pages.

Meeting Minutes

As the name implies, the Meeting Minutes tool allows you to take minutes during a meeting pertaining to your presentation or even during your slide show. If you choose to use this tool during your slide show, you can keep track of discussions from the audience or speakers. Later, you

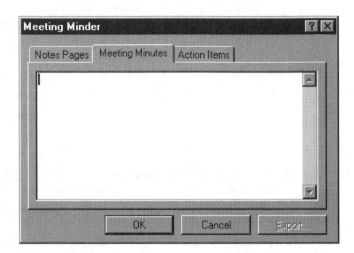

Figure 28.1 **Meeting Minder dialog box**

can export your Meeting Minutes to Word for printing. As with Notes Pages, each slide has its own set of Meeting Minutes.

Action Items

Action Items is a handy tool that allows you to track specific items you need to attend to as a result of the presentation. You can write specific tasks that need to be completed or even areas that may need attention in the future. When you add an item to the Action Items tab in Meeting Minder, PowerPoint creates a final slide in your presentation entitled "Action Items," which outlines in bulleted form those specific tasks you placed in the Meeting Minder. You can see an example of an Action Items slide in Figure 28.2. As with Notes Pages and Meeting Minutes, you can export Action Items to Word for editing and printing. However, unlike Notes Pages and Meeting Minutes, all slides in a presentation share the same Action Items. For instance, if you add an Action Item while editing slide 1 in your presentation, it will also be present when you add another item in slide 3.

NOTE   PowerPoint creates only one slide at the end of your presentation. If you enter too many items, they will not fit on the slide. Try to limit yourself to placing five or six items under Action Items.

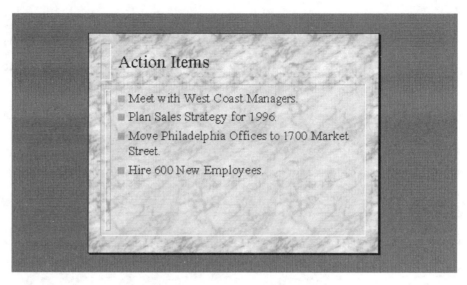

Figure 28.2   *Action Items slide created by PowerPoint*

Using Meeting Minder

To use Meeting Minder in Slide view, select Tools ➤ Meeting Minder. If you want to add notes to this particular slide, click on the Notes Pages tab and type the information you want to be able to use for that slide. If you want to add any minutes for this slide, just click on the Meeting Minutes tab and type. To add specific items that will become bulleted in a final slide, click on the Action Items tab, and enter one line for each specific task. When you press Enter, PowerPoint automatically starts a new bullet item for the slide.

> **NOTE** Meeting Minder does not work in Outline view. If you want to use Meeting Minder, change your view to Slide, Notes, or Slide Sorter view. You can also use Slide Show view to edit Meeting Minder items.

To use Meeting Minder, follow these steps:

1. Select Tools ➤ Meeting Minder.
2. Click on the Notes Pages tab and type your notes.
3. Click on the Meeting Minutes tab and enter your minutes.

4. Click on the Action Items tab and type a list of items you want to appear on a final bulleted slide. Use the Enter key to separate bulleted items.

5. Click on OK to save your changes to Meeting Minder.

6. Select another slide and repeat steps 1 through 5.

After you have entered all the Notes Pages, Meeting Minutes, and Action Items for your presentation, you can create a Word document based on the items entered into Meeting Minder:

1. Select Tools ➤ Meeting Minder.

2. Click on the Export button to see the Meeting Minder dialog box shown here:

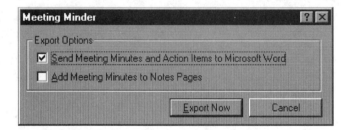

3. Make sure the Send Meeting Minutes and Action Items to Microsoft Word checkbox is selected.

4. Click on Export Now. Microsoft Word opens and a document based on your Meeting Minder items is created. You can now print this document or save it.

5. Exit Word and return to PowerPoint.

> **NOTE** Even if you have entered text into Notes Pages, if you have not entered any items into Meeting Minutes or Action Items, you will not be able to export to Word. To print out your Notes Pages, choose File ➤ Print and select Note Pages.

You can also choose to have your Meeting Minutes added to your Notes Pages from this dialog box. If you do so, your Meeting Minutes will be added to your notes for easy retrieval in Notes view and for printing from PowerPoint. To choose this option, make sure the Add Meeting Minutes to Notes Pages checkbox is highlighted.

Write-Up: Exporting to a Word Table

You can choose to have all the notes and slides for your presentation exported to a Word table. Each slide will appear as a picture next to any notes for that slide. The Write-Up tool is quite useful. Unlike Notes Pages, which prints one slide per page, Write-Up lets you easily fit several slides onto a page in Word. Likewise, handouts (hard copies of the slide presentation) in PowerPoint can print only two, three, or six slides on each page, without notes. To access Write-Up, follow these steps:

1. Select Tools ➤ Write-Up to display the dialog box shown in Figure 28.3.

2. Select the layout for your notes relative to the slides.

3. Choose whether you want to paste or paste link.

4. Word opens, and a table with your slides and notes is created. You can edit this document and then print it.

5. Exit Word to return to PowerPoint.

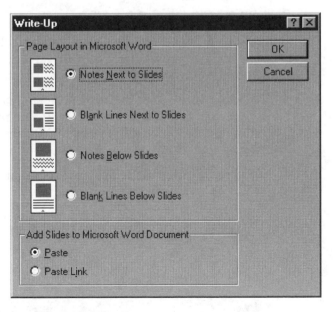

Figure 28.3   **Write-Up dialog box**

Part
4

Presenting with
PowerPoint

Slide Meter:
Rehearsing Your Presentation

Before you give your presentation before an audience, it's a good idea to rehearse your slide show and make note of slide timings. PowerPoint allows you to time your presentation and then rehearse subsequent shows using your previous times. You can choose to use the Slide Meter, a timing device that shows you whether your presentation is running too slowly or quickly according to the times you recorded previously. You can also let PowerPoint automatically advance each slide according to the times you record for a dry run.

Let's run through the procedure for creating a base time for your slide show and then see how you can use several of the tools in PowerPoint Slide Show view to enhance and speed up your presentation. If you don't already have a presentation open, open one now. If you don't have any presentations, use one of the complete template presentations from PowerPoint.

1. Select View ➤ Slide Show to see the dialog box shown in Figure 28.4.

2. Click on Rehearse New Timings.

3. Click on Show. The first slide appears, along with a Slide Timer in the lower right-hand corner of your screen, as shown in Figure 28.5. Also note the dim pointer in the lower left-hand corner of the screen.

4. Advance through each slide by clicking on the "next" arrow in the Slide Timer box or clicking on the slide. If you make an error, you can repeat the slide, and the timer will start from 0:00 again. You can also pause the timer if you need to by clicking the Pause button in the Rehearsal dialog box.

5. When you have finished your show, a dialog box appears, asking whether you want to record the new times for your slide show:

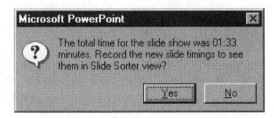

Click on Yes.

When you have completed your dry run through the presentation slide show, PowerPoint automatically switches you to Slide Sorter view, where you can see each of the slides in your show, along with the times recorded for each slide (see Figure 28.6).

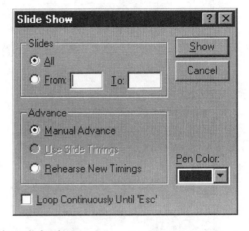

Figure 28.4 **Slide Show dialog box**

Figure 28.5 **Recording new slide times**

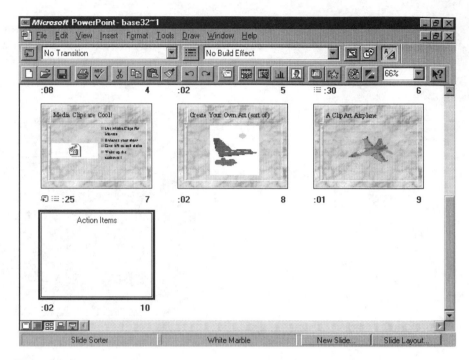

Figure 28.6   *Slide Sorter view with new times*

After rehearsing your presentation, you might choose to delete or edit some slides. However, you may first want to see how the slide show will be affected before you make the changes permanent. You can hide any of the slides in your presentation from the Slide Sorter view that PowerPoint opens for you. To hide a slide, select Tools ➤ Hide Slide.

Once you have recorded your time for the slide show and hidden any slides you decided you no longer need, you can rerun your slide show, timing yourself against your original time to see whether you can repeat your performance. If you find you have to talk too quickly or there are too many pauses between slides, you can always rerun your slide show and record new times.

Once you are satisfied with your times, you can let the computer rerun your slide show using the times you recorded. PowerPoint automatically advances your slides. All you have to do is give your speech for each slide.

To let the computer run the slide show, follow these steps:

1. Select View ➤ Slide Show.

2. Click on the Use Slide Timings radio button.

3. Click on Show.

4. Deliver the script for each slide as you normally would.

When the slide show has finished, PowerPoint returns you to your original view. Using the Slide Meter tool, you can see whether your original times are too slow or too fast. Or you can choose another approach entirely, to still use the slide times as a guideline but to manually advance each slide in the show. To do this, follow the steps above for an automatic show, but this time click on the Manual Advance radio button.

To access the Slide Meter during a Slide Show, click your right mouse button and select Slide Meter from the shortcut menu. Within a few seconds, PowerPoint places the Slide Meter in the lower right-hand corner and the pointer in the lower left-hand corner of your screen, as you can see in Figure 28.7. To advance through the slides, either press N or click on the slide.

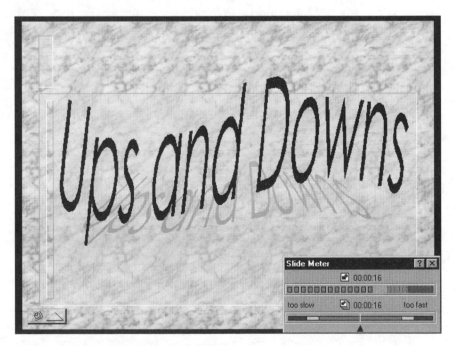

Figure 28.7 **Slide Meter in the slide show**

As you give your slide show, you will notice that the black arrow in the Slide Meter moves either to the left, indicating that you are taking too long with your presentation, or to the right, meaning that you are moving too quickly. The meter updates itself as soon as you advance to the next slide. You can use the running clock in the Slide Meter to see how long you have taken with each slide.

The Pointer: Your Toolbox during Presentations

You have seen the pointer in the lower-left hand corner of the screen in Slide Show view. Think of this pointer as your toolbox to use during a presentation. You can access several items that may come in handy during your presentation. Available from the pointer are

▶ A pen for writing on slides in several colors.

▶ Access to the Slide Meter and Meeting Minder tools.

▶ A Slide Navigator that permits you access to hidden slides during a presentation.

▶ The option of blacking out the screen to take the audience's attention off the present slide and onto something else in your presentation.

If your pointer is not visible in Slide Show view, click the right mouse button, select Pointer Options, and uncheck the Hide Now option, as shown here:

If your pointer is still not visible, click the right mouse button again, select Pointer Options, and make sure the Hide Always option is not checked. If it is, uncheck it.

If you are not already in a slide show, switch to Slide Show view and activate your pointer.

Navigation

The first three selections on the Pointer popup menu, shown in Figure 28.8, deal with slide navigation. The first and second selections on the menu permit you to go to either the next or the previous slide. Of course, if you are at the first slide in your presentation, you cannot go to a previous slide. If you are at the last slide in your presentation, choosing Next exits you from the slide show.

The third option on the menu is Go To, which allows you either to go to a specific slide in your slide show or to reveal hidden slides. If you choose Hidden Slide from Go To, you will go to the next hidden slide. This option is available only if the next slide is hidden. If you need to go to an indiscriminate hidden slide, use the Slide Navigator.

If you choose Slide Navigator from Go To, you see a dialog box like the one in Figure 28.9, displaying the names of all your slides in the order in which they appear in your presentation. If the number is enclosed in parentheses, that means the slide is hidden. From this dialog box you can go to any particular slide in your presentation. For instance, if you are on slide 1 and you choose to go to slide 4, you will skip slides 2 and 3. Likewise, if you are on slide 6 and you choose to go to slide 3, you will move directly to slide 3.

If you choose to move through your slide show using Slide Navigator, you will *not* return to the slide from where you activated the Navigator. If you go back through your slide show, you will have to use Slide

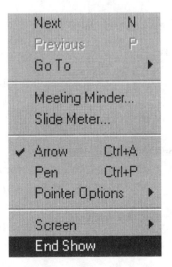

Figure 28.8   *The pointer and its shortcut menu*

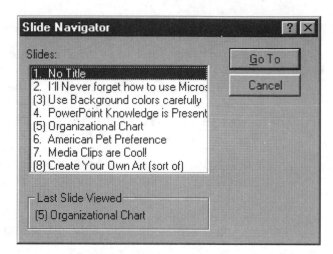

Figure 28.9   Slide Navigator dialog box

Navigator to return to your previous position. Likewise, if you move ahead in your presentation, you will have to navigate back to your starting point using Go To.

NOTE   If you want access to either the Meeting Minder or the Slide Meter during a slide show, you can do so from the Pointer popup menu. Just remember, your Meeting Minder and Slide Meter will appear to your audience if you use these tools during a live presentation.

Pens and Arrows

The third set of tools available from the Pointer popup menu consists of the Arrow, Pen, and Pointer Options choices. You can choose to use an arrow as a pointing device during your slide show, or you can switch to a pen. If you choose a pen, you will still be able to access different tools from the Pointer popup menu by clicking the right mouse button to open the shortcut menu. However, you will not be able to advance to a slide by clicking on the present slide, and you will not be able to activate any of the text-building options of interactive programs you may have associated with objects on your slide.

You can use the pen to write on the surface of your slide without making any changes to the slide itself. For example, you can circle important items or draw the audience's attention to another item by underlining it. You can change the color of the pen and use several different color "inks" on the same slide. When you have finished marking your slide, you can erase everything you did with the pen and have your slide appear as it originally did when you opened it.

> **TIP** If you have access to a Pen Pad, you might experiment with it to see whether you can use it effectively during your presentation. The mouse does not offer a great amount of agility; consequently, when you use the pen, your handwriting appears uneven, not unlike the contestant sign-ins on *Jeopardy.*

To use the pen, click on the pointer and choose Pen. You can write anywhere on the slide; it will not affect the slide's transition in the show.

If you want to change the color of the pen, follow these steps:

1. Select Pointer Options ➤ Pen Color from the Pointer menu.

2. Select a new color for your pen.

When you need to erase any marks you have made on your slide, follow these steps:

1. Click on the pointer.

2. Select Screen.

3. Select Erase.

Go to Black

You can black out the screen at any time during your presentation by selecting Screen ➤ Black Screen from the Pointer popup menu. You can still use the pen to write on the black screen if you wish. To return your slide to its normal view, select Screen ➤ Unblack Screen from the Pointer popup menu.

Presentation Conference: Adding Other Computers

To use Presentation Conference you first have to take note of a few items. If you are unsure about the information, contact your network administrator or Help Desk staff. They should be able to help you in creating your Presentation Conference.

First, you need to make sure your computer is on a network. You will know whether you are networked with other computers if you double-click on the Network Neighborhood icon on the desktop and can browse your entire network. If your computer is not networked, contact your systems staff to either correct the problem or find a computer that is on your network.

Second, you need to know the addresses or "names" of the computers you wish to join to your presentation. For some offices, this is usually the same as a person's logon. For others, it is a special inventory code. And for still others, it is a personalized name for the computer. It's traditional with network administrators to pick a theme for a network. If you have any trouble locating the names of the computers, again, talk with your systems staff.

Starting a New Conference

To begin a new conference, select Tools ➤ Presentation Conference to see the Presentation Conference Wizard dialog box shown in Figure 28.10.

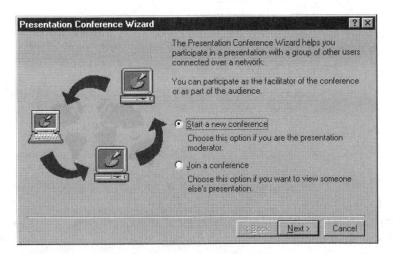

Figure 28.10   *Presentation Conference Wizard dialog box*

Make sure the Start a New Conference radio button is blackened, and click on Next to see the dialog box shown in Figure 28.11.

You can select the tools you would like to use during your Presentation Conference. When you have made your selections, click on Next to see the dialog box shown in Figure 28.12.

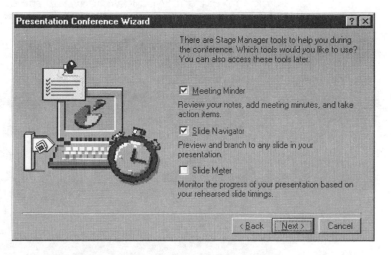

Figure 28.11   **Presentation Conference Wizard, second dialog box**

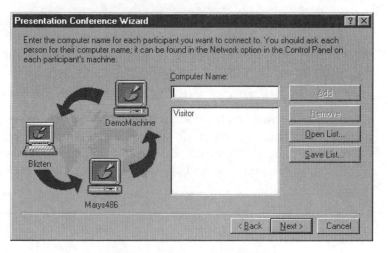

Figure 28.12   **Presentation Conference Wizard, third dialog box**

Now you can choose those computers you wish to invite to your Presentation Conference. Type in the name of the computer (not the user's logon, but the computer name) and click on Add. PowerPoint searches your network to find the computers. You can add just one or several computers to your conference. If PowerPoint cannot find the computer on your network, contact your systems staff for assistance. Click on Next once you have added all the computers you want in your conference, to see the dialog box shown in Figure 28.13.

Now click on Finish so PowerPoint can find the computers on your network.

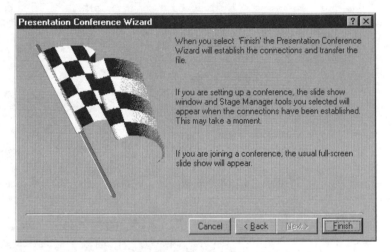

Figure 28.13   *Presentation Conference Wizard, fourth dialog box*

Joining a Conference

Once you have invited your viewers' computers to join your conference, they must then do so from their workstations. To join, they need to open the Presentation Conference Wizard by selecting Tools ➤ Presentation Conference and choose the Join a Conference radio button.

Click on Next to see the dialog box shown in Figure 28.14.

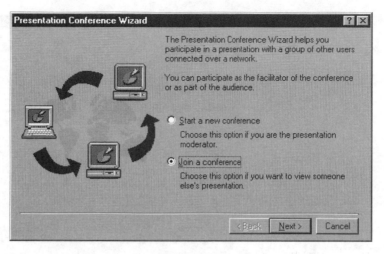

Figure 28.14 **Presentation Conference Wizard dialog (joining)**

Once the final dialog box in the Presentation Wizard comes up, as shown in Figure 28.15, click on Finish to allow the computer to join the conference you started. The computer then displays this message:

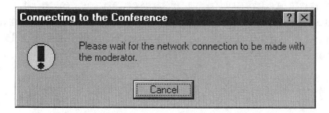

and searches for the moderator (the computer that created the Presentation Conference). If you have any problems connecting, you may have to restart PowerPoint and rejoin the conference.

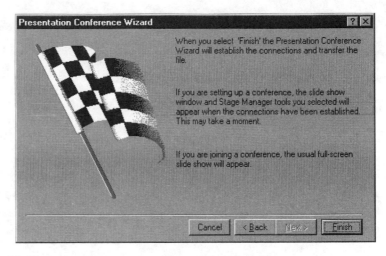

Figure 28.15　**Presentation Conference Wizard Finish dialog box**

What's Next

Making a success of one presentation is an accomplishment; providing consistent quality in your presentations, even at a moment's notice, should be the quest of anyone relying on PowerPoint as a key ingredient to getting their job done. Chapter 29 delves into the PowerPoint features that allow you to provide the desired consistency.

Chapter 29

Master Templates and Reusability

Featuring

Spending hours perfecting your presentation, placing graphics and tables in their proper positions, and customizing text and colors mean little if you can never re-create that exact look. At times you will want to be able to use a format that you found very successful before. You can always use one of the numerous design presentations or complete presentations PowerPoint provides, but sometimes you might want to modify the appearance of the slides to suit your presentation or organization.

With PowerPoint, you can create your own templates or complete presentations for your own use or for PowerPoint users in your organization. Although the process can take time to perfect, it is well worth the effort: Future presentations will be easier to create and edit.

Reusability Terminology

To take full advantage of the reusability features in PowerPoint, a primer of the terminology involved is in order.

Templates

A template is a slide that has predefined properties, such as background color, text color, text font and size, and interactive settings. A template can either contain no slides, such as the templates in Presentation Designs, or have numerous completely formatted slides, with text and bullets. PowerPoint includes several templates that already contain slides in Presentations, as shown in Figure 29.1.

Layouts

Slide layouts contain the number and placement of objects on the slides themselves. When you create a slide, AutoLayout prompts you for a layout for your slide. You can choose from 24 different layouts. Sometimes you need to create a custom layout for your presentation. In this case you can either use the blank layout and place those objects you need on the slide or modify a formatted layout to fit your slide's needs.

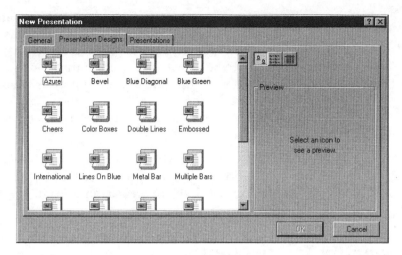

Figure 29.1   **Master menu in PowerPoint**

Title Slide

The term *Title Slide* is somewhat misleading. It does not refer to the first slide in a presentation or to the slide that contains the name of your presentation. It refers only to a particular layout, the Title Slide layout. You can have as many Title Slides as you want in your presentation. Although this may at first seem redundant, having one layout to control the Title Slide is important if you want to break down your presentation into several sections and introduce each section with a Title Slide.

NOTE   The Title Only layout is *not* considered a Title Slide. If you want to create a Title Slide without any subtext, do not place any text in that object. Remember, the dotted lines surrounding objects do not appear in the presentation; they are used only for reference in editing slides.

Masters

Masters control the appearance of slides, handouts, and notes in a presentation. Select View ➤ Master to select the Master you want from the Master menu, shown here:

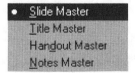

Masters control the appearance of the footer, date, page number, and any graphics or lines you want to add to all your slides, handouts, and notes. Masters also control the color of your text and background and the interactive settings for objects.

 NOTE Although you can change the Interactive settings for a Master, you cannot change the Slide Transition, Build Slide Text, or Animation Settings options here. You must activate these settings from the individual slides and objects.

Slide Master

Slide Master, shown in Figure 29.2, contains the formatting that controls how layouts will appear for existing or new slides in a presentation. Slide Master controls the appearance of all the slides in a presentation or template, except for one: the Title Slide.

Figure 29.2 **Slide Master**

Title Master

Title Master, shown in Figure 29.3, changes the formatting for only the Title Slide layout. You can have numerous Title Slides in a presentation, and they can appear at any position in a presentation. However, PowerPoint considers

Part
4

Presenting with
PowerPoint

only the Title Slide layout as a Title Slide, so if you change the Title Master, it will not affect any other slide layouts in the presentation.

Figure 29.3   **Title Master**

Handout Master

Handout Master, shown in Figure 29.4, controls the appearance of the handouts you choose to distribute to your audience or presentation staff. You can include a header, footer, date, and number in your Handout Master. You cannot control the number of slides that will appear on a handout from the Handout Master. You choose the number of slides that will appear on a handout from Print.

Notes Master

You select Notes Master, shown in Figure 29.5, by clicking the right mouse button and selecting Notes Master Layout. Notes Master controls the placement of the header, footer, date, number, notes body area, and slide image on your notes. Additionally, you can choose to crop or cut a slide image so that all or only part of your slide will appear on your notes.

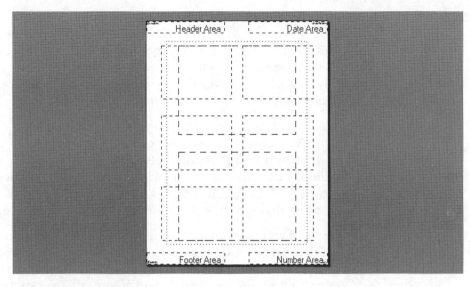

Figure 29.4   **Handout Master**

Figure 29.5   **Notes Master**

Master Layouts

Each Master also has a layout. The layout is visible only when viewing a Master, and then only the layout for that master is accessible. To view the layout of any Master, just click on the Master Layout button on the status bar. Figure 29.6 shows the Notes Master layout.

A dialog box appears showing the objects that are currently available on the Master. Although you can delete any object from a Master by selecting it and pressing Delete, you cannot delete it from the Layout dialog box. Likewise, if you want to add an object such as the date object to your Master, you cannot add it directly. You must access the Master Layout dialog box, select any object you wish to add, and choose OK.

Even if you have an object on your Master, it will not appear unless you activate it from the Header and Footer dialog box. Figure 29.7 shows the Header and Footer dialog box for Notes and Handouts, and Figure 29.8 shows the Header and Footer dialog box for Slides.

To activate an object on a Master, follow these steps:

1. Select View ➤ Header and Footer from the menu bar.

2. Make any changes you want by activating checkboxes for those objects under the Notes and Handouts tab.

3. Click on Apply to All.

4. Click on the Slides tab.

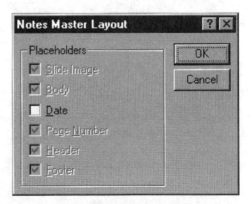

Figure 29.6   **Notes Master Layout without the date object chosen**

5. Repeat step 2 for Slides.

6. Click on either Apply to change the current slide or Apply to All to change all the slides in your presentation.

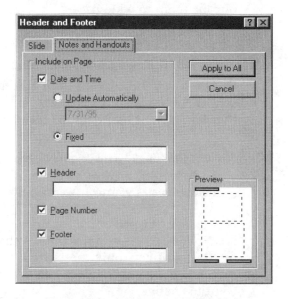

Figure 29.7   **Header and Footer dialog box for Notes and Handouts**

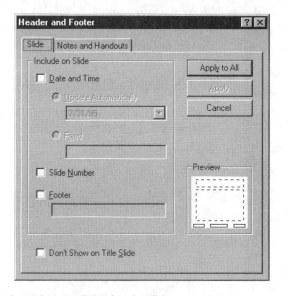

Figure 29.8   **Header and Footer dialog box for Slides**

Editing Masters is almost as easy as editing a layout or individual slide. But because Masters affect all slides in a presentation or for a template, take care when making changes to any Master. You can always undo them, but make sure your template and Master look as you wish before putting them to wide use.

Existing Templates

Before you jump in with both feet and try to create a template from scratch, let's work through the steps required to edit an existing template that PowerPoint has included for you.

NOTE   If you did a minimal or laptop install of Office or performed a custom installation, you may not have templates on your computer. If you don't have these templates, you might want to install them now so you can work with them.

If you have any presentations open in PowerPoint, it is probably a good idea to close them all at this time. Although making changes to a template or Master affects only the current presentation, you could mistakenly switch between open presentations and alter a presentation you don't want to change.

TIP   When you edit a template, PowerPoint prevents you from overwriting an existing template accidentally by prompting you for a name. Because of this, you can feel free to experiment.

Deciding on a View

First, you need to decide on the view for your template. You don't want any of the slides already in your presentation, so choose from the list of blank templates:

1. Select File ➤ New.
2. Click on the Presentation Design tab.
3. Select the Splatter template.
4. Because you want a template with no slides, do not choose a layout. Click on Cancel.

Now you should have a blank presentation on your screen. This particular template is useful to work with because it reveals some of the mystery about templates. Notice the two large, colorful "splatters" on the slide. These two splatters are actually just one large piece of clip art. You can replace these splatters with a different graphics image. Let's walk through the steps to do this.

Replacing Graphics

At this point you need to switch your view so you are viewing the Title Master. Remember, this is a Title Slide, so if you want to make changes to the images on the Title Slide, you have to view the Title Master. Also remember that even though you can change the background color and color scheme from Slide view, those changes will affect only this individual slide. To create a new template and make changes that will affect all the slides you create in any future presentations based on this template, follow these steps:

1. Select View ➤ Master ➤ Title Master from the menu bar.
2. Click on the slide background. The graphics image should be selected.
3. Press Delete. The image should disappear.
4. Click on the Insert ClipArt button on the toolbar.
5. Choose a piece of clip art you like and click on Insert.
6. Repeat steps 4 and 5 if you want other pieces of art.

You should now have the Title Master on your screen with clip art, like the example in Figure 29.9. You can copy, move, or resize the clip art to suit your needs. You can even resize the clip art to fill the entire slide. However, if you choose to do this, be careful to pick clip art that doesn't interfere with the text on the screen. The text will appear on top of the background and image, but if the colors conflict or there is too much clutter, the text will be difficult to see.

Changing the Font

Let's also change the font for the title on the Title Slide:

1. Select the title for the slide by pressing Shift and clicking on the title.
2. Select Format ➤ Font from the menu bar.

3. Select a font you like from the dialog box, and also change the color. Figure 29.10 shows the example Title Slide with a new title font.

Figure 29.9   **Title Master with new clip art**

Figure 29.10   **Title Slide with new title font**

Adding a Name and Logo

Finally, let's put a company name and logo on the Title Master. If you have your own company logo that you have used before in another application, you might want to see how it will look on this slide. If not, just choose any piece of clip art. To add a logo, follow these steps:

1. Click on the Insert ClipArt button on the toolbar.

2. Locate your logo or choose a piece of clip art you like and click on Insert.

3. Resize the image if needed.

4. Place the image in the lower right-hand corner of the slide.

Now that you have added the logo for this slide, you need to add your company name to the footer on the Title Master. Do not add any text to the text objects on the slide. Since this is the Master, the text would appear on every Title Slide in your presentation, and you would not be able to use titles. To add your company name, follow these steps:

1. Select View ➤ Header and Footer from the menu bar.

2. Click on the Slide tab.

3. Click on the checkbox next to Footer.

4. Type the name of your company.

5. Click on Apply to All.

> **NOTE**   You will not see your company name in the footer. You will see the <footer> field code instead. If you want to see how your logo appears on a slide, you can switch to Slide view and add a new Title Slide. Afterwards, remember to delete the new slide, since you want no slides in your template.

If the text does not fit in the footer, you need to adjust the footer so it accommodates your text:

1. Select the footer.

2. Select Format ➤ Text Anchor from the menu bar.

3. Check the Adjust Object Size to Fit Text option by clicking on it.

Figure 29.11 shows the example Title Slide with a company logo and name.

Figure 29.11   **Title Slide with company logo and name**

The term *footer* is somewhat misleading. You don't have to keep the footer at the bottom of the slide. You can move it anywhere on the slide and even make a copy of it so you can have it appear in two places on your Title Master. This may be a good idea if you want to distinguish a division of your company from the entire company. You will have to edit the copy of the footer, replacing the <footer> field with your own text.

The identifying names of the objects will not appear on the slide. They are there only to help you refer to the objects as you work on the Title Master.

Now that you have created a Title Master, you need to create a Slide Master so that all the slides in your presentation will have the same format. When you create a Slide Master, you can change the attributes for all the slides in a presentation without affecting the Title Slides.

Creating a Master Slide

To create a Slide Master, follow these steps:

1. Select View ➤ Master ➤ Slide Master. Notice that you are back to your original format.

2. Choose Format ➤ Custom Background.

3. Click on the drop-down arrow next to the color box and choose Patterned.

4. Select a pattern. Be sure to select one that will not interfere with the text on the screen.

5. Click on Apply to change the background of the Slide Master without changing that of the Title Master.

6. To show the Slide Master with new formatting, as shown in Figure 29.12, select File ➤ Open ➤ MS Office ➤ Templates ➤ Presentation Designs.

If you want to include your company logo, you need to add it again on the Master Slide. If you placed your company name in the footer, you need only format the font and position it again.

At this point you should save your template:

1. Select File ➤ Save from the menu bar.

2. Change the file type to Presentation Templates.

3. Type the name of the template.

4. Click on Save.

Figure 29.12 **Slide Master with new formatting**

Now, close out this template so you can create a new presentation based on it. You should be able to find it alongside the other templates under Design Templates. If it's not listed there, open the template again by selecting it from the most recently used file list under the File menu, and then repeat the steps above for saving a template.

Creating a New Presentation

To create a new presentation based on the template:

1. Select File ➤ New from the menu bar.
2. Click on the Presentations Design tab.
3. Select the template you just created.
4. Select the Title Slide layout.
5. Click on New Slide.
6. To select a different layout from Title Slide, click on the Slide Layout button and then choose a different layout.
7. Click on Apply.

If you are not in Slide view, switch to it. Then switch between your two slides to confirm that they are formatted the way you want. The Title Slide should be as you formatted it. It should be different from the second slide you created. If you are unhappy with the formatting or need to change something, you can always delete the slides you just created and repeat the steps above to reformat the Masters.

You can use Masters to change the settings not only for templates, but also for existing presentations. Now that you have learned how to edit the Slide and Title Masters, you might want to reopen a presentation you created previously and redesign the slides. Don't be afraid to tinker; you can always close your presentation without saving, preserving you original presentation.

Design Presentations

PowerPoint has created numerous templates for you. You should open each and see how the Masters are designed. Feel free to copy any graphics images you like onto another Master for a different presentation. Browse freely; you might find that certain effects you cannot create yourself have been created for you.

You might also look at the stylish Marble template, shown in Figure 29.13. The bevel is created by placing a large graphic on the Slide Master. Because of the color of the template and the background texture, the marble appears to have been chiseled. The text object is oriented over the graphic to give this sculpted appearance.

Although we created a template based on an existing design presentation, don't feel limited to using a predesigned template. You can always create a template from scratch, but you might want to wait until you are thoroughly familiar with PowerPoint before attempting this.

Experiment with different patterns and textures to see how they will work with different text colors. Create your own colors. Use your imagination and be creative. Remember, it will take some time to become comfortable with everything you can do with slide layouts, Masters, and templates.

Figure 29.13 **Marble template**

What's Next

With the reusability techniques covered in this chapter, you are now versed not only in creating powerful presentations, but in how to recycle the pieces of your presentations that will aid you in making future presentations easier to create with the same level of quality.

The next chapter explores the considerations you need to take into account when making presentations out of the office, possibly without the comfort of the computer that was used to create the presentation. The chapter also reviews basic file-management techniques that will focus on where and how you keep your presentations on your computer.

Chapter 30

File Management and Taking It on the Road

Featuring

Changing the Default File Location

Using the Pack and Go Wizard

n this chapter we focus on two major aspects of file maintenance: locating files and taking presentations on the road.

Changing the Default File Location

Windows 95 provides a folder named My Documents. Many people, especially new users, will want to save their files here so they know where they are. When you save a presentation in PowerPoint, however, the default folder shown in the File Save dialog box (see Figure 30.1) is the folder to which you *most recently saved* in PowerPoint. If you saved your last presentation to your floppy (or A) drive but now want to save a new presentation to your C drive, you must remember to change your drive and folder.

You can change this PowerPoint option of defaulting to the most recently saved folder by defining a path, or a place for PowerPoint to save all your files. This simple process takes just a few seconds. Follow these steps to change this option so you will know from now on where your files have gone:

1. Select Tools ➤ Options from the menu bar.

2. When the Options dialog box appears, click on the Advanced tab.

3. With your mouse, click in the Default File Location field and type the name of the folder where you want your presentations always to be saved. For example, if you wanted the default to be the My Documents folder, you would type **C:\My Documents** into the field.

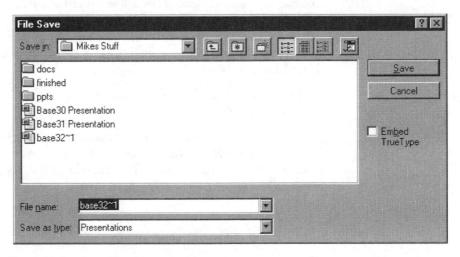

Figure 30.1   *File Save dialog box in PowerPoint*

Using the Pack and Go Wizard

One of the most useful tools now available in PowerPoint is its ability to "pack up" all your work for you. Not surprisingly, the tool responsible for this is called the Pack and Go Wizard. Pack and Go compresses your presentation and any files you have linked to it to a floppy disk so you can make your presentation on another computer. This Wizard also gives you the option of installing the PowerPoint Viewer on the floppy so you can view your presentation on a computer that does not have PowerPoint installed.

 NOTE   The PowerPoint Viewer *will* work on a computer running Windows 3.1 or Windows 3.11. However, the Viewer does not support all the functionality of the full PowerPoint product.

Packing Up

To use the Pack and Go Wizard, first be certain your presentation is in its final form. If you use the Wizard and later make changes to your presentation, you will have to rerun the Wizard to repack your presentation in its new form.

To start saving your presentation on a floppy disk, select File ➤ Pack and Go from the menu bar. The Pack and Go Wizard asks you a few easy-to-answer questions, then it asks whether you want to include linked files and embed TrueType fonts (see Figure 30.2). If you have linked any files, make sure this box is checked. If you also have any special fonts on your machine that may not be available on the machine where you will be doing the presentation, you should also check the Embed TrueType Fonts box.

Once you have made your selections, click on Next to see the screen shown in Figure 30.3.

You should check the Include PowerPoint Viewer checkbox in this screen if you will be taking your presentation to another computer that does not have PowerPoint. Click on Next to see the final screen in the Pack and Go Wizard, as shown in Figure 30.4.

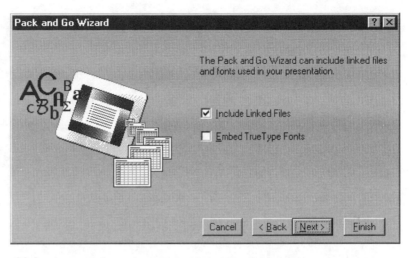

Figure 30.2 **Pack and Go can keep track of linked files and fonts.**

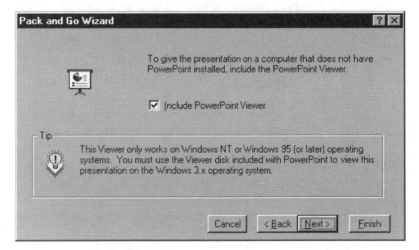

Figure 30.3 **Fifth screen in Pack and Go**

The final screen asks to go back, cancel, or finish. If you are satisfied and wish to continue creating your compressed presentation file, click on Finish.

PowerPoint now creates a compressed file on your floppy drive, or another drive if you chose one, that you can run, or execute, when you arrive at the location where you are going to make the presentation.

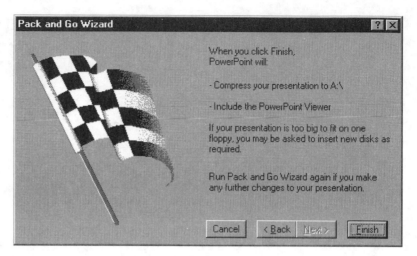

Figure 30.4   **Final screen in Pack and Go**

Unpacking the Presentation

Once you have reached your destination, run the file PowerPoint created while packing up your presentation. To do so, from the Start button on the Microsoft window, select Run. Then type **A:\PNGSETUP.EXE** and press Enter.

The dialog box in Figure 30.5 asks you for a destination for your presentation. After browsing for the folder or typing it directly into the destination field, your presentation will be uncompressed for viewing (see Figure 30.6) and a dialog box will open checking to see whether you want to view the presentation now.

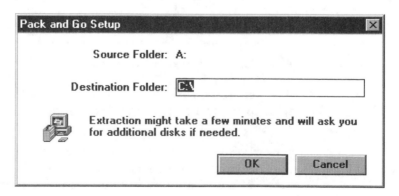

Figure 30.5   **Pngsetup at work**

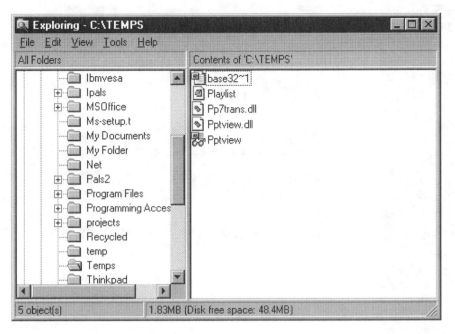

Figure 30.6 **The uncompressed files**

If you decline to view the presentation at the time of decompression, you can double-click on the Pptview file at any other time to begin viewing your presentation.

What's Next

The presentations you will be making, whether they are on the road or in house, will at one time or another benefit from the other Office applications you use. The next chapter illustrates how you can greatly increase the functionality of PowerPoint and significantly reduce the duplication of effort by incorporating the other Office applications into the creation of your presentations.

Part
4

Presenting with
PowerPoint

Chapter 31

Office Connections—The "Whole Office" Presentation

Featuring

One of the most powerful features of PowerPoint is its ability to share information between the other programs in Office. You can copy and paste between any of the other Office programs with the same ease with which you would copy and paste from within PowerPoint. You can either create a working copy of an object from another program or create a link to the original file so all changes will be updated in your PowerPoint presentation.

To Link or Not to Link

One of the biggest questions you will face as a writer of a presentation is whether you should link or embed objects you place on your slides. Up to this point, we have addressed only embedding an object in a presentation—that is, placing a complete copy of the file within your presentation. However, this technique has some drawbacks.

One problem is that your presentation file can become rather large if you embed enough objects in it. Another problem is that you have no access to updated information. If you embed an Excel spreadsheet in your presentation and someone later comes along and updates the data in that spreadsheet, your presentation will still reflect the old data. The same is true if you plan to embed a graph based on a spreadsheet or Access table.

However, when you link the original file instead of embed it, the original file is always being referenced and updated in the link. When someone updates the original spreadsheet, your presentation will reflect the new data.

Of course, there is an advantage to embedding a file. If someone moves or deletes the original file, your copy is still securely embedded in your presentation. Also, you don't have to worry about accidental changes in your presentation, because you have "locked" the copy of the file by embedding it.

Another problem with linking is that it does not work over networks. You must still embed any objects you want in your presentation, even if you have permission on a network to access and edit information in that file.

Also be aware that if you plan to use the Pack and Go Wizard, your embedded or linked objects will work only if your presentation computer has the resident Office program installed. For instance, if you attempt to show a presentation with an embedded Access table on a slide on a computer that does not have Access installed, you will not be able to use that table. If you do not plan to take a computer with you for your presentation at another location, be sure to request a computer that has all the necessary programs already installed. When in doubt, it is always best to carry with you one laptop that has a complete version of Office 95, just in case.

Consider these issues as you develop your presentations using data from other applications.

> **TIP**   If you move a linked file, Access will not be able to locate it. You must delete the object and reinsert it with the new link.

Up to this point, when you created a new slide, you embedded objects rather than linking them. It is a good idea to continue to create your slides in this fashion until you feel secure enough with PowerPoint to break with tradition and explore the options associated with objects in presentations.

A Review of Embedding an Object

Let's quickly review creating a slide with a simple object, such as a graph:

1. Create a new slide from the New Slide button on the toolbar.

2. Select an AutoLayout based on a graph.

3. Double-click on the graph icon.

4. Highlight the existing data and press Del.

5. Enter your new data.

6. Choose a format for the graph and edit it if you like.

7. Close the Datasheet to view your finished slide with the embedded graph.

Now that you know how to create a slide with a graph embedded in it, take a closer look at what has just happened. You created a graph from scratch with new data that you entered onto a datasheet. You then chose a form for the graph and, optionally, edited it.

When you closed the datasheet, PowerPoint automatically updated your slide by inserting your graph into an object. You really didn't have to worry about files, their locations, or linking and embedding.

This is the simplest way to create an object on a slide. Every time you created a new slide with an object, what you were really doing was either creating a new object from scratch, such as your graph or organizational chart, or embedding an existing object, such as clip art. But now you need to look at creating a slide with existing objects by linking and embedding them.

You can embed or link an object in PowerPoint in two ways. One way is to copy just the portion of the file you want and then paste it on a slide. The other way is to insert an entire file into the slide. Let's look at both ways.

Copy-and-Paste When Embedding and Linking

Perhaps the easiest way to insert an object into a slide in PowerPoint is to switch to the application in which the object was created, select the object, copy it, and then paste it onto the slide. You have two choices of insertion when you create objects on slides in this manner:

▶ Pasting

▶ Pasting with a link

If you paste without a link, you are creating a copy of that file on the slide. If you paste with a link, you are only directing PowerPoint to the file so it can create the slide. Since you have not made any copy, your data can refresh as needed. In Office Connections for Word, you copied and linked a graph to a Word document. You use the same process to insert a chart into a PowerPoint document (slide), first without the link and then by linking the Excel chart.

Copying a Graph

Here are the steps for copying a graph:

1. Enter Excel and open a spreadsheet. If you do not already have a graph made for this sheet, create one now using the Graph Wizard.

2. After you have placed the graph on a sheet, select the graph and press Ctrl+C, choose Edit ➤ Copy, or right-click the mouse on the selected graph (see Figure 31.1).

3. Switch to PowerPoint, and if you have not already done so, create a new slide based on the Blank layout and choose OK.

4. Press Ctrl+V or choose Edit ➤ Paste.

When you copy and paste a graph in this fashion, you are creating a copy of it on the slide. If you edit the original graph, your slide will remain unchanged. This would, of course, be advantageous if you were making a graph of a spreadsheet that changed daily but only wanted to graphically reflect the data as of one date—for example, if the data was replaced every day but you needed to see only one particular day's graph. In this instance, you would want to embed the graph with no link.

Linking a Graph

But what if you wanted to have your presentation updated every time the original spreadsheet changed? Then you would create a link between your slides and the original files.

Once again, we'll work with an Excel graph. Try to work with the same graph you used in the preceding example so you can see the difference between the two slides you have created.

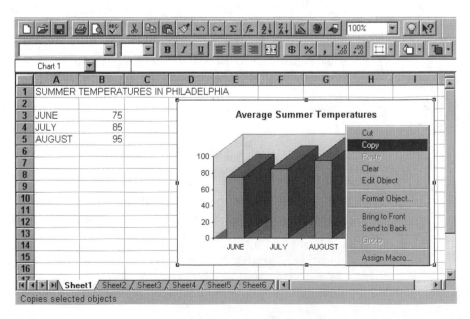

Figure 31.1 Copying a simple graph from Excel to PowerPoint

Here are the steps for linking a graph:

1. Enter Excel and open a spreadsheet. If you do not already have a graph made for this sheet, create one now using the Graph Wizard.

2. After you have placed the graph on a sheet, select the graph and press Ctrl+C or choose Edit ➤ Copy.

3. Switch to PowerPoint, and if you have not already done so, create a new slide based on the Blank layout and choose OK.

4. Choose Edit ➤ Paste Special. You will see the Paste Link box shown in Figure 31.2.

5. Select the Microsoft Excel Chart Object choice.

Now go back to your original Excel spreadsheet and change some of the data used to create the graph. Notice that in Excel, the graph will automatically update to reflect the changes in the data. If you now switch back to PowerPoint, you'll see that your original slide, with the embedded (pasted without a link) chart, is unchanged. However, the graph you pasted with a link back to the original Excel spreadsheet has changed to reflect the new data.

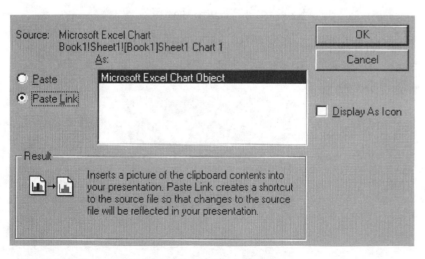

Figure 31.2 **Pasting an Excel graph with a link into PowerPoint**

Inserting an Entire File

You can also insert an object into a slide in PowerPoint by using the Insert ➤ Object menu. When you place an object on a slide in this manner, you are not selecting one section, such as a graph, sheet, or page, to be inserted into the slide. You are placing the entire document on the slide. This technique is advantageous if you want a user to have access to a copy of a file. For instance, you may want to actually show the spreadsheet that produced a particular graph, or you may want to enter the spreadsheet to view other data that you did not use to create your graph.

As with cutting and pasting, you have the option of creating a link when you insert an object into your slide. Just click on the Link checkbox in the Insert Object dialog box (see Figure 31.3).

Here are the steps for creating a link:

1. Choose the Insert ➤ Object menu.

2. Click on the Create from File radio button.

3. Click on Browse.

4. Select the file you want to insert.

5. Click on the Link checkbox.

6. Click on OK to insert the file.

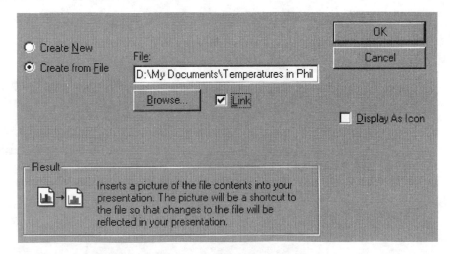

Figure 31.3   Check the Link box to create a link.

TIP You can display the file as an icon, which will allow you to enter the file and edit information, but the file will appear only as an icon on your slide. You can choose this option to speed up the painting of a slide with linked information on it. If an object is large, it can take several minutes to appear.

You can also insert a new object that you create from scratch using this method. In this case, instead of clicking on the Create from File radio button, you would click on the Create New radio button and choose the object type you wish to insert.

The advantage of using this method to insert objects is that you have greater control over the creation process. Instead of relying on PowerPoint to choose a layout for you based on clip art, a graph, an organization chart, a media clip, or an object, you can automatically request a Microsoft Equation or WordArt object. Some users like to use this method of object insertion. Others prefer using AutoLayout. The method you choose will not affect your object's appearance or behavior.

Real-Life Situations

Now let's take a look at a Visitor's Service Center in Philadelphia, where one of the managers, Susan, must create a presentation bringing together elements already created by other employees in the company.

Susan needs to create a simple presentation to welcome employees moving into Philadelphia. This product will be provided free of charge to any company that needs to orient new employees. But Susan has just moved to Philadelphia herself, and she doesn't know much about the city or its attractions. She decides to put her thoughts down in outline form first, before jumping into PowerPoint.

Susan uses Word's Outline view to create an entire document representing the order in which she thinks the information should be presented (see Figure 31.4).

Using a Word Outline as a PowerPoint Presentation

Susan knows she can use Word outlines as the basis of PowerPoint slides, and she decides to create the slide show presentation directly from the

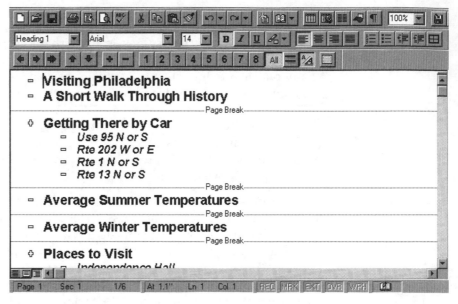

Figure 31.4   **Outline view of document**

outline. She uses Word's Outline view (View ➤ Outline) to create a few headings. Heading 1 items will become new slides. Heading 2 items will become bullet points under Heading 1. Heading 3 items will become subitems under Heading 2. She then saves the Word file and closes it.

Here are the steps for creating the PowerPoint presentation from the Word outline:

1. Create a blank presentation in PowerPoint.

2. Select Insert ➤ Slides from Outline from the menu bar.

3. Choose the Word file containing your outline and click on Insert.

4. Save your presentation.

Copying Excel Data to a PowerPoint Slide

After Susan has created the slides from the outline, she notices that each slide is a little empty. She thinks the slide show needs something more. She has included summer and winter temperatures but not the supporting data. Susan decides to create a workbook in Excel with two charts that graphically display the winter and summer temperatures in Philadelphia. To integrate the data from Excel into the PowerPoint slide will require Susan to open her new presentation in PowerPoint so she can edit the slides. Next, she will need to start Excel and open the workbook containing the charts. Then she can start to insert her charts.

Here are the steps:

1. After opening both Excel and PowerPoint, move to the slide where you want the chart and delete any empty text boxes.

2. Switch to Excel using the taskbar.

3. Click on the chart in Excel that you want to insert. Sizing handles will appear around the chart to indicate that it is selected.

4. Press Ctrl+C to copy the chart.

5. Switch back to the PowerPoint slide using the taskbar, and press Ctrl+V to paste the chart.

6. Place and resize the chart as needed on the slide.

   The slide should resemble the one shown in Figure 31.5.

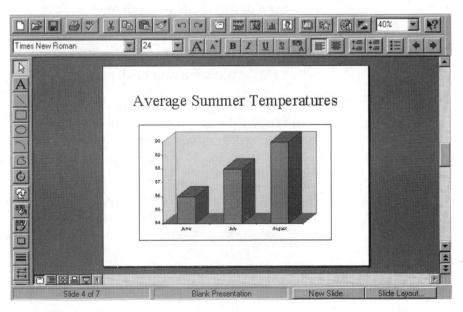

Figure 31.5   *Excel Chart data in PowerPoint slide*

Part 4

Presenting with PowerPoint

Susan has placed her charts on the appropriate slides, but she decides that the slide showing how to get to Philadelphia should have a map to give the employees a good idea of where Philadelphia is in relation to other cities. She creates a map using Microsoft Map in Excel. After including major cities on the map and some geographic features and highways, she saves the workbook. Susan launches both PowerPoint and Excel. She opens the workbook she created. She then starts to work through the steps of copying the map onto her slide:

1. If there is an empty text box on the slide, delete it.

2. Switch to Excel using the taskbar.

3. Select the map and press Ctrl+C to copy it.

4. Switch to PowerPoint using the taskbar.

5. Press Ctrl+V to insert the map.

6. Place and size the map as needed.

7. Save your presentation.

Susan now has a completed slide ready for the employee orientation. She decides to make some minor changes before her presentation by applying a design template to change the look of her slides. She does this by using the following steps:

1. Choose Format ➤ Apply Design Template from the menu bar.

2. Select a style you want and click on Apply.

3. Save your presentation.

Susan shows the slide presentation to members of the Visitor's Service Bureau board, and they decide to include the disk with other marketing materials provided to companies and individuals seeking information about Philadelphia.

The entire slide show, shown in Slide Sorter view in Figure 31.6, was created in PowerPoint using elements from other Office 95 applications.

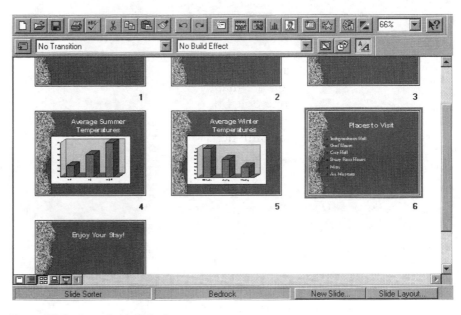

Figure 31.6 **PowerPoint Slide view**

Power Moderation

In this part of the book, you have learned how to create a new presentation, create and edit slides, use the powerful tools included in PowerPoint, such as organization charts and clip art, create templates, make presentations, use the Pack and Go Wizard, and share information between other applications in Office 95. Of course, no text can be exhaustive in its exploration of a program as powerful and flexible as PowerPoint. From here, you should practice your art.

The best way to learn more about PowerPoint is to jump in and start creating new presentations. Try using all the concepts introduced in this part, even if you don't think you will be using them immediately. You will learn more from trial and error than you could ever gain from one textbook. If you aren't sure whether something will work, try it. You can always undo your work later. Keep a backup copy of your presentation on hand, just in case you cannot undo any changes to your file. Soon you will find that you have become a PowerPoint expert, and people will be coming to you for advice and help in creating their own presentations.

Business Processing: Organizing with Schedule+

In this part the features of the newest member of the Office are introduced, with special attention devoted to its vital integration with Word. The features of Schedule+ are explored to provide you with the ability to create and manage appointments, projects, and to-do lists.

The integration chapter of this part details the process of importing contact information from other Office applications and how to use the contacts stored in Schedule+ for mass mailings.

Chapter 32

Organizing with Schedule+

FEATURING

Microsoft's Schedule+ helps you keep track of your busy life. Whether it is keeping tabs on meetings and appointments or remembering the thousands of little tasks you must complete, Schedule+ includes the tools you need to stay organized. In Schedule+ you'll find a calendar based on the familiar desk calendar. In addition to allowing you to keep track of meetings, appointments, or anything else you do at a certain time, Schedule+ also allows you to schedule appointments with coworkers who use Schedule+. In addition to being a full-featured scheduling program, Schedule+ also keeps your to-do list and contact information. All this is available on your computer's desktop whenever you need it.

In the next few chapters you'll learn the basics of the following Schedule+ features:

- ▶ Calendar
- ▶ To Do List
- ▶ Reminders
- ▶ Contact List

Starting Schedule+

You can start Schedule+ by selecting Schedule+ from the Office group. Click on the Start button on the Taskbar and choose Start ➤ Programs ➤ Schedule+. If you are a member of a network, Schedule+ will ask whether you want to work in group mode or alone. Group-Enabled Mode allows you to perform group scheduling for meetings; working alone allows you to work only on your personal calendar. Click on OK to continue. The Exchange Profiles dialog box appears; choose your Exchange Settings and click on OK. The Schedule+ window appears showing a daily calendar, as you see on the next page.

 TIP You can use File ➤ New to create additional Schedule+ files. One common use of additional Schedule+ files is to keep track of office resources, such as a conference room.

Looking at the Calendar

You will probably find yourself spending most of your time using Schedule+'s calendar features. Schedule+ gives you all the features of a paper calendar —with some very useful additions. Schedule+ can pop up reminder dialog boxes on your computer screen a specified amount of time before an appointment. You can also easily schedule recurring appointments such as biweekly staff meetings or monthly management meetings. With Schedule+ you will always know your time commitments.

Changing Views and Navigating around Your Calendar

When you first start up Schedule+, you'll see the Daily view of your schedule. In addition to seeing your appointments for the day, you'll also see a small calendar of the month in the upper-right corner of the window and a list of the active items on your To Do list in the bottom-right corner. Along the left of the Schedule+ window are six tabs; click on a tab to pick a different calendar view. The most common ways to view your schedule are:

▶ Daily

▶ Weekly

▶ Monthly

▶ Planner

> **NOTE** You will learn about the bottom two tabs, To Do and Contacts, in a later chapter. They are used to access the To Do list and contact list features of Schedule+.

Daily The Daily view shows you what you have planned for any given day. It is a very useful view for scheduling new appointments. You can change the day displayed by using either of the arrows near the top of the calendar or by clicking on a date on the calendar (see Figure 32.1).

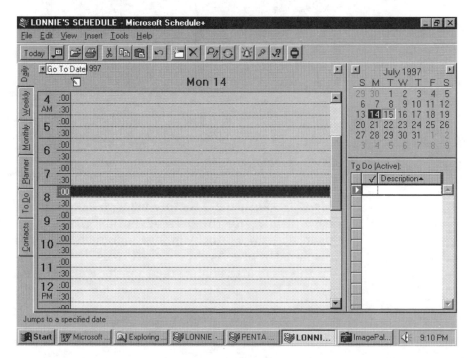

Figure 32.1 *When you are viewing your calendar in Schedule+, you can change dates either by using the two arrows near the top of the screen or by clicking on a date on the calendar.*

Weekly   The Weekly view gives you a good overview of what you have scheduled for the upcoming five days. When you are viewing an entire week of your schedule, you can change the week by clicking on either arrow button near the top of the window. You can also use the Today or Go To Date buttons on the toolbar to move the window of days displayed (see Figure 32.2).

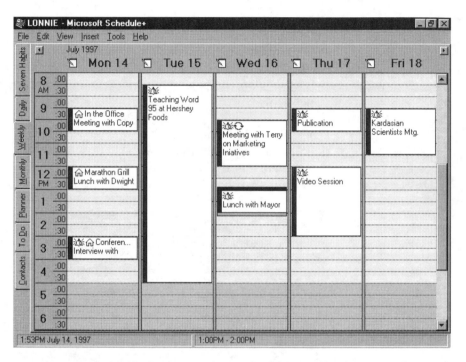

Figure 32.2   *In the Weekly view you see what you have scheduled for the next five days.*

Monthly   With the Monthly view you get a picture of everything you have planned for the current month. Clicking on either of the arrows near the top of the window increments or decrements the month displayed by one. As always, you can use the Today or Go To Date buttons on the toolbar to change the month displayed (see Figure 32.3).

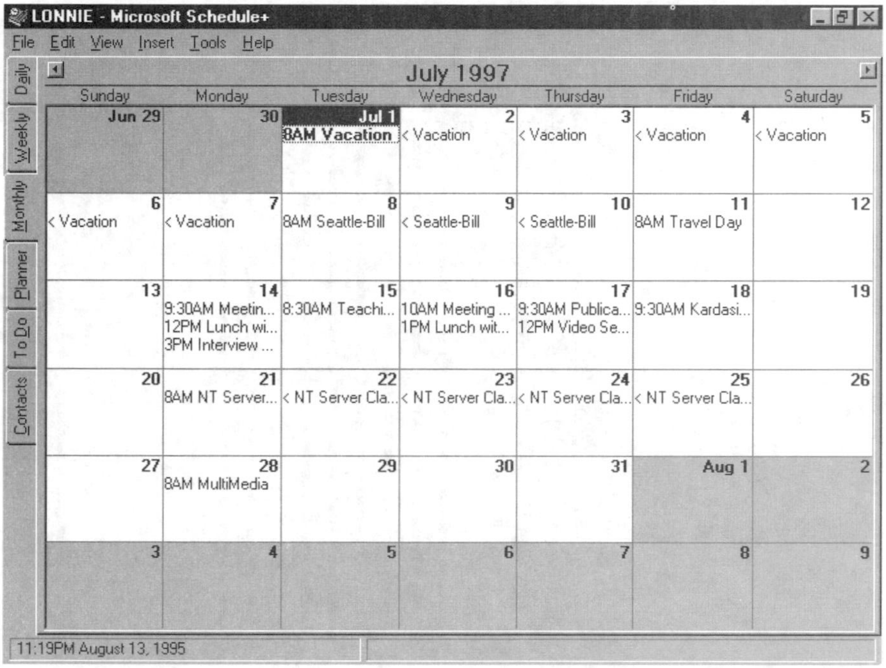

Figure 32.3 *The Monthly view shows you everything you have planned for an entire month. Because of the small amount of space available, only the first few words of each appointment are displayed.*

Planner   The Planner view is similar to the Weekly view, except it displays many weeks on the screen at once, includes a calendar, and lists the other attendees at your meetings. The calendar appears in the upper-right corner, just like in the Daily view. The other attendees list appears in Attendees box in the lower-right corner. You can use the two arrow buttons at the top of the window or the Today and Go To Date button on the toolbar to change the days shown; you can also click on a date on the calendar (see Figure 32.4).

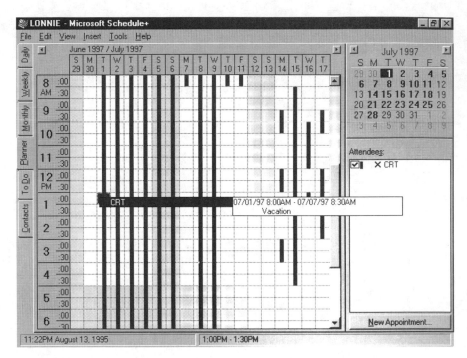

Figure 32.4 *The Planner view shows the most information of any of Schedule+'s views. You can see your upcoming appointments for a few weeks.*

Viewing the Tab Gallery

The tabs listed on the left side of the calendar can be edited, removed, added to, and reordered by choosing View ➤ Tab Gallery from the menu bar. The Tab Gallery dialog box appears with the different viewing possibilities.

One of the more interesting additions you can make to the Tab Gallery is the Seven Habits Planner. Based on Stephen Covey's *Seven Habits of Highly Effective People*, the Seven Habits Planner view combines the Weekly view with the To Do list. From the Tab Gallery, click on Seven Habits Planner in the Available Tabs box and then click on Add to display it with the other tabs (see Figure 32.5).

The Seven Habits Planner is also listed on the Tools menu; the Seven Habits Planner Tools and Wizard help you prioritize important tasks. Choose Tools ➤ Seven Habits Tools. When the Seven Habits Tools dialog

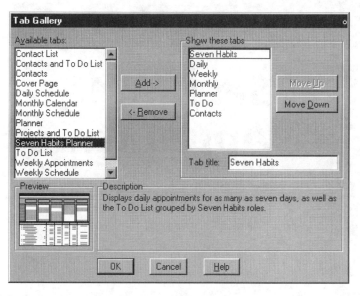

Figure 32.5 **You can add more tabs and change the name of existing tabs.**

box appears, click on the Wisdom tab and choose a bit of wisdom from
the possibilities (see Figure 32.6).

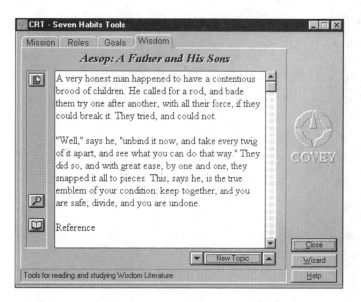

Figure 32.6 **The Seven Habits Tools is a welcome addition to Schedule+.**

Part
5

Organizing with
Schedule+

Chapter 33

Setting Up Appointments

FEATURING

The easiest way to mark an appointment on your calendar is while viewing your schedule in the Daily view.

1. Click where you want the appointment to appear on the schedule (you can also right-click drag over a block of time if the appointment is longer than 30 minutes). For example, to schedule a 12:30 pm to 2:00 pm lunch appointment, point at the block of time next to 12:30 pm and right-click drag down to 2:00 pm.

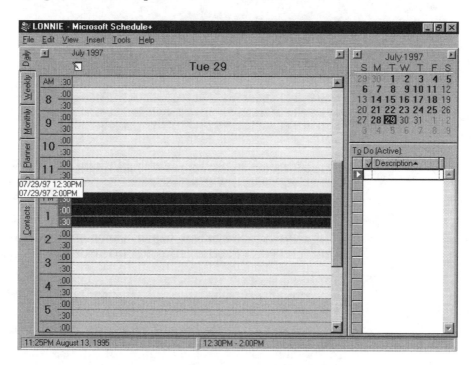

2. You can now either right-click on New Appointment from the menu that appears or select Insert ➤ Appointment from the menu bar, or press Ctrl+N. The Appointment dialog box will appear.

3. Near the top of the Appointment dialog box is a box for the start time and another for the end time of your appointment. If you highlighted a block of time before you opened up the Appointment dialog box, these boxes will already be filled in. (You can make an appointment for the entire day by selecting the All Day box on the right.)

4. Now type in a description of the appointment in the Description text box. This description will appear on your calendar and on your reminder dialog box, so be sure your description really will remind you what the appointment is about.

5. In the Where text box you can enter the appointment's location, which is useful if you attend meetings in many different offices.

6. If you would like Schedule+ to display an on-screen reminder before the appointment, click on the Set Reminder box. Two boxes will appear to the right where you enter the amount of time before the appointment that you want the reminder to appear on your screen.

7. In the first box enter the number of minutes, hours, days, weeks, or months before the appointment you wish the reminder to appear. In the second box, pick the units used in the first box. For example, to have a reminder box appear one hour before an appointment, enter **1** in the first box and select *hours* from the list in the second box.

8. You can mark the appointment as a private affair by checking the Private check box. When you mark an appointment as private, anyone else you share your schedule with will only see that you are busy in that block of time. They will not be able to see who you are meeting with or the description of the meeting.

9. If you are not sure that an appointment will really happen, you can mark it as tentative by checking the tentative box. A tentative appointment shows up in your calendar with a light gray background and the tentative icon near the top.

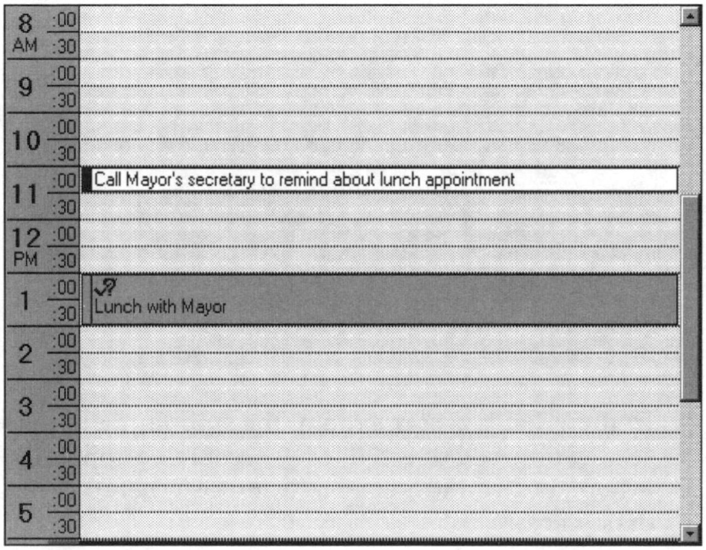

Once you have entered all the information for your appointment, click on OK. You will be returned to the calendar window. You will now see the appointment you just scheduled along with its description and its icons if you set a reminder, made the appointment private, or made it tentative.

Recurring Appointments

With Schedule+ you can add recurring appointments—like those staff meetings every other Wednesday or the department meeting on the last Friday of the month. To schedule a recurring appointment, follow these directions:

1. Follow steps 1-9 above, but don't click on OK yet.

2. Now click on the Make Recurring button at the bottom of the dialog box. The Appointment dialog box will change to the Appointment Series dialog box as shown below.

Part
5

Organizing with
Schedule+

3. In the What box at the top of the Appointment Series dialog box, you'll see the time you selected for the recurring appointment. You can't revise it here, but you can change it in the When box near the bottom of the dialog box.

4. In the This Occurs area, specify how often the recurring meeting happens. You can select Daily, Weekly, Monthly, or Yearly.

5. Depending on the meeting's frequency, different options will appear to the right. This is the area where you specify the precise frequency of the appointment. For example, when you select Weekly, this area allows you to pick the day of the week for the recurring appointment.

6. In the Duration area, you now pick how many weeks, months, or years the recurring meetings will happen. The default is that the meeting starts on the day you scheduled the first appointment and occurs indefinitely. You can enter a new starting date in the Effective box. To specify a stopping date, select the Until box and enter the end date in the text box that appears to its right.

    Once you have all of the settings correct, click on OK to return to the calendar window. The new recurring appointment will appear every day for which it is scheduled, all the way until the ending date you specified (if you did specify an ending date). You can tell an appointment is recurring because the recurring icon (circular arrow arcs) appears next to the description.

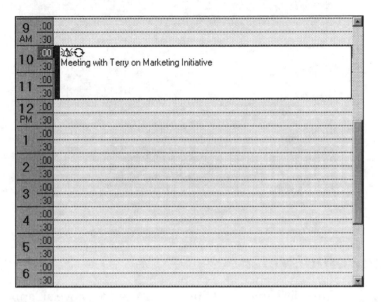

Deleting Appointments

You can delete an appointment in any of the views by right-clicking on the appointment to be deleted and choosing Delete Item from the shortcut menu. There is no confirmation on the Delete. You can Undo the deletion by pressing Ctrl+Z or choosing Edit ➤ Undo from the menu bar.

You can also delete an appointment by double-clicking on the appointment to activate the Appointment dialog box. Click on the Delete button at the bottom of the screen. Again, there is no confirmation of the appointment being deleted.

Moving an Appointment

You will sometimes find it necessary to move an appointment to another time or day. To move an appointment from any view, right-click on the appointment time. The Move Appointment dialog box will appear, and you can type in the new time and date. Alternatively, click on the drop-down list arrow to the right of the date displayed and change the date on the tiny pop-up calendar.

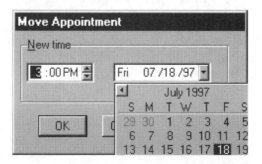

In the Daily and Weekly views, you can also drag and drop an appointment from one time to another.

Scheduling Meetings

Using the Planner, you can see your schedule across multiple days and weeks, making it easy to find free slots that could be used for meetings. In group-enabled mode, you can see the schedules of other individuals on your network. To schedule a meeting with other people, follow these steps:

1. Click on the Planner tab. The option for inviting attendees is only shown here.

2. Click on the Invite button on the right side of the Planner screen. The Select Attendees dialog box appears.

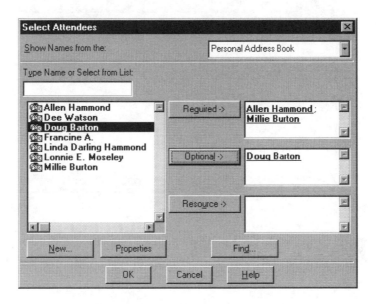

3. Select the name of the first attendee and click on either the Required, Optional, or Resource buttons. Required attendance signifies that the attendee must come to the meeting. Optional allows you to invite someone, but they do not have to attend. Resource is used for names that represent a resource, such as a specific meeting room or data show and projector.

4. Once you have finished the list of attendees, click on OK and return to the Planner Tab, where the attendees will be listed on the right in the appropriate group.

Part
5

Organizing with
Schedule+

5. Now request the meeting by sending a message to the attendees. Click on the Request Meeting button at the bottom of the attendee list and compose an Exchange mail message inviting the individuals and/or requesting the resources for the meeting. When you have finished composing a message, choose File ➤ Send or press Ctrl+Enter to send the Meeting Request. The meeting will now be added to your schedule.

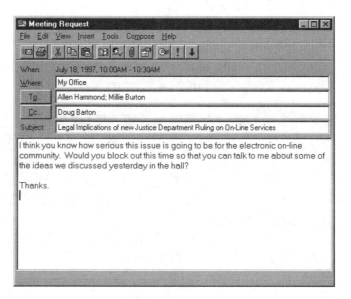

 TIP You can use the Meeting Wizard to walk you through the steps for scheduling meetings. Choose Tools ➤ Make Meeting from the menu bar and follow the Wizard's steps and prompts.

Chapter 34

Managing Projects and Tasks

FEATURING

n addition to allowing you to schedule appointments on your calendar, Schedule+ helps you keep track of your ongoing projects and tasks. Schedule+ includes a To Do list, which allows you to create projects and assign tasks to each project. You can create alarms that will sound at certain times for a project, as well as reminders that will pop up on your computer screen to remind you of your tasks.

To view tasks, select the To Do tab along the left side of the Schedule+ window. The window will change to display a list of Projects (as shown below).

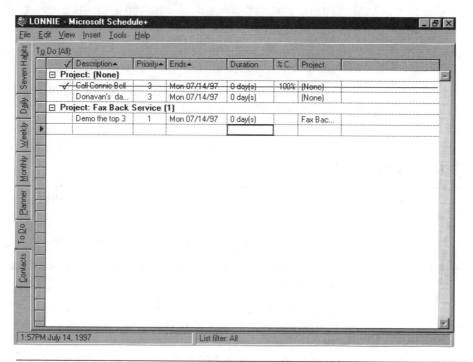

 TIP Schedule+ comes with a project called (None) already set up. When you have a task that stands alone—that is not part of a bigger project—you can assign it to this project. (None) is Schedule+'s miscellaneous project.

Adding a Project

To add a new project to your task list, you need to have the To Do window displayed on your screen. Then follow these steps:

1. Either right-click on the To Do window and select New Project from the menu that appears or select Insert ➤ Project from the menu bar. Either way, the Project dialog box will appear.

2. In the Name box, type in the name of the project.

3. In the Priority box, select a priority for the project. You will later be able to sort your tasks based on priority.

4. If the project is private, check the Private box. This will prevent other people who share your schedule from seeing the project.

    Once you have entered all of the information for the project, click on OK to create the project. You will now see your project listed in the To Do window.

Adding a Task

Once you have created a project, you can add tasks associated with the project.

1. First click on the project in the To Do window to highlight it.

2. Now either right-click and select New Task or select Insert ➤ Task from the menu bar. The Task dialog box will appear, as shown below.

3. If the task has a definite ending date, you can select the Ends button and enter the date into the text box on the left. Indicate the duration of the task in days, weeks, or months by selecting a duration in the Starts box. If you are confident that when the end date passes the task will have been completed, check the Mark as Done after End Date box. Schedule+ will automatically cross it out as a completed task after the end date.

4. Now type a description of the task in the Description box. This description will appear in your To Do list, so make it something you will understand.

5. Click on OK. The To Do list will appear again, now including your new task.

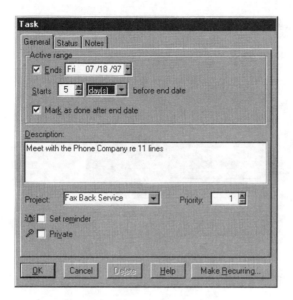

Keeping Tabs on Tasks

Use the Task dialog box to mark a task as partly—or even completely—finished. Right-click on the task and choose Edit Item. When the Task dialog box appears, select the Status tab (see next page). In the Percentage Complete box, type or use the arrows to indicate how much of the task you've completed. If you wish to track the amount of effort the task required compared to what you thought the amount of effort would be, enter this information in the Actual Effort and Estimated Effort boxes. Seeing the difference in amounts helps you to be more realistic about the requirements for getting something done or to find the bottlenecks in a process. When you have finished entering the information, click on OK.

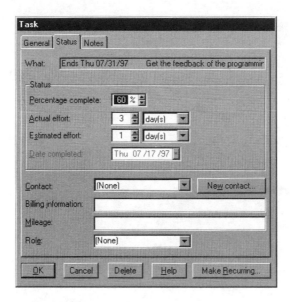

Creating a Recurring Task

There will be times when your schedule will include tasks that recur on a regular basis. These may be tasks that don't need to be completed during any specific time frame but do need to appear on your To Do list every day, week, month, or other regular interval.

To create a recurring task:

1. Select Insert ➤ Task from the menu bar to open the Task dialog box in Figure 34.1.

2. Enter the information for the task and click on the Make Recurring button.

3. The Make Recurring button opens the Task Series dialog box, which has three groups of options.

4. The This Occurs buttons allow you to specify whether your recurring task is daily, weekly, monthly, or yearly.

5. The option group to the right of This Occurs changes according to your previous choice so you can provide details about the recurring task (see Figure 34.2).

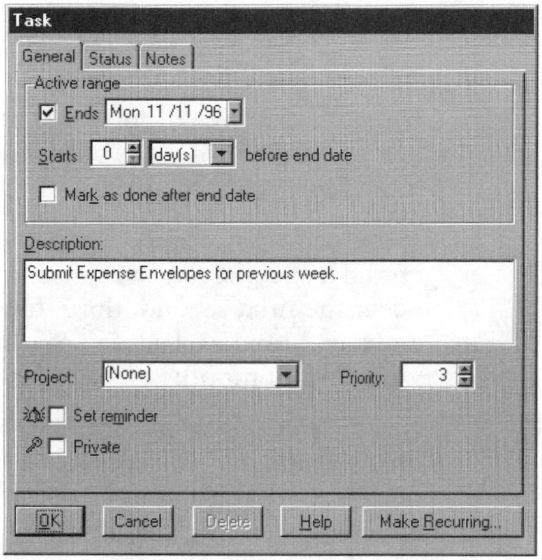

Figure 34.1 **Entering the basic information for a recurring task in the Task dialog box.**

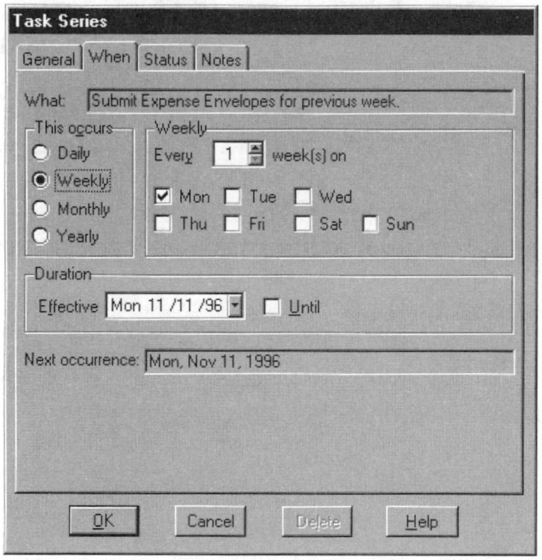

Figure 34.2 **The Task Series dialog box shows the options for the recurring details of a task.**

Part
5

Organizing with
Schedule+

- If you choose Daily, you can specify that the task occur every x number of days.

- If you choose Weekly, not only can you specify that the task occurs every x number of days, but you can specify which day(s) of the week you want it to appear on your To Do list.

- If you choose Monthly, you can either choose to have the task occur on a specific day every x number of days or you can have it occur the first, second, third, fourth, or last day, weekday, weekend day, Monday, Tuesday, Wednesday, Thursday, or Friday every x number of months.

- If you choose Yearly, you can either choose to have the task occur on a specific day of a specific month or you can have it occur the first, second, third, fourth, or last day, weekday, weekend day, Monday, Tuesday, Wednesday, Thursday, or Friday of a specific month.

6. The last option group, Duration, has a box where you can input the first day of the task and an Until check box that, if checked, makes visible a box where you can specify the date the task should cease recurring.

7. Once you have set the options to fit your specific task, click on OK.

8. The recurring tasks will appear in your To Do list on the appropriate days. If you do not mark a recurring task as completed and enough time goes by that another occurrence of the task is triggered, a second reminder of your task will appear on your To Do list.

Chapter 35
Contacts

FEATURING

You can use Schedule+ to keep the names, addresses, and other information about all of your business contacts.

To use Schedule+'s Contact feature, click on the Contacts tab along the left side of the window. Schedule+ will display the Contacts window as shown below.

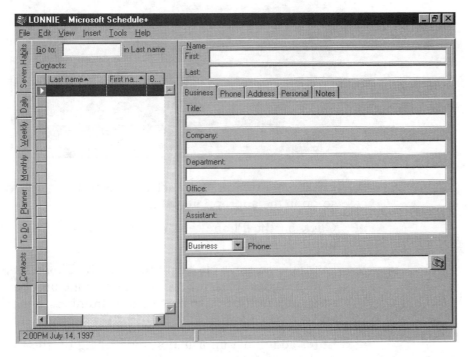

Adding a Person

To add a person to the Contacts database:

1. Select Insert ➤ Contact from the menu bar. The Contact dialog box will appear (as shown below).

   You can enter different types of information by selecting the appropriate tab from the top of the Contact dialog box. The Business tab is already selected; its dialog box displays fields used to enter basic information about the person's name and business.

2. Enter the person's name in the Name area's First and Last fields.

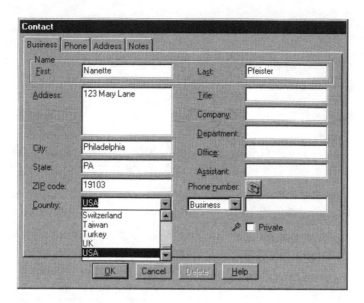

3. Enter other information such as their address, title, company name, and so on in the appropriate fields.

4. Click on the Phone tab. You will now see fields for entering phone numbers.

5. Enter the person's phone numbers in the Phone Number fields. Schedule+ provides space for two business phone numbers, a fax number, an assistant's number, two home phone numbers, a mobile phone number, and a pager number.

6. Enter additional information by clicking on the two remaining tabs—Address and Notes. The Address tab allows you to enter personal information about your contact, such as a home address and phone number. You can also enter birthday and anniversary information, which will automatically appear as an appointment on your calendar. Use the Notes tab to enter miscellaneous information about the contact. After you've entered all the information you have about the person, click on OK to return to the Contacts window. Your new contact will be visible on your screen.

TIP You can see and edit a list of annual events—such as birthdays and anniversaries—by choosing Edit ➤ Edit List ➤ Annual Events and double-clicking on the event you wish to edit.

TIP Notice the telephone icon that appears next to the phone number as you are looking through your contact database. As long as you have a modem attached to your computer, you can call any displayed phone number by clicking on the telephone icon.

Customizing Contact Columns

You can customize the column selections and their order in your Contact List. You may want to see the contact's last name, first name, business phone, and birthday; or company, last name, first name, and business phone.

With the Contacts tab selected, choose View ➤ Columns ➤ Custom. The Columns dialog box appears with the list of available fields on the left and the current columns on the right, as shown below.

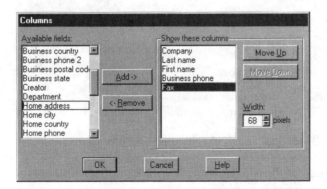

To add a column from the Available Fields list, select it on the left and click on Add. The column will be moved to the Show These Columns list on the right and no longer listed on the left. If you change your mind, click on Remove, and the column will be moved back to the Available Fields list.

If you wish to change the column order, select a column on the right in the Show These Columns list and choose the Move Up or Move Down button to reposition the column. When you're done, click on OK.

To view all your columns in the Contacts section, widen the Contacts List area by dragging to the right the vertical separation line between the contact list and the contact form. You can also widen individual columns by dragging the separation line between each column, as shown below.

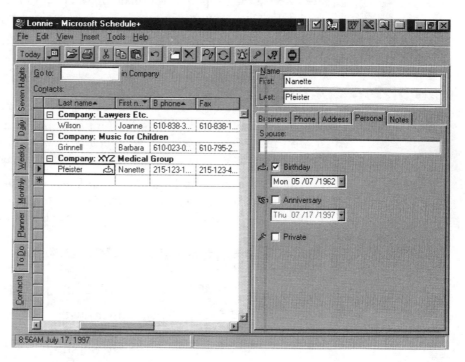

Grouping in a Column

Once you have customized your columns, you can sort your contact list by a particular column.

Choose View ➤ Group By from the menu. When the Group By dialog box, shown below, appears, select a column from the Group Contacts By box; the columns are listed in alphabetical order. If you choose Company, which is a logical choice for your first grouping, future additions will also be grouped by company name. You can then apply two additional groupings within the main grouping (such as sort by last name, then first name). You can also choose to sort in ascending or descending order: ascending sorts from low to high alphabetically (A to Z), and descending sorts from high to low.

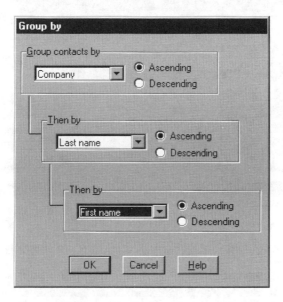

Once you have designated your groupings, click on OK. The listings will be displayed in the order you chose.

Setting an Appointment for a Contact

If you need to schedule an appointment with a person in your Contact List, use Schedule+. Click on the Contacts tab and right-click on the gray box next to the contact's row. On the shortcut menu, choose Appt. from Contact, as shown on the next page. When the Appointment dialog box appears, fill in the particulars of the appointment and click on OK. The appointment is set.

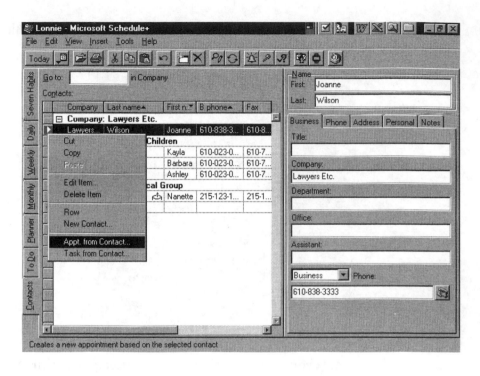

Chapter 36
Printing

FEATURING

S chedule+ allows you to print out copies of your schedule, To Do list, or contact database so you can take it with you as you move about your office or travel. Schedule+ can even print your schedule in a format suitable for putting in a Filofax book.

Printing from Schedule+

To print your Schedule+ data:

1. If you are printing your schedule, display the day you want to print.

2. Select File ➤ Print from the menu bar. The Print dialog box will appear (Figure 36.1).

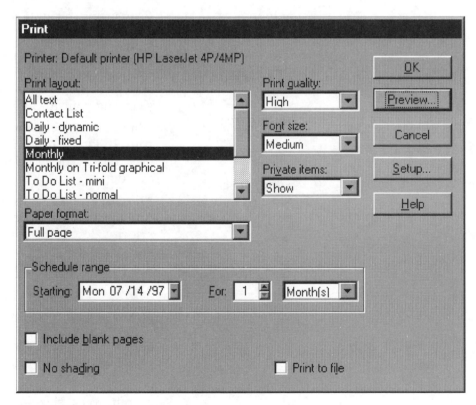

Figure 36.1 *The Print dialog box is rich with printing options.*

3. In the Print Layout box select the type of report you wish to print. Your choices are:

All Text	Prints your schedule in text-only form
Contact List	Prints your contact list
Daily - dynamic	Prints only your schedule for the day
Daily - fixed	Prints your schedule for the day, the To Do list, and your appointments outside of the normal work hours
Monthly	Prints your schedule for the month
Monthly on Tri-Fold Graphical	Prints out a compact schedule for the day with your daily appointments, a calendar of the year, and your to-do items
To Do List - mini	Prints the active items on your To Do List showing only task priority, description, and due date
To Do List - normal	Prints the active items on your To Do List showing task priority, description, start date, and end date
To Do List - text	Prints the active items on your To Do List showing only task description
Weekly—5 day	Prints your schedule for the current week, only showing Monday through Friday
Weekly—7 days	Prints your schedule for the current week, showing all seven days

4. Once you have selected the type of report you want to print, choose the paper format. If you wish to use standard paper, just leave the Full Page default setting. To select from a number of Avery forms and sizes suitable for Filofax books, click on the drop-down list arrow.

5. In the Schedule Range boxes select the range of dates you wish to print. The default value here is the day that was active when you selected File ➤ Print from the menu bar.

6. You can now click on the Preview button to see what your report will look like; one possibility is previewed below. To return to the Print dialog box, click on Close.

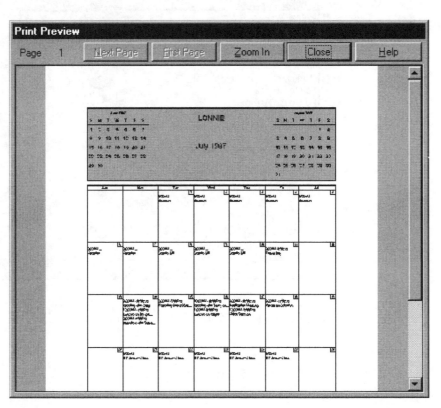

7. Now click on Print to print out your report.

Printing a Contact List

You can easily print your Contact List. To bring up the Print dialog box, click on the Print button on the toolbar, or choose File ➤ Print from the menu bar, or press Ctrl+P. Select Contact List from the Print Layout list. Choose Full Page from the Paper Format list.

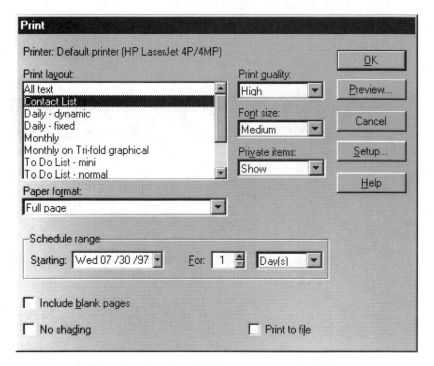

Click on the Preview button to preview the contact list fields that will print. Click on Zoom In or Zoom Out to adjust the viewing size.

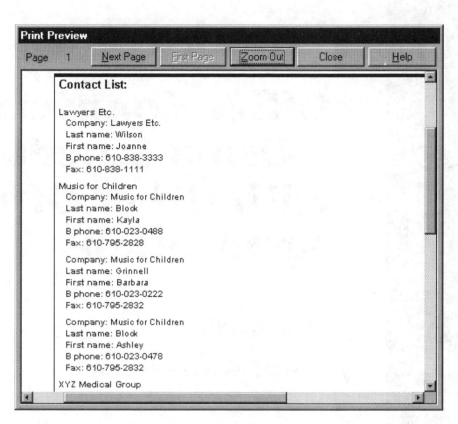

Click on Close when you have finished previewing and choose OK to print.

Exiting Schedule+

To leave Schedule+, select File ➤ Exit from the menu bar. However, once you have exited Schedule+, your appointment reminders will not appear on screen. Instead of quitting Schedule+, you can minimize it by clicking on the Minimize button; your reminders will still appear on screen.

Chapter 37

Office Connections —Using Schedule+ with Other Office Applications

FEATURING

Using Schedule+ and Word Together

Getting a Quick Letter Out

Mass Mailings with Word

Importing Data into Schedule+

The benefits of including Schedule+ with Office 95 become apparent when you discover just how easy it is to print form letters or mailing labels using Schedule+ data as the source. You won't encounter the inconvenience of exporting data into a compatible format; simply specify Schedule+ when getting data from within Word's Mail Merge Helper. If you're working in Access, for example, and all that you require are a couple of contact addresses that you saved in Schedule+, clicking the Insert Address button on the Standard toolbar lets you pick from those stored addresses.

Using Schedule+ and Word Together

Schedule+ and Word work efficiently together whether you want to get a letter out to one or one thousand of the contacts that you are keeping track of in Schedule+.

Getting a Quick Letter Out

When you want to send a letter from Word to a contact whose address is stored in Schedule+, follow these easy steps:

1. Open a new document in Word.

2. Press Enter three times.

3. Type the current date or select Insert ➤ Date and Time from the menu bar.

4. Press Enter three times.

5. Click the Insert Address button on the standard toolbar. The Select Name dialog box appears, as shown in Figure 37.1.

6. Select Schedule+ Contact List from the *Show Names from the:* combo box at the top of the dialog box.

7. Select the name of the person whose address you want to insert into your letter and click OK. The name and address will be inserted into your letter.

Once you have used a name from Schedule+, clicking on the drop down arrow to the right of the Insert Address button will reveal the name for quicker access along with other names that you previously inserted from Schedule+.

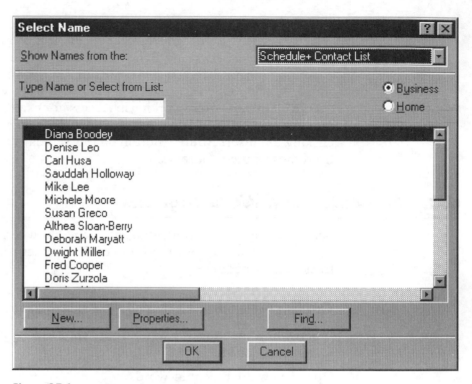

Figure 37.1   **The Select Name dialog box**

Mass Mailings with Word

On-demand availability of addresses while in your word processor provides a big leap in productivity; and with Office 95, you can also merge contact information with form letters or mailing labels. Those who have previously had to use two separate software packages for such tasks—one for letter writing and one for keeping track of contacts—will find the process of merging Schedule+ data with Word documents seamless.

1. Open a new document in Word.

2. From the menu bar, select Tools ➤ Mail Merge from the menu bar.

3. The Mail Merge Helper dialog box, shown in Figure 37.2, opens.

4. Click the Create button.

5. Select Mailing Labels from the list of possible merge formats.

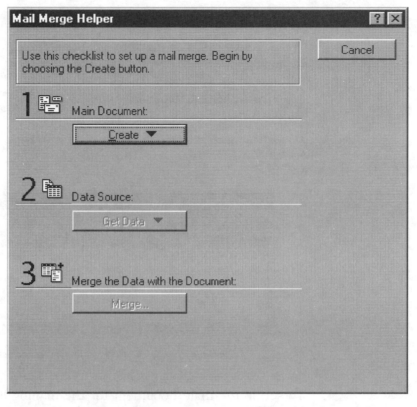

Figure 37.2   *The Mail Merge Helper dialog box*

6. You will be asked where you want to create the merge document. Select New Main Document from the dialog box shown in Figure 37.3.

7. Click the Get Data button on the Mail Merge Helper dialog box, and select Use Address Book from the list that appears.

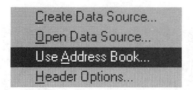

8. The Use Address Book dialog box appears next (see Figure 37.4). Select Schedule+ Contact List from the Choose Address Book list.

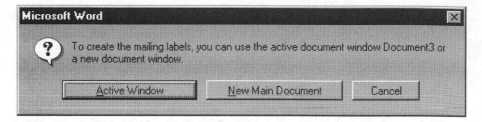

Figure 37.3   Select New Main Document to have Word create a new document for the merge document.

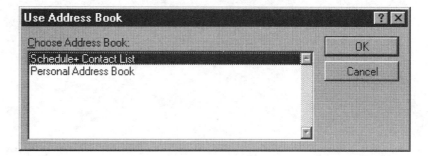

Figure 37.4   Selecting Schedule+ Contact List in the Use Address Book dialog box.

9. To set up the main document for the mailing labels, click the Set Up Main Document button on the dialog box shown in Figure 37.5.

10. Select the mailing label specifications from the Label Options dialog box (see Figure 37.6). Click OK with you're through.

11. In the Create Labels dialog box (see Figure 37.7), insert the fields that you want on your mailing labels. Click OK when finished.

12. Once you've set everything up, the third button of the Mail Merge

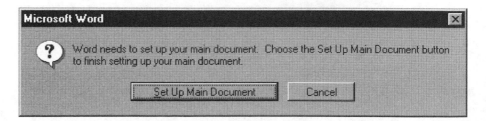

Figure 37.5   Set Up Mailing Main Document

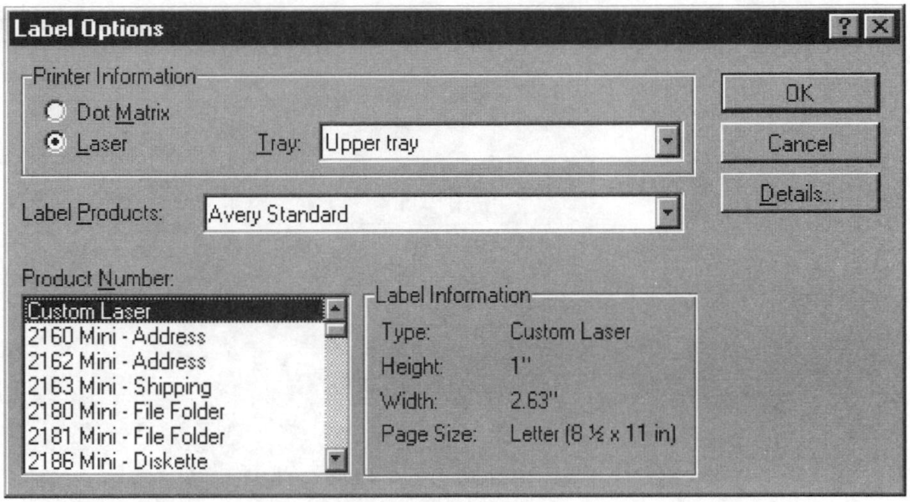

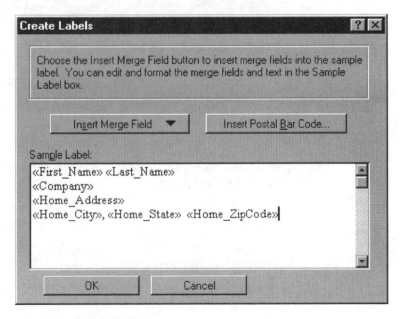

Figure 37.6   Match the information given on the actual label box with the choices in the Label Options dialog box.

Figure 37.7   Create label dialog box

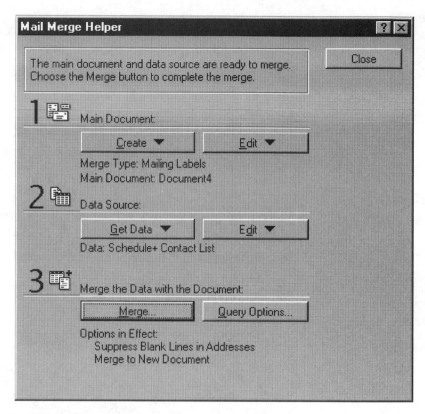

Figure 37.8   **Merge button enabled in the Mail Merge Helper.**

Helper becomes enabled. Click the Merge button now (see Figure 37.8).

13. The Merge dialog box opens next (see Figure 37.9). From here you can choose to either print to a New Document or directly to the printer.

If you do not want to include all of the people stored in your Schedule+ for a specific merge, you can limit the merge by one of these two methods:

▶ By simple record number: Specify your from and to values for the Records to be Merged group.

▶ *Or* by specifying criteria and sort order for certain fields: Use the Query Options dialog box, opened by clicking on the Query Options button.

Being able to use Word and Schedule+ together in the above fashion provides a seamless link between Personal Information Manager (PIM) and word processor previously unavailable.

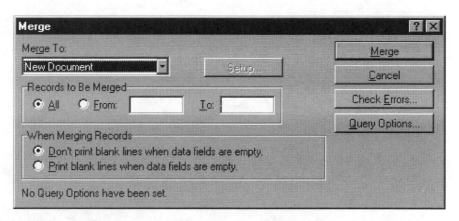

Figure 37.9   Merge dialog box ready to bring together Schedule+ and Word.

Importing Data into Schedule+

Schedule+ can easily import information in text format; this means that you can import existing data from just about any software on which you currently store your contact information, including any of the Office applications. Before importing into Schedule+ you will want to export the data into text delimited format.

To export data stored in any of the other Office applications, select File ➤ Save As from the menu bar. Using the Save As menu option you can export a Word table, Excel worksheet, or Access table to text format.

Once the data is in text format, you are all set up to use the Schedule+ Text Import Wizard.

1. Select File ➤ Import ➤ Text from the menu bar to start that Text Import Wizard.

2. The first step in Figure 37.10 allows you to browse for the file that you want to import. Once you've identified the file, click Next.

3. The second step checks to see if the first row contains field names. The file in Figure 37.11 does not.

4. The third step in the Text Import Wizard (see Figure 37.12) allows you to verify the field and text separators. Click Next after you have verified this information.

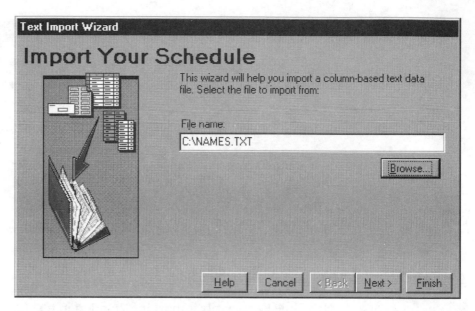

Figure 37.10   *First step of Text Import Wizard*

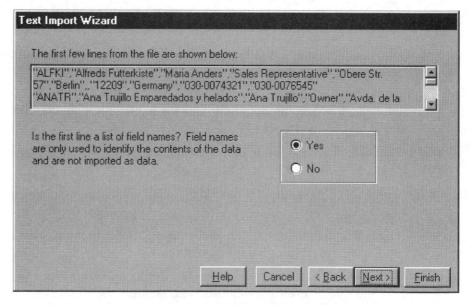

Figure 37.11   *Checking to see if the first row of your data contains field names.*

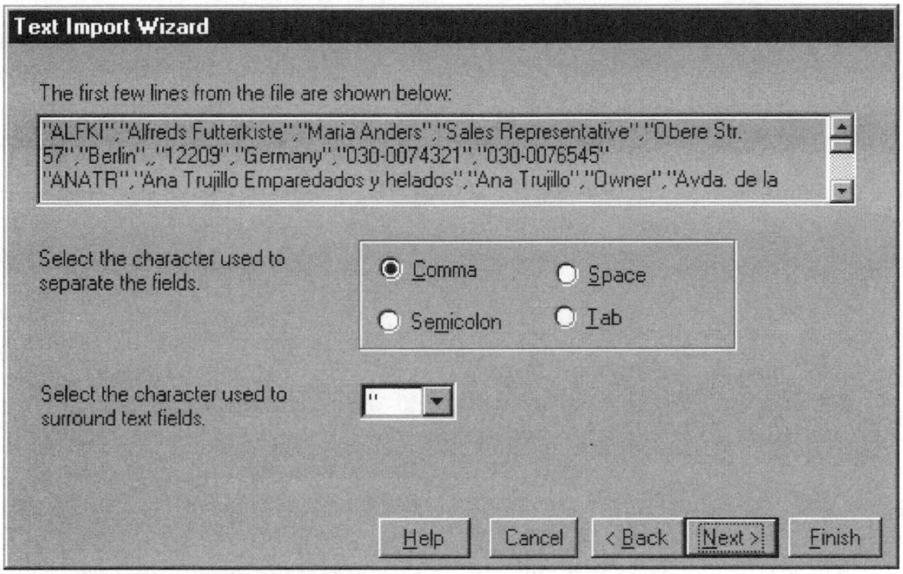

Figure 37.12   Verifying field separators

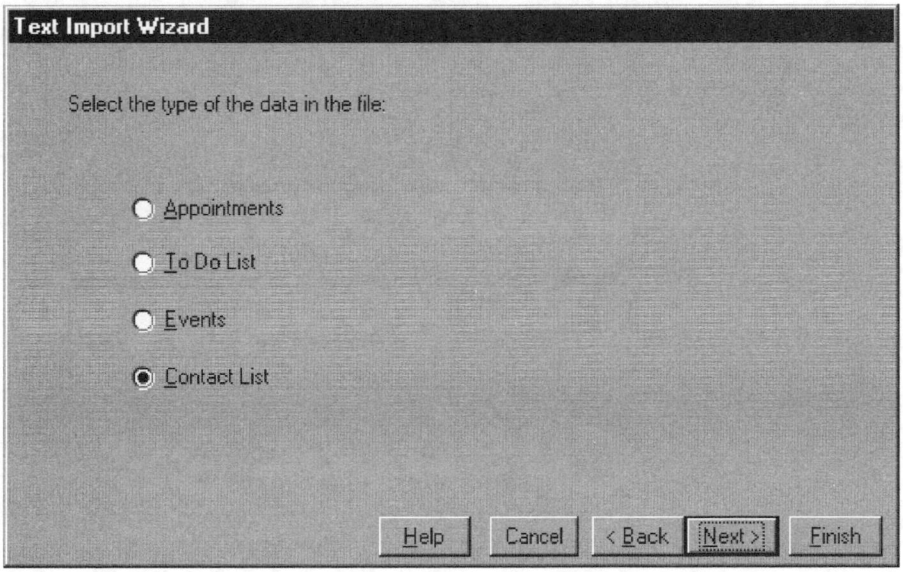

Figure 37.13   Options allowing you to choose what list to import the information into.

5. The fourth step of the Text Import Wizard asks you to select the Schedule+ area into which you want to import the data (see Figure 37.13).

6. The fifth and final step lets you match up records in your data file on the left with those available in Schedule+ on the right (see Figure 37.14). If you need to change the Schedule+ field in the right column that you want to match to your data file field to the left, click on the Schedule+ field to get a combo box that will help you pick whatever Schedule+ fields are available to match up to your field. Click Finish when you're through. Your data should now be imported.

Incorporating Schedule+ with your other Office applications allows you to take advantage of their functions for your contact and time management. The tight integration, especially with Word, gives Schedule+ a leg up on any other contact or schedule management software. Schedule+ is a welcome addition to the Office suite of packages and helps to extend the reach of the Office into your daily routines, allowing you to benefit with higher efficiency and a greater return for your efforts.

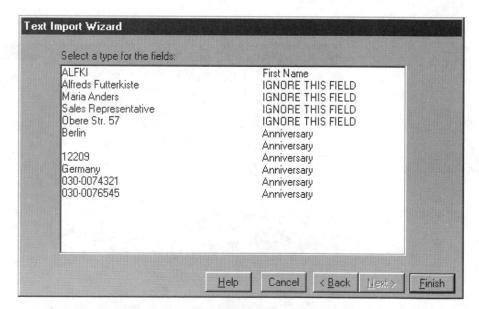

Figure 37.14 **Choosing the Schedule+ fields to match up with the fields that you are importing.**

Business Processing: Data Management with Access

Making a relational database has never been easier than it is now with this most recent release of Access. This part explains how you can create very powerful relational databases. From basic concepts and helpful Wizards to advanced tips, we cover basic database design and implementation. Quicker and easier development of forms, reports, and query development are the hallmark of this release. The integration part examines the possible needs of the fictional NorthWind Traders company, addressing the company's needs to merge Access data with Word for a monthly mailing, to substantiate presentation points using data stored in Access, and using an Excel pivot table on an Access form to analyze the data stored in Access.

Chapter 38

The Road Map / Jump Start

FEATURING

The Main Elements of Access

Creating a Quick Database with the Help of Access Wizards

Access is a Relational Database Management System (RDMS) that you can use to store and manipulate large amounts of information. Because its tools are user friendly and because it is a powerful development environment, it is equally appropriate for novices and for MIS professionals. Bernadette User, who works primarily with Microsoft Word to produce documents, can use Access to quickly and easily create a database of mailing list information that she can merge with Word documents. Nadine Professional can use Access to develop a database application that tracks customer and order information, which data entry people can operate without ever knowing they are in Access.

Beginners can use Access to:

▶ Store and manage various types of inventories such as recipes, stamps, records, or other hobby collections.

▶ Keep log information such as auto repairs for one or more cars, doctor visits for multiple family members, or daily exercise history for everyone in a training program.

▶ Create contact management databases that can track not only contacts, but phone calls to contacts, meeting with contacts, and any other interactions with contacts.

Developers and MIS professionals can use Access to develop:

▶ Order-entry systems.

▶ Applications that manage survey results.

▶ Front ends for enterprise-wide databases such as SQL server.

▶ Help-desk applications.

▶ And any other database application that departments in their organizations might need.

The above are, of course, only suggestions; the possibilities for end-user and developer use of Access are limited only by the needs of an organization and the imagination of the user or developer.

The Main Elements of Access

Access is an object-oriented program; that is, everything in Access is an object, including the application itself. Each object has properties that define how the object looks and performs.

In this chapter we will define the main object types and then use the Wizards to build a basic database that utilizes most of the objects. In the following chapters, we will delve deeper into the individual objects.

The Database Window

In Access, all objects of a database are stored in a single file, and the filename has an MDB extension. You manage objects through the Database window (see Figure 38.1).

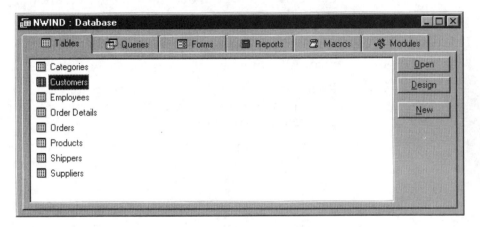

Figure 38.1   The Database window of the Northwind sample database

At the top of the Database window are six tabs, each representing one of the main object types. Selecting a tab switches the view of the window to reveal a list of the objects of the type selected that are stored in the current database.

On the right side of the window are three buttons.

▶ The first button is labeled Open, Run, or Preview, depending on which tab is selected. Clicking on the first button activates the selected object.

▶ The second button is labeled Design. Clicking on it opens the selected object in Design view so that you can modify its structure and properties.

▶ The third button is labeled New. Clicking on it starts the process of creating a new object of the type of the selected tab.

TIP To quickly bring the Database window to the front, on top of other windows that are currently open, press F11.

Tables

Tables are the primary building blocks of any Access database. All data is stored in tables. Every table in your database should focus on one subject, for example, Customers, Orders, or Products. Every row, or record, in your table is a single unique instance of that subject (for example, every record in a Customers table would provide information about one customer). The characteristics of each customer are separated into the fields. For example, First Name, Last Name, Address, City, State, Zip, Phone, and Birthday would all be fields that could make up a record in a Customers table.

Figure 38.2 shows a table in Design view. The top pane of the window lists the individual fields of a table, the type of data those fields can store, and, optionally, a description of the fields. The bottom pane shows the properties of the current field in the top pane. Field properties determine how data is formatted in the field and whether that data must meet any specific criteria. You build the structure of your tables in Design view, telling Access which fields and which types of fields you want to store in the table.

You enter or view data in Datasheet view. Figure 38.3 shows a table in Datasheet view. In Datasheet view, every row is a record in the table, and the columns are the fields of the records. Using this view, you can add, modify, delete, view, sort, find, filter, and format the data in the table. Although accessing table data through the Datasheet view is the most direct method, you can also access table data through forms that you create—a more visually appealing experience. Once you have the table datasheet looking the way that you want it, you can print the datasheet. Because formatting is limited in Datasheet view, however, you'll generally want to print from Report view.

Queries

A query is a question that you ask of the data that is stored in the tables of your database. For example, you can create a query that asks for only those customers in the state of California or that finds all employees who

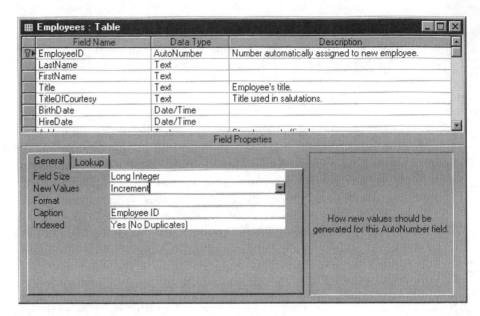

Figure 38.2 *To open the Design view of a table, click on the Design button on the Tables page of the Database window.*

Employees : Table				
Employee ID	**Last Name**	**First Name**	**Title**	**Title Of Courtesy**
1	Davolio	Nancy	Sales Representative	Ms.
2	Fuller	Andrew	Vice President, Sales	Dr.
3	Leverling	Janet	Sales Representative	Ms.
4	Peacock	Margaret	Sales Representative	Mrs.
5	Buchanan	Steven	Sales Manager	Mr.
6	Suyama	Michael	Sales Representative	Mr.
7	King	Robert	Sales Representative	Mr.
8	Callahan	Laura	Inside Sales Coordinator	Ms.
9	Dodsworth	Anne	Sales Representative	Ms.
(AutoNumber)				

Record: 1 of 9

Figure 38.3 *To open the Datasheet view of a table, click on the Open button on the Tables page of the Database window.*

have birthdays in the current month. You can also use queries to determine which fields of a table will be included in a new datasheet. Most Access databases contain more than one table, and you can use queries to pull specific fields from multiple tables into one datasheet. The datasheet that a query returns is called a recordset.

Some queries do not provide recordsets. The job of these special queries, called Action queries, is to perform bulk updates on your data. For example, you can use Action queries to find and delete the records of customers with no sales activity in the past year. You use Action queries to update, append, or delete records in tables or to construct new tables from the results of the query.

Figure 38.4 shows the Design view of a query. The top pane lists the table(s) that are supplying the data for the query. The bottom pane shows the QBE, or Query by Example, grid in which you place fields from the table(s) in the top pane that will be included in the results of the query. The QBE grid is also the place where you can specify any criteria or sorting that will be applied to any fields.

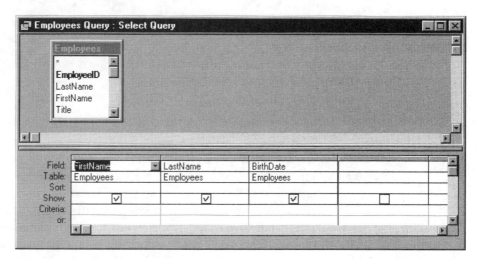

Figure 38.4   *Design view of a query*

To view the answer of a query, you open the query in Datasheet view. The Datasheet view of a query looks just like the Datasheet view of a table, and you manipulate the data in a query datasheet in the same way you manipulate data in a table datasheet. One primary difference between the two, however, is that the fields in a query datasheet may not always be updatable. This situation may occur when you are using more than one table in a query and do not include enough fields in the query to make a valid record in the table(s) it was built on or if you include calculated fields that are based on expressions that use values from multiple fields. An unupdatable query can also occur if that datasheet is the result of a totals query, a query that groups data instead of providing the detail. Figure 38.5 shows a query datasheet.

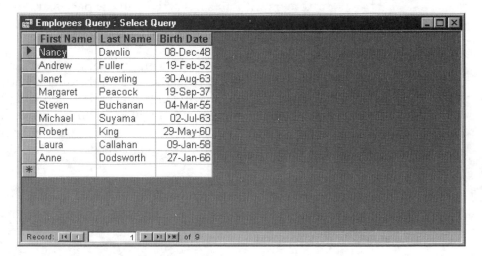

Figure 38.5   *A query datasheet*

NOTE   An important concept to remember about queries is that you are storing the question and not the datasheet. If you run a query that asks for all companies in the state of Oregon, you will get a datasheet of those records that match your criterion. If you close the query, add records of Oregon companies to the table(s) on which the query is based, and then run the query again, the datasheet will reflect your changes because every time you open the query, it is run anew, and it asks the question of the current data.

Forms

Access forms serve two functions. The first is to present the data in a table or a query in a format that is easy to view or update. Forms can be bound to a table or to a query. The fields in that table or query are then available to place on that form. You can edit the form just as you would edit the datasheet of the bound table or query, or you can set parameters that restrict the form's use to only viewing data, only adding data, or only editing data without the ability to add records.

The second function of forms is primarily for people who are developing applications with Access. The forms in this category do not need to be bound to a table or a query. They are used to create the interface portion of an Access application. You can, for instance, create forms called Switchboards that aid in navigating to other forms and functions of the application, you can create forms to use as dialog or message boxes, and you can create forms on which a user can enter information and then click on a button that dynamically creates a report or a query based on the information.

The easiest way to design forms bound to a table or to a query is to use the Form Wizards. Whether you are a novice or an advanced user, you can use the Form Wizards to design the bulk of a form and then make any necessary changes in Design view. Figure 38.6 shows a form in Form view. Figure 38.7 shows the same form in Design view. To learn more about the Design view of a form, see the chapter on forms. Finally, Figure 38.8 shows an example of a Switchboard form that you can create to open other forms and to provide a central focus for an application, for example, a Main menu.

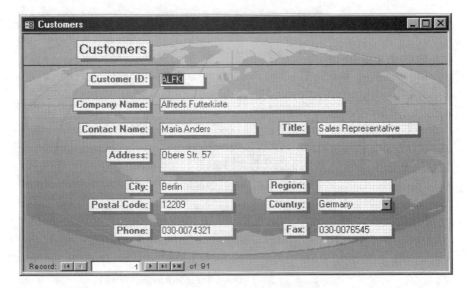

Figure 38.6   *The Form view of a form*

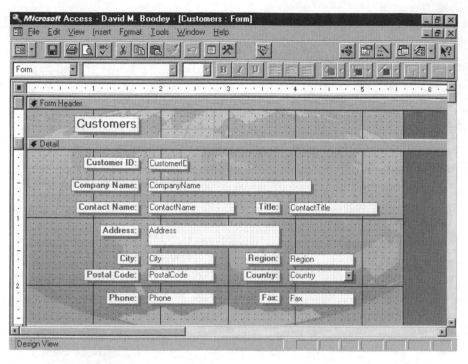

Figure 38.7 **The Design view of a form**

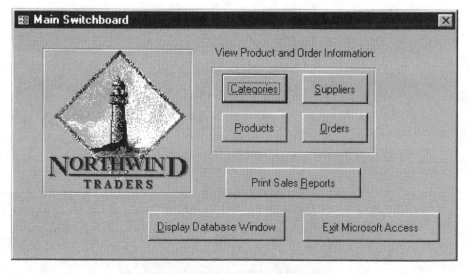

Figure 38.8 **A form called a Switchboard can be used as the control center of a database.**

Reports

Whether we like it or not, we are still a paper-based society; printing the results of the data we store—reports—is still necessary. With Access, you can quickly and easily design reports based on your data.

Like forms, reports can be bound to a table or to a query that could incorporate the fields from one or more tables. Report Wizards can help make report writing a cinch. Like the Form Wizards, Report Wizards may not provide exactly what you want, but you can always make adjustments in Design view. See the chapter on reports for more detailed information about designing reports.

An Access report is not restricted to your basic row and column format. It can be a catalog of products, mailing labels, a graph, or any other form that can take advantage of the WYSIWYG (what you see is what you get) capabilities of the Design view of a report. Figure 38.9 shows the preview of what many consider a basic report, and Figure 38.10 shows a preview of a mailing label report.

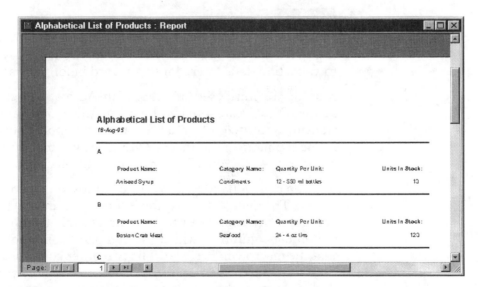

Figure 38.9 *A basic columnar report preview utilizing the formatting capabilities of the Access report Design view*

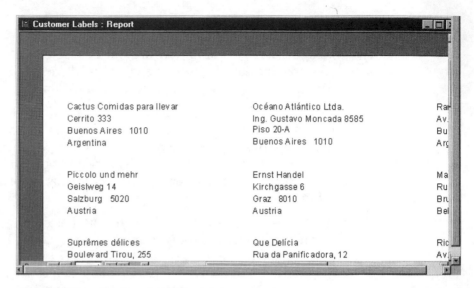

Figure 38.10 **A preview of a mailing label report**

Macros

Macros provide an easy, effective method for automating many database tasks. You can use macros for everything from displaying message boxes to validating data entered into a record before it is saved.

Macros are composed of actions. In Access, you can choose from 49 actions. You create a macro by listing the actions in the order that you want them to be performed. Each action appears in an individual row in the top pane of the macro Design view. The bottom pane shows the arguments or the specifics for the current macro action in the top pane.

The top pane is divided into four columns; only two of which are visible at first. The main column is the Action column, in which you specify the action for the row. The other column visible from the beginning is the Comment column, in which you can place comments about the actions that the macro will perform. The two other columns are labeled Condition and Macro Name. To open either column, you can click on its toolbar button, choose it from the View menu, or right-click the mouse on the Design view title bar. You can use the Condition column to test an expression. If the condition returns true, the action on that row is run; if the condition returns false, the action is skipped. The Macro Name column provides a way to group a number of small macros into one macro design window, thus reducing the number of macros listed in the Database window.

Macros can be run from a number of places in the database. To run a macro from the Database window, select it and click on the Run button or simply double-click on it. You can also run a macro by selecting Tools ➤ Macro from the menu bar. The most common place to run a macro, however, is from the Event page that contains the properties of an object.

When you design forms and reports, the forms and reports and the other objects that you place on them all have event properties. An event is something that can happen to an object. For example, a form has a Before Update property that gets triggered right before a record on the form is saved. If you have placed the name of your macro in the Before Update property of the form, your macro will run right before the current record of the form is saved. If you place a button on a form, the button has an On Click event that is triggered whenever the button is pressed. If the name of a macro that opens the Employees form is set to the On Click event of a button on another form, the Employees form opens when the button is clicked on. More discussion of events and examples of using them to automate your database are in the chapter on macros.

Macros can be as simple as the one in Figure 38.11, which displays a message box that says "Hello World!" Or they can be as complicated as the one in Figure 38.12, which validates the postal codes entered into a form and displays a message box informing the user if they are incorrect.

Modules

Modules are the containers for any programming code written in an Access database. The two types of modules in an Access database are global and form or report.

Global modules are listed in your Database window. The code that you store in these modules is available everywhere in your application; hence, the name global.

Every form or report that you design has its own module that can store code. If you import or export the form or report to another database, the code travels with the form or report. The code in the form or report modules is available only when the form is open and, even then, can only be called from the form or report in which it is stored.

Macro1 : Macro
Action
Comment
MsgBox
Opens a Messgae box displaying Hello World!
Action Arguments
Message
Hello World!
Beep
Yes
Type
None
Title
Greeting
Enter the text to display in the message box title bar. For example, 'Customer ID Validation.' Press F1 for help on this argument.

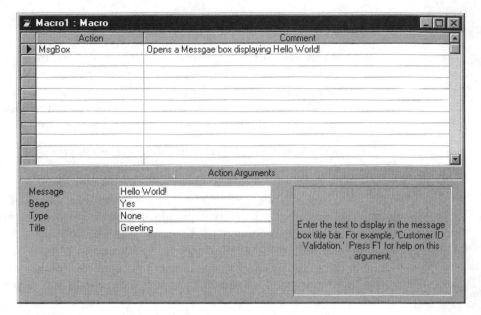

Figure 38.11 **Design view of a macro that opens a message box**

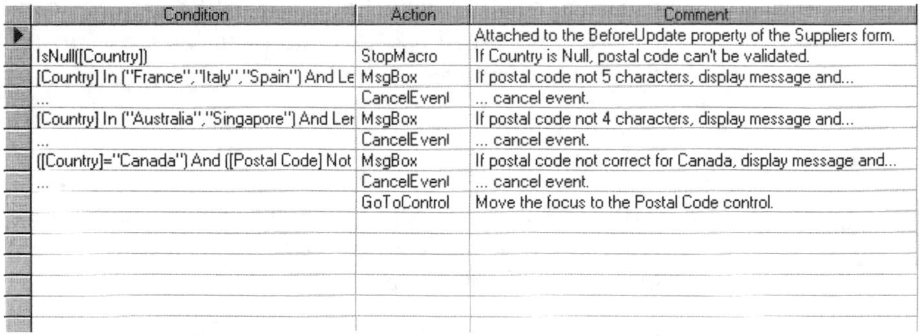

Condition
Action
Comment
Attached to the BeforeUpdate property of the Suppliers form.
IsNull([Country])
StopMacro
If Country is Null, postal code can't be validated.
[Country] In ("France","Italy","Spain") And Le
MsgBox
If postal code not 5 characters, display message and...
...
CancelEvent
... cancel event.
[Country] In ("Australia","Singapore") And Ler
MsgBox
If postal code not 4 characters, display message and...
...
CancelEvent
... cancel event.
([Country]="Canada") And ([Postal Code] Not
MsgBox
If postal code not correct for Canada, display message and...
...
CancelEvent
... cancel event.
GoToControl
Move the focus to the Postal Code control.

Figure 38.12 **Design view of a macro that validates the data entered into a form**

The language that Access uses for code is VBA, or Visual Basic for Applications. If you have written code for previous versions of Access using Access Basic, the transition should be relatively smooth. The syntax changes are minor, and with only a slight bit of tweaking, most of your code should run without problem with VBA.

Data Management
with Access

NOTE   Programming with VBA is generally the preserve of intermediate level users to developers. Although the scope of this book does not allow for the depth necessary to cover VBA completely, the chapter on automating Access will provide you with a foundation.

Relationships

When working with Access, you can create and use multiple tables, which helps reduce redundancy in a database. For example, to track customer orders in a spreadsheet program, you would have to repeat the customer information, such as Name, Address, and so on, for every order. In Access, you can create a table to store customer names and another table to store order information. In the Customers table, you create a field, called a primary key, that uniquely identifies each customer. In the Orders table, you need store only the ID, or the primary key, of the customer in the Customers table. Because you will have multiple tables that need to be connected in some way (for example, the Orders table needs to know which field in the Customers table to refer to in order to select the correct customer), you create relationships between tables. You use primary keys all the time in your day-to-day life. In your wallet you are probably carrying a card that has a primary key embossed on it. Your driver's license number, your frequent flyer account, and your credit card numbers are all examples of primary keys. The institutions that assign you these numbers use them to uniquely identify you among the thousands, possibly millions, of people that they track. Their databases use your primary key to track all your transactions, for example, traffic violations, flights, or purchases. Creating and working with relationships requires a bit more explanation, and you can find it in the chapter devoted to relationships.

Creating a Database Quickly with the Help of Access Wizards

Now that you are familiar with the basic components of Access, we can run through a couple of exercises that, when finished, will produce a complete Access database. With the help of the Access Wizards, these exercises will be swift and will demonstrate that with almost no knowledge of Access one can create a fully functioning database.

> **TIP** The following exercise uses the individual object Wizards to generate a table. If you are really new to creating databases and have no idea where to start, you might want to create a database by selecting the Database Wizard from the opening Microsoft Access dialog box instead of clicking on the Blank Database button. You can also access the Database Wizard by selecting File ➤ New Database from the menu bar. The Database Wizard handles everything from selecting the tables and fields to building the forms and reports you will need.

Starting Access

The first step is to start Access and begin a new database.

1. From the Start button menu, select Programs ➤ Microsoft Access.

2. In the Microsoft Access dialog box (shown in Figure 38.13), select the Blank Database option button and click on OK.

3. In the File New Database dialog box (shown in Figure 38.14), type **My Application** in the File name text box and then click on Create.

Figure 38.13   *The opening dialog box in Microsoft Access*

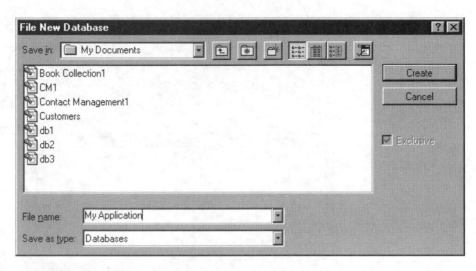

Figure 38.14   *The File New Database dialog box*

After you specify the database name, you are presented with an empty Database window. Your job now is to create all the objects you want in your database. Our example database will track basic phone book entries.

Building a Table to Store Phone Book Entries

The first step in creating a database is to design the table(s) that will hold your data. Using the Table Wizard, this is a snap.

1. Be sure that the Tables tab of the Database window is selected.

2. Click on the New button in the Database window.

3. The New Table dialog box opens.

4. Select Table Wizard from the list and click on OK.

5. After a couple of seconds the Table Wizard dialog box opens (see Figure 38.15).

6. You can choose which types of tables you want to use as samples: Business or Personal. Select Personal.

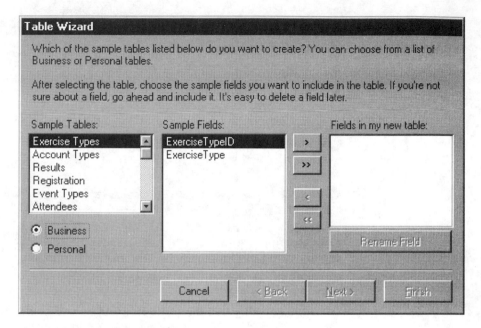

Figure 38.15   **The Table Wizard dialog box**

7. Now scroll through the Sample Tables list box until you find Friends and select it.

8. In the Sample Fields list box, select the following fields and click the > button after each one to send them to the *Fields in my new table* list box: Friend ID, FirstName, LastName, SpouseName, Address, City, StateOrProvince, PostalCode, HomePhone, WorkPhone, Birthdate, and Notes.

9. Your Table Wizard dialog box should look like the one in Figure 38.16.

10. Click on Next, and the second Table Wizard dialog box opens (see Figure 38.17).

11. Accept Friends as the name of your table and leave the button pressed that is telling Access to create a primary key for you. (Primary keys are discussed in the chapter on tables.) Now, click on Next.

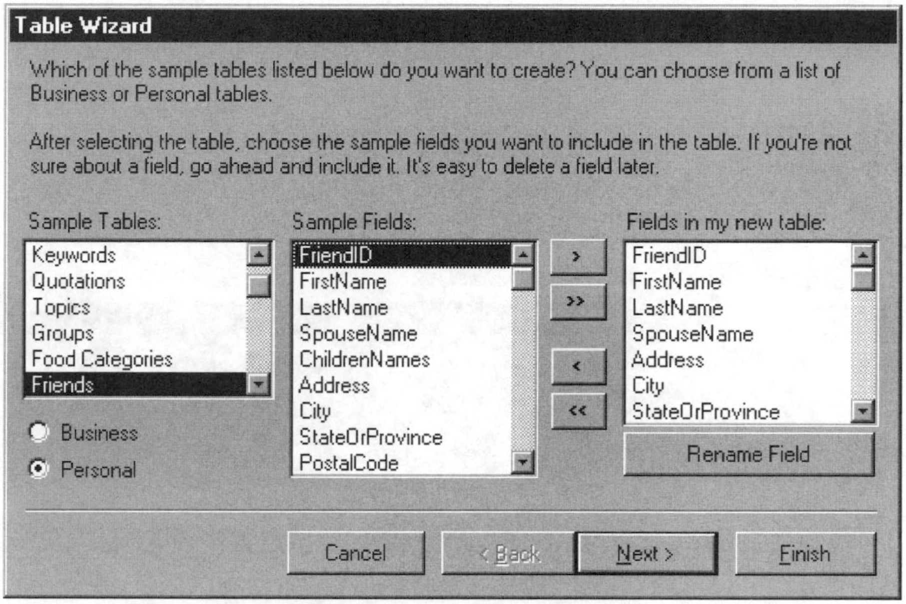

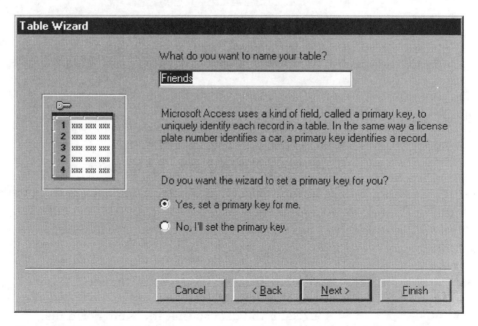

Figure 38.16 *Building a Friends table with the Table Wizard*

Figure 38.17 *Defining the name of your table and allowing Access to create a primary key with the Table Wizard*

12. In the last dialog box for the Table Wizard (see Figure 38.18), select *Modify the table design* radio button and then click on Finish.

13. The Wizard generates the table and then displays the Design view of the Friends table as shown in Figure 38.19.

14. After investigating the design, select File ➤ Close from the menu bar or click on the close button in the title bar.

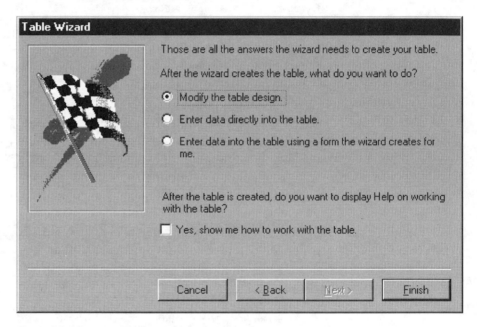

Figure 38.18 *The last dialog box of the Table Wizard*

Making Data Entry Easy with a Form

The next object that we want to create is a form so that entering data in the table will be easy.

1. In the Database window, select the Forms tab.

2. Click on the New button.

3. In the New Form dialog box, select Form Wizard from the list box at the top and select the Friends table in the combo box in the middle as the source for the data so that the New Form dialog box looks like the one in Figure 38.20. Click on OK to continue.

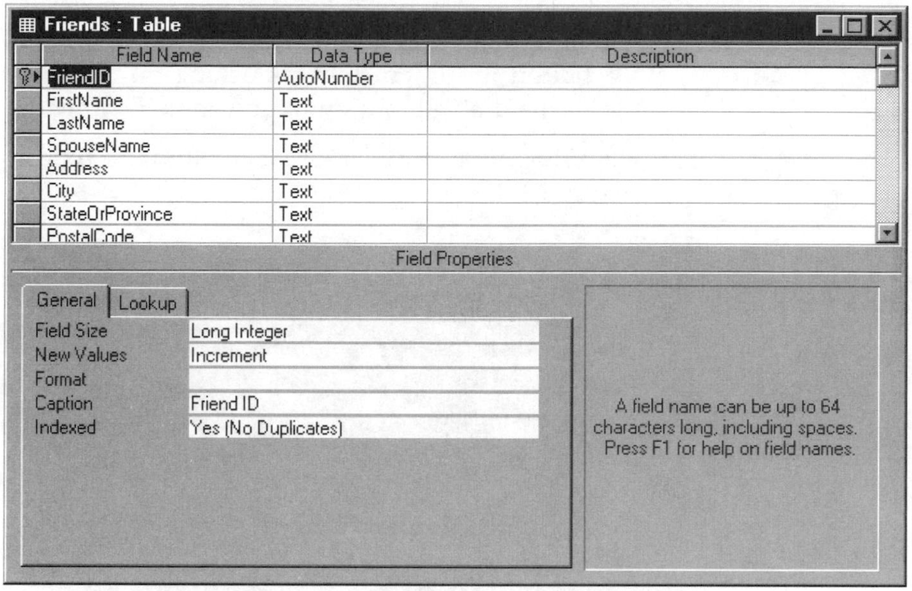

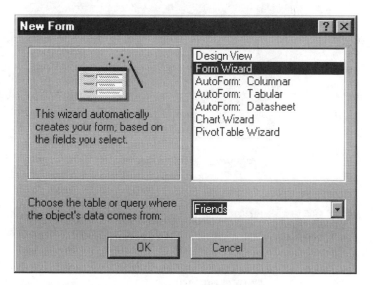

Figure 38.19 *The Friends table in Design view*

Figure 38.20 *The New Form dialog box set for the Form Wizard to use the Friends Table as the data source*

4. In the first Form Wizard dialog box you select the fields to include on the form. Send over all the fields except for FriendID by clicking on the >> button and then double-clicking on the FriendID field to send it back. The dialog box should now look like the one in Figure 38.21.

5. Click on Next and choose a Columnar report layout as shown in Figure 38.22

6. Click on Next.

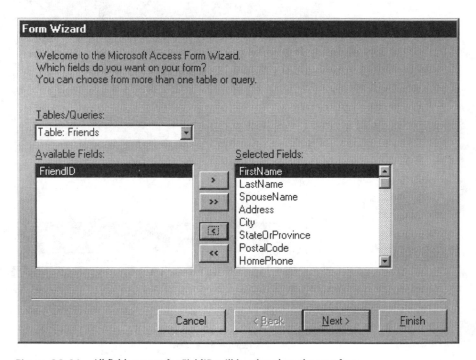

Figure 38.21   *All fields except for FieldID will be placed on the new form.*

 NOTE We left FieldID off the form because it is an automatic number field that Access increments on its own. There really is no reason for it to be on this form since the user does not need to enter the number. The number is being used to uniquely identify each friend. This is explained later in the chapter on forms.

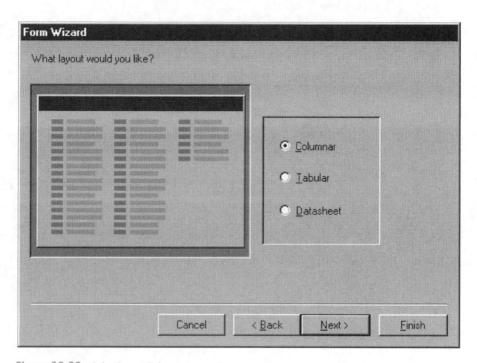

Figure 38.22 **Selecting a Columnar report**

7. The Form Wizard prompts you for a style for your report. Select Win95 and click on Next.

8. The last dialog box will ask for a name for the form that you want to create and what you want the Wizard to do when it finishes designing the form. Leave the default of Friends for the name and the *Open the form to view or enter information* radio button selected as in Figure 38.23.

9. Click on Finish.

Your form will open in Form view so that you can enter some records. To enter your first record, click on the First Name text box and type the name of your first friend. Now press Tab to move from field to field and press Shift+Tab to move back field by field. When you reach the last field on the form, in this case the Notes field, press Tab; Access moves you to the next record. Some basic data entry techniques are listed below. Refer to the chapter on forms for more detail.

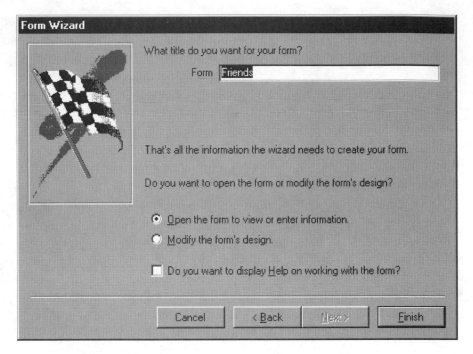

Figure 38.23 *The last step of the Form Wizard*

NOTE   You can also use the Enter key to move from field to field. When doing so, be sure that the Enter Key Behavior property of text boxes is set to Default Behavior and not to New Line in Field. If it is set to New Line in Field, pressing enter will not move to the next control but will insert a new line in the field bound to the text box. If the Enter Key Behavior property of text boxes is set to Default Behavior, pressing enter while in the text box will perform one of the three Move After Enter options (Don't Move, Next Field, Next Record) set by selecting Tools ➤ Options ➤ Keyboard.

▶ To add a new record, choose Insert ➤ Record from the menu bar.

▶ To delete the current record, choose Edit ➤ Delete Record.

▶ To move from one record to the next, press PgUp and PgDn.

▶ To undo changes to the current field or record, press the Esc key once.

After entering the information about some of your friends into your database, close the form by choosing File->Close from the menu bar or by pressing Ctrl+W.

Creating a Query to Question Your Data

You might want to generate a list of only your friends' names and phone numbers. You can do this by using a query to select only those fields that you want to view.

1. From the Database window, select the Queries tab.

2. Click on the New button.

3. In the New Query dialog box, select Simple Query Wizard and click on OK.

4. In the Select Query Wizard dialog box, send the FirstName, LastName, and HomePhone fields to the Selected Fields list box using the > button or by double-clicking on them. Click on the Next pushbutton when you are ready to continue.

5. In the last Select Query Wizard dialog box, change the name of the query to Phone Numbers, but leave the radio button selected to *Open the query to view information* as shown in Figure 38.24. Click on Finish.

6. Your query will run, showing you only the three fields that you chose from the Friends table. You will see information based on the records that you entered. The query datasheet/recordset shown in Figure 38.25 reflects that there is one record in the Friends table.

7. When you are finished viewing the datasheet, choose File ➤ Close.

Generating a Report to Print Your Data

You could, if you wanted to, print the datasheet that results from the query. Doing so, however, limits the amount of formatting. Creating a report from which to print the data is a more attractive option.

1. From the Database window, select the Reports tab.

2. Click on the New button.

Figure 38.24 *The Phone Numbers Select Query Wizard*

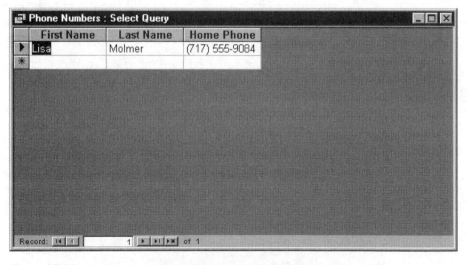

Figure 38.25 *The Phone Numbers query datasheet/recordset shows three fields of one record.*

3. In the New Report dialog box, select Report Wizard and the Phone Numbers query as the data source, as shown in Figure 38.26.

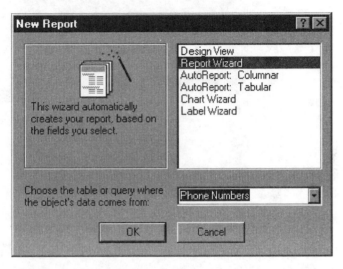

Figure 38.26 *Creating a new report for the Phone Numbers query using the Report Wizard*

4. Using the >> button, send all the Available Fields of the query to the Selected Fields list box so that the Report Wizard dialog box looks like the one in Figure 38.27. Click on Next.

5. The Report Wizard will ask if you want to group anything in your report. For this example we don't, so click on Next.

6. The Report Wizard then prompts you for report layout information with some defaults already chosen. Accept the defaults of Tabular Layout and Portrait Orientation by clicking Next.

7. Figure 38.28 shows the Report Wizard requesting that you choose a style for your report. Select Bold and then click on Next.

8. The last stage of the Report Wizard requests a name for the report. Leave Phone Numbers as the name and leave the radio button selected to *Preview the report*. Click on Finish.

9. Your report will open in Print Preview.

10. When you are finished looking at the report, select File ➤ Close from the menu bar.

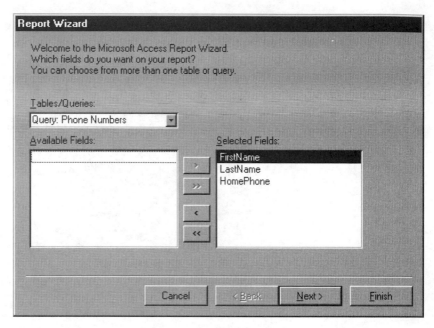

Figure 38.27   Selecting all fields from the Phone Numbers Query

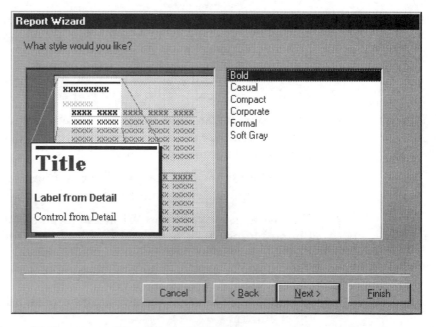

Figure 38.28   Selecting the Bold style for the report

Setting Database Startup Options

You now have a functional database. You have a table to store the data, a form to make data entry easier, a query to select only certain fields from your table, and a report to print the data from your query—in this case a nice phone list.

There are, of course, more advanced uses for all these objects, and you can choose from among many other options to determine how your database will perform. The detail about the objects we have just touched upon can be found in their respective chapters. One last exercise for our quick database does, however, set an option that polishes your Access database.

Generally, you have one main form that you use to start working with your database when you open it. It would be nice for that form to open automatically when you open your database. To do this in Access, you simply set a database option.

1. Select Tools ➤ Startup to open the Startup dialog box.

2. In the Display Form combo box, select the Friends form.

3. Click on OK.

4. From the menu bar, select File ➤ Close.

5. Select File ➤ 1 My Application from the most recently used file list at the bottom of the screen.

6. Now, when your database opens, the form you specified opens automatically.

Chapter 39

Working with Data in Tables

FEATURING

Designing a Table

Designing a Table in Datasheet View

Working with the Table Datasheet

As mentioned in the previous chapter, all your data is stored in tables. Tables are made up of records, and records are made up of fields. You can do quite a bit with tables using the Wizards while not really understanding the structure beneath the datasheet. If you plan to work with Access and not use the Wizards, however, a small primer on the types of fields you can use and the properties available for the field types is necessary.

The goal of this chapter is to help you understand Access table design and to introduce you to the navigation tools with which you maneuver the resulting datasheet.

Designing a Table

You can design a table manually, and you can design a table using Wizards. This chapter focuses on the manual approach so that you have an opportunity to look closer at the options.

To create a new table, you first select the Tables tab from the Database window and then click on New. The New Table dialog box appears (see Figure 39.1). The options are Datasheet View, which allows you to enter sample data and have Access define the field type; Design View, which you use if you want to build a table from scratch, defining all your fields and their properties; Table Wizard, which steps you through the process; Import Table Wizard, which brings in existing tables in other file formats; and Link Table Wizard, which aids you in attaching to tables outside your current database (we'll talk about that in a later chapter). Because you want to build a table from scratch, select Design View and click on OK.

The Design view window consists of a top pane and a bottom pane. In the top pane you enter/name each field needed and decide on its data type; in the bottom pane you specify properties for each field.

Field Names

In the Field Name column in the top pane, you type the name of the field you are adding to your table. The field name can have as many as 64 characters and can contain any characters, numbers, and spaces except for the period <.>, an accent grave <'>, square brackets <[ ]>, and exclamation marks <!> because these characters have reserved meanings in conjunction with filenames in Access. Leading spaces are

Figure 39.1   *Selecting Design View to create a table*

also not allowed, so you will need to begin each field name with a valid character or number.

Although you can have 64 characters in the field name, keeping your field names as small as possible is advisable. Smaller names are easier to remember and to type when you need to refer to the field in a form, a macro, or an expression or in code. Even though spaces are allowed in a field name, try to avoid using them; they only make working with the field more cumbersome.

Data Types

The data type of a field determines the kind of data the field can store. You can choose from 9 data types, ranging from Text, which stores characters, to OLE Object, which stores OLE objects such as Word documents, Excel workbooks, bitmaps, sounds, and even video files.

Text

The Text data type can store as many as 255 alphabetic or numeric characters. You use this data type to store data such as names, addresses, and descriptions and numbers that will not be used in calculations, for example, phone numbers.

Memo

The Memo data type can contain the same type of data as the Text data type, but it can hold as many as 64,000 characters. You do not, however, have as much flexibility with this data type as you do with the Text data type. You cannot sort or index a table using a Memo data type field.

Number

The Number data type stores numbers that will be used in mathematical calculations. The size of the number that you can store in a field is determined by the Field Size property (discussed later in this chapter).

Date/Time

The Date/Time data type is a special number data type that allows you to store dates and times in a field. The Format property of this data type allows you to specify how the date will appear in a field (for example, 4/10/70, April 10, 1970, 4/10/70 8:00:34AM, or some other form).

Currency

The Currency data type stores numbers representing currency that will be used in calculations. This data type has special built-in logic that corrects rounding errors.

AutoNumber

If you select the AutoNumber data type for a field, Access handles the entry for that field in every record. You can set AutoNumber to increment 1 number at a time or to generate random numbers. You can have only one AutoNumber data type per table. If an AutoNumber data type field is used, it is usually the primary key of the table (discussed later in this chapter).

Yes/No

The Yes/No data type is a logical field that can store either True or False. The field accepts True/False, On/Off, Yes/No, -1/0 for its values although you can use its Format property to customize what it shows for True and False.

OLE Object

The OLE Object data type stores large binary OLE objects such as Word documents, Excel workbooks, bitmap files, sound files, and video files.

Lookup Wizard

The Lookup Wizard, although not a data type, assists you in defining the data type and properties of a field whose values can be chosen from a static list or from values in an existing table or query. Selecting the Lookup Wizard from the Data Type combo box of a field in Table Design view initiates the Lookup Wizard. It steps you through filling out the properties on the Lookup page in the properties pane in Table Design view. The Lookup properties define the default display control to be used for the field and the properties associated with control.

Field Properties

Although data types broadly define a field, field properties specify the characteristic of a field such as size, format, and data restrictions. Depending on the data type, a field may or may not have certain properties. The list of properties below includes the data types to which they apply and any special considerations.

Field Size

Text, Number, and AutoNumber data types have Field Size properties. For the Text data type, you can specify a length from 1 to 255, which is the number of characters the field will hold. The Field Size property of a Number data type is actually a subtype that determines the range of numbers allowed. The table below lists the Field Size options for the Number data type.

Field Size	Range
Byte	0 to 255
Integer	−32,768 to 32,767
Long Integer	−2,147,483,648 to 2,147,483,647
Single	−3.402823E38 to 3.402823E38

Field Size	Range
Double	−1.79769313486232E308 to 1.79769313486232E308
ReplicationID	Globally Unique Identifier (GUID) used with AutoNumber for Replication

When choosing a Field Size property for a number, be careful. You don't want to choose a number that is too small, but you also don't want to choose a number that is needlessly large. The larger the number a field can hold, the more space the field takes up in your database.

> **NOTE** If you need to work with decimals, you must choose either a Single or Double Field Size property because the other Field Size properties do not have decimal precision.

Although the AutoNumber data type has a Field Size property, it is almost always set to Long Integer. If it is not set to Long Integer, it is being used for a process called replication, which is beyond the scope of this book.

Format

All data types except for the OLE object data type have a Format property. The Number, Date/Time, AutoNumber, Currency, and Yes/No data types all have predefined formats. If none of the predefined formats is suitable for your situation or if you are formatting a Text or a Memo field, you can create custom formats. To get a list of formatting codes available for different data types, click on the Format Property of a field in Table Design view and Press F1.

A format is applied after the user enters information into a table or a form. For example, if you have an ID field that formats all characters in uppercase letters and the user types all lowercase, the table stores the entry in lowercase. But whenever that entry is viewed in a table, a form, a report, or a query, it appears in all uppercase.

Input Mask

Text, Number, Date/Time, and Currency data types all have an Input Mask property. The Input Mask property is similar to the Format property except that it formats the text as the user enters it and can even provide a little template as to how the data should be entered. A phone number Input Mask, for instance, could look like

(XXX)-XXX-XXXX

The easiest way to apply an Input Mask to a field is to click on the Input Mask property of the field and then click on the Build button or the button with three periods on it that appears directly to the right of the property. When you click on the Build button for either a Text or Date/Time data type, the Input Mask Wizard, as shown in Figure 39.2, opens. Simply follow the steps.

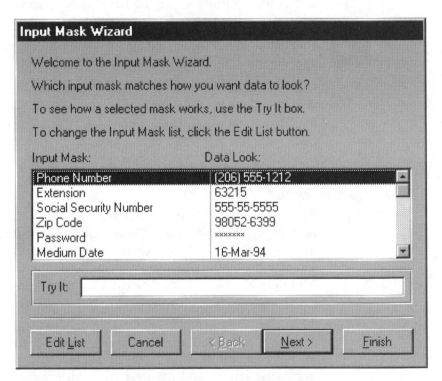

Figure 39.2 **The Input Mask Wizard**

Caption

All data types have a Caption property. The Caption property provides an alternative name for Access to use for your fields when creating labels or references that the user will see, for example, the column headers in

Datasheet view. For example, a field called FNAME on a form could be labeled as First Name if First Name was the caption for the field. Captions help keep field-name size small while providing users with meaningful names.

Decimal Places

The Number and Currency data types have the Decimal Places property, which determines how many decimal places are shown with a number. Remember, only Number data types with a size of Single or Double have decimal precision.

Default Value

All data types except AutoNumber and OLE Objects have a Default Value property, which specifies the value of a field when a new record is started. Default Values are not permanent; they can be changed. You use Default Values when the value of a field is almost always the same, with few exceptions. Declaring a Default Value reduces the amount of data entry.

Validation Rule and Validation Text

The Validation Rule and Validation Text properties are available for all fields except AutoNumber and OLE Objects. A Validation Rule specifies criteria that make the data entered into a cell valid. If, for example, you had a Quantity field that must never accept quantities less than 100, you could place >=100 in the Validation Rule. Access would then not allow any numbers less than 100 to be entered into the field. Validation Text is the text that you want a message box to show when a user violates the Validation Rule. If you have a Validation Rule, be sure to have Validation Text; otherwise, Access will present its own cryptic message.

Required

The Required property specifies whether a field must contain a value before the record is saved. This property does not apply to fields with the AutoNumber data type because Access always provides a value for AutoNumber data types.

Allow Zero Length

Applied to the Text and Memo fields, the Allow Zero Length property determines whether a zero length string qualifies as a valid value.

Indexed

If a field has the Indexed property, Access stores it in a special table, much like the index listing in the back of a book, that makes searching the records easier. Running a query that searches for all customers in a specific zip code goes much faster, for example, if the zip code field has the Indexed property. The three possible values for the Indexed property are No, Yes (No Duplicates), and Yes (Duplicates OK). The No value obviously tells Access not to store an index on that field. The Yes (No Duplicates) value tells Access to index the table on the field and not to allow duplicate values in the field. For example; if one record has ABC as an ID number, no other record can have ABC. The Yes (Duplicates OK) value tells Access to index the table based on the field and to allow multiple records to have the same value in the field.

Primary Key

The primary key of a table is the table's main index. In addition, the field or fields that make up the primary key are used to uniquely identify each record; no two records can have the same value stored in the primary key field(s).

Although Access does not require a primary key, it strongly suggests that you have one. Every time you try to modify the structure of a table without a primary key, Access prompts you to create one or to allow Access to create one. If you are new to working with databases, letting Access set the primary key for you might be a good idea.

When Access sets the primary key of a table, it uses a field with the AutoNumber data type. If you already have a field in your table of this type, and you can have only one, Access uses that field as the primary key . If the table does not have an AutoNumber field, Access inserts one, names it ID, and sets it as the primary key.

The Index property of the field(s) set to be used as the primary key is automatically set to Yes (No Duplicates) to ensure that the value in the primary key field(s) is not duplicated.

To set the primary key manually, follow these steps:

1. From Design view, open a table.

2. To select the field that you want to be the primary key, click on the gray field selector to the left of the field name so that the field row is selected as shown in Figure 39.3.

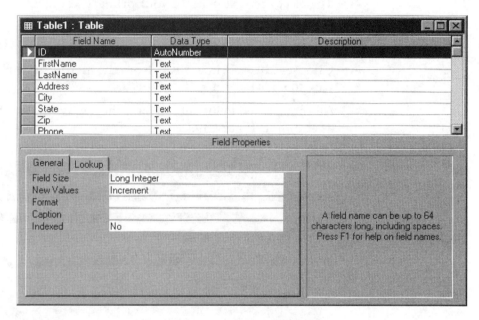

Figure 39.3   Selecting a field to be the primary key

NOTE   Fields with the Memo or OLE Object data types cannot be indexed and therefore cannot be primary keys.

3. From the menu bar, choose Edit ➤ Primary Key or click on the Primary Key button on the toolbar or right-click on the field selector and choose Primary Key from the shortcut menu.

4. A key appears in the field selector to signify that the primary key has been selected.

A primary key can be made up of more than one field if you do not have any one field that can uniquely identify a record. To have more than one field make up a primary key, select all the fields to be included before setting the key.

1. From Design view, open a table.

2. To select the first field for your primary key, click on the field selector.

3. While holding down the Ctrl key, select the other fields to be included. In Figure 39.4, three fields are selected to be included in the primary key.

4. Choose Edit ➤ Primary Key from the menu bar or click on the Primary Key toolbar button.

5. All the selected fields should have the key symbol in their field selectors, as shown in Figure 39.5.

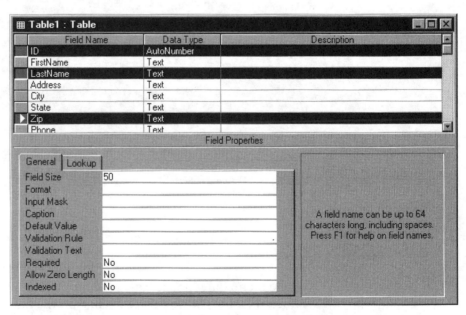

Figure 39.4   *Selecting multiple fields for a primary key using the Ctrl key and the mouse*

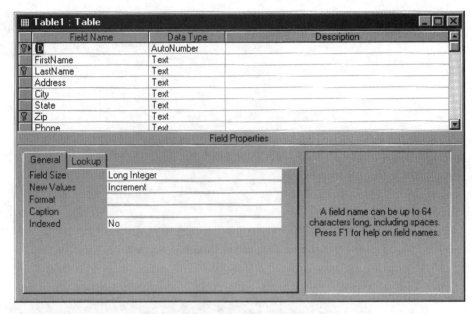

Figure 39.5 *The fields of the primary key all have the key symbol in their field selectors.*

Designing a Table in Datasheet View

If selecting data types and field properties seems a little daunting for your first time out, you might want to try creating a table by using the Datasheet view. Using the Datasheet view is slightly different from using the normal datasheet. When designing a table with the datasheet, Access gives you a blank datasheet with generic fields and default field names such as FIELD1, FIELD2, and so on. Your job is to fill the first row of the table with sample data so that Access can determine the data types.

1. Open a database and select the Tables tab.

2. Click on the New button.

3. In the New Table dialog box, select Datasheet View (see Figure 39.6).

4. The datasheet shown in Figure 39.7 opens.

5. In the first row of the datasheet, type Mickey under Field1, Francis under Field2, 208 Morris Ave. under Field3, Lockhart under Field4, PA under Field5, 19000-2822 under Field6, and 10/20/46 under Field7 so that your datasheet resembles that in Figure 39.8.

Figure 39.6   *Selecting Datasheet View in the New Table dialog box*

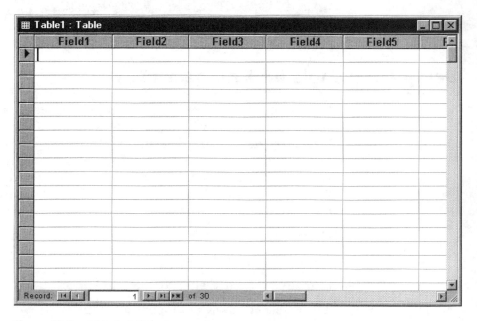

Figure 39.7   *A blank datasheet*

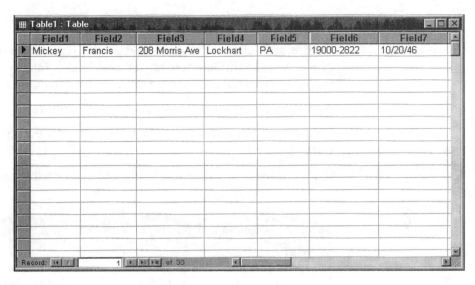

Field1	Field2	Field3	Field4	Field5	Field6	Field7
Mickey	Francis	208 Morris Ave	Lockhart	PA	19000-2822	10/20/46

Figure 39.8 **Entering data to design a table in Datasheet view**

6. From the menu bar, choose File ➤ Save Layout. Accept the default name of Table# (where # is the next number in the succession of tables that you have created during your current session of Access), and answer Yes when asked if you want Access to define a primary key.

7. From the menu bar, choose View ➤ Table Design or click on the Table View button on the Table Datasheet toolbar.

8. Notice that Access has defined the data types and properties for you. You can now make any changes you feel are necessary; for example, you might want to alter the field names.

Working with the Table Datasheet

Once you have designed your tables, you will need to know how to navigate your datasheet so that you can add, edit, and delete records, sort records on specific fields, search for records containing specific information, and apply formatting.

Navigating the Datasheet

Figure 39.9 shows the datasheet of the Customers table that is in the North Wind sample database located in the Samples folder under your main Access folder. To view a table in datasheet view, follow these steps:

1. From the Database window, select the Tables tab.

2. Select the table you want to see in Datasheet view and click on the Open button.

3. The datasheet opens and is similar to the one in Figure 39.9.

Figure 39.9   The Table datasheet of a table

Moving from Field to Field and Record to Record

In the datasheet, you can move from field to field and from record to record using the arrow keys or Tab and Shift+Tab. Pressing Tab is the same as using the right arrow key, and pressing Shift+Tab is the same as using the left arrow key. Notice that when you move up and down a triangle marker is in the record selector, indicating that it is the current record.

Editing

To edit the contents of a field, press the arrow keys until the field that you want is highlighted and then press F2. Pressing F2 removes the highlight and allows you to edit the field. If you are using the mouse, simply click on the field you want to edit. If you are replacing the entire contents of the field, you need not press F2. Instead, position the highlight on the field you want to change and start typing. Your new entry replaces the entire contents of the field. When you are editing a field, a picture of a pencil appears in the gray record selector for that row (see Figure 39.10).

Customer ID	Company Name	Contact Name	Contac
ALFKI	Alfreds Futterkiste	Maria Anders	Sales Repre
ANATR	Ana Trujillo Emparedados y helados	Ana Trujillo	Owner
ANTON	Antonio Moreno Taquería	Antonio Moreno	Owner
AROUT	Around the Horn	Thomas Jon	Sales Repre
BERGS	Berglunds snabbköp	Christina Berglund	Order Admin
BLAUS	Blauer See Delikatessen	Hanna Moos	Sales Repre
BLONP	Blondel père et fils	Frédérique Citeaux	Marketing M
BOLID	Bólido Comidas preparadas	Martín Sommer	Owner
BONAP	Bon app'	Laurence Lebihan	Owner
BOTTM	Bottom-Dollar Markets	Elizabeth Lincoln	Accounting I
BSBEV	B's Beverages	Victoria Ashworth	Sales Repre
CACTU	Cactus Comidas para llevar	Patricio Simpson	Sales Agent
CENTC	Centro comercial Moctezuma	Francisco Chang	Marketing M
CHOPS	Chop-suey Chinese	Yang Wang	Owner
COMMI	Comércio Mineiro	Pedro Afonso	Sales Assoc
CONSH	Consolidated Holdings	Elizabeth Brown	Sales Repre
DRACD	Drachenblut Delikatessen	Sven Ottlieb	Order Admin
DUMON	Du monde entier	Janine Labrune	Owner

Record: 4 of 91

Figure 39.10 Editing a record

Undoing Changes

If you begin changing a field and make a mistake, press the Esc key to undo the change. If you continue to make changes in other fields of the same record without moving to another row, pressing the ESC key undoes the changes to the entire record. This works only if you have not moved off the current record because Access saves the changes to your record whenever you move off the record after changing it.

TIP   If you move to another row or record and find that you made an error, press the Esc key to restore the last record you edited. Be careful, however, not to rely on this because it only works for the last record saved, and if you make even a minor change in another record before noticing your error in a previous record, you will not be able to undo the change.

Adding New Records

When you want to add a new record to a table, you first need to get to the very last row of the datasheet. You can do this in a several ways (see Figure 39.11).

► Use the down arrow key on your keyboard to move to the last row

► From the menu bar, choose Insert ➤ Record.

► Click the New Record button on the Table Datasheet toolbar.

► Use the Goto New Record navigation button at the bottom of the datasheet.

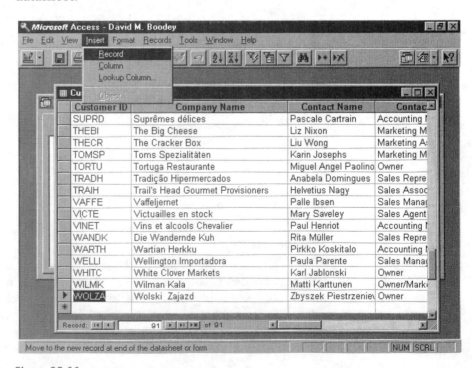

Figure 39.11   Options for inserting a new record

If you look at the blank row before you enter data into it, you will notice an asterisk in the record selector. This signifies that the row is really not a record yet, but a place to add new records to the table. Once you begin typing in the row, the asterisk turns into the normal triangle current record marker.

Deleting a Record

To delete a record in the table, make it the current record and follow the steps below (see Figure 39.12).

▶ From the menu bar, choose Edit ➤ Delete Record.

▶ Click the Delete Record button on the Table Datasheet toolbar.

▶ Select the current record by clicking on the record selector and pressing the Delete key or right-click on the record selector and choose Cut from the shortcut menu.

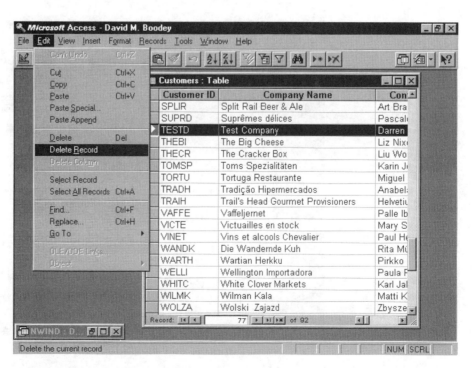

Figure 39.12   Options for deleting the current record

Sorting and Filtering Your Data

You don't necessarily enter information into a table in the order that you need to view it. You may also need to view only certain records at a time. Using the sorting and filtering functions in Datasheet view gives you this flexibility.

Sorting

Sorting data in Datasheet View is a snap. First, click on the field column by which you want to sort, and then do one of the following: (1) Click on one of the sort buttons in the toolbar (see Figure 39.13); (2) choose Records ➤ Sort ➤ Ascending or Records ➤ Sort ➤ Descending from the menu bar; or (3) right-click on a field and choose either Sort Ascending or Sort Descending.

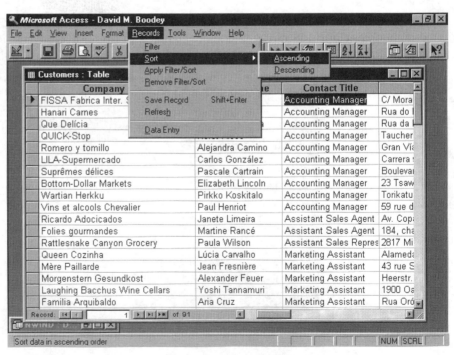

Figure 39.13   *Sorting by Contact Title, using either the toolbar or the menu bar*

You can also sort by multiple columns, but the columns must be adjacent, or side by side (see the section later in this chapter on changing column layout). If the field columns are adjacent, select the first column by clicking on the column header; then hold down Shift and click on the last column header of the columns by which you want to sort. Your datasheet now resembles that in Figure 39.14, and you can use any of the previously mentioned methods for sorting.

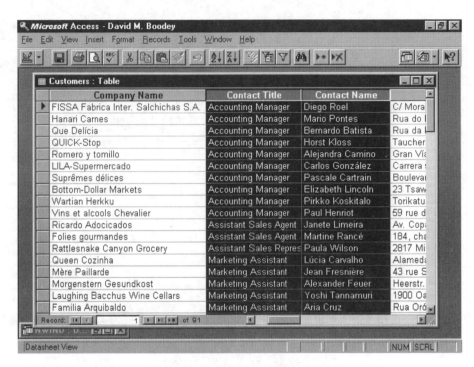

Figure 39.14   *Sorting by Contact Title and Contact Name*

Filtering Your Data

You can filter the information in your datasheet in three ways:

▶ Filter By Selection

▶ Filter By Form

▶ Advanced Filter/Sort

Filter By Selection is the quickest and easiest method, albeit the most limited. First, place the insertion point in the field that has the data value that you want to extract, and then do one of the following: (1) Choose Records ➤ Filter ➤ Filter By Selection from the menu bar; (2) press the Filter By Selection toolbar button; or (3) right-click on the desired value and choose Filter By Selection from the shortcut menu. Figure 39.15 points out two of the options.

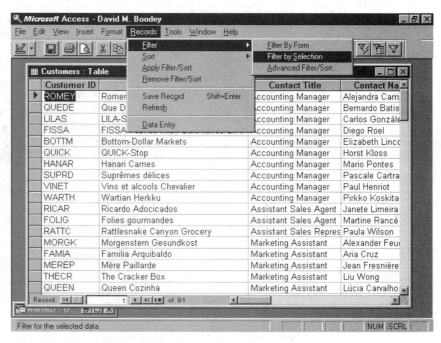

Figure 39.15   *Filtering By Selection*

Figure 39.16 shows the entire, unfiltered Customers table in the sample North Wind database.

Suppose we want to see the records for only those customers in Oregon. The first step is to find a record that has Oregon in the Region field and then click on that field. Figure 39.17 shows a record with Oregon in the Region field.

Figure 39.16 *The unfiltered Customers table*

Figure 39.17 *A record with Oregon in the Region field*

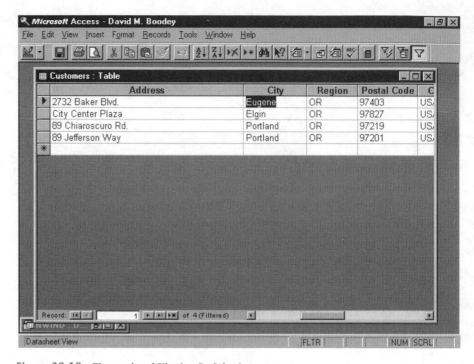

Figure 39.18   *The results of Filtering By Selection*

Next, choose Records ➤ Filter ➤ Filter By Selection from the menu bar. Figure 39.18 shows the results.

To clear a Filter By Selection or to clear any filter applied to a datasheet, do one of the following: (1) Choose Records ➤ Remove Filter/Sort from the menu bar; (2) click on the Remove Filter toolbar button; or (3) right-click on any field and choose Remove Filter/Sort from the shortcut menu.

Filtering by Form in a datasheet allows you to filter the records that you want by selecting field filters from a combo box. To filter by form:

1. In Datasheet view, open a table.

2. From the menu bar, choose Records➤ Filter ➤ Filter By Form, or click on the Filter By Form button on the toolbar.

3. Your datasheet will reduce to one row (see Figure 39.19). When you click on any field, a combo box arrow appears.

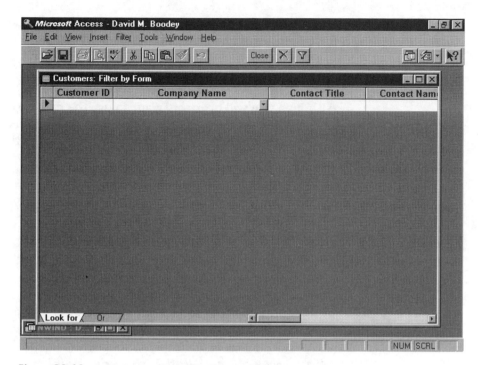

Figure 39.19 *Setting up a Filter By Form in Datasheet view*

4. To select a filter value for the current field, click on any of the drop-down arrows.

5. You can select criteria from other fields.

6. After the criteria for the filter are chosen, choose Filter ➤ Apply Filter/Sort from the menu bar or right-click on the title bar of the Filter By Form window and choose Apply Filter/Sort from the shortcut menu.

 To modify the above filter, choose Records➤ Filter ➤ Filter By Form from the menu bar and make the changes in the filter row. To clear the filter and see all records, choose Records ➤ Remove Filter/Sort from the menu bar or right-click on a field or the window title bar and select Remove Filter/Sort.

 Using Advanced Filter/Sort is similar to creating a query except that you do not specify the fields to show or hide; instead, you specify criteria. To learn how to use the Advanced Filter/Sort option, review the chapter on designing a query with the QBE grid.

Formatting the Datasheet

Although you will probably want to use the formatting abilities of forms and reports instead of formatting the datasheet, a couple of formatting techniques can make working with datasheets a little more effective.

Changing the Font

If the font in your datasheet is too small, too big, or just not right, you can modify it.

1. From the menu bar, choose Format ➤ Font.

2. In the Font dialog box, select the options you want and click on OK.

> **NOTE**   You cannot change the font for only one field column or row. The whole table must use the same font.

Changing Column Widths and Row Heights

At times you will want to change the height of rows or the width of columns to facilitate viewing the data.

To change the column width:

1. From the menu bar, choose Format ➤ Column Width.

2. In the Column Width dialog box, specify the number of characters you want to see in the column.

3. Click on OK.

> **TIP**   You can also change the width of columns by placing your mouse pointer over the top right border of the column you want to change and clicking and dragging the border until it is the desired width. Double-clicking on the column header's right border will "Best Fit" the column to the largest entry in that column, which occasionally will be the field name/caption in the header itself.

To change the height of rows, choose Format ➤ Row Height from the menu bar, type a number, measured in points, in the Row Height dialog box, and click on OK. Changing row height changes all rows; you cannot specify different row heights for only some rows.

> **TIP** You can change the row height by clicking and dragging the top border of one of the gray record selectors on the left side of the datasheet.

Changing the Column Layout

To change column order while viewing the datasheet, you need only click and drag the columns that you want to move.

1. In Datasheet view, open a table.

2. Position your mouse pointer over the the gray column header of the column that you want to move and click once.

3. Position your mouse pointer back over the column header and click and hold the left mouse button.

4. A box is now attached to the bottom of your mouse pointer.

5. Drag your mouse pointer until the black column separator that moves with it is in between the columns where you want to place the column you are moving.

6. Let go of the left mouse button, and your column moves.

Freezing Columns

If you have a large number of fields in a table and you need to keep one or more columns in view as you scroll through the other fields, you can freeze those columns.

1. In Datasheet view, open a table.

2. Click anywhere in the column that you want to freeze, and choose Format ➤ Freeze Columns from the menu bar, or select the column, right-click on the column header, and choose Freeze Columns on the shortcut menu.

3. The column that you were in will move to the far left and freeze.

4. If you scroll to the right to view the other fields, the frozen column always stays in view.

5. To freeze more than one column, simply repeat the steps above for each new column.

6. To unfreeze columns, choose Format ➤ Unfreeze All Columns from the menu bar.

> **NOTE**   When you unfreeze columns that were not originally on the left side of the datasheet, Access keeps the columns on the left side and does not move them back to their original position.

Hiding Columns

To hide a column in datasheet view so that you have more room to focus on the other columns, click on the column you want to hide and choose Format ➤ Hide Columns from the menu bar or select the column and right-click on the column header to choose the Hide Columns option on the shortcut menu. To unhide a column, choose Format ➤ Unhide Columns from the menu bar, check the column you want to unhide in the Unhide Columns dialog box, and click on the Close pushbutton.

> **TIP**   The easiest way to hide multiple columns is to choose Format ➤ Unhide Columns from the menu bar, uncheck all the columns you want hidden in the Unhide Columns dialog box, and click on the Close button.

Inserting Columns

Access allows you to add fields or columns to a datasheet.

1. In Datasheet view, open a table.

2. Click on any column and choose Insert ➤ Column from the menu bar, or select the column and right-click on the column header to choose the Insert Column option on the shortcut menu. The column is inserted to the left of the selected column.

3. Type a sample of the data for the field in a record.

4. Switch to Design view by choosing View ➤ Table Design from the menu bar.

5. Notice that your field is added to the structure and that a data type is chosen.

Renaming Columns

You can change a column name in Datasheet view.

1. Click on the column whose name you want to change.

2. From the menu bar, choose Format ➤ Rename Column.

3. Type the new name of the column in the header and press Enter. Or double-click on the column header and edit the name. Or select the column, right-click on the column header, and choose Rename Column from the shortcut menu.

Chapter 40

Using Forms with Your Data

FEATURING

Access provides a number of methods that you can use to generate forms. This chapter focuses primarily on the Form Wizards and AutoForms. If you're a beginning user, these methods are for you. If you're more adventurous or if you're an advanced user, you'll probably want to use the Design view to create forms or to modify a form that was created with the Wizards. This chapter also includes an overview of the Design view.

Designing a Form

When creating new forms, you have seven options. Figure 40.1 shows them as they are presented in the New Form dialog box. To see them for yourself, click on the New button on the Forms page in the Database window.

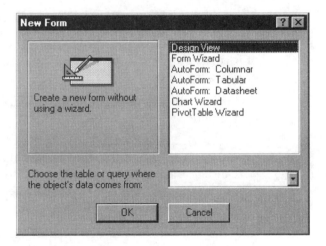

Figure 40.1   The New Form dialog box

▶ Design View is for the experienced user who wants to create a form from scratch.

▶ Form Wizard takes a user step by step through the creation of Columnar, Tabular, and Datasheet forms.

▶ AutoForm automatically creates a Columnar, Tabular, or Datasheet form without any user interaction, except for selecting a particular AutoForm.

▶ Chart Wizard helps a user easily create a form that displays a graph of the chosen data.

▶ Pivot Table Wizard steps a user through placing an Excel Pivot Table, based on Access data, on a form. (For more information on pivot tables, see the chapter on Excel database capabilities.)

When specifying the method by which to create your form in the New Form dialog box, you must also specify the record source. The record source is the table or query from which the form will get its data. A form can have only one record source.

The Form Wizard and AutoForms

With Form Wizard or one of the AutoForms, you can create three kinds of forms: columnar, tabular, and datasheet. Let's walk through the steps of using the Form Wizard.

For this example we will use the NWIND database in the SAMPLES folder under your main Access folder.

NOTE   If you cannot find the sample databases, you may not have chosen to include them during installation. It is strongly recommended that you run setup again and add the sample databases. For the beginner and the seasoned Access user, all the sample databases provide a wealth of information via examples.

1. Open the NWIND database.
2. From the Database window, select the Forms tab.
3. Click on the New button.
4. Select the Form Wizard option and select the Customers table for the record source, as shown in Figure 40.2. Click on OK.
5. Select the fields you want on your form.
6. Click the >> button to send all the fields from the Customers table to the selected fields list, as shown in Figure 40.3. Click on the Next button.

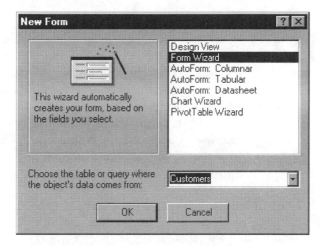

Figure 40.2   Selecting Form Wizard and the Customers table

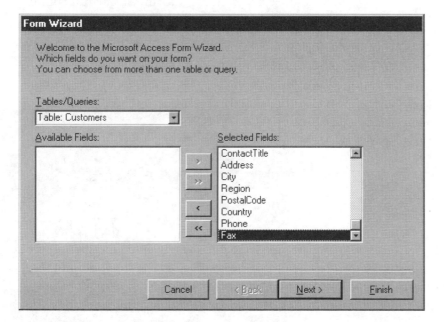

Figure 40.3   Selecting all fields from the Customers table for the form

NOTE You can choose fields from multiple tables or queries. Selecting fields from multiple tables or queries does not mean you can have more than one record source per form, however; if you select fields from more than one table or query, Access creates a Main form with a subform or a Main form with a Linked form. You choose fields from multiple tables or queries when you want to show the relationships between the tables or queries. For example, you might want the Customers fields on a Main form and the fields from the Orders table on a subform or a Linked form. Then, when you view a customer, you see only that customer's orders.

7. Next, the Form Wizard asks you to choose a layout (see Figure 40.4). The choices are Columnar, Tabular, and Datasheet. Select Columnar. (We will see samples of all three later.) Click on the Next button to continue.

8. Choose a style for the form. Select International (see Figure 40.5) and click on Next.

9. Now title your form (see Figure 40.6) **My Customers**, without changing any of the other options, and click on Finish.

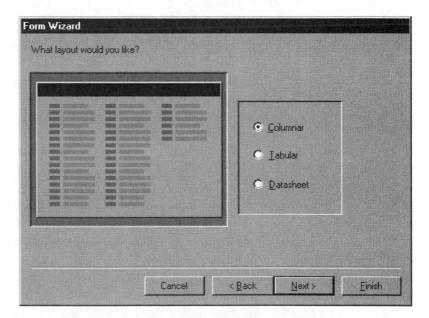

Figure 40.4   Selecting the Columnar layout for your form

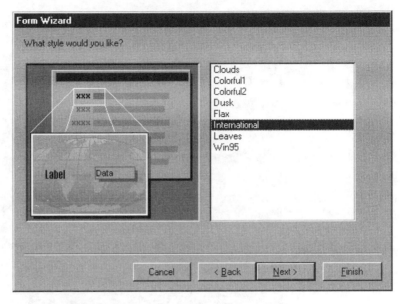

Figure 40.5　*Selecting the International style to apply to the form*

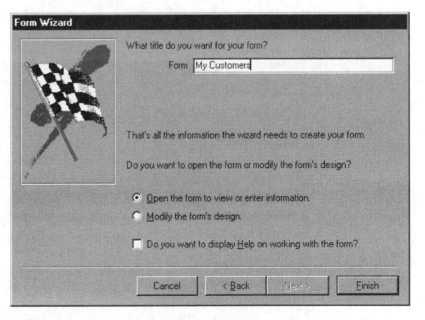

Figure 40.6　*Titling the form My Customers and clicking on Finish*

10. Your form opens for use and is similar to the one in Figure 40.7.

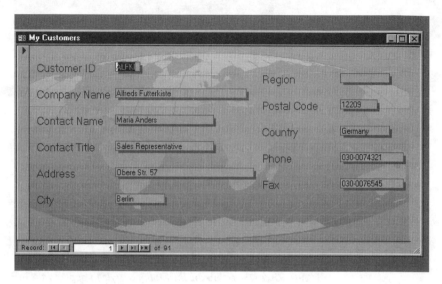

Figure 40.7   The resulting form

If you had chosen Tabular layout, the result would resemble that in Figure 40.8. If you had chosen Datasheet layout, the result would resemble that in Figure 40.9.

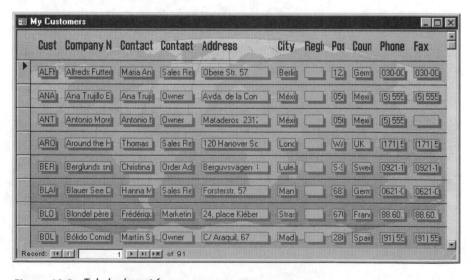

Figure 40.8   Tabular layout form

Data Management
with Access

Custo	Company Name	ContactName	ContactTitle
ALFKI	Alfreds Futterkiste	Maria Anders	Sales Representative
ANATI	Ana Trujillo Emparedados y helad	Ana Trujillo	Owner
ANTO	Antonio Moreno Taquería	Antonio Moreno	Owner
AROU	Around the Horn fff	Thomas Hardy	Sales Representative
BERG	Berglunds snabbköp	Christina Berglund	Order Administrator
BLAU:	Blauer See Delikatessen	Hanna Moos	Sales Representative
BLON	Blondel père et fils	Frédérique Citeaux	Marketing Manager
BOLIC	Bólido Comidas preparadas	Martín Sommer	Owner
BONA	Bon app'	Laurence Lebihan	Owner
BOTTI	Bottom-Dollar Markets	Elizabeth Lincoln	Accounting Manager
BSBE	B's Beverages	Victoria Ashworth	Sales Representative
CACTI	Cactus Comidas para llevar	Patricio Simpson	Sales Agent
CENTI	Centro comercial Moctezuma	Francisco Chang	Marketing Manager
CHOP	Chop-suey Chinese	Yang Wang	Owner
COMN	Comércio Mineiro	Pedro Afonso	Sales Associate
CONS	Consolidated Holdings	Elizabeth Brown	Sales Representative
DRAC	Drachenblut Delikatessen	Sven Ottlieb	Order Administrator
DUMC	Du monde entier	Janine Labrune	Owner
EASTI	Eastern Connection	Ann Devon	Sales Agent

My Customers

Record: 1 of 91

Figure 40.9 **Datasheet layout form**

If you choose one of the AutoForms in the New Form dialog box, Access automatically (without asking you any questions) creates the form by using all the fields in the table or query that you choose.

The Form Design Screen and Its Components

You use the Form Design Screen to create a form from scratch or to modify a form that was created with a Wizard. Although the Access Form Design Screen is easier to use than many of the form design utilities in other databases, it takes practice and time to become adept and effective at using it. The best way to learn to use the Form Design Screen is to practice modifying existing forms. Once you are comfortable with modifying forms, you can take the plunge and create a new form using only the Form Design Screen and no Wizards.

TIP   Even if you become extremely adept at creating forms, you will probably find that using the Form Wizard, at least to get your form started, will save time—even if the only things that the Wizard-created form and your final form have in common are the controls that are bound to fields.

In our example design screen, we use an existing form in the NWIND database. Open the NWIND database and select the Forms tab.

1. Select the Employees form and click on Open. Or right-click on the form name and choose Open from the shortcut menu. Or simply double-click on the name.

2. The form opens and is similar to the one in Figure 40.10.

3. Click on the Personal Info button to go to the next page.

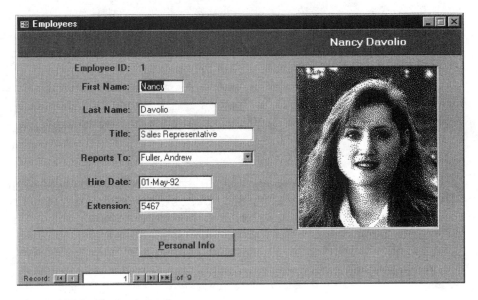

*Figure 40.10 **The Employees form***

4. Click on the Company Info button to return to the top of the form. To see how this form was constructed, we need to look at it in Design view. Using one of the methods described below (see Figure 40.11), switch to Desgin view.

▶ From the menu bar, choose View ➤ Form Design.

▶ Click on the Form View button on the Form View toolbar, or click on the down arrow button next to it and select Design View from the list.

Figure 40.11 *Switching to Design view*

Sections

Forms are divided into sections, and a form can have as many as five sections. Each section begins with a gray section header that contains the name of the section. The five sections in the blank form shown in Figure 40.12 are:

▶ **Form Header.** The items you place in the Form Header appear once and only once at the beginning of the form. Information stored here is not printed out. When you create a new form in Design view, the Form Header is not visible by default. To make the Form Header visible, choose View ➤ Form Header/Footer from the menu bar while in Design view or right-click on the window title bar and choose Form Header/Footer from the shortcut menu.

▶ **Page Header.** The information you place in the Page Header does not appear on the screen. It only appears in the printed form.

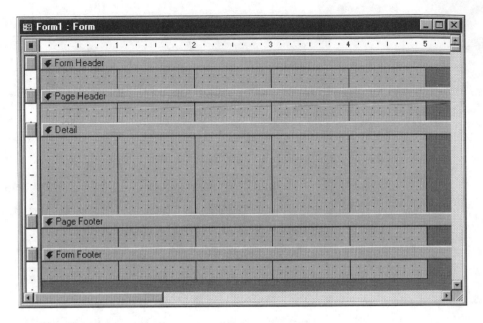

Figure 40.12 **The sections of a form**

▶ **Detail.** A form always has a Detail section. In it you place the fields of records that you want to view or anything else that you want to be the focus of the form.

▶ **Page Footer.** The information you place in the Page Footer does not appear on the screen. It only appears in the printed form.

▶ **Form Footer.** The items placed in the Form Footer appear once and only once at the end of the form. Information stored here is not printed out. When you create a new form in Design view, the Form Footer is not visible by default. To make the Form Footer visible, choose View ➤ Form Header/Footer from the menu bar while in Design view or right-click on the window title bar and choose Form Header/Footer from the shortcut menu.

Figure 40.13 shows a form that has information only in the Form Header and Form Detail sections.

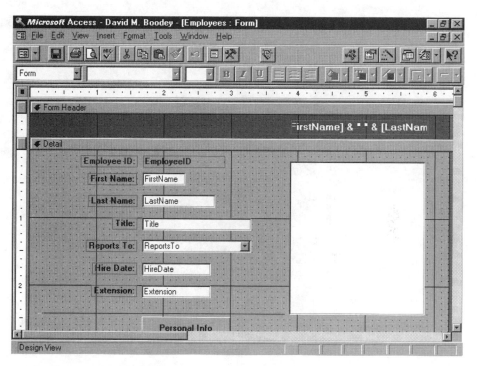

Figure 40.13 *The Employees form has information only in the Form Header and Form Detail sections.*

Field List

When working with a form that has a record source, you can open a field list window that shows a list of fields. You can click and drag any of these fields onto the form. To view the field list of the Employees form shown in Figure 40.14, choose View ➤ Field List from the menu bar or click on the Field List toolbar button.

The Toolbox and Controls

The Toolbox is a special toolbar that contains every type of object that you can place on a form. The objects that you can place on forms are called *controls*. If you want to place a control on a form, click once on the control in the Toolbox and then click on the section of the form in which you want the control. Figure 40.15 shows the Toolbox that you can view by choosing View ➤ Toolbox from the menu bar or by clicking on the Toolbox toolbar button.

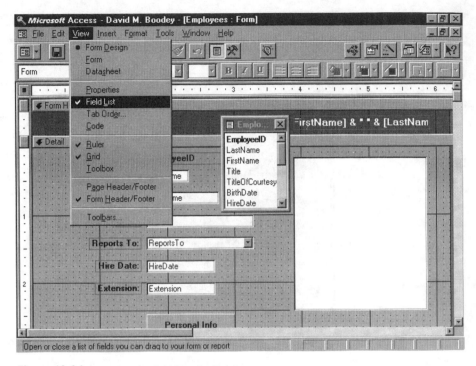

Figure 40.14   *Viewing the field list of a form*

Properties

As mentioned earlier, everything in Access is an object, and objects have properties. Properties determine how an object looks and performs. To view the Properties window shown in Figure 40.16, choose View ➤ Properties from the menu bar or click on the Properties button on the Form Design toolbar. There is only one Properties window. To view properties for different controls, select the control; the Properties window changes to show you the properties for the selected object. You can see the change in the title bar of the Properties window. Remember that the form itself is an object, and you can select it by clicking the intersection of the two rulers in the top left corner of the Form window.

TIP **If you want to know what a particular property does, click on the property's value in the Properties window and press F1.**

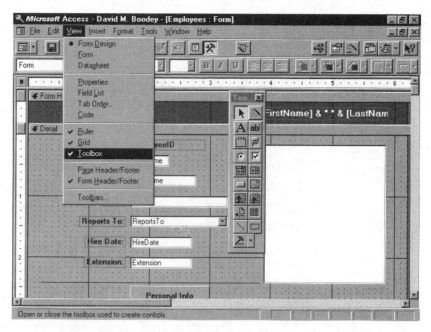

Figure 40.15 The Toolbox holds all the controls that can be used on a form.

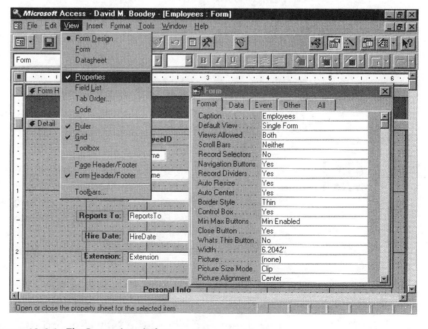

Figure 40.16 The Properties window

The Form View of a Form

Once you create a form, whether with Wizards, from scratch in Design View, or by a combination of the two, you can use the form to add, edit, and view the data in the table or query that is the form's record source. The way you work with data in a form is similar to the way you work with data in the Datasheet view.

Navigating Your Data in a Form

To open a form in Form View, select the form in the Database window and click on Open or select View ➤ Form from the menu bar while in the Design view of a form.

Editing

To edit fields on a form, use Tab, the arrow keys, or the mouse to get to the field that you want to edit. Once the contents of the field are highlighted, press F2 to begin editing.

Undoing Changes

If you change a field and than want to restore it to its original state, press the Esc key. If you want to undo changes to an entire record, press the Esc key as well.

Moving from Record to Record

To move from record to record, you can use PgUp and PgDn or the record navigation buttons in the bottom left corner of the Form window.

NOTE   If you use PgUp or PgDn to move from record to record and a form has multiple pages in the detail section, PgUp and PgDn switches pages before changing records. If you are on the last page of a form for the current record and you press PgDn, you will go to the next record, on the last page of the form. The Employees form in the North Wind database is an example of a form that has two pages in the detail section.

Adding a New Record

To create a new record using the form, choose Insert ➤ Record from the menu bar or click on the New Record toolbar button. You can also use the Go To New Record navigation button on the bottom left corner of the Form window if it is available.

Deleting a Record

To delete a record in a form, choose Edit ➤ Delete Record from the menu bar or click on the Delete Record toolbar button. Or right-click on the record selector and choose Cut from the shortcut menu.

Filtering Records

You can filter the information in a form using Filter By Selection or Filter By Form.

Filter By Selection

When you choose Filter By Selection, you filter the records displayed in a form based on the value or part of the value in the field of the current record.

1. Open the Employees form of NWIND.

2. Notice the number of records available to the right of the navigation buttons at the bottom left of the form.

3. Tab to the Title field of Nancy Davolio so that it is selected, as shown in Figure 40.17, and then do one of the following:

    • Click on the Filter By Selection button on the toolbar.

    • *Or* choose Records ➤ Filter ➤ Filter by Selection.

    • *Or* right-click on the field containing the value on which you want to build a filter, and then choose Filter By Selection from the shortcut menu.

4. The number of records available is reduced to include only those in which the employee is a sales representative. To the right of the navigation buttons is the term (Filtered), as shown in Figure 40.18.

5. To restore all records, do one of the following:

    • Click on the Remove Filter button on the toolbar.

    • *Or* right-click anywhere on the form and choose Remove Filter/Sort in the shortcut menu.

    • *Or* choose Records ➤ Remove Filter/Sort from the menu bar.

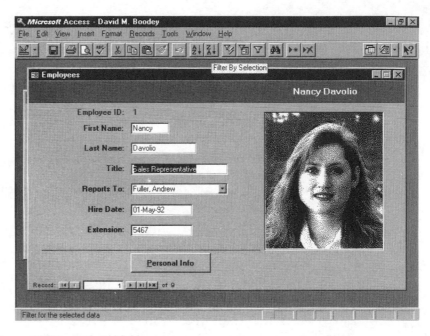

Figure 40.17   *A selected field*

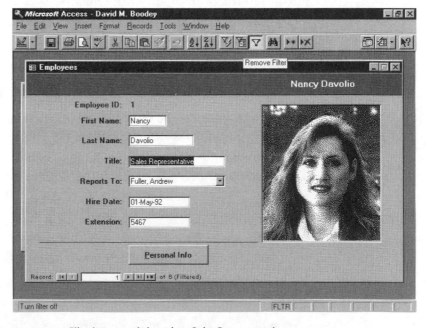

Figure 40.18   *Filtering records based on Sales Representative*

TIP   If you select only part of the value in a field, for example, Sales instead of the entire Sales Representative, Access filters only the selected part. In this example, you would get Sales Representative and Sales Manager.

Filtering By Form

When you use Filter By Form, you specify the values of all fields that you want to filter by right in your form and then you apply the filter based on your criteria.

1. Open the Employees form of the NWIND database.

2. Choose Records ➤ Filter ➤ Filter By Form from the menu bar or click on the Filter By Form toolbar button. Or right-click on an open area of the form and choose Filter By Form from the shortcut menu.

3. The controls on your form will all go blank, as shown in Figure 40.19, so that you can specify criteria.

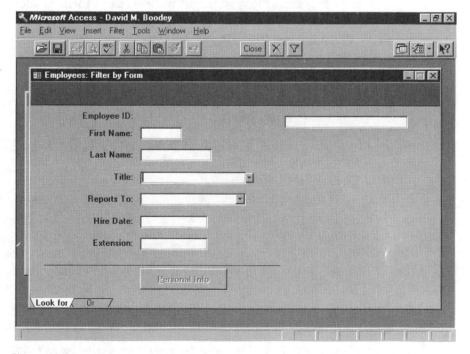

Figure 40.19   *Filtering by Form*

4. If you click on the field for which you want to specify criteria, a drop-down arrow appears to allow you to choose from a list of values.

5. After you specify the criteria, choose Filter ➤ Apply Filter/Sort from the menu bar or click on the Apply Filter toolbar button. Or right-click on an open area of the form and choose Apply Filter/Sort from the shortcut menu.

6. The recordset is extracted/sorted based on the criteria you specified.

> **TIP** If you need to specify OR criteria—for example, you want to see everyone that has the title of President or Chairman—you can use the OR tabs at the bottom left of the Filter By Form window and specify separate pages of criteria for OR conditions.

Forms without Data

You may want to create some forms that will not have a record source. For example, you might want to use a form to access all the other forms in your database, or you might want to use forms as message boxes or dialog boxes. The NWIND database form Main Switchboard, shown in Figure 40.20, is a good example of a form that is used for interface purposes rather than for direct data access. These types of forms must be created from scratch using the Design view without the help of any Wizards.

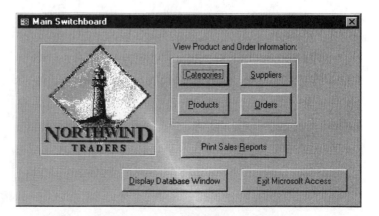

Figure 40.20   The Main Switchboard form does not have a record source and is used to access other forms.

Chapter 41

Asking Questions of Your Data with Queries

FEATURING

Designing a query has never been easier than it is now with Access. The five Query Wizards step you through the query creation process, asking which fields you would like in the final datasheet/recordset and how you want to sort the resulting datasheet/recordset.

Designing a Query

Modifying the queries created by the Wizards is elementary using the Query Design Screen and its QBE (Query By Example) grid.

At the root of all query-building interfaces is SQL, or Structured Query Language. SQL is command-line-like language that requires a user to select fields from a specific table where certain conditions are true. Microsoft has gone to great lengths to provide interfaces to shield the user from SQL for a reason: It Is Hard to Learn! Unless you are an adventurer at heart or an experienced SQL database person, put this aspect of Access on the back burner until you fully understand the other parts.

Using the Wizards

Previous versions of Access relied on the Query Design Screen for the creation of all queries except for the four more difficult queries that were and still are supported with Wizards of their own. The Simple Query Wizard has been added to help with creating basic queries. You now have six ways to design a query.

▶ **New Query.** Opens a new Query Design Screen and allows you to create your queries from scratch.

▶ **Simple Query Wizard.** Asks which fields you want in the resulting datasheet, whether you want the information grouped, and whether you want to perform a function such as sum, count, or average on any field.

▶ **Crosstab Query Wizard.** Creates a spreadsheet-like result from three fields: a field to use as the row headings, a field to use as a column heading, and a field to perform a function on at the intersection of the row and column headings. If, for example, you want to know how many orders each employee has in each country where you have customers, you take the following steps: (1) Specify the Employee ID field as the row heading so that all employee IDs are listed down the left column.

(2) specify the Country field as the column heading so that all the countries you deal with are listed across the top in the column headings; and (3) specify the count of the Order IDs as the value that you want at the intersection of Employee ID and Country.

▶ **Find Duplicates Query Wizard.** Helps you generate a query that looks to see if records in a table have duplicate values in specific fields.

▶ **Find Unmatched Query Wizard.** Looks at two related tables to see if there are any records with values in a specific field that do not appear at least once in the related field of the other table.

▶ **Archive Query Wizard.** Helps create a query that takes certain records from a table or tables and copies them to another table &or archival purposes.

You will use the Simple Query Wizard to create or at least start most of your queries. The following walk-through is indicative of how to use most Query Wizards.

1. Open the NWIND database in the Samples folder under your main Access folder.

2. From the Database window, select the Queries tab.

3. Click on the New button.

4. In the New Query dialog box (see Figure 41.1), select Simple Query Wizard and then click on OK.

5. The Simple Query Wizard (Figure 41.2) asks you to select the fields for the query.

The first window of the Simple Query Wizard has three parts: the Tables/Queries combo box, the Available Fields list box, and the Selected Fields list box. In the Tables/Queries combo box, you select the table or query from whose fields you want to choose. The Available Fields list box shows you the available fields for the table or query you selected in the combo box. The Selected Fields list box holds the fields you want to include in your query.

A nice feature of this Wizard step is that from this window you can select all the fields from all the tables that you want to include. Once you select all the fields from one table or query that you have chosen in the combo box, you can select another table or query from the combo box and choose the fields from that table or query that you want to include.

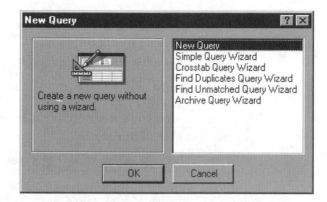

Figure 41.1 *The New Query dialog box*

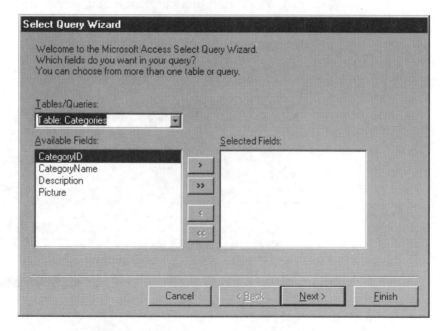

Figure 41.2 *The first step of the Simple Query Wizard*

You can continue to select tables, queries, and fields until you have chosen all the fields you want in your query.

> **WARNING**　Be aware that if there are no relationships between the tables that hold the fields that you choose for your query, Access will prompt you to either change your relationships and then restart the Wizard or remove the fields of the tables that are not related.

When all the fields you want to include are listed in the Selected Fields list box, you can continue.

6. From the Tables/Queries combo box, select the Customers table.

7. Send the Company Name field from the Available Fields list box to the Selected Fields list box by clicking the > button. Or simply double-click on Company Name.

8. From the Tables/Queries combo box, select the Orders table.

9. Send the OrderID, OrderDate, and ShippedDate fields to the Selected Fields list box.

10. When your screen looks like the one in Figure 41.3, click on Next.

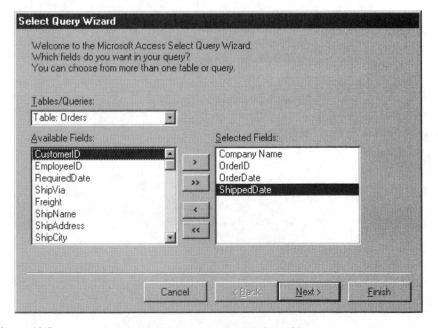

Figure 41.3　*Fields selected from the Customers and Orders tables*

In the next step the Wizard asks whether you want detail (Show me all of the records in their entirety) or a summary (Summarize my information for me).

11. Leave the default of *Show me all of the records in their entirety* as it is in Figure 41.4 and click on Next.

12. Next, the Wizard asks for a title for your query (see Figure 41.5). Type **My Query** and click on Finish, leaving the other settings in the window with their defaults.

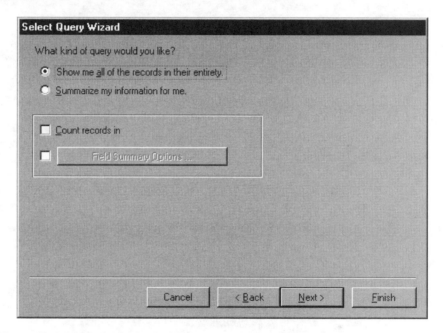

Figure 41.4   *The Wizard asks whether you want detail or summary information.*

Figure 41.6 shows a maximized view of the datasheet that results from the query you just created. Note that it lists the name of the company every time there is an order. If you wanted a cleaner presentation, you could create a report from this query and sort, group, and format the information.

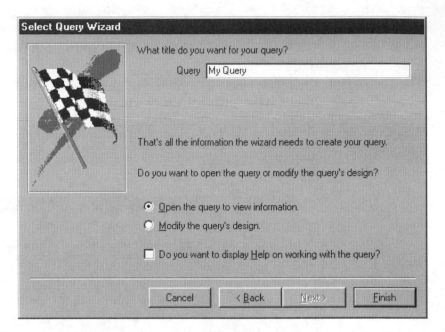

Figure 41.5   Providing a title for your query is the last step of the Simple Query Wizard.

Although the Simple Query Wizard makes query creation a breeze, a few restrictions will generally require that you modify the query using the Query Design Screen. Using the Simple Query Wizard you cannot:

- Sort.
- Specify criteria.
- Create calculated columns.
- Limit to Top Values.

Using the Query Design Screen, you can modify queries that were created with the Simple Query Wizard or you can create new queries from scratch that have the above features.

The Query Design Screen and the QBE Grid

The Query Design Screen, as shown in Figure 41.7, consists of the top pane that holds the field lists of the queries or tables being used and the

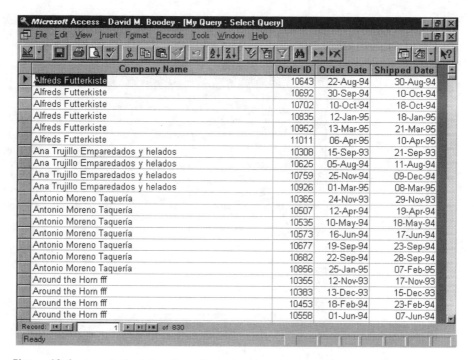

Figure 41.6 **A maximized datasheet of recordset/datasheet for My Query**

QBE grid. In the QBE grid you specify the fields to be included in the query and any sorting or criteria that you want to apply to the fields.

Field Lists

The field lists in the top pane of the Query Design Screen show the tables or queries that you are using in the query as the data source. Selecting New Query from the New Query dialog box creates a new query in Design view and opens the Show Table dialog box. From the Show Table dialog box, you can add the tables or queries to be used in the query. If you need to add tables after you close the Show Table dialog box, you can always open it by choosing Query ➤ Show Table from the menu bar or by clicking on the Show Table toolbar button. Or right-click on the top pane and choose Show Table from the shortcut menu.

If you are using more than one table in the query, any relationships that have been created are reflected in the top pane. If a relationship does not exist between a table you are using in the query and at least one other

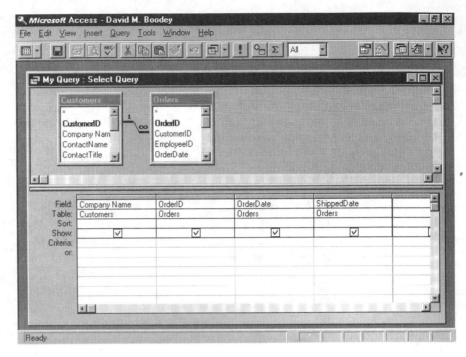

Figure 41.7 **The Query Design Screen**

table, you can join the tables by clicking and dragging from a field in the unrelated table to a field in another table. For more information on relationships and joins, see the chapter dedicated to helping you understand them.

WARNING   Never run a query if there is a field list in the top pane of the Query Design Screen that is not related to another field list with at least a join. If the query is run and there are field lists that are not joined to other field lists, the datasheet will reflect what is called a Cartesian Result. For example, assume you have two unconnected tables in a query and you run it. If one table has 100 records and the other table has 10 records, the resulting datasheet will consist of 1000 records. Because the query does not know how to relate the two tables, it matches every record in one table with every record in the other table—a meaningless result that can be costly in terms of time and memory if tables are large.

The QBE Grid

Once you have the field lists in the top pane of the Query Design Screen, you need to specify which fields to use with the query. The idea is to take the fields from the top pane and place them in the QBE grid. Here are some ways to do so:

▶ Click and drag the desired field from a field list in the top to a column in the QBE grid.

▶ Double-click on a field in a field list to place it in the next available column.

▶ Click on the field row of a column and then click on the drop-down arrow to choose from a list of available fields.

▶ Click on the field row of a column and then type the expression of a calculated field that you want to use in the query.

TIP If you want to use all the fields from a field list, the quickest way to add them is to place the asterisk (*) located at the top of a field list into one of the columns of the QBE grid. The asterisk represents the entire record, and when the query runs, all fields in that field list are included in the datasheet. The only downside to using the asterisk is that you cannot specify criteria for individual fields. To quickly get all fields from a field list in their own individual columns, double-click on the title bar of the field list to select them. Click and drag the selection to the QBE grid, and the fields are placed into their own columns.

Once the fields are in the QBE grid, you can specify sort order, set criteria, and determine whether a field will be shown or used only to set criteria or for sorting.

Building the Query

To demonstrate the capabilities of the Query Design Screen, we will rebuild the query we constructed with the Simple Query Wizard and expand on it in ways not possible with the Simple Query Wizard.

1. Select the Queries tab of the NWIND Database window.

2. Click on the New button.

3. From the New Query dialog box, select New Query and then click on OK.

4. In the Show Tables dialog box, select the Customers table and click on Add.

5. Select the Orders table and click on Add.

6. With the two tables added to your query, click on Close in the Show Tables dialog box.

7. Your Query Design Screen should look like the one in Figure 41.8.

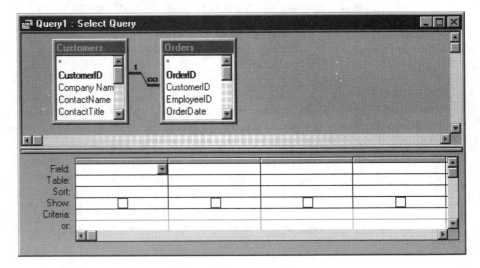

Figure 41.8   Customers and Orders are added to the new query.

8. Point to the Company Name field in the Customers field list and drag the field to the first column of the QBE grid.

9. Double-click on the OrderID field in the Orders field list. The field appears in the second column of the QBE grid.

10. Click on the field row of the third column and click on the drop-down arrow that appears. Select the Orders.OrderDate field from the list, as shown in Figure 41.9.

11. Add the ShippedDate field from the Orders field list using one of the above methods.

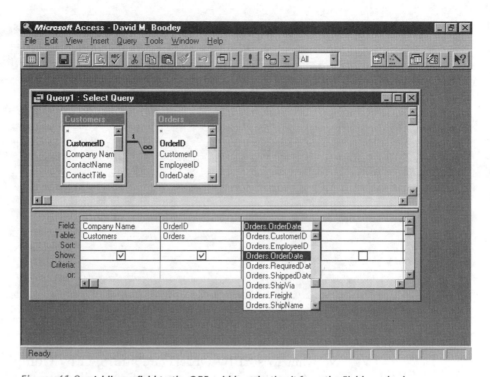

Figure 41.9   Adding a field to the QBE grid by selecting it from the Field combo box

12.   Using the Query Design Screen, you can add calculated fields to your query. Click on the Field row of the fourth column.

13.   In the fourth column, type the following, with no spaces:

```
DAYS ELAPSED:[SHIPPEDDATE]-[ORDERDATE]
```

The text to the left of the colon is the caption, or the name of the calculated column, and the expression to the right of the colon generates a value for the column. When referring to fields, field names are enclosed in square brackets.

14.   Your Query Design Screen should look like the one in Figure 41.10.

> **TIP**   If you find it hard to type in the limited space of the column cell when creating calculated columns or specifying criteria, you can press Shift+F2 to zoom in on the cell, or you can right-click on the Field row cell and choose Zoom from the shortcut menu.

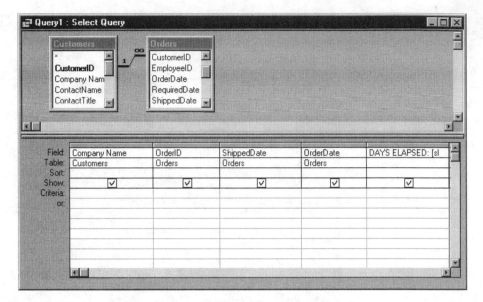

Figure 41.10   New Query with a calculated column to figure the days elapsed between Order-Date and ShippedDate

15. We want to sort by OrderDate and then by Company Name, but we want Company Name to appear first in the datasheet view of the query, and Access sorts from left to right. All is not lost though. We can bring OrderDate down to the grid a second time, this time placing it before Company Name. To do so, click and drag the OrderID field from the Orders field list on top of the Company Name field in the QBE grid. All columns shift right.

16. Click on the Sort row under the OrderDate field in column one, and choose Ascending from the drop-down list displayed by clicking the down arrow button. We also want to sort by Company Name after OrderDate, so choose Ascending in the Sort row under Company Name as well.

17. Even though we needed OrderDate in the first column for sorting, we do not want it to show in the query datasheet; so uncheck the checkbox in the Show row under OrderDate in the first column.

18. In the Criteria column under the DAYS ELAPSED column, type >10. This criterion restricts the records to only those whose orders took more than 10 days from the order date to ship. Figure 41.11 shows the finished query in design view.

When you are ready to view the results of your query, choose View ➤ Datasheet from the menu bar or click on the Datasheet View button on the Query Design toolbar. Or click on the Run button on the same

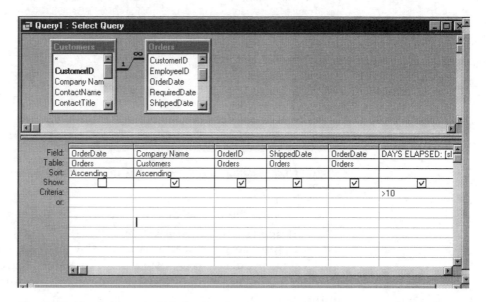

Figure 41.11   Our query to find all orders that took longer than 10 days to ship from order date sorted by date and company name

toolbar. Figure 41.12 shows the result of the query that we just created.

Remember that although this query was created from scratch with the Query Design Screen, you can redesign any query created with the Simple Query Wizard and add sorting, specify criteria, or create calculated columns.

Top Values

You can easily set the properties of a query so that it returns only the top percentage or some top number of records. If you click in an open area of the Query Design Screen and choose View ➤ Properties from

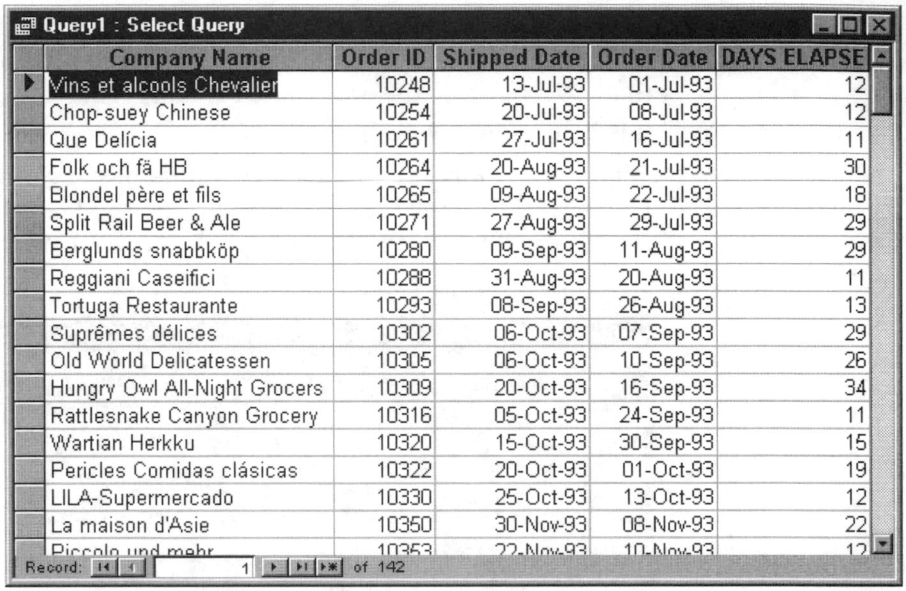

Company Name	Order ID	Shipped Date	Order Date	DAYS ELAPSE
Vins et alcools Chevalier	10248	13-Jul-93	01-Jul-93	12
Chop-suey Chinese	10254	20-Jul-93	08-Jul-93	12
Que Delícia	10261	27-Jul-93	16-Jul-93	11
Folk och fä HB	10264	20-Aug-93	21-Jul-93	30
Blondel père et fils	10265	09-Aug-93	22-Jul-93	18
Split Rail Beer & Ale	10271	27-Aug-93	29-Jul-93	29
Berglunds snabbköp	10280	09-Sep-93	11-Aug-93	29
Reggiani Caseifici	10288	31-Aug-93	20-Aug-93	11
Tortuga Restaurante	10293	08-Sep-93	26-Aug-93	13
Suprêmes délices	10302	06-Oct-93	07-Sep-93	29
Old World Delicatessen	10305	06-Oct-93	10-Sep-93	26
Hungry Owl All-Night Grocers	10309	20-Oct-93	16-Sep-93	34
Rattlesnake Canyon Grocery	10316	05-Oct-93	24-Sep-93	11
Wartian Herkku	10320	15-Oct-93	30-Sep-93	15
Pericles Comidas clásicas	10322	20-Oct-93	01-Oct-93	19
LILA-Supermercado	10330	25-Oct-93	13-Oct-93	12
La maison d'Asie	10350	30-Nov-93	08-Nov-93	22
Piccolo und mehr	10353	22-Nov-93	10-Nov-93	12

Figure 41.12 ***A datasheet with five resulting columns, including the calculated DAYS ELAPSED column***

the menu bar, the Properties window for the query will open. The Top Values property has a combo box list of suggested top values, for example, top 5, top 25%, and ALL. By selecting the value directly in the Top Values property or by using the Top Values list box on the Query Design toolbar, you can restrict the records returned to a certain number.

For the previous query, you might want only the top 10 orders with the worst elapsed shipped time. To get the 10 worst, you remove the other sort parameters previously entered and then sort by the ELAPSED DAYS column in descending order and specify a Top Values property of 10. Figure 14.13 shows the changes to the Design view of the above query for this scenario, and Figure 14.14 shows the results in Datasheet view.

NOTE **Figure 14.14 shows 11 records even though it is a Top Values query set to 10. The reason is a tie for last place. If there is a tie for the lowest value, Access does not cut off any records because it has no way of determining which records take precedence over others since they all meet the same criteria.**

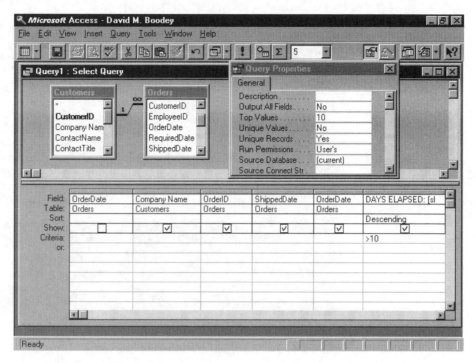

Figure 41.13   *Modifying the previous query to show the top 10 worst elapsed ship days*

Behind the Scenes with SQL View

Once you have finished designing a query, you might want to see what you were really creating, a SQL statement. You can view the SQL of a query by choosing View ➤ SQL from the menu bar or by clicking on the drop-down arrow of the Query View button on the toolbar and choosing SQL View, or by right-clicking on an open area of the Query Design Screen and choosing View SQL from the shortcut menu. Figure 41.15 shows the SQL view for the query we just created.

> **TIP**   You can switch from Design view to SQL view, and you can switch from SQL view to Design view. This feature is useful when you are learning SQL. You can write the SQL statement first in SQL view and then switch to Design View to see if your statement results in what you were expecting.

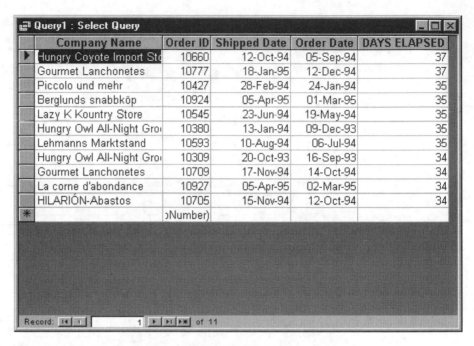

Figure 41.14 *The results of the modified Top Values query*

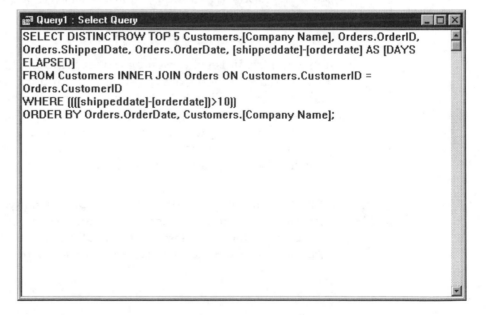

Figure 41.15 *The SQL view of a query*

Query Datasheet

You maneuver a query datasheet in the same way you maneuver a table datasheet. Refer to the chapter on tables to review how to work with a datasheet.

Chapter 42

Publishing Your Data with Reports

FEATURING

Clicking on the New button on the Reports tab of a Database window opens the New Reports dialog box, which gives you six options:

▶ **Design View** opens a new blank report on which you can build a report from scratch.

▶ **Report Wizard** steps you through the creation of a report, asking which tables and fields you want to use. It also allows you to specify levels of grouping, for example, grouping all orders by customers. The Report Wizard also asks whether you want a columnar or tabular layout, whether you want to sort in groups, which type of style you want, and so on.

▶ **Columnar AutoReport** generates a columnar report based on the table or query you choose in the New Report dialog box and a set of report defaults.

▶ **Tabular AutoReport** generates a tabular report based on the table or query you choose in the New Report dialog box and a set of report defaults.

▶ **Chart Wizard** assists in creating a report that requires a chart.

▶ **Label Wizard** makes creating labels of any size based on a table or a query a complete snap.

Designing a Report

In this version of Access, the Report Wizard is now so user-friendly that the beginner need not create a query to include fields from multiple tables. If you do not specify a table or a query to use in the New Report dialog box, the first step of the Report Wizard is to ask which tables and fields you want. It then creates a SQL statement for you to use as the recordsource for the report.

To use AutoReports, you must first specify a table or a query; however, after you do so, the rest of the report is generated using default settings. You don't have to answer a single question.

If you want a report that includes graphics, you use the Chart Wizard.

If you and your word processor or report program have labored to create mailing labels or any other type of label, be prepared to be amazed. With the Label Wizard, you can take an existing table or query and fashion a report to print any size label. Most of the time, you can select a size from the Avery Label collection. Avery is the most popular brand of computer-generated labels; even most of Avery's competitors put a reference to the corresponding Avery label number on their packages. If your label format is not available, you can always easily specify a custom format.

Using the Wizards

The Wizards provide a fast and easy path to report creation. The two Wizards that you will probably use most often are the Report Wizard and the Label Wizard. All the Wizards are by nature easy to use and generally self-explanatory.

Report Wizard

You can use the Report Wizard to create most of the reports you will need. In our example, we will create a report without using a preexisting table or query. Creating a report from a preexisting table or query would eliminate several of these steps.

1. Open the NWIND database found in the Samples folder in your main Access folder.

2. Select the Reports tab and click on the New button to open the New Reports dialog box as shown in Figure 42.1.

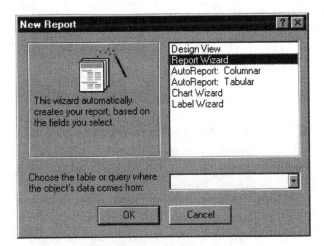

Figure 42.1   *The New Reports dialog box*

3. You do not need to specify a query or a table that is already created to use the Report Wizard as you do to use the other Wizards; so select the Report Wizard, leave the table/query combo box empty, and click on OK.

The first window of the Report Wizard has three main focus points: the Tables/Queries combo box, the Available Fields list box, and the Selected Fields list box. In the Tables/Queries combo box, you select the table or the query that contains the fields you want. The Available Fields list box changes to show the available fields for the table selected in the combo box. The Selected Fields list box will hold the fields that you want to include in your report.

One of the nice functions of this step is that from this one window you can select all the fields from all the tables you want to include. Once you select all the fields from one table or query that you have selected in the combo box, you can make another selection from the combo box and choose the fields from that table or query. You continue to select tables/queries and fields until you select all the fields to be included in your report.

> **NOTE** The Report Wizard uses the relationships that you create in the Relationships window to determine which tables to include in the query that it creates as the source for your report. To view the relationships for the NWIND database, select Tools ➤ Relationships from the menu bar. See the chapter on relational databases for more details on relationships.

Once all the fields to be included are listed in the Selected Fields list box, you can continue.

4. From the Tables/Queries combo box, select the Categories table.

5. Send the CategoryName, Description, and Picture fields from the Available Fields list box to the Selected Fields list box as shown in Figure 42.2 by clicking on the > button or by double-clicking on the field names in the Available Fields list box.

6. From the Tables/Queries combo box, select the Products table.

7. Send the ProductName, UnitsInStock, and UnitsOnOrder fields from the Available Fields list box to the Selected Fields list box.

8. Once you have all the fields selected as shown in Figure 42.3, click on Next.

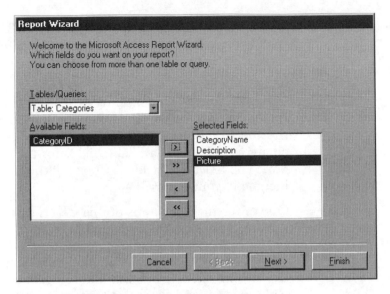

Figure 42.2   Fields from the Categories table selected

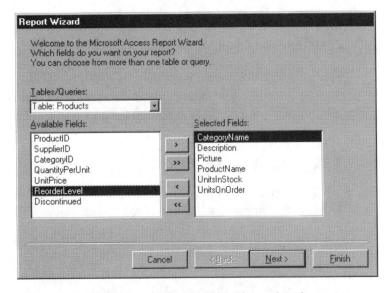

Figure 42.3   All fields for the report being created have been selected.

9. Next, the Report Wizard asks how you want to view the information on your report. In our example, each product listed in our Products table is related to a category in the Category table by CategoryID; so if we choose to view our report by categories, all the products for specific categories will be grouped together. In this report that is the effect we want; so select *by Categories* as your viewing method, as shown in Figure 42.4, and click on Next.

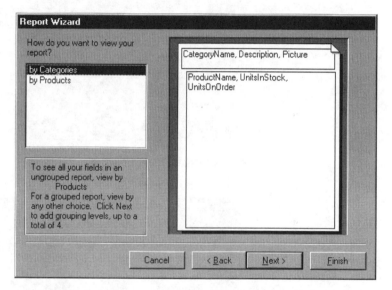

Figure 42.4 **Selecting to view our report by Categories**

10. Next, the Report Wizard wants to know if you want to create any additional grouping. We have no need for another grouping in this example, so click on Next.

11. The Report Wizard now needs you to tell it how you want the detail section of your report sorted. You can have as many as four levels of sorting, as shown in Figure 42.5. Select ProductName in the first sorting combo box. Notice the sort buttons on the right of the sort combo boxes that you can click to change the sort order from ascending to descending and then click on Next.

12. Next, the Report Wizard asks about the layout of your report. Select Outline 1 and click on Next, leaving all other options as their defaults. Figure 42.6 shows this step and provides a sample preview of the layout.

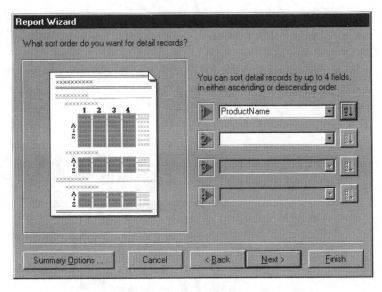

Figure 42.5   Sorting by ProductName using the Report Wizard

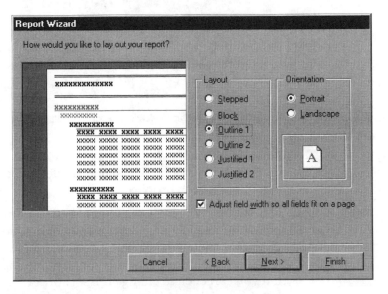

Figure 42.6   Selecting a Layout for your report

13. The next to last step in creating a report with the Report Wizard is to choose a style (see Figure 42.7). Click on each of the views to see how the different styles appear. We'll use Corporate in our example; so select it and click on the Next button.

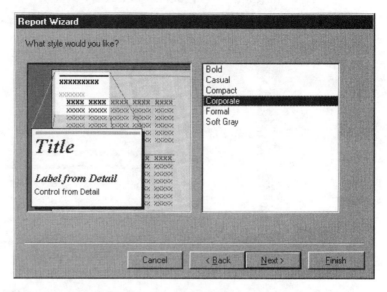

Figure 42.7   Selecting a style for a report with the Report Wizard

14. The final step is to enter a title for the report. Replace the default title Categories with **Products by Category Report** and click on Finish, leaving all other options with their defaults. Your report should look similar to that in Figure 42.8.

Label Wizard

The Label Wizard takes you by the hand to help you create perfect labels almost every time. The Label Wizard, like the other Wizards except for the Report Wizard, requires that you already have a table or a query to use for your report.

1. Open the NWIND database.

2. Select the Reports tab and click on the New button.

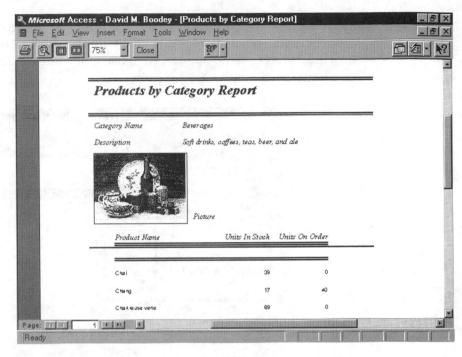

Figure 42.8 **Print Preview of the beginning of the report created with the Wizard**

3. In the New Report dialog box, select Label Wizard and choose the Customers table in the combo box, requesting a table or a query for a data source.

4. Figure 42.9 shows the first step in the Label Wizard. The label size list box provides descriptions of labels for which it already has dimensions: the Avery number (which can be found on almost every box of laser or ink jet labels), the dimensions, and the number of labels across a page per row. This list contains most of the labels that you should ever need. You can modify the list to display a Metric Unit of Measure or a Label Type of Continuous by changing the appropriate option button below the list box. You can also click on the Customize button to define your own label if by chance it is not listed. Select Avery number 5160, which is a sheet-fed label, and click on Next.

5. Figure 42.10 shows the next step—choosing a text format for your labels. The options you choose will be applied to all text, fields, and data. The preview on the left of the dialog box will change to reflect the changes that you make to the options on the right. Remember, you are generally

working with small labels, so don't make your font size too large. For this example, you can simply accept the defaults and click on Next.

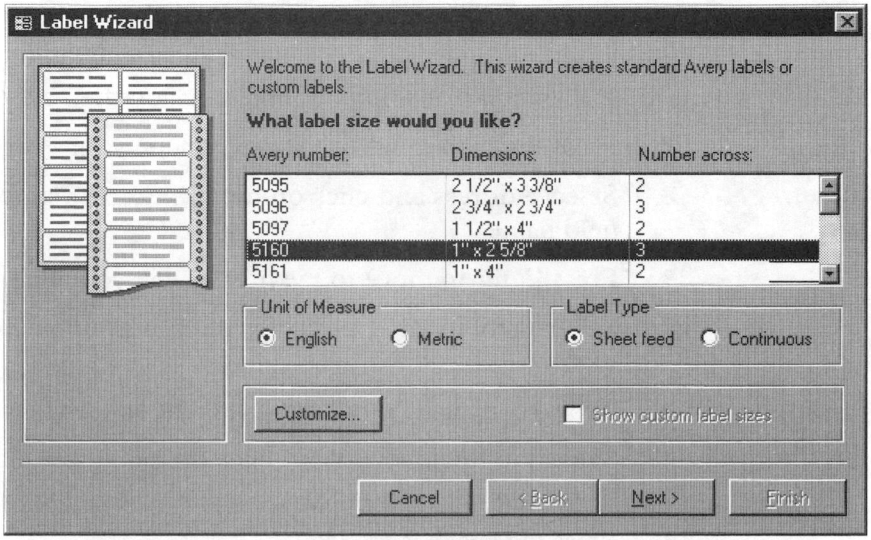

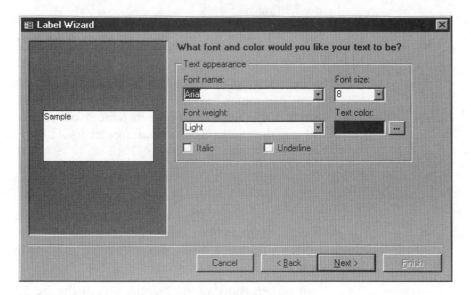

Figure 42.9 *Selecting a label size with the Label Wizard*

Figure 42.10 *Selecting the format for all the text in a label*

In the next stage, you design a template for your label using the fields from the table or the query that you selected earlier. If any extraneous punctuation marks or text should appear on every label, you can type them directly into the Prototype label.

6. From the Available fields list, select CompanyName and then click on the > button or simply double-click on the field name.

7. Press Enter to move to the next line in your Prototype label.

8. Select Address and click on the > button or simply double-click on the field name.

9. Press Enter to move to the next line in your Prototype label.

10. Select the City field and press the > button or double-click on the field name.

11. Type a comma (,) and then press the spacebar once.

12. Select the Region field and click on the > button or double-click on the field name.

13. Press the spacebar twice.

14. Select the PostalCode field and click on the > button or double-click on the field name.

15. When you're done, your screen should like that in Figure 42.11.

16. Click on Next.

    In the next step, the Label Wizard asks if you want to sort the information in any particular order. If you choose to sort by more than one field, the report is sorted in the order in which you selected the fields. Since we will use these labels for a mailing, let's sort by PostalCode and within each PostalCode by CompanyName.

17. Select PostalCode from the Available fields list box and click on the > button to move it to the Sort by list box or double-click on the field name.

18. Select Company Name from the Available fields list box and click on the > button to move it to the Sort by list box or double-click on the field name.

19. Your screen should look like the one in Figure 42.12. Click on Next.

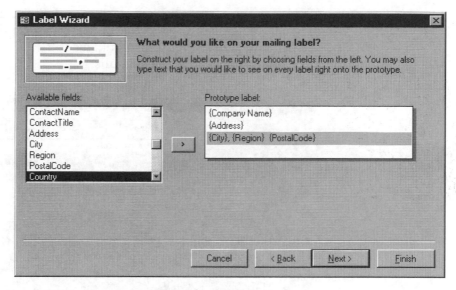

Figure 42.11 *Designing a label with the Label Wizard*

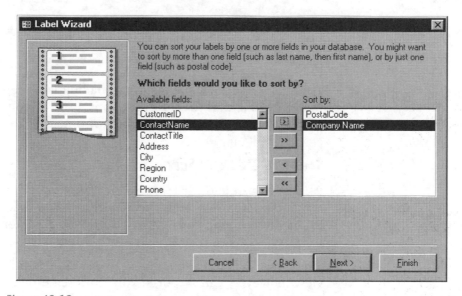

Figure 42.12 *Selecting the fields to use for sorting the mailing labels*

20. Change the title/name of the report from Label Customers 1 to a more meaningful name of Customer Mailing Labels so that the last screen of the Label Wizard looks like that in Figure 42.13. Click on Finish, leaving the other options with their defaults.

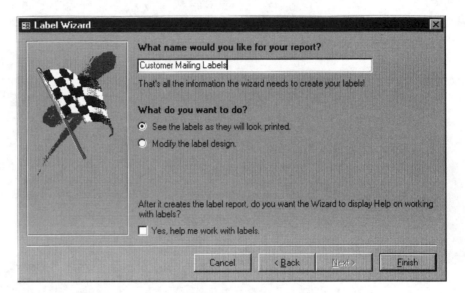

Figure 42.13 Changing the title of the mailing label report to Customer Mailing Labels

Figure 42.14 shows the resulting mailing label report in Print Preview mode. Notice that the information is in three columns, as is the Avery label sheet to which we would be printing.

Report Design Screen

As helpful as the Wizards are for creating reports, they could not possibly accommodate everyone's specific needs. You meet these special needs by modifying reports created with the Wizards or by creating reports from scratch. You do both in report Design view.

The Design view of a report is in five sections, similar to the form Design view; however, with reports, you can create new sections in which to group data to allow for subtotals or for formatting reasons.

The main tools for building the report in Design view are the same as those used in building forms: the Field List, the Toolbox, and, as always, Properties.

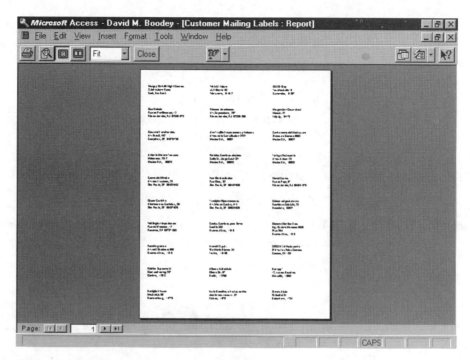

Figure 42.14 Print Preview of a label report created with the Label Wizard

Sections

Each section begins with a gray section header that contains the name of the section. The five primary sections in a report are:

▶ **Detail**. A report always has a detail section. In it you place the fields that repeat for every record.

▶ **Report Header/Report Footer**. The items you place in the Report Header and Report Footer appear once and only once—the Report Header at the beginning of the report, and the Report Footer at the end of the report. You place controls that calculate grand totals in the Report Footer. When you create a new report in Design view, the Report Header and Footer are not visible by default. To make the Report Header and Footer visible, choose View ➤ Report Header/Footer from the menu bar while in Design view or right-click on the Report window's title bar and choose Report Header/Footer from the shortcut menu.

▶ **Page Header/Page Footer**. The Page Header holds information that you want to appear at the top of every page in your report, and the Page

Footer holds information that you want to appear at the bottom of every page in your report. You can set the Page Header and Page Footer properties not to print on the first and last pages of the report.

Sorting and Grouping

If you elect to group the report by specific fields, you can add new sections to a report. If you group a report by a field, you can set the group to have a header and/or footer section of its own to hold section totals.

1. Open the NWIND database.

2. Select the Reports tab and click on New.

3. In the New Report dialog box, select *AutoReport: Tabular* and the *Customers* table, as shown in Figure 42.15.

4. Click on OK.

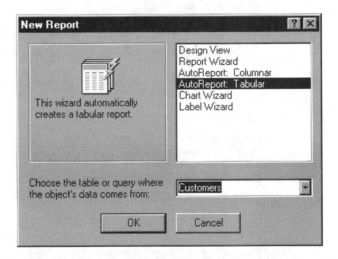

Figure 42.15 **Creating a Report using AutoReport:Tabular and the Customers table**

5. A new report based on the Customers table opens in Print Preview.

6. Click on the Close button on the Print Preview toolbar.

7. The report is now is Design view, as illustrated in Figure 42.16.

8. From the menu bar, select View ➤ Sorting and Grouping to open the Sorting and Grouping dialog box as shown in Figure 42.17.

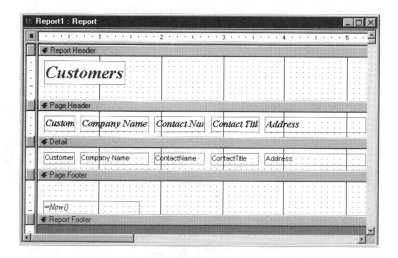

Figure 42.16 *Design view of our Tabular Report*

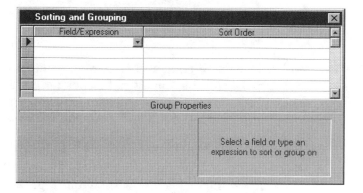

Figure 42.17 *The Sorting and Grouping dialog box*

9. In the top pane of the Sorting and Grouping dialog box, click on the first row of the Field/Expression column.

10. Click on the drop-down arrow and select the Country field from the list.

11. When you select a field, the Grouping Properties for that field are listed in the bottom pane.

12. In the Group Header and Group Footer properties, change the setting to Yes by typing over what is there or by clicking on the down arrow button and selecting from the drop-down list.

13. Select the CompanyName field in the second row of the Field/Expression column in the top pane.

14. Since we want to sort by CompanyName after Country, leave the Group Properties with their default settings.

15. Your dialog box should look like that in Figure 42.18.

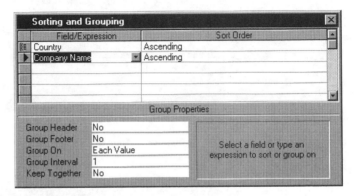

Figure 42.18 **Sorting and Grouping on the Country field**

16. Close the Sorting and Grouping dialog box by clicking the close button on the title bar or by right-clicking on the title bar of the dialog box window and selecting Close. Or simply type Alt+F4. Notice the new sections created in your report design.

17. From the menu bar, select View ➤ Field List.

18. Click and drag the Country field from the Field List to the left center of the Country Header, as shown in Figure 42.19.

19. Dragging the field from the field list will also bring a label for the Country field. The name in the label is meaningless for our report, so point to the label, click on it, and press Delete.

20. From the menu bar, select View ➤ Print Preview or File->Print Preview or click on the Print Preview toolbar button. The report is now grouped by country, as shown in Figure 42.20.

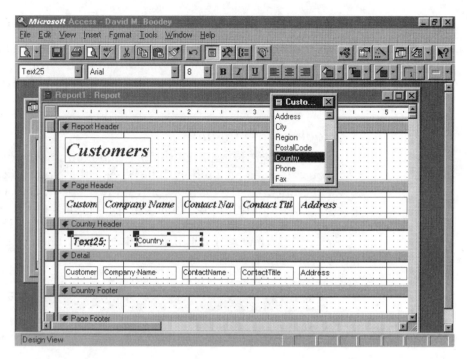

Figure 42.19 *Dragging the Country field from the field list to the Country Header*

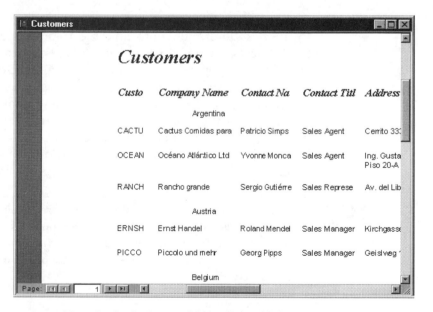

Figure 42.20 *Grouping by the Country field has been added to our report.*

Field List

When working with a report that has a record source, you can open a Field List window that shows a list of fields. You can click and drag any of these fields onto the report. To view the Field List, select View ➤ Field List from the menu bar or click on the Field List toolbar button.

Toolbox and Controls

The Toolbox is a special toolbar that contains every type of object that you can place on a report. The objects that you can place on reports are called *controls*. To place a control on a report, click once on the control in the Toolbox and then click on the section of the report in which you want the control. Figure 42.21 shows the Toolbox that you can view by selecting View ➤ Toolbox from the menu bar or by clicking the Toolbox toolbar button.

Figure 42.21   *The Toolbox holds all the control types that can be used on a report.*

Properties

Properties determine how an object looks and performs. To view the Properties window, select View ➤ Properties from the menu bar or click on the Properties button on the Report Design toolbar. There is only one Properties window. To view properties for different controls, select the control; the Properties window changes to show you the properties for the selected object or section. You can see the change in the title bar of the Properties window. Remember that the report itself is an object, and you can select it by clicking on the intersection of the two rulers in the top left corner of the Report window.

NOTE   The chapter on Forms provides more details and figures that illustrate the Field List, the Toolbox, and the Properties window. Remember the design screens for forms and reports work the same except for some minor differences that depend on whether you are printing to paper or formatting for the screen.

Previewing Your Report

Instead of opening reports, you preview them. The sole function of reports is to generate output suitable for printing, so there is no "screen view" other than Print Preview, which shows you exactly how the report will print. Figure 42.22 shows the Print Preview screen and points out some of the buttons on the Print Preview toolbar, whose functions you will want to use when previewing a report.

WARNING   When exiting from Print Preview, be sure to click on the Close button on the Print Preview toolbar or press Esc. Selecting File ➤ Close from the menu bar or the close button on the window's title bar closes the report object completely, not just the preview.

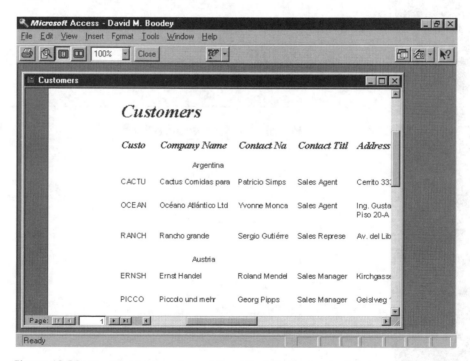

Figure 42.22   *The Print Preview of a report and the Print Preview toolbar*

Chapter 43

Making the Access Parts a Whole

FEATURING

Macros

Visual Basic for Applications

Bringing all parts of your database into an efficient whole is the job of Access macros and the programming language of Access, Visual Basic for Applications (VBA). Unlike the other applications in Office, Access differentiates between macros and VBA. In Access you create macros using Macro Design view, from which you can choose from 49 actions for each step of the macro. Macros provide most of the automation that most users ever need. Developers and more advanced users, however, can use VBA, which provides faster execution of automation procedures. You can use VBA to manipulate other applications, including Word and Excel, and to tap into the core functions of Windows.

Both macros and VBA code center around the event properties of objects. An event, as we've mentioned, is something that can happen to an object. For example a Command Button on a form has an On Click event that is triggered when you click on it. The event properties hold the name of the macro or code that you want to execute when a particular event occurs. By using events to trigger when macros or code run, you can create a database that fits seamlessly into an application.

Macros

Access macros allow you to automate tasks step by step. In Macro Design view, you list the actions that you want to perform in the order that you want them to be performed.

Designing Macros

The Macro Design view screen, like many of the design screens, is divided into a top pane and a bottom pane. In the top pane you list the actions to be performed, and the bottom pane reveals the arguments for the current action, which is marked by the cursor in the top pane.

The top pane has four columns: Macro Name, Condition, Action, and Comment. The Macro Name and Condition columns are not visible by default, because they are not necessary for basic macros. To view all the columns, do one of the following: (1) Select View ➤ Macro Names and View ➤ Conditions from the menu bar; (2) click on their corresponding buttons on the Macro toolbar; or (3) right-click on the title bar in Macro Design view and choose View Macro Names and/or View Conditions from the shortcut menu. Figure 43.1 shows Macro Design view with all columns in view.

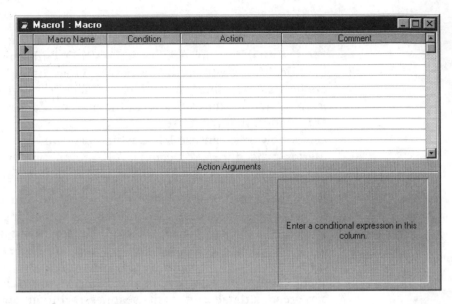

Figure 43.1 Macro Design view with all columns in the top pane in view

Actions

An action is a command that has a specific function. Forty-nine actions are available to use in each line of a macro. Some of the actions are:

▶ **OpenForm, OpenReport, OpenQuery,** and **OpenTable.** Each opens its respective object.

▶ **MsgBox.** Displays a message dialog box.

▶ **ApplyFilter.** Applies a filter to a form, a report, or a table.

▶ **OutputTo, TransferDatabase,** and **TransferSpreadsheet.** Exports, Imports, or Links Access objects to certain file formats.

▶ **RunCode** and **RunMacro.** Run other automation routines from within a macro.

▶ **Quit.** Exits Access from a database.

By listing the actions one after the other in successive rows, you can easily automate your database.

Arguments

For every action you specify in the top pane of the Macro Design view screen, corresponding Action Arguments appear in the bottom pane. The arguments in the bottom pane change as you move from action to action in the top pane. Figure 43.2 shows the arguments for the Open-Form action.

Form Name	
View	Form
Filter Name	
Where Condition	
Data Mode	Edit
Window Mode	Normal

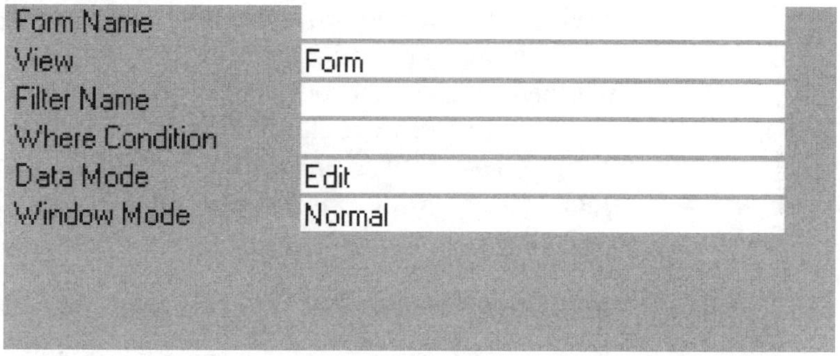

Figure 43.2 **Arguments for the OpenForm action**

TIP After you select an action in the top pane, a short description of the action is displayed in the area to the right of the action arguments. If you need more information about the action, press F1. Help opens directly to the section on the selected action. You can get the same kind of help for the individual arguments for each action.

Conditions

The Condition column is not visible when you start a new macro because you don't need it to build a macro. If all the actions in your macro execute every time the macro runs, the Condition column can remain hidden. The Condition column provides a way to test the result of an expression that returns either True or False. If the expression returns True, the action executes; if it returns False, the action does not execute. Here are two ways to use Conditions:

▶ Checking to see if a form is open before referring to a control on the form that would result in an error if the form is closed.

▶ Checking the current value of a control on a form before saving the record, to ensure data integrity.

Macro Names

You use the Macro Name column to group small macros into a logical whole. For example, you have a bunch of small macros that are used to respond to the On Click event of four buttons on a form. If you create an individual macro for each button, four macro icons are displayed in the Database window. In the Macro Name column, you specify the name of each macro within the current Macro Design view screen, the name of which will be the only one listed in the Database window. When the first action of a macro is listed in Macro Design view, a Macro Name is specified in the Macro Name column. The Macro Name column remains empty until the next macro begins. Figure 43.3 shows Macro Design view with four small macros, each having two actions. Each macro opens a different form and closes the form from which the macro was called—more than likely a Switchboard form of some sort.

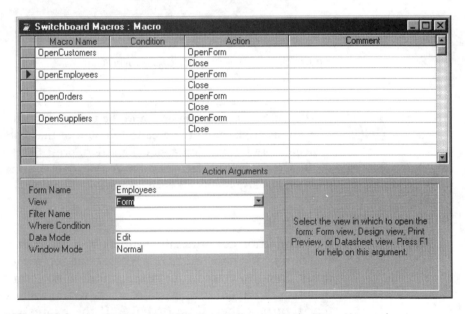

Figure 43.3   Macro Design view with four small macros in the Macro Name column

Running Macros

You can run macros from a number of places in your database: from the Macro Design view of the macro, from the Database window, in response to events on forms and reports, and from other macros or code modules.

Running a Macro from Macro Design View

It is sometimes desirable to test a macro as you build it so that you do not go too far without verifying that your macro works. To run your macro from Macro Design view, you need to save it first or be prompted to do so by selecting Run ➤ Start from the menu bar or by clicking on the Run button on the Macro toolbar that has an exclamation point on it.

Running a Macro from the Database Window

Although most of the macros that you create are not meant to run from the Database window, if need be, they can. To run a macro from the Database window, select the macro on the Macros page and click on the Run button.

Running a Macro in Response to Events

The purpose of most macros is to respond to the events of various objects: the click of a Command Button, the opening of a form or a report, and before the update of a record in a form. Figure 43.4 shows the Event properties of a Command Button control that you can place on a form, and Figure 43.5 shows the Event properties of a form.

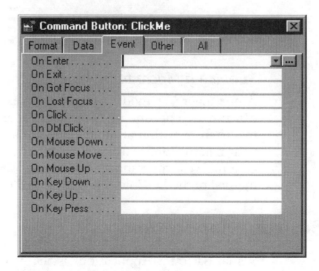

Figure 43.4 **The Event properties of a Command Button**

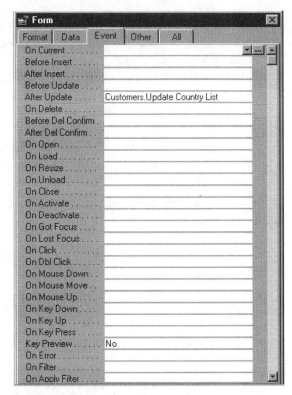

Figure 43.5   **The Event properties of a form used for data entry**

Running a Macro from Another Macro or From a Code Module

If one macro or module triggers the execution of another macro, you can use the appropriate macro action or VBA statement. To execute a macro from within another macro, make the macro action of a line in your macro RunMacro and specify the macro in the arguments for the action. To execute a macro from within VBA code, you use the RunMacro method of the DoCmd object, followed by the necessary arguments.

Visual Basic for Applications

Visual Basic for Applications is the programming language of Access, Excel, and Project. Eventually, all applications in Office will provide VBA. You move from macros to VBA when macros no longer provide the functionality your database needs.

Functions and Procedures

When you write VBA code, you create either a procedure or a function. The main difference between a function and a procedure is that the function returns a value and the procedure does not.

A function begins with Function NameofFunction and ends with End Function, and a procedure starts with Sub ProcedureName and ends with End Sub.

Modules

A module is a generic term for a container object that holds the VBA code that you write for your Access database. The two types of modules are Global and Form (or Report).

Global Modules

Global modules are the modules listed in your Database window. The procedures and functions in these modules are available from anywhere in your application.

Code Behind Form

Code written for use with specific forms or reports is stored in special form and report modules that are saved with the form or report. This code is available only within the form or report in which it is stored and while the form or report is open.

To create CBF (Code Behind Form), click in the Event property of an object on a form or report and then click on the Builder button. Selecting Code Builder opens the form or report module and places you in an event procedure, where you can enter the code, called an event procedure, that you want to execute when the event is triggered.

Code Sampling

The following example procedure will give you a taste of working in a Code window. The code that we create will be stored in a Global Module that is available anywhere in your application.

1. Open the NWIND database.

2. Click on the Modules tab.

3. Click on New.

4. In the new module (as shown in Figure 43.6), type **Sub SayHello** and press Enter.

Figure 43.6   **The new module opened by clicking on the New button on the Modules tab**

5. Figure 43.7 shows the procedure header and footer in which you type the code for the procedure.

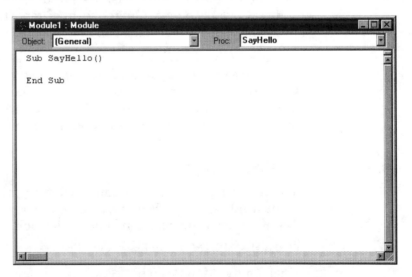

Figure 43.7   **The procedure header and footer for SayHello**

6. Type **A$=InputBox$("What is your Name")**

7. Press Enter.

8. Type **MsgBox "Hello " & A$ & "! Here is the Employees Form."**
   (Be sure to space between Hello and the closing quotation mark.)

9. Press Enter.

10. Type **DoCmd.OpenForm "Employees"**

11. Your Code window should look like that in Figure 43.8.

12. To test the macro, we can use the Debug window. Select View ➤ Debug
    Window or press Ctrl+G.

13. In the Debug window, type **Sayhello** and press Enter.

14. Your procedure should run, ask your name, say hello to you, and open
    the Employees form.

15. Since we are running this procedure from the Debug window, the Debug
    window will cover up the Employees form when it is opened. The Debug
    window is used primarily for debugging programs and not for real-life
    execution of code.

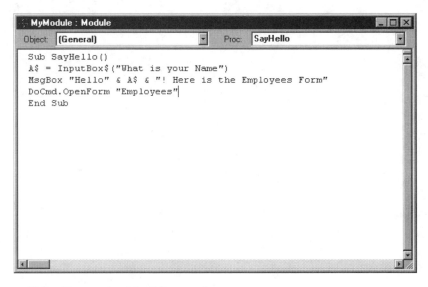

Figure 43.8   The completed SayHello procedure

16. To run this procedure from a Command Button on a form, you use the Code Builder to write code for the event, using the Builder button to create an event procedure in which you could specify SayHello as the only line of code in the procedure.

17. When you are finished, select File ➤ Close from the menu bar.

This sampling of VBA code is by no means meant to be anything more than a demonstration. To learn more about VBA and how you can use it in Access, see one of the books devoted to Access, VBA, or Access and VBA.

Chapter 44

Connecting Access to the Outside World

FEATURING

Importing Data

Linking Tables

Exporting Data

Although it would be wonderful if all the data that we need to access was in the same format, the truth is, it isn't. Data stored in older programs, data we receive from organizations that utilize various database programs, and data that we need to connect to on larger mainframe and SQL platforms are all in different formats. Access can deal with external data in two ways: by importing it and by linking to it.

Importing Data

When importing data, Access reads a file in another format and saves a copy of it as a table in your database. When you import a table, there is no connection between the original data and the new table in Access.

Many people import data when they know that they'll never again need the data in its original format. A mailing list is an example. Mainframe data is often imported because it is not accessible from the machine that has the Access database. When data is being imported from a mainframe or a large database system, the importation is generally automated with macros because the tables containing the mainframe data will probably need to be frequently updated and replaced with fresh data.

To import data, you take the follow steps:

1. While you have a database open (whether empty or containing tables), select File ➤ Get External Data ➤ Import from the menu bar.

2. In the Import dialog box, select the type of file that you want to import from the Files of type combo box in the bottom left corner (see Figure 44.1).

3. Locate the folder that contains the file you want to import and select the file.

4. Click on the Import button.

5. If successful, you will receive a message similar to that in Figure 44.2.

6. The imported data is listed as a table.

Depending on the file type that you are importing, other steps may be involved. A spreadsheet program, for example, will need to know if you want to import an entire worksheet or only a specified range. If you are importing delimited or fixed-width files, Access may require additional information. Figures 44.3 through 44.5 show a few of the possible screens you may come across when importing a spreadsheet file or an ASCII text file.

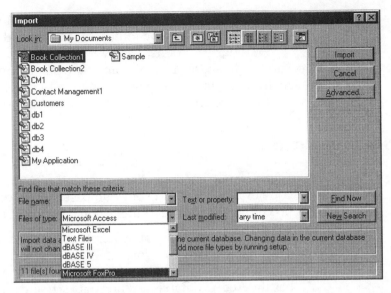

Figure 44.1 **The Import dialog box, which you open by selecting File ➤ Get External Data ➤ Import from the menu bar**

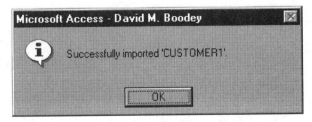

Figure 44.2 **Data has been successfully imported to a new table in your Access database.**

You can also import objects other than tables from one Access database into your current database. When importing from Access, the Import Objects window shown in Figure 44.6 opens to allow you to select the object.

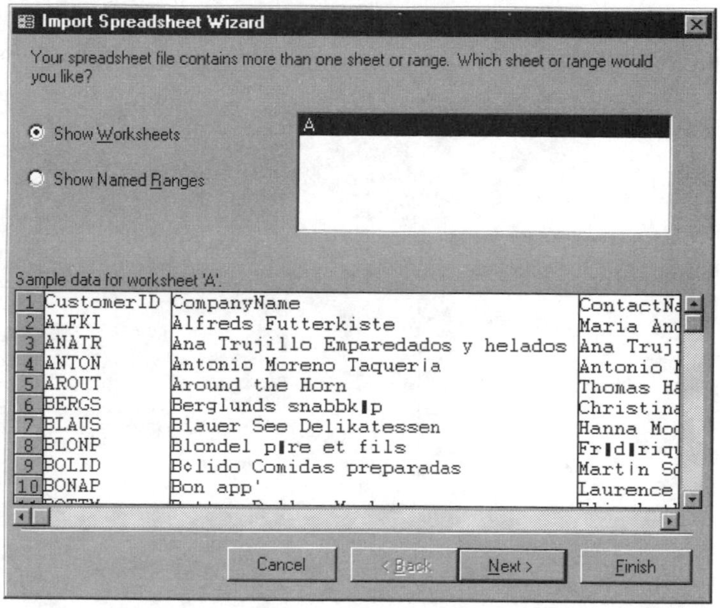

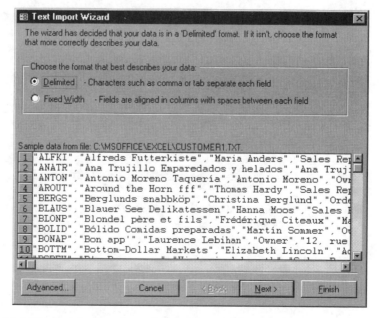

Figure 44.3   The Import Spreadsheet Wizard dialog box for spreadsheet files containing multiple worksheets

Figure 44.4   The Text Import Wizard dialog box for delimited text files

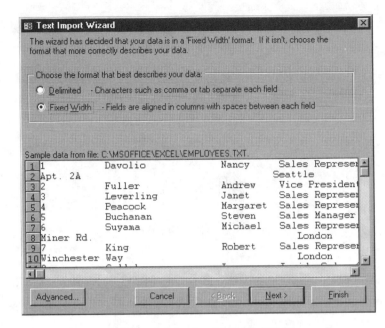

Figure 44.5 *The Text Import Wizard dialog box for fixed-width files*

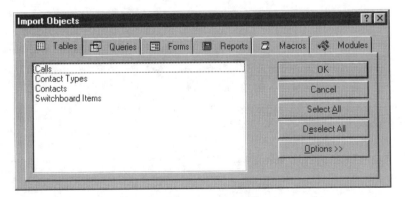

Figure 44.6 *You use the Import Objects window to import objects from one Access database to another.*

Import Errors

If Access encounters errors while importing tables, it will display an error message and create an Import Errors table that tracks the records not imported and the error that caused their exclusion. The table includes the field names and row numbers of the data that caused the errors.

If Access reports errors, open the Import Errors table and try to determine the reason for the errors. The following are some possible reasons:

▶ **Field Truncation.** An imported field value is too large for the specified field width.

▶ **Type Conversion Failure.** An attempt was made to import the wrong data type for a field.

▶ **Key Violation.** A record's primary key value duplicates a record that already exists.

▶ **Validation Rule Failure.** The value of a field in a record would break rules set using the Validation Rule property for this field or for the table.

▶ **Null in Required Field.** A null value appears in a field where null values aren't permitted because the Required property for the field is set to Yes.

▶ **Unparsable Record.** Access cannot understand the value of a field.

Linking Tables

When you are working with external data that needs to remain in its original format (perhaps the original application still needs to use the data), linking to the external data is the way that you want to go.

Linking to a table, previously known as attaching, allows Access to perform as a front end to the data, writing and reading it in the original format and application. While linked to the external data, Access is working with the original data. If Access changes the data, the original application sees the changes; if the original application changes the data, Access can see the changes.

To link to a table outside your Access application:

1. From the menu bar, select File ➤ Get External Data ➤ Link Table.

2. In the Link dialog box (shown in Figure 44.7), specify the file type that you want to import in the File of type combo box and find the file using the dialog box options. To select the file, click on the filename once and then click on the Link button.

3. If you are linking to a spreadsheet or to text files, Access presents you with a Linking Wizard. If you are linking to a dBase or a Paradox file, Access may ask if there are index files that it will need to keep updated.

4. When you are finished, Access confirms a successful link with a message box.

5. Linked files appear on the Tables page of your Database window. The little black arrows to the left of the filename signify that the file is linked, and the little icon indicates the file type. Figure 44.8 shows a Database window with three linked tables.

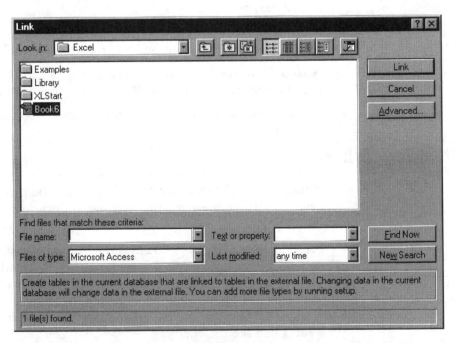

Figure 44.7   **The Link dialog box opens when you select File ➤ Get External Data ➤ Link Tables.**

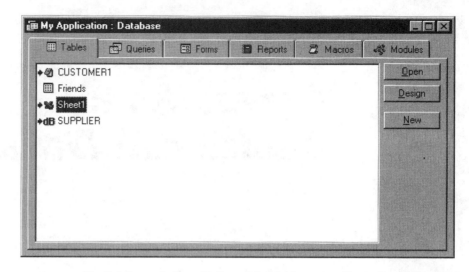

Figure 44.8 *The Database window with three linked tables: a text file, an Excel spreadsheet, and a dBase file*

ODBC

To link to foreign data sources, Access takes advantage of ODBC, or Open Database Connectivity. ODBC is a data access standard that acts as an interpreter from the foreign data source to Access or to any other database that supports ODBC. Every database format needs its own ODBC driver—the program that you install so that programs supporting ODBC can read and write in the driver's format. To install an ODBC driver, select Start ➤ Settings ➤ Control Panel. The Control Panel window contains a 32-bit ODBC icon that you double-click on to access the install procedure. When attaching to a database format supported by ODBC, select ODBC Databases as the file type.

Exporting Data

On occasion you will want to give the information that you are storing to someone that does not have Access. To export a table or a query to another file type, select File ➤ Save As/Export from the menu bar. In the Save In dialog box, you specify the folder in which you want to store the exported file, the filename, and the file type. After you specify these options, you click on the Export button to create the file.

Chapter 45

Access As a Relational Database

FEATURING

Access is a *relational* database. A relational database consists of multiple tables or subjects of data and joins those tables by common fields or characteristics. Using multiple tables instead of a single table (a flat file database) improves speed and makes storage more efficient.

For purposes of example, let's compare how a flat file database (Excel) and a relational database would track customers and orders.

Excel can track customer information without much problem. But if you try to use Excel to also track the orders that a customer places, you run into problems.

One problem is redundancy. Every time that you want to enter an order for a customer, you must enter not only the order information but also the customer information. You end up with a table or a flat file that stores customer information every time it stores order information. On the other hand a relational database creates a table for every subject. Customers, for example, is a table, and each customer has one record of information in that table. Another table holds information pertaining to the order subject, and every order has one row in that table storing information about it. A relational database uses relationships to associate the Orders in one table with the Customers in the other table.

Relationships provide a logical link from one table to another. In our Customers and Orders example, a relationship exists between the Customers table and the Orders table. The relationship is based on the primary key of the Customers table, which is a field that uniquely identifies one Customer in the table and a field in the Orders table, which stores the identification number, or primary key value, of the customer who placed the order. Once this relationship is defined, Access can determine the address of a customer who placed an order even though that information is not stored in the Orders table. Access simply follows the relationship from the value of the Customer identifier in the Orders table back to the record with that value in the primary key field of the Customers table, which holds the basic information for each customer.

Types of Relationships

Three types of relationships can exist: one-to-many, one-to-one, and many-to-many.

One-to-Many

Perhaps the most commonly used relationship, the one-to-many relationship, allows a main subject in one table (Customers) and multiple instances of related records in another table (Orders). One customer can have many orders, just as one parent can have many children, and one author could have written many books.

In a one-to-many relationship, the "one" table has a primary key field that is indexed and that allows no duplicates values so that it can serve as the unique identifier for the records in that table. The "many" table can have multiple records that relate to a single record in the "one" table and an index on a field that references the primary key in the "one" table, but the "many" table is indexed to allow for duplicates, because one customer can have multiple orders.

One-to-One

In a one-to-one relationship, one record in Table A corresponds to one record in Table B. You use a one-to-one relationship when some fields in your records are not used by a good percentage of the records. For example, an Employees table tracks employee information, including benefits. If 40 percent of the employees are part-timers who are not eligible for benefits, 40 percent of the records in the table have blank fields.

To relieve this inefficiency, you can create a second table and call it Benefits. The primary key field for the Benefits table is exactly like the one in the Employees table. The only difference occurs when the primary key data type in the main table (Employees table) is AutoNumber; in that case, the data type of the related table (Benefits table) is a Long Integer. The data type cannot be AutoNumber because you will need to enter values that match the primary key of the other table and Autonumber is self-numbering.

In a one-to-one relationship, both sides of the relationship must have a unique field that identifies the records in the respective tables, and the second table can be considered an extension of the first table. Each record in the first table can have no more than 1 record in the related table. The related table, however, is not required to have any records that relate to the main table. For example, the 40 percent of employees who are part time do not have records in the Benefits table because they are part time.

Many-to-Many

The many-to-many relationship cannot directly exist in Access, but you can form individual one-to-many relationships that give the effect of a many-to-many relationship.

For example, the Orders table and the Products table have a many-to-many relationship. Many Orders can include many products. The solution is to create an intermediary table that has one-to-many relationships with each of the two tables. The relationship of the Orders table to a new table, Order Details, would be one-to-many; and the relationship of the Products table to the Order Details table would be one-to-many, because one product can be on many Order Detail lines. The two direct one-to-many relationships have created an indirect many-to-many relationship.

Creating Relationships in Access

You create relationships using the Relationship window. In this window, you can add or delete tables and click and drag from the primary key of one table to the foreign key of another table to set relationships.

To open the Relationship window, select Tools ➤ Relationships from the menu bar or click on the Relationships toolbar button. Figure 45.1 shows the Relationship window of the NWIND database.

All relationships in the NWIND database are one-to-many. The symbols on either side of the relationship indicate its type. The 1 represents the "one" part of a relationship, and the infinity symbol (∞) represents the "many" part. If a relationship has a 1 on both sides, it is a one-to-one relationship.

To delete a relationship, click on the middle of the line joining the two tables and press Delete. Deleting a table (by clicking on the title bar and pressing delete) simply removes the table from the layout screen and does not remove the relationship.

When you click and drag from one table to another in the Relationships window, the Relationships dialog box, as shown in Figure 45.2, opens.

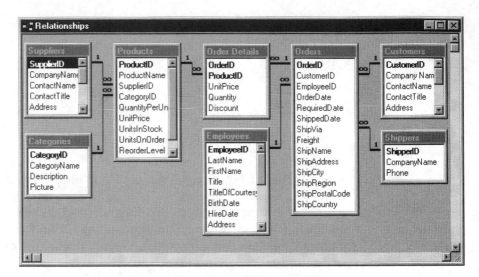

Figure 45.1   **The Relationship window of the NWIND database**

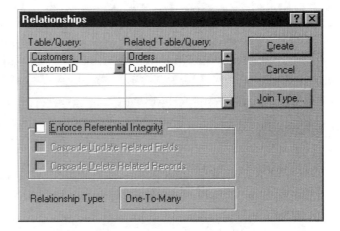

Figure 45.1   **The Relationships dialog box**

In the Relationships dialog box, you indicate whether you want to enforce referential integrity, turn on Cascading Updates and Deletes, specify the type of join you want for your relationship, and click on the Create button to create your relationship type, which Access automatically determines.

How Access Determines Relationship Types

Access determines the type of relationship you will be creating by following some rules of thumb:

▶ If only one of the related fields is a primary key or has a unique index, Access creates a one-to-many relationship.

▶ If both of the related fields are primary keys or have unique indexes, Access creates a one-to-one relationship.

▶ If neither field is a primary key or has a unique index, Access creates an undefined relationship.

Referential Integrity

When you elect to Enforce Referential Integrity, you are instructing Access to watch over your tower of data. When referential integrity is enforced, the relationships created will insure the integrity of your data.

You cannot enter data, using any method, into a table on the "many" side of a one-to-many relationship if the value in the foreign key relating to the table does not have a corresponding value in the table on the "one" side. You cannot, for example, add orders for a customer that does not exist.

You cannot delete records in a table on the "one" side of a one-to-many relationship if records on the "many" side refer to that record. Doing so would create the orphan record syndrome—child records without a parent; orders without a customer. Unless the Cascade Delete option is set, you would have to delete the "many" records before you would be allowed to delete a record on the "one" side.

Cascade Update

Cascade Update is an option of referential integrity. If Cascade Update is engaged for a relationship, when you change the primary key value of a record on the "one" side of a one-to-many relationship, Access cascades the change in number to the child, or to the "many" records. For example, if a Customer with the ID of ABC123 must be changed to 789XYZ, all orders for that customer must reflect the change. In most situations, this is a must-have option.

Cascade Delete

You do not want to be as quick to use the Cascade Delete option as you would to use the Cascade Update option. Cascade Delete deletes all records on the "many" side of a relationship if you delete the record in the table on the "one" side. Although this takes care of having to delete "many," or children, records before deleting the "one," or parent, record, there are consequences. Be sure that the information stored in the tables that you would delete with a Cascade Delete is not needed elsewhere in the database even if it is not necessary for the section that you are deleting. For example, an accounting application uses the data in the Orders table for its calculations; past data may be needed even if a customer ceases to buy in the present.

Joins

To open the Join Properties dialog box, you click on the Join Type button in the Relationships dialog box. You can choose from three types of joins: the inner join, the left outer join, and the right outer join. The join type of a relationship determines which records from the tables involved in the relationship will be included in the recordsets of the queries that use the tables.

The inner join is the default. When two tables are connected with an inner join, only those records that have equal values in the joined fields appear in the results of a query. For example, if you create a query based on a Customers table and an Orders table that are related on the Customer ID field, the only customers that will be included are those that have orders in the Orders table.

In a left outer join, all records in a table on the "one" side of a relationship are listed at least once, and only those records that have a value in their foreign key that equals the joined primary key of a record in the table on the "one" side are included in a query. For example, if you have a one-to-many relationship between the Customers table and the Orders tables, every customer, even those that do not have an order record in the Orders table, is listed once, and only those orders in the Orders table that match an existing customer are included in a query. If a customer does not have a corresponding record in the Orders table, any fields included in a query from the Orders table will be blank.

In a right outer join, all records in a table on the "many" side of a relationship are listed at least once, and only those records that have a value in their primary key that equals the joined foreign key of a record in the table on the "many" side will be included in a query. For example, if you have a one-to-many relationship between the Customers table and the Orders table, every order, even those that do not have a customer record in the Customers table, is listed once, and only those customers in the Customers table that have order record(s) in the Orders table will be included in a query. This join type is popular for finding "orphan" records—those records in tables on the "many" side of relationships that do not have a corresponding record in the table to which they are related.

The toughest part of creating a database application is the design process—deciding which tables are needed and determining the relationships. Some people devote their lives to studying how to make databases more efficient and how to better the design standards. If you are serious about developing applications with Access, be sure to refer to one of the books devoted solely to Access that has a substantial section on table design.

Chapter 46

Office Connections—Using Access with Other Office Products

FEATURING

Access and Word

Access and PowerPoint

Access and Excel

Access is a real powerhouse member of Office. If you are taking advantage of all the programs, chances are good that Access is the center of your Office world.

Access makes an excellent hub to the spokes of the other applications. You can merge letters created in Word with current mailing lists and other data stored in Access. Making sense of the information stored in Access is a snap whether you need to include it in an Excel workbook or on a form right in your database; and PowerPoint, an unlikely compatriot, can siphon out the figures to use in maps or charts that serve as visual confirmation of the points made in a presentation. Not only can Access provide data to the other applications, but you can use Access forms in Excel.

To illustrate how you can use Access with other applications, let's look at what the folks at Northwind Traders Company can do with the data stored in the NWIND database, which is located in the Samples folder in the main Access application folder.

Access and Word

Northwind Traders is planning a monthly mailing to customers who placed orders that month, thanking them for their continued business. First, we will create a totals query that groups sales of the past 30 days by customer, and then we will create a merge letter in Word that we can print every month.

Creating the Query

The first step is to create a query that asks the data, "Which customers have ordered in the past 30 days and how much did they spend on all orders?" To create the query, take the steps that follow.

1. Open the NWIND database.

2. Select the Queries tab and click on New.

3. Select the New Query option, as shown in Figure 46.1, and click on OK.

4. In the Show Table dialog box (see Figure 46.2), select Customers and click on Add.

5. Now select Orders and click on Add, and then select Order Details and click on Add.

6. Click on the Close button.

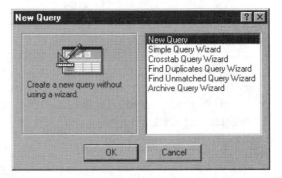

Figure 46.1   **Select the New Query option in the New Query dialog box.**

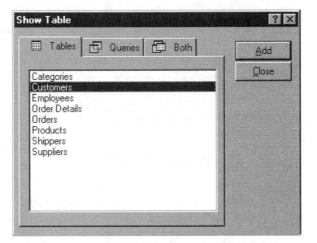

Figure 46.2   **The Show Table dialog box**

> **TIP**   You can select all the tables that you want to add at one time. To do so, select the first table with your mouse. Now hold down Ctrl and continue clicking on the other tables you want to add. When all the tables are selected, click on **Add**.

7.   Your Query Design screen should now have three tables in the top pane.

8.   Point to the title bar of the Customers table field list and double-click to select all the fields except the asterisk (see Figure 46.3).

Figure 46.3   *All the fields for the Customers table have been selected by double-clicking on the field list title bar.*

9.   Click and drag the selection from the field list to the QBE grid in the lower pane. Your QBE grid should now have in it all the fields from the Customers table.

10.   From the Orders table field list, click and drag the OrderDate field on top of the Customer ID field in the QBE grid. The Customer ID and other fields shift to the right.

11.   Click anywhere in the OrderDate column of the QBE grid and select Insert ▶ Column from the menu bar.

12.   Your design screen looks like that in Figure 46.4.

   We need a column in our query for the total amount spent on orders for the month. To do this, we create a calculated field.

13.   Your insertion point should still be in the Field row of the blank column. If it is not, click there now.

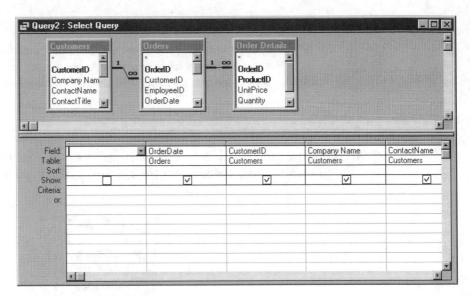

Figure 46.4 *The Query Design screen after adding the OrderDate field and inserting a blank column*

14. In the cell, type **Total:[unitprice]*[quantity]**. The result will be the value of the current quantity from the Order Details table multiplied by the value of the current records' unit price, also from the Order Details table.

15. Because we want one line per customer with a grand total in the Total row, select View ➤ Totals from the menu bar or click on the Totals button (which has a sigma symbol on it) on the Query Design toolbar to create a totals or grouping query.

16. A Total row appears in the QBE grid with Group By in each column.

17. Change the value of the Total row under the first Total column to Sum and the value under the second OrderDate column to Where.

18. Your Query Design screen should now look like that in Figure 46.5.

19. We want to total records only for those orders placed during the past 30 days. Normally, you would place >Date()-30 in the Criteria row under OrderDate to specify orders with order dates that are greater than 30 days prior to the current date on which the query is run. Because we are using data that has order dates that may not fall within the past 30 days, we will place >11/30/94–30 in the Criteria row under OrderDate.

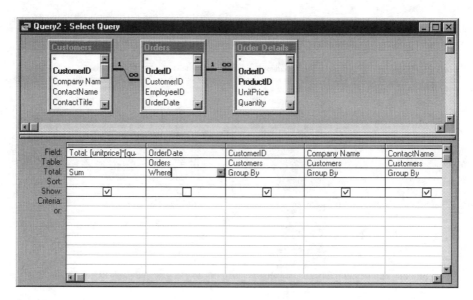

Figure 46.5   *The Totals query with Sum in the Total column and Where in the OrderDate column*

20.   The completed design of your query should look like that in Figure 46.6.

21.   From the menu bar, select File ➤ Close or press Ctrl+W and name the query **Monthly Customer Sales Merge**.

We now need to link Word and Access so that Word can merge letters using the Access data. Thankfully, an Access Wizard makes this a breeze.

Creating the Merge Document

To perform a merge with Word, you need not exit Access and open Word. Access and the Word Mail Merge Wizard will walk you through all the steps.

1.   Be sure the cursor is on the Queries tab of the Database window.

2.   Select the query that you want to use for a merge to a Word document, in this case Monthly Customer Sales Merge, and select Tools ➤ Office-Links ➤ MergeIt from the menu bar or click on the OfficeLinks button on the toolbar.

3.   The Microsoft Word Mail Merge Wizard opens, as shown in Figure 46.7.

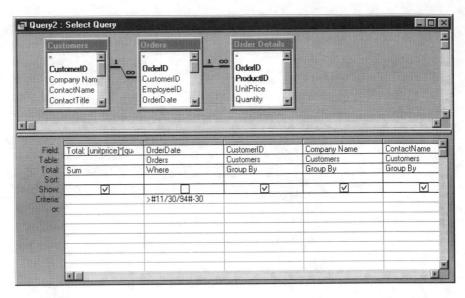

Figure 46.6   *The final Query Design screen*

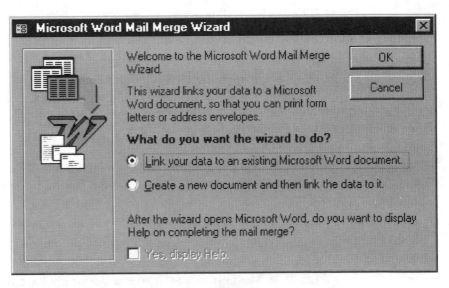

Figure 46.7   *The Microsoft Word Mail Merge Wizard*

4. You can merge the query with an existing document or with a new document. Select *Create a new document,* link the data to it, and then click on OK.

5. After a bit of hard drive churning, Word opens a new document that has a data source of your query. The Word window looks similar to that in Figure 46.8.

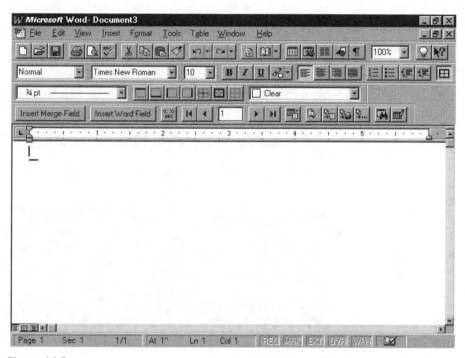

Figure 46.8 **The Word window as it appears when you link a merge document with an Access**

6. Your insertion point should be at the top of the new document. Press Enter five times.

7. From the Word menu bar, select Insert ➤ Date and Time. From the Available Formats list, select the date format you want in your letter. Be sure that the Update Automatically checkbox is checked and then click on OK.

8. Press Enter three times.

9. Click on the Insert Merge Field button on the Mail Merge toolbar, as shown in Figure 46.9, and choose Company_Name from the list. Press Enter.

10. Click on the Insert Merge Field button again and choose ContactName and press Enter.

11. From the Insert Merge Field button list, select Address and then press Enter.

12. Now, add the City field, type a comma and a space, add the Region field, type two spaces, and add the PostalCode field. When finished, press Enter twice.

13. Your Word document should look like that in Figure 46.10.

Figure 46.9   **The Word Mail Merge toolbar**

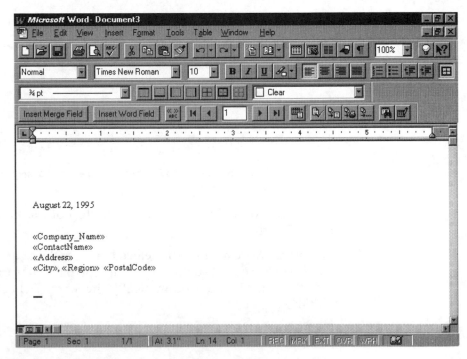

Figure 46.10   **Merge fields inserted for the opening of our letter**

14. Because we do not have a field for the first or last name of our contact or even an honorific so that we can address the person properly as Mr., Ms., and so on, we will type **Dear Customer:** instead of Dear with specific field information. Press Enter twice.

15. Type the following:

    Greetings from Northwind Traders! Everyone here would like to express their thanks for your business.

    (blank line)

    This is just your monthly reminder of our appreciation for your business. This month you have spent

16. After the word *spent*, press the spacebar and insert the Total field using the Insert MergeField button on the Mail Merge toolbar.

17. Now, press the spacebar again and finish the sentence with:

    worth of our products.

    (blank line)

18. Start a new paragraph and type:

    As always, if there is ever anything that we can do to make your experience with our company any better, please do not hesitate to call and speak with anyone here.

    (blank line)

    Thank You,
    (blank line)
    (blank line)
    (blank line)
    (blank line)
    Northwind Traders

September 22, 1995

<<Company_Name>>
<<ContactName>>
<<Address>>
<<City>>,<<Region>> <<PostalCode>>

Dear Customer:

Greetings from Northwind Traders! Everyone here would like to express their thanks for your business.

This is just your monthly reminder of our appreciation for your business. This month you have spent <<Total>> worth of our products.

As always, if there is ever anything that we can do to make your experience with our company any better, please do not hesitate to call and speak with anyone here.

Thank You,

Northwind Traders

Figure 46.11   **The merge document ready to be merged**

19. The final merge document should look like that in Figure 46.11.

The final stage is to test the merge document by performing a merge to a new document.

1. From the menu bar, select Tools ➤ Mail Merge.

2. In the Mail Merge Helper dialog box, as shown in Figure 46.12, click on the Merge button.

3. The Merge dialog box, as shown in Figure 46.13, is set to merge with a new document. If you are certain that the merge is correct, you can merge with a printer instead of a new document.

4. All customers in the Access query merge with your form letter into a single document called Form Letters1, separated by section breaks so that every merged letter starts on a new page.

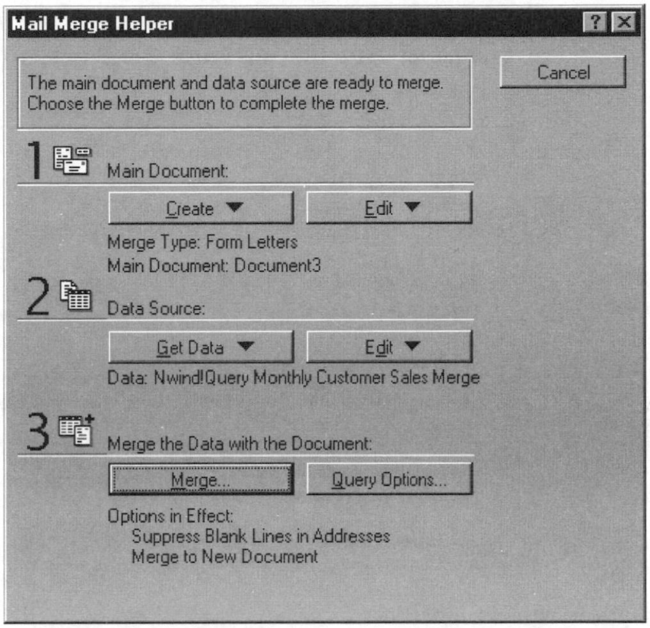

Figure 46.12   The Mail Merge Helper

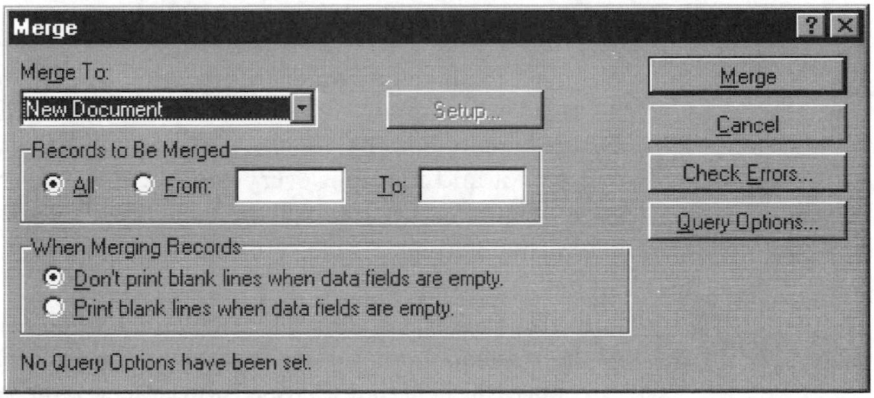

Figure 46.13   The Merge dialog box

5. You can now print the form letters from the document or **close the merged document and** rerun the merge **and direct the output to** the printer once you are certain that everything is printing correctly.

Figure 46.14 shows Form Letters1 with one of the letters that has customer information from the Access query.

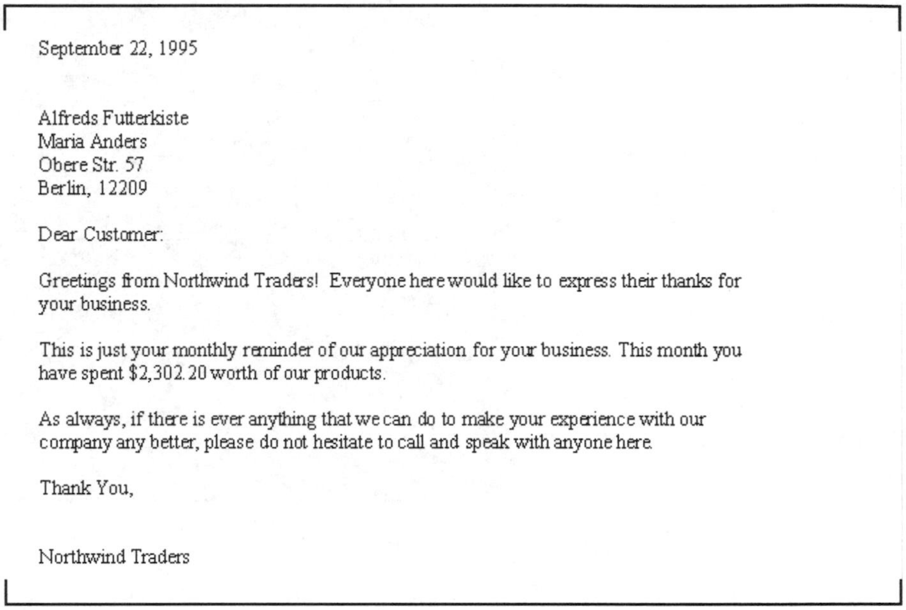

September 22, 1995

Alfreds Futterkiste
Maria Anders
Obere Str. 57
Berlin, 12209

Dear Customer:

Greetings from Northwind Traders! Everyone here would like to express their thanks for your business.

This is just your monthly reminder of our appreciation for your business. This month you have spent $2,302.20 worth of our products.

As always, if there is ever anything that we can do to make your experience with our company any better, please do not hesitate to call and speak with anyone here.

Thank You,

Northwind Traders

Figure 46.14 **Form Letters1 showing one of the merged letters**

No need to store customer information in a Word table *and* in Access, no need to manually insert monthly numbers into merge fields—the Office is truly coming together. Once you have written the letter, you can save it and merge it every month. Because the document is linked to your query, the data will be as up-to-date as your Access database every time you merge the letter.

NOTE   When saving documents in Word that you want to merge, never save the resulting Form Letters# document. Save the original document that contains the field codes. Saving Form Letters# is the same as saving the result of the merge and will do you no good when you want letters with new data.

Access and PowerPoint

Let's suppose you are the sales manager for Northwind Traders and it is your job to make the yearly presentation to the board, briefing the board members on sales progress. If you already have the sales data in Access, you will not have to spend time collecting the data for your presentation.

If you need a visual representation of European sales figures, for example, you can create a query that groups sales by country and then use the data map feature to place a map on a PowerPoint slide.

Creating the Query

The first thing we need to do is build the query to gather sales by country.

1. Open the NWIND database.

2. Select the Queries tab and click on New.

3. Select New Query and click on OK.

4. In the Show Tables dialog box, add the Orders and Order Details tables to your query and then click on Close.

5. From the Orders table, bring down the OrderDate and ShipCountry fields to the first and second columns of the QBE grid in the lower pane of the Query Design screen.

6. In the third column, click on the Field row.

7. In the Field row of the third column, type

   Total:[unitprice]*[quantity]

8. Change the query to a totals query by selecting View ➤ Totals from the menu bar or by clicking on the Totals button on the Query Design toolbar.

9. In the Total row of column three, change Group By to Sum.

10. Change the Total row of the OrderDate column to Where.

11. In the Criteria row of the OrderDate column, type

    year([orderdate])=year(date)

    and uncheck the checkbox in the Show row so that only orders from the current year are included in the query result.

12. Save the query as **Yearly Sales by Country** once it looks like that shown in Figure 46.15, and then close the Query Design screen.

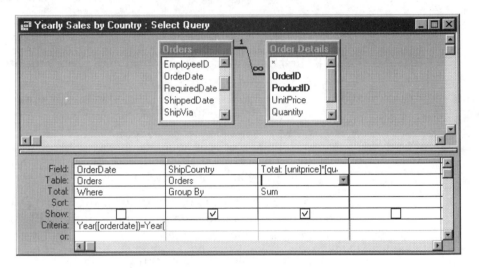

Figure 46.15 *The query to group sales by country for the current year to date*

Creating the Slide with a Data Map

We now need to create a slide in PowerPoint and place a Large Object on a slide to use for a data map.

1. Open PowerPoint and start a Blank Presentation.

2. In the New Slide dialog box (see Figure 46.16), find the Large Object slide and click on OK.

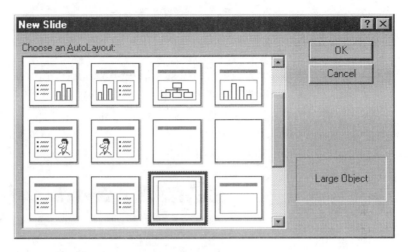

Figure 46.16   *The New Slide dialog box*

3. Double-click on the Large Object in the middle of the slide.

4. In the Insert Object dialog box, select Microsoft Data Map and click on
    OK. Figure 46.17 shows the PowerPoint screen before inserting a chart.

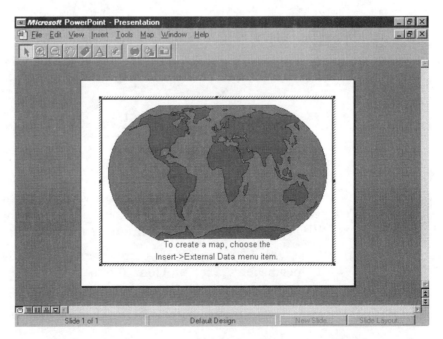

Figure 46.17   *The PowerPoint slide awaiting data for the data map to be added*

5. From the menu bar, select Insert ➤ External Data.

6. Select Microsoft Access as the External Data Source and click on OK.

7. In the Open Database dialog box, find and open the NWIND database in the Samples folder that is in your main Access folder.

8. In the Select External Data dialog box (shown in Figure 46.18), select the Yearly Sales by Country query and send all the fields to the *Fields to display in map* list box.

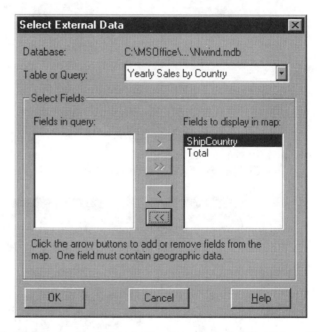

Figure 46.18 **Selecting the Yearly Sales by Country query in the Select External Data dialog box**

9. The data map will begin generating; however, it will not recognize the abbreviation *UK* which is used for the United Kingdom. In the Change To text box, type **United Kingdom** and then click on Change.

10. The recordset is read only so that the United Kingdom change will not be permanent. Click on Continue to ignore the error.

11. The abbreviation *USA* will cause the same error, so change the reference to United States and then click on Continue.

12. Figure 46.19 shows the global map with shadings that represent our numbers.

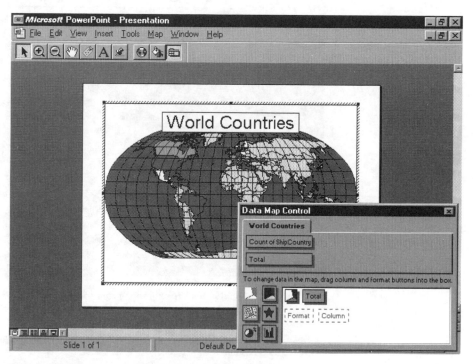

Figure 46.19 **The Data Map that results from our query**

We will zoom in on the European countries so that we can make out the shading that is being applied to the countries with sales.

13. Click once on the Zoom In control toolbar button, which is the second button on the Data Map toolbar.

14. Position your mouse with Zoom In attached to it over the center of the European countries, as indicated in Figure 46.20. Now click a couple of times to get a better view of the European counties.

15. Double-click on the World Countries label, type **Europe,** and delete the remaining text.

16. Double-click on the Total compact legend and remove the checkmark from the Use Compact Format checkbox. Your Edit Legend dialog box now looks like the one in Figure 46.21.

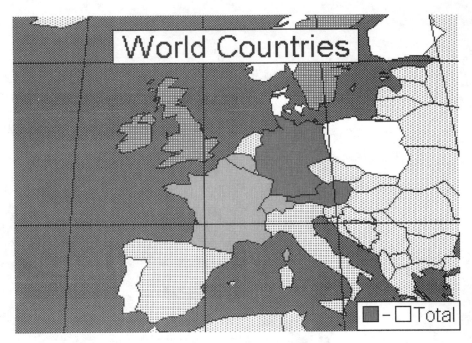

Figure 46.20   *Zooming into the European countries*

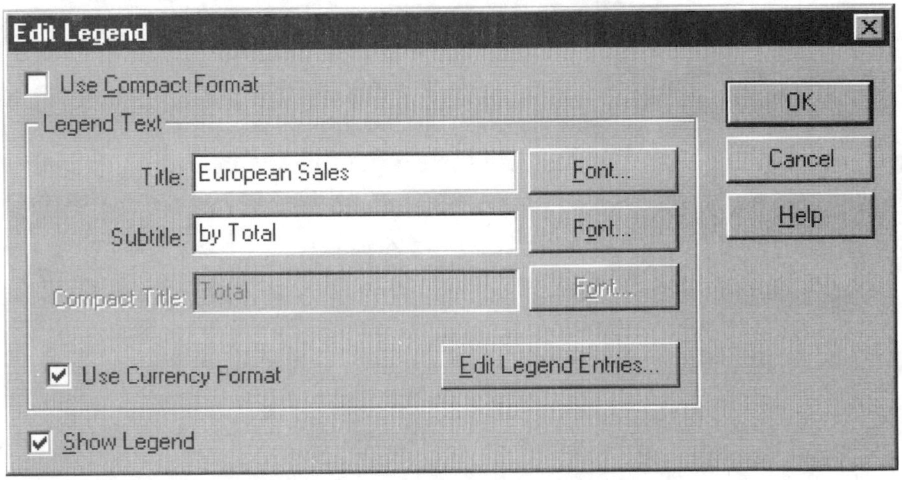

Figure 46.21   *The Edit Legend dialog box*

17. Resize the legend, using the frame handles, and adjust the level of zoom to make the map look close to the one in Figure 46.22.

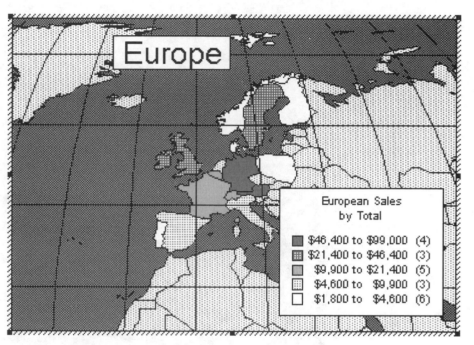

Figure 46.22　*The European Countries Sales map with detailed legend*

18. Click the fifth button on the Data Map toolbar to get the Map Labels dialog box shown in Figure 46.23. Choose OK. Click on the European countries that you want to label.

19. When you are finished, click outside the map area onto the border of the slide to end the editing of the Map object and see the final slide, as shown in Figure 46.24.
You can now use the map in your presentation. If you ever need to update or modify the information, you can simply double-click on the map on the slide and make the changes.

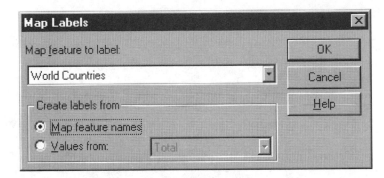

Figure 46.23   The Map Labels dialog box

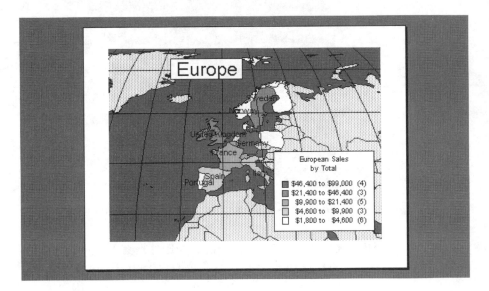

Figure 46.24   The final PowerPoint slide

Access and Excel

As efficient and powerful as Access is, if you want to summarize your data every which way from Tuesday, you will need to rely on the PivotTable, which is available through Excel.

In Access, the Form Wizard helps you generate a form on which you can view a PivotTable.

Creating the Query

The first step is to create a query whose results you want to analyze with the PivotTable.

1. Open the NWIND database.

2. Select the Queries tab and then click on New.

3. In the New Query dialog box, select New Query and click on OK.

4. Add the Categories, Products, Order Details, and Orders tables to the query.

5. In the Show Table dialog box, add the Category Name Field from the Category table to the first column of the QBE grid and then click on Close.

6. Add the OrderDate field from the Orders table to the second column of the QBE grid.

7. In the Field row of the third column, create a calculated column by entering

   Total:[order details].[unitprice]*[order details].[quantity].

8. Save the query as **Category Sales**.

Creating the Form
with the PivotTable Wizard

Once we have the query on which we want to base the PivotTable, we can create a form using the PivotTable Wizard.

1. In the Database window, click on the Forms tab and then click on New.

2. In the New Form dialog box, select PivotTable Wizard and click on OK.

3. Select the Category Sales query and all its fields as the Field Source for the PivotTable (see Figure 46.25). When you're finished, click on Next.

4. A form will be generated with a PivotTable object on it. You will be presented with a PivotTable Wizard dialog box in which you place the fields on the PivotTable layout.

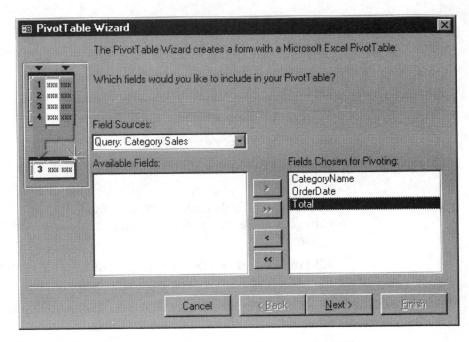

Figure 46.25 **Selecting Category Sales and its fields for your PivotTable**

5. Drag CategoryName to Row, OrderDate to Column, and Total to Data. Click on Next.

6. The PivotTable Wizard asks you to confirm the name and some check-box options. Leave the defaults and click on Finish.

7. When you are prompted that the entire table will not fit, click on OK.

8. Once the pivot table is created, click on the gray OrderDate cell with your right mouse button. Choose Group and Outline ➤ Group from the shortcut menu.

9. Change the Starting date to 1/1/1994 and select quarters and years in the Grouping dialog box, as shown in Figure 46.26. Click on OK.

10. Save the form as **Category Sales**.

11. Look at the form in Form view.

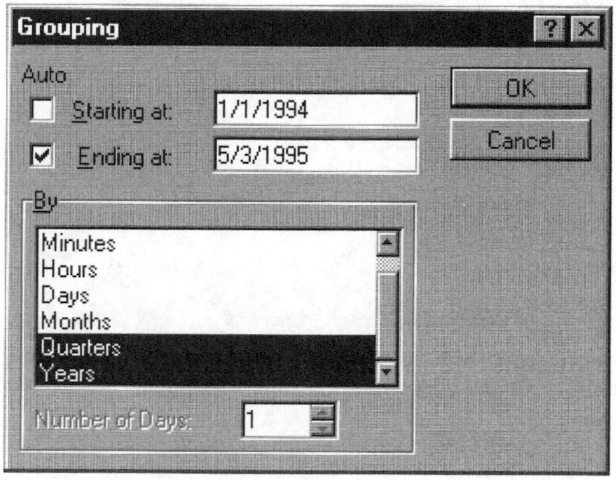

Grouping

Auto

☐ Starting at: 1/1/1994

☑ Ending at: 5/3/1995

By

Minutes
Hours
Days
Months
Quarters
Years

Number of Days: 1

OK

Cancel

Figure 46.26   **The Grouping dialog box**

TIP   You may want to change the format properties to remove record selectors, navigation arrows, and maybe even the control box. You may also want to set the AutoCenter and AutoResize form properties to Yes. Doing so will improve the look of your form.

WordMail and OLE (Object Linking and Embedding)

In this short part we explore how to use electronic mail within

Office, with tips on using Word as your mail editor, and we

explain the powerful features afforded by object linking and

embedding (OLE).

Chapter 47

Using Electronic Mail and WordMail

FEATURING

A**n** electronic mail program allows you to send and receive documents across a network and while using online services such as CompuServe, America Online, or MSN (Microsoft Network). You can even receive and send messages via the Internet.

You can use any Windows 95 compatible mail program, including Microsoft's Exchange Client, Microsoft Mail, and cc:Mail, with more becoming available soon. This chapter focuses on Exchange Client, which we'll refer to as *Exchange*. The first section will get you up and running quickly on Exchange, and demonstrate how to use Word for Windows 95 as your *mail editor* for composing and replying to messages.

Starting Exchange

To start your mail program, double-click on the Inbox icon on your desktop (you might have to minimize your applications in order to see the desktop). Unless you've installed another mail program, Exchange is the program that starts.. Figure 47.1 shows the Exchange messaging screen.

Figure 47.1 *The Microsoft Exchange program*

Composing a Mail Message

Click on the New Message button on the toolbar or choose Compose
▶ New Message, or press Ctrl+N to start a new message. When the New
Message dialog box appears, click on the To: button on the left to see a
list of individuals contained in your address book.

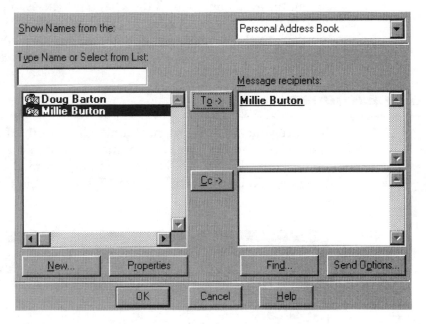

Select the name of the person or entity to which you are sending the
message and click on the To: button to the right of their name to add
them to the Message Recipient text area. Click on OK and you will be
returned to the New Message dialog box.

In the New Message dialog box, click on the CC: option if you wish for
someone to receive a copy of the message. Fill in the subject area. This
is important as the Subject of the message is prominently displayed when
a person receives their mail. It will help the recipient to know the subject
matter. Click on the blank white message area to type your message.

When you are finished composing your message, click on the Send
button or choose File ▶ Send from the menu bar.

Adding New People to the Address Book

If you wish to add a person to your list of recipients, start by composing a new mail message. When you click on the To: button to designate the recipient, you will be shown the Address Book dialog box. Click on the New button at the bottom of the Address Book dialog box. Choose the Entry type from the New dialog box. (Usually this will be a Personal Distribution.) Click on OK.

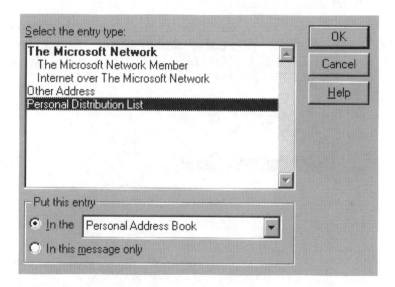

When the New Personal Distribution List Properties dialog box appears, type in the name of the new person and click on the To: or CC: or OK button at the bottom of the dialog box.

Using WordMail as
the Editor While Composing

When you compose a mail message, there is the blank typing area below the Subject line that is used for typing the mail message. Usually the default editor is a good, no-frills editor. You have basic formatting available such as bold, underline, italics, etc. If you decide to use Word as your editor instead of the default editor, you will have available to you most of Word's additional functionality and features. For example, most of the commands are available to you. Word's Standard and Formatting toolbars become available. You can now use features during Mail composing that were never possible before. You can insert a table in the middle of a mail message, create bulleted or numbered lists, use the highlight feature to draw attention to a tract of text, etc. The automatic spelling feature can be activated so that you are conscious of typos as you create your message. You can select specific paragraphs to change the font size and typeface.

To make Word your editor, start the Exchange program and choose Compose ➤ WordMail Options from the Exchange menu bar. The WordMail dialog box appears with the name of the template that is being used for the WordMail editor.

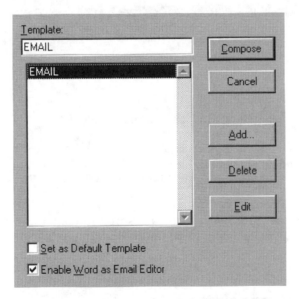

To enable Word as the Email Editor, check the box at the bottom of the WordMail dialog box. If you would like for EMAIL to become the default template for whenever you compose mail messages, also check that option. You can compose the new message right here from the WordMail dialog box. Click on the Compose button on the right side of the dialog box to create your new mail message using Word as your editor.

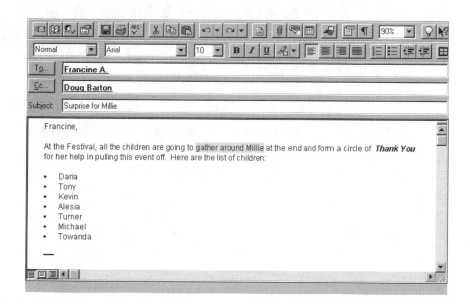

WARNING You need at least 12MB of memory to use Word as your electronic mail editor. Microsoft Exchange and Word must also be installed before this capability is available. Even with 12MB of memory, using Word-Mail as your editor can be a slow process. The benefits are tremendous but you might want to judge if using WordMail slows your system down.

Attaching and Sending Documents

You can attach and send an existing document in two ways:

▶ Start your mail program, compose a message, and then look around in folders for the document you wish to attach and send.

▶ *Or*, from within your application (Word, Excel, PowerPoint, etc.), open the file on the screen that you wish to attach to a mail message and choose File ➤ Send from the menu bar. The mail program will start automatically and allow you to compose a message for your attachment.Figure 47.2 displays a message with an attached document.

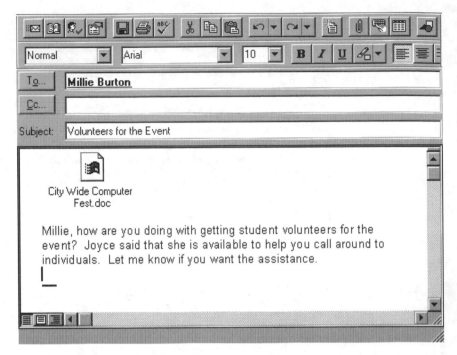

Figure 47.2   *When you use the Send command from within an application's File menu, the Message Compose screen is activated for you with the document attached.*

Viewing a Mail Message's Properties

To see additional information about your mail message, choose File ➤ Properties from within Exchange while you have the mail message open. Figure 47.3 displays the properties screen for this mail message. You can change the message's priority from Normal to High and check a check-box to specify that you wish for a Delivery Receipt (this lets you know that the mail was delivered and read by the recipient).

Receiving Documents

When someone sends you a mail message with a document attached, your Inbox will show the name of the sender and a paper clip on the same line that has the name of the mail message.

Double-click on the mail message to open it. When you see the attachment icon, double-click on the attachment icon to launch the program

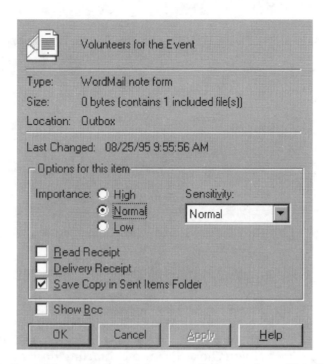

Figure 47.3 **To set different priority levels for your mail message, choose File ➤ Properties while the mail message is active.**

that created the attached document. Once you have activated the attachment, it is just a regular file and you can perform all of the commands you would normally: view, edit, re-save to another folder, etc.

Saving and Printing Attachments

If you do not wish to immediately open an attachment but wish to save it or print it immediately, open the mail message that contains the attachment. Click once on the Attachment icon to select it. Choose Edit ➤ File Attachment Object and then either Save As or Print from the Mail menu bar.

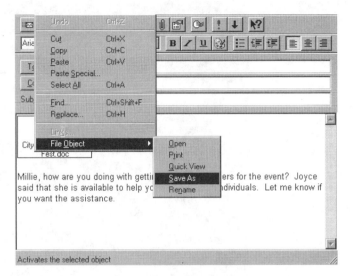

If you chose Save, the Save As dialog box appears with the default folder being the WordMail folder. Type a name for the attachment or use the existing name. You can store all of your attachments here in one place. If you chose Print, the attachment is quickly opened, the Print feature activates, and the file is closed. You are returned to the mail message. Figure 47.4 displays the Save As dialog box for saving your attachments.

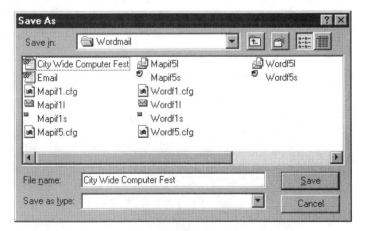

Figure 47.4 *The Attachment Save As dialog box saves your attachments into the WordMail folder.*

Deleting a Mail Message

After you have viewed a mail message and its attachments, if any, you can delete it. From the Inbox, click on the file to be deleted and press Ctrl+D, or choose File ➤ Delete from the menu bar, or right-click on the file and choose Delete from the shortcut menu.

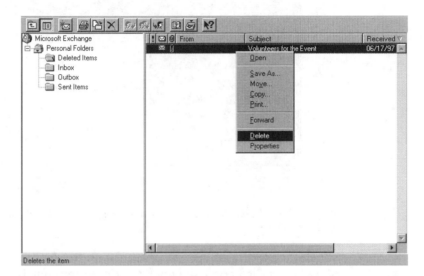

Deleted messages are stored in the Deleted Items folder on the left. To permanently delete a message, delete it again from this folder. There is no Undo for a Deleted Item. You can, however, restore a deleted message by opening the Deleted Items folder and dragging the message back onto the Inbox folder.

Routing a Document

Routing a document through electronic mail allows you to distribute a single copy of a document to individuals to review in sequence. Each reviewer sends the document to the next person on the list. You avoid getting five copies back of a document because you had to send it as an attachment to five different people. When the last person reviews the document, it is sent back to you.

If your mail program is MAPI-compliant, the mail routing commands will automatically appear on your application's File menu. To route a document, open it on the screen and choose File ➤ Add Routing Slip. Figure 47.5 shows the File menu options.

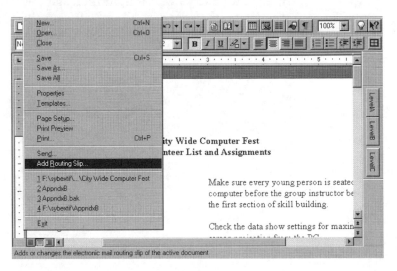

Figure 47.5   *The ability to easily route a single document to multiple reviewers is available on the File menu.*

When the Routing Slip appears, click on the Address button to see a list of names of the people to which the document will be routed. Select each name and click on the To: button to the right side of the name until you compile a list of reviewers. When you have added all of the names, click on the OK button at the bottom of the screen.

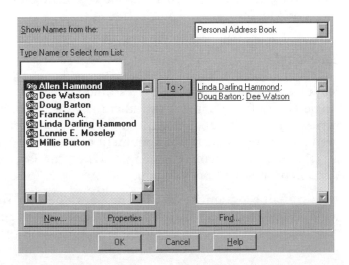

When you return to the Add Routing Slip dialog box, you can reorder the names with the Move Up and Move Down arrows to the right of the names selected for routing. When you have the order you wish, type a subject and the message text. Decide on your options at the bottom of the dialog box. The default is to let each reviewer send to the next. Figure 47.6 shows the final result before sending.

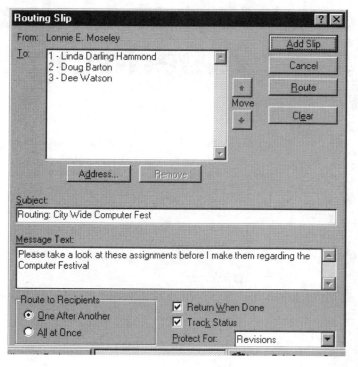

Figure 47.6 *You can change the document routing options so that all of the reviewers receive the document at once.*

Chapter 48

Understanding OLE: Object Linking & Embedding

Featuring

A s introduced in Chapter 3, OLE is what makes the integration of the Office applications possible. Although OLE is an acronym for Object Linking and Embedding, it has grown over the last couple of years to now provide much more power than simple embedding or linking of data. OLE is also used to provide *automation*, or the ability to manipulate one program's objects from within another program through the use of code. And with Office 95 you have the addition of a new OLE feature, the Binder, which harnesses the power of OLE to provide unique functionality, making it possible to store objects from multiple programs into one file.

The Elements of OLE

Linking

Linking from one application into another means that a connection to data from within one application is provided to another, keeping any references to that data up to date without the assistance of the user (except for the initial linking). An Excel chart, for example, could be linked in a Word document that is used for monthly status reports and, as the data changes from month to month, the Word document is updated automatically.

Embedding

Embedding an object from one application into another enables one program to utilize the objects of another program without the need to independently run the other application. A Word document may need to have a table in it with the power of an Excel worksheet, but you do not want a separate file for the worksheet. An Excel worksheet can easily be embedded into a Word document so that the Excel functionality is available and all of the information is stored directly in the Word document.

Automation

OLE automation provides the ability to manipulate obects from within OLE's programming code. Automation provides the developer with the resources to transfer information from one program into another. An application written with Access keeps track of a user's contacts. When the user wants to write a letter to a contact, she should not need to open a Word document and manually enter the address stored in Access. With OLE automation, a user could click on a button that launches Word, creates a new document, inserts the opening portions of a letter including the address and the *Dear:* line, and presents the user wi4h a letter fully addressed ready for her to add the body.

Binder

The Binder provides a container for your Office objects, including Word documents, Excel worksheets and charts, and PowerPoint slide presentations. By adding sections to a Binder as new objects or from existing files, Binder facilitates the creation of a true *Office* document. Suppose you are working on a project for an account that, like most large projects, requires the use of more than one Office program. What better way to organize the lot than in a Binder that allows for one-file access to all of your project documents?

Linking

You will want to link data from one file to another when you need to keep data in one application while providing constantly updated information to another.

When linking, the path of the linked data is stored within the application receiving the information. Since it is the *path* of the information stored and not the actual information, you must make certain that the linked file is not moved from the original folder in which it is stored. If it is moved, then the application that needs access to the information will not be able to update the data, because it will contain an erroneous path.

Although you should make every effort *not* to move linked files, you can correct a problem with a moved link's path by modifying it via the Edit ➤ Links command from the menu bar of the application containing the link.

Methods of Linking

Linking can be initiated by using the copy and paste functions of the Windows clipboard or by selecting Insert ➤ Object from the menu bar of the application in which you are storing a link to another application.

Linking Data Using Copy and Paste

1. Select the information in the original application to which you want to link.

2. Switch to the application where you want to link the data.

3. Select Edit ➤ Paste Special from the menu bar.

4. The dialog box in Figure 48.1 opens. Select the Paste Link radio button and the object type to which you are linking. Click on OK.

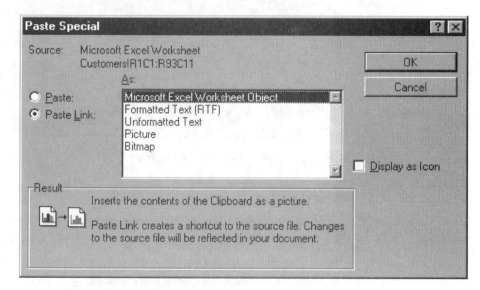

Figure 48.1   *The Paste Special dialog box*

To Link Using the Menu Bar

1. Select Insert ➤ Object from the menu bar.

2. The Object dialog box in Figure 48.2 opens.

3. Select the *Create from File* tab. Specify the file that you want to link to: Either enter the path and file name here or click on the Browse button and select the file from the Browse list.

4. In the Object dialog box, check the *Link to File* checkbox, then click on OK.

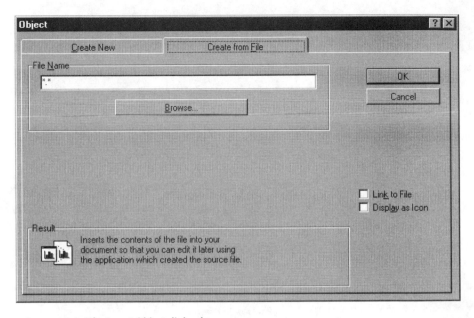

Figure 48.2 **The Insert Object dialog box**

Examples

Here are some situations in which you would use linking:

▶ Linking to Excel information from within Word, so that any reports will have current numbers when printed, without your having to manually update the document every time you need to print it.

▶ Linking to Word from Access in a document-management system that manages document files on a local machine or network.

▶ Linking to Word, Excel, or Access files from within PowerPoint to keep presentations up to date.

Embedding

You will embed data when you need to keep all of your data, including data that is stored in other applications' objects, within one file.

When embedding information into your document, the entire object is embedded. Thus, the increase in size of your host application is quite significant. Embedding an Excel chart, for example, requires the embedding of the entire workbook in which the chart is created.

The increase in size, however, must be weighed against the need to keep track of external files when linking. If you needed to transport a file with embedded data, you would only need the one file; if the same information were linked, you would need to ensure that you also transport the linked files containing the data, *and* modify the path in each link.

Methods of Embedding

You can copy and paste embedded data or select Insert ➤ Object from the menu bar of the application in which you are storing a link to another application

Embedding Data Using Copy and Paste

1. Select the information in the original application from which you want to embed.

2. Switch to the application where you want to embed the data.

3. Select Edit ➤ Paste Special from the menu bar.

4. The dialog box in Figure 48.3 opens. Select the Paste radio button and the object type into which you are embedding. Click on OK.

To Embed Using the Menu Bar

1. From the menu bar, select Insert ➤ Object.

2. The Object dialog box opens.

   - If you want to embed a new object that has not been created in an existing file, select the *Create New* tab and specify the object type.

   - If you want to embed a new object from an existing file, select the *Create from File* tab and specify the file name without checking the Link to File checkbox.

3. Click on OK.

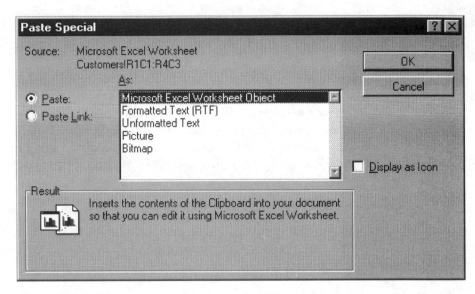

Figure 48.3 *Embedding a Microsoft Excel object using the Paste Special dialog box*

The Drag-and-Drop Option

If you want to embed part of a file already created, you can also click and drag from one application to another with both applications open. Alternatively, you can do the same with only the application in which you will be embedding data open, as long as you have access to the source file in a folder window.

To drag-and-drop from one open application to another open application:

1. Select the object to be embedded in one application.

2. Move the pointer to the selection. The white mouse arrow should appear.

3. If the receiving application is open, click and drag directly into the application window.

4. If the receiving application window cannot be seen because the application from which you are dragging the selection is maximized, click and drag the selection to the Taskbar button bearing the destination application's name, keep the left mouse button down until the destination application opens, and finally let go of the left mouse button within the application.

> **WARNING**   When you drag-and-drop a selection from one open application to another, the application that originally holds the selection incurs a Cut effect: the data will be cut, not copied, from the original application. You can overcome the loss of the data by switching back to the originating application and selecting Edit ➤ Undo from the menu bar. Curiously enough, the Cut will be undone but the Paste into the destination application will not—the information will exist in both places. (You can also overcome the effect of the Cut by simply closing the file in the original application without saving.)

To drag-and-drop from a file object to an open application:

1. Open the application in which you want to embed data.
2. Locate a file either on the desktop or in an Explorer window.
3. Click and drag the file icon into the application.
4. Your selection will be embedded.

Examples

You may want to embed when:

▶ You want to embed an Excel worksheet into Word so that you don't have to manage another file to store the worksheet.

▶ You want to embed pictures, sound files, or other objects into Access fields, to help to identify a subject being stored in a record.

▶ You want to include Word Art in a PowerPoint slide presentation, in order to add flair to your text.

Automating through Programming

Automation requires programming. To see code samples and a more in-depth explanation of automation, turn to the Answer Wizard in the Help menu of any of the Office programs. Ask it, "What is OLE automation?," and refer to the *Programming and Language Reference* section of the returned help listing.

Examples

You may want to use OLE automation if you need to:

▶ Integrate Word's word-processing features with data being stored with Access or Excel.

▶ Automate the creation of pivot tables based on your Access data.

▶ Have an Access application automatically create customized Excel workbooks with multiple worksheets from queries and/or tables.

The Binder

The Binder is a container object that will allow you to create multiple sections to store different Office objects. When you have one section selected, you can work in the Binder as if you were in the original application.

Using the Binder

To create a new Binder:

▶ From the Taskbar, select Start ➤ Programs ➤ Microsoft Binder.

Figure 48.4 shows what a Binder may look like after adding some sections.

To add a section to the Binder:

1. From the Binder's menu bar, select Section ➤ Add or Section ➤ Add from File.

2. Select the Object type that you want for the new section from the Add Section dialog box (shown in Figure 48.5), and click on OK. Alternatively, select the file to insert as a section from the Add from File dialog box shown in Figure 48.6, and click on Add.

To modify the sections:

1. On the left, click on the section you want to modify.

2. The toolbars and menu bar of the Binder will change to reflect the section's application.

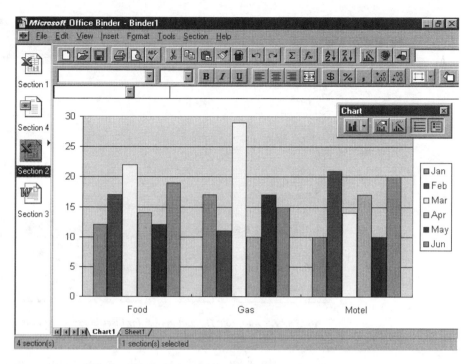

Figure 48.4 **A Binder with multiple sections added**

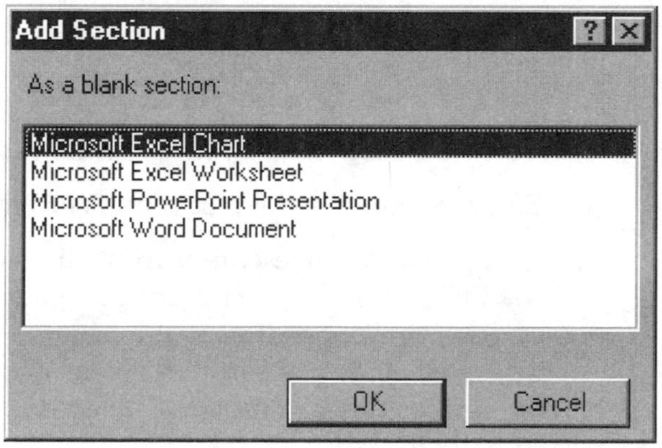

Figure 48.5 **Add Section dialog box**

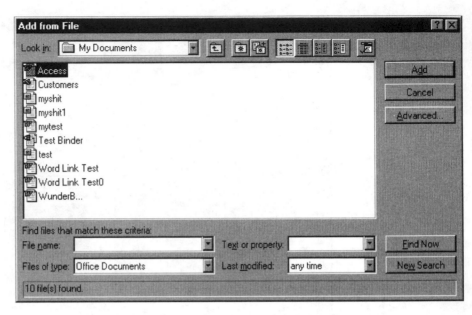

Figure 48.6   *Add from File dialog box, for inserting sections from existing files*

3. Work in the section as you would in the original application.

    To work on the section outside of the Binder:

1. Select Section ➤ View Outside from the menu bar.

2. Edit the object.

3. Select File ➤ Close from the menu bar.

    To save a section as a self-contained file:

➤   Select Section ➤ Save Section As from the menu bar.

    The power of OLE comes from the fact that it can be used throughout the Office. Unless you never share your information between documents or even drag and drop within documents, it is inevitable that you will take advantage of its power. Getting to know OLE and the features that it provides means that you'll learn how to put the full potential of Office to work for you.

Appendix

In this appendix we walk you through the installation process for

Microsoft Office Professional for Windows 95.

Appendix

Installing Microsoft Office for Windows 95

Th**here** are two editions of Microsoft Office for Windows 95: Standard and Professional. The Standard Edition includes Word, Excel, PowerPoint, and Schedule+. The Professional Edition adds Access to the group.

If you are upgrading from a previous version of Office, you don't need to remove the existing version of Office. Office 95 will install itself to a new location on your hard disk and you can choose later whether to remove the existing version. Your documents, templates, and other files created using the other Office version are preserved.

If you know from the beginning that you wish to overwrite the old version, select the same directory folder when prompted for where Office should be installed. Make sure that you have backed up important templates (especially Normal.dot). Even though there are assurances that old templates will be preserved, take no chances.

Before you begin the actual installation, you should take a moment to do a little inventory to make sure the installation will be easy and hassle-free.

▶ Make sure you have all the installation diskettes or CD-ROM.

NOTE   Important: On the back of the CD there is a CD key number that you will be required to provide at some point in the installation. Write it down so you have it handy before you begin installation.

▶ Be sure your computer is already running Windows 95 or Windows NT. Office 95 will not run under earlier versions of Windows.

▶ If you are installing from a CD, make sure your CD-ROM player is working properly in Windows 95.

▶ Make sure you have enough space on your computer to install Office 95. For a typical install without Access you need 55 megabytes of space on your hard drive. Access requires an additional 39 megabytes. Regardless of the type of installation you choose, you will also need about 20 to 40 megabytes of free space *after* installing Office 95, to allow space for Windows 95 to work properly and space for you to save your files.

If you do not have enough disk space, you can install parts of Office now, and install more later, after you use the Windows Explorer to find files that can be deleted or sent to a floppy in order to make room on your hard disk.

 TIP If you're really tight on free space, Office 95 can be run from the CD, so that you are actually using the files on the CD instead of having the programs installed on your hard disk. With this approach, Office will still need to copy approximately 30 megabytes of files to your Windows 95 folder, but not the entire Office Suite of program files.

A few last things to do before you start installing:

▶ Close any open programs.

▶ Disable any virus-detection programs. (This might involve typing **REM** at the beginning of the line that loads the antivirus program in your Autoexec.bat or Config.sys files, then restarting your computer.)

▶ Set aside enough time to complete the installation. A typical Office 95 installation can take anywhere from 30 minutes to an hour, depending on your machine.

Running Setup the First Time

To start the installation of Office for Windows for 95:

1. The first step depends on the format of the installation medium:

    • **Installing from the CD:** Insert the Microsoft Office CD in the CD-ROM drive.

    • **Installing from Floppy:** Make sure that you have inserted the disk labeled **Disk 1** into your floppy disk drive (A or B).

    • **Installing from a Network Location:** Make sure that you connect to the proper network location. Use Network Neighborhood from the Windows desktop to search for shared drives. Your network administrator can be of assistance to you. You can also find additional information about installing across the network by reading the network Readme file (Network.txt) in the Office folder on a network drive. If it isn't already there, refer to the Network.txt file on your setup disk or the CD.

2. Click on the Start button on the Taskbar and choose the Run command. Designate the drive letter from which you will be installing Office, and

type the word **Setup**. Figure A.1 shows the Run dialog box for a CD-ROM installation.

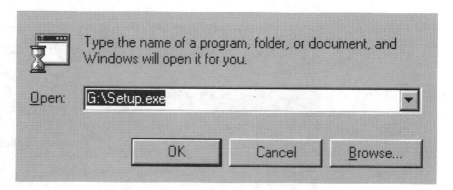

Figure A.1   *The Run dialog box for installing*

3.   When the Setup Welcome screen appears, Microsoft reminds you to close any open files before continuing with Setup. Once you are ready to continue, click on the Continue button at the bottom of the dialog box, as shown in Figure A.2.

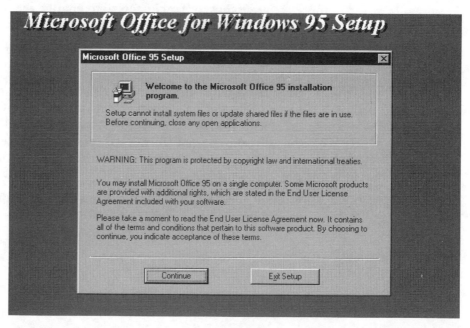

Figure A.2   *The Setup Welcome screen reminds you to close all applications before running Setup.*

4. Enter your name and company or organization in the Name and Organization Information dialog box. Microsoft uses this information for future installs.

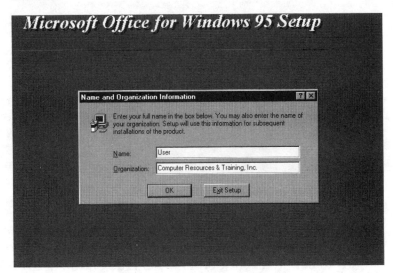

You will be asked to confirm the name and organization information. If there are any typos, or you just wish to change the information, click on the Change button and Setup will redisplay the dialog box.

5. This step differs, depending on if you are installing from a CD or from a floppy or a network.

   • **Installing from the CD-ROM:** An ID or key number is needed to authorize the installation. Enter your 10-digit CD Key number in the slots provided if you are installing from a CD-ROM and click on the OK button (see Figure A.3). You will be presented with a Product ID verification dialog box. Click on the OK button.

   • **Installing from Floppy or from a Network Drive:** A dialog box will appear with your Product ID number. This information will be important if you need to contact Microsoft about any problems you are having with Office 95. If you do not already have a

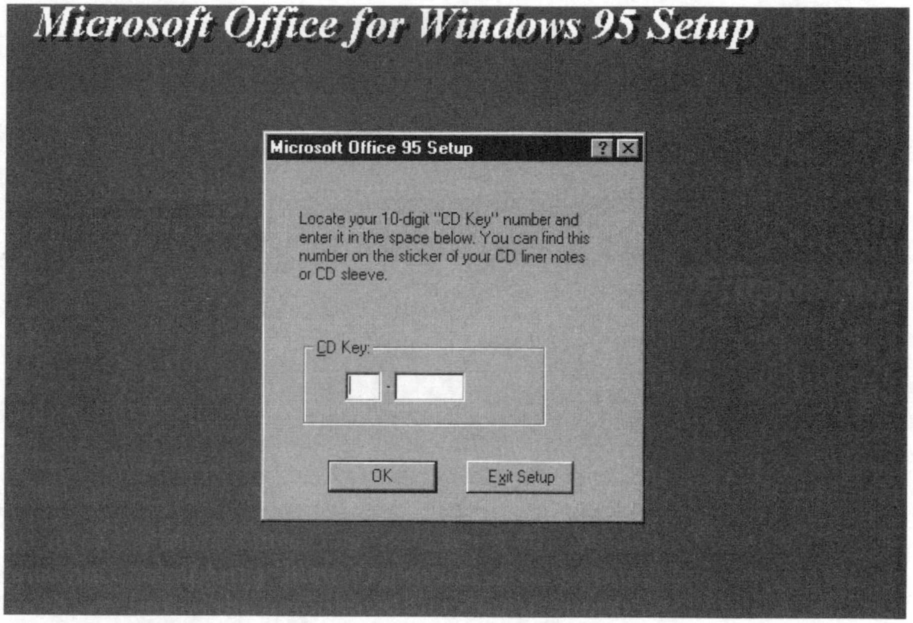

Figure A.3   **The key number ID is required for CD-ROM installations.**

copy of the Product ID number, take a moment to write it now on both your Office for Windows 95 manual and the box for your software. After you have recorded the information, click on OK.

Designating the Installation Folder

When prompted to verify the folder into which Office for Windows 95 will be installed, check to see if the default folder is agreeable to you. You can choose to change the folder, exit Setup, or choose OK to continue. If you choose to change the folder, you can install Office to another folder on the same drive or on another drive, even a network drive. Figure A.4 shows the Change Folder dialog box.

Appendix: Installing

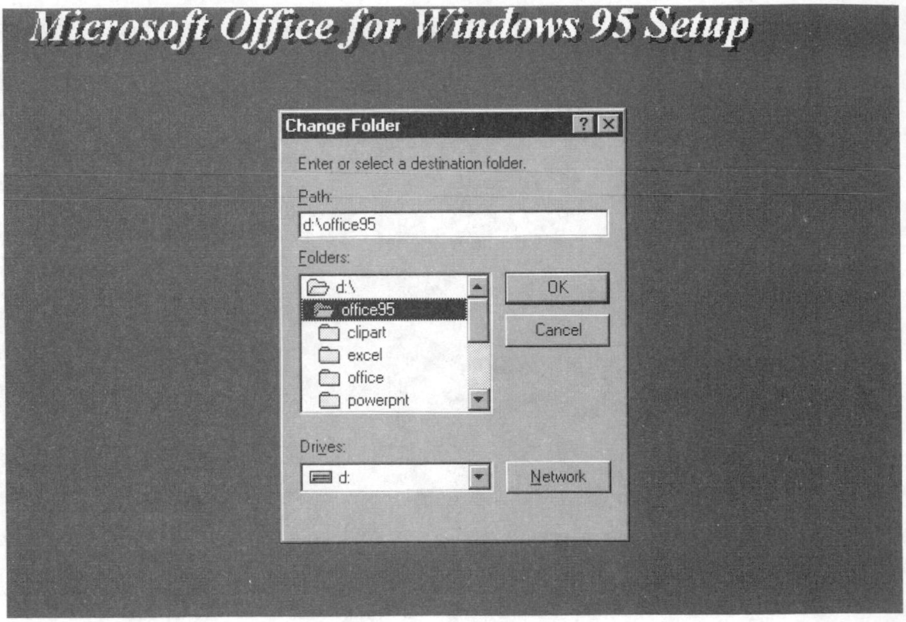

Figure A.4 *Office allows you to change where you want the installation to occur.*

Another verification dialog box appears displaying the folder name that you selected in the Change Folder dialog box. If the settings are correct, click on the OK button.

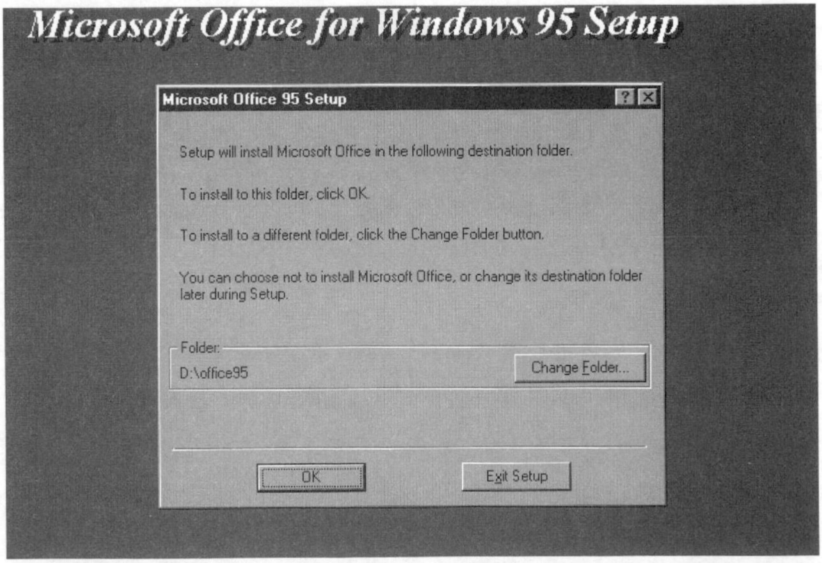

Choosing a Type of Install

Office now asks you what kind of installation you want to perform. There are four choices: Typical, Compact, Custom, or Run from CD-ROM. The Typical installation is generally the wisest choice, but you'll need to assess the amount of disk space required. Figure A.5 shows the installation options and the disk space required for each.

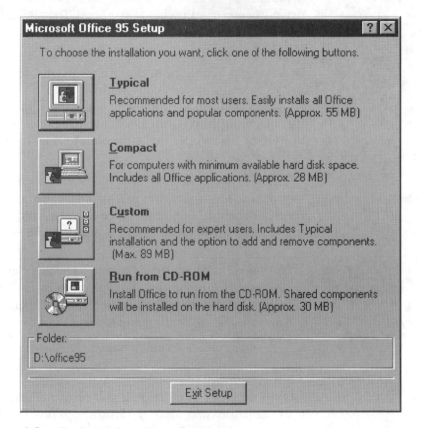

Figure A.5   Office for Windows 95 Installation options

  TIP If you want *everything*, you must choose the Custom installation, which allows you to install more components than the Typical installation.

Appendix: Installing

The Compact installation is ideal for laptops or machines with limited disk space. Remember, you can always reinstall later when you have more disk space (at which point you should choose Custom install to add the components you need).

If you do not want the Office for Windows 95 programs on your hard disk at all, you can run the entire suite from the CD. Only a few important files will be copied to the hard disk. Of course, to run any of the Office programs using this installation method, you must keep the CD in the drive whenever you wish to use the Office 95 suite of products.

Typical

In a Typical installation, the programs and tools most commonly used in Office will automatically be installed on your computer. Your main programs will install along with some frequently used tools. Choose this installation option if you are a first-time user of Office, or if you plan to use Office using only the most common features.

Compact

Choose the Compact option if you have limited hard-drive space. If you have less than 40 megabytes free on your hard drive, you should choose this option, or delete or move unwanted files to free up space.

> **TIP**   When in doubt, DON'T delete! If you don't know what a file is, chances are, you didn't put it there—which usually means it was put there by (and is needed by) Windows95 or another installed program. Only delete items that you *know* are no longer going to be of use to you or are already copied to another disk.

Custom

Choose Custom installation if you plan to install either less or more than the installations provided by the other options. For instance, you can choose this option to install everything that comes in the box. You can also use this option if you want to install certain tools but leave out others. Use this latter option only if you are experienced with Office, and know what a particular tool or item does. One particularly good use of Custom is to spread out your programs to several drives. For instance, if your C drive is nearly full, but you have a D drive that is almost empty, you can install some files on C, and the rest on D. Figure A.6 displays the Custom/Maintenance dialog box.

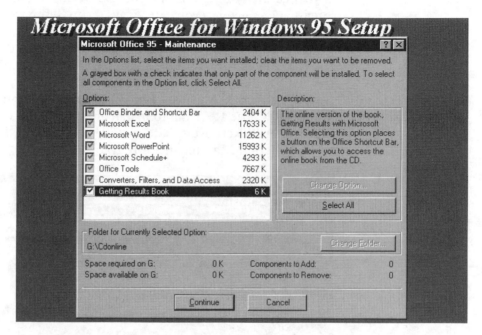

Figure A.6 *The Custom Installation allows you to add/remove install options.*

If you want to install everything for Office 95 by choosing Custom, just click on Select All. Alternatively, to install just certain tools, select the main item that would include the tools you want, and then click on Change Option.

Run from CD-ROM

If you do not have the space to install Office, use the Run from CD-ROM option so that the Office suite will reside primarily on the CD and not on your hard disk. There is still a minimum requirement of 30MB of disk space for files that Office needs to keep on your hard disk, which is actually a little more than a Compact install without Access. Because it is usually faster to run the suite from a hard disk instead of the CD-ROM drive (depending how fast your CD-ROM is), if you can plan to keep your disk usage to 30MB you should opt for the Compact install instead.

Reinstalling Office 95

If you leave anything out of Office 95 in this initial setup, and you find later that you need it, you can always rerun Setup from the original disks or from the network folder where Office was installed. Click on the Start button and choose Run from the Start menu. At the Open prompt of the Run dialog box, type the drive letter to tell Windows where to find the floppy, the CD-ROM, or the network folder, then type the word **Setup** and click on OK. The Installation Maintenance dialog box appears. Choose Reinstall to install another entire version of the Office Suite, or Add/Remove to add or take out options. Figure A.7 displays the Installation Maintenance Program screen.

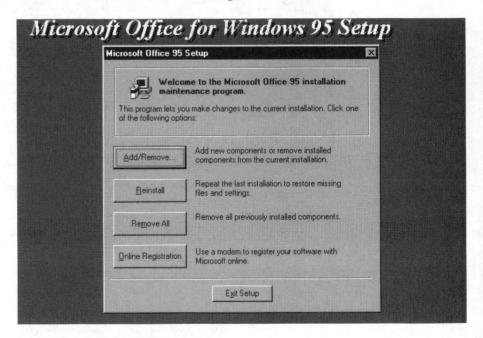

Figure A.7   Reinstalling Office 95 Setup

Installation Announcements

After you have started the installation, a meter shows how much of the installation process has been completed up to that moment, and changes to show the progress as Setup continues to copy files from your source drive onto your hard drive or network.

If you chose a typical Setup, Office will ask you if you want to install map information. This information is for use in Excel to create maps based on spreadsheets. If you have no space problems on your hard drive, choose Yes. If you are unsure about the amount of space you have, click on No. You can always install it later, if you need it.

If you are running the installation from floppies, Setup will install all of the files from the first diskette and then prompt you to load another diskette into your floppy drive. If you did not choose to install the entire Office 95 program, Setup may skip a diskette in the series. Don't be alarmed. Setup knows where to find the proper programs, and will prompt you for the needed diskette to insert in your floppy drive. If you place the incorrect diskette in the drive, Setup will let you know and let you try to insert the proper diskette.

During the installation process, you will be presented with colorful dialog boxes describing features in the program that you will enjoy using, as shown in Figure A.8.

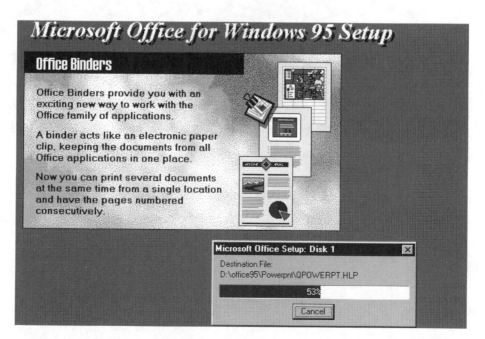

Figure A.8 *While Office is installing, there are colorful messages to describe the exciting features of the program.*

Appendix: Installing

After Office has completed its installation, a dialog box informs you of the fact and reminds you to fill out and send (or transmit via modem) your registration of the software (see Figure A.9). After this, there's nothing left but to start using Office as you like. Click on the Start button on the Taskbar and then choose Programs to find the Office95 folder that contains your Office 95 programs.

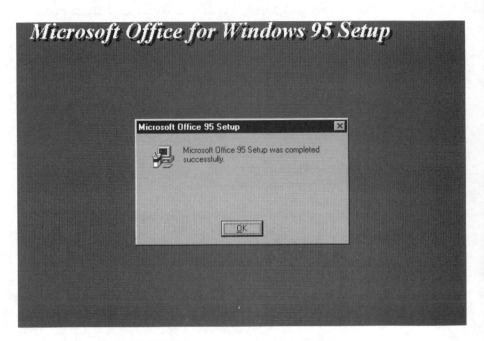

Figure A.9   Finish Installation dialog box.

Installing Access Separately

Access is part of the Professional Edition of Office, and can be installed from scratch using any of the options presented above. If you do not have the Professional Edition of Office 95 (i.e., you bought the Standard Edition instead), you may purchase Access separately and install it separately. The following instructions will help you to do just that. Access requires approximately 39 MB of disk space.

The procedures for installing Access are identical to those for installing the Standard Edition of Office. Insert Disk 1 or the CD-ROM version of Access into the appropriate drive. Click on the Start button on the Taskbar and type in **Setup** in the Run dialog box. The Access installation will begin. Figure A.10 displays the Access Startup dialog box. Click on the Continue button.

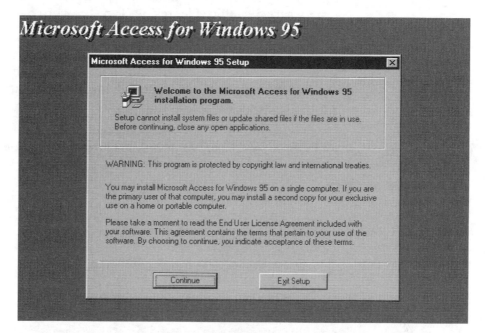

Figure A.10   *The Access installation follows the same pattern as the Standard Edition installation.*

The Name and Organization dialog is presented with the information you previously entered during the Standard Edition installation. If this information is still the same, click on the OK button. Access verifies that the information is correct and shows you the Product ID dialog box.

After searching for installed components, the Setup menu returns for one final verification of the drive on which you want Access to be installed. Click on OK and begin the installation.

Installing Office 95 from the Network

If you have a license from Microsoft to install Office 95 on more than one client computer, there are two ways you can approach the installation. You can distribute the Office disks to each end-user, or you can install Office on a network and have each end-user install from there.

Tell each user which network drive contains the software files or the shared CD-ROM drive. Choose Start from the Taskbar and click on the Run command. At the Open text area, type the letter of the shared Network drive where the Office files reside. Type the word **Setup** and press Enter, or click on the OK button.

Alert the user as to the folder they should direct the installation to occur. When prompted, the user must also know which drive letter to use for their hard disk in the case of there being multiple hard disk drive letters. The installation will proceed normally.

If you want additional information, read the file Network.txt in the Office folder or look up *network readme file* in Office's online table of contents.

Index

Note to the Reader: Throughout this index **boldfaced** page numbers indicate primary discussions of a topic. *Italicized* page numbers indicate illustrations.

X

Y

Z

What's New in Office

▶ *Office Shortcut Bar* replaces Office Manager, providing quick access to Office programs.

▶ *New* dialog box lets you create a new document from any application.

▶ *Office Binder* allows the creation and storage of documents from multiple Office applications in one file.

▶ *AnswerWizard*, available in all Office applications, giving help based on common language questions.

▶ *Schedule+* provides personal or group scheduling and contact management.

What's New in Word

▶ Better file management, including the ability to create a new folder for a document when you save it.

▶ Enhanced AutoFormat both after you have finished your document and automatically as you type.

▶ Better AutoCorrect, with a new Exceptions feature that allows correction in one situation but not another.

▶ Tight integration with Schedule+ that facilitates easy merges for a single letter or mass mailings.

▶ Tip Wizard that watches you as you work and makes suggestions on how you can use Word more efficiently.

▶ New Highlighter tool makes highlighting documents for on-screen viewing or printing as easy as selecting text.

▶ The ability to Find and Replace word forms.

▶ Automatic Spell Checking that notifies you of misspellings as you type, by underlining the errors with a wavy red line.

▶ Word can now be used as the mail editor for Exchange.

What's New in Excel

▶ Multi-user editing of workbooks using the new Shared Lists feature.

▶ Cell Notes can now be viewed simply by placing the mouse pointer over a cell with a note indicator.

▶ The new Data Map enables you to analyze geographically related data with different types of maps.

▶ You can now find the top or bottom values of a list by using AutoFilter and the "Top 10" option.

▶ Excel can finish typing your cell entries using AutoComplete, based on previous entries in a column.

▶ Better Drag-and-Drop that allows dragging and dropping from sheet to sheet, and scroll tips to indicate row and column for long-distance dragging.

▶ New Templates that help make even the most complicated spreadsheet a breeze with easy customization.

▶ Template Wizard helps you link worksheet cells to a database.

▶ Quick answers to common functions are no longer a problem with AutoComplete; simply select the cells that contain the values and view the Status bar for your answer.

▶ Number formatting has been made easier, with more options and built-in formats to match your everyday needs.